MW00423890

HEMINGWAY'S WIDOW

The Life and Legacy of
Mary Welsh Hemingway

TIMOTHY CHRISTIAN

PEGASUS BOOKS
NEW YORK LONDON

HEMINGWAY'S WIDOW

Pegasus Books, Ltd.
148 W 37th Street, 13th Floor
New York, NY 10018

Copyright © 2022 by Timothy Christian

First Pegasus Books cloth edition March 2022

Interior design by Maria Fernandez

Library of Congress Cataloging-in-Publication Data is available.

ISBN: 978-1-64313-883-1

10 9 8 7 6 5 4 3 2 1

Printed in the United States of America
Distributed by Simon & Schuster
www.pegasusbooks.com

To my family

CONTENTS

Preface by H. R. Stoneback   vii

Prologue   xxi

1   Chatting with Lords: 1904–1937   1

2   You May Sleep Quietly: September: 1938–June 1940   10

3   It Would be Just Like That Bloody Hitler to Try His Invasion on Christmas: July 1940–November 1941   17

4   A Glamorous, Globe-Trotting War Correspondent: December 1941–April 1943   25

5   A Deft, Tricky Way with Men: August 1942–May 1944   33

6   Beautiful as a May Fly: May 1944   40

7   Railway Trains Across the Sky: May 1944–June 1944   46

8   She Was Mad For Shaw: June 1944–July 1944   51

9   I Cannot Understand this Chest-beating: August 1944   56

10   We Lived in Those Days Far Beyond the Usual Reach of Our Senses: August 1944–September 1944   63

11   I Also am Committed, Horse, Foot, and Guns: August 1944–September 1944   70

12   Irwin, Are You Going to Marry Me?: September 1944–November 1944   78

13   I Could Never be a Simone de Beauvoir to Papa's Sartre: November 1944–December 1944   85

14   A Complicated Piece of Machinery: December 1944–February 1945   94

15   This is Like Being a High-Priced Whore: March 1945–June 1945   101

16   I Bleached My Hair Lighter to Please Him: June 1945–July 1946   109

17   How Did a Beat-up Old Bastard Like You Get Such a Lovely Girl as That?: August 1946–July 1947   120

18   That Was a Day of Triumph for Me: September 1947–September 1948   129

19   Platinum-Blonde at Torcello: September 1948–November 1948   137

20   He Has Become the Most Important Part of Me: November 1948–May 1949   145

21   Ernest Taunts Me with This: May 1949–March 1950   154

22   It Lays Me Open, Raw, and Bleeding: March 1950–January 1951   166

23   People Are Dying That Never Died Before: January 1951–March 1952   177

24   Every Real Work of Art Exhales Symbols and Allegories: April 1952–August 1952   190

25 Safety Off, Hold Steady; Squeeze: August 1952–December 1953   199

26 A Plague Began to Descend Upon Us: December 1953–March 1954   215

27 The Swedish Thing: January 1954–February 1955   226

28 She Knows How to be Lazy as a Cat: March 1955–September 1956   235

29 If You Have a Message, Call the Western Union: September 1956–
    September 1958   243

30 I Wished for a Room of My Own: October 1958–July 1959   253

31 Smashed Like an Eggshell: July 1959–January 7, 1960   262

32 Lots of Problems but We Will Solve Them All: January 1960–
    September 25, 1960   270

33 A Vegetable Life: October 8, 1960–April 24, 1961   279

34 Good Night, My Kitten: April 25, 1961–July 2, 1961   289

35 The Sun Also Ariseth: July 2, 1961–July 4, 1961   296

36 This in Some Incredible Way Was an Accident: July 5, 1961–July 10, 1961   304

37 Picking up the Pieces: July 15, 1961–October 16, 1961   312

38 A "Vastly Different Outcome": October 1961–January 1963   325

39 You Are Rated as Politically Unreliable: December 1961–July 1962   337

40 A Moveable Feast: November: 1956–2015   349

41 Defending Papa's Reputation: February 1964–August 1966   359

42 No, He Shot Himself. Shot Himself. Just That.: March 1966–
    September 1968   372

43 Who the Hell is He Writing About?: July 1966–February 1975   379

44 I Never Especially Liked the Killing: July 1970–August 1974   388

45 Have Success in Something Instead of Talking About Equality!:
    February 1975   397

46 Ernest's Gift Was Joy: 1951–1977   402

47 How It Was: May 1966–July 1977   410

48 It's a Beautiful Place of Bougainvillea and Poinsettia, but the Heart of it
    is Gone: May 1977–July 1977   419

49 Life is Ruthless: September 1979–June 2019   423

    Acknowledgments   433
    Bibliography   437
    Endnotes   445
    Index   495

PREFACE

"This is the Hemingway book we've all been waiting for so long."
—H. R. Stoneback

Today is one of those sudden-sun-glory afternoons in the Hudson Valley when the chill finally lifts and you can see the first hints of spring. It is the perfect weather to spend the afternoon sitting in the unshaded spot near the head of my driveway and read while I wait for the mail. I greet neighbors and other people taking advantage of the quiet side street in our small village leading downhill to the Hudson River. It has been a pleasant ritual during this strange pandemic year of various states of isolation and conversational quarantine.

My last public lecture on Hemingway was on a ship sailing the Caribbean in February of 2020, a ship that barely made it home to port before the lockdowns started. Since then, about a dozen of my Hemingway lectures worldwide, from New York to New Orleans to Wyoming, from Florida to Ireland to France, have been canceled. I miss the passing conversations about Hemingway with strangers in far places. In this strange year of Covidian metamorphoses, my travels have mostly been to my mailbox and my conversations have mainly been with passersby.

I've lived quietly and mostly anonymously in my village, but some neighbors have seen announcements of my public lectures or reviews of my books in local newspapers. They know I'm a professor and some kind of writer, and some of them seem to think I'm so ancient that I used to hang out with Hemingway in Paris or Cuba or some old war or sporting glory. Neighbors are not to be held accountable for their flawed chronology. Most know me only as "the writer-guy" or "the Hemingway professor" or "the old writer-dude that lives in the big haunted house above the river and loves to garden and talk about his garlic and leek crops and give his garlic and leeks away to neighbors." That is fine with me; it reminds me of long ago when I lived in a French village where people still believed what they read in the newspapers, and still gardened, and respected writers, and the only American writer they'd heard of was Hemingway.

I have long observed that our first reading of really good books is mysteriously and inextricably bound up with the place where we did the reading. All good things are suffused with Place, and it is as if the Deus Loci summons us to read certain good books in certain numinous places. Today then, I was sitting by my driveway reading what had come in the mail two weeks before—a large fat heavy manuscript of 623 pages in the form of a spiral-bound Staples print-job. I lost the first week after the manuscript arrived to the vaccine-quest runabout and other daily necessities and interruptions. I lost most of the second week to urgent round-the-clock communications with editors about the publication of my Memorial Ode for Jerry Jeff Walker, the legendary Texas singer-songwriter and my old hitchhiking buddy in the early sixties, and working out my role in the grand Jerry Jeff Memorial Show in Luckenbach later this year, where I will take the stage and sing with the likes of Ramblin' Jack Elliott, Emmy Lou Harris, Jimmy Buffett, Steve Earle, and other music legends who love Jerry Jeff as I do. My life and work is not all Hemingway all the time—it never has been. However, delightful crossovers do occur, such as the historic occasion when Mary Hemingway met Jerry Jeff Walker, described later in this book.

With other pressing matters settled, I started reading the manuscript slowly, in the after-midnight hours, jumping around in the text checking sources, doing the sideways scholarly recon often deployed in approaching a book. It was the final draft of another Hemingway book, a biography. I had known every Hemingway biographer since Carlos Baker; and even before Carlos and his first full-dress biography of Hemingway, I had known A. E. Hotchner and his *Papa Hemingway* meditation. I was still in mourning for Hotch since we lost him, aged 102, last year as the pandemic started, and lately regretting that I had to cancel my last invitation to visit Hotch again at his home in Connecticut. I personally knew many of the primary sources, Hemingway's family and friends. And I knew the main character of the manuscript entitled *Hemingway's Widow: The Life of Mary Welsh Hemingway*. I knew Mary Hemingway not as a subject for academic inquiry and scholarly interviews, but as a social friend to be cherished. Nothing written before brought to life the person I knew. That conviction, together with the more than forty years spent on the front lines of the Hemingway lit-critical wars and scholarly skirmishes, led to a certain jaded and glutted feeling of satiety at the frontier of ennui; a place where there is nothing new under the sun (when it came to all Hemingway books). This made my first approaches to this manuscript peripheral. I started at the back, jumping around here and there, source-checking, writing brief marginal annotations, taking the temperature of the book, seeing if it tested negative or positive. But that's no way to read a good book. A good book deserves and demands more than circuitous post-midnight perambulation, or even the more devout higher circumambulation. Besides, I prefer to read in natural light.

Seeing that the forecast called for two consecutive warm sunny days, I canceled everything, turned my phone off, and started really reading the book straight through. The first long afternoon, on my porch and in my mail-awaiting driveway, I read 253 pages. I stopped when the natural light dictated and resisted reading into the night because the feeling of reading outdoors seemed right for this book that was a rare breath of fresh air in Hemingway studies. Then in the bright clean early spring light of the second day of plein air reading, I finished the last 311 pages of the narrative without even a coffee break. I closed my eyes in the late afternoon sun and thought, *there is something new under the sun. This is a stunning achievement. Perfectly organized, impeccably paced, well-written in clean crisp prose, free from academic jargon and critical gibberish and psychoanalytical balderdash.* My eyes still closed in meditation, I thanked my grandmother for that word—she was the only person I ever knew who could say the word "balderdash" five times in a conversation and give the word its appropriate authority and force—and Mary Hemingway reminded me of my tough, enduring, librarian-teacher grandmother who dealt admirably with the complexities and burdens of marriage to a talented husband who drank too much, among other excesses. I kept thinking about the heavy manuscript in my lap: *some revelations here, things we did not know before; perspicacious throughout in its search for and interpretation of evidence; exactitude and amplitude; meticulous research, more than fifty pages of notes and documentation; always judicious in its assessments and judicial when it needs to be; and how good it is to have at last a writer who brings to bear his vast legal experience on matters such as Hemingway's contracts and lawsuits and wills, something never before dealt with adequately. Most importantly, the real Mary Hemingway is brought to light and life and walks through these pages.*

I had been so absorbed in finishing my excited reading of the manuscript that I hadn't even opened my mail, delivered hours before, and I was still sitting by my driveway where the last afternoon sun slanted on my property. A voice broke into my reverie: "Beautiful day, ain't it now. You finish writing another one of your books, Mr. Writer?"

I opened my eyes.

"No, this one's not mine. It's the manuscript of a new Hemingway book."

"So you got your Professor Hemingway hat on today."

"Semper fi." I touched the Marine Corps cap I was wearing. He got my double meaning.

"Semper," he said and still standing mask-less six feet away, he let enough leash out so his hound dog could wag-tail prance up and lick my hand the way he always did when these conversations happened in passing once a month or so from spring through fall. I don't know the dog's name or the man's name and I don't think they know my name. He always calls me "Mr. Writer" or "Professor Hemingway," and the dog seems to agree. They live somewhere in the village, not in my immediate neighborhood, and he walks his dog past my house down to the Hudson several times a week when the weather is good. One thing we do know is that we are both ex-Marines. Correction: there are no "ex" Marines—*once a Marine always a Marine* as the band-of-brothers watchword goes—and we always recognize each other. I vaguely know that he has held all kinds of jobs, mostly in construction, and that he retired early, in his fifties, on disability from his last job as a heavy-equipment operator. The only thing I know for sure about him is that he loves Hemingway and reads everything he can find by and about Hemingway. (That's one of the great things about Hemingway—the *only* American writer who compels readers of all kinds, not just writers and academics and English majors and crusaders looking for a strawman writer to hate.)

"So what's that-there Hemingway book about?"

"It's actually about one of his wives."

"I might ought to skip that one then. I've had it up to here"—he lifted his dog-free hand making the usual gesture at his throat—"with all them Paris wives and Key West wives and all them *wifeographies* and all that damn I don't know what—emotional crap, well not that exactly just romantic greeting card stuff or the opposite which is just as stupid and I don't know what to call any of it—"

"Sentimental?"

"Yeah that's it. And it smells like toxic waste." (He used to operate the bulldozer at the town dump.)

"Sentimentality can be just as toxic as cynicism."

"You said it brother."

"You might like this *wifeography*. It's the first one about Hem's last wife."

"What's it like? I never read anything but uh—bull-crap about her." In his avoidance of the word *bullshit*, he was being genteel and polite to his distinguished neighbor. I couldn't think exactly what to tell him—I did not want to say *impeccably written and meticulously researched, anchored in exactitude and open to amplitude*. So I just said:

"This is the Hemingway book we've all been waiting for so long."

"If you say so I might better read it."

"You'll learn a lot of new things about Hem. And his last wife, his most enduring and important mate, really comes alive in these pages."

"Then I'll get the book when it comes out. Something I know you won't remember 'cause I was just a scrawny pimple-pocked kid just out of high school, but I was in the audience when you brought Mary Hemingway here and introduced her talk forty-some years ago."

"Really? That lecture at the university?"

"Yep. That and her talk at the village library, too. I liked her a lot. I tried to buy her book but she *gave* it to me and signed it and I took it with me when I went away to the Marines. I remember all that like it was yesterday. I liked her a lot."

I was happy to be reminded of Mary's village library visit. I always saw Mary in Manhattan, except for her one visit eighty miles north to my village at the end of her grueling year-and-a-half tour plugging *How It Was*. I reckon maybe I talked her into what she called her "last public talk"—(and I think it was her last, in late November 1977)—at my university. She agreed to give the talk for the pittance my institution offered, about one-tenth of her normal lecture fee. I took that as an act of friendship. Driving her north to my home, I mentioned that the local village librarian asked if I could bring Mary by to sign a few of her books. It would only take a few minutes, I said, and we'd have plenty of time to relax and to eat something before her big evening lecture. To my surprise, she said enthusiastically, "Let's do it." Mary was a real trouper. I had arranged with Sparrow, my wife, that if Mary said *yes* to the library-stop we'd be there at a certain time and if Mary said *no* we'd go on to our house so she could rest and I'd call Sparrow from home. So we stopped at the village library, really a modest old house with cramped quarters and tight-packed bookshelves.

I looked at my neighbor standing in my driveway and said, "I remember vividly Mary Hemingway's lecture at my university but I'd forgotten all about the village library event. And I'm amazed that you were there. Tell me what you remember."

"I reck-lec' like it was yesterday. I see you bringing Missus Mary in and taking her over to your missus and then you went back outside. I was there before anybody else come and I was carrying my guitar coming home from a music lesson. Missus Hemingway says to me *may I please borrow your guitar for a minute* and she did and she played a few chords then her and your Missus that everybody called Sparrow started singing and it was that French lady's song about no regrets that was my momma's favorite song. That Piaf-lady and her theme song."

"*Non, je ne regrette rien.*"

"That's the one. Then you come back inside and stood there towering over the both of 'em and them the same height and neither of 'em a hair over five-foot-two and them singing their voices blending like sisters and both of 'em had that low voice with the mystery-thing in it standing there singing like sisters thirty years apart and then your Missus Sparrow took the guitar and played what I know was your theme song with her because I heard you open many shows with 'I wisht I was some little sparrow' and that about 'come all ye fair and tender ladies' and then you harmonized with 'em on the next line."

"*Take warning how you court your men* . . . Where did you see the shows I did with Sparrow?"

"Ever' time I seen the ads in the papers about a show you was doing nearby. Maybe a dozen times over the years. Been meaning to tell you this ever' time I walk by and we talk. And once on stage you told the story how your wife got the name Sparrow. And that brought tears to my eyes 'cause Piaf was my mama's favorite singer."

His hound dog looked sad. Maybe we all did.

"That was one of Mary Hemingway's favorite songs, too," I said.

The reason this matters is because in Tim Christian's biography, one of the small but important pleasures and satisfactions, among all the major ones, is the plethora of references to Mary Hemingway's love of singing. I even think there is a reference to Mary's singing Piaf, though I may have dreamed that. I just leafed through all the many pages where I penciled a checkmark next to references to Mary's joy in singing but I can't find the ostensible Piaf reference now. The point is that if a biographer does not report his subject's love of singing, the life story remains untold. And maybe we should never trust a biographer who does not sing.

In late 1963, my wife and I were onstage performing at a nightclub when the MC came on stage to report tearfully the news of the death of Piaf, "The Little Sparrow." Then, dipping his fingers into his gin and tonic, the MC christened my wife "The New Sparrow." At first it was her stage name, but soon everybody around the country and the world called her Sparrow. We sang our way around the world, performing in forty states and forty countries, and for more than forty years together singing was a way of being. The reporter who does not know and understand that, even if he knows all my books, even if she knows all my hundreds of published essays and thousands of poems, knows nothing about my life. In this biography, I'm happy to say, I can hear Mary singing, and Ernest, too (even if he is somewhat off-key but never mind).

After reading this biography, with its pervasive evidence of Mary's joy in singing, I will always remember her songfulness, especially when I read and hear the usual invidious comparisons of Mary with Hemingway's other wives. For Mary, singing was a form of social discourse and connection, singing was fun, singing was joy. And I do not mean art-song, performance-song—I mean folk songs and popular songs sung in the spirit of singing along together. I have read all there is to read and heard all the gossip about Hemingway's other wives and I'm not sure if any of them really liked to sing or if they were the kind of song-shunners who retreated into silent corners or spouted weary witticisms while others sang. I could make a few untuneful suggestions about the singing identities of the other wives, but I won't. I do feel confident in saying that none of them would, like Mary, visit a local library and in an idle moment ask a local teenager if she could borrow his guitar and then play and sing with others, not as performance, but for joy. Is there anything better to do with idle moments than fill the silence with song? Singing *is* a way of being, of *being together*.

Delighted with my dog-walking neighbor's memories, I asked, "What else do you remember about Mary Hemingway's visit?"

"Well, maybe twenty people crowded into that small room where she sat at a desk and talked. She said a few words about Ernest and about her book. Then you announced that she would have to leave in a few minutes and that we were all welcome to come to her talk in the big lecture hall at New Paltz. You said she'd be happy to sign her book if we wanted to buy a copy from the librarian.

Missus Hemingway was sitting at that desk with a cardboard box wrapped in green tissue paper with a slit in the top and a sign that said *Donations for Library Book-Buying Support*. I watched her rub her fingers over that sign on the box then she said, 'I will give you these books and ask you to consider putting the purchase price in this library donation box.' I think most of us did that. I know I did. I did not have much money and I was about to spend almost all I had on her book but I put it all in the donation box. It was the first charity gift I ever made and I felt good about it. And after she'd signed all the books she gave away I watched her reach in her purse and put a wad of bills that looked like mostly twenties in that box."

If I noticed that then I had forgotten it. So Mary was a trouper, and a benevolent and generous trouper.

"What else do you remember?"

"Well, after that signing of books you all left the library and two or three hours later you arrived at that big lecture hall where the standing-room-only crowd was waiting and you gave your fancy introduction of her and then she talked some about Ernest but talked much longer about what it was like living in London during the Nazi Blitz. It was better than any talk or program or movie I ever heard or watched about that war. It made me feel like I had lived through the Blitz. She must have been one hell of a war correspondent."

"Some say she was. Anything else you want to say about her?"

"I thought she was perky, tough, a grade-A talker, and right on. And I'll bet she was sexy as hell in her prime."

"I think you'll like this biography a lot."

"I got your word on that and I'll be there with bells on to buy that-there book when it comes out. I might even buy a copy to give to my strange estranged wife. She's like one of them whiny snobbish Hemingway wives and the whiny biographers who write about them. Somebody needs to tell them whiners to just SITFU. Excuse my Marine-mouth but you know what I mean."

"Yes."

Marines like acronyms, the pinnacle of pared-down prose and economy of speech. Unfortunately, decorum seems to forbid printing here what the acronym stands for.

"Just hand all the whiners a straw and don't even say SITFU," my neighbor continued. "You'd have to carry a lot of damn straws these days with whiners coming out of the woodwork everywhere. I'll bet nobody ever had to tell the one true tough Missus Hemingway to suck it up."

"Yeah, you'll like this biography. Makes the best case ever for Mary as the most important wife of all, with the toughest gig when Hemingway was alive and started falling apart; and after his death she spent decades defending and advancing his literary legacy. Always faithful."

"The Semper Gumby Semper Fi wife. "

"You got it." I had not heard anyone say *Semper Gumby* in decades. It is the other Marine Corps *semper—always flexible.*

"And I've heard she could handle her liquor, too. Some folks in these parts still talk about how much she drank with you before she gave that great talk. Bartenders talk. Well, me and my old hound better move on to get home before dark. Semper my good Mister Professor—Semper."

"Semper." I watched him walk away and I thought, *Well, there's another Hemingway interview done. I'd like to add him to all the other audiences I've had for Hemingway, write for him, lecture for him, teach him, and learn from him.*

But there it was again, the story of Mary's drinking, and a particular story still alive in regional oral tradition forty-three years after it happened. That day long ago, after our stop for the local library program, Mary and Sparrow and I went to our house for a spell. Sparrow had carefully put the gin and all other bottles of kindred spirits out of sight. She offered Mary some coffee and fruit juice and they talked in the living room, then sang and played guitars again, while I got on the telephone to New Paltz, calling the restaurant where I planned to take Mary for something to eat before the evening program. I wanted to make sure Barnaby's was open and not too crowded, and I reserved a booth in the back corner as far from the bar as you could get, on the theory that the farther from the bar we were, the longer it would take to get drinks. In the time since Mary and I became friends, all the social and cultural events where we were together had an inclination toward and generous affection for alcohol. My main concern was keeping her reasonably sober before her big talk—and keeping myself reasonably sober enough to make an eloquent and elegant introduction. And like anyone who had visited Mary at her penthouse apartment, I knew she drank hard and fast there. I was one among many who worried about those priceless paintings and the even more priceless Hemingway manuscripts scattered around her apartment. Like that shopping bag with *The Garden of Eden* manuscript on the floor beneath the edge of a table with a large ash tray and an assortment of liquor bottles perilously perched above. We all hoped they would be removed to the archive soon. But my concern the night of her much-anticipated "last public talk" was just keeping the speaking-under-the-influence index reasonably favorable.

With our bar-distant table reserved, I hung up the phone and went into our living room where Mary and Sparrow were both playing guitars and sister-singing folk songs.

"What's your pleasure, Mary? Another hour of rest here and then grab a bite to eat before your talk?"

"Let's have a bite now if we may."

So Mary and I left Sparrow, who was driving to the lecture hall separately to pick up the grad student crew that would help set up the reception after Mary's lecture.

Mary and I entered the restaurant and were met by the maître d' who started to lead to our back-corner table but Mary said, "I'm not hungry yet. Let's just sit here at the bar."

So we sat at the bar and drank for about an hour. In depth. On empty stomachs. And we never did get any food. Mary had five or six very dry double or triple martinis. It was the first time I'd seen her shun her usual gin and tonics and the mammoth martinis worried me a little, especially when she ordered two at a time. My poison of choice in those days was double Jack D on the rocks. I had two of those in the time that Mary consumed at least five of her killer martinis. We talked about travel, about New Orleans and Paris, about everything but her late husband. And then the clock swam into view and I knew we had to leave to get over to campus for her talk.

After my introduction, Mary took the podium and made some opening remarks about her life with Ernest, then talked for an hour with no notes about living under the London Blitz, holding her standing-room-only audience spellbound, and pleasing them even more after her talk was over with the gracious acuity of her answers to questions from the audience. She got two standing ovations, the first when the talk ended, the second after the question-and-answer session. It was an exemplary performance in every respect.

That night, she out-drank and out-performed me. She was in her late sixties, petite; I was in my mid-thirties, with more than twice her body mass and in those days a reputation for drinking hard and handling it well. As my literary generation often says of the literary generation that preceded us—*Giants walked the earth in those days*. For me, those elder *Giants* included friends and mentors like James Dickey, Allen Tate, Robert Penn Warren, and many others known for drinking mythically before performing admirably for their public. And in my witnessed knowing, Mary was of that company, that literary generation—any one of them likely to drink more than a busload of MFAs today, and perform far more admirably.

For decades now, I have been wary of speaking with interviewers and biographers about any of the Hemingway family and friends I have known, perhaps under the code that discretion is the better part of alcohol-fueled valor—or something like that. Or really just the much more fundamental code that when it comes to friends, discretion is the rule. And when it comes to Mary Hemingway, any conversation, any biography, must deal with what many who knew her—as well as those who did not know her—characterize as her decline and disintegration into drunkenness and dementia. In my view, she was, during the years 1976 to 1980, more than competent and capable, indeed sometimes charming and witty, sometimes joyful, always faithful, and devoted to Ernest Hemingway's literary legacy. In those years we had many good conversations. She invited me several times to Ernest's annual birthday party in Idaho. I never went, but I should have.

Just as she, of all people, should have gone to the grand opening ceremony of the Hemingway Room at the Kennedy Library in July 1980. It was a grand occasion as well as the first time I was truly troubled by the vicious gossip I heard about her—for example, she was "too drunk," too "incompetent" to make the trip to Boston to celebrate the event that would not have happened without her. Without Mary Hemingway and her friend William Walton—and his friends the Kennedys—the most extraordinary literary archive in the United States would not exist. That 1980 ceremony was very fine, and I enjoyed my conversations with George Plimpton and Jacqueline Kennedy and other glitterati and Hemingway family members, and enjoyed meeting many others who would be my colleagues in a new generation of Hemingway scholars and critics. We also enjoyed the excellent wines and cognac that were served—and enjoyed taking surplus bottles back to Thompson Island with us on the boat. My only regret was that Mary was not there.

By then I had become friends with Bill Walton, my seasonal neighbor in the Hudson Valley. He had inherited a remarkable old stone house in Stone Ridge, New York, twenty miles or so up the road from my place. We were friends and neighbors and he was not, for me, a subject of academic inquiry, a source to be interviewed. Our friendship was anchored by our mutual love of gardening. From my garden, I took him rare varieties of French leeks and garlic, not just the harvest, but the seedlings and cloves for him to plant. From his garden, he gave me bulbs and cuttings to plant and bouquets of flowers to take home to Sparrow. We talked as much about clematis and azaleas and hollyhocks and leeks as we did about Hemingways and Kennedys. Oh we talked about them, to be sure. And about Gertrude Stein, who had visited Bill's aunt Emily at that very place, the historic stone tavern-turned-home his aunt bequeathed him. In the dim light, he showed me letters from Stein to his aunt, and some letters to him from Ernest and Mary.

When I told Bill that Hemingway's Nobel Prize medal was missing from the Cuban shrine to the Virgin Mary where Hemingway had given it as a gift, an offering, and I had been told by a Chilean diplomat who knew Fidel Castro well that Fidel carried Hemingway's medal in his pocket as a good luck charm, Bill got excited and said, "We must get it back to its proper place." It became our cause, in a kind of *Mission Impossible* way. I told Bill I would get to Cuba as soon as I could and investigate. (And I did, but that's another story.) But our deepest admiration was for Hemingway's work. Bill was not just an accomplished journalist and painter, but a good literary critic. I have a copy of one of his Hemingway books from his college days. In the margin, the young Bill Walton had written, "The secret of Hemingway's prose is this: it is often perfectly wrought blank verse."

Because my interest in Hemingway was a matter of story and style, the art of fiction, I never "interviewed" Bill, but all through the 1980s I told everybody who had Hemingway biographical inclinations and interests they had better talk to Bill Walton. I urged my friend Mike Reynolds, Hemingway's definitive biographer (to date), to talk to Bill, and I even set up an extended visit but it never happened. Finally, two interviews were recorded with Bill Walton shortly before his death in 1994. Bill was a great conversationalist and loved to gossip. When those interviews, much cited in this biography, were about to happen, Bill described them as, "academics, you know, and I'll do the usual Hanseling-and-Greteling, a few white pebbles, lots of bread crumbs and all that."

In more than a decade of conversations with Bill it became clear to me that he admired both Ernest and Mary, but his views had hardened as he aged. Mary was now just an "old drunk" and so forth. I saw Mary at least once in the early eighties—after the 1980 Kennedy Library celebration that she missed—when she was quite lucid and witty and not drunk at all. And then in the summer of 1983, I went to see her as a kind of farewell visit because I was going abroad to live in France and then China for more than a year and I feared she would be gone before I returned to the States. She was not lucid. Alfred Rice was there, doing surveillance and sentry duty. I have known many people who knew Alfred Rice, and I have never heard anyone say they liked him. I didn't. But the image that lingers from my last visit with Mary is the blankness in her eyes. I do not think she recognized me. By the time I settled back in the States a few years later she was gone.

In assessing a biography of someone you knew, a biography which draws on many source-persons that you also knew, there are many intricacies and treacherous seas to navigate. The printed record, which is mostly what a biographer writing in the year 2021 has as a guide, is very different from the human record, the flesh-and-blood lived record. I must say that I cannot imagine any biographer navigating these waters better than Timothy Christian does here. And as for those I did not know personally, for example, the Buck and Pete Lanham situation (where treachery is the apt word): I am grateful for the acute illuminating analysis provided in these pages, and I hope every student of Hemingway will pay close attention and adjust accordingly their views of Carlos Baker's biography.

Again I say, this book is a stunning achievement. It is the custom to say in these introductory remarks that this volume belongs on the bookshelves of every scholar and student and fan of Hemingway. And it does. That includes Hemingway aficionados like my neighbor the bulldozer man. He will appreciate Timothy Christian's superb skills as a heavy-equipment operator in biography. And I'm certain he will echo what I told him the other day: *This is the Hemingway book we've all been waiting for so long.*

H. R. Stoneback
Distinguished Professor Emeritus
The State University of New York
President (past): The Ernest Hemingway Foundation & Society

PROLOGUE

In August 1946, a famous writer and his wife, a former *Time* reporter, drove from Key West toward Sun Valley, Idaho. The backseat of their apple-green Lincoln convertible was packed with fishing gear and a couple of shotguns, a case of wine, and picnic hampers. Her portable typewriter was lodged between two large duffel bags stuffed with clothing, and there was no room left to sit. They planned to hunt in the hills and fish in the streams of the valleys of the Sawtooth Mountains. She was three months pregnant and wanted to be with her mother when the baby arrived.

The couple was in love and talked excitedly about their expected child. Though he had three sons from two previous marriages, he longed for a daughter. They agreed to name a girl Bridget after her grandmother and a boy Thomas after her father. She made snacks of rye bread, cheese, and sliced onion, and they drank red wine from a bota as they drove from Florida to Louisiana and then north and farther west. She sang songs to amuse him, imitating Edith Piaf with her low alto voice, and they talked about the changes in scenery and accents and local habits. They stayed at roadside motels and ate in diners, exploring America from the road.

When they reached Kansas the temperature rose sharply, and they put up the top to find relief from the sun's searing rays. She sucked on chunks of ice but felt dizzy. "Maybe it's my baby protesting the heat," she thought. Two days later, having traveled through Nebraska, they reached a ramshackle motel in Casper, Wyoming. After a dinner of pork chops and mashed potatoes, they retired to their linoleum-floored room, and she fell into a deep sleep and dreamed of the sport of pig-sticking in India. She was riding a cantering horse, hunting for a pig to spear with her beribboned lance. Without warning, one of the other riders stabbed her in the stomach, and she fell from her horse and writhed shrieking on the ground.

She woke from the nightmare to a burning pain in her belly, and he went to find a doctor and ambulance. It seemed to take forever for the ambulance to arrive, but when it did a nurse gave her a painkilling shot and she lapsed into unconsciousness.

When she woke ten hours later, she saw her husband milking a plasma tube into a vein in her arm. He smiled at her and said, "Welcome back, Kitten."

She learned from the doctor and nurses that her husband had saved her life. One of her fallopian tubes had burst and the resulting hemorrhage filled her abdomen with blood, "like she was gut shot," with no place for the blood to go. Before he could operate, the surgeon had to inject plasma and blood to restore her fluid levels. When he tried to insert the intravenous needle her veins collapsed, and he could not inject the lifesaving liquid. It was hopeless. The surgeon said, "Sorry," and took off his gloves. He told the man to say goodbye.

Instead, the husband took over. He told an assistant to cut an incision in her forearm so he could grab a vein. The cut was made, and the man pushed his finger and thumb into the slit in her flesh and managed after several tries to pinch a vein and pull it to the surface. He inserted the intravenous needle directly into the vein and squeezed on the sack of fluid, coaxing it into her. After one pack she seemed to recover slightly, and he ordered the surgeon to operate at once. The man alternated plasma with pints of blood and fed them into his wife's arm. The surgeon opened her belly and sutured the ruptured fallopian tube. Over the next few hours she hovered between life and death. When she came to, she saw her husband looking at her tenderly.

He had refused to give up on her. She owed him her life, and he admired her courage—she kept going after pit bulls would've quit. He had never seen a stronger will to live, and the bond they formed that day was more robust than any wedding vow. As her father later remarked, they had discovered genuine friendship, "the best thing, the most lasting thing in one's life."[1] She was distressed to have lost the baby, but she loved her husband for saving her, and she hoped to become pregnant again.

This could be a Hemingway short story, but it isn't. Mary and Ernest forged an unbreakable friendship in the face of certain death. Ernest saved her life, and she thanked the fates he was with her in her time of danger. She forgave every misdeed and cruel act of the past and felt renewed faith in his love for her. Mary was beholden to Ernest and could never desert him. And Ernest felt responsible for her very being.[2]

ONE

Chatting with Lords

M ary Welsh was born and raised in the Paul Bunyan country of Minnesota. Oversized statues of the mythical giant lumberjack and his blue ox, Babe, stand on Lake Bemidji's shore in the heart of Mary's hometown. This is the story of her escape from the land of lumberjacks.

Mary's father, Thomas, was the son of Irish Protestant immigrants who settled in L'Anse, Michigan. Thomas saved enough money by working in logging camps to attend Valparaiso College for one year. He became a bookkeeper with a large logging company and entered the timber business on his own in 1904. That same year, thirty-four-year-old Thomas married his childhood sweetheart, Adeline Beehler, the daughter of a miner and granddaughter of German immigrants from Baden. Adeline was fêted at a party at her friend's house which "was prettily decorated with asparagus vine and carnations, and the guests, who were all office associates of Miss Beehler, were very enjoyably entertained with cards and music." [1] A week later, Reverend J. M. Shank performed the marriage ceremony in the bride's home. The wedding "was a very quiet affair, only relatives being present. The bride is accomplished and highly respected in this county, where she has lived most of her life." Thirty-five-year-old Adeline worked in the Department of State's office, and friends were sorry to see her leave the capital. Fellow workers said Thomas was "the happiest man in town." [2]

The couple settled in Walker, Minnesota, in a log cabin on the shore of Leech Lake, named for the bloodsuckers that dwell along its shore. The population of

Walker was 917, only seventeen fewer persons than reside there today.[3] Thomas harvested timber from the forests surrounding the lake, and his fortunes rose and fell with the volatile lumber industry. His autobiography retraces the trail he followed "through millions of acres of pine-covered forest, always searching for something better to feed my hungry body and mind."[4]

Thomas befriended lumbermen, townsfolk, and members of the Chippewa tribe. He railed against rapacious logging practices and the theft of Indian lands. Ahead of his time, he advocated conservation measures, including the re-planting of forested tracts. Thomas was a progressive thinker who got on well with the Chippewa people, respected their religious beliefs in the great Manitou, and advocated on their behalf.

Adeline was lonely in Walker and missed the social life of Lansing. Her favorite memory was of the two years she spent working in a state senator's office when her older brother chaperoned her at the city's fancy balls. Adeline's life changed on Sunday, April 5, 1908, when she gave birth to a healthy baby girl they named Mary, after Thomas's mother. When Thomas heard Mary's first cry, "A beautiful feeling of fatherhood came over me and a flood of love for your mother and you, that seemed to come like a burst of sunshine from heaven."[5]

Two years later, Adeline gave birth to a boy they named Otto, after her brother. There must have been great joy, for Thomas wanted a son to help in his business. Eight months later, on a Sunday morning, Otto died after a weeklong illness. Funeral services were held in the family home before interment at the Greenwood cemetery. Adeline blamed their doctor for giving the baby the wrong medicine; she lost faith in doctors and became captivated by the teachings of Christian Science. In her home, reading religious tracts came to replace medical treatment.

The family moved to the town of Bemidji when Mary was six so she could attend school. Thomas bought a large white house on the corner of Bemidji Avenue and 12th Street, which still stands, though it has been converted to apartments. Adeline maintained a neat, disciplined home filled with canned vegetables, fresh-baked bread, and solid, if not exciting, food. Over the years, perhaps because of Thomas's frequent absences on business, Adeline became more involved in the Christian Science congregation. Mary remembered her mother as a proper Victorian lady who arranged her hair and attached her hat with pins before dressing for her weekly round of visits to other homes, where she left engraved calling cards. She also became active in the Charities Society and chaired the Relief Committee charged with helping people find work. Ads appeared in *The Bemidji Pioneer* inviting "anyone needing assistance in finding work" to phone Mrs. T. J. Welsh.[6]

Thomas incorporated the T. J. Welsh Land and Lumber Company to purchase timberlands, real estate, and wood products.[7] He launched the *Northland* to haul log booms, carry passengers on lake excursions, and transport cargo. A slowly rotating paddlewheel propelled the boat through the water at the dignified speed of one knot. From the age of eight, Mary spent her summers aboard the *Northland* with her father, cruising the waters of Leech Lake and exploring streams on camping trips in birchbark canoes. Thomas taught Mary to read the stars and talked to her about the meaning of justice and charity, illustrating his points with Bible stories and Shakespeare's plays. She learned to respect the Chippewa people who had been displaced from their lands by settlers moving westward. "They liked my father because he never broke his word to them. A couple of times, our Indian friends saved us both from certain death, once by drowning, once by freezing."[8]

Thomas was no ordinary lumberjack. He had studied Shakespeare at Valparaiso College, learned *Hamlet* by heart, and sometimes wished he could have been an actor instead of a logger. He recited passages to his daughter as she sat with him in the *Northland*'s wheelhouse on trips across Lake Leech. Mary joined as he sang Irish ballads in his rich baritone, learned his repertoire, developed a low alto voice, and loved singing for the rest of her life.

Thomas became active in Progressive Republican politics and was elected to attend state conventions.[9] He read widely, wrote tracts for progressive causes, and in 1920 put himself forward as a candidate for Congress on the National Labor Party ticket.

Mary opened her heart to her diary. "My father, nearly 6 feet tall, slim, wiry, quick in his movements, with his wavy auburn hair, long, straight nose, and quick sharp blue eyes, was my biggest hero during all of my childhood, and a hero always." Mary found him "indomitable, valiant, and always ready to take a risk." She was "grateful that he treated me both with attention and as an incipient adult."[10] When the *Northland* moored for the night, its salon became an island of high culture in the backwoods of Minnesota. A windup phonograph played scratchy Mozart sonatas and Chopin piano concertos, the music wafting through screened windows into the night. Coal oil lamps cast a golden glow over the pine paneling and sparkled off the shiny brass barometer. Thomas and Mary sat in comfortable wicker chairs reading from the ship's library, which contained Shakespeare's complete works, volumes by Tolstoy and Galsworthy, and books borrowed from the Bemidji library. Thomas cared about Mary's intellectual development and prepared her for the challenges she would face in a man's world. He treated his pretty, curly-haired daughter as an honorary boy, training her to be independent and self-confident.

Two Chippewa boys, Bob Cloud and Jim Thunder, both twice Mary's age, became her summer friends. They called her "Manee" and taught her Chippewa phrases. One hot summer day, Bob fished from the lower deck of the *Northland*. He baited a hook with a piece of bacon and tied it to a string attached to a green willow stick. As Mary watched the line trailing in the water, Bob's rod bent, and he flung it upward. "A shiny brown-green pickerel flopped on the deck beside us. Bob picked it up by its tail, bashed its head against the deck, and it lay there inert. Except for flies, I had not seen many creatures killed."[11] Mary took her consternation to her father in the wheelhouse. "It was so alive and shining. And then so quick, it was dead, and the shine faded." Her father nodded. "Let's let things live, Papa. I don't shine, but I like living."[12] Mary could not bear the killing of animals, even for food, and eventually became a conservationist like Thomas, who refused to hunt for deer because he did not like killing them.[13]

During the winter, Mary practiced Chopin études and accompanied the Sunday school choir. In March 1920, she played Beethoven's piano solo "Minuet in G" for the Women's Study Club.[14] On a Sunday in November that same year, Mary went to the church early to practice an unfamiliar hymn. She overheard a heated argument between her mother and a Sunday school teacher, each claiming to be in charge of the Sunday school. Mary was disturbed by the hypocrisy of her mother and the other lady. How could they teach children to love and respect their neighbors when they did not? When she got home, twelve-year-old Mary announced she was resigning from Sunday school. Her mother protested, saying she was being cruel and breaking her heart, but Mary would not relent and never went to Sunday school again.[15]

Mary came to prefer her father's world, filled with outdoor adventures, music, reading, and reflection. Her mother focused on household chores and centered her social life around the Christian Science congregation in Bemidji. Mary's expectations for male behavior owed much to the standards she observed in her youth. Her father treated her with respect, encouraged her to see the wider world, and fostered her ambition to write. Mary could not have had a more secure foundation than her father's love. His unwavering support created an inner expectation that all men would adore her.

Thomas Welsh continued to be proud of Mary, and he cheered her climb through the male-dominated field of journalism. After he retired, Thomas taught himself to type, and he wrote short stories, completed an autobiography, and drafted political tracts supporting Progressive causes. He enjoyed a glass of Irish whiskey but controlled his intake. Mary's memoir pays tribute to her father and the lessons he taught her. While she felt love from her mother and appreciated her kindness, she did not want to become like her—trapped in a house in a remote town.

◆

Carl Sandburg's poem "Chicago" was published when Mary was six years old, and she read it several times in her youth. His homage to the city "with lifted head singing so proud to be alive and coarse and strong and cunning" pulled her like gravity. She knew she had to leave Bemidji, the "soft little city" of her childhood, and face the "strong, husky, brawling" reality of Chicago. [16] In grade school, influenced by *The Bemidji Pioneer* editor who often dined with her parents, Mary decided to become a journalist. This was an unusual ambition for a young girl in those times, but the courage of the suffragettes succeeding in getting the vote for women inspired twelve-year-old Mary. In grade eight, she received first prize "for the use of correct words" and finding the right word became an obsession for the rest of her writing life. [17]

After graduating from high school, Mary spent a year at the Bemidji teacher's college. Then, she persuaded her parents to send her to the journalism program at Northwestern University in Evanston, just north of the city of her dreams. Professor Melville Herskovits, a noted American anthropologist, inspired her with his lectures about the trading economies and culture of West Africa. He opened her eyes to the world beyond her small town and raised issues of ethnic and racial equality in America. Herskovits created a hunger for travel to far-off places to discover and question, understand and describe. [18]

Mary attracted male attention and flitted from boy to boy, taking none of them seriously. At Northwestern, she fell in love with a drama student who won her heart with his poetic eyes and gentle manner. Larry Cook drove her to meet his parents in Ohio, and on their way they found a justice of the peace who married them in his sitting room on May 30, 1930. Mary had just turned twenty-two, and they soon realized they had very different expectations for their lives. Mary found her husband selfish and self-centered. He was not solicitous of her, as her father had been, and her first marriage ended almost as casually as it had begun, without rancor or nastiness.

The Great Depression which began in 1929 devastated the timber industry, and Thomas could no longer afford to support Mary in college. She took part-time catering jobs, serving the wealthier students, but she questioned the value of a college degree and decided it made more sense to get a job in journalism. In 1930, she dropped out of Northwestern to edit a trade journal, *The American Florist*. Mary worked long hours and stayed for two years, earning seventy-five dollars a week. She impressed the publisher, who wrote a laudatory letter of reference, noting she "Capably and competently disposed of every division of her work and unsparingly disregarded the hours involved."[19]

In 1932, Mary became a reporter for a company that published five weekly neighborhood newspapers on Chicago's north side. Later that year, she landed a job at the *Chicago Daily News*, and her dream of becoming a journalist came closer. Mary wanted an ordinary reporter's position but was assigned to the "society department" under its imperious editor, Miss Leola Allard, who tried to make the women's pages the finest in the country. Mary recalled, "She had a voice that was frequently irritating. You could hear her from quite a distance, and work used to stop when Leola had someone on the carpet. I think she really felt a day in which no tears were evoked from someone on her staff was a worthless day."[20]

Mary's colleague, Adeline Fitzgerald, described the society pages as "a young" department, and Mary "was our baby. She was little and elfin and cute, with extraordinarily small neat ears which the women's editor alternately praised and pinned back. Her fluffy yellow dandelion head survived, where weightier heads fell. Stamina, we called it."[21] The reporters worked long hours, and Mary learned to write under pressure and became braver. She adopted the nom de plume of "Margot, Jr." and wrote a daily column reporting on Chicago's society weddings and dinner parties. Her friend Sarah Boyden remembered, "within a few months she knew more people in Chicago society than did many of its members." Mary cut her curly hair very short and achieved "an aureoled appearance, much more striking than the more conventional bob she had worn before."[22]

Leicester Hemingway, the famous author's younger brother, was also a reporter at the *Chicago Daily News*. Though Leicester was seven years younger than Mary, they became friends, and she went sailing with him a few times. In his memoir, Leicester recalled, "Mary was a cheerful, petite blonde from Minnesota who kept her stockings nicely pulled up and liked to sit on a desk swinging her legs while she talked." Fascinated by Ernest, she would say, "Gee, it must be wonderful to have a famous brother. Come on, tell us about him."[23] Mary read everything Ernest wrote, and she pestered Leicester to tell her about his older brother.

◆

In the spring of 1936, just after her twenty-eighth birthday, Mary spent her life savings on a ticket, boarded a steamer in Montreal, and made her way to London. She wandered the streets of London and fell in love with the city. Days later, in Paris, "after an all-night toot on the left bank," Mary lunched with journalists who told her stories of the impending war with Germany.[24] Mary decided on the spot that she wanted to stay and report on the action. One of her new friends gave her the telephone number for Canadian millionaire Max Atkin, known by his formal title Lord Beaverbrook, who owned several British newspapers.[25] Mary had nothing to lose and phoned the "Beaver" the following morning. "I just called him up as though I were in the habit of hanging on international telephones and chatting with Lords." Mary talked fast, and the idea that a young woman would travel from Paris to meet him persuaded the Beaver to grant a fifteen-minute interview. "I dug up practically my last cent and flew to London to visit the greatest newspaper tycoon in the world. He turned out to be a genuinely friendly guy."[26]

Mary made it to his home for four o'clock tea, and they had a brief chat about her wish to be a London-based journalist covering the coming war. He dismissed the idea there would be a war but told her to see the editor of his *Daily Express*, then the largest circulation English-language daily newspaper in the world. The butler called a cab and Mary shot to Fleet Street, where the editor informed her that as he already had an American girl on staff, he had no use for another. Defeated and deflated, Mary boarded a ship to New York the next day. She wrote to the Beaver, thanked him for his consideration, and asked him to remember her if a vacancy arose.

Mary returned to her old beat, "covering dog shows and murder trials, Gold Coast weddings, and raids on burlesque houses."[27] The arbitrary rule of Leola Allard seemed all the more aggravating. Mary tried to persuade the managing editor to give her a chance to work in the Paris or London bureaus. He noted her deficiency in French and said the man in London was doing an excellent job on his own. Mary spent a frustrating winter working at the paper, but in the spring her luck turned. Lord Beaverbrook's secretary called to say the Beaver was in Chicago, and he invited Mary to dine with him in his private suite that very evening. She agreed to meet him for lunch the next day at the Drake Hotel. A series of lunches and dinners followed, and it emerged that the old man was smitten with Mary. He was almost twice her age and asthmatic. His grand head rested on a weak body, and his legs were like sticks, and though Mary was not attracted to him, he was relentless. Mary kept asking him to find a place for her on the staff of the *London Daily Express*.

Perhaps to further his pursuit of Mary, the Beaver shared his philosophy of how a young woman ought to advance her career in Europe. Nothing would be gained through innocence or virtue. Instead, a young woman should realize her path would be easier if she had a powerful man as her sponsor and supporter. And how to find such a supporter? She must learn how to please men and bring those secrets to the bed of her sponsor. Her influence would grow, and her career would blossom. Romantic love was a waste of time.[28] The Beaver's pale blue eyes sparkled as he imparted this advice. In her memoir, Mary said the Beaver did not change her mind. Many years later, Mary counseled Valerie Hemingway that "to be a successful female journalist it was advantageous to sleep your way to the top. I found that very amusing. It had not been in any of the handbooks I had consulted."[29] Whether Mary took her own advice in the case of Lord Beaverbrook, we cannot say.

Before Beaverbrook returned to England, he tried to persuade Mary to accompany him on a trip up the Nile, but she declined and pressed him for a real job. He agreed that if she came to London, he would help her find work. Mary didn't trust the Beaver, but she took a risk, sold her furniture, and scraped together enough money for a one-way ticket across the Atlantic. The Beaver invited her to lunch at his country estate in Surrey and offered her a job on one of his three papers. She chose the *Daily Express* and turned up for work on July 2, 1937, the same day the world learned Amelia Earhart had disappeared over the Pacific. The editor asked Mary to write a thousand-word piece about Earhart's misadventure.

◈

Despite the *Daily Express*'s grand facade, the newsroom was cramped, and Mary shared a rough plank table with four other reporters. They covered news in London and the country south of Birmingham. Her favorite assignments were those needing pictures when she was able to travel with the friendly photographers in their cars. Driving through the countryside, she learned about rural England over pints of beer and bangers and mash in village pubs. Mary also enjoyed her social life in London, partying with fellow reporters and lunching at the pubs surrounding the *Express*'s offices. An Australian journalist, Noel Monks, began paying attention to her. He was bulky but fit from his swimming days in Australia and carried his large frame in well-pressed suits. His bullet-shaped head was prematurely gray, and his ruddy face cleanly shaved. Noel extended a protective shield around Mary, which she found comforting and attractive. He was stern and ponderous but Mary discovered his gentle, private side. Noel had an underlying lack of confidence because he had stuttered as a child. Even as a young reporter, Noel continued to stammer, and when he got excited he stuttered until he could settle down.

Though only thirty-one, Noel was already a seasoned war correspondent. He had reported on the Italian invasion of Ethiopia in 1935 and was the first correspondent to reach Guernica after the Germans firebombed the Basque town on April 26, 1937. Noel reported in the *Daily Express*, "I walked this evening through the still-burning town. Hundreds of bodies were found in the debris. Most were charred beyond recognition. At least two hundred others were riddled with machine-gun bullets as they fled to the hills. . . ." He estimated "Of the four thousand bombs dropped by the raiders, a thousand were incendiary, and one thousand were aerial torpedoes."[30] Noel was haunted for weeks by the sight of the blackened bodies of fifty women and children huddled together in a cellar. He told Mary they thought they had found a safe refuge, but the fires burned them alive. Mary felt sickened by this story, and it fed her hatred of fascism.

Mary had come a long way from the backwoods of Minnesota to the cosmopolitan diversions of London. Exhilarated to be in the center of things, she was happy to be dating a famous foreign correspondent who shared stories of his adventures.

TWO

You May Sleep Quietly

September 1938–June 1940

As Mary and Noel dated, the war came closer and interrupted their lives. In late September 1938, the *Express* sent Mary to Munich to report on Prime Minister Neville Chamberlain's meeting with Hitler, Mussolini, and Daladier of France. She watched the crowds chanting "Heil, Heil" as Hitler drove slowly to the meeting in an open car. He responded "with a handwave that looked bored, languid, foppish."[1]

The next morning, Chamberlain waved to cheering crowds from the balcony of the Fuhrerbau. The people of Munich did not want war and yelled, "Heil Chamberlain."[2] After further talks that afternoon, Chamberlain called a press conference in his suite. Mary watched him, wearing a scraggly mustache and stiff wing collar, announce in his posh accent that Britain and France had agreed to Hitler's demand for the Sudetenland's annexation in exchange for a treaty of peace. Chamberlain flew back to England, and cheering crowds greeted him as he read the letter he and Hitler had signed promising to never go to war again. Later, Chamberlain appeared in the window of 10 Downing Street to greet the happy crowds and utter the infamous words, "You may sleep quietly; it is peace for our time."[3]

After Mary reported the news of Chamberlain's Munich press conference, the *Express* ordered her to the Czech border to observe the German occupation of the Sudetenland. She crossed the Danube and saw columns of German troops waiting for orders two miles from the border. The German major commanding the operation greeted Mary graciously and sent her to a country house where she could wait until they finished the process. His refined manners underlined her powerlessness and made her feel hopeless. She shared her anger toward Chamberlain with her friend Herbie Clark: "This anger runs along my nerves and brain like a flame—fury at the injustice toward the Czechs, fury that Chamberlain runs this country into God knows what shame without giving them a chance to speak, even in Parliament." Mary said she had transformed from "a violent pacifist into a violent fighter. That's what's happened to most of the people around here." The things they said about Chamberlain infuriated her: "Hells delight if thoughts could kill. He made me sick at my stomach this morning, repudiating all responsibility for everything."[4]

A week later, Mary returned to London and Noel. They had been dating for a year, and they married at the registry office in Chelsea Town Hall on December 31, 1938.[5] Noel was thirty-two and divorced from his former wife, Susan, with whom he had a son, John, and Mary was twenty-nine. For many months of their courtship, Noel had failed to mention to Mary that he had a son from his first marriage. When he later apologized for this "oversight," he told Mary, "the boy meant nothing to him and never would."[6] Noel was a mild-mannered man who abstained from drink and delighted in provisioning their marital nest. Mary told her parents she enjoyed being called "Mrs. Monks."[7] They moved into a small house in Chelsea with gilt chairs and red velvet cushions and carpets, and from the upstairs windows they could look into a walled garden bright with flowers and singing birds. On Sundays, they slept until noon and finished their breakfast at 3:30 P.M. They read the Sunday papers, went for walks in Hyde Park, and watched children feeding the swans on the beach of the Serpentine. Walking home, arm in arm, they talked about the future. Noel wanted Mary to move with him to Australia, but she wanted to return to the States to be close to her mother when they eventually had children.

Meanwhile, the war grew closer and threatened to pull them apart. In March 1939, Chamberlain promised the Polish government that if the Germans attacked Poland, the British and French governments would immediately provide all necessary support to the invaded country. Beaverbrook warned against the guarantee to Poland, but Chamberlain ignored his advice.[8] In April, the British government instituted compulsory military service. Over the following weeks, Mary's reports in the *Daily Express* sketched London's poor and powerless as they prepared for war. Mary interviewed Mrs. Edith Spong, who decorated her ARP (air raid precaution) shelter with curtains and a toy elephant on the roof. Mrs. Spong said, "We will be live sardines, tin and all . . . It doesn't look big enough to hold us all." A photo showed a large woman holding a small child on her knee in the doorway of a tiny, corrugated shed.[9] Mary reported on four young unmarried couples who were "blazing with indignation" because their landlord would not permit them to build an ARP shelter in their back garden. The landlord refused to tear up the paved terrace. "Who will pay to replace the tarmac?" he asked. One of the young women appeared less angry and more fatalistic, asking, "but are these shelters so important? Would they really save us if one of the big bombs dropped on the street?"[10] Mary's stories capture the spirit of the people she met.

In May 1939, the *Express* dispatched Noel to Gibraltar and Tangier to cover the German fleet in the Mediterranean, then to Morocco to report on France's preparedness. Next, he covered the Spanish camps at Perpignan, France, where some three hundred thousand refugees from Franco's fascism lived, forgotten by the world. Then, they sent him to Jerusalem to report on the chaos in Palestine. Finally, the *Express* assigned him to Cyprus and the British General Headquarters for Middle East Land Forces.

Meanwhile, Mary continued to write prosaic stories about life in London. In late June, she met Sam Cotton, a pensioner from the Isle of Wight who had traveled to London to present a petition requesting an increase in the old-age pension. Afterward, he drank tea at the Houses of Parliament. "A very nice tea, this," he said. "I think it is costing more than I have to live on in a week. Such a lot!"[11]

The *Express* ordered Noel back to London, and the couple took a romantic vacation on the wide sandy beaches of France's Saint-Jean-de-Luz, the fashionable resort town. They spent hours lying in the sand and playing in the surf. A giant sea wall, started by Napoleon but finished thirty years later, protected the port from violent Atlantic storms. The rolling surf lapped at the edge of the town and Mary thought it spectacular compared to Bemidji and the bloodsucker-infested beaches of Leech Lake. They ate fresh seafood brought to restaurants by the flotilla of fishing boats moored in Port de Pêche, strolled along plane tree-lined streets, walked to the lighthouse, and retreated to their bed. They tried their luck in the casino and took a car to Biarritz to dine in splendor and play baccarat at the magnificent Hotel du Palais, frequented by the Spanish aristocracy since the Spanish Civil War.

The next move in the international chess game came on August 24, 1939, when Stalin signed a Non-Aggression Pact with Hitler's foreign minister. The agreement paved the way for Hitler's attack on western Europe, for he knew the Russian bear on his eastern flank would remain in hibernation. Hitler could now fight a one-front war and only twelve days of peace remained. On Friday, September 1, the BBC reported German troops had crossed the Polish border. The Luftwaffe firebombed Warsaw using the same brutal technique they perfected at Guernica's expense. Chamberlain's promise of "peace for our time" became a naïve failure to appease Hitler's ruthless ambition. Mary waited in Downing Street for a reaction from the prime minister's office. None came. Instead, Chamberlain went to the House of Commons that evening to deliver an ultimatum: the Germans were to withdraw their troops from Poland or the British government would fulfill its obligation to Poland. The Germans did not reply.

That afternoon, Noel's editor summoned him to Fleet Street. "Monks, we will be at war on Sunday. The War Office and Air Ministry have asked us for names of two correspondents to represent us. I have put you down for the RAF. Is that all right?"[12] Noel was delighted and took a taxi to Moss Brothers to buy a tailor-made uniform. Two days later, at 11 A.M. on Sunday, September 3, 1939, just as Mary was preparing breakfast, Chamberlain came on the radio to announce that, given the German failure to comply with the British ultimatum, a state of war was in effect.

A week later, Noel set off for Reims in the heart of France's Champagne country. He stayed at the luxurious Lion d'Or, next to the suite the Duke and Duchess of Windsor used when they visited the front. For the next seven months of what became known "as the phony war" (that period between the declaration of war by the United Kingdom and the German invasion of France), Noel covered the operations of the RAF's Advanced Air Striking Force, made up of two British squadrons of Hurricane fighters. They were to hit the German forces when and if they entered France. The French were optimistic about repelling a German invasion, believing the defensive positions making up the Maginot Line would protect them.

Noel found the French attitude appalling, and he told Mary the Maginot Line was the biggest hoax of the war because the guns pointed in the wrong direction. Several correspondents wrote pieces critical of the Maginot Line, and one suggested they should strengthen fortifications at Sedan, the very place where the

Germans would soon enter France. French censors deleted all references in the press to the vulnerability of French defenses.

Using Noel's connections, Mary traveled to join him in France to report on the British Expeditionary Force's living conditions. During Christmas 1939, the much-loved Gracie Fields, decorated by the king for her services to entertainment and recuperating from cervical cancer, came to entertain the troops. "Officers not invited. Only petty officers, Tommies, and aircraft-maintenance crews could come. Spirits ballooned."[13] Mary and Noel watched Gracie's inspired performance at the Reims Opera House. After the show, soldiers climbed into lorries and hundreds of voices sang "Roll out the barrel" as they drove home in the frosty air. Little did they suspect that five months later, they would be on the verge of extinction on the beaches of Dunkirk.

In January, Mary returned to London to interview the American Ambassador to Britain, Joseph Kennedy, Sr. (the future president's father). Having returned from a visit to Germany, he didn't believe the French and English could hold out against the mighty German forces and Kennedy encouraged appeasement. Mary filed a story describing the ambassador's views but editors eviscerated her piece, stifling the unwelcome news that the American Ambassador did not believe Britain could defend herself. Mary persuaded the *Daily Express* to send her back to France and she found a pleasant flat in Paris near Les Invalides. She enrolled in French classes, spent time at the Ritz bar meeting journalists, and wrote pieces she considered merely decorative. The French officials she interviewed seemed oblivious to the threat posed by Germany and deflected questions. During that spring, Mary met a fellow journalist, Kenneth Koyen, at the French language class for foreigners given by the Alliance Française at the Sorbonne. Koyen provided a snapshot of Mary: "rather stocky at about 5'2". She had brown hair, blue eyes, sharp features, and a self-assured manner." Koyen and Mary nodded at each other during the classes, but they did not chat, instead giving their attention to the instructor, who spoke English as well as she spoke French.[14]

Mary thought the French were living in denial of the German menace. Meanwhile, she and Noel visited between Paris and Reims, and she felt secure when she was with him. The French illusion of security fractured on May 10, 1940, when the Germans began a thorough and devastating bombing campaign against the Allies in France. German forces executed a rapid attack at Sedan, the weakest point of the French defenses, and drove to the Channel, encircling and trapping

British troops. The Luftwaffe vastly outnumbered Noel's Hurricane squadrons, which retreated deeper into France, and the correspondents left their comfortable lodgings in Reims and followed the squadrons south. Over the next month the German attack became relentless and they pushed the British Expeditionary Force closer to the sea. When France's defenses collapsed, the British had to save themselves, abandoning their equipment and evacuating Dunkirk in hundreds of small civilian boats. In four days, from May 28 to May 31, 1940, some three hundred and fifty thousand troops retreated to Britain.

Noel visited Mary in Paris on June 10. They dined with friends at the elegant Cascades in Le Bois, and Mary and her friends enjoyed two bottles of an exquisite Château Mouton Rothschild. Noel drank only water. They could hear the rumble of massive artillery explosions in the distance as the fighting came closer. Taking a cab back to Mary's flat, they saw convoys of trucks loaded with file cabinets and office equipment abandoning the city of light. The French government was pulling out of Paris, and they realized the time to leave had arrived. Mary packed in twenty minutes, leaving most of her clothes, books, and all her grandmother's silver in the care of her landlady.

They caught a taxi to Gare Austerlitz and ran down the platform alongside the train, already filled to bursting with desperate Parisians fleeing the city. Finding space on the last coach, Mary sat on her suitcase next to a spaniel and his old master who had been a curator at the Louvre. Mary and Noel got off at the city of Blois in central France where the French government planned to re-establish itself. They found a hotel and spent a restless night. In the morning, it became apparent the collapsing French government would move to Bordeaux. Mary saw no reason to stay in Blois and found a ride to Biarritz with a wealthy American woman she had befriended in Paris. Noel stayed behind.

After an arduous drive, Mary arrived at the coastal resort town of Biarritz and found a pleasant hotel near the central square. Suffering from a cold and fever, she slept for two days. On the third day, she strolled the beach and watched the relentless waves break against the ancient rocks. Eons of crashing water had carved them into jagged sculptures standing in the turquoise sea surrounded by salty spray. Mary walked to the Hotel du Palais, lingered at the outdoor café, sipped an espresso, smoked a few cigarettes, and watched the pounding waves. She had abandoned all her worldly goods in Paris and realized she might as well get back to London. A man at the next table told her a few ships were still carrying passengers from Bordeaux to England, and this might be the last chance to escape from the German troops.

Late that afternoon, Noel arrived, his clothes caked with dust and his eyes bloodshot from lack of sleep. Mary felt relieved to see his smiling face through the stubble of his gray beard. He told her about walking the roads to Biarritz, clogged with refugees carrying all they had. After Noel cleaned up, they walked to a restaurant and bumped into the same man who had driven them several times from Saint-Jean-de-Luz to the casinos in Biarritz the year before. Luckily, they had tipped him well, and he agreed to drive them to Bordeaux for only twice the regular tariff.

The following day, they arrived in Bordeaux and found the city teeming with people desperate to escape the Nazis. Mary and Noel managed to buy tickets on the last ship to leave Bordeaux, the *Madura*. Over sixteen hundred people jammed into the small steamer designed to carry two hundred and fifty passengers—among them many of the journalists Mary and Noel had befriended in London and France, plus the staff of the British embassy. They stood at the rail watching nervously as the boat cleared the harbor while bombs fell around them. The *Madura* zigzagged for five days and nights to avoid torpedoes. Despite the ever-present risk, Mary slept well on the deck, under the stars, on an air mattress provided by a generous crewman. On June 25, 1940, the *Madura*, escorted by a British destroyer, reached Falmouth's quiet harbor. "The ordered greenery of England never looked so hospitable and comforting, verdant hills sloping down to the neat town of Falmouth, as it did that June morning when we drew into the quiet harbor."[15]

THREE

It Would Be Just Like That Bloody Hitler to Try His Invasion on Christmas

July 1940–November 1941

M ary was delighted to be back among feisty Londoners and away from the depressed, surrendering French. She found a flat in their old Chelsea neighborhood and Mary resumed shopping with her local butcher, greengrocer, and provisioner. Despite the rationing and frugality, Mary felt at home. On the zigzagging *Madura*, Mary had decided it would be better if she reported for an American rather than a British newspaper. Shocked by the speed of the German advance, she felt the urgency of persuading her fellow citizens to come to Britain's aid. "Nearly all of the correspondents I knew held similar estimates of England's desperate plight," Mary recalled, "and hoped by their dispatches to indicate to the American people that they must take the honorable risk and quickly send the British help."[1]

Mary phoned Walter Graebner, the bureau chief for *Time* magazine in London, with whom she had worked at the *Daily News* in Chicago. Graebner regarded Mary so highly he asked her to come in at once, but she wanted a day off to arrange her things. On July 10, 1940, she began working at *Time*'s offices in Dean Street,

Soho—the first day of the air war over Britain.* At the *Daily Express,* each reporter wrote and filed stories published under their byline. *Time*'s formula was different because it was a weekly magazine rather than a daily paper. *Time* reporters sent in their material by cable and editors rewrote "the cablese" and blended it with wire service reports to create a coherent story covering the last week. The magazine stories were usually combined efforts and *Time* published few pieces with bylines. Despite this policy, *Time-Life* published several articles during the war under the byline "Mary Welsh."

Mary contributed to many stories about the threatened German invasion. *Time* reported the Nazis aimed to close the coast of Southeast England to British shipping. German submarines attacked convoys and docks, and massive German bombing raids trapped British airplanes on the ground.[2] Convinced an invasion was imminent, British authorities evacuated all women, children, and foreigners from areas within twenty miles of the coast. Winston Churchill replaced Chamberlain as prime minister and he concluded that to stop the German invasion, the British needed to achieve air superiority.[3] He appointed Lord Beaverbrook as minister of aircraft production in his National Coalition Government. *Time* approved the appointment of "the bumptious result-getting, self-made man, Lord Beaverbrook, the impish 146-pound" owner of the *London Daily Express.*[4]

Mary worked on the *Time* cover story about Beaverbrook, published on September 16, 1940. She toured aircraft and ammunition factories and interviewed the men in charge. Then, she visited the Beaver at his office on the embankment. As he escorted Mary through his outer office past rows of male secretaries, he asked in a loud voice, "And tell me, is your husband giving you sexual satisfaction?" Mary supposed the Beaver wanted to embarrass her because he had not forgiven her for refusing to cruise the Nile with him.[5] The cover story asserted, "Even if Britain goes down, it will not be Beaverbrook's fault. If she holds out, it will be his triumph. This is a war of machines. It will be won on the assembly lines."[6] The story lauded the Beaver's unconventional but effective methods. "By nagging, harrying, wheedling, the Beaver got underlings to assume responsibility." The appointment of an unelected "bowling, boasting, gauche little man from the

---

* The *Time* offices were at 2-4 Dean Street, just off Oxford Street, in an undistinguished red brick five-story building, now converted to a Tesco Express grocery store. Farther down the street sits The French House, a bar that served as the unofficial headquarters of General Charles de Gaulle and the French resistance in London.

colonies" to a position second only to Churchill was as unbelievable—even to the Beaver himself—as if they had appointed him the Archbishop of Canterbury.[7]

Throughout Britain, civilians trained in self-defense, preparing to defend their homeland. Mary joined a women's rifle brigade and drilled with them until she lost interest because they couldn't practice with live ammunition, which was being saved for the real war. The fear of invasion was palpable, and the saleswoman in Mary's greengrocers shop kept a long knife under a folded newspaper next to the coin box. "If I ever meet one of those Germans, I'll swish his head off," she said, lifting the paper and showing Mary her weapon.[8]

◆

In August and September, the Germans launched massive daylight raids, first targeting naval bases and coastal air defenses, then RAF bases and aircraft factories. Mary traveled to the bomb sites to report on the damage. She recalled Londoners slept in the Underground, "where at least the noise of the bombs and ack-ack guns was muffled." Some nights when she had worked late and Soho was the primary target, "those few of us in our office who still lived in London moved down to pallets in the airless shelter of our building and Dean Street." Mary remembered, "I only slept there once; walking home through the noise was so much preferable to public sleeping."[9]

Hitler's Operation Sea Lion, the plan for invading Britain, assumed German mastery of the air over the English Channel to protect invasion barges ready to depart along the Dutch and Belgian coasts. The Luftwaffe began daylight raids to wear down the RAF in a war of attrition. Relying on "neutral experts," *Time* reported the Germans had twice as many bombers and fighter planes as the British. The Germans had eleven thousand pilots, the British only seven thousand. While RAF pilots flew back-to-back missions, the Germans took a full day's rest after each day of flying. *Time* concluded, "On paper, the outcome looked inevitable, only a matter of time."[10]

The Germans planned the invasion for September, assuming the Luftwaffe would have achieved air superiority by then. On August 16, two thousand five hundred German planes attacked the London docks and munitions stores near Tilbury on the southwest, killing a thousand civilians. Two days later, they flew up the Thames estuary and attacked London again, endangering the city's water supply. Mary filed reports detailing the death and destruction.[11] The Germans launched daylight raids of eighteen hundred to two thousand planes in the following days. As German losses grew, they reduced the flights' size, deploying one thousand planes a day in groups of fifty or sixty aircraft at a time. The Luftwaffe expected the constant pressure would cause the collapse of the British forces. However, as *Time* reported, railway lines suffered no significant dislocation, and Lord Beaverbrook claimed the production of fighters and bombers had reached an all-time high.[12]

On September 6, the British bombed Berlin. This tactic surprised and enraged the Germans, and they stopped bombing radar stations and airbases and began attacking London. The German response allowed the British to repair their airbases, and by September 12, most of the airfields were operational and many of the aircraft had been replaced.[13] The civilians of London now lived on the front line of the war, and Mary wrote about the impact of the bombing on a typical Londoner: "The crudest, most cruel, and least effective attacks of the Nazi Luftwaffe have been in its indiscriminate bombing of the homes and properties of the people of Britain."[14]

Mary told of Mrs. Lillian Hart and her husband, George, who lived in the working-class district of Bethnal Green in the city's East End. George, a cabinet-maker since he was fourteen, had made all the furniture in their flat. After attending the National Day of Prayer, Lillian walked down the road with her dog, Gyp, to meet George coming home from work. As the church bell rang eight o'clock, an air raid siren wailed, and she rushed back to her flat to show people the way to the shelter under the vicarage. She heard a screamer coming down, and then another, and another. After sending Gyp upstairs to the kitchen to hide under the table where he stayed during raids, Lillian ran back to the shelter and stood inside. She heard a dull thud, followed by a giant explosion. A shower of broken glass fell around her, but miraculously, she escaped injury. Children screamed, and a woman moaned in the debris. Lillian scrambled to the shelter's front door to help the people coming in. Glancing up, she saw her flat was gone. The sky appeared where her bedroom had been. Feeling numb, she went looking for her cat, Timmy, and Gyp. She returned to work at the shelter until late that night when George came. They embraced and looked over the pile of rubble that had been their home.

In the morning, while Lillian looked for Timmy, she found her black pleated skirt slashed and torn hanging from a bush on the other side of the vicarage. She spotted their ration cards and a pair of pajamas George had just bought, still in the cellophane wrapper. Losing the flat and all the furniture he had crafted devastated George, and Lillian tried to comfort him, saying they could start again. Amid the rubble, they turned up the biscuit tin holding all their savings. They found Gyp's body draped over a rafter, but discovered no trace of Timmy. [15]

◆

The Luftwaffe launched two massive bombing raids on London on September 15, 1941, now commemorated as Battle of Britain Day. The Germans believed the RAF lay crushed on the brink of defeat, but British pilots were rested. Crews had repaired their aircraft, and Bomber Command brought in squadrons from around the country to defend London. The first wave of about two hundred and fifty bombers arrived over the Channel just before noon. Swarms of RAF Hurricanes and Spitfires attacked, breaking up bomber formations, allowing only about half to deliver their bombs over the city. The rest of the bombers scattered and dropped their loads over a wider area, doing less damage than intended. A second wave came in the early afternoon, and the attacking Spitfires and Hurricanes again broke up the formations. Harried by the pursuing fighters, bomber crews dropped their loads at random, hoping to lighten their aircraft and make a safe retreat across the Channel.

In an optimistic account of the conflict, the *Daily Telegraph* reported the RAF destroyed one hundred and seventy-five German planes but lost only thirty. [16] These figures proved to be incorrect but did wonders for morale. As *Time* later reported, the Germans lost sixty-one aircraft, and the RAF lost thirty-one fighters. The RAF had managed a two-to-one kill ratio. [17] Since the dogfights took place over Britain, police or citizens captured downed German pilots. British pilots who had to bail out, or crash-land, could return to duty. Churchill visited Bomber Command's bunker at the height of the battle and observed that all the squadrons were flying. Churchill asked Air Vice-Marshall Keith Park, "What other reserves have we?" Park replied, "There are none." There was not one squadron left in reserve. [18]

The war of attrition settled in Britain's favor that day, and the Luftwaffe never had the strength to launch another massive daylight raid—Operation Sea Lion was postponed. However, the Germans had sufficient power to bomb London each night from October 1940 until May 1941. The Blitz was terrifying but did not break the will of the British people.

Mary and her friends had plenty of close calls during the extended bombings. One evening, Mary walked home alone from the Savoy in a fine new black suit. When she got to her flat and looked in the mirror, the suit was gray. "It was a night of incendiaries. I had flung sandbags on a couple of them that were burning along my way and had thrown myself prone on the pavement five times, during the mile or more when the descending screamers sounded too close."[19] A few nights later, Mary and Noel enjoyed drinks at home with three RAF friends when the air raid sirens sounded and anti-aircraft guns started firing. The young RAF men left for a club, and Mary began undressing for bed. She heard the scream of an incoming bomb and rushed into the hallway, just as an explosion blasted shards of glass through the curtains in her bedroom. The electricity went off. Noel found a flashlight and they went down two floors to the mattresses kept under the stairs for such a night. In the morning, Mary tasted dust in her mouth, and her eyes were red and stinging. A fine layer of combined dust and ash coated everything in the house. Burglar alarms sounded in the neighborhood, and fires burned on the horizon. When the bombing stopped, the resulting inconveniences proved intolerable. Everything was a mess. However, Mary grew closer to her neighbors through the shared experiences, and they managed with good humor and small kindnesses.

One night, a fragment of shrapnel blew through the window and sliced through Mary's ear lobe before blasting apart a sugar bowl. Mary saved the sugar before tending to her ear.[20] She felt terrified as she realized how close death had come. When Mary interviewed ordinary Londoners to assess the Blitz's effects on morale, she found stubborn pride and resilience, and she wrote a story for *Time* about "blitz business." She reported, "the measure of British sangfroid, and the 'business as usual' spirit in London, was shown by a crowd of several hundred women shoppers." They rushed for bargains at one of the big West End stores; at the same time, firefighters were digging through tons of debris in frantic efforts to release two hundred clerks entombed in the basement the night before by a bomb. Each day, thousands of shoppers and window-gazers flowed down Oxford Street, ignoring air raid alarms until German bombers appeared overhead. "They dawdled and browsed over displays of goods ticketed 'For Christmas,' in no hurry to pick up presents."[21] Mary contributed to a *Time* story on December 30, 1940, about "Blitzmas," describing how Londoners celebrated Christmas under the constant bombing. They abandoned traditional door-to-door caroling because of the blackout; carrots replaced fruit in Blitzmas pudding, and beef or mutton stood in for Christmas turkey or goose. They hung holly without mistletoe, which came from France, and British children scoffed at peacetime toys and asked for dolls wearing gas masks or toy war equipment. The British dared not let down their guard, for as one woman said, "It would be just like that bloody Hitler to try his invasion on Christmas."[22]

In early 1941, Noel attended a party at the home of the colonial secretary, Oliver Stanley. He spent "the most wonderful half hour of my life"[23] chatting with King George VI. They talked about the effect of the Blitz on the morale of the people. The king acted as an ordinary person might when visiting the home of a friend. During their talk, the king stammered, and so did Noel, fearing that as his old curse resurfaced, the king might think he was mocking him.

Mary and Noel continued spending Sundays in bed until noon, reading the papers and chatting about the news. Noel busied himself writing his first book, and Mary helped edit it.[24] *Fighter Squadron* traces the exploits of the pilots of the two Hurricane fighter squadrons Noel had followed in France. He writes in a sensational style about dogfights and heroism and high adventure, focusing on the feats of New Zealand's ace "lion-hearted" Cobber Kain. "No one ever heard Cobber Kain brag. No one ever knew him to go about with his chin stuck out, looking for trouble. Out of the cockpit of his fighting machine, he was mild-mannered and peace-loving." However, "In the cockpit, he was a killer. What more could a nation at war ask of a son?"[25] The final paragraph of *Fighter Squadron* is sheer propaganda. "There is a difference between unloading bombs on worker's homes in the dead of night and fighting it out in God's sky with the courageous dare-devil fighting pilots of the Royal Air Force. On that difference hangs the fate of Britain."[26]

While Noel worked on his book, Mary made broadcasts to America from the BBC building's bombproof basement. "We used to meet in the dank and smelly cafeteria deep in the roots of the building for tea and a final reading of scripts before we went on air at 3 A.M."[27] Mary met J. B. Priestley, the Yorkshire novelist, who, in his nightly "Britain Speaks" series, sketched a forceful portrait of a unified Britain waging a people's war.[28] He criticized the class system in England, arguing for social reform when they had won the war. He likened the struggle for independence from Nazi invasion and slavery to George Washington's battle for American freedom from tyranny.

Graham Greene, the famous author, later remarked that in the months following Dunkirk, Priestley became a leader second in importance only to Winston
Churchill.[29] Mary found him pedantic and arrogant, though he did advise her
that the most important quality in speaking is sounding sincere. She also worked
with actor Leslie Howard, star of *Gone With the Wind*, whose broadcast followed
hers. She enjoyed chatting with him and Priestley in the BBC cafeteria, deep
underground. Mary remembered walking home with Howard "in the black and
trembling streets beneath the noisy sky, listening everywhere, all the time for a
bomb scream to end in its bursting, watching the fires, washing off and sham-
pooing out the stench of the sheltering tubes."[30] A year later, Howard was dead
after the plane in which he flew on a diplomatic mission to assist British intelligence was shot down by enemy aircraft.[31]

FOUR

A Glamorous, Globe-Trotting
War Correspondent

December 1941–April 1943

I n her weekly letters to her parents, Mary extolled Noel's decency and her love
for him. She bragged to her mother that Noel served her Sunday breakfast in
bed and challenged her to get Tom, as she affectionately referred to her father, to
serve her toast and tea. Mary celebrated their domestic bliss.[1] On the evening of
December 7, 1941, Noel and Mary dined with friends at a fashionable restaurant
in Park Lane. A reporter from the *Express* rushed in with news: the Japanese
had bombed Pearl Harbor. Everyone realized the Americans might now enter
the war as combatants. Mary wrote in her diary, "My country is at war. May
her victory be speedy and decisive, her peace worthy of the fight."[2] Over the
Christmas holidays, the Monks spent a long weekend at *Time*'s country house,
Time Out, a stucco and timber house with large living rooms and many bedrooms
set among great trees near High Wycombe in the rolling hills of Buckinghamshire.
They hiked and talked about the impact of the war. Since the summer, some thirty
thousand civilians had died in German bombing raids, mainly in London. Bombs
had destroyed many homes but Noel and Mary had been lucky, and as 1941 ended,
they counted their blessings.

In early January, the *Express* ordered Noel to Singapore, but while he made
his way there the island city fell to the Japanese. The *Express* redirected him to
Australia, where he spent the next year covering the war in the Pacific. Mary could

not help wondering if he spent time with his first family during his Australian assignment, but Noel said nothing about it in his letters.

Mary told her parents she missed Noel "in all the little things—whistling at me in a special way he has, whenever I come in the door, snuggling on his lap, seeing his cheerful face smiling at me in the mornings, watching him prowl around the house like a flat-footed bear." She missed "the balanced judgment he lends our mutual life, and the protective barricade of love and affection, with which he surrounds me, and blocks out so much of the dreariness and pettiness, of the world outside."[3] She accepted his absence was necessary and did her best to cope by keeping herself busy with background assignments on the British economy and politics.

During the early years of the war, Mary was the only female correspondent accredited to the RAF. After she joined *Time-Life*, she became one of the first women accredited to the US Army, and she wore a regulation uniform while on duty. Dozens of American women reporters had tried but failed to achieve this status, and Mary felt justifiably proud of the distinction. Though she was bound by army rules and regulations, she had access to top officers and was on hand to write about US military operations. Her identity card showed she was five feet three inches tall, weighed one hundred twenty pounds, and enjoyed the rank of captain—likely one of the most petite officers in the US Army. Her rank did not convey power to command but allowed her access to the clubs reserved for officers. The black-and-white photo on her identity card was taken before she could have a uniform made by the tailor she and Noel shared. The lacy white collar of her blouse flowed over a dark sweater. Her hair color, described as "light," shines with a blonde luster. Mary became one of the women correspondents writing under fire in bombed cities and on battlefields, covering what used to be a man's assignment. They were "a capable, gutsy, and inquisitive bunch."[4]

In late January 1942, Mary took an overnight ferry across the Irish Sea to Belfast to cover the first American troops landing in the European theater. Though they were a small contingent, the "Red Bull" division members were important symbolically. They arrived less than two months after the Japanese attack on Pearl Harbor and signified America's commitment to defeating the Axis powers. Mary's byline featured on the piece she wrote for *Life* and the lead photo shows a helmet-wearing American sergeant hugging her. Mary reported that "the Yanks," as the Irish called them, were having a hard time keeping clean and warm in their

Nissan huts—"elongated igloos of corrugated iron, with cement floors."[5] She interviewed Irish girls who were most interested in meeting the soldiers. "A hotel chambermaid, aged nineteen, with the blue-black hair of the Normans and the blue eyes and white skin of the Celts, breathed, 'Ah, twill be lovely to see them.'" Local businessmen built wooden dance halls where soldiers met Irish girls, "for respectable colleens still don't go to pubs." Mary concluded, "in the Ulster mists, sensible boys from the Midwest should grow no more discontented than armies anywhere, and fonder than ever of home—unless Nazi bullets interfere."[6]

On her return to London, Mary worked on short pieces for *Time-Life* and completed a lengthy study on the economic effects of the war on Britain which traced the advance of socialism in the country. She met Harold Laski, a professor of economics and political theory at the London School of Economics, who came to be her hero. Laski was the intellectual leader of the non-communist British left, and he believed that only a socialist state could bring about a free society.[7] In her draft memoir, Mary described Harold Laski as "the brilliant, leftist political scientist whose contemporary pronouncements I cherished as near dogma."[8] She developed a keen interest in British politics and was influenced by her friends Laski and Michael Foot as her political views moved left.

Mary told her parents she was working steadily, but she was also eating well. The generosity of her friends allowed her to live beyond her means. Soon after Noel left, Mary realized it wouldn't do any good to shut herself away moping.[9] One general who took a romantic interest in Mary was Brigadier General Robert McClure, the military attaché to the American embassy in London. In 1942, General Eisenhower appointed him chief of intelligence for the European theater of operations.[10] McClure was eleven years older than Mary and possessive of her. She did not see the relationship going beyond the war or affecting her marriage, but she appreciated McClure's doting.

In May 1942, Noel cabled Mary telling her they might transfer him to Washington. She was excited by this news because she was planning a trip to America in July and she hoped they could synchronize their visits. Mary told her parents that nothing could pry her away from London if it weren't for them. "It's not disloyalty, this feeling, or being un-American. . . . it's that London is the most interesting city in the world . . . despite my affection for so many things and people at home, my interests and my friends are here."[11] Mary asked them to look at the cover story for *Time* on June 15, 1942, which she had written about General Brehon

Somervell, the man in charge of organizing the vast supplies to invade Europe.[12] "Somervell has plenty of ways of getting action. . . . He also knows where to go when he needs big things, but other agencies block his path." Somervell had two potent friends in Washington—Harry Hopkins and Franklin Delano Roosevelt.

In July 1942, Mary traveled to New York on the *Atlantic Clipper*, a British Overseas Airways flying boat, a luxurious, single-hulled plane capable of landing and taking off from water. *Time*'s P. I. Prentice reported, "two of America's top-flight generals saw her off: General Dwight 'Ike' Eisenhower, Commander of US Forces in Europe—and Brigadier General Robert McClure, the US Military Attaché in London."[13] This was enduring evidence of Mary's tight connections with the high command. *Time* brought Mary to New York to learn about the operations of the magazine. Once she understood the office culture, she discovered she had attained greater privileges than other women in the company. She told her parents the office "is working me steadily as a *Time* writer—that is, one of the little squad of people (supposed here to be very exalted) who polish off the cables from abroad and the news as it comes in the papers." The edited material "appears in *Time*. I am the first woman they've ever had writing foreign affairs (though there are lots of women around as secretaries and researchers)." Therefore, "everybody is watching me and the stuff I turn out very closely."[14]

Mary was well-qualified because she had reported about the war from London for years and had more experience than the men in the New York office. She worked hard and wrote several published pieces. The female researchers who didn't feel intimidated by her success were friendly. Men in the office ignored her and did not include her in their business lunches or drinks after work. An exception was William "Bill" Walton, who would become a lifelong friend. Born to a prosperous newspaper-owning businessman and his artistic wife, Walton was two years older than Mary.[15] Tall, blonde, and handsome with an endearing lopsided smile, Walton had a self-assured easy-going manner and a talent for friendship others found attractive. Years later, Walton was called "the epitome of a life-enhancer, someone who always added to the joy of life, someone who made any group of people snap and crackle."[16] With the onset of the war in Europe, *Time-Life* began building up its team of reporters and they invited Walton to join the company. He worked in the New York headquarters and when Mary arrived he shared his office with her. Soon she called him "Willie" and he called her "Welshie," and they enjoyed snappy chats about life and became close. Walton told Mary his wife suffered from depression and mental instability, and he worried how she would manage with their children if *Time* posted him to London.

Meanwhile, Mary informed her parents, several publishers had asked her to write books and articles about her war experience in Britain. Tom shared his pride at her recognition as a serious journalist. Adeline thought Mary had done enough for the war effort and that she should stay home in the safety of America. Mary rejected her mother's appeals, writing, "I know how you feel about it, Mommy, that I've done my bit about the war and ought to able now to sit back and take it easy." She couldn't do that because "[t]here is a tremendous job to be done by my generation toward winning this war, and particularly toward winning the peace afterward . . . my place is going back to London and writing about it for America."[17] Mary displayed as much commitment as any soldier. She would do her vital job—writing about the war so Americans would understand the stakes.

Mary visited her parents in Thief River Falls, Minnesota, finding them healthy but agitated about how little money they had. She deposited funds in their account from her small salary and said she would help provide for them—and she kept her promise. Mary felt lucky in her parents. "None of my friends' fathers, benign as they might be, were as graceful or poetic as my father, and few of my friends' mothers were as pretty or witty as mine."[18]

The Bemidji Pioneer reported that Mary was fêted at neighborhood gatherings when she visited Thief River Falls and Bemidji. "Her job is to make sure *Time*'s editors and readers get the insider's viewpoint, and for that purpose, her friendships with so many of the great and near-great are invaluable."[19] The *Fargo Daily Tribune* declared, Mary lived the life of "a glamorous, globe-trotting war correspondent." She had married the famous war journalist Noel Monks, "and there was a Hollywood touch to her career."[20] The local papers celebrated Mary's escape from small-town life.

In late November, Noel arrived in New York and Mary moved to a larger apartment overlooking the skyline for his one-month visit. They went to plays, dined out with friends, and enjoyed the city as far as their budget allowed. Mary wrote to her parents, "Everything seems to come alive when we are together, and when we are apart, no matter how nice things are, life seems awfully dead."[21] She told them, "Noel has not stopped growing in mental and spiritual breadth and depth, and each time we come together again after a separation, I find more things to love and be proud of. We have so much to be thankful for."[22] Their month together had been like a honeymoon. Mary was delighted when the *Express* posted Noel back to London.

On January 1, 1943, Mary left on a flying boat and Noel followed in the refurbished coal bunker of a British steamer, the *Red Duster*. Mary's trip was extended when authorities "pushed [her] off one plane at Bermuda to make way for people with higher priorities." Mary told her parents she stayed in Bermuda for thirteen days "of wonderful hot, bright sunshine, palm trees, bananas ripening, and sea and sky even bluer than Minnesota's."[23]

Mary was glad to arrive in London and see everyone looking so fit and healthy, despite the rationing. She wrote to her father that the British wanted to "turn the war to good account—to improve all the people's health and freedom from want and fear."[24] Even the big corporations held meetings and put out reports on improvements to the national economy. Mary thought Americans, in contrast, were less optimistic and were fighting to get back something they had lost. Austerity became a way of life for the Monks, and they stayed in their tiny flat each night while Noel worked on his book and Mary did odd writing jobs. Mary told her parents she bothered Noel by snuggling her nose under his second chin or chewing his ear.[25] There were still splurges, and on her birthday they went out with friends to a revival of *Showboat*.

During the spring, Mary and Noel began drifting apart. While he traveled around Britain covering the British Army, she wrote about American strategic and political issues in London. They had less in common, and their incompatible work schedules meant even when they were both in London, they had little time for long walks together. Quiet evenings at home became rare, and they shared fewer confidences. "Among our friends, a dozen other couples appeared to be having similar difficulties."[26] Earlier, Mary had hoped to get pregnant, but now the time was not right. In mid-June 1943, Noel left England aboard a British destroyer to report on US troops landing on Sicily. He followed as they fought their way across the island, then Noel went to Algiers. Mary did not know when he would return but hoped to join him in the Mediterranean for the summer.[27] She took a small one-room apartment at 32 Grosvenor Street. Though it was too small for two people, she didn't bother looking for a larger flat because her future with Noel seemed uncertain.

Over the next year, Noel covered all the hot spots in the European theater. He landed with US troops on the beaches of Salerno, Italy, and followed the soldiers, reporting on the fighting as they moved toward Naples. Then, he landed with US troops on the beaches of Anzio.[28] The landings were dangerous and Noel narrowly escaped death several times. Following the Italian campaign, the *Express* assigned Noel to cover the Cairo Conference where Churchill, Roosevelt, and Chiang Kai-shek discussed plans for postwar Asia.

Mary missed Noel. When she came home from the office she heard no cheeky wolf-whistle as she walked into the room. There was no hulking bear to navigate around, no lap to cuddle on, and no one to wrap her in his arms at night when the bombs fell and the explosions came closer. Mary lay awake frightened, knowing she could not carry on alone, for she needed intimacy—not solitude. She began socializing with her set of men friends. Her feelings about Noel changed dramatically when two of his buddies on leave in London let it slip he was "enthusiastically" escorting a pretty girl about Cairo.[29] Mary was surprised, then angry, after she heard the news. Noel had betrayed her trust, and her affection for him vanished as she realized his absence involved more than geographical distance.

Once she was over the shock of Noel's infidelity, Mary decided the news gave her permission to sleep with other men. The driving ethic of wartime London was "eat, drink, and be merry, for tomorrow we may die," and many people had long ago added "and have a bit of fun on the side" to the list. Among Mary's friends, "she knew few 'war widows' who had not made friends from overseas."[30] Mary joined London's vibrant social life. As the war turned in favor of the Allies and they prepared for an invasion of Europe, everyone who was anyone passed through London.

As a journalist, Mary interviewed the men who played vital roles in the war effort and used her unique access to spice up her personal life. Drawn to strong military leaders, she had no qualms about using her charms to pry information from them. Most evenings, she hung out with reporters and newsreel producers arriving from the States to witness the coming Allied invasion of France. Rumors of the attack buoyed everyone's spirits.

Mary's protector was Charles Wertenbaker, a novelist and *Time*'s forty-one-year-old foreign editor. Wert was a big man with a booming voice, permanent bags under his eyes, and an appetite for the finer things in life.[31] He was a warm, egalitarian soul, and he stood by Mary when the men in the New York office of *Time* had questioned whether a woman could, or should, hold a writer's job. Wert believed in Mary's ability and ignored the prejudices of the male establishment.

It was thanks to him that she became the newsmagazine's first female foreign correspondent. [32]

Wert's attitude toward female journalists was refreshing but not surprising, as Mary was not the only one at *Time*'s London office. Wert had married another, curly-haired Lael Tucker. It was the third marriage for each of them. [33] Wert and Lael were a lively couple in the small world of expatriate journalists and went for dinner and drinks with Mary and their other friends. Like Mary, Lael had enrolled at university but never completed her degree. Lael told Wert that Mary was so attractive to men because she wasn't intimidated by them, no matter how high their social or military rank. Lael said she was "able, and tough, in a good sense." [34]

Mary was delighted when her New York colleague Bill Walton arrived at the London offices in late April 1943 to cover the American Air Force for *Time*. On many weekends, she and Walton traveled together to Time Out. As close as they were, it's doubtful they had an affair. In one of her letters to Walton following the war, Mary scolded him for having shown no romantic interest in her. "Willie beloved, I still consider I know you better than your wives or those many not very enchanting females you chose for your favors. The other night I was feeling very degraded because you never made a pass at me—it practically makes me an un-woman." [35]

The war pulled Mary and Noel apart, and they each found comfort in the arms of others. It was too soon to know if the rupture could be repaired.

FIVE

A Deft, Tricky Way with Men

August 1942–May 1944

I n her memoir, Mary described wartime London as "a Garden of Eden" for single women. "There was a serpent dangling from every tree and streetlamp, offering tempting gifts and companionship, which could push away loneliness, and warm, if temporary, affections." This provided relief from "the hovering, shadowy sense of mortality."[1] Bill Walton said it was a marvelous time for Mary, "Perhaps the best time in her life, full of laughs and full of lovers." She was "very little, very attractive, and always seemed to be the one to dash out into the blackout for the taxi." Confident in her dealings with men, she never ran after anyone. "If the chase was on, it was the guy's chase."[2] Walton recalled, "Mary was really a very liberated woman. She had such strings of lovers."[3] Lael Tucker admired Mary's "absolute guts" in any situation. Her courage was "one reason she was so attractive to men. And she . . . had a lovely torso and marvelous curly hair. You could do anything with that hair."[4]

As the first woman reporting on foreign affairs for *Time* magazine in wartime London, Mary was strongly supported by her editor, Walter Graebner. He wrote she was "without doubt, the ablest female journalist in London."[5] Bill Walton commended her "first-class, creative journalism," recognizing "what a long road she had traveled on her own from Bemidji to *Time*" in an occupation that had been a male preserve until then.[6] *Time*'s publisher, P. I. Prentice, told his readers that Mary's job meant getting the inside story. Any day in London, she might be seen having tea with the American ambassador, eating fish pie with the archbishop of

Canterbury, playing tennis with the minister of labor, or dining at the Savoy with the foreign minister.[7] Mary had deep connections inside the British government and within the American military command.

She became friends with Pamela Churchill, the estranged wife of Randolph, the prime minister's reckless, drinking, gambling son.[8] "For nearly twenty years, Pamela lived as a courtesan," and she invited Mary to lunches and dinners with American and British generals and leading political figures.[9] Mary recalled, "At some of her dinners, Pamela and I were the only women, she presiding, always soft-voiced and gentle, always glowingly beautiful, with what I considered the town's most interesting men surrounding her."[10] Mary noted, "For a single woman Pamela, without apparent effort, gathered together the most attractive people to be found."[11] Winston Churchill continued to dote upon his daughter-in-law and Pam remained an excellent source of news about the government's inner workings. Mary also gained insight into the British leadership through Lord Beaverbrook. The Canadian millionaire-turned-press baron counted Churchill as a close friend, and after serving as his minister of aircraft production became minister of state.

Mary knew General Dwight Eisenhower, the Commander of US Forces in Europe, and was friendly with his driver and companion, Kay Summersby.[12] American generals routinely invited Mary to dinners in London. Her hosts included Carl "Tooey" Spatz, Commander of Strategic Air Forces in Europe, Sam Anderson, Commander of the Air Materiel Command, and Omar Bradley, Commander of the 12th Army Group. Mary's connection to the American military could not have been closer, especially given her affair with Brigadier General Robert McClure, Chief of Intelligence for the European Theater of Operations. Mary told her parents that though she was working steadily, she enjoyed "getting free meals from my boyfriends, especially generals who like having a gal who's young and passing decent looking to take to dinner."[13]

◆

One evening, Mary and Connie Ernst went for dinner after work to the White Tower, a Greek bistro popular with journalists. Mary first met Connie when she arrived from New York to work for the Voice of America at the United States Office of War Information (OWI) on Wardour Street, just a short walk from the *Time* offices.[14] Connie was the daughter of Morris Ernst, a prominent Jewish

Democratic trial lawyer in New York. He was a dedicated defender of freedom of speech and a friend of FDR. [15] Connie had absorbed her father's liberal values and was a dark-haired beauty with a sharp sense of humor, exuding the energy of a string of ponies. Mary loved Connie's optimistic personality and they quickly became confidantes. Nine years younger than Mary, Connie sought her advice as she would from an older sister, and in return Connie trusted Mary and told her juicy details about many of the recent arrivals from New York.

In those days, Mary spent many evenings with Michael Foot talking about politics. (He would become a Labour MP and leader of the British Labour Party.) He loved that Mary was perky to the point of impudence, and he laughed at her witty denunciations and irreverent sketches of the high and mighty. As Mary and Connie entered the White Tower they ran into Michael, who asked if he could join them. He was smitten by Connie even before the Spam á la Grecque arrived because her liberal values and belief in a free press resonated with his own. The next day, Michael enlisted Mary in his romantic pursuit of Connie. [16]

There were a few dank days of rain that spring, and on one of them, Mary and the American novelist Irwin Shaw found a seat by the flickering fireplace in the lobby of an old hotel near the Houses of Parliament. Shaw was handsome, with powerful shoulders, a muscular chest, strong arms, and the close-cropped head of a boxer. He had arrived in London after spending a few months with a documentary unit filming the end of the African campaign. Shaw had enlisted in the army in July 1942 when he was thirty years old and already a well-known literary figure in the United States. He had published eighteen short stories in the *New Yorker*, written two anti-war plays which were produced on Broadway to critical acclaim, and written scripts for Hollywood. [17] He was working on a story about a soldier's loss of identity amid the interwoven mechanisms of army regulations and transport. The setting was the stopover barracks in North Africa for personnel awaiting transport to or from the European Theatre to the US. [18]

Mary recorded the episode in a draft of her memoir but omitted it from the final version. "As Shaw read me this one aloud, I felt he was entering a new country of his work, where further refinements of observation and intuition became apparent." Though Mary never claimed "to be a student of writing, and certainly not a critic or authority, she thought the new story a most effective job of work and said so." They had a drink to the new work before putting on their coats. "It had been an hour of quiet and thought. Very rare in those bustling days." [19] They saw each other often over the next few months. "Soon enough, Shaw was paying regular visits to Welsh's penthouse apartment . . . and in that war-torn time, conducting a more serious relationship than many."[20] Mary later told Bill Walton, "Irwin was the best lay in Europe."[21] When not frolicking in bed, they discussed writing and Shaw read his stories to Mary. She liked them and told him so. After each reading they drank to the new work, sometimes celebrating late into the night. Mary "read most of his short stories, which she found gutsy, gutsy, ebullient, tensile."[22] She liked Shaw's writing so much that she recommended his short stories to her father.[23] In her diary, Mary noted, "Noel seems so far away. Shaw is entertaining—says I'll manage all right if I stay in Europe."[24] Mary took Shaw on weekend visits to Time Out and they talked about writing. Shaw admired the work of Ernest Hemingway and told Mary he "reread every one of his books four times, several of them a dozen times."[25] He studied Hemingway's technique for setting scenes, introducing characters, and describing action.[26]

Their relationship did not remain exclusive, for Mary continued to see the jealous General Bob McClure. This meant she had to schedule the visits of the two men to her flat carefully. One morning when she entered the *Time* office, Bill Walton commented she looked like hell. Mary flopped into her chair, facing Walton behind his adjoining desk, and told him it could have been worse. The previous evening, Shaw had come over at about nine to read her a new story—they opened a bottle of wine, and the story proved intoxicating. They drank to Irwin's success before falling into bed. Mary drifted off to sleep and awoke at midnight to a loud banging on the front door. She told Shaw to stay in bed, pulled on a nightdress, and went to investigate. McClure stood outside, holding a bottle of Pinch whiskey, and wanted to come in. Mary had to think fast, for she knew McClure would be furious to find Shaw in her flat, let alone in her bed.[27] She told him she felt miserable from the curse, but he wanted to come in for a drink anyway. Mary put on a show of wretchedness, and finally he gave up. She returned to bed and found Shaw sitting up, smoking. He said she should have let her little general in because he would've enjoyed pounding his ass. Walton laughed at the story and smiled when Mary implored God to save her from the male ego.

Shaw alluded to Mary a few years later in his successful wartime novel, *The Young Lions*, in which he created Louise M'Kimber as the avatar for Mary. Louise had a small elegant body and a husband someplace in the Pacific. She seemed to know every bigwig in the British Isles and had "a deft, tricky way with men."

Louise spent weekends at country estates with talkative high-ranking military officers who revealed essential secrets—she knew the date for D-Day and which sites in Germany were targeted for bombing. Louise even knew when Roosevelt would next meet with Churchill and Stalin. [28]

Shaw's avatar, Michael, described Louise as "small and clever-looking . . . warm and undemanding." Louise attracted Michael, and he may have channeled Shaw's feelings when he admitted Louise was dearer to him than his wife. Although Michael and Louise talked about ending their affair and knew they really ought to, neither of them wanted to give up sleeping with the other, and they continued to see each other for months—just as Mary and Shaw did. [29]

◆

The military's strict segregation of the social lives of officers and lower "other" ranks frustrated Mary and Connie. Mary's rank of assimilated captain allowed her access to the exclusive officers' clubs, but her friends of lower rank in the film units and the press were barred. There was no place where the two women could socialize with the newcomers from America and their English friends except at crowded, noisy pubs. Connie suggested they start a lunch club at the White Tower to get around the rules. The Greek bistro sat minutes away from their offices, up Rathbone Place at 1 Percy Street. Connie talked to the Greek Cypriot owner, John Stais, who agreed to set aside a lunch table for eight each Friday in a second-floor room. [30] The club became a smash hit and every Friday the reserved table filled, and people not invited came anyway and sat at adjacent tables. The arrangement pleased Stais for the guests often selected the most expensive items on the menu. Sometimes the club met all afternoon and into the evening, filling the room with chatter, laughter, and cigarette smoke, all of which wafted into the street. It helped make the restaurant *the* place for American ex-pats to eat. Mary and Connie invited pilots, officers, enlisted men, journalists, and secretaries from their offices. They wanted happy people who could laugh despite the difficult times.

On November 10, 1943, the *Times* published a review of the film *For Whom the Bell Tolls*, starring Gary Cooper and Ingrid Bergman. It was playing at the Carlton Cinema in the Haymarket. The reviewer noted, "Hemingway had found a people, which in their passions, their acceptance of death, and the mystic working of their instincts, he could honor."[31] Mary and Connie had read the novel and went to see the movie.

Throughout the spring of 1944, the nightly incendiary raids of the Baby Blitz unnerved Mary. The Luftwaffe's revenge attacks for the bombing of German cities were frightening. Mary listened to the thudding explosions of bombs stitching through the city, trying to discern a pattern in case it pointed to her flat. Some nights the bombs fell far away in the docklands of eastern London, but on others the explosions came near Grosvenor Square and the American embassy. She could never tell how close the raid was, and like her neighbors she decided safe was better than sorry, even though it meant no sleep and too many cigarettes. Those nights, Mary left her bed and huddled with her neighbors in a foul-smelling shelter below the street. Mary remembered, "the stench of all those bodies parked together, looking like badly wrapped bundles in a warehouse, never dispersed."[32]

Mary's thirty-sixth birthday was on April 5, and she decided to celebrate with a cocktail party in her tiny flat. Mary and Connie scoured Soho for supplies, finding three bottles of expensive Scotch in two Italian shops and enough bread, Spam, and watercress to make three plates of dainty sandwiches. Mary expected about twenty people but was delighted when over fifty turned up. Most guests brought fifths or entire bottles of Scotch or rum, and they had more than enough to go around. Mary's flat, perched on the top floor of a brick row house six hundred yards from the American embassy on Grosvenor Park was a convenient spot for senior officers to visit.

The guests talked and drank into the evening while cigarette smoke streamed out the windows. Despite the close quarters, the amount of liquor consumed, and the mixing of ranks, there was no acrimony. Generals Omar Bradley and Sam Anderson talked with men of lower status—her friends from the BBC and the world of journalism. Mary monitored Shaw as he chatted up a young woman newly arrived from New York, and Michael cornered Connie next to the fireplace and told her about the Churchill government's latest efforts to censor the press. The overflowing flat testified to the many friends Mary had made in London.

A few weeks later Mary noted in her diary, "I walked home alone across the park in my new Jaegmar suit, feeling I've had the best of my life and made little of it." She had "no children, no fame, no money."[33]

Friday, May 26, was a bright, warm day, and Mary strolled with Shaw up Rathbone Place to the lunch club at the White Tower. Instead of her correspondent's
uniform, Mary wore a tailored jacket and skirt her seamstress had cut from one
of Noel's civilian suits. When she put on her sunglasses, Shaw said she looked
fresh from Hollywood, and Mary appreciated the compliment. As they neared
the restaurant on Percy Street, several men cast admiring glances. One romantic
soul swept off his hat and bowed. Mary felt good about herself.

SIX

Beautiful as a May Fly

May 1944

E rnest Hemingway arrived in London on May 17, 1944, as the accredited
RAF correspondent for *Collier's Weekly* to report on the invasion of France.
He was forty-four years old and one of the most famous writers in the world.
Announcing his arrival, the *Daily Mail* claimed he would be the only man in
military uniform with a large beard because his doctors had forbidden him to shave
it off for two months. Questioned about the state of the war, Hemingway said,
"Sorry to be so dull; I am bad at generalizations. I think any writer—especially a
war correspondent—is dull in conversation. It's only the phonies that are personally
colorful." Giving the lie to that remark, he said of the film version of *For Whom
the Bell Tolls*, "It seems to me rather like an animal that you have seen in your rifle
sights, shot, and then get delivered home by the taxidermist."[1]

Ernest was a star, but his private life was in shambles. His third marriage to war
correspondent Martha Gellhorn was falling apart. Ernest had replaced her as the
Collier's correspondent in London and taken her place on a flying boat which carried
him over the Atlantic. Martha was making her way to England across the stormy sea
on a leaky ship carrying dynamite, passing her days thinking about divorcing Ernest.
She wrote to her friend, Hortense Flexner, "As far as I am concerned, it is all over,
it will never work between us again . . . I only want to be alone. . . . I want to escape
from him and myself and from this personal life which feels like a straitjacket."[2]
Martha declared, "I want my name back, most violently, as if getting it back
would give me some of myself. Please use it always from now on, writing to me."[3]

Ernest regretted the failure of his marriage, but he couldn't abide Martha's independence. She wanted to travel to war zones to write about armed conflict—he wanted a wife in his bed at night. Ernest thought about finding a new woman, but not for a casual affair; he wanted to make up for the time he had lost with Martha. He wanted a woman who would be an emotional anchor, allowing him space and freedom to ruminate and create—someone who could appreciate and support "that thing in his head," as he called his creative power. [4]

For the last two years, Ernest had hunted German submarines off Cuba aboard his fishing trawler *Pilar*. The American Navy provided radio equipment, fuel, and weapons to outfit the boat, and Ernest grew an enormous beard to protect his skin from the searing tropical sun. The photojournalist Robert Capa told Ernest's brother Leicester, who was in London with a film crew, "Papa's got troubles, that bloody beard scares off all the girls." [5] Leicester remembered his old friend Mary Welsh, who had often spoken about Ernest and had read his novels. [6] Leicester guessed she might see the man despite the beard. Bill Walton told him Mary was reporting for *Time* and dating Irwin Shaw. Leicester learned Mary would be at a lunch meeting that coming Friday at the White Tower, and he urged Ernest to go and check her out. She was blonde, buxom, and fun, and he bet Ernest would like her. Taking Leicester's advice, Ernest walked to the bistro and took a chair at a table with a view of the room. People were seating themselves at a reserved table. Glad he had come early and anticipating Mary's arrival, he leaned back and drained a glass of ouzo.

◆

John Stais tended tables in front of the White Tower. He greeted "Miss Mary" with a wave, and she blew him a kiss. The beautiful weather was drawing people outside, and Mary expected a full house at the lunch club. Inside the restaurant, they climbed the stairway to the first floor. "Coming up!" Shaw shouted. Ernest turned to watch. He stared at Mary as if trying to fix her features in his memory, and the intensity of his gaze made her turn away.

Shaw followed Mary across the room to the reserved table, and she took a seat against the wall. When she looked up, she saw the imposing stranger continuing to stare at her. His temples showed gray, and he had oiled his longish hair. A gigantic beard formed a dark brown hedge with white sideburns extending under his jaw. Mary thought his brown eyes were beautiful, "lively and perceiving and friendly."[7] Shaw saw her looking at the big fellow and casually mentioned he was Ernest Hemingway.

The room was so hot Mary removed her jacket. She had refused her mother's advice to wear bras since the age of twelve because she found them uncomfortable.[8] As Mary slipped off the tight jacket, a passing airman commented, "the warmth does bring things out, doesn't it?"[9] Mary took a long drag on her Camel cigarette, and as she exhaled she noticed Hemingway's eyes trained on her. He smiled, stood up, and came over to her table. Hemingway was a big man, as tall as her father. He had broad shoulders, a barrel chest, and slim hips; he looked fit and moved on the balls of his feet with the rhythm of a big cat.

Hemingway towered over the table. "Say, Shaw," he said, addressing Irwin, but looking at Mary, "introduce me to your friend." Ernest was fourteen years older than Shaw and curt with the younger man. Shaw had recently told Mary that Hemingway's days at the top of the literary ladder were numbered because young writers, including himself, were writing about the war in a riveting style that would overtake the older novelists. Shaw introduced Ernest, who spoke softly and directly to Mary. Ernest told her he was a stranger in London and wondered if she could brief him on the state of hostilities. Ernest had a midwestern accent, and his voice was younger sounding than Mary had expected. He asked shyly if she would have lunch with him the next day.

Mary was busy that weekend but agreed to meet him on Monday. Ernest beamed with the happiest face she had seen in a long time then left, turning sideways to negotiate the narrow staircase. Mary's friends gossiped the second he disappeared, and Shaw feigned jealousy, saying it had been nice knowing her.[10] Mary regarded Ernest as another lonely man in a city full of lonely men, and it was not unusual for visiting journalists to ask her for a briefing. Still, celebrity is an aphrodisiac, and Mary had felt his commanding presence and was pleased he had asked her out. Ernest became infatuated with Mary. To him, she exuded self-confidence and sexual appeal, and he could not wait to see her again. His mood improved dramatically, and Leicester noted, "in a couple of days, Ernest was feeling personally admired again, and life was very pleasant around him."[11]

Mary spent the weekend at Time Out. In good weather, Mary and her friends sprawled on blankets on the lawn and read or rode bicycles or hiked through the countryside. She went for a walk with Bill Walton and mentioned her upcoming lunch with the famous novelist. Walton revealed that Leicester had earlier asked about Mary's whereabouts to arrange a meeting with Ernest. Slowly, Mary realized the meeting with Hemingway was far more intriguing than she had first imagined, and she wondered what Ernest had in mind.

Monday morning dragged slowly until noon when Mary ran out of the office, glad for the bright spring day. On her way to the restaurant, she noticed a rose bush budding amid the rubble and three daffodils hiding behind a rain barrel. She took them as good omens. At the White Tower, John Stais chatted with Ernest at a small table outside. They both turned and smiled at her as she approached, saying, "Miss Mary" in unison. Ernest stood, pulling out a chair. He had combed his hair, slightly trimmed his beard, and wore a cravat, but otherwise his outfit was unchanged from the Friday before. It was Ernest's first time in London, and he didn't know much about the war in Europe. He hoped to get an aerial view of the action in France by riding along on a few RAF missions.

Mary had grown used to her fast-talking fellow reporters who peppered their speech with military acronyms. Ernest spoke slowly, joked about hearing British English over aircraft intercoms, and performed a hilarious impersonation of a commander giving orders. He hoped to join the Allied invasion force to report for *Collier's*, and he pressed Mary for information. She told him everything she knew, even sharing her guess about the date for the invasion, all the while feeling odd about revealing this much to a competing journalist. She realized later she was trying to impress him.

Ernest mentioned his wife was on a supply ship somewhere in the mid-Atlantic. She would arrive in a week, but their marriage was over and had been for some time. Mary told Ernest that she and Noel had grown apart during the last year when he was in Cairo, but she hoped they would get back together. Ernest wished her luck and told her he had met Noel in Spain and thought he was a classy guy. Then he added that if she ever wanted to talk, he was staying at the Dorchester. The lunch ended; they shook hands and said goodbye. Ernest said he wanted to see her again, but Mary was busy with work and preoccupied with Shaw and deflected his request.

Two days later, Mary and Connie decided the nightly bombings by the Luftwaffe were becoming more dangerous. They moved into a room in the Dorchester, the first hotel built of reinforced concrete in London and reputed to be the city's safest building. General Eisenhower lived in a suite on the first floor as he planned Operation Overlord. Decorated in an Art Deco style, the hotel had twenty-foot ceilings, black-veined white marble floors, and gold-leaf-plated Corinthian columns. Mary and Connie believed the Dorchester would offer better protection from a German bomb than the slate roof of the flat on Grosvenor Street. They were right; during the entire war, the Dorchester suffered nothing more than a few shattered windows.

After moving their things, they went down to the lounge to meet their dates for the evening—Michael Foot and Irwin Shaw. Charles and Lael Wertenbaker, who also lived in the hotel, had invited them for a drink, and when they entered their room, they found Ernest sitting in a chair. He said he was an old friend of Wert's. The two women sat on the bed and listened to Ernest mourn the loss of his lucky stone from Cuba. He seemed lost in his world, full of self-pity, and Mary found his self-absorption unattractive. He told them he hoped to accompany the D-Day landing force and joked his mother had never forgiven him for not being killed in the last war and would be pleased to become a Gold Star mother in this one. Mary had heard enough and left for dinner with Shaw, putting Ernest out of her mind.

Mary arrived home at about nine to find Michael and Connie sitting on Connie's bed, having a drink. The windows were open to admit the fresh evening air and the lights were out to maintain the blackout. Mary sat on her bed and chatted with them. They were laughing at a joke when there was a knock at the door. "I had to see you again, Miss Mary," Ernest said, brandishing a bottle of champagne. Michael poured a round of bubbly, and Ernest made himself comfortable next to Mary. Michael criticized Churchill's efforts to control the press through sweeping censorship, and Ernest listened without interest. He launched a story about his own family, and after portraying his brilliant sisters, he returned to the theme of his overbearing mother and downtrodden father. Mary felt both fascinated and appalled that he raised the subject of his mother, whom he repeatedly referred to as "that bitch." Though forty-four years old, he was still obsessing over her. He stopped talking, and silence came to the dimly lit room. Then he turned to Mary and said, "I want to marry you. You are very alive. You're beautiful like a May fly." [12]

Stunned by his declaration, Mary sat quietly, not daring to look at him. He said, "I want to marry you now, and I hope to marry you sometime. Sometime, you may want to marry me."[13] Mary said nothing for minutes. Finally, she looked at him and told him not to be silly because they were both already married and hardly knew each other. Ernest ignored her objection and plowed on, saying although the war might keep them apart for a while, they should begin their "combined operations." He sounded optimistic, but Mary told him he was premature. At this second rebuff, Ernest stood up to leave. Before he did, he asked her to remember that he wanted to marry her, here and now, and declared he would still want to marry her next month or next year. Mary said nothing, but she wondered how he could be so sure so quickly.[14] Michael also got up to leave, and after they let the men out, Connie turned on Mary, wanting to know why she had been so hard on Ernest. Why couldn't she have been more gracious? She might end up being sorry for brushing him off. After all, it wasn't every day Ernest Hemingway asked to marry you.

SEVEN

Railway Trains Across the Sky

May 1944–June 1944

When Noel left for Cairo, he expected to be away a few months but he stayed on assignment for almost a year. Mary wondered if the postponements had something to do with his woman in Cairo, and she became indifferent to his absence. In late May 1944, Noel phoned to say he was in England to cover the Allied invasion of France and was coming to London the next day. Mary had mixed feelings about his arrival, for she didn't know how they would handle their intervening infidelities. Mary rushed to the Dorchester to pick up her things, bought some groceries, and returned to the small flat to welcome Noel. His gear covered a quarter of their floor space, but they ignored it and Mary briefed him on what she knew about their British friends.

They snuggled in the small bed, "but something was missing in one or both of us."[1] Noel didn't mention his lover in Cairo, nor did Mary ask. She assumed he must have heard of her parties with Connie and their boyfriends, but Noel didn't comment. Mary recalled, "Maybe we hoped for simple dispersion of our difficulties."[2]

◆

Robert Capa threw an extravagant party to show his "devotion and prosperity" to Papa on the evening of May 24, 1944. He invited Mary, and she wanted to go, but it would have been awkward to have Noel and Ernest in the same room.

Mary decided it was better to stay away but she urged Bill Walton to go, hoping he would fill her in later.

On the day of the party, Capa placed brandy-soaked peaches in the bottom of a giant fishbowl and poured champagne over them. Leicester Hemingway recalled, "Capa was a master at organizing, scrounging, and liberating" and supplied "the finest bottles from various officer's messes."[3] The free booze drew journalists and members of the film units. After the hard-drinking crowd finished the scotch and gin, they began on the champagne punch. As Bill Walton looked out a window, Ernest came up from behind and asked if he had the "black ass"? (Ernest's term for depression). Walton explained he didn't feel like partying because he had heavier things on his mind—he planned to parachute into occupied France with a typewriter strapped to his chest. After three grueling weeks of calisthenics and practice jumps with the 82nd Airborne Division, Walton had qualified for the mission. He would be the only civilian to do so.[4] Impressed, Ernest pumped Walton for information about the invasion, and Walton told him some of what he knew but didn't feel very conversational.[5]

Ernest wandered off to talk to Capa's doctor friend Peter Gorer and his beautiful wife, Gertrude, a German refugee. Ernest asked Gorer to confirm that his beard protected him from skin cancer, but Gorer, a specialist on tissue transplantation, was skeptical. Later, Ernest swapped stories with Leicester in the kitchen. "We put down our glasses and sparred for a while, trading stomach punches and practicing tensing up, and we let the others who had come in punch us in the gut." By 4 A.M., they reached the peaches in the punch bowl, signaling the end of the party. The guests filed down the stairs into the dark street. "I'll drive you to the Dorch," Gorer said to Ernest. "You can't get a cab this time of night. Not even a general could."[6] Capa ate the peaches and went to bed. Gorer was no more sober than Ernest, and in the blackout he drove at speed into a water tank. Ernest launched headfirst through the windshield, and the glass carved a deep wound in his scalp. Gorer received severely bruised legs, and Gertrude's face was cut from the broken windshield.

At 7 A.M., Capa's phone rang, and a nurse asked him to come to the St. George's Hospital casualty ward. He rushed there to find Ernest stretched out on a gurney, "his scalp split open, pink and gaping," and his beard full of blood. Leicester recalled, "Ernest looked like a great bear that had just had a meat cleaver removed from its skull."[7] It took two-and-a-half hours of surgery and fifty-seven stitches to repair his scalp. His knees were bruised and swollen from ramming into the car's dashboard. The scalp would heal, and the bruises disappear, but Ernest received a severe concussion that caused intense headaches, ringing in his ears for months and, as he later discovered, made him impotent.

Mary heard from Connie that Ernest had been in an accident so serious that he was first reported dead. A later report in the *Times* said, "he was slightly injured . . . when a car crashed into an emergency water tank at Lowndes Square during the blackout."[8] Mary wanted to check on his condition, and she walked to the hospital carrying a bouquet of daffodils and tulips wrapped in newspaper. She entered Ernest's room and found him sitting on the bed, his back resting against a raised pillow and his hands over his head holding onto the white metal bed frame. He wore striped hospital pajamas, and a turban fashioned from a wide bandage covered everything above his bruised eyelids.[9]

Ernest smiled when he saw Mary, and his "lively brown eyes" followed her. She found a water jug and arranged the bouquet on the windowsill, bringing some cheer to the dull room. When Ernest thanked her, Mary replied, "flowers are good for everybody." He said, "You're good for me."[10] Despite his injuries, Ernest remained cheerful. The lovely blonde bearing flowers undoubtedly helped his mood, and a shot of morphine induced a pleasant fog. He told Mary it looked worse than it was, and he would be back at the "Dorch" in two days. Ernest asked her to come and see him. Mary promised she would and calculated how much longer Noel would be in London.

Mary and Noel spent little time together over the next few days. Noel lined up the kit he needed to accompany the invasion force and Mary spent time at the office dealing with reports about the expected battle. The hospital released Ernest on May 29, and he returned to the Dorchester.

On June 1, Noel left the tiny flat to wait at Newhaven for the order to embark. He was to follow the commandos clearing Ouistreham beach of mines. On June 4, Mary wrote to her parents, telling them the last two weeks had gone by "like a flash." She put on "a happier face than I was wearing"[11] about Noel's visit, "so that they would not worry from afar."[12] Mary said, "he was so much more silent and reserved than I had remembered him." Now he was off again. She couldn't tell them where, but she hoped to see him again in three or four months. Mary told them not to worry about her, for she was "working hard and happily, glad to be where I am."[13] She continued to keep them in the dark about Irwin Shaw, Ernest Hemingway, and her generals.

◈

The first step in the plan (Operation Overlord) to defeat the Germans called for the invasion of Normandy (Neptune). Preparations began in 1943 with a massive buildup of men and equipment in the UK. There were fewer than 150,000 US troops in Britain at the end of May 1943. A year later, the number had grown to over 1.65 million. The date and location for the landing in Normandy remained a tightly guarded secret, and troops began boarding ships at various British ports up to a week in advance. General Eisenhower set the invasion to launch on June 5, 1944, but the English Channel was too rough to allow landing craft to ferry troops to the Normandy beaches. He rescheduled D-Day for June 6 when experts predicted a break in the weather.

◈

On June 6, Mary received a call at 4 A.M. from a military friend who said, "Take the curlers out of your hair and get going," meaning, in their code, the invasion of France had started. [14] Mary toured tactical fighter and bomber bases around England to see the air side of the campaign. She knew her story would be second-class in news value and might make page ten in an account of local air action. Mary confessed to her diary, "it had been a worthless disappointing day for me," and she fell asleep, "hoping the Allied toehold in France would last through the night." [15]

In the early hours of D-Day, the most massive armada in history arrived off the Normandy coast and at first light naval guns fired a thunderous barrage against the German positions. To Ernest, it sounded as though the big naval guns were "throwing whole railway trains across the sky." [16] Hundreds of landing craft carrying troops made their way to designated beaches. Despite the bombing and naval barrages, most German defensive positions survived, and gun crews fired mortar, artillery, and heavy machine guns toward the landing craft and beaches. Capa recalled, "The water was cold and the beach still more than a hundred yards away. The bullets tore holes in the water around me, and I made for the nearest steel obstacle." [17] When he reached the beach, he shot photos with trembling hands as "a new kind of fear shook his body from toe to hair." [18]

Despite his head wound and bruised knees, Ernest took an attack transport ship, the *Dorothea Dix*, across the Channel. He had been aboard the *Dix* since June 1, enjoying the privileges of a US navy lieutenant.[19] On the morning of June 6, he clambered down a rope ladder to travel to the Fox Green sector of Omaha Beach in a landing craft, the *Empire Anvil*. It was a foolhardy mission for a man in his condition.

In the article he wrote for *Collier's*, Ernest described "the frontal assault in broad daylight, against a mined beach . . . defended as stubbornly and as intelligently as any troops could defend it. . . . No boat was lost through bad seamanship. . . . And they had taken the beach."[20] Ernest placed himself in the heart of the action. After the officer in charge of the landing craft, Lieutenant Robert "Andy" Anderson, lost his map overboard, he was unsure where they were to land. Ernest had memorized the map and directed Andy to the Fox Green sector. Ernest noticed the crossfire coming from two machine-gun nests and told Andy to delay their landing until a destroyer bombardment took out the guns, then Ernest guided the landing craft to the right beach. After the men disembarked, the bullet-pocked boat made its way back into the Channel. The crew hauled Ernest aboard the *Dorothea Dix* in a boson's chair.

Waves of men landed on the rocky shore. "The living lay beside the dead and fought with flamethrowers, grenades, bazookas, and Bangalore torpedoes which blasted holes in barbed wire entanglements."[21] They secured some beaches by late afternoon. All that night the naval guns boomed and explosions flashed along the coast.

The next day, Mary had tea with Pam Churchill. There was not much news from Normandy, and Mary hoped Pam would have heard something from Churchill or Ed Murrow, the American newsman with whom she was having an affair.[22] Pam stressed they should not be optimistic about the invasion's success, for the weather was poor and it remained difficult to land supplies.

EIGHT

She Was Mad for Shaw

June 1944–July 1944

A week after D-Day, Hitler launched the first buzz bombs against London. Mary thought they sounded like "an Evinrude outboard motor" cruising through the sky, then suddenly stopping and falling with their explosive loads. [1] About a hundred of the German vengeance weapons—the V-1 flying bombs—came in daily, and Londoners feared the rockets. They had no discernible pattern, their routes were unpredictable, and they brought arbitrary death and injury from the air, falling on crowded restaurants, hospitals, churches, apartments, houses, shops, and buses. The buzz bombs packed the terrible explosive power of 2,300 pounds of TNT. Even far from the point of impact, the explosions shattered glass and sent debris flying. Londoners became obsessed with the buzz bombs, and the V-1s became harder on their nerves than the bombs of the Blitz at its worst. [2]

The rockets flew toward London rather than military installations because terrorizing civilians was their sole purpose. Mary recalled, "There was something macabre about this wholly mechanical enemy and about the idea of being killed by a machine." [3] Like most Londoners, she left pubs or restaurants when she heard the buzz of an incoming bomb or the repeated wail of an alarm because the streets seemed safer from shattering glass. After an attack, everyone went back inside and resumed eating and drinking.

Ernest flew in a formation of six B-25 Mitchell bombers on a sortie to take out the V-1 launch sites in Drancourt, France. He saw black smoke from flak exploding around him and watched the bomb bay doors of a nearby B-25 open. He wrote for *Collier's*, "with the smoke rings forming along her side, the belly of this kite . . . opened, pushing out against the air, and the bombs all dropped out sideways as if she were having eight long metal kittens in a hurry."[4] Ernest asked the commander to fly back over the site to check for damage, but he refused because of retaliatory flak. And he proved correct, for flak downed the leading aircraft in the next flight. Ernest wrote in a faux-humble way of the courage it took for him to accompany the pilots chasing rockets or bombing V-1 sites. He said he was not a man who had "a perpetual urge to seek peril in the sky" but he found himself on flights because he had trouble understanding English accents over the telephone.

Mary wrote to her parents on June 13 telling them the invasion of France "for which everyone on this island has been working so long is merely making your child work harder than ever."[5] She put in fifteen-hour days flying around England to air stations, camps, and hospitals, and then back to her typewriter to pound out the news. The intensive work was exhilarating. To keep up appearances, she told them Noel was in France with the British forces and sending back stories for the *Daily Express*.

◆

Ernest invited Mary to lunch on June 15. She wanted to show him some of her favorite streets in Chelsea and then have lunch at one of the pubs, but Ernest had no curiosity about the city and they settled on a French restaurant in Jermyn Street. Ernest said he wanted to know more about her, and Mary described childhood summers aboard the *Northland* and told him about her father's logging business and their canoe trips. Mary claimed water had become as natural to her as land and she felt comfortable on boats of all sizes. Ernest told her about *Pilar* and the dawn's pink skies above the Gulf Stream. He promised she would love *Pilar* and became animated as he described the thirty-eight foot New England–style fishing trawler.

Ernest told Mary her strong legs reminded him of Prudy Boulton, the Chippewa girl who had been his first lover. After a couple of drinks and a bottle of wine, Ernest announced he would dedicate his next book to Mary. She asked if he would dedicate the book "with love"?[6] He replied he had never done that before, but he would do it for her.[7]

After the boozy lunch, they strolled back to the Dorchester. Ernest's room sat empty, and he pulled her to him. They kissed, and she stretched her arms to hug him and felt his muscular back and chest. One thing should have led to another, but it didn't. "Mr. Scrooby," as Ernest called his penis, wouldn't cooperate. Ernest blamed his head injury which was still causing blinding headaches. Mary sensed Ernest's embarrassment but she talked to him matter-of-factly about his inability to perform, as she later explained in a letter to friends. "Poor guy, there he was trying to impress a new girl healthy enough sometimes to have that inescapable urge to wiggle. And he could do nothing—nothing normal, that is, about it." Ernest asked, "how long I thought I could go along on faith in him, and I consid-ered carefully and, ruling out assists from outside, told him six months precisely." Mary noted, "Although he was floored by my arbitrary straightforwardness, he was impressed, I guess by my honest intent—none of that squealing about 'Oh darling, forever.'" [8]

Ernest knew Irwin Shaw and General McClure were in the background. He decided to assert his masculinity by turning to his art and writing news stories for *Collier's* and letters to Mary, emphasizing his manliness and importance to the war effort.

Mary waited for permission to travel to Normandy to report on the medical side of the invasion, and an RAF flight surgeon grounded Ernest because of his head injuries. With little to do except recuperate and see Mary in the evenings, Ernest wrote his "First Poem to Mary in London." He described his homesickness and the blinding pain of his headaches. He wrote of his desire to reunite with *Pilar* and take up his life on the water and his longing for Mary. In the evening, he watched the clock tick toward the hour when she would come, "small-voiced and lovely to the hand and the eye to bring your heart back that was gone." [9]

Ernest shaved off his huge beard to fit the military style in London, and Mary liked the strong chin and high cheekbones that emerged. [10] On July 1, Noel came to London for a few days and stayed with Mary in the tiny flat. They found no joy this time, and though Mary didn't tell Noel about Ernest, he must have sensed her detachment. A week later, Mary wrote her Sunday letter to her parents, maintaining the fiction of a happy marriage with Noel. She told them, "it has been nice having him these nights when the buzz bombs make me restless. I must say they are not conducive to sound sleeping." Noel was "out-rightly optimistic" about the campaign in France, and she expected to be going to France herself for a few days to cover the medical side of the war.[11] Mary was seeing Ernest, but she felt it necessary to pretend to her parents she was continuing to enjoy Noel's company. It must have been a confusing time for her, with her husband popping in and out, General McClure standing by to spoil her, and Ernest pursuing her vigorously despite his impotence. Then there was the underlying reality that, as she confessed to Bill Walton, "sexually, she was mad for Shaw."[12]

◆

While she waited to travel to France, Mary filed several stories for *Time-Life* on the medical side of the battles. In "Invasion Surgeon," she wrote about the efforts to reduce the number of deaths from wounds. There were many men who, had they been injured in 1918, would have been permanently invalided. In 1944, men with the same injuries recovered rapidly, entirely thanks to "a solid, freckle-faced surgeon named Paul Ramsey Hawley."[13] His watchword was, "Get the surgeon to the patient, not the patient to the surgeon."[14]

In mid-July, her approvals came through and Mary flew to Normandy to cover the care and evacuation of the wounded. It remained cold in the transit station near Ste. Mère-Église, and the chill from the soil penetrated her sleeping bag and clothing. She had a fitful sleep and felt groggy in the morning. "The dried scrambled eggs we got for breakfast helped me thaw, but the tepid coffee was so uncoffee that I wondered why they had bothered with it."[15] The army assigned Mary a jeep and a driver who was young enough to be her son. Frightened about the possibility of hitting a mine, he stayed on the roads plugged by armored vehicles heading south. Mary persuaded him to take a shortcut, and they headed down a road she had found on her map. The boy drove slowly, and Mary could smell death. They found an American soldier dead in a ditch with his blue eyes open to the sky, his body putrefying, and they found two other dead boys farther up the road. They left them where they'd fallen in case their bodies were booby trapped.

At the battalion aid station, Mary saw doctors working under tents with the sides rolled up. The surgeons focused on their work and moved quickly from patient to patient, and Mary walked down the rows of the wounded men—some of them just boys. Their awful anonymity disturbed her. Charts listed their names, serial numbers, blood types, and army units, but nothing mentioned what they had done before joining the army. "Nobody knew, and who cared, which of the bodies had been high school football captains or presidents of the local drama club or hot men on the guitar."[16] Mary wished she could gather them in her arms and say some comforting words until she realized how little one could say to console a boy who had lost his leg.

Mary returned to London and met Ernest for whiskey in Frisco's, a notorious club where white women danced with black GIs to the latest American jazz tunes. Mary watched the dancers swaying to the music and told Ernest about her trip to France. "I mentioned the smells of the dead . . . and he agreed with me."[17] They headed back to Ernest's place at the Dorchester, and he told her that while she had been in France, the London-based society matron Lady Emerald Cunard and her friends had visited him. The London upper class seemed immoral to Ernest because the women wanted to stay all night and yet be home in the morning before their husbands left for the office. They were thrill-seekers.[18] Mary saw the notes and trinkets Lady Cunard had left about Ernest's room to stake out her territory. When she protested, Ernest told her he was only the diversion of the week, and they would hunt for fresh game when he left for France.

Mary was discouraged, but Ernest took her in his arms and asked her to write to him while he was in France. Mary woodenly agreed to perform any favor for the troops. He complained "the shits" at *Collier's* rarely forwarded his mail, and he had heard nothing from his sons in weeks.[19] The next day, Mary noted she had "a wonderful lunch with Hemingway at the White Tower, though I was terribly sleepy."[20] This was their goodbye lunch, and Ernest flew to Normandy on July 18 and stayed at "a hideously ugly German-modern-1930s-kind-of-brick-and-concrete place" in a suburb of Cherbourg.[21] There, Ernest found Bill Walton and gave him the bundle of mail he had carried.[22]

Mary missed Ernest and began to think, despite all his wives, he seemed to be a conscientious father because he felt sad that he hadn't heard from his sons.[23] The war had changed all the rules, and few marriages were holding. Men and women alike were lonely, frightened, unmoored from peacetime obligations, and seeking comfort where they could find it. Mary felt no guilt about her affairs and doubted whether anyone else did about theirs. It did not seem reasonable to count on promises, and there was no point staying loyal if it meant being lonely.

NINE

I Cannot Understand this Chest-beating

August 1944

M ary felt vulnerable and lonely in London in August, as V-1 flying bombs continued to fall from the sky, leaving death and destruction in their wake. "With so many of my friends in France, the buzz bombs continuing their harassment, and most London news seeming mere footnote to Normandy," Mary wanted to return to France.[1] Most of her male friends were already there. Bill Walton parachuted into Normandy behind enemy lines the night before D-Day and was reporting on the American forces under General Patton. Noel, Charlie Wertenbaker, and Robert Capa landed with the troops on Normandy's beaches on June 6. Noel was covering General Bernard Montgomery and the British and Canadian troops under his command. Capa took dramatic photographs of the landings and worked with Wert to bring out a quick book on the Normandy Invasion. Shaw made it to France several days after the invasion, and his camera team photographed Cherbourg's destruction and liaised with General Patton's group as it fought toward Paris. Ernest left for Normandy on July 18.

Two of Mary's female friends had also traveled to France to report on the action. Despite the rules against women entering combat zones unless escorted by a male officer, brave women filed stories about the battles through France. Lee Miller photographed the fight for Saint-Malo, the ancient walled city on the coast of Brittany, and wrote a riveting tale of her time in a German dugout.[2] Helen

Kirkpatrick, the London bureau chief for the *Chicago Daily News*, reported on the Free French Forces.

Meanwhile, stuck in London, Mary wrote stories on the supply chain that provided the weapons and equipment for Allied troops. She wrote a cover story on "the miracle of supply." The Allies landed well over a million men, a million tons of supplies, and 100,000 vehicles in France, and repaired docks, laid pipelines, built railways, and paved truck routes. The Germans sacrificed thousands of men trying to slow the advance. Mary's piece featured a human-interest angle, highlighting the man in charge of the effort, Lieutenant General John Lee, "a man of exceptionally friendly and attractive personality."[3] While the supply chain proved vital to the Allies' success, Mary wanted to be reporting breaking news in France.

During August, Mary wrote one whimsical letter to Ernest but he wrote to her often. Despite his passionate pleas, Mary reserved judgment. Thirty-six years old, having married twice and known many men, Mary was pragmatic. She didn't fall for his romantic overtures and Ernest's impotence troubled her, for she hoped to have children. As we shall see, Ernest overstated his role in intelligence gathering, military planning, and firefights—perhaps to assert his masculinity and compensate for his impotence.

Ernest found a comfortable field home in the infantry regiment of Colonel Charles "Buck" Truman Lanham. Three years younger than Ernest, Buck had graduated from West Point, written training manuals, produced Hollywood training films, and composed poetry. Buck admired the famous writer because he considered himself a man of literary sensibilities, having published three poems in *Harper's Magazine* in the early 1930s.[4] Buck told Ernest's official biographer, Carlos Baker, "I was spellbound by this magnificent human being—simple, gentle, direct, unaffected. No man before or since has ever struck so swiftly and so deeply into my mind and affections."[5]

Ernest followed the troops and collected souvenirs. He retrieved a canvas belt—the buckle inscribed with the words, "Gott Mitt Uns" (God is with us)—from the body of a dead German soldier and wore it outside his belt loops to carry two canteens. In his 1949 *Life* story building up the Hemingway legend, Malcolm Cowley wrote that one canteen contained gin and the other vermouth, but as Ernest later wrote to Buck, no one gave canteen space to vermouth in a war. Ernest kept the belt and wore it daily, without canteens, for the rest of his life.

In his letters to Mary, Ernest became an intelligence officer instead of a journalist as the division moved south. On July 30, he snatched a German motorcycle and sidecar and a Mercedes staff car convertible which the motor pool painted olive drab. A red-headed grade school dropout from Potsdam, New York, Private Archie "Red" Pelkey, became Ernest's driver. The vehicle's capture was featured in a letter Ernest wrote to Mary and he promised to drive her around in the convertible when she arrived. As if on a swashbuckling adventure, Ernest told Mary, "The division has killed a great many Germans, and we have gotten excellent cognac from the armored vehicles."[6] He reported the general in charge (R. O. "Tubby" Barton) is "an educated, talented and charming man and a fine soldier. He was very gay and pleasant just now when he saw me driving in the Mercedes."[7]

Ernest worried he might lose Mary, and he wrote to her almost daily, asking, "Please write because I miss you totally."[8] On July 31, he wrote, "I wish I could talk to you: preferably in bed. More than preferably as you well know. . . . Small friend, I love you very much."[9] He expressed his joy in combat. "We have a very jolly and gay life full of deads, German loot, much shooting, much fighting, . . . dead cows, dead horses, tanks, 88's, dead US guys." And he described the harsh conditions, "sometimes don't eat at all, sleep in the rain, on the ground, in barns, on carts, on cots, on one's ass and always moving, moving."[10] As evening came, he faced danger. "It's getting dark now, and the little machine pistols go trrrrrut-trrrrrut—like a Kitty cat purring but hard and metallic." He told Mary, "the only bad thought I ever have in the night is of landing in London and finding you are gone somewhere. So, keep good contact and write."[11]

Ernest boasted to Mary of the close rapport he enjoyed with his "good friend" General Barton. Since Ernest was "an old soldier and spoke French," he proved useful to the general. When he was dead tired, Barton shared Ernest's blanket on the grass, and Ernest gave him "the gen on how it actually is at all the places we go by motorcycle." Barton referred to Ernest's motorcycle and sidecar as his "irregular cavalry" and he relied upon the intelligence he gathered. At the end of one intelligence briefing, General Barton gave Ernest a bottle of bourbon and said, "Ernie, I will miss you very much. Both personally and officially."[12]

Years after Ernest's death, Carlos Baker showed Buck Lanham copies of Ernest's letters to Mary, and Lanham told Baker that Ernest had inflated his role in military matters. He'd never made a wartime suggestion, nor did he ever contribute to any plan, nor offer any intelligence upon which Lanham relied. Buck also doubted General Barton ever relied on any intelligence provided by Ernest.[13] "He certainly wrote a lot of crap to Mary in those days," Buck said. "I cannot understand this chest-beating. Why, of all people, did he feel he had to inflate himself in this way? . . . His reputation was secure in every way. It is a sad thing."[14]

Ernest feared losing Mary, and he portrayed himself as a laid-back hero on a quest to defeat the Germans, prove his manhood, and earn her love—despite his impotence. The hero he created advised Buck on strategy, gathered intelligence for General Barton, and helped plan operations.

On August 4, Ernest ran into Robert Capa and suggested they investigate an unusual attack a few miles away. Reluctant to get ahead of the main force, Capa followed from afar. Ernest and Pelkey sped along a road, and a German antitank shell exploded in front of them. The motorcycle and sidecar flipped and threw Ernest headfirst into a rocky ditch. He hit his head and received a new concussion before the pain from the last one had faded. Writing about the incident to Mary, Ernest said, "their jolly future was on the bum yesterday." While he was "ahead of the infantry, I was knocked down by a tank shell, and then fired on by tank machine gun and two people with machine pistols on each side of the road." He had "to pretend to be dead until quite a while later and could hear Germans talking on other side of hedge at about ten feet. They spoke very disrespectfully of your big friend, who they considered dead." He hurt his back, received a new bump on his head that brought double vision, and he began "urinating blood." Mary worried about him and had trouble sleeping. Yet, Ernest bragged, "Have been cited for something moderately impressive, but probably nothing will ever come of it because of irregularity of actions."[15] The concussion did further damage and prolonged Ernest's symptoms—terrible headaches, ringing in his ears, double vision, impotence, and outbursts of anger coupled with depressive moods.[16]

Mary pleaded with a SHAEF (Supreme Headquarters Allied Expeditionary Force) Public Relations Officer (PRO) for permission to go on an airborne operations job. Walter Graebner told the PRO that Mary should do the story because no one else in the office wrote as well. Mary wrote to Ernest, "Those bloody poops, constipated with their orthodoxy, said no because I'm a dame."[17] Mary told Ernest not to apologize that his letters seemed dull. If he did that, she would have to compare hers, asking herself, "what's a little squirt like me doing, presuming to love a big hotshot like you."[18]

Pelkey drove Ernest to Buck Lanham's new headquarters in a Norman strong-
hold, Château Lingeard. Buck invited Ernest to stay for a banquet to celebrate his
wedding anniversary, but Ernest declined. The next morning the Germans shelled
the Château, killing several officers. Many, including Buck, suffered injuries.
When Ernest next spoke to Buck, he asked, "Do you know why I didn't accept
your invitation to dinner on the 9th? I replied, 'No.' He said, 'That place stank of
death.'" [19] Ernest wrote to Mary about his premonition and told her it saved his life.

Ernest rejoined Buck Lanham's group and became more active, working with
members of the Office of Strategic Services, the intelligence service before the CIA,
and the French Maquis (Free French Interior). The German forces maintained strong
defensive positions, and the shattered German Seventh Army lashed out in desperate
counterattacks. Ernest wrote for *Collier's* of his involvement in the skirmishes around
the village of Rambouillet in the rolling countryside southwest of Paris. The precise
role he played is a matter of conjecture, but he helped get arms for the Maquis and
translated American officers' orders. Whether he engaged in armed combat is the
question. [20] Ernest set up a command post at the Hôtel du Grand Veneur, taking
over two rooms, and he liaised between divisional headquarters and the partisans.
Colonel David Bruce of the OSS was pleased to see the Maquis because there were
not enough regular troops to defend the town against an expected German attack.

Bruce (later ambassador to France during the Kennedy administration) recorded
his view of Ernest's command post in his diary. "Army gear littered the floor. Carbines
stood in each corner; revolvers of every nationality were heaped carelessly on the bed."
Even "the bathtub was filled with hand grenades, and the basin with brandy bottles,
under the bed was a cache of Army rations and whiskey." [21] Since the Geneva Convention prohibited Ernest from bearing arms, Ernest asked Bruce for a handwritten
note allowing him to convey orders to the Maquis. He and the colonel then assigned
the men to defensive positions just outside of town, but the Germans did not attack.

Ernest told Mary a group of Maquis placed themselves under his command.
"Clothed them with clothing of cavalry Recon unit which had been killed at the
entrance to Rambouillet. Armed them from Division." [22] They took and held
Rambouillet and ran patrols to gather intel about the German positions. "I was
very scared twice," Ernest admitted. "Some of the patrols we made would scare
you worse than Grimm's fairy tales even if there had been no Krauts." [23] Making
the risk of death seem even closer, Ernest confided, "Have strong feeling my luck
has about run out but I'm going to try to pass a couple of more times with dice." [24]

Though Ernest remained busy on the battlefront, he claimed Mary was never far from his thoughts. He wrote of his longing for her, weaving his loving phrases among the scenes of dread. "Wish I could see you. I miss you very much and would like to be in bed and make jokes." In the coming days, the number of Maquis reporting through Ernest to Colonel Bruce increased. Ernest distributed Sten guns and grenades, and the Maquis harassed German patrols and gathered intelligence on German positions for the imminent march on Paris. Ernest described the action for *Collier's*: "the German tanks roamed around the roads ahead of us. They took hostages in the various villages. They picked up the French resistance forces and shot them. They went where they pleased." But "all this time, they were followed and kept track of by French guerrillas on bicycles who came back with accurate information on their movements."[25] Ernest assisted Colonel Bruce in interrogating prisoners and translating the reports of the guerillas and local country people.

On August 21, Mary told her "big friend" the New York bosses had approved her going to France as *Time's* representative at SHAEF. She expected to arrive in Paris in mid-September and stay until the war ended. Meanwhile, Mary hoped she might come to Paris on a quick four- to five-day job, and if she did, she would ask everywhere for him. She looked forward to seeing him but asked for nothing: "no tie, no obligation—you know that." After a buzz bomb landed close to her, Mary told Ernest he shouldn't worry for "they only make me wish I could crawl inside your arms."[26]

By August 23, the Allied forces had established an armed arc around Paris. Eisenhower did not rush the attack to liberate the city but took time to make sure of a tight grip on the surrounding countryside, and he put the right actors in place for a dramatic victory parade. For diplomatic reasons, Eisenhower decided a French general should have the honor of leading the advance on Paris. He assigned General Philippe Leclerc, the hero of the Fighting French African campaign.[27] Leclerc directed the Second French Armored Division toward Rambouillet on the road to Paris. With 16,000 battle-hardened troops and 4,000 vehicles under his command, the outcome of the fight to take Paris was not in doubt.[28] The only concern was the amount of damage the city would suffer.

Ernest and resistance leaders attempted to brief General Leclerc on the German defenses around Rambouillet. Ernest wrote for *Collier's*, "Accompanied by one of the big shots of the resistance movement, a gallant officer who had held the town ever since they could remember, they advanced toward the general. His greeting—unprintable—will live in my ears forever." The general's printable greeting, "Buzz off, you unspeakables," outraged Ernest, and the men withdrew.[29] He wrote, "But for your correspondent, that was the high point of the attack on Paris. In war, my experience has been that a rude general is a nervous general."[30] Later, the division's second-in-command invited Ernest and his colleagues to dinner and focused on their intelligence reports. These allowed the division to work in relative safety on its approach to Paris.

In his piece, Ernest criticized General Leclerc for refusing to meet with him and the Maquis leaders, even though the second-in-command met with them, received the information, and acted upon it. Not for the first time in a *Collier's* piece, Ernest implied he was at the center of the action. On the eve of the march on Paris, General Leclerc probably had other things on his mind than meeting with an American journalist.

The French army insisted the guerrilla forces give way to the column of regular troops. Ernest wrote that a young French lieutenant pushed the Maquis to the rear, insisting "the guerrilla rabble" not go ahead until the column passed. Ernest and the Maquis advanced parallel to Leclerc's column to the edge of Versailles. Then they took a series of side roads to Paris while Leclerc's column halted. Ernest's aim at this stage "was to get into Paris without being shot. Our necks had been out for a long time. Paris was going to be taken." He took cover in the street fighting, "the solidest cover available—and with someone covering the stairs behind me when we were in houses or the entrances to apartment houses."[31]

In the early afternoon of August 25, General Leclerc's column crossed the Seine and entered Paris. Soon after, Red Pelkey drove David Bruce and Ernest at racing speed along the deserted Champs-Élysées and they pulled up in front of the Travelers Club "where several Old Guard had collected, including the President of the Club." As they were "the first outsiders to come there since the taking of Paris . . . the Club celebrated by opening champagne."[32] They drank toasts and walked through the Place de l'Opéra, already crowded with jubilant Parisians. After kissing "several thousand men, women and babies," they arrived at the Ritz in the Place Vendôme.[33] As David Bruce remembered, "except for the manager, the imperturbable Auselio, the Ritz was completely deserted, so we arranged to quarter there." Then Auselio asked what he could do for them, and they ordered fifty martini cocktails. "They were not very good as the bartender had disappeared, but they were followed by a superb dinner."[34]

TEN

We Lived in Those Days
Far Beyond the Usual Reach
of Our Senses

August 1944–September 1944

Mary had been traveling in her correspondent's uniform since the day before Paris fell. She flew to a military airfield on the coast of France and, after spending the night in an uncomfortable barracks, made her way to Paris by jeep. Her young soldier-driver weaved in and out of the heavy traffic, and his driving became erratic the more he drank from bottles of Calvados offered along the route. They arrived as evening fell, a few hours after the German surrender. The jeep made slow progress, so she stepped off and carried her knapsack and typewriter through the noisy, happy crowds of singing, shouting Parisians. She walked to the Hotel Scribe, the Allied press headquarters, which was full of journalists, although Noel was not among them—he was still up north with Montgomery's forces. [1]

The Scribe had no vacancies, so Mary checked into a shabby, second-rate hotel across the street. Then she headed out with friends to explore the bars full of celebrating Parisians. She ran into her old boyfriend, Herbie Clarke, and they walked arm in arm down the Champs-Élysées, and the Parisians applauded them—or their uniforms. They had a drink at an outdoor café and absorbed the atmosphere. Later, Clarke gave an interview about the mood in Paris that day. "I can't stay at my typewriter; I can't stay off my balcony away from the spectacle of all the delight that's outside. Words can't describe Paris today." He continued, "You need music for it. Some tune that is a cross between the spine-tingling 'Marseillaise' and the rollicking roll of 'Turkey in the Straw,' and the rhythm of the Brazilian samba."[2]

Mary went to bed late but did not sleep well. In the morning, she left her bags with the concierge, walked across the street, and found Wert having breakfast in the Scribe. "Get us a piece on Paris fashion," Wert asked, and Mary left to research her story.[3] Later that day, Mary strolled through the exuberant crowds to the Ritz. She asked the concierge whether Monsieur Hemingway had arrived, and he waved to a white-uniformed bellboy who escorted her on the lift to chambre 31. He knocked on the door and a red-headed man Mary recognized from Ernest's letters as Red Pelkey opened it. She asked if Mr. Hemingway was there. Pelkey yelled, "A dame is here." Ernest strode into the hallway, hugged her, and then picked her up and twirled her around. The bellboy and Pelkey stood back and watched the show.[4] Inside Ernest's room, Maquis comrades cleaned rifles and drank champagne. Ernest told Mary he received her letter in Normandy and read it every day until he lost it. He wondered if she wrote more letters that might have gone astray. She told him frankly, "No."

They drank champagne, and Ernest described the action he'd seen at Rambouillet and wanted to take her there. Mary still had work to do and managed to extract herself after promising to meet Ernest later for dinner. On her way out of the hotel she asked the concierge if she could get a room, and to her delight he gave her chambre 86, which became her home for the next seven months. The room was elegant compared to her flat in London. Gold-patterned rose brocade covered the chaise longue which sat next to the window looking onto the gardens behind the Ministry of Justice. Hitler had declined to bomb Paris, because it surrendered early, and the city looked untouched, especially in contrast to London. Mary appreciated this even more when she walked past the shops full of delightful displays tempting the American visitors. Though the high-end fashion houses looked beautiful from the outside, they had barely survived the conflict because the Germans were poor customers. As Mary wrote for *Life*, "The first day Goering arrived in Paris, he roared up to the door of Paquin in Rue de la Paix and bought two scarves." After that business, "a half-dozen of the best couturiers agree that German trade totaled not over 2% of the total during the four years of occupation."[5]

After pounding out her impressions of Paris, Mary passed her work to the censors and sent the piece on to New York, hoping to make the next edition's deadline. Though Paris escaped being bombed, the German occupation had ruined daily life and Mary observed the dislocation and depression. Paris looked "poor in everything: poor in money, poor in food, soap, tobacco, and hard liquor, poor in men to make things, and in transport to bring things from elsewhere." It was so bad, "Pretty women dive for cigarette butts on the street."[6]

Mary rushed through the surging crowds up the Champs-Élysées to the Arc de Triomphe. She arrived at 3 P.M., just before General Leclerc's column began its march along the broad avenue lined with emotional Parisians. Generals Charles de Gaulle and Omar Bradley reviewed the troops from a stand in the Place de la Concorde. Mary had last encountered Bradley at her birthday party, and he gave her a subtle wave. De Gaulle led the march, and thousands of voices yelled, "Vive la France" as the soldiers passed. Simone de Beauvoir described the parade as "a magnificent if chaotic, popular carnival show."[7]

The parade ended at Notre-Dame, where the troops dispersed into the crowds. Parisian women had put on their finest clothes to welcome the soldiers. Some wore extravagant hats covered with imitation fruit and lace. Mary wrote, "Shopgirls in printed frocks, bright sweaters, and the tricolor in their hair, as well as elegant women, make the GIs realize how much they have been missing in unimaginatively dressed Britain and the damp fields of Normandy."[8]

In a crowd of thousands, led by General de Gaulle, Mary walked toward Notre-Dame Cathedral to attend a thanksgiving mass. The high doors stood open and light streamed inside. At 4:20 P.M. members of the Vichy militia hiding in the roof of the Cathedral began firing. As the shots rang out General Leclerc tried to hustle de Gaulle through the door, but de Gaulle shook him off and walked slowly down the aisle. A machine pistol fired from above. The BBC's Robert Reid reported, "Firing started all over the place . . . General de Gaulle walked straight ahead into what appeared to be a hail of fire . . . but he went straight ahead without hesitation, his shoulders flung back . . . even while the bullets were pouring about him." Reid recounted, "It was the most extraordinary example of courage I've ever seen; there were bangs, flashes all about him, yet he seemed to have an absolutely charmed life."[9] After the shooting stopped, Mary got in close enough to hear the choir and smell the incense.

After the service Mary walked through the thronging streets to the Scribe, wrote a long cable, and dispatched it at the Western Union office. She made her way to the Ritz and found Ernest alone, sitting in the twilight before his open window. They embraced and kissed, and Ernest suggested they dine at a Left Bank restaurant he knew. Although tired, Mary agreed, and they walked along the rue Castiglione to the Tuileries, the famous gardens damaged in the fight to liberate Paris. They found the restaurant where Ernest's friends sat eating, drinking, and talking in excited voices. Mary's weariness soon returned, and the red wine did not revive her.

After the meal, they walked out onto the silvery moonlit street. Gunshots sounded from buildings not far away and Ernest suggested they walk in the shadows. The soft air smelled fresh without the ever-present odor of cordite one breathed in London and Mary celebrated the freedom of walking without the fear of buzz bombs. Ernest spoke of his first days in Paris, his marriage to Hadley, and their son, John. Hadley had nicknamed him "Bumby" because he waddled like a fat teddy bear. Mary asked why he had left Hadley, and Ernest confessed he'd been foolish. He'd fallen in love with Hadley's friend, Pauline Pfeiffer, and killed Hadley's trust and respect for him. Mary understood the topic troubled Ernest, but he did not shift blame, and she expected it to come up again. She shared the story of her failed marriage to Larry Cook.

As they neared the Ritz, the doorman recognized Ernest and saluted him with a friendly wave. In Ernest's room, Mary fell into the deepest sleep she had enjoyed in weeks. The next morning, she awoke to the pop of a champagne cork. Ernest smiled and carried two glasses to the bed, commenting on her melodic snoring. As Mary propped herself up on the pillows, she accepted a glass of Perrier-Jouet Brut and glanced over at the next bed, where she saw a pile of grenades and revolvers. Pelkey, brewing coffee on a GI stove in the empty fireplace, turned and smiled at her. The armed camp did not please Mary, and no matter how brave the men considered themselves, she did not wish to share their room. She left for chambre 86 and told Ernest he would be welcome if he came alone. Ernest brought his two extra shirts and necktie to Mary's room, where they enjoyed time alone as a couple for the next few days.

Mary and Ernest declared a break from the war. He stayed in Paris while the 4th Infantry Division headed east, and she avoided the duties of *Time-Life*, much to Wert's consternation. They wandered the streets of Paris, sharing their special places. When not vertical they were horizontal in Mary's shiny brass bed, creating a world filled with laughter and playfulness and lovemaking within the limits of Ernest's continuing impotence. During this interlude, the war seemed far away and they grew closer. Mary wrote, "We lived in those days far beyond the usual reach of our senses," and on one of their precious mornings together, Ernest summed it up: "This is it. Our one and only life."[10] Mary found Ernest's regard for her captivating. He looked upon Mary as his equal, listened to her ideas, and treated them with respect. The famous writer valued her opinions and focused his full attention on her, and she grew to expect his esteem and hoped he might always treasure her. Mary did not recognize that absolute adoration formed but the first step in Ernest's infatuation with women.

Ernest showed Mary where he and Hadley had lived at 74 Rue Cardinal Lemoine in the Latin Quarter and the room he rented and worked in across the street. They wandered through the Luxembourg Gardens and sat on the bench where Ernest had relaxed while Bumby rested in his stroller. Ernest explained that the once-adorable Bumby was now serving as a counter-intelligence officer near the front lines.

On the Rue de l'Odéon, Ernest pointed out number 12, where Sylvia Beach's bookshop, Shakespeare and Company, stood before the war.[11] He had spent hours in the shop reading the latest magazines from America, often with Bumby on his lap. Ernest told Mary that Sylvia had allowed him to borrow books, and he read Tolstoy and Chekhov thanks to her. Sylvia even sat and listened while he read one of his early short stories, and she loved it. Her encouragement mattered in the days when publisher's rejection slips cluttered his desk.[12] At Sylvia's place he met his mentor Ezra Pound and James Joyce, the latter always willing to go out for a drink. Wonderful conversations took place around the little table upstairs.[13]

Farther along the street they wandered into a bistro and the waiter waved them to a table after warning there was no gin, whiskey, or fine wine. Ernest ordered two glasses of a young red wine, almost too tannic to drink, and Mary soaked the heel of a baguette in her glass like a biscuit in tea. As Mary began to consider she and Ernest might have a future together, she wanted to understand his political beliefs. To Mary, Ernest seemed apolitical, for he never analyzed events from a left- or right-wing point of view, as did her British friends. He professed anti-authoritarian and anti-fascist opinions but showed no signs of interest in conventional political parties, focusing instead on individual motives and actions. Mary had supported

Roosevelt in the last presidential election and wondered how Ernest had voted. Not at all, he reported, because he lived in Cuba, but he would have supported FDR. The last presidential candidate he voted for was Eugene Debs because he cared for the little man.

This news relieved Mary, and she called Ernest a political soulmate of her father. Tom Welsh had supported Debs for years. Ernest backed the common people—and ordinary soldiers. He railed over the officer class's pretensions, especially French officers, and complained again about General Leclerc. The couple sat watching the passersby until Ernest declared the wine too poor to keep him there for another glass, and they returned to the Ritz for a late lunch and a loving nap.

One evening they visited the studio of Pablo Picasso, who welcomed Ernest with open arms. Mary stayed in the background with Françoise Gilot, Picasso's "slim, dark, quiet girl with serpentine movements." Picasso showed Ernest "his big, chilly studio" and the work he had done over the past four years despite the German occupation. "*Les boches* left me alone," Picasso said. "They disliked my work, but they didn't punish me for it."[14] Picasso's studio occupied an apartment building's upper story, with rough wooden floors and high walls that reached to a loft. Tall windows let in the pink light of the setting sun, which glowed on the half-finished pieces hanging on the walls. Picasso showed them over five hundred "canvasses, abstractions, two- and three-profiled portraits, some more or less representational landscapes, some few paintings on cardboard or wood, many compositions which I did not even dimly understand." As the Paris sky turned violet, Picasso took them to an open window and showed them a view of rooftops and chimney pots. "'There,' he said. 'That is the best picture in my studio.'" The tour ended, and, as they left, Picasso pointed to the handlebars of a bicycle, turned forward, and called it his bull. They had seen several canvasses reminiscent of bullfighting, and he used the bicycle handlebars to model the shapes of bull horns.

As they walked home, Mary thought out loud about the story she would write. "His colors are bolder and stronger than I remember. No Blue Period. No longer the soft sand colors. But many of the forms I don't understand at all."[15] Ernest replied that Picasso was pioneering, and she shouldn't condemn his pieces because she didn't understand them. A few nights later they dined with Picasso and Gilot at a place on the Boulevard Saint-Germain. Mary missed a third of the apparently amusing interchange because her ears were too slow to understand their French. Ernest told Pablo about his adventures with the US Army in France, and they reminisced "rather solemnly," Mary thought, about the old days in Paris. "Françoise Gilot and I mostly held our tongues, she, it seems to me, watchfully or critically, I, because I had little but goodwill to contribute."

Ernest asked Pablo if he would do a nude portrait of Mary from the waist up. Taken aback, Mary said nothing. For the first time, Picasso gave her his full attention. He examined the bone structure of her face, her eyes, and her nose. He studied the curve of her lips, the line of her brow, and the shape of her breasts. Mary thought she could not be as exciting as the exotic Françoise. "Picasso's enormous black radar eyes turned onto me, shrouded in my uniform, for a moment, smiled and said, 'Bien sûr. Have her come to the studio.'"[16] It did not occur to Ernest to consult Mary, and his lack of consideration shocked her. He told Picasso on her behalf that it would be her honor to pose for him. It was as if she were his property, and he could have his friend paint her in the nude if he wished.

Ernest traveled to the front to join Lanham's Regiment, and without him to prod her into modeling for Picasso, Mary kept postponing her visit to his studio. "It seemed so presumptuous of me," and she never saw Picasso again.

ELEVEN

I Also am Committed, Horse, Foot, and Guns

August 1944–September 1944

Allied officers and journalists took advantage of Paris's thriving black market in food, liquor, and wine and threw wild parties. Fine restaurants which a few days before had served officers of the German army now welcomed members of the Allied forces. American journalists assembled at the Hotel Scribe. Floyd Davis captured the bar scene in a piece commissioned by *Life*, now hanging in London's National Portrait Gallery. Caricatures of Dave Scherman, Janet Flanner, Lee Miller, Robert Capa, Charlie Wertenbaker, and Hemingway carouse in the Scribe bar in the days following the liberation. Capa captured the atmosphere of the place: "I was . . . sitting at the bar trying to teach Gaston to mix that most potent of pick-me-ups, the 'Suffering Bastard.'"[1] Gaston, a former Maquis fighter, had exchanged his rifle for a cocktail shaker.

Caught up in the giddy atmosphere and sensing the war's end, Mary decided to chart a new course. In the early years of their relationship, Mary had enjoyed Noel's praise for her journalism. After consorting with Shaw and Ernest, she found Noel less impressive and his colonial mindset embarrassed her.

Mary found Ernest exciting, curious, and questioning, and she enjoyed his sense of humor—though he was moody. She felt vibrant with Ernest but dull with Noel. Life with Noel moved in a predictable pattern but living with Ernest would be an adventure, and she could not help but feel the allure of his celebrity and wealth.

Noel had never made any real money. Paid at American instead of British rates, Mary had long earned more than her husband, but Ernest had enough money to change her life. And the promise of living in a tropical paradise with access to the water on a fast boat suited her bold spirit. Five days after arriving in Paris, Mary decided she would leave Noel. Not that she committed to Ernest, but she freed herself from a marriage going nowhere. In her memoir, Mary dispatched Noel in a paragraph, but her letters and journals show the protracted and sad end of their relationship.

On August 30, Mary wrote to Noel, "I've been trying for a long time to think of some kind and gentle way of putting it down." She had "lost all faith in the future, lost it reluctantly but entirely. And, therefore, I think it will save us both pain and further hurt to make a clean and complete break now, without waiting longer." Mary added, "I am in no hurry for legalities. But I think the matter must be settled now between us."[2] She was sorry to be putting this in a letter because it would sound cold and hard. Mary thanked Noel for the "fine years of affection," but she didn't mention Ernest. The next night at 11 P.M. Noel wrote, telling her he had phoned twice but missed her. "If by some kind and gentle way of putting it down you mean telling me that you have dumped me overboard," he could, "only say I'm glad you didn't think of the hard way. But . . . that's what you want, Mary and I accept it."[3] Noel promised to get his things out of the flat, and he offered to help with the legalities. Her "vote of non-confidence in him was carried," and he apologized, "I had not the necessary qualifications to stay the distance with you." In her memoir, Mary quoted only Noel's "apology" for his lack of "qualifications." This version of the story distorted the painful reality of the split.

Mary realized she had hurt Noel but didn't know what else to say.[4] She told Ernest that Noel's note, "makes me shaky and sad and needing to check my navigation. It makes me proud of him." Mary lectured Ernest, "you and I have to look, and if what you see is ugly, or simply tarnished or unclean or petty, you still have to look . . . [at] what's coming to you from your own censure and your conscience."[5] Ernest did not respond well to Mary's fit of conscience, and she expressed her frustration with him. "From the roots of his being . . . Ernest's streak of forefathers had . . . been subscribers to the truth." But in this case, Ernest was not truthful, and Mary grew impatient with him for dismissing Noel as a chump and ignoring the questions troubling her. She protested, "perfidy and rationalization" were easier for him than the truth. She was "outraged that he thought he could impose

such childish substitutes on . . . my adult brain."[6] They argued, but Ernest did not
stop mocking Noel. The argument escalated, and Ernest's jealousy of Irwin Shaw
resurfaced in harsh criticism of the younger man. Mary defended Shaw's writing
and her friendship with him and landed a low blow. Shaw's biographer claims
Mary said Irwin had a larger penis than Ernest.[7] Since Mr. Scrooby remained
dysfunctional, Ernest could only swear. Later that night, Mary wrote an anodyne
letter to her parents about her trip to Paris, saying she lived at the Ritz while Noel
stayed with the army at the front.

In early September, Mary woke from a deep sleep to find Ernest missing from
his bed. She found him, overcoat over his shoulders, sitting on the lid of the toilet,
writing on rough wartime toilet paper with a pencil. Mary later typed the "Poem
to Mary (Second Poem)" on loud pink paper scrounged from the office. She presented the draft to Ernest when they met for drinks after work at the Ritz bar.
As he read to her, he noticed something missing and asked to check the toilet
paper draft. Mary ran up to her room, found her wastebasket empty, and chided
herself for not having kept the scroll. She sprinted down the corridor in search of
the chambermaid, who told Mary the staff had taken the garbage downstairs and
burned it. Filled with foreboding, Mary came back to the bar and confessed to
Ernest. He remained nonchalant as he was missing only two or three lines. This
counted as nothing compared to the trouble he had suffered at Hadley's hands back
in 1922, and he told Mary the story. Away from Paris for a few weeks, covering
the Peace Conference in Lausanne for the *Toronto Star,* Ernest missed Hadley.
He invited her to fly to meet him, but she took the train instead. She brought his
manuscripts, typescripts, and carbon copies in a small valise. Ernest's life work
rested in the bag. Hadley put the bag in a storage area when she left the compartment to buy a bottle of water.[8] The valise went missing. Mary lit a Camel as she
waited for Ernest to tell her the outcome.

When Hadley arrived in Lausanne, she was afraid to tell Ernest what had
happened. Instead, she sobbed. He pleaded with her to tell him the awful thing,
and when she finally did, Ernest found the news incomprehensible. He asked
if she had checked lost and found, whether she had packed the carbons too,
whether she had checked the other cabins on the train. Distressed, Ernest took
the next train to Paris, went straight to their flat, and checked the old Vuitton
suitcase he used to store his work. He checked the drawers but found nothing.
The words and thoughts he had struggled over for years had vanished. Ernest did

not recover, and he never fully trusted Hadley again. As Ernest told Mary this story, the oblong scar on his forehand inflamed with anger even after twenty-two years. Mary empathized with both Ernest and Hadley and realized Hadley must have known he could not forgive her. Mary promised never to lose another piece of his writing and assured him his archives would be safe with her.[*]

A few days later, Mary received a handwritten note from Ernest complaining she ran away from him that morning. She should have waved or "given me a wink with your ass."[9] Mary had glimpsed him chatting with the concierge while she scrambled to meet an urgent request from the office. Enthralled by Ernest when they were alone, Mary found her personality melted away when they were with others because his charisma drew everyone's attention to him. She doubted the wisdom of a long-term commitment, and she expressed her doubts in a letter on pink paper. "Maybe it is true that I turned my head away from you and ran, wanting an escape, wanting a four hours pass from your domination because you are so big, and you absorb me so that I lose myself." Mary found herself "wanting only the soft, easy business of flattery and admiration and gaiety that matters not, and nothing intense."[10] Ernest's "bullshit detector" sensed she didn't want to consider their future together. He knew "wimmys like gifts" so he bought her a white imitation angora sweater they had seen in a shop window on the Boulevard des Capucines. Mary tried on the garment when they got back to chambre 86. Ernest remembered the first time he met Mary at the White Tower, and they embraced.

Mary observed that Ernest used his money to win over people, including her. He didn't let others pay, and his friends came to expect him to pick up the tab. Ernest tipped well to make sure waiters, doormen, concierges, and even chambermaids remembered him and showed delight when they next met him.

With Ernest in Paris, Mary's work became difficult because they held opposing views about how to present the news. Ernest complained about "the drab colors" in which *Time* reporters "visualized the news." Mary defended the magazine's approach, maintaining they pursued "the truths of the many-faceted life of the city

---

[*] Hilary Justice contends the loss of the manuscripts was not a complete loss for Ernest. "Their ideas—their structures, themes, and phrasing, their stories—were not lost at all, nor could they have been, at least to Hemingway." Indeed, as Paul Smith suggested, "the loss of the manuscripts was the best thing that ever happened to Hemingway's writing." Ernest himself decried the loss of his papers in *A Moveable Feast* and in more detail in his short story, "The Strange Country."

and its surrounding military headquarters." They were "not writing thrillers." [11] Mary defended *Time*'s method in her draft memoir. "Our principal aim was to paint in perspective backgrounds, forms, colors, people and their problems and their right or wrong solutions." Though Mary seldom argued when friends asked how she could work for "*Time* with its biases and inaccuracies," she felt *Time* "averaged out about as well in the truthful presentation of the news as any other outfit." [12] Ernest interfered in Mary's work by discussing with Wert how she should handle her assignments. Mary felt stifled, and her resentment built until it exploded and she told him to leave her alone. She had survived on her own for many years before he came along, and she didn't need or want his help. Though she missed him when he was out of town, his absence made her work more manageable.

On September 7, Archie Pelkey drove Ernest in a small convoy to meet Buck Lanham's 22nd Infantry Regiment, which was beginning the push into Germany. The next day, Ernest wrote to Mary saying, "I love you very much and could not have been happier and am still happy from being with you." [13] A stream of letters filled with lovers' talk followed, and Ernest asserted his masculinity by describing his exploits in battle.

From Mary's memoir it appears that only Ernest wrote loving letters, and he comes across as needy. But Mary left her letters to Ernest during this period in Cuba, and she made no mention of them. When we include the letters found in the Museo Hemingway collection, their attraction appears mutual, though Mary needed convincing. The letters show Ernest fell in love with Mary, and he pursued her, hoping to make her his wife and life partner. Though Mary was skeptical in the beginning, she began to succumb to his insistent pleading.

On September 11, Ernest wrote, "Pickle, this has been the truly happiest month I've ever had in all my life. . . . and you, my true own beloved, lovely to touch, lovely to feel, lovely to be just with you and know you were there." He closed, "Dearest lovely, I love you so." [14]

Mary replied to Ernest's first letter, assuring him she loved him and him only but making him aware she had other suitors. General McClure had arrived from London, bringing her "an extra skirt, a carton of cigarettes, and some stockings from my room at the Dorch." They spent a long evening together, "from 6:30 until

1:30 and he behaved, not as I was telling you all men behave when they renounce a doll, bosom-beating, deep throated and big-gestured, but really beautifully—worried about my reputation." He wanted "to have me back with all forgiven and not snide." McClure told her, "no man would love me as much as he had," and Mary conceded, "no one has spoiled me more, being good or more generous and always." But then she assured Ernest where her affections lay: "I'd like to be your woman; I want to be your woman; please let me be your woman, please."[15]

Ernest wrote about his finances, assuring Mary he had enough money to allow them to live well until he finished his next book. He knew this was a winning argument with Mary, telling her he was better off than he'd ever been, and he intended to write a fine novel. Only the dedication existed: "To Mary Welsh: If you don't like the novel, you can dedicate it to anybody you want as it is your property."[16] A day later he wrote, "We loved each other with no clothes on at all, no lies, no secrets, no pretenses, no underwear." He closed, "Small friend—I like to remember us in the dining room of the Ritz within our own world."[17]

During the rest of September, Ernest wrote to Mary often to push for a long-term partnership with "combined operations." She slowly realized "combined operations" meant he wanted her to be both his lover and his manager, although he would control the checkbook. Ernest made sure Mary knew he was facing danger and suffering in the cold and wet. He told her he wore "a battle jacket held together by safety pins—socks worn through—same two shirts, both on, no raincoat."[18] Ernest drew a heroic portrait of himself to win Mary's heart, and it began to work.

On September 15, Mary told Ernest she spent an evening at the Scribe with Irwin Shaw and two journalists and drank brandy until she got slightly tight. She rushed home to flop on her bed, wanting "to wrap myself around you, warm almost to slipperiness." She wanted "to ease this ache that grows up from my feet through my loins and especially in my loins and in my stomach and shoulders."[19] Like Ernest, Mary became explicit in her yearning. One can't help wonder whether Shaw, rather than the absent and impotent Ernest, stimulated the condition she described and whether Mary knew that invoking Shaw's name would make Ernest burn with jealousy.

Ernest was with Buck Lanham as the 22nd Regiment fought its way through Belgium and into Germany. Lanham's headquarters was a plywood trailer which troops hauled, parked, and defended near the front. The trailer provided protection from the rain, but not from the cold or bullets. Ernest and Buck spent hours together, cursing, laughing, and drinking, like two guys on a big-game hunting trip. Ernest wrote for *Collier's* that Buck's courage on the battlefield inspired his men to rally and follow him into combat. In a story Buck later labeled as "completely false," Ernest exaggerated Buck's role. With his men pinned down by German fire, Buck, armed only with his pistol, "came up the hill and out over this terrace where they were all laying." He said, "Let's go get these Krauts. Let's kill these chickenspitters. Let's get up over this hill and get this place taken." Ernest implied he saw the attack. "He had his goddam .45, and he shot 3-4 times at where the Kraut fire was coming from." Buck said, "Goddam, let's go get these Krauts! Come on! Nobody's going to stop here now!" Buck got them moving, "And he kept leading them deeper into the forest."[20]

Buck's men broke through the Siegfried Line near Grosshau and Ernest wanted the world to know the brave men of the infantry, not the air force, cracked the line. With every path mined and every crossing covered by machine guns, the battle proved exhausting and expensive. On the second day of the conflict, the 22nd lost 10 officers and 129 enlisted men. The losses were demoralizing and it took all of Buck's strength to keep his men moving forward. In his *Collier's* piece, in an account Buck later called "invented," Ernest described the fighting to clear a bunker of a nest of SS troops. "I yelled at Roger to get down, and right then, they shot him. I saw the goddam hole, and I threw the grenade to go in, but you know how those apertures were beveled, and it hit and bounced out." There was a slit trench on the left. A "Kraut stood up, and Smith shot him with his carbine." Ernest wrote, "You can tell how fast this happened because just then the grenade went off, and they all ducked."[21] Unable to force the Germans from the bunker, they brought in a wump gun and fired six rounds to blast off the steel door. The Germans inside moaned, screamed, and surrendered, yelling, "*Kamerad!*"

Later, Lanham made it "absolutely clear" to Carlos Baker that Ernest missed the attack on the Siegfried Line. "Not until your manuscript reached me did it ever occur to me that EH was trying to create the impression that he was present. He wasn't." Buck wrote, "the account he gave . . . was (shall we say) not the true gen. . . . The account of the battle was completely inaccurate."[22]

As Mary read Ernest's dispatches, his writing took her on an adventure showing his view of the action and amplifying the danger. He admitted his fear. Irresistible in person, Ernest overwhelmed her in his letters. She had no way of telling he was shaping the narrative to prove his manliness. Mary wrote to him on September 20, saying, "two envelopes and five wonderful letters arrived today." She "dropped all work and came back here to the hotel and spent most of the afternoon reading them and loving them . . . in a great big bloody orgy of happiness."[23]

When Mary prepared to leave for London, she told Ernest she had hidden the letters she'd received from him. She didn't want Martha to find them if she moved into her husband's room. "In case Mrs. Hem moves in there," they are, "in my room, in a sealed envelope in the cupboard where my clothes are stored."[24] Mary worried Ernest might go back to Martha. She told him, "Mrs. Hemingway" was "enquiring everywhere tenderly for you." That "scares the be-Jesus out of me, but only darling if you decide you want her, and not me." Mary asked him, "please do this one little thing for me—please tell me straight and at once. I promise you I will behave okay: but Mr. Big Friend, please don't fool around about it." In the meantime, Mary said she was behaving like "a businesslike virgin, with never even slight consideration of being otherwise because I love you and I'm your woman until you say, 'no.'"[25] She had merged into him, "as deeply as a blood transfusion." She asked nothing, "except that if you change your mind, you tell me truthfully. Because, as you wrote, I also am committed, horse, foot, and guns."[26] Mary began having nightmares about Ernest's involvement in the fighting. "I woke up one-night rigid and cold and wet with a dream you were caught alone and hurt. Please let nothing bad happen to you, darling."[27]

Ernest wrote a troubling letter to Mary on September 18. "Casualties were fairly heavy . . . certain amount of battle fatigue. Many more than they should be." Ernest was "getting sort of mixed up on a lot of things again." He told her, "I think about you. . . . I write you awfully dull letters, darling because I get tired and sort of emptied out. And all I have to tell you that I can write is that I love you."[28] After receiving this letter, Mary stood on her balcony in the dimming September light: "I prayed that he would survive the ballroom bananas, however, our personal alliance developed."[29] She wrote to Ernest, concerned he was participating in the fighting. "It's fine—fine and splendid—you've got a good mob. . . . But you've said something about going in with the platoon. Are you going in every day with your platoon?" She confessed, "I don't know who is expendable and who isn't or the right and wrong of your throwing grenades . . . But I hope you don't go in, up in the line with your infantry fellows every day."[30] Ernest's letters had the desired effect—preoccupying Mary with thoughts of his bravery and concern for his safety.

TWELVE

Irwin, Are You Going to Marry Me?

September 1944–November 1944

E rnest wrote of his wish to be with Mary in a house away from the war. "I want to get out of this hawk and cough and spit area, and somewhere we can sleep good and talk and put our loneliness out of business." He professed to her, "true and straight; I have never been happier, true, solid, knowing, confident, happier . . . than I ever was in all my life." [1] On the back of the envelope, he wrote, "Please deliver in case of casualty," leading Mary to worry that he faced mortal danger. The hairs on the back of her neck stood up as she read, "Will be here a while now, my dear beloved. . . . Love me very hard and very much and take good care of me for a while." Ernest sent a poem about the terrible conditions: "So now/Losing the three last night. /Taking them back today, /Dripping and dark in the woods. . . ." [2] Mary worried about him even more. Some men would have spared their lovers the frightening and horrible reality of war—not so Ernest, who described the danger he faced, and according to Buck Lanham, even exaggerated.

◆

In mid-September, Mary saw a notice on the Ritz concierge desk: "The Hotel Ritz provides accommodation for V.I.P. personnel only," and she feared she would have to move. To her great relief, the major in charge of US housing in Paris told her the rule did not apply to her because she was an "original inhabitant." Ernest's great friend, Marlene Dietrich, showed up as one of the Ritz VIPs. Ernest and

Marlene had met on a transatlantic crossing in 1934 and become close. They never coordinated the times when they were not married to others, so they never became lovers. Ernest called it "an unsynchronized passion." "The Kraut," as Ernest called her, never hesitated to call him a great artist, and Ernest found her style and flair intoxicating. Mary realized they loved each other but didn't find Marlene a threat.

Marlene knew Irwin Shaw from Hollywood and invited him to use her bathtub one evening. The Ritz was famous as the only hotel in Paris with hot running water in the weeks following the liberation. Mary suffered a pang of jealousy when she visited with Marlene and Shaw in the bar afterward and they mentioned his bath. Forty-three-year-old Marlene enjoyed the company of the much younger Shaw. Mary told Ernest that Marlene was sensitive about her age, which was not a subject for jokes. She went on to say she loved Ernest's bigness and the way he moved around the room, "and your slim boys' sized behind, and how you always greet me, warmly and sweetly."[3] At the end of September, Ernest received permission to leave the front and return to Paris to continue writing for *Collier's*. Mary was delighted to see him, despite his hacking cough and fever. Ernest qualified as a VIP at the Ritz, and he continued nightly visits to chambre 86.

When Mary met Marlene, she was already famous for her roles in *The Blue Angel*, *Shanghai Express*, and *Desire*. A well-loved frontline entertainer of the troops, Marlene looked as gorgeous in a khaki outfit as in her body-hugging sequin dresses. A practical businesswoman, Marlene supervised every detail of her performances, from lighting and staging to makeup and costume. She called Ernest her anchor, sage, advisor, and "the Pope of her personal church."[4] Marlene sang her favorite songs for their private enjoyment in Ernest's rooms, and they sang together. Sometimes, Mary teased Marlene by singing "Falling in Love Again" in her style and accent, warbling before landing on a note, or missing it, to make Marlene and Ernest laugh.

In early October, a group of American politicians visited Paris to investigate the US Army's European Theater of Operations, and Mary met them for an early "brain-stimulating, but gastronomically boring dinner." She returned to her room to help Ernest host four officers from the 22nd Regiment on a short leave in Paris. Ernest had passed the word in the Regiment that they should regard his rooms at the Ritz as their command post.[5] Marlene joined them. She wore a modest civilian outfit that did not disguise her charms, and she awed the men of the 22nd. After one of them said his dream would be to write home that he had shared a bed with her; she stretched out on the satin bedspread and patted the bed beside her. The nervous soldier lay next to her at rigid attention. Everyone laughed, drank another round of champagne, and by the time they arrived in the dining room, the soldiers were slurring their words. Mary worried because she saw Clare Boothe Luce, her boss's striking wife and a member of Congress, dining with an air force officer at a nearby table.

As Mary tried to speak to the man next to her, his eyes closed, and his head pitched forward. His comrades escorted him away, returning to the table just as Mrs. Luce wandered over to chat. Impressed by the stories she had just heard about the vital role the air force played in the European campaign, Luce supposed the infantry helped by pinpointing targets for air attacks. The angry men told her she understood nothing because the infantry did far more than target air attacks, complaining that Mrs. Luce had diminished the sacrifices of their dead and wounded comrades. They were so vehement that Mary feared Mrs. Luce might mention the incident to her husband and have her fired from *Time-Life*. After Luce left the table, the party descended into drunk talk. Marlene slipped away, and Mary followed.

Relieved to be alone, Mary got ready for bed after cleaning up the vomit a soldier had left in her bathroom. Ernest arrived and paced around her room. Mary told him goodnight, but Ernest was furious and claimed she had insulted his friends all evening. Mary exploded. She said Ernest's friends were "drunks and slobs." They threw up all over her bathroom and might get her fired. "They might be heroes in Germany, but they stink, stink, stink here."[6] Ernest boiled over and struck her face. No one had hit Mary in anger since her mother whacked her with a hairbrush for childish misconduct, and she fell onto her bed, covering her stinging jaw with her hands. Then her fury surged, and Mary danced around the room calling Ernest a fat coward, a woman-hitter, and a bully. She challenged him to "knock my head off" to show his friends the kind of man he was. Ernest's eyes bulged. He put his hands behind his back and sat on the bed. "Hold it," he said, "hold it now."

"You big slob," Mary said. "Break my jaw, you coward."

She pushed him down on the bed, straddled his hips, and beat his chest with her fists. He became detached and said she was pretty when she was mad. That made her even angrier. She pushed him out the door and threw his shirts, socks, and tie after him. "Good night and goodbye!" Mary shouted and slammed the door.[7]

Mary brushed her teeth, crawled into bed, slept well, awoke refreshed, and resolved to live her life to the full—without Ernest Hemingway. A young battalion commander knocked on her door. He relayed the message that Papa felt very sorry. Mary told him, "Papa be damned. He is a coward." Mary wanted nothing to do with him. A few minutes later, another hapless officer knocked on her door, and Mary made short work of him, too. She had no interest in continuing any relationship with Ernest, and she wanted to be alone. Then Ernest dispatched the most charming emissary of all—Marlene. Ernest had already confessed to Marlene that Mary "considered him a 'pitiful lover,' and only I could help him out of this fix by having a talk with the girl."[8] Marlene stood with her elbow on the fireplace, looking elegant and making Mary feel like a country mouse. Marlene drew calmly on her long black cigarette holder and exhaled smoke to punctuate her sentences. She said she understood Mary's anger, but Ernest loved her, and he was a good and responsible man. Marlene recalled, "Mary Welsh didn't love Hemingway, of this I'm certain. Yet this modest, inconspicuous woman war correspondent had nothing to lose."[9]

Mary told Marlene she didn't want Ernest, and she "turned a deaf ear" to arguments in his favor. Marlene listed the advantages of a marriage with Ernest, asking Mary to compare life with and without him at her side. She would live far better with him than as a reporter. By lunchtime, Mary's resistance crumbled, and she said she would consider Ernest's proposal of marriage. "I was trembling all over when the evening arrived," Marlene wrote. "Mary Welsh showed up wearing a radiant smile and accepted his offer, in the presence of a single witness, namely me." Marlene said, "I've never seen anybody as happy as Hemingway. His huge body seemed to emit sparks whose light fell on us and was reflected in our eyes."[10]

Later, Ernest told Buck about the fight, saying he "made a false accusation and Mary poked him twice and gave him the old knee." Ernest "gave her two Hollywood slaps on the right side of her lovely puss." After Marlene's work as a peacemaker, things were better between them than before the fight.[11] This initiated a pattern of behavior between Ernest and Mary. He acted cruelly, hitting her or making nasty comments; she threatened to leave him, and he capitulated, apologized for his behavior, promised to do better, and bought her gifts or gave her checks or cash.

Ernest received a letter on October 2 commanding him to appear before Colonel Park, the Inspector General of the Third Army, at the city of Nancy. Park was investigating whether Ernest had breached army regulations governing the conduct of correspondents in his actions around Rambouillet. Ernest railed about the unfairness of it and the cowardice of the journalists whom he assumed had filed the charges. Colonel Kent A. Hunter, the PRO for General Patton's Third Army, launched an investigation after hearing journalists' gossip and rumors about Ernest's actions. On October 6, Colonel Park held a hearing to decide whether any of the charges merited a full court-martial. The allegations were that Ernest "stripped off correspondent insignia and acted as a colonel, [to] French Resistance Troops; had a room with mines, grenades, and war maps; and had directed resistance patrols, which action is believed to violate credential rights of the correspondents."[12] Ernest read a prepared statement denying the allegations and responded to questions under oath. The inspector general found there were no grounds for a court-martial and released Ernest. Since the charges rested on hearsay, gossip, and rumors of journalists, the result made sense. Indeed, Major Owens, one of the two officers who fed the rumors to Lt. Colonel Hunter, faced discipline—he was admonished for relying upon hearsay and wasting everyone's time.[13]

Bill Walton doubted Ernest was ever in any combat. "They realized that it was a puff of wind."[14] Carlos Baker wrote that after the inquiry what Ernest "wanted most was a drink in the crowded bar on the Rue Cambon side to forget, if possible, that for the first time in his life he had committed perjury."[15] Baker's statement must be the most offhanded conviction for perjury in the history of American literature. Perjury is a grave charge and difficult to prosecute. Baker did not say which of Ernest's statements under oath amounted to perjury, nor did he analyze the evidence to reach his decision. There is a complete absence of legal reasoning, and Baker's conclusion is unjustified. Given the hearsay evidence against Ernest and the eyewitness testimony supporting him, Colonel Park's decision was correct.

◆

On October 20, Ernest's oldest son, John, also known as Jack (Bumby), assisted the OSS to locate a farmhouse used as a letter-drop by friendly underground forces behind enemy lines. A German patrol stumbled upon them, and in the ensuing firefight Jack received a wound in his right arm and shoulder. They took Jack for questioning before an oberleutenant of the German Army. Through an interpreter, he asked Jack his name, rank, and serial number. The oberleutenant looked puzzled and asked to see Jack's dog tags, and after examining them, asked whether Jack had ever visited Schruns. Jack said he visited long ago as a child. The oberleutenant asked his nurse's name, and Jack told him he called her "Tiddy." The German officer broke into a broad grin, saying in French, "We drink a toast to Tiddy. She is my girlfriend!" They drank a glass of schnapps. [16]

When Ernest learned of Jack's capture, he became frantic and wanted to know where Jack was wounded and how much blood he had lost. He tried to determine which German outfit had captured him and whether the army planned a parachute drop to rescue him. Ernest and Mary arranged for her to do a reconnaissance mission. At Mary's insistence, Wert ordered her to do a story about the countryside where the Germans captured Jack and she traveled with a driver to Jack's last known whereabouts and questioned locals.

◆

After returning to Paris, Mary covered the trials of the French traitors and collaborators taking place at the Ministry of Justice on Île de la Cité. A wave of revenge swept France and courts sentenced thousands of suspected collaborators to death. Mary found the whole proceeding depressing because she considered the punishments excessive for the crime of succumbing to greed or pressure during the Nazi occupation. In a piece for *Time* titled "For Whom the Bell Tolls," she wrote, "the trials were almost social events. Crowds jam-packed La Cour d'Assises, in Paris' Palais de Justice, where Marie Antoinette heard her death sentence pronounced." Some prisoners awaiting trial in France's crowded jails and concentration camps were guilty. Others suffered arrest "on the denunciation of personal foes, business rivals, even discontented wives. Many were obscure men." [17]

◆

Mary did not tell Ernest she met Irwin Shaw for drinks on November 14, and she also left that meeting out of her memoir. Before Shaw departed France Mary wanted to know his true feelings for her to decide whether her future lay with him or with Ernest. She loved Shaw's personality, admired him as a writer, and found him more attractive physically than Ernest. They met at the Ritz bar where Shaw sat drinking with Bill Walton. Walton overheard the conversation between them.[18] Mary got straight to the point. "Irwin are you going to marry me?" she asked. "No, whatever made you think that!" Shaw replied. "All right then, I think I'll marry Ernest," Mary responded.[19] Walton recalled, "both of the participants told me the story, so I think it's true. She was conscious of Ernest's position. Sexually, she was mad for Shaw. And Ernest was all right, but not that hot."[20] Shaw returned to New York a week later to restart his marriage with Marian.

THIRTEEN

I Could Never be a Simone de Beauvoir to Papa's Sartre

November 1944–December 1944

After breaking through the Siegfried Line near Aachen, the US Army pushed into Germany. On November 15, 1944, Ernest and Bill Walton arrived at Lanham's regimental command post on the western edge of the Huertgen Forest. For the next eighteen days, they covered what the US Army's official historian later called "a misconceived and basically fruitless battle that could and should have been avoided."[1] A quarter of the force of 120,000 American soldiers—33,000 men—were killed, wounded, went missing, or were put out of action by trench foot or respiratory disease.[2] Lanham's Regiment suffered near-destruction, sustaining 2,678 casualties out of his complement of 3,200 men.

The Germans defended the forest using mines to boobytrap every path, fire-break, and road. Fortified emplacements protected machine gunners. German artillery barrages poured down, and shells sometimes lodged in trees, exploding later and raining shrapnel and splinters. Ernest described the battle as "Passchendaele with tree bursts."[3] The trees shut out the sun, and the weather turned cold and wet. The GIs suffered hacking coughs, and men broke down from the constant noise and bloodshed. Many of the fresh recruits became disabled by fear. In a piece for *Life*, Bill Walton described the conditions. "Then it snowed. A wet, suffocating blanket sifted through the trees, weighting heavy-branched firs," and "roads, already pale brown rivers, remained quagmires that sucked down tanks, trucks, and jeeps struggling toward the front."[4]

Walton and Ernest lived in a woodcutter's hut. They spent hours talking into the night with the lights out to avoid being shot by their sentries. Ernest spoke of the writers who had educated him, including Flaubert, Stendhal, Balzac, de Maupassant, Tolstoy, and Turgenev. A few officers from nearby outposts came by the hut looking for conversation and drinks, which Ernest always supplied. Ernest acted "happy except for a moody spell or two. He admired the men, and the men admired him. Gone was the braggart Hemingway, the chip on his shoulder, barroom fighter, the master of the provocative remark. Instead, he was downright avuncular."[5]

In the mornings, Walton and Ernest walked around the camp and the GIs called out, "Hi Ernest" or "Hi Papa." "And he just loved it; he really did," Walton recalled. They often visited Buck Lanham in his trailer headquarters and reviewed the maps and battle formations. Walton found Lanham "a plucky little guy." He went in for drama and acted out his role in arguments with "fat-assed" General "Tubby" Barton. Lanham despised Barton, and he later told Carlos Baker that Barton visited his command post only once because he was "terrified of death or injury."[6]

Ernest found Lanham fascinating but Walton did not, and he slipped away when they talked about their manhood or what soldiers should or shouldn't do or why Lanham's role required him to send men to their deaths. When Walton returned, they asked him to take photos of them together, and Lanham showed his pride at having befriended the famous writer. After the war, Walton said Lanham "bored him stiff. . . . He always wanted to have long, soulful, heart-to-heart talks about the war and Ernest. He fell madly in love with Ernest." Walton considered that Ernest ruined Lanham. Buck confided all his problems to Ernest, and then Ernest "pumped him dry every day for literary purposes."[7]

Between November 11 and November 30, 1944, Ernest wrote sixteen letters to Mary, some containing separate entries covering single days.[8] The letters span the time Ernest spent with Bill Walton and Buck Lanham in the battle for Huertgen Forest. Ernest's letters to Mary provide a horrifying glimpse of the ugly conflict, and it is easy to imagine the fear Mary must have felt upon receiving some of them. Ernest used his literary skills to assert his bravery and coolness under fire. When not pleading with Mary to love him and professing his love for her, he described the danger facing him almost every day. His account to Mary differed entirely from Bill Walton's light-hearted recollection. The tone of his letters also differed remarkably from those Ernest wrote to his family during the First World War in which he joked about his circumstances, downplayed danger, and minimized the extent of his serious wounds. He hoped the cable to his family about his wounding "didn't worry you very much." "I am all OK and include much love to ye parents." Trying to relieve them, he reported, "Everything is fine, and I'm comfortable, and one of the best surgeons in Milan is looking after my wounds."[9] He drew a cartoon of himself, bandaged with 227 wounds, and cheerfully saying, "gimme a drink!" Ernest abandoned the mollifying approach in his letters to Mary and instead stressed the danger.

Ernest recounted the hazards of traveling by jeep on his way to Huertgen through the snowy, rainy weather. "Yesterday, Jeep with the windshield so muddy and snowy practically unseeing came within twenty feet of running into a mine-field on road being told was OK." They were told the route to the town was fine but it turned out it was "held by Krauts. Sort of thing could produce unfortunate results."[10] Once they arrived at the command post, the danger did not diminish. "Had the what do you call it shelled out of us last night—not really bad but would impress a visiting fireman fairly. Germans have about 19 Battalions of artillery around here."[11] Ernest said he could write "damned interesting letters" if he wasn't so security minded. "So simply picture your man riding in a Jeep (Boom) trudging through snow (Boom) mud up to knees (Boom) in forest (Boom) trees fall down (Boom) in renewed house outgazing over Kraut land (Boom Boom)." He continued his chilling account, "in partly Kraut villages (Boom Boom Tot Tot Tot) in bed (Boom Boom Double Boom)." Each morning, he laid still for half an hour before getting up, saying to himself, "I will think of absolutely nothing and lie here quietly, neither asking nor hoping, just straight not thinking and rest my fucking heart."[12]

Five days later, he dramatized his vulnerability "For your files, copy of letter to be sent in case of my death." He withdrew coverage of Collier's life insurance policy from his wife and children and transferred it to Mary.[13] He told Mary the value of the policy was fifty thousand dollars. Then he returned to the battle unfolding before him. "Today we could have killed six Krauts—they got away across a field and into a ravine right under our noses—but so much Brass around we could not intervene—Krauts galloping—strong, sound, husky Krauts—getting away to fight another day."[14]

Two days later, Ernest told Mary, "to beat the Krauts" they still needed to "punch through the crust." "But it is like facing the pitching of an old pitcher who knows everything and has four fine innings in his arm—or an old boxer who can go 4 of 10 rounds—or even 6." He told Mary it was like being back on the Piave in 1918, suggesting he was taking part in the fighting. "Have almost cut out drinking on account need head very sharp and mean. Also, would like to be fine for you. Also, would like many Krauts to be done away with."[15]

The next day, he hinted he was in the fight himself. "Today big fight in woods; ditto yesterday, day before same . . . Krauts tough, smart, very professionally intelligent and deadly. We will kill and destroy some." He described the harrowing scene in words which he must have known would cause her to fear for his safety. "Mines, mines, boobytrapped, booby traps, boobytrapped—all fire breaks through woods tabbed for mortar and m.g. [machine gun] fire. Smart Krauts infiltrating."[16]

He conveyed more horror the next day. "This is one of the bitterest and worst fights in history. . . . The artillery and mortar fire is most intense I've known since I was a kid on Piave in 1918." Ernest said, "I suppose right now the most useful thing a man could do, besides the most pleasurable, is killing Krauts," again implying he was personally shooting German soldiers. And then, almost to double the unease Mary must have felt, "There's a little matter of putting it all on the line tomorrow."[17]

Ernest used more frightening imagery the next day. "Every day in the woods is like Custer's last stand if that distinguished leader had fought his way out of it and slain the red men." During an attack, "The Kraut counter-attacking, attacking, attacking, attacking - moving like the Lemmings in a migration into death - The guys wait until they are at 20 yards - and you can walk knee-deep in them."[18] In a second letter that same day, he told Mary, "This is the toughest fight I've ever known . . . The fire rolls like the sea."[19]

The next day was "the toughest day of toughest fight ever."[20] He was detached from human empathy. "You can walk in the woods knee-deep through dead Krauts. Nobody will ever know how many Krauts we've killed because there's no way to count them, and they get a lot of their dead away too." He told Mary, "I get the old feeling of immortality back like I used to have when I was right in the middle of a really bad shelling."[21] Of course, he was not immortal, and that was his real point.

The next night, November 25, Ernest wrote words that must have sent a shiver up Mary's spine. "I'm so damned anxious not to be killed. Pickle on account of loving you that knowing I'm at the end of my tour of duty it makes me hurt where

I don't usually."[22] Toward the end of the battle, he told Mary he was glad Bill Walton was with him, "because if anything happens, he can write the story of the fight."[23] These words were not meant to calm Mary.

◆

Mary sent Ernest a careful letter reporting on the capture of Bumby. The general in charge of the forces in the vicinity turned out to be an old friend of hers from London. They enjoyed a little reunion, drinking whiskey in his trailer. She added, "not an intimate friend—never had a date with him in my life but rather an acquaintance." From then on, everyone cooperated with her mission. Mary described her findings: Bumby received a shoulder wound, but not a serious one; he did not try to escape because his buddy suffered severe injuries. The commander considered mounting a rescue effort but feared that might draw attention to the intelligence work being carried out by Bumby. They hoped he would receive routine treatment from the Germans. He wore his dog tags, but nothing to identify him as an officer of the OSS.

Mary visited the place where they captured Bumby. The colonel handled the thing "as wisely as possible in the midst of that freezing jungle fighting hell over there." The outfit that captured Bumby belonged to the regular army and treated people right, and after his capture, Bumby seemed in excellent spirits. "Altogether, I feel encouraged about the whole business and considerably more optimistic than we did here." Mary prayed, "God grant, I am right about it and not being either fooled nor stupid." She underlined, "One thing you know, my darling, darling dearest—I'm not soft soaping to save you anguish." She ended her report, "I am your woman, my dearest, for as long as you will have me, and I will try to make that forever." Ernest could not have hoped for a more complete and detailed report from anyone.[24]

In his next batch of letters, Ernest told Mary of his pride in her excellent work. He missed her "fine, clear intelligence to put me right, as necessary to me as a compass. You are so much better a reporter than I am." He confessed, "I am so involved and mixed up in it what with knowing the people that one day knocks another out of my head." Ernest missed her "lovely clean, sound un-lying competent head" as much as he missed her "pocket-size miracle of a body and your beautiful face that breaks my heart every time I see it."[25]

Ernest's compliments about Mary's intelligence and exceptional reporting must have boosted her self-confidence. The great Hemingway respected her intellect and competence and found her as vital to him as a compass. Mary took pride in her work and came to accept that their relationship rested on mutual respect. The famous writer wanted to rely upon her to navigate life, and Mary found this a compelling overture. Ernest's confession about his difficulty keeping facts straight helped to explain how he wrote. He didn't create an accurate factual record but allowed his creative talents to take over and embellish reality. Years later, Bill Walton said Ernest was "a storyteller. He didn't know when the truth and fiction stopped." Sometimes when they sat together, "he'd tell me a story, and then I'd look sort of strangely, and he'd say, 'You don't believe me, do you?' And I'd say, 'No, I don't.' He'd say, 'You're absolutely right.'" [26]

The letters from November 1944 are full of lover's talk juxtaposed with imminent danger. Ernest claimed to "love you more and steadier than always." [27] He asked Mary, "please love me very much the way I love you, and I will be back, and we will start our fine life. My dearest blessed most beautiful and lovely." He wanted to spend time in bed, telling her anything that came into his head. "I love you, my dearest most beautiful, most true, most complicated, most simple, and most lovely." Ernest wanted to write better, to be a credit to Mary, and he wanted "to be straight partners with you and try to make you happy and be a good husband and father and writer."

◆

In the chronology he wrote for Baker, Buck told the biographer that he delighted in Ernest's company. It helped cure his loneliness as a commander. Buck had to hold back information, even from his second-in-command, but "With E.H., I could talk. I could get all manner of things off my chest, and I had a hell of an accumulation." [28] Buck reported he and Ernest spent hours together in Buck's trailer. They told each other their life stories and they bonded, locking themselves into "a species of brotherhood that both of us knew would last as long as we lasted." [29] In these talks, Ernest referred to his mother as "a bitch," called his father "a coward," and complained that Hadley lost his papers. His rage mounted as he retold the story. Though it hadn't been her fault, Buck got the impression "Ernest thought it was, and that he had never forgiven her for it and never would." [30]

◆

Walton credited Ernest with saving his life on the last day of the Huertgen campaign. Pelkey was driving Ernest and Walton around the dugouts and command posts to say goodbye to the men. On a straight patch of road, Ernest threw his head back, listening. "Stop, quick!" he yelled at Pelkey, who jammed on the brakes. The three of them jumped into a ditch just before a plane "stitched our jeep with machine-gun bullets." They sat in the ditch and drank martinis from Ernest's canteens, and he told them he recognized the distinctive sound of the Henkel biplane from his days in Spain.[31]

◆

Ernest unleashed his talent as a writer to win over Mary in the stream of intimate and persuasive letters magnifying his role in combat and intelligence gathering. He used every weapon in his arsenal to arouse her empathy for the danger he faced with the troops, and she came to subscribe to his vision of their "combined operations." The attention and praise from the literary giant flattered Mary. She was also attracted to Ernest physically. "Have I told you lately how much I love you and the way you walk, rolling like a sailor and confident and away." She liked "the pensive way" he looked "putting on his boots and the color of the morning light in his eyes." And she loved his "competence for love, . . . and always the enormity and intensity of you." When she heard steps coming along the hall that sounded like Ernest's, Mary said she felt "inert with emotion."[32]

◆

By mid-December 1944, the worst of the Huertgen Forest battle ended, and the decimated 22nd Regiment moved to a rest camp near Luxembourg. Ernest suffered from pneumonia, aggravated by his constant exposure to the forest's dripping wet and sub-zero temperatures. He retreated to recover in luxury at the Ritz. Mary greeted him and, with Marlene Dietrich, tried to discourage visitors so he might rest and defeat the infection. While glad to have Ernest safe and home, Mary found him a difficult patient because he was often in a foul mood when not diverted by admiring visitors. He drank too much and Marlene didn't help Mary's efforts to stem the flow of champagne. She said it turned every day to Sunday.

The French philosophers Jean-Paul Sartre and Simone de Beauvoir came to visit. Younger than Ernest by six years and shorter than Mary, Sartre was unable to speak more than a few English words and relied upon Ernest's French. He had a wandering left eye in a face of pale pockmarked skin and his smile showed the twisted, discolored teeth of a pipe smoker. He wore heavy-rimmed glasses and looked like he needed a bath and a good sleep. It amazed Ernest that he attracted female affection. In contrast, Beauvoir appeared striking. Her elegant suit was tight-fitting, her hair swept into a chignon, her piercing blue eyes sparkled, and her lively smile displayed even white teeth.

Sartre and Beauvoir had become the intellectual leaders of their time in part because of their impeccable academic credentials. Sartre had ranked first and Beauvoir second in their graduating class from the École Normale, founded after the Revolution to train the brightest students in France. The couple worked with the Resistance during the German occupation and after the liberation of Paris they wanted to meet the famous American author. They had spoken of Hemingway's technique and pondered whether it might serve their purposes—Sartre wondered if they might put existentialist ideas into novels written in Hemingway's spare style. A year before the visit, Beauvoir had published her first novel, *She Came to Stay*, a barely disguised autobiographical account of a ménage à trois she and Sartre enjoyed with one of her young female students. Beauvoir wanted to meet Hemingway, because as she told *The Paris Review*, "In writing, *She Came to Stay*, Hemingway certainly influenced me." He "taught us a certain simplicity of dialogue and the importance of the little things in life." [33]

Mary wanted to attend the meeting and to write a story for *Time* about Sartre and existentialism, the ideas that had attracted the postwar generation in France. She mentioned the article to Wert but he told her to forget it because Henry Luce didn't want to give any space in his magazine to promote the ideas of the godless existentialists. [34] Luce regarded Sartre's philosophy as part of the problem with the postwar world, not the answer.

Mary envied the attention Beauvoir received from both men, but she misjudged her. She wrote to Carlos Baker that Beauvoir took notes and recorded the words of Sartre. "I could never be a Simone de Beauvoir to Papa's Sartre (we called her Someone de Pouvoir)." Mary "refused to spoil our fun by rushing for notebooks and breaking the spells."[35] Mary failed to appreciate that Beauvoir was not only Sartre's intellectual equal, but she was destined to be as famous as a thinker and writer. While Sartre's existentialism spoke to a postwar generation, his sophisticated style and flirtation with communism limited his appeal. His work became sidelined to classrooms while Beauvoir's feminist writing placed her in the mainstream of the authors who inspired the late twentieth century.

Leicester Hemingway acted as bartender during the visit. He recalled that after the third bottle of champagne, Beauvoir, nicknamed "Castor" (Beaver) by Sartre, asked about Ernest's health. "'I'm this sick . . . healthy as hell, see?' Ernest kicked back half the bedclothes, flexed a well-muscled leg, and grinned. In the next hour, he repeatedly insisted he was feeling tremendous."[36] Leicester left after serving the sixth bottle of champagne. The next morning, Ernest told Leicester he sent Sartre home soon after that bottle. Castor, whom he found delightful, stayed to chat.

Six months later, Sartre asserted that the most significant literary development in France in the prewar years was the discovery of Faulkner, Dos Passos, Hemingway, Caldwell, and Steinbeck. When the Germans prohibited the printing of American books, the French themselves wrote in the American manner. The novel which caused the greatest sensation between 1939 and 1945 was *The Stranger* by Albert Camus. He had borrowed Hemingway's technique from *The Sun Also Rises*, using the same short brutal sentences, lack of psychological analysis, and heroes. Sartre said, "We learned from Hemingway to depict, without commentaries, without explanations, without moral judgments, the actions of our characters." Hemingway showed his characters from the outside "and he is only the witness of their conduct. It is from their conduct that we must, as in life, reconstruct their thoughts."

FOURTEEN

A Complicated Piece
of Machinery

December 1944–February 1945

I n mid-December, Mary prepared to make the break with Noel permanent. She wrote to Connie Ernst, asking her to contact Mary's solicitor in London to answer several questions: must she divorce Noel in England or might she divorce him in the States, how much would it cost, and how soon might it be done?[1] The next day, Mary was plagued with doubts about her relationship with Ernest. Stuffed up and miserable with a cold, she sat on her rose brocade chaise longue, looked out her window at the green lawn of the Ministry of Justice, and wrote in her diary, "Pop Hemingway and I were not made for each other."[2] Mary's other men had spoiled her with gifts and kindness, and now she was "too bloody independent." She liked her work and managed on her own. She had detected no genuine kindness from Ernest and his manners in public seemed better than at home. When he was good, she found him "more endearing, more stimulating of mind and gaiety and wisdom and love and rock loyalty than anyone I've ever known." But when Ernest was bad, he became "wildly, childishly, and weakly bad." Overdrinking produced it "like a boat sailing freely and suddenly crossing into a current of black, menacing water." The chief feature of the badness was "egocentricity which he well controls when good." His monumental ego dwarfed everything. The night before, Ernest became annoyed because Bill Walton didn't emphasize how courageous and intelligent he had been in a battle.[3]

Ernest invented excuses for drunkenness with evasions but he never admitted to weakness or failure. Mary wondered "why other women want to hang on to him—and if he made them into bitches as he's doing to me."[4] From the episodes she'd already observed, she imagined the problems she would face living with him. Yet she put these concerns to one side and worked to tame him, starting a campaign against Ernest's overdrinking and believing her love could make him a better man.

That evening, Mary went to a dinner hosted by General Carl "Tooey" Spatz, the Commander of Strategic Air Forces in Europe. He was known for his aggressive public relations campaign on behalf of the "high octane" air force in London, where he hosted lavish dinners, "wining, dining, and playing poker with important Englishmen and visiting Americans."[5] Kay Summersby, who later wrote she had been General Eisenhower's lover, described walking into Spatz's headquarters.[6] It resembled "entering a crowded cocktail lounge—lots of people, lots of smoke, lots of chatter, lots of flirtation."[7] Some nights, Tooey brought out his guitar and "the American officers were like boys—sitting around, their heads thrown back, singing rackety old songs they had learned at West Point."[8] As a regular at Spatz's London dinners, Mary brought her alto voice to the parties.

At Spatz's December 16 dinner in Paris, midway through a generous meal, aides interrupted Spatz, advising him of the German counterattack that would become known as "the Battle of the Bulge." Mary excused herself and Spatz sent an armed airman and chauffeur to escort her back to the Ritz, where she found Ernest. Rumors claimed German soldiers wearing GI uniforms had infiltrated Paris, and Mary and Ernest tried to imagine the scale of the fighting. The Germans might cut off troops in the north, launch parachute troops, or even retake Paris. Ernest left in the morning to rejoin Lanham's Regiment despite his heavy chest cold and hacking cough. He asked Mary to destroy a canvas sack of papers if she was forced to leave Paris. Mary worried over the news of the invasion by the Germans, recalling her retreat from Paris four years earlier. Army PRO's briefed journalists that the Allied forces had contained the German attack but rumors persisted of a breakout drive to the English Channel.

Before Ernest left he gave Mary a check for two thousand dollars, and she soon began missing him and regretting their fights. She wrote a long letter apologizing for being "asinine and childish" in insisting he stay with her for Christmas. She was "happy to have all that money to spend any way I want." This was a relative fortune, equal in purchasing power to twenty-eight thousand dollars in 2020 and four times larger than Mary's life savings.[9] Ernest's generous gift was an act of contrition for his boorish behavior over the last couple of months, and Mary responded warmly, writing, "I love you so very much." They should avoid "stinking little misunderstandings" which were insignificant compared to their love for each other. They knew this when forced to be apart; they had to see it when together. "Living without you would be only a matter of drying up slowly until I died." She adored him with "a devotion, dearest beloved that will last as long as I live."[10] The extravagant gift became a practice, and Ernest gave Mary jewelry, cash, minks, and even a convertible to atone for his sometimes-cruel behavior.

By the time Ernest reached the Fourth Division at Luxembourg, the German offensive had ended. He and Bill Walton moved to Buck Lanham's command post in a luxurious rectory near Rodenburg and spread their bedrolls on a double bed they shared. Lanham's regimental doctor filled Ernest with sulfa drugs and prescribed rest. Ernest found a cellar full of sacramental wine, ignored the doctor's advice, and drank several bottles. On December 24, Martha Gellhorn arrived at the command post. At first Ernest ignored his wife, but later he drank brandy with her next to General Barton's Christmas tree. Buck Lanham gave the married couple his bedroom for the night, and the next morning Buck took them on a jeep tour of his command. Martha used the occasion to scold Ernest in French, unaware of Buck's fluency. Buck recalled Martha speaking of personal matters and switching to French to exclude him from the discussion, a move which Buck found "inexcusably rude." After a while, Ernest said to Martha, "Buck speaks better French than you." As Buck told Carlos Baker, after Ernest's rebuke, "She did not discuss the intimacies of the preceding night."[11]

On Christmas night, Ernest found time to write to Mary in Paris. He told her Martha had arrived, but he didn't mention he spent the night with her in Buck's bedroom. He told Mary he had been "good and kind" to Martha because it was Christmas. He informed Martha he would love Mary forever, and he hoped to have children with her—a boy named Thomas Welsh Hemingway and a girl named Bridget Welsh Hemingway. Ernest mentioned, "Mr. Scrooby has risen at this point."

Mary spent Christmas at the Ritz, enjoying lovely boozy lunches with Leal Wertenbaker and Bill Walton, who had returned to Paris for a few days. Charlie Wertenbaker thrilled Mary when he gave her a five-hundred-dollar bonus for Christmas. Mary appreciated Ernest's gift of an Iron Cross he'd cut from the uniform of a dead German soldier in the Huertgen fight, and she expressed delight again with his check for two thousand dollars. No man had ever given her so much money, and it impressed her. Ernest wanted to marry her and be the one who worked, and she would be his "wife, partner . . . and the mother of our children." He planned to give up journalism and write books again. She should be happy "to have a husband and be healthy and economically sound," and when they visited London and Paris, she could talk to the people whose "minds bring you pleasure."[12] Mary found this an intriguing promise but worried about giving up her career in journalism.

In mid-January, Ernest returned to the Ritz. Mary bought him a fancy utility knife for Christmas, but Marlene Dietrich gave him something more useful—her double bed. Mr. Scrooby had started working again, and Mary and Ernest enjoyed Marlene's gift. The impotence caused by the concussions had lasted eight months, two months longer than Mary said she would wait. Although they had found pleasure in sexual experiments short of full intercourse, when Ernest could perform again it did wonders for his self-confidence, and the delights of their shared bed drew them closer. According to Walton, Ernest was glad about his lovemaking with Mary. "He was proud of her, this cute little girl on his arm as he swept into the Ritz dining room. Mary treated him as the hotshot warrior, macho man, great in bed."[13]

Mary grew so sure about Ernest that she told her parents about him. She explained she'd left Noel but didn't give reasons, preferring to tell them in person. She might have told Noel sooner but couldn't do so before D-Day because she didn't want to send him into battle with any extra burdens of sadness or trouble. Mary did not "feel mistaken, wicked, or foolish and had suffered no attacks of conscience." She had "found a friend, a great man, but she couldn't tell them his name." Mary felt devoted to him, and she wanted to marry him. The saving grace Mary dissembled was that she didn't meet him until long after she'd left Noel. She asked them not to judge her until they talked it over when she got home.[14] Mary's parents replied by cable. Although surprised, they would reserve judgment until they could talk to her. Mary assured them she would do her best to behave as they had taught her—with "courage, fairness, dignity, and grace."[15]

In late January, Mary returned to London to help the short-staffed London office. When she went to the Bank of Australia to withdraw cash for expenses, she received a shock. Noel had drained the account, taking all five hundred dollars of her hard-earned savings. Later, he broke the agreement about their flat, selling off her furniture and book collection. She burned with fury. On February 8, 1945, Noel wrote a letter to her, shouting in uppercase (Mary did not mention these letters in her memoir). Noel had just heard about Ernest. "TO A SIMPLE BUSH-BRED SOUL LIKE ME, ALL OF THIS IS A REV-ELATION. BEING YOUR HUSBAND, IT IS ONLY NATURAL THAT I SHOULD BE THE LAST TO HEAR ABOUT IT." Noel didn't know "WHETHER TO CONGRATULATE YOU OR BE SORRY FOR YOU. I'M SURE YOU MUST BE ONE OF THE MOST ENVIED WOMEN IN ALL THE WORLD." Noel had long suspected someone had caused Mary "to lose confidence" in him. He guessed it might have been "the pipsqueak" gen-eral again (the five-foot six-inch General Robert McClure) or the film unit guy (Shaw) or "a queer-looking guy" (now forgotten) whose picture Mary carried in her wallet. Noel had matched himself against these suitors, expecting Mary to tire of them and return to him. That sentimental streak died when he learned Ernest Hemingway had stolen her heart.

Noel said his life would now be as meaningless as the promise Mary had made to love and honor him forever. "MAYBE I'LL FIND SOME WOMAN WHO WILL LOVE ME FOR BEING JUST MYSELF—AND NOT THE HUS-BAND OF THE WOMAN THE GREAT HEMINGWAY LOVES—I'M AT LEAST ENTITLED TO THAT BREAK."[16] Noel's anger and jealousy burned through the pages.

Noel wrote again on Valentine's Day, asking Mary if she had not hurt and humiliated him enough. She had offered to pay him for the gifts he had given her. He saw her offer as a plan to "GRIND OUR MARRIAGE AND ALL REC-OLLECTION OF ME TO DUST." He told her she should throw the rings in the Seine or down one of the Paris sewers along with everything else connected with their marriage. "YOU'VE PAID ME OFF IN A MANNER THAT COULDN'T HAVE BEEN ANY MORE GROTESQUE IF I'D BEEN THE GREATEST SCOUNDREL OF A HUSBAND A WOMAN EVER HAD. . . . YOU OWE ME NOTHING. . . . I CLAIM NOTHING."[17]

Noel wrote in lowercase a week later, apologizing for "a letter unworthy of a man who so loved you, he married you."[18] When Mary showed Ernest his letters, he scowled, called Noel a jackass, and said good riddance. On February 14, Ernest wrote to Buck. "Mary's husband is becoming faintly difficult." While he expected things would be tough for a while, he assumed "the divorce would be ok."[19]

◆

In late February 1945, Buck Lanham and several of his men visited Ernest at the Ritz. Mary felt uneasy given the disaster that had ensued when Ernest's friends from the 22nd Regiment had dropped by the last time. She hoped a colonel would have a sobering effect on the men's behavior. Colonel Lanham turned out to be shorter than Mary had imagined. With a graying brush-cut and round black spectacles, he appeared studious for an army colonel and looked more like a poet wearing a uniform. The impression was shattered when Buck spoke brashly and profanely. Mary needn't have worried about the behavior of the troops—the problem came from Ernest. Buck presented Ernest with an elegant wooden, velvet-lined case containing two German machine pistols, complete with ammunition. Thrilled, Ernest wanted to try them. Like a child, he loaded one and "pranced around the room regretting there were no Krauts within range, aiming though his French windows at an imaginary enemy in the back garden of the Ministry of Justice."[20] He aimed into the fireplace, but Buck placed his hand on Ernest's arm, cautioning against a ricochet.

Ernest seized a photograph of Noel and Mary from the mantelpiece. He called Noel an idiot for his letters to Mary and took the photo into the bathroom. Mary "followed him muttering, 'Don't be a bloody fool,' and watched in feeble, hypnotized revulsion as he set the picture into the bowl of his toilet and shot it with half a dozen bullets."[21] He fired at Noel's mouth, creating a gaping hole, shattering the porcelain bowl, and water leaked everywhere. Ernest later joked that Noel's mouth made a perfect target. His action horrified Mary, but he laughed as the hotel staff shut off the water. He stood next to the shattered fixture and gave a speech in French, expressing the shock of soon-to-be-General Lanham at the poor state of French plumbing.

Mary retired to her room for the rest of the evening. She had thought the future looked bright, but yet again, Ernest's behavior distressed her. The next morning, Ernest came to Mary's room, apologized for shooting up the toilet, and promised he would drink moderately when they were pursuing their "one and only life" in Cuba. Mary wanted to see the war to its end and didn't want to leave her work, which had become her lifelong companion. He told her he wanted her to quit working, that he would be the writer in the family, and he didn't want her competing with him as Martha had done. Mary protested she didn't compete with him because she wrote cablese, not bloody literature, and she didn't pretend to have his memory or prickly genius. Ernest insisted she quit working for *Time* and come work for him, keeping him organized, typing his work, doing his correspondence, helping to entertain, and managing the Finca. If she kept her job with *Time,* they wouldn't be together because he couldn't stay in Paris any longer. He had to get the phlegm and blood out of his lungs, ditch the hacking cough, and clear his head. He wanted her to come to Cuba to share his life, and he would take care of her parents. They would be fine on the money front.

Mary asked what would become of her, reminding him she liked her life in London. She would miss her friends and the action. Unless Ernest quit his heavy drinking, she did not want to be with him. He assured her they would travel, and she would not lose contact with her friends, but things would fit in around the writing. She would love the weather and the vegetation and being out on the sea on *Pilar,* where they would be alone. Cuba had no rationing, and it cost little to live well. It would be a different life for her, but he promised she would like it. Friends might visit, but not so often as to destroy his work. And she might continue to write articles, but not full-time. He would stop drinking when he got away from the war and settled at the Finca with his work.

Mary wondered about entrusting herself to the "philosophies and habits and whims" of the "complicated piece of machinery" making up Ernest.[22] Despite her qualms, she succumbed to Ernest's insistent pleas and requested a one-year sabbatical from Wert, telling him she and Ernest "thought they had something which deserved a chance." She told Ernest Wert became "sweet and sympathetic." He agreed to press New York for the leave, and she "wished she could crawl inside [Ernest's] arms to celebrate."[23] On February 27, Mary wrote to her parents, saying that she had asked for travel orders and expected to return to the States in about a month. She told them of rumors circulating that she planned to marry "Ernest Hemingway," the writer, and asked them not to say anything to anybody about it until she got home so they might talk it over.[24]

FIFTEEN

This is Like Being a High-Priced Whore

March 1945–June 1945

O n March 6, 1945, Ernest hitched a flight across the Atlantic in a bomber with
Major General Orvil Anderson. The general had helped plan the Anglo-
American Combined Bomber Offensive against Germany and was returning
under orders. Ernest was struggling with bronchitis, and the change in air pressure
inside the bomber as it descended caused him unbearable pain. The experience
"put an end forever to what he had once thought of as 'the romance of the air.'"[1]
Though he was tired of the war and longed to get back to his estate in Cuba,
Ernest had to attend to business in New York. He met with his editor, Max
Perkins, and dined at the Stork Club with his sixteen-year-old son Patrick
and Mary's friend Connie Ernst. Patrick had come to see his father from his
boarding school, and he followed Ernest to the places he liked in New York.

Patrick remembered his father "was in terrible shape . . . with very bad lung
trouble, and coughing blood, and drinking a lot, and I realized that he had been
through a lot."[2] Soon after he arrived, Ernest wrote the first of a torrent of letters to
Mary, promising to be faithful and a good husband. "I love you always and always
will. Now go to get our life started. Don't let anything bother you. I'm sorry to
be so sticky getting off." He said it would be wonderful to meet her in Cuba,
and he promised "to be truly faithful to you every minute I am away. In my heart and
my head and my body."[3] A few days later, Ernest's old sparring partner, George

Brown, saw Patrick and Ernest board the train to Florida. Patrick remembered that in those days before antibiotics, Papa was treating his bronchial condition "by drinking heavily as a home remedy he believed in." Patrick was "in charge of a very valuable bottle of Scotch, and as the three of us ran, heavily loaded with baggage down the station platform to catch the train, I tripped and fell, and the bottle of Scotch smashed to pieces on the concrete." It was, "a long, dry, and very sad trip . . . we didn't talk much and slept little."[4] He "felt very sorry because . . . [Papa was] alone for a long train trip."[5] Along the way, Ernest told Patrick about Mary, "a wonderful girl whom I know you will like."[6] Reflecting back, Patrick told me his father "was in generally bad shape, overweight, and with bronchitis. It's a good thing he came back when he did because he probably would've died."[7]

◆

Just after Ernest left, Mary received a letter from Noel. He objected to her proposal that they use his desertion of her as the reason for their divorce. Her plan left him speechless since he claimed she had deserted him. He might use other grounds to get a divorce, implying her adultery, but he did not wish to do so, if only for her parents' sake, and he warned, "I've heard nothing but bad of Hemingway in regard to women all my life. One only has to read his books. Be careful, my dear."[8] Mary wrote back, apologizing for making Noel feel bad, and telling him she proposed the ground of desertion only to make things simpler for him. He could divorce her on any ground he wanted, but she wished to have his decision.[9] In his reply, Noel refused to acknowledge any shortcomings on his part, and Mary let him blame her for everything just to finish it. She didn't even mention he had stolen her life savings.

◆

On April 2, Ernest returned to his Cuban estate, the Finca Vigía (Lookout Farm). Martha Gellhorn had found the property years earlier and persuaded Ernest to rent it so she wouldn't have to stay in Havana. He later purchased the twenty-acre farm, featuring a rambling one-story Spanish colonial house perched on the highest point of land in the area, overlooking Havana fifteen miles away. In the fall of 1944, a hurricane passed by the Finca, ripping up trees and casting them around the property, and Ernest supervised the repairs. Though happy to be home, he began missing Mary so much he became "black-assed and temperamental." [10] Ernest went to have his head examined by Dr. José Herrera Sotolongo, his surgeon-friend who had become his doctor when they met during the Spanish Civil War. Herrera told him the London doctors should have drained the hemorrhage from the concussion he received in the car accident and that he should have convalesced in bed for a month. The second concussion from the motorcycle accident, coming so close to the first, had created a dangerous condition. In Herrera's opinion, many of Ernest's "unlovely traits" were symptoms of his brain injury. Herrera ordered him to rest and do only light intellectual work each day. Ernest had suffered five concussions over the last two years, and he blamed them for his offensive behavior and his impotence. Hoping to placate Mary, he told her about Herrera's diagnosis. [11]

◆

At the end of March 1945, Mary started her sabbatical leave and crossed the Atlantic on a British troopship, the *Aquitania*, bound for Halifax. Still under military command, the ship could not serve liquor, and the days at sea seemed long. Michael Foot was a fellow passenger on an errand to Washington for the British government and a vital personal mission—he planned to see Connie Ernst and propose marriage. [12] Mary and Michael chatted on deck to ease the monotony of the crossing. To give herself something else to do, Mary read the morning and evening news over the ship's loudspeakers.

On their arrival in Halifax, Mary and Michael headed to a tavern and enjoyed a few glasses of gin to celebrate the end of the abstemious voyage. They boarded a train for New York and arrived on April 12, the same day President Roosevelt died. *Time* asked Mary to do a piece on the radio about the reaction in the army to his death. She found herself in a numb fog, wondering what to say, and phoned Michael to get his views.

That evening, the radio host introduced Mary as one of *Time's* correspondents in London. She was more qualified than most to present a picture of how American soldiers and the people of Europe would react to Roosevelt's death. She began, "Sudden, unexpected death is nothing new to American soldiers by now." The "average Joe" did not often think of the president who was even more remote than their regimental colonel. But they considered him a good guy, and the more they talked to Europeans, the more they understood his importance. She quoted "the eminent British journalist and my friend, Michael Foot," who said, "No statesman of another land ever held so firm a place in the hearts of the British people."[13]

While Michael journeyed on to Washington, Mary took the train to Chicago. She stayed for a few days with her parents in the small South Side apartment they'd moved to from Bemidji and found it filled to overflowing with souvenirs of their earlier life. Glad to find them both healthy and in good spirits, Mary noted their bickering had become routine. In these minor disputes, Mary almost always sided with her father because he seemed rational and well-meaning. Adeline, rooted in Christian Science doctrines, masked her aggression with platitudes. Mary slept in the sitting room and sat up late talking with her father, marveling at his well-ordered memory and recall of events from long ago. Hard at work on his memoir, he reminisced with Mary about their summers together on the *Northland*. On this visit, she sensed his mortality for the first time. Although he was still energetic and stoical, he showed his seventy-five years, and his strides were now less powerful. Mary kept up with him without difficulty.

Mary gave her "darlings" a sanitized version of the breakdown of her marriage with Noel, and to her great relief, they accepted her account and supported her decision about Ernest. Her father became almost keen at the prospect of Ernest becoming his son-in-law, believing the famous author would help him to get his autobiography published. Thomas, an occasional drinker but a lifelong abstainer from tobacco disliked Mary's chain-smoking, which became a point of friction between them. Before long, Mary felt cramped in their tiny apartment, and she moved into a flat on the North Side near her favorite cousins, Homer and Beatrice Guck. Mary visited her parents but enjoyed getting back to her place where she might smoke and drink as she pleased.

Mary received more of Ernest's pleading, lonely letters, but she didn't understand his anxiety, which seemed to amount to desperation. She held to the idea that the coming year would be a trial run, and she had made it clear to Ernest he must reduce his drinking for their relationship to have a chance. Ernest wrote to Buck, telling him he had quit drinking in the morning and at night. His chest had cleared up, he no longer spit blood, and his headaches had disappeared. He remained faithful to Mary, and he said he had reduced his drinking by ninety percent to impress her.[14]

Ernest asked Mary to meet with Hadley to give her a full report on Jack's capture and rescue. Ten years earlier, Mary had met Hadley at a Christmas reception for the *Chicago Daily News* staff when Mary reported for that paper and Hadley's husband Paul Mowrer was its editor. Now Mary and Hadley drank tea at the Ambassador East Hotel, and Mary told her "all I could of the Vosges country, the people of his unit and how he had been treated well after his capture, feeling sorry that I could not give any assurance of his subsequent welfare."[15] Hadley was grateful to hear Mary's firsthand account of what had happened to her son.

Ernest told Mary he lived in an "imitation of purgatory." He had last seen her a month and three days ago, and he missed her as though his heart had been cut out "with one of those things, you take the cores out of apples."[16] Five days later, he wrote again, letting her know he had honored his earlier promise to take over the financial support of her parents. He had put a thousand dollars in her father's bank account.[17] Mail delivery in Cuba remained unreliable at the best of times, and Ernest fretted over gaps in their correspondence. On April 16, he complained he had received no letters from her and he was counting the days until her arrival.[18] Ernest lamented the next day that although he stayed home because he hoped there might be mail, none came. And nothing arrived in the morning. He asked her to please write to him for "it's tough as hell without you." He missed her so much "I could die" and if anything happened to her "I'd die in the same way an animal will die in the zoo if something happens to its mate."[19]

The tone and frequency of the letters unsettled Mary—"the importuning seemed to be putting a lien on my independence." She failed to understand "how a man in his own house with his books and animals and friends and sports could feel so frantic."[20] Ernest was desperate to restart his life in Cuba with Mary because she would provide emotional stability and create a climate in which he might write. He believed Mary would be as supportive as Pauline, though without her money. Ernest hoped he would not suffer from the terrible jealousy and loneliness he endured at Martha's efforts to pursue her remarkable writing career in diverse hotspots.

In late May, Ernest received a letter from Martha, addressed to him as "Bug," and signed by her as "Mook." She told him various media in the States had announced their separation, and she asked him to find a lawyer in Cuba to get busy on the divorce.[21]

In early June, Mary flew to Havana, and Ernest met her at the airport. He had shaved, combed his hair, and wore a white *guayabera* (a pleated white shirt fashionable in Cuba). She wore her war correspondent's uniform, designed for Northern Europe's climate and much too heavy for the tropics. Ernest had instructed her to wear it to smooth her passage through customs. He introduced his driver, Juan, who collected her few bags and put them into an apple-green Lincoln Continental convertible. As they drove to the Finca, Mary delighted in the vistas of royal palms and green hills against a cloudless blue sky. They passed through the village of San Francisco de Paula and turned into the Finca's drive under a bower of scarlet flowers. Bougainvillea arched around the door, and the moist air smelled of tropical plants.

Mary came to love the place, even though she found the house somber as a funeral parlor. When Ernest opened the door to Martha's bedroom, Mary received a shock. The bright blue walls were painted the same color as the large desk, chest of drawers, and dressing table. [22] It looked like they had covered everything with a can of paint purchased on sale. It was certainly not the Ritz, or the Dorch, or her flat on Grosvenor Street. After Mary changed out of her hot uniform, Ernest took her on a tour of the estate. His favorite cat, Boise, purred and rubbed himself against Mary's leg. On the terrace, Ernest pointed to the blue sea beyond the brown buildings of Havana to the north. They strolled down the hill from the house to the swimming pool, filled with ice-cooled water, and Mary checked with her toes and wanted to dive in. Ernest seemed tense, and identified some of the plants, and told her, "sounding like a real estate agent," she would grow to like the place. He pointed out a tamarind and described it as an exotic tree with a romantic name. Feeling tense herself, Mary replied brusquely, "We could use a little romance." She recalled, "Ernest's face stiffened as though I had slapped it; I could have bitten off my tongue." [23] After months of courting her assiduously, Ernest was strangely unromantic when the woman of his fevered dreams appeared in the flesh at his estate. They sipped gin and tonics and talked about how they spent their time during the separation. She found him remote and preoccupied until the gin loosened his tongue, and he told her how much he had missed her. The ice melted.

A few days later, Ernest drove Mary to the tiny fishing village of Cojímar, a few miles east of Havana. Gregorio Fuentes, the first mate, brought the glistening *Pilar* to the pier next to the village's old stone fortress. Over the past month, Ernest had overhauled the boat, replacing the cushions, varnishing the woodwork, and painting the hull. Mary loved the lines of the sleek trawler, and after stepping aboard, she explored the boat from stem to stern. Ernest took the controls on the flying bridge, seven feet above the deck, and Mary had to discover her route there, standing on a horizontal strut, hooking her foot onto the bridge, and then pulling herself up. They motored to a small bay with a golden beach and anchored and swam off the boat. Later they lunched on Gregorio's fresh-caught tuna simmered in seawater and herbs. Mary recalled, "Lolling in the shade of *Pilar*'s afterdeck, I felt, after the gray years of the Blitz in London and the frozen winter in Paris, that I had returned to the remembered paradise of childhood summers."[24]

Soon after Mary arrived in Cuba, Ernest hired a young woman, also named Pilar, to teach Mary Spanish, and a distant relative of Reymundo, the deaf gardener, to be her maid. Ernest engaged Lily, a hairdresser from Havana, to come every Wednesday morning to fix Mary's hair and nails, and suggested Mary bleach her hair as a present to him. Mary accepted Ernest's request, and Lily lightened her hair from peanut butter to platinum blond. Ernest seemed "entranced with the result." Over the years, he insisted she keep her hair bleached platinum or ivory, and when they could not find a hairdresser, Ernest colored and styled her hair himself, creating soft, shining, golden curls that contrasted with her suntanned face.

All of Ernest's wives, except Martha Gellhorn, wore short boyish haircuts, and all of them, including Martha, bleached their hair to enhance his sexual pleasure. In his early childhood, Ernest's mother, Grace, had dressed Ernest as a girl and presented him in public and at school as a twin to his older sister Marcelline. They wore identical dresses, and until Ernest turned six, Grace cut his hair in the same style as his sister's. This left the adult Ernest with a fetish for short hair, dyed ivory or red, and Ernest's hair fetish figured in his writing. Mary may not have understood why Ernest wanted her to keep her hair short and platinum-colored, but she knew his sexual pleasure depended on it, and she accommodated him.[25]

Mary's happiness at being on vacation and away from the war wore off. The reality of Cuba replaced the fantasy, and Mary began missing her old life as one of the few female war journalists writing important news stories. Despite modest wages, she had managed her affairs carefully and lived well. In London and Paris she belonged to a fast crowd of writers, politicians, academics, and military leaders, and her friends and lovers cared about her. She cut them off when she left London, thinking it the right thing to do to start a new life with Ernest in Cuba. Like many women of her generation, Mary believed finding the right man to marry and then starting a family trumped being a working girl, but her doubts resurfaced.

During Mary's first months in Cuba, we find a tension between her inner life, as revealed in her journals, and the happy public face she portrayed in her letters and published in her memoir. She boasted to her friends and parents about her good fortune and lavish lifestyle in the tropical paradise. However, as Mary confessed to her journal, she regretted giving up her independence. She wished "the hell I were out of here and near my household and my own life—with no dictatorship, and [with] my own privately earned responsibilities and usefulness. This is like being a high-priced whore."[26] She put on a contented face in public but harbored dreadful private reservations about her relationship with Ernest. The account of these days in her memoir is innocuous, but her journals reveal private torment.[27] Undoubtedly, the end of wartime intensity would itself have caused Mary to feel emptiness or loss of purpose. However, nothing prepared her for the dramatic change in circumstances she faced in Cuba, where she no longer felt in charge of her life.

As Mary didn't speak Spanish, she couldn't converse with the local people or the Finca's staff, and none of Ernest's friends appeared to be intellectual or even interested in world events. They enjoyed fishing, shooting, and sports—the bloodier, the better—long boozy lunches and late boozy dinners. No one talked about anything of interest to Mary. She felt trapped and turned to her journal to unburden herself. "All of June 5, I wept . . . for a future which looked good, tasted good, and went sour in my stomach. This is not my métier, and it is time, now, I admitted it."[28] Two days later, she wrote, "I am inadequate to this and might as well admit it. It is too tough for me." Nothing belonged to her. It was all his. "His writing, his children, his cats." She owned a little silver jewelry and a few clothes but no books. Even the bed where she slept was not hers. "The room belongs to Marty . . . I am a guest in a room that was never intended as a guest room."[29] Ernest expected her to be present with his guests and converse with them, and she felt on-call, nothing more. "How little to ask. And if one forgets her name, how unreasonable that she weeps. I was busy and cheerful, an entity. Now I have become Welshie the weeper." Whenever a guest asked about her bracelets and anklets, she felt tempted to say, "Sorry, I can't take them off, to show you better. You see, they chain me to this place here by the wall." She wanted to get a room in the servant's quarters, "where nobody could enter without knocking so I could earn my way decently, without waiting above stairs?"[30]

SIXTEEN

I Bleached My Hair Lighter to Please Him

June 1945–July 1946

In early June, Ernest's twenty-one-year-old son Jack (Bumby), fresh from celebrating his release from a German prisoner-of-war camp, arrived in Cuba. Ernest met him with open arms at the airport, and on their drive to the Finca, Ernest talked about Mary, making it clear to Jack he had "fallen completely under her spell."[1] In his memoir, Jack recounted his unusual introduction to Mary. Ernest told him to meet her at the swimming pool, and Jack walked straight there. Just as he reached the edge of the pool, Mary climbed out of it and turned to face him. She was naked. Startled, Jack swiveled away, but Mary told him to come ahead and introduced herself as she wrapped in a towel. Thus began the long and sometimes troubled relationship between Jack and Mary.

In the beginning, Jack laughed at Mary's quips and appreciated her efforts to guide the cuisine of Ramón Wong, their Chinese cook. Mary described Jack as "a handsome, jolly young man" who seemed "marvelously undisturbed by his having been wounded and imprisoned."[2] Still sporting a military brush-cut, Jack was lean and fit, taller than his father, and would always be taller than his half-brothers. He was the son who most resembled his father physically, but he had inherited or adopted the gentle personality of his mother, Hadley. At first, Jack liked Mary and believed they would become friends, but later he would write, Mary was "the only one of my three stepmothers I never loved."[3]

Two weeks later, Patrick (Mouse) and Gregory (Gigi), Ernest's sons with Pauline, arrived at the Finca. Patrick had taken time off from school to prepare for the college entrance exams for Stanford. He was seventeen years old, slender, shorter than his father, and the most bookish of the boys. Thirteen-year-old Greg attended a Catholic prep school in Connecticut and he was free for the two months of his summer vacation. Though he wished he looked like his father, Greg resembled his mother. When Greg was a young boy, his mother disappointed him by telling him flatly he and Ernest did not "look at all alike." From an early age, Greg believed that his mother preferred Patrick.[4]

Greg recounted his first impressions of Mary, comparing her to Martha Gellhorn. "If anything, she was prettier than Marty and even more fun for us children because we were older and could share so many more things with her." Mary "brought order to the domestic chaos that Marty left behind."[5] Patrick recalled, "Mary straightened things out." The household "had really gotten in pretty poor shape because Martha was away." Mary "got things going again, and under a routine, and things got back to normal, and [my father] started writing again."[6] Patrick told me, "Mary struck me as a sort of BBC announcer. She was very young in comparison with Marty. When I was ill, I referred to her as the Tin Kid." Patrick said, "We were a family, and I loved Mary."[7] "I think we got on with her very well. It was a surprise that she replaced Martha, and we made the usual accommodations."[8]

Mary was learning to work with their cook Ramón Wong in a mix of English and Spanish, and she began producing spicy dishes which Ernest and the boys loved. Family lunches lasted from two until four o'clock or even later with "Bumby lilting and gay, Mousie thoughtful and bright, and Gigi sardonic, muttering gleeful gibes."[9] Mary enjoyed the boys' company and learned Spanish with them, studying the names of plants and animals and trying to memorize twenty words a day. In mid-June, Ernest wrote a friendly letter to Mary's father, thanking Thomas for the three books he had sent and assuring him of his love for Mary. Ernest added he had been faithful to her since he first told her he loved her. "My only ambition is to make her a good husband."[10] He told Thomas to remember him if he needed a son and that Thomas might also count on Ernest's three sons.

Mary was to fly to Chicago to complete the divorce from Noel, and Ernest drove her to catch her plane so Juan wouldn't have to confront the drivers on strike at the airport.[11] According to both Mary and their majordomo, René Villarreal,[12]

Ernest had been drinking. Mary described the scene in her memoir, but left out her concern about Ernest's drunk driving—facts she recorded in her handwritten notes.[13] Juan warned Ernest to drive slowly because of the drizzling rain, and they passed along the back road on the outskirts of Havana. The rain made the dirt road greasy, and as they came over a rise, the heavy car began sliding. Ernest lost control and said, "Oh, this is bad, Pickle."[14] The Lincoln skidded off the road and crashed into a bank of earth. Ernest's forehead hit the rearview mirror, and his ribs rammed into the steering wheel. The impact threw Mary forward, her head smashed through the windshield, and her lacerated cheek bled profusely. Mary remembered "the warmth of her blood." Despite his injuries, Ernest got Mary out of the car and carried her fifty yards to a roadside first-aid station.

A nurse wiped Mary's face, using the same piece of cheesecloth to remove both dirt and glass splinters without once rinsing it. Mary wrote, "I could feel her grinding glass bits into my skin, and my legs felt cold in my bloody dress."[15] Mary's limited Spanish didn't allow her to give the woman instructions, so she screamed instead. The people at the aid station feared the police would take away Ernest for driving drunk and causing the accident. Mary begged him to phone Cucu Kholey, their doctor friend, who came and picked them up from the first-aid station and drove them home. He then contacted the best plastic surgeon in Cuba, who was away on a quail shoot. Kholey ordered Mary to stay in bed without smiling, talking, or crying for two days until the surgeon could repair her face. She spent a miserable time in her blue bedroom and found Ernest's attempts to cheer her up unsympathetic, for he believed she should tough it out without complaint. Mary blamed him for drunk driving and insisted that in the future they hire drivers.

Three days later, at a clinic in Havana, the surgeon gave Mary a local anesthetic. He stitched up her many cuts while she watched his hands wielding the needle and thread. Afterward, exhausted and dying for a cigarette, Mary asked for one, but the nurse refused her request.[16] When Jack walked into the room and told her she looked pretty, she asked him for a cigarette. He lit one and placed it between her lips, and Mary remembered this as an unparalleled act of kindness. Jack later described her reaction when he held the cigarette to her mouth: "The closest thing to gratitude I ever had from her."[17]

Mary was struck with the irony that she had survived the Blitz but suffered disfigurement in a stupid accident. When she looked at her face in a mirror, she had to resist the urge to break into tears because she feared the scars would frighten children. She applied the cream prescribed by her surgeon, and after weeks the swelling subsided, and within a year the scarring was unnoticeable.

Two weeks after the accident, Mary joined Ernest at the shooting club for a luncheon, "hideous in its disorder and raucousness." Later that evening, she wrote in her diary, "I'd be an idiot to stay on here or marry Papa." She couldn't make herself into the woman he wanted because their values "were exactly opposite."[18] Not once since coming to Cuba had she heard a serious discussion of politics. She missed her London friends who were articulate about political affairs. When Ernest mentioned politics, he dismissed any argument with oversimplifications. He put "a premium on bad manners, on violence, on killing (war, animals, fish) on toughness, on death." Mary valued "gentleness, conversation, nonviolence" and thought it was "childish to pursue animals."[19] She had disliked Noel's tendency "to have everything either jet black or snow white." Now she saw the similarity between Ernest and Noel; she should go "while the going is possible and can be without too much bitterness." But she stayed and reported none of these doubts in her memoir.

A few days later, Mary's mood improved, perhaps because she had persuaded Ernest to make improvements to the Finca, and she spun a positive story in a letter to her friend Pam Churchill. Pam would not believe life at the Finca, "so idyllic, so lush, so leisured with everything so plentiful, especially after all those years of stringency and chill and high explosive." Every morning she woke to discover palms shining in the sun against the brilliant blue sky. They kept over twenty cats of varying shapes, colors, and personalities—all named after poets (though they weren't). The Finca housed five dogs and a parrot that spoke Chinese, Spanish, and fragments of English. His favorite phrases were "I'm going to take the bus to Havana" in Spanish and "I want to be a fighter pilot" in English.[20] Ernest's three sons were charmers, and they accepted her without formalities or embarrassment.

In late August, Mary flew to Chicago, visited her parents, and divorced Noel in a ten-minute court proceeding. Relieved to be Miss Welsh again, Mary celebrated her freedom by spending a week with her cousins Bea and Homer at their log cabin on Lake Superior's shore. Meanwhile, Buck Lanham and his opinionated wife, Mary, known as "Pete," arrived for a two-week vacation at the Finca, paid for by Ernest. Buck later thanked him for "the best two weeks I ever spent in my life."[21] Pete had a jaundiced view of their visit and later sent an account of it to Carlos Baker when he was writing Ernest's authorized biography. Pete said she and Ernest often stayed at the lunch table drinking wine after Buck retired for a siesta. Ernest talked about himself and his life without reservation, to a degree that surprised her. Pete never heard him say anything good about any woman, except Mary, "the current favorite," and Pete concluded Ernest "disliked all women except the one who seemed best in bed at any given time."[22] He especially hated his mother and Martha. "My feeling was that she was the one woman in his life—besides his mother—who had ever stood up to him and defied him."[23] In Pete's view, "Ernest Hemingway was a heel, the garden variety type."[24] When Ernest told her how Pauline stole him from Hadley, she considered it "the most colossal exhibition of smugness of the male variety." He claimed he could not stop it because "when women start on that sort of thing, they can't be stopped." He said he needed Pauline's wealth and that any man would have taken her over Hadley. When Martha came along, and Pauline protested the proposed divorce, Ernest told her, "My dear, those who live by the sword must die by the sword. You stole me from Hadley; what made you think another woman would not steal me from you?"[25] Pete and Ernest clashed during her stay, causing her to have a sour view of her host. As we shall see, Pete may have had her own reasons for disparaging Ernest.

Ernest wrote to Mary almost daily describing the improvements being made to the Finca and declaring his love for her. He realized how much she missed her old life and seemed to understand life at the Finca did not satisfy her. Ernest admitted that he, too, "missed the lovely simple Paris restaurants, where you could eat just what you wanted . . . and have the wine with it that you wanted." He expected France would recover quickly from the war, and the exchange rate would allow them to spend the next year there.[26]

Mary returned to Cuba in better spirits, and this time the Finca felt like home. A pragmatist at heart, Mary resolved to make the best of her new life. Ernest had made clear what he wanted and she agreed to marry him, knowing that meant subsuming her life to his, though it came at a more substantial emotional cost than she had imagined. Still, it seemed a significant step up for a country girl from Minnesota to be the indispensable right hand to a rich, famous, and virile writer who loved her. Now, to make the best of things.

Ernest and the Lanhams picked up Mary at the airport, and Mary soon reported Pete's odd behavior in a letter to her parents. "I never met any woman who could be so critical of things in a house where she is a guest." Pete "got as

excited over the appearance of a mosquito or a moth as though it were a lion."
She also "kept bossing Buck around all the time, and correcting him as though
he were a child, poor guy."[27] Though Pete was only three years older than Mary,
she was prematurely gray and suffered from poor health. Buck had complained
to Ernest about her constant badgering.

A few days after the Lanhams left, Mary and Ernest went for a cruise on *Pilar*,
lounging in the cabin and drinking daiquiris as Gregorio drove the boat. Most
likely at her instigation, they convened what Mary called "a conference" about her
role in managing Ernest's affairs, and they came to an agreement. Mary would
type his drafts and take care of the correspondence he did not wish to answer. She
would supervise the shopping and gardening while guarding his privacy during
the hours he worked each day. Finally, Ernest had found the woman he wanted.
Mary would look after his home and estate, protect his privacy, and be in his bed
at night.[28] It may not have been the arrangement Mary once hoped for, but now
she settled for it, and in the coming years she would defend the accord to her
female friends and interviewers.

Mary confided to her journal that for two months after she got back from Chicago, Ernest settled down to writing, and they enjoyed "an almost idyllic existence."[29]
She took over more and more duties, "organizing meals and checking food prices,
directing the gardening, combing cats, and writing letters for Papa." She worked
on his income tax and checked household expenditures, calculating that they spent
three thousand dollars a month. Mary noted in her diary, "I bleached my hair lighter
to please him, painted my nails darker to please him, exercised to get thin to please
him." She "looked after his clothes, persuaded him to buy a dinner jacket, got the
shirts he didn't like altered by Josephine, wrote to Chicago for a radio and caviar."
Mary "improved their meals, read his stuff at regular intervals and criticized only
favorably, manicured his hands and feet, and cut his hair."[30]

As the manager handling correspondence Ernest did not wish to deal with,
Mary wrote to Martha Gellhorn. She provided a complete inventory of the furniture and belongings Martha had left behind. Mary noted Cuba's wartime restrictions and customs delays made sending Martha's things to London complicated,
and she asked if Martha could arrange shipping. Ernest would cover the costs.
Mary explained Ernest had not finished going through Martha's papers yet, so she
could not send them. While Mary may have enjoyed writing the letter, Martha
did not enjoy receiving it.

On July 25, Martha wrote to thank Mary for being "the labor in the small and tedious transactions." Martha upbraided Ernest for "what strikes me as a piece of absolutely unnecessary nonsense, of forwarding at great expense such vital and personal items as one box of corn pads." Martha did not want Ernest "going over" her papers, and if he were looking for his letters, it would be a waste of time, for she had already returned them. "He wants the record; I do not." Martha imagined nothing could be more distasteful to Mary than "winding up the affairs of the previous occupant."[31] Mary sent Martha two boxes of papers, and some of her china, much of which arrived broken. Bill Walton said Martha tried for years to get her belongings back, including her notes, papers, and letters. Ernest refused to return any of it,[32] and he appalled Pete Lanham when during her visit "he gloated" about using Martha's cutlery, which was engraved with her family crest.[33]

Mary bragged to her parents about her improved circumstances. She had become the mistress of an estate and was living glamorously, or so she made it seem, with one of the most famous men in the world. She directed gardeners, carpenters, and kitchen staff. "Papa doesn't want me to cook for us—thinks it would be too much 'drudgery'!!!" She had her own yellow Plymouth convertible with a chauffeur, Juan, who loved to sing with her as they drove to Havana and back.[34]

In mid-December, Mary received a warm letter from Michael Foot. He missed her and Connie so much that each Friday, which would have been a White-Tower-lunch-club day, became "a Black Friday." He was so delighted with the letter Mary had sent to him, he took it to share with their friends at the White Tower. "It was fine, in the best Welsh style." He continued to tell people, "Welsh is without question the best female journalist on either side of the Atlantic, apart altogether from being the most agreeable and amusing."[35]

In her ongoing effort to develop a friendly relationship with the boys, Mary wrote a warm, newsy letter to Patrick, telling him she regretted that he and Gregory would not be at the Finca for Christmas Day. She dreamed of an old-fashioned celebration with a tree, many presents, and Ernest in his red sweater as Santa.[36] Ernest had become sweet, and Mary recorded the fact in a draft of her memoir. "Papa is doing just swell—working steadily every morning, and it reads fine—no 'drinkly' at all in the mornings, no matter how bad he feels or what kind of good excuses there might be for one." He is "being lovely and considerate and delightful to me."[37] On December 19, Ernest's divorce from Martha came in the mail. He called it a true Christmas present and made plans for a wedding with Mary.

As Christmas approached, Mary found "a spindly, exhausted tree" which she resuscitated for their celebration of the first peacetime Christmas in six years. Jack joined them, and Patrick and Greg arrived on Boxing Day. Mary spent New Year's Eve drinking Cuban beer with the boys at a small local bodega, and she wondered about London, which, after years of wartime austerity, would be alive again with dance music and conversation and pretty dresses. In his Christmas card that year, Ernest wrote, "To my dearest blessed Kitten who makes Christmas and the other 364 days, Big Kitten." He enclosed a ticket, "For Miss Mary, A trip to France when she wants it, Ernest Klaus."[38] Ernest worked hard on the manuscript that would become *The Garden of Eden* for two months, writing every morning, and he continued to be kind, thoughtful, and loving toward Mary. As she grew more comfortable with life at the Finca, she relaxed, admitting to her diary that Ernest might be better for her than any man she ever knew. "In bed, he has certainly been better for me than any man I ever had."[39]

Ernest gave Martha's Winchester shotgun to Mary, and fourteen-year-old Greg taught her how to use it to shoot the blackbirds which flew in a flock of thousands over the Finca every evening. In his memoir, Greg said he enjoyed "positioning her trim body" and putting his "cheek against hers just for a second" to ensure the gun's sights were aligned correctly. Mary's speed in learning to shoot impressed him. Greg admitted to having a crush on Mary, "and I felt then that she had a crush on me too."[40]

❖

In March 1946, Mary went to Miami to buy a wedding dress. Mary surprised her friends in Miami, Maruja Braden and her husband, Bill Lyson, when she sought their opinion about whether she ought to proceed with the planned marriage. Maruja, who had known Ernest for years, told Mary she must decide whether she loved him enough to stick with him even when he became beastly, as all men were from time to time.[41] In her draft memoir, Mary replied, "Sure he's beastly. Sometimes. But I want to marry an angel if I get married. An ever-loving angel."[42] Meanwhile, Ernest sent Mary flowers and cables, declaring his love. They helped resolve Mary's lingering doubts, and the wedding date was set on her return to Cuba.

Under Cuban law, marriage required signing a marriage contract before the wedding ceremony could take place. They had to itemize each asset brought into the marriage, and it took two sessions at the somber office of Ernest's lawyer in Havana to complete the property depositions. Mary understood little because Ernest and his lawyer discussed the documents in Spanish. When they presented the contract for Mary to sign, they gave a summary. She learned that gifts from one spouse to the other must be returned in the event of the marriage's dissolution. She had purchased an antique gold and diamond engagement ring with Ernest's money, and the idea she would have to give it back upset her, but she signed the contract anyway.

Mary might have been more troubled had she understood more about the Cuban laws governing marriage and divorce, which had been in place since the Spanish Civil Code of 1899. Wives could not acquire or dispose of any property or enter any contracts without their husband's consent. Apart from ordinary family items such as food and clothing, a wife did not have the legal capacity to buy anything. She could not give gifts or make donations without the consent of her husband. [43] The Code defined "community property" to include property gained during the marriage or obtained through the work or salary of either spouse. The husband retained the power to administer the community property after a separation unless he caused the separation. That is why Ernest believed he did not have to return Martha's property. She had caused the separation by leaving him.

Mary understood none of this, but Ernest almost certainly did. Fluent in Spanish, he also had experienced American divorce laws, and he had complained about his treatment when he divorced Pauline because she retained ownership of their house in Key West. The court ordered Ernest to pay her alimony of five hundred dollars a month, even though Pauline's father and her Uncle Gus were much richer than him. He thought he shouldn't have had to pay anything. [44] With three marriages behind him, Ernest probably realized he gained a legal advantage over Mary that he wouldn't have had if they married in the United States. Mary signed a misogynist contract; she had no rights over his property, and if she left him, she could take nothing, not even his gifts. Ernest would not be subject to an American divorce again.

Mary told her parents they were finally getting the thing done, "Observing all the funny, strict, complex Cuban laws (which many people don't observe—but Papa Hem wants to do it with complete legality)—next week." [45] They were holding the wedding in Havana and the reception would follow at the home of Colonel Dick Cooper and his wife, Marjorie, in Havana. Mary told them Dick

Cooper was a British army officer and an old friend of Ernest's. "They hunted in Africa together, etc., quite nice, very rich." Mary explained she would not be sending her mother a formal announcement to give to the Chicago papers because the wire services would report the story straight from Havana.

On March 20, 1946, six days after the wedding, Mary wrote to her parents describing a bright and lovely wedding day. She hadn't known exactly when she married Ernest because the judge read the Spanish vows so quickly. Mary told them, "the ceremony went swimmingly . . . and the party afterward was gay and pleasant."[46] To ensure reporters wouldn't bother them, they told everyone that they were going on a cruise on the boat, but they stayed at the Finca.

The wedding was not the happy occasion Mary described to her parents. After they signed the marriage contract in his lawyer's office, Ernest said, "Let's take the cup of hemlock now." That started a quarrel which left Mary feeling "more like a middle-aged sparring partner than a bride."[47] On the drive home from the reception, a misunderstanding over something Mary said (which she has not shared with us) made Ernest release "a furious earthquake of incrimination and abuse."[48] Back at the Finca, Ernest went straight to bed. Mary considered the marriage over, and she packed to leave for New York. Overcome by fatigue and indecision about what to pack, she fell asleep, determined to finish in the morning. The next day, when Ernest saw her luggage, he offered peace, and they resolved never to get married again, especially not to each other.[49] Ernest wrote a long letter to Mary's father describing the wedding and the guests in some detail but leaving out the unpleasant bits. He concluded, "please know I will love Mary and look after her as best I can and make her as happy as I can. I have no other aim except to write well and truly and try to raise my children well. All very difficult."[50]

On March 27, Mary wrote a chatty letter to Connie, who was now married herself but not to Michael Foot. After the war, Connie decided she no longer wanted to live in Britain, which was subject to the ongoing deprivations of rationing. Instead, she married a New Yorker, the book editor Simon Michael Bessie, who later became friends with Foot. Indeed, after Bessie founded his own publishing house, Atheneum, in 1959, he published several of Foot's books.[51] Mary wished she could see Connie in Paris so they could trundle around looking at fabric for dresses and eating and drinking in the workmen's cafés. She always felt happy in Paris. Mary painted a rosy picture of her life in Cuba, mentioning that Ernest's new novel was coming well. She described the bougainvillea that climbed the walls of the house, the winter nasturtiums and zinnias, her rose garden, and the sweet white snapdragons by the pool. She enjoyed fishing off *Pilar* in the exciting undersea world of the Gulf Stream. [52]

Despite Mary's account to Connie, life at the Finca was not all sunshine and flowers. Mary resented her loss of independence, and she experienced constant tension with Ernest over money. She purchased everything for the home, including Ernest's fine wine and alcohol, from a small allowance he gave her. Mary noted in her journal, "Spent hours adding columns of figures—he counts every penny every Sunday and thus feel forever pinched—while he never considers the cost of anything he actually wants himself and drinks two bottles of expensive wine daily." [53] Mary kept accurate records of all purchases, and tensions rose because the stream of income from Ernest's writing was intermittent and unreliable. Like any small business owner, Ernest worried about the amount he earned on projects and his tax liability.

After an argument about money, Mary wrote to her "Dearest Mountain." She apologized for suggesting he did not earn enough, for he earned impressively according to any standard. Mary felt "pinched" because she no longer made her own money and didn't feel in control. For the first time since being a teenager, she had to depend on somebody else, which felt awkward. However, she didn't give a damn about her personal security because she'd only ever had jobs that afforded her a small savings. Mary confided her concerns to her journal. "I had thought—knowing how generous he is, innately, that I would not mind having no money of my own, that it might be fun to be the pampered darling, asking for money and getting it whenever I needed it." However, it didn't work out that way. "I find I don't like the idea of all money being given me, for myself, as presents and that nothing is mine through grace and having earned it—it all makes me feel like a poor relation." [54]

Since they first met, Ernest and Mary had talked about having a baby, and during May, they made love often. Mary wrote to her doctor, James A. Gough, for advice about how to get pregnant, and he replied he was sorry his "work, pills, advice, etc." had not "borne fruit." He suggested "restricting relations to once or twice a week increases the vigor of the sperm." [55] Mary underlined this with a red pencil. In mid-July, her gynecologist confirmed she was pregnant, and Mary and Ernest were both delighted at the news. They would have their own family.

SEVENTEEN

How Did a Beat-up
Old Bastard Like You Get
Such a Lovely Girl as That?

August 1946–July 1947

Ernest and Mary set off for the hunting and fishing trip in Sun Valley, Idaho, (described in the Prologue) on August 7, 1946. It was during this trip that Mary suffered the life-threatening rupture of one of her fallopian tubes from an ectopic pregnancy in Casper, Wyoming, where she would've died, but for the quick action of Ernest.

A few days later, Ernest wrote to Buck, "it was the closest one I've ever seen. The doctor had given her up and taken off his gloves." A good thing they stopped in Casper. While it was awful luck to have that sort of pregnancy, "Mary [had] been brave and patient and good as hell. . . . Very impressed on missing Boot Hill last Monday night. Was closest I've ever seen with anybody."[1] Ernest wrote to his journalist friend, Lillian Ross, about the incident. He considered Mary a hero "for the way she fought on the operating table and wouldn't die . . . long after pit bulls would have quit . . ."[2]

Mary and Ernest arrived in Sun Valley three weeks later and came to Lloyd and Tillie Arnold's for dinner. Tillie recalled she was roasting doves in the woodstove "when Ernest came in carrying Mary like a doll. He put her in a rocking chair Lloyd brought into the kitchen, and within minutes she visited with us like an old friend."[3] Though tired and weak after her three-week stay in the hospital, Mary's spirit impressed Tillie.

Ernest was far too fat in Tillie's opinion, and Dr. John Moritz, the Sun Valley Resort doctor, put him on a strict diet, which meant reducing his drinking. He also forbade Ernest from hunting at high altitudes because of his soaring blood pressure. While Ernest and the boys explored the streams and hills, Mary rested, and her strength returned. Twenty-three-year-old Jack recalled Ernest was torn between his wish to be with his sons and his need to care for Mary. Jack found his father's "absorption" with Mary became "almost total," and the boys couldn't spend as much time with him as they would have liked. The younger boys didn't seem to care as much as Jack. He "sensed acutely the distance that comes between fathers and sons and realized that these days were precious." He knew "[t]he hours we spent laughing with Papa and sharing experiences were to be important ones for all of us." [4]

As Mary recovered, she ventured out with the boys into the rugged country, and it captured her "as simply as a trout takes a Mayfly." [5] The town of Ketchum, next to the Sun Valley Resort, came from the old west. False-fronted wooden buildings lined the two blocks of the main street, and wooden sidewalks ran along each side of the road. Mary loved the town, and it is not surprising they returned to live there when they were forced to leave Cuba. Ketchum had a relaxed, small-town atmosphere that reminded her of Bemidji, and she formed friendships with the locals.

After the boys returned home to go to school, Mary began accompanying Ernest on pheasant-hunting trips. They walked through irrigation ditches bordering the land of potato farmers Ernest had befriended before the war. Mary welcomed the fresh air and long walks with Ernest, and thanks to his patient teaching, she became more confident with her shotgun and missed less often. She overcame her childhood qualms about hunting for food and came to appreciate the skill and joy involved in anticipating and shooting the fast-flying pheasants.

Ever since their wedding, Mary had wanted Ernest to meet her parents. She was reluctant to invite them to Cuba because the Finca did not operate well enough to sustain them, and she feared that her mother's Christian-Science-inspired prejudice against smoking, swearing, and drinking might clash with life at the Finca. She found a solution by planning, with Ernest's agreement, a Thanksgiving Day rendezvous with Tom and Adeline in New Orleans on the drive back to Cuba. All went smoothly and Ernest charmed Adeline who, dressed in her Sunday finest, giggled at his stories as she sipped from a flute of champagne. Tom was delighted to meet the famous author, but he resisted calling Ernest his son-in-law. He and Ernest swapped stories of their adventures in the woods, and Mary glowed with pride because she'd never heard her father sound more eloquent.[6]

Ernest arranged for them to attend the Thanksgiving Day horse race at the local track, and the plan delighted Tom, for he had not seen a horse race in years. In France, Ernest had learned how to play the horses, and he spent time at the stables and paid for a few tips from a stable boy. He knew which horses to back and which to avoid, and he won most of the bets he placed. Ernest gave the winnings to Adeline to hold, and soon the bills bulged from her small purse as she beamed with delight. Adeline asked why Ernest wrote for a living when it seemed so much easier to place bets on the horses. He told her she brought him luck and that it would be tedious just to attend races. On the way home from the racetrack, Adeline announced from the back seat that the winnings amounted to over four hundred dollars. Ernest astounded Adeline when he insisted she keep the small fortune, and she handed the bills to Tom for safekeeping. After a turkey dinner served at the luxury hotel and an evening of storytelling, Mary and Ernest retired to their room. The kindness Ernest displayed toward her parents touched Mary, and she showed her gratitude. "'Mmmmmm, like the early days in Paris.' Woven together, we slept all the night in his bed."[7]

In December, Mary and Ernest returned to Cuba and spent a quiet Christmas celebrating with a tough Cuban turkey. The next day Patrick and Greg came from Key West, and a few days later, Ernest's sister Sunny and her son, named for the author and known as "Young Uncle Ernie," arrived. Fishing trips on *Pilar* and swimming parties around the pool followed. Ernest served champagne in the afternoon and wine at dinner, and a wine glass rested at young Ernie's place. Sunny asked, "'What about the boy drinking wine?' 'Wine's fine for him,' Ernie said. 'But don't give him hard liquor until he's thirteen.' We all laughed heartily."[8]

During this Christmas visit, Greg's infatuation with Mary grew, and he recalled a trip aboard *Pilar* with his father and Mary. Ernest allowed his sons to drink as much alcohol as they wanted, expecting they would learn their limits. After a dinner with drinks, Mary said she wanted to sleep with "Mr. Gig" on the flybridge that night. Pleasantly drunk, Ernest agreed, and Greg recalled the evening in his memoir. He blew up the air mattress, placed it on the flying bridge, and covered it with blankets. He changed into his pajamas and drank a beer, not knowing what was expected of him but thinking he might have to perform sexually. Greg lay on the mattress, waiting for Mary, and recalled his father's advice about sex. "The key to making a woman happy in bed . . . is to stroke [her clitoris] gently, over and over, like you're petting a cat."[9] Greg was not sure what it was or where to find it.

When Mary arrived, she lay on the mattress and talked about the constellations in the cloudless night sky. She wondered how Greg felt after drinking several beers, then rolled over and fell asleep. Greg remembered he did not enjoy a sleep "of the innocent." Fearing if he fell asleep, he might "inadvertently roll over and put my arm around her or do God knows what else," he didn't fall asleep until four A.M. He remembered Mary nudging him around seven and saying, "Better get up Gig. . . . You're an excellent sleeping companion; you didn't make a sound all night."[10]

Sunny, young Ernie, and Greg left Cuba, and Patrick stayed for the semester, studying for the Harvard College Board exams. Life at the Finca returned to a routine of reading, writing, gardening, tennis, swimming, and fishing. Mary discovered her expensive French lingerie had disappeared, and she accused her maid of theft and fired the poor woman despite her denials. Two weeks later, as Mary cleaned the little house where the boys stayed, she discovered her lingerie under Greg's mattress. Her shock turned to anger, in part at herself, as she regretted having falsely accused her maid. She complained to Ernest, who became worried about Greg because he had caught him trying on Martha Gellhorn's white stockings two years earlier.[11] Ernest decried Greg's offense and suggested he apologize to Mary, which he did—six years later. "Give my love to Miss Mary and tell her if I see her again, I sure as hell would like all to be forgiven. I did a terrible thing in lying about that clothes business, and I make no excuses for it (except to say that the whole business is my least rational aspect), but everyone's life is not Simon says, I'm sure, and I used to like her a hell of a lot."[12] Greg explained his attraction to women's lingerie resulted from Pauline's abandonment of him as a little boy. She did not like being a mother, found small children odious, and wanted to travel with Ernest. They often left Greg with Ada Stern, a strict governess who instilled fear in the boy by threatening to leave him if he misbehaved. Traumatized by her threats, Greg ran to his mother's lingerie drawer and soothed himself by touching and rubbing her things.[13] Patrick remembered Greg stole Mary's lingerie "and he stole every woman's lingerie. He even stole my daughter's lingerie."[14]

Firing her maid was an exception to Mary's typically good relations with the staff, and she played a more active role than Martha Gellhorn in the life of the Finca. According to Norberto Fuentes, Martha showed no interest in running the house and complained to Bill and Annie Davis of "the servant problem," which made her jittery and wretched. If they got rid of their possessions, they would not need servants to care for them, "and then I would not have to make myself into a fury trying to find and instruct domestics."[15] Martha preferred playing tennis and sunning herself at the swimming pool, and she delegated domestic duties to the gardener and the carpenter. Martha spent time with her friends in Miramar, the Havana district where wealthy Cubans and Americans lived. As Norberto Fuentes remembered, "then one day, she was gone, soon to be replaced by a more sympathetic woman."[16]

That woman was Mary. She took a keen interest in the day-to-day affairs of the Finca, directing the gardeners and kitchen staff and working herself. As Fuentes recalled, Mary took over the house. The townspeople remembered Mary "affectionately . . . for her charm, her efforts to learn Spanish, and the energy she bestowed on her rose gardens." She'd return from the garden, said Pichilo, the former gardener, "covered with sweat." "And full of mud," added Herrera Sotolongo. Mary "would be the one remembered as the true mistress of Finca Vigía."[17] Mary engaged with the household staff as friends, not as members of a serving class. René remembered that Mary visited his house, met his family, and took a particular liking to his nineteen-year-old sister, whom she invited to visit the Finca. Mary walked his sister home and spent time talking with his mother. She worked hard to understand the cultural differences.[18]

Mary convinced Ernest they ought to build a tower featuring a room with a view toward Havana where he might work undisturbed. There would be a carpentry shop and a residence for the growing population of cats on the lower levels. Mary took measurements, learned Spanish architectural terms, designed the tower with amateur drawings, and engaged a local building firm. Construction started. She planned a deck on top where she might suntan in the nude without the gardeners seeing her. Ernest liked Mary's skin to contrast with her platinum hair. He wanted her to look as brown as Cuban mahogany, as brown as Catherine or Marita—the gender-switching-lovers Ernest was then creating in what would become *The Garden of Eden*.

Mary's mother interrupted their happy life in April 1947 when she wired, asking Mary to come north to help with her father, who had been hospitalized after having collapsed unconscious. He was suffering extreme rectal pain from cancer in his prostate. Adeline had been treating his condition according to the teachings of Christian Science, which meant reading religious tracts to the patient rather than seeking medical treatment.

A second disaster struck the same week when Patrick returned to the Finca after a quick trip to Key West to visit Greg. Patrick had struck his head when he fell off a bicycle.[19] Back at the Finca, Patrick began showing signs of a concussion. He was supposed to write his college board exams in Havana on April 12, and with Ernest helping him manage the stress of the exams, Patrick passed, but he got a very poor grade. Two days later, Patrick displayed the symptoms of a severe concussion, becoming delirious and talking nonsense. Ernest put aside his novel about the sea and the *Eden* manuscript to attend to Patrick. He kept watch over his son and administered the anti-convulsant Seconal while he sent for the doctors. Ernest did not want to send Patrick to the hospital, and they moved him to Ernest's room and provided round-the-clock care at the Finca. For a time, Ernest fed his son rectally. Patrick told me that while his father was looking after him, they weren't getting anywhere. "My mother made inquiries in New York about psychiatric help available in Cuba. They recommended a German who was not in the United States because he had been a communist as a young man, and he refused to give that up." Dr. Stetmeyer "came on board and recommended electric shock for me. They gave me electric shock down by the swimming pool, and that brought me back." Patrick recalled, "I am the one person in the family where it [electric shock therapy] really worked." To this day, he doesn't know "what he actually suffered from. Was it physical from the bike accident, or was it something else?"[20]

Mary felt some guilt about leaving but booked a flight to Chicago on April 15 to be with her parents, who needed her more. She found her father in his hospital bed, reduced to skin and bone. Mary arranged for sedatives and advocated for treatment on his behalf. Discharged after a week, Tom moved home to their tiny flat, and Mary sat with her father, reading to him and trying to cheer him up while her mother shopped and prepared his favorite foods. Mary hid her anger at her mother's faith in Christian Science, which had caused her father to suffer needlessly. She decided that challenging her mother's faith of thirty years would be pointless and do nothing for her father.

Meanwhile, Pauline Pfeiffer, Ernest's second wife and the mother of Patrick and Greg, wrote to Mary saying she was so worried about Patrick's condition, she had traveled to Cuba to be with him and help Ernest care for him. She hoped

Mary didn't mind her staying at the Finca. Mary replied, inviting Pauline to help herself to her wardrobe.

During the month Mary stayed in Chicago, Ernest wrote loving letters, reporting on Patrick's recovery, his own exercise regime in the swimming pool, and reviewing their finances. He expected an injection of income from film royalties and urged Mary to buy some new clothes. By mid-May, Mary felt she could leave her parents to manage on their own, and she flew home to Havana. Pauline, looking "cool, crisp and chic," met her at the airport, and Mary became her instant admirer. Over that first day, the women bonded as alumnae of the same alma mater—marriage to Ernest. They giggled over drinks next to the pool, and Pauline complimented Ernest on his choice of a new wife. Ernest reported this news to Buck and told him of a conversation he overheard between Pauline and Mary when Pauline described her feelings for Martha Gellhorn. "I haven't a thing in the world against her except, possibly, for her being self-centered, self-seeking, quite stupid, childish, almost without talent, and a phony." Pauline concluded, "Outside of that, I haven't a thing in the world against her. Of course, I thought Ernest was rather stupid about her, but then he was upset by the Spanish Civil War." [21] Patrick recalled Mary and his mother "became very good friends, but it didn't last. I think probably it was my mother's fault. She was very upset by her divorce. She was much less an independent woman than Mary or Martha." Though "she was a journalist, she was a woman's journalist for *Vogue* in Paris. She was never on the level of Mary as a journalist." [22]

Two weeks later, Mary's father, improving and putting on weight, wrote that he had buckled his belt to the last hole. He thanked Ernest for sending Mary to look after him, saying it appeared the Heavens opened and that an angel came to care for him. Patrick also improved, and Pauline returned home. Mary took her to the local airport in her bright yellow convertible and waved goodbye as Pauline took off on the quick flight to Key West.

On June 17, Ernest's longtime friend and Scribner's editor, Max Perkins, died of pneumonia at sixty-three. This news was a stunning blow, and two weeks later Ernest wrote to Charlie Scribner that they needn't "talk wet" about Max. "The bad was for him to die. I hadn't figured on him dying; I'd just thought he might get so completely damn deaf we'd lose him that way." [23] Ernest reflected, "Max was my best and oldest friend at Scribner's and a great editor—he never cut a paragraph of my stuff nor asked me to change one." Though Max, who was highly sensitive to the artistic integrity of Ernest's work and deferential to his authorial judgment, may not have cut paragraphs, he had insisted Ernest remove or alter obscene words and phrases.[24] Ernest called him his "wisest counselor in life as well as in writing."[25]

Just after they received the news of Max's death, Mary woke up choking and with a high temperature. Dr. José Luis Herrera visited and diagnosed a fever which he suggested came from drinking contaminated cow's milk. Despite a course of penicillin and sulfa drugs, Mary's temperature did not fall. One feverish morning, Mary wrote her will in pencil with an unsteady hand on a scrap of brown paper and left it on her bedside table.[26] In the will, she left her jewelry to her cousin and expressed the hope Ernest would continue looking after her parents. In a gesture of friendship, Mary left the cash in her London account to Pauline. The little scrap of brown paper is a sad testament to Mary's acceptance of her imminent death. When Ernest found the paper, he insisted that Mary go to Havana for more sophisticated laboratory tests. It turned out she was suffering from undulant fever, and the doctors prescribed more antibiotics. As Mary's temperature dropped, Pauline phoned and suggested that Key West's invigorating air might speed her recovery.

At the end of June, Mary flew to Key West and joined Pauline at her house on Whitehead Street, where she took the room over the carriage house. Ernest had used that room when he wrote *The Green Hills of Africa*, *To Have and Have Not*, *For Whom the Bell Tolls*, and several short stories. Mary loved the house, which had been decorated with care, and she enjoyed lounging by the pool and chatting with Pauline. Ernest phoned daily to report on Patrick's progress. He wrote on July 8 that Patrick had improved "like he was coming to high ground." Mary returned home and found Patrick recovering, but Ernest failing. Discovering his blood pressure measured an alarming 215 over 125, Mary implemented booze rationing and adjusted their diet. Ernest grumbled but started exercising, and his blood pressure fell. He recorded his weight daily on the bathroom wall in the Finca, and we can read his scrawling pencil notes to this day.

Ten days later, Pauline returned to the Finca to celebrate Ernest's forty-eighth birthday, and she helped Mary decorate the pool area with colored tissue paper and ribbons. They served the guests champagne followed by two birthday cakes. Mary had picked up gifts on her earlier trip to Chicago, and a battery-operated radio became a particular hit with the birthday boy who declared it his best birthday ever. He considered it a bonus that his fourth wife was cooperating nicely with his second wife and wrote to Charlie Scribner, "Pauline thinks Mary's a wonderful girl, and they've made good friends."[27] Ernest reported to Buck that Pauline had asked him, "How did a beat-up old bastard like you get such a lovely girl as that?" He went on to declare, "Mary looks beautiful and is behaving like a god damn fucking Angel—she has ever since Casper, which was the town that gave her the confidence."[28] Mary added a note to Ernest's letter, telling Buck that Ernest was proving very durable, "and I love him very much. I wish nothing better for you and Pete than that you could enjoy each other as much as we are doing. If this all sounds a little fatuous—forgive—and best love—Mary." The next day Pauline turned fifty-two, and thirty-nine-year-old Mary improvised with a cake on which she wrote in colored icing, "We Love You, Pauline." Mary later wrote of Pauline, "she was a high-spirited sharp-minded woman, an accidental friend to me, both generous and loving."[29]

EIGHTEEN

That Was a Day of Triumph for Me

September 1947–September 1948

I n mid-September, Ernest bought a new royal blue Buick Roadmaster convertible with red leather lining and seats. He flew to Miami to pick up the car and meet his old friend, "man Friday and general factotum" from Key West days, Toby Bruce.[1] They meant to take the vehicle on a leisurely drive through Michigan, visiting Walloon Lake, Beartooth Pass, and Red Lodge—all places unique in Ernest's childhood—before heading to Sun Valley. Once they reached Sun Valley, Mary would fly out with their rifles and shotguns. In the meantime, Mary arranged a tour of the roads west of Havana in her yellow convertible for Pauline and Patrick.

A few days after Pauline's departure, Mary was working in her room when the dogs started barking. She investigated and found Cuban soldiers emerging from the bushes, rifles drawn. Frightened, Mary demanded the reason for the action, and a junior lieutenant arrested her and produced a search warrant. Despite difficulty reading the document, Mary recognized the dangerous allegation that Hemingway was "antipático" to the Cuban government. René reviewed the official-looking paper and told her it appeared to be legal and that the soldiers had the right to search the Finca for weapons.[2] In the ensuing search, the soldiers found rifles, shotguns, pistols, and thousands of unused shells and ammunition—all of which they confiscated—despite Mary's protests. The soldiers took Mary and the weapons to the local police station. René gave her the phone number of Paco Garay, an old friend and official in the Cuban government. After Mary complained to him, Garay spoke to the commanding officer, and he released Mary and a soldier drove her home. A judge later allowed her to leave Cuba on her assurance that she would return in the spring to face charges.

Mary learned a Miami newspaper had published a story describing the arrangements between two American pilots and their Cuban accomplices to free Dominica. The report said the headquarters for the plotters was the home of an American writer near Havana. Mary discovered that an editor of *Reader's Digest* owned the house where the plotters met. The army mistakenly identified the Finca as the arms cache for the proposed operation. Two weeks later, Mary flew to Idaho and settled in with Ernest at the Sun Valley Lodge. The hunting party included Ernest's old friend, Gary Cooper, who had starred as Frederick Henry in the film adaptation of *A Farewell to Arms* and as Robert Jordan in *For Whom the Bell Tolls*. His unpretentious wife, Rocky, became Mary's friend. The Hemingway's wedding reception hosts, Dick and Marjorie Cooper, also came to the Lodge. Guests and key staff partied together in the warm log cabins, and Tillie Arnold became the social spark plug while her husband, Pappy, photographed the famous friends socializing. The guests downed cocktails at the sizable dinner parties, feasted on game, and drank robust red wine out of wineskins. Ernest performed better than Gary Cooper, squirting the red wine down his throat even while singing. "Coop" brought on laughter as he sprayed red wine all over his white shirt. Often the evenings ended in singing, and they called Mary, with her extensive repertoire and low voice, "their *basso profundo*."[3]

Dr. John Moritz maintained that it would be risky for overweight Ernest to trek through the mountains to pursue deer. Ernest obeyed doctor's orders and worked on the manuscript for *The Garden of Eden* while the hunters walked the fields and irrigation ditches looking for ducks and pheasants. Mary hunted with Ernest's old friend and guide, Pappy Arnold, and shot her first buck. Pappy saluted her endurance because she kept up with him as they climbed a rugged trail to a ridge high in the mountains. When they spotted a buck far below, they climbed as close as they could without alerting the handsome beast, and Mary killed him with a tricky downhill shot. The venison provided a welcome change to their diet. "That was a day of triumph for me," Mary wrote to her parents. While her buck didn't have the biggest antlers in the world, it measured "a darn good size," and she promised to send them a small roast and steaks.

Pauline invited Mary to come to San Francisco to spend Thanksgiving with her and Patrick and her sister, Jinny. Patrick recalled this was the time when "Mary and my mother got along very well. My mother was a great lover of San Francisco, and she gave Mary a very good time."[4] Mary was happy for the break, and Pauline's aunt and uncle invited them to Thanksgiving dinner. As Pauline parked the car in front of their large house, she cautioned Mary that her relatives were serious practicing Catholics. She added, "If I hadn't been such a bloody fool practicing Catholic, I wouldn't have lost my husband."[5] Mary wished the conversation could continue, but it didn't, and she dared not ask Pauline what happened after Greg's caesarean birth. Pauline's doctor had warned she should not risk another pregnancy,[6] and deferring to church doctrine, she refused to use birth control and insisted that Ernest abstain, adhere to the rhythm of her menstrual cycle, or practice *coitus interruptus*.[7] Ernest told Mary that Pauline's decision drove him to have affairs with Jane Mason and Martha Gellhorn. Greg later wrote that Ernest gave the same justification to his sons. When Ernest fell in love with Martha Gellhorn, he repeated the excuse of Pauline's two caesarean births and the fact the doctor had told her she must not become pregnant again. Greg considered that "alibi absurd," for his father often said "too much intercourse was counterproductive to good literature. To put it simplistically, he felt he had to save some of his creative juice for his writing."[8]

After the trip to San Francisco, Mary rejoined Ernest in Idaho and began preparing for Christmas. She auditioned for a choir and enjoyed singing with the altos, and spent four or five hours a day preparing dinners and practicing a new skill—pie baking. "'Sure smells good in here,' Gary Cooper would say, sniffing my pastry as it lay on top of the refrigerator."[9] In the years since her marriage to Ernest, Mary had taken cuisine and cooking seriously. She learned several Chinese dishes from their cook and she managed the Finca's vegetable garden carefully to ensure she had fresh produce. Mary began to enjoy cooking and baking, and she collected recipes on her travels.

A black dog followed Ernest home from a bar and the dog too appreciated Mary's cuisine. Ernest tried to find the dog's owner, but it seemed he was abandoned. Deciding the dog was a rare "Alaskan" springer spaniel, Ernest named him "Blackie" and he took up residence, sleeping next to their bed, becoming a loyal friend, and staying thirteen years—the rest of his life. Christmas 1947 passed in front of a tree decorated with lit candles in a home filled with the smell of delicious

baking. Mary was delighted to unwrap a gift from the boys, for she had worked
hard on developing that relationship. They gave her a western leather belt with
a silver and gold buckle, which she wore the next year in a photo with Ernest in
front of the Gritti Palace Hotel in Venice (the cover photograph).

Many friends came to visit, and they received so much of Ernest's attention, Mary
began to feel like a worthless piece of his backdrop. She wondered how important
she could be to him when he occupied himself with others, but she decided not to
raise her concerns with Ernest after receiving a letter from her father. He complained
that, even after forty years of marriage, Adeline's stormy moods caused "terror in
his heart." Mary resolved to work harder on her own marriage. [10]

In January and February, Mary tried to take ski lessons but the warmth from
the sun that winter turned the runs to muck, and in late February they began
their thirteen-day journey back to Cuba. Even before they started packing the
car, Blackie sensed changes afoot and installed himself on the front seat. Outside of Sanderson, Texas, Ernest took Blackie to the café near the cabins where
they had stayed and ordered breakfast. The waitress objected when she noticed
Blackie—dogs were not welcome in the restaurant. Offended at the treatment of
his friend, Ernest left without touching his breakfast or paying. Mary bought him
a ham and egg sandwich for the road.

They drove down the coast, over the bridges joining the keys, and reached Pau-
line's house in Key West. Happy to see each other, Mary and Pauline embraced.
Over drinks, Pauline started needling Ernest. Now that Patrick had recovered,
Pauline no longer required Ernest's cooperation, and bitterness bubbled from her.
Mary felt so uncomfortable she dropped a book on the floor to break the mood,
but her apologies for the banging book did little to interrupt Pauline's attack.
Not until guests arrived for dinner did Pauline become a charming hostess. Mary
confided to her journal, "I imagined I had mistakenly entered the wrong movie.
The next morning the air of Whitehead Street was calm and friendly, even gay." [11]
Ernest and Mary took the ferry to Cuba, and René and the gardeners greeted
them as they pulled up to the Finca. Mary had worried about how the menagerie
of pets would react to Blackie, but after two quick fights, Blackie established his
authority and ruled as first dog.

A week later, the trial over the weapons stored at the Finca took place in the
local courthouse. Jack came to help, and he testified the German pistols were
souvenirs he had retrieved from dead German officers and that he had left them at

the Finca. The judge accepted the explanations tendered by the Hemingways, and the hearing ended in twenty minutes. Still angry, Mary considered legal action against the Cuban government before realizing it would be futile.

On March 7, Malcolm Cowley, the literary critic and specialist on American literature, arrived for a two-week visit to interview Ernest for a portrait in *Life*. Cowley received an expense-paid vacation to Havana for himself and his family in exchange for writing the piece. Ernest was "sickened of the idea of a piece about me after ten minutes and just gave him the names of my friends that he could ask about me." This, instead of "getting a lot of crap from me which would nauseate me to give out and to read."[12] Cowley found that Ernest lived like "old Father Abraham, among his entourage of servants, wives, children, friends, and dependents." He spent his time "[w]atching out for them, teaching and advising them, writing them letters—and meanwhile screwing the big motion-picture people so he can get money to maintain his retinue." On his return from Havana, Cowley wrote to his friend Nathan Asch, "I thought that Papa, as everybody calls him now, was an extremely nice person. He regards himself as a great man, which is irritating." He was willing to pay the high cost of greatness—"not only the financial cost but also the emotional cost, the sheer labor of being continually attentive to the people around him, of giving himself at much expense to his work."[13]

On April 5, Mary turned forty. Ernest forgot her birthday, but when he remembered, he gave her a painting by André Masson from his collection. Extravagant gifts had become his way of making up for overlooking anniversaries and birthdays.[14] Mary's father did not forget, and he typed a touching note on paper, out of which he cut curlicues highlighted in pink. He wrote that Sunday, April 5, 1908, when he stood beside the bed and heard Mary's first cry, "was the happiest morning and day in my life. I thank God that you have the strength of body, heart, and mind to keep the sunshine you brought into our dear little home in Walker forty years ago."[15]

Ernest wrote every morning as Mary supervised the installation of the windows and staircase for the tower. She designed, and their carpenter Pancho crafted, a set of bookcases and a large table from indigenous majagua wood, tan and streaked with gray and olive tones. She matched the wood with olive green floor tiles, and her designs created a space that is welcoming to this day. Mary enjoyed the challenge of designing and supervising the construction of the tower and the finer detail involved in creating the furniture and selecting woods and colors.

In June, Ernest met with Ed Hotchner, a representative from *Cosmopolitan* who'd been sent to persuade Ernest to write a piece on the future of literature. Red-headed and freckle-faced, Hotchner, then in his late twenties, waited for the famous author in the Floridita, where photographs of Ernest and his famous friends, including Gary Cooper and Ava Gardner, hung on the walls of the old fashioned bar. Ernest entered and shook hands with Hotchner, and they sat at the spot reserved for Ernest, where a life-size bronze statue of Papa now leans against the bar. They ordered Papa Doblés, a daiquiri named in honor of Ernest, comprising two-and-a-half jiggers of Bacardi White rum, the juice of two limes, half a grapefruit, and six drops of maraschino, all mixed with ice and shattered in an electric blender. They drank while Ernest told stories which charmed the young man. Hotchner became a faithful retainer, producer of dramatizations of Ernest's work, promoter of the Hemingway legend, and keeper of his legacy. He kept a journal of his conversations with Ernest, supplemented by recordings he made on his pocket tape machine—sometimes secretly, according to Valerie Hemingway.

The next day, Ernest introduced "Hotch," as he had renamed him, to Gregorio Fuentes, who took them out on *Pilar* for a cruise. Hotch and Papa were sipping tequilas when Gregorio spotted the dark purple fins of marlin and yelled, "Feesh." "Let's go," said Ernest as he grabbed a baited rod from Gregorio and handed it to the stunned Hotch, who had never caught anything larger than a ten-pound bass. Ernest coached him, and Hotch landed the marlin, leading Ernest to suggest the creation of "Hotchner and Hemingway, Marlin Purveyors." Flattered by the suggestion of an ongoing relationship with Ernest, Hotch courted Hemingway.[16] Ernest convinced Hotch he would write the piece about the "Future of Literature," or something, but insisted on an advance of fifteen thousand dollars, which Hotch arranged.

In August, Ernest wrote to Buck Lanham bragging about his lovemaking with Mary and saying, "we fucked the hell out of May, June, July, and August. It is like six-day racing. The more you do it, the better you are at it." He said Mary had figured their sexual frequency "since we met, including the time I was impotent with head injuries and the time of her blowing gaskets and tubes, was around 100 a month which makes a bum out of Dr. Kinsey's report."[17] Ernest told Buck he really loved Mary and was going to be faithful to her. "She has been so damned wonderful to me, Buck, ever since Casper that I've been so happy that I really did not give a shit about anything else at all except my duty." Mary was solid and dependable, "and yet every night the damned ecstasy is wonderful as first time ever together."[18] Ernest understood Buck was having marital problems with Pete, and his bragging letter could not have been well-received by Buck. Baker makes no mention of this correspondence in the biography and omits it from the *Selected Letters*.

◆

Ernest and Mary decided to tour the Cézanne country of Provence that fall rather than returning to Sun Valley, which was becoming overrun by tourists. Ernest thought they should take the Buick so they might travel comfortably through the French countryside. A few days later, as Juan drove her home from Havana's markets, Mary noticed a smartly painted ship, the *Jagiello*, moored at the docks. She toured the first-class cabins and learned the boat, staffed by Polish officers and an Italian crew, would be back in Havana in September before departing for Cannes and Genoa. Mary rushed home with the news, and they made plans for a fall sea voyage.

In July, Ernest decided he would like to celebrate his forty-ninth birthday onboard *Pilar*, and Gregorio and Greg helped Mary stow caviar, champagne, and birthday cake on the boat. Gregorio waited at the city dock while Ernest, Mary, and Ernest's old friend, Sinsky, a Basque captain of merchant ships sailing between Cuban and US ports, stopped in at the Floridita for a couple of Doblés. Mary and Ernest chatted with friends, and Mary, accompanied by the band, sang a few songs, including one for which Ernest had written the lyrics. Two Doblés turned into several more, and they didn't get to the dock till 2 A.M. Loyal Gregorio rowed them in *Pilar*'s dinghy across the bay to Casa Blanca, where *Pilar* rested at her mooring ball. Exhausted, Mary fell into her bed and slept for twelve hours until awakened by Gregorio, shouting, "Feeesh, feeesh!" Ernest hooked a large wahoo on his line, and after landing it, delighted in this birthday present from the sea. He wrote to Lillian Ross that he celebrated his birthday drinking champagne starting from 6 A.M. and felt superb. He told her Mary had prepared gifts with presentation cards from the dogs and cats and smuggled aboard a beautiful birthday cake. "I was so proud and happy to have made 49"—much like a golfer who breaks 49—"I was just stink happy all day."[19] After the birthday party, Ernest returned to his diet and exercise regime and got his weight down to 210 pounds and his blood pressure almost to normal.

Mary flew to Chicago to make sure her parents were settled before she and Ernest headed off for Europe in the fall. She found her father, having recovered from his surgery, was now seeking a job as commissioner of lands for Idaho. He refused to take the medication prescribed by his doctors, and Ernest weighed in, advising Tom that he had worked hard enough in his life, deserved rest, and should devote himself to reading and looking after Adeline. Tom took Ernest's opinions to heart. Mary longed to return to her life at the Finca with Ernest, the man she loved almost despite himself. She missed their witty conversations, his profound dedication to his art, her chance to share in editing, occasionally expressing her opinions, and watching his stories evolve. Mary had become attached to the people and animals of the Finca and enjoyed her role as chatelaine of the estate.

◆

In early August, grim news came in a cable advising that Ernest's lawyer of twenty years, Maury Speiser, had died. Though their relationship had been tricky, Speiser's death marked the loss of another pillar of Ernest's infrastructure. Ernest had once blamed a hangover on his lawyer, whom he could not visit without the help of alcohol,[20] and he had removed Speiser's authority to discuss permissions or reprints of Ernest's work[21] because his negotiating skills were so weak.[22] Alfred Rice, Speiser's partner and a specialist in copyright law, became Ernest's new lawyer.[23] Rice would play a pivotal role in advising Ernest about his literary, radio, television, and motion picture properties. In the coming years, he would travel to Cuba often to meet with his client. Mary and Alfred became close friends, and Mary helped Alfred and his wife find and adopt a Cuban son, Felipe.

◆

Mary looked forward to being alone with Ernest and was excited at the prospect of their voyage on the *Jagiello*. This would be their first trip to France since the war, and she thought of it as a honeymoon cruise. Despite their disagreements and Ernest's fluctuating temper, Mary loved her husband and was optimistic about the future. She believed they were an effective partnership, and she hoped to become pregnant again. Mary couldn't wait to cast off, and she rushed to complete the minor jobs that needed doing before they could leave.

NINETEEN

Platinum-Blonde at Torcello

September 1948–November 1948

Mary and Ernest left the Finca at ten o'clock on the morning of September 7 after saying goodbye to René, the staff, and the pets. Mary noted Blackie became "too desolate to move." [1] They reached the Havana docks and the crew of the *Jagiello* lashed the blue Buick convertible to the foredeck and covered it with tarps. After boarding the boat, Mary and Ernest hosted an onboard farewell party for many friends. Champagne flowed, and the party got louder and louder until they sailed at 1500 hours. Once underway, and after more drinks at the bar, they dined with the Polish captain, who looked to Mary like Pinocchio, with a smooth face and sharp nose. She later thought she'd been harsh, for he gave her tips about places to see in Florence and shared the ship's log.

At the bar a few nights out, the drunk Polish chief engineer stood next to Mary and muttered, "But what are you—what are you?" Ernest introduced himself and asked, "How are the engines?" The engineer must have believed Ernest made fun of him, for he seemed to resent the question. When Mary said she would "like to see the engines—he snorted [she] couldn't." [2] After Mary left, the engineer became belligerent. He nudged Ernest in the chest, calling him "a capitalist, bourgeois pig" with "no right to have big motorcar." Ernest told him he had never killed a chief engineer before but would now like to do so and challenged him to a duel. Tension filled the air as the blustering engineer accepted the dare. The next morning, Mary wanted to come and watch, but Ernest told her to stay back and that he would only shoot the man in the leg.

"The engineer came to apologize, eyes rimmed with bright pink," and asked Ernest, "would it go any further, and Papa assured him absolutely not."[3] The disappointed Italian crew had offered to intervene because they didn't like the engineer, who stayed drunk in his cabin for days at a time. The crew suggested unusual ways of disposing of the engineer to save Ernest the trouble of shooting him: shoving him overboard, hitting him with a blacksmith's hammer, or pushing him into the moving parts of the engine. The crew recited these methods in a poem they read to Ernest and Mary at a wine and cheese party in the engine room. Mary noted, drunk or sober, the engineer "still looks like a swine to me. I'm afraid I would not have been so generous with him as Papa was."[4]

◆

They were delighted with the ship and slipped into a leisurely routine of reading, writing, studying French, and eating. The food was excellent, and a rich Orvieto Secco accompanied the sumptuous lunches. The steward served "dreamy" ice cream with dinner, after which they went to the bar for coffee and ended up opening a bottle of champagne. Mary and Ernest talked to the captain or the other passengers until midnight when, having had a little too much to drink, they wandered to their cabin and bed. A week into "the honeymoon voyage," Mary wrote they "made lovely gay full-bodied love this afternoon, then slept like thistle-down until dinner."[5]

As they entered the Mediterranean and passed Gibraltar, Mary watched five sperm whales spouting plumes of water. While she sunned herself, Ernest chatted with his friends from the engine room. The thirteen-day voyage came to an end too soon.

A storm had twisted the narrow wooden dock at Cannes and they decided it would be too difficult to land the Buick. Instead, they sailed on to Genoa, off-loaded the car and Ricardo and the Hemingways began driving through the countryside of northern Italy. At Stresa, the hotel's doorman welcomed back "Signor Hemingway" after an absence of thirty years. Mary suspected Ricardo had phoned ahead but the welcome was still impressive and pleased Ernest.

They were invited to the opera but Ernest didn't want to go. Mary rushed to put on her rust-colored silk dress and Ricardo whisked her off to the opera house where gentlemen in black tie greeted her, made compliments, and took her to a box. The director of La Scala, who was visiting Stresa, came to Mary's box, and she found him to be a charming man, fluent in English, French, and Italian. The production was magnificent, and she enjoyed the rich voice of the bass, who they said was "breaking himself" for that minor house.[6] A director of the local opera apologized to her for the rough apparel of the audience. He explained the house had been *plus chic* on the opening night. In her journal, Mary commented that the locals' clothing ranged from boys in corduroy pants to girls wearing satin and ermine. There was "a fat debutante bursting out of pink taffeta, and guarded by her mother, father, and aunt." And there were many housewives with "the kind but undistinguished face and coiffeur of Flo Atkinson of Picabo, Idaho, in their poorly cut black evening dresses." Mary dropped this cutting description in her memoir because homely Flo became an invaluable friend after Ernest's death.

A week later, Oxford-accented Count Federico Kechler, a sportsman from Cortina D'Ampezzo and a fan of Ernest's writing, invited them to fish at his private lake across the Austrian border. They set out on a perfect fall day, with the bright sun in a deep blue sky above the mauve and beige mountains covered with pines, poplar, and birch.[7] The blue Buick followed Federico's wine-colored Lancia, and they climbed from Cortina north through the Dolomites to the low valley where Kechler's lake contrasted with tea-leaf green and mustard fields. A delicious lunch of pork chops and spaghetti was followed by fruit and coffee. Though the fishing was not exciting, with Ernest catching only one trout from the shore, the company was friendly. The invitation led to others from Federico's brother, Carlos, and their friends in Venice.[8]

The region around Cortina was so agreeable they decided to stay for the winter. Mary and Ricardo took the car and surveyed the valley for the perfect home. She found the Villa Aprile on the edge of town, overlooking gentle slopes, allowing them to ski from their front yard. Dogs herded sheep from one pasture to another, and a stream flowed through the valley floor. Mary could not imagine a more pastoral scene. Yet, visible across the vale, commanding the peak, was the massive, gray-stone tower of the Sacrario Militare, a shrine built in 1935 to the memory of the thousands who lost their lives in World War I on the Dolomite front. Mary felt overwhelmed and miserable at the thought of the men wounded and dying in the frozen landscape.

As soon as Ernest saw the chalet, with its verdant views and gentle ski slopes, now spring green, he liked it. The chalet was bright and spacious, and they rented it, even though it was a mile from the center of town. Mary began shopping for sheets and towels, soap, dried mushrooms, and caviar. She noted they slept late on October 15, still exhausted from their lovemaking the day before. After lunch, they went to inspect the Sacrario Militaire, where General Antonio Cantore lies in a crypt surrounded by the bones of six thousand soldiers. Back in Cortina, as if responding to the memories of conflict prompted by the massive monument, Ernest's old foot wound opened wide. The local doctor removed pieces of shrapnel that had worked their way to the surface and applied sulfa dressings.

◆

After last minute packing, generous tipping, and elaborate farewells, they left Cortina for Venice on October 18. The big blue Buick was a striking *bella machina* that never failed to impress the local folk as it moved along the winding roads lined with lemon trees and grapevines. Women walking barefoot under wide-brimmed straw hats waved, girls on bicycles smiled, and men nodded encouragement. No one displayed the resentment of the Polish engineer. They drove through the old town of Bergamo, warm in the sunshine, and stopped at the piazza for drinks. When they reached Federico's house at San Martino, he was standing outside and greeted them warmly. They enjoyed a light lunch accompanied by excellent regional wines. Later that afternoon, as Ricardo drove to Venice, Ernest dozed while Mary watched the countryside transform under the orange and pink light of the setting sun. They entered the city at night, and Mary found it more beautiful than she could have imagined.[9] After dining, they went to bed in their magnificent room in the Gritti Palace Hotel, across the Grand Canal from the Basilica of Santa Maria della Salute.

Mary toured with a sculptor, Ennio Peltellino, who opened her eyes to the exceptional beauty and diversity of the architectural styles and ornamentation. After a morning walking with Ennio through "the profusion of color and movement and motion and strength," she became exhausted and found the Academy of Arts a luxurious tropical garden of delights in which to rest. For several mornings while Ernest wrote, she toured with Ennio.

The mood of the city captivated Mary. Water lapped against the canals as ornate gondolas ferried well-dressed passengers beneath bridges, clocks chimed through time, and gondoliers sang arias. Even the bells which sounded at day-light and rang until well after dark were resonant and less tinny-sounding than those she had heard in other towns. On Friday, Ernest came with her, and they took photographs across the Grand Canal from the Basilica di Santa Maria della Salute. She wore her western belt with the silver-gold buckle. He wore his old tweed jacket, a sweater vest, and tie. Mary spent several pleasant days shopping for crystal goblets and lace table settings and napkins for the dining table at the Finca. She picked out some glass after days of pondering—glass or crystal?—decorated Venetian, or simple?—to fit in at the Finca. She was trying to select unique pieces they would enjoy forever. And she tried to find the best prices, bargaining and keeping meticulous records of her purchases.

Mary rushed out to buy wool socks and then dressed for a trip to the country on October 22. After lunch at the home of Florian Franchetti, they traveled to Fossalta di Piave, close to the place where Ernest was wounded in the First World War.[10] He walked along the riverbank, lingered over the spot where he'd avoided death, and imagined where the Austrian mortars, which had filled his leg with shrapnel, must have been placed. Just as Colonel Cantwell would later do in *Across the River and Into the Trees*, Ernest stooped to cut a slit in the sod on the spot where he was wounded and inserted a 10,000 Lira note. Mary noted that Ernest paid for his new Scott double-barreled shotgun on October 25. The 12-gauge over and under was inlaid with silver and had a hammerless tandem trigger mechanism with a separate trigger to fire each barrel. Ernest couldn't wait to try it out. This was the very gun Ernest would later use to end his life.[11]

They attended a hearty dinner in the lodge of the shooting club, featuring a massive square open fireplace next to the table where they dined on delectable local game. After dinner, the village band members puffed on their polished horns and a thin priest led the village children in song as he pounded on a drum to keep time.[12] Early the next morning, wearing three sweaters and two shirts, Mary sat beside Ernest in a punt. An oarsman poled them along the canal to their duck blind in the middle of the shallow lake. Sportsmen had sunk large wine casks into the bottom of the marsh to provide hiding places, and the hunters climbed into them, carrying their shotguns and chairs. It was just as Ernest later described in *Across the River and Into the Trees*. Clouds of ducks passed overhead, wings whirring, and some brushing close to them while they held fire, waiting for the horn, which would signal the start of the hunt.[13]

As dawn broke and the mountains became visible on the horizon, the ducks flew just out of range overhead. The horn sounded, and flashes erupted from the guns of the hunters hiding in the wine casks. Instead of shooting, Mary knocked down the spiders, slugs, worms, and frogs trying to get into the lunch basket or crawl up her leg.[14] Ernest shot eighteen ducks with his new gun, but Mary hit only one and worried Ernest would chastise her performance. Instead, he was exuberant about his kills with the Scott and happy she had accompanied him.

When they returned to Venice a couple of days later, they walked from the Gritti for a few streets and found Harry's Bar, which would become Ernest's office for the next few months. Mary so enjoyed the home cooking and the paralyzing Negronis, made from gin, vermouth, and Campari, she recorded the recipes in her journal. The owner, Giuseppe Cipriani, was hospitable and invited them to visit Locanda Cipriani, his inn on the island of Torcello.[15]

Mary and Ernest took a gondola through the little canals of Venice to the Fundamenta Nuova where they boarded a Vaporetto for the trip across the big lagoon. The water bus passed the glassblowing island of Murano, which appeared industrial, and they saw the leaning tower on Burano, the island of lacemakers. They got off at Torcello, walked along the path beside the canal, passed the Devil's Bridge, and reached the lovely inn, Locanda Cipriani. Giuseppe welcomed them, sat them at a table close to the fireplace, and brought two Negronis and later bottles of Amarone to accompany their excellent lunch. Giuseppe asked if they would like to look at the best room in the inn, which he could rent to them for the winter, even though he usually closed the inn, for the season.[16] They climbed the stairs and walked down a hallway as Giuseppe told them about the craftsman on Murano who made the room's furniture. He opened the door to the Santa Fosca suite and explained they named it in honor of the young girl who suffered martyrdom for refusing to renounce her Christian faith. Legend said her bones were buried in the basilica which they could see from the French doors that opened onto a balcony. The other balcony looked over a flower garden. Bookcases, a dining table before the fireplace, two large beds, and a modern bathroom with yellow fixtures made this the most comfortable suite Mary had seen since they left the Finca.[17] Ernest suggested, after looking at the rooms, they ought to move to Torcello.

Mary and Ernest sat and sipped more Amarone with Giuseppe. He told them the island had once been home to tens of thousands of people. However, after a mosquito-borne-malarial fever struck in the Middle Ages, they abandoned Torcello in favor of Venice. Boats carried the stones of many dismantled structures on Torcello to form the buildings of Venice. Fewer than twenty people now lived on the island. Ernest later studied the history of Torcello and wrote of it in *Across the River*.

The sun was sinking into the sea, side-lighting in gold the buildings on Burano as they churned across the water back to Venice. Darkness fell as they entered the Grand Canal and Ernest, warm and confident from the Amarone he had sipped along the way, sang passionately but off-key to the gondoliers they passed.

The next day they hired a motor launch. Ricardo loaded it with their baggage and they left for Torcello in a dense fog Mary found charming and mysterious. "The boatman, it soon became obvious, was spooked for he started a series of quick switch-abouts, turnings, and sudden engine retardings. Ricardo, with his eagle eye, went to help him."[18] Mary watched the black, scythe-like bows of gondolas cut through the fog, springing up and disappearing. They reached Torcello and the boatman navigated along the canal to the Locanda Cipriani standing at the end. As they passed under the Bridge of the Devil, Mary imagined the ghosts of the malaria victims in the vapors rising from the marsh.

Giuseppe offered them a table close to the crackling fireplace. They sipped Negronis as they waited for a delicious veal stew which came with a bottle of Amarone. Ernest was developing a taste for the potent wine and the waiter brought more bottles which Ernest shared with Ricardo and the boatman. Mary was not sorry to leave the men to their drinking, and she went to bed early. The mattress was firm, and she slid under the fresh sheets, pulled the feather comforter to her chin, and fell into such a deep sleep she didn't hear Ernest when he came in later.

In the morning, Mary unpacked their books and put them on the shelves above their beds and over the fireplace. She moved the table and chairs to the side and pulled the reading chairs closer to the fireplace. They treasured their new home over the next few days. The place stimulated Ernest, and he woke fresh with ideas. While he worked in the mornings, Mary explored the island, walking along the paths through the fields bordering the marsh and the lagoon, finding ponds left by the tide teaming with fish. On the horizon, just over the water, she could see the leaning tower of Burano and she resolved to shop on the island of lacemakers.

Mary began practicing her guitar when Ernest was napping. She had found "a woman's guitar" in Venice, "about half the size of the standard European instrument and delicately inlaid with three types of wood, with charming dulcet tones," and she began strumming along to folk melodies.[19] They took afternoon naps, and Ernest later remembered the days on Torcello were the most torrid of their sexual relationship. Ernest wrote in Mary's journal (as he did sometimes), "she was a platinum-blonde . . . at Torcello, where we lived one fall and part of the winter and made love at least every morning, noon, and night, with beech log fires, and had the loveliest time Papa ever knew."[20]

TWENTY

He Has Become the Most Important Part of Me

November 1948–May 1949

M ary's old friends Lucy and Alan Moorehead invited her to visit them at the house they had rented near Florence. Poised and elegant, Lucy had been editor of the women's pages at the *Daily Express* before she married Alan. Noel Monks and Alan were fellow Australians who befriended each other before traveling to Britain to become foreign correspondents for Beaverbrook's *Daily Express*. Alan became one of Britain's most renowned war correspondents, a prolific author of articles in the *New Yorker*, and an award-winning author of several books. In 1965, Winston Churchill presented him with the Duff Cooper Memorial Prize for his book *Gallipoli*. Lucy had retired from her position at the *Daily Express* to become mother to their two children.[1] Mary and Lucy became friends at the *Daily Express* in the days before they married the two Australians.

Mary was reluctant to leave Ernest on Torcello, but he said he didn't mind because he would be able to concentrate on his work and she could have fun and bring back stories for him. The conversation between the husband and wife in Ernest's short story "Get Yourself a Seeing-eyed Dog" reads as if it were drawn from Ernest's effort to persuade Mary to go for a vacation with the Mooreheads. Early on the morning of November 17, Ernest came downstairs in his bathrobe to wave goodbye as she headed toward the lagoon. She took the Vaporetto to Venice and met Ricardo at the garage where they stored the Buick.

Two days later, they arrived at Lucy's house in Fiesole, and she looked "every bit as fresh and pretty and alert" as when they were girls in London.[2] Mary, Lucy, and her two children lunched in the sunroom off the terrace of the big house filled with heavy furniture. The daughter, Caroline, appeared to be a sweet girl, and the son a very adult small boy. Caroline would mature into the author who would write an award-winning biography of Martha Gellhorn.

Lucy and Mary dined in the grandeur of the living room and chatted late into the night. They knew each other's secrets from years earlier. Alan had never been particularly faithful, his biographer noting, "his strong libido was an aspect of his personality that Moorehead indulged throughout his life."[3] Lucy, "the clever daughter of a country doctor in Dorset," was "a reticent and reserved Englishwoman" who was deeply in love with him. The two women had a lot to talk about during their visit.

Over the next few days, Lucy and Mary visited the galleries in Florence. They ate lunch at an expensive restaurant, and Mary picked up the tab. She bought presents for the children and paid for Lucy and her to have a manicure—noting the disbursements in her journal. One theme of their ongoing conversation was whether Mary ought to have given up her job in journalism to become Ernest's wife. Lucy had been proud Mary occupied a prominent position and had done so well in a man's world. Mary was at the top of *Time,* and everyone said how good a journalist she was. Mary admitted that she missed it sometimes but pointed out "the advantages of being simply a wife, and not a harried and competing career woman."[4] She did not have to report to a boss or put up with the male egos in a newsroom, though she had never felt mistreated. "It was such fun being a wife," Mary told Lucy.[5] She was a partner with Ernest, creating an environment in which he could write, typing drafts, and subtly influencing him. She was vital to his work and believed if she had not come to Cuba, he would have drunk himself to death. Keeping him focused and healthy was a full-time job, for which she felt well-compensated. She was leading a life she could never have afforded on a reporter's income. Her life with Ernest was thrilling—they traveled, associated with fascinating friends, and had an agreeable sex life. She loved being the mistress of the Finca and boating with her man on *Pilar* as they fished the Gulf Stream. She could have had none of this if she'd stayed in London reporting for *Time.* Anyway, she could still write pieces for magazines and would enjoy those jobs. And, she confided, she was hoping she would become pregnant and have the daughter she and Ernest both wanted.

Mary told Lucy their voyage to Genoa was like a honeymoon, and she was happy with her decision to leave Noel and take up with Ernest. She probably did not share with Lucy how difficult Ernest could be, how cruel and even vicious he became with too much drink. Instead, she painted a charming picture of their life together, which for the last few weeks had been close to the truth. Ernest wrote the next day, saying how much he missed Mary, and he felt "pretty damn lost and lonely" after she left.[6]

Ricardo drove Mary and Lucy to Pisa, and they climbed the leaning tower, surprised at how far over the tower tilted. At the top, they could have fallen off but for the metal railing. They bought ham, cheese, bread, and wine for a chauffeur's lunch and stopped to eat in a forest between Pisa and La Spezia. Mary missed Ernest as she realized how much he would have enjoyed the pine trees, and she confided to her journal, "missing Papa badly now. A week without him is about all I can stand—then my battery needs recharging. . . . I'm devoting most of my attention to wishing for him, worrying if he is okay and heartily needing and loving him."[7] She continued to note her expenses, including the amount paid to Pisa beggars and the purchase of a turtleneck sweater for Ernest that he would later wear in Yousuf Karsh's photograph.

Ernest wrote he had "been working hard and missing you harder." He also told Mary friends had invited him to a big duck shoot in the next few days and concluded, "I love you dearest Kittner and miss you very, very, very, very, very, very much."[8]

Mary was delighted to return to Torcello. Ernest seemed well, and they ate a delicious lunch, retired to their suite, and made love next to the fireplace. Ernest had befriended the parish priest, Don Francesco Tagliapietra, who had guided him around the monuments. They had talked for hours about theology and the astonishing mosaic representation of the last judgment featured on the west wall of the basilica of Santa Maria Assunta. When leaving the building, worshippers who could not read would still understand the images displayed like a comic strip in the vivid gold mosaic. The dead are resurrected, angels weigh their souls, and the sinful are punished in a frightening variety of tortures. Christ, cloaked in a blue robe, saves some souls from the limbo of Hell.

Two days after Mary's homecoming, Ricardo drove Ernest to Fossalta di Piave to look at the old battlefields. Perhaps Ernest was beginning to imagine Colonel Cantwell contemplating the spot where he was wounded. While Ernest was away,

Mary invited the schoolmaster and his wife to a dinner of roast chicken and crêpes suzette. He was charming and spoke in accented English. She was shy and quiet until they started singing, and her forceful personality emerged. The schoolmaster taught Mary a new folksong and changed the words to suit a blonde. "Tutti mi-chiamono bionda. /Ma bionda io non sono. /Porto capelli neri." ("They all call me blonde. But I'm not blonde. I have black hair.")[9] The words were silly in English, but the melody was lovely, and Mary taught Ernest to sing the last line. She sang the first two lines, and he came in with the last line. They sang it over and over, and it became their love duet. Whenever they sang it, they remembered their romantic days in front of the fireplace in the Santa Fosca suite. These were some of the happiest days of their relationship, before either of them knew a beautiful black swan would bring discord.

◆

Ernest went duck hunting with Carlos Kechler on December 11. Mary decided she would stay home because the morning sky was overcast with a light rain falling. Carlos drove Ernest's big Buick toward the marsh, while Ernest sat in the front passenger seat and three of Carlos's friends sat in the back. Unknown to Ernest or Mary, a teenaged countess, Adriana Ivancich, was to join the hunting party. She stood by the side of the road trying to keep out of the persistent rain, and when she saw the blue Buick, one of Carlos's friends stuck out his hand and shouted her name. She ran to the car, and after seating herself in the back, Carlos said, "Adriana, this is Hemingway." As she recalled, "Only then did I notice that big man with the gray hair who, seated in the front, turned around to look at me. 'I'm sorry, Adriana, for this delay. It was my fault,' he said with a smile."[10]

The next morning at 4 A.M., it was still raining when the hunting party awoke and prepared to go by boat to the hollow barrels among the reeds in the marsh. They hunted for several hours, but Adriana, still wet and cold, did not enjoy the experience. At the end of the hunt, the party returned to the country house where a brilliant fire burned under the chimney, and the hunters ate, drank local red wine, and told stories of their adventures. Adriana recalled Ernest stimulating everyone's imagination, telling stories about Africa, Spain, and Cuba. He also noticed Adriana, and she described their first encounter: "annoyed by my long hair, which continued to fall across my forehead, I asked for a comb." No one heard her, so she asked again. "Suddenly, Hemingway's massive figure appeared next to me. He dug a hand in his pocket, took out his bone comb, broke it in two, and gave me half."[11] They began talking, and when it was time to leave, he asked if he could see her the next day. She agreed, and another day followed, and then others. At first, Adriana was bored to be with a man so much older whom she could not understand. However, he seemed pleased to have her near him, and whenever she arrived, his face broke into a smile and he swung to his legs "like a great bear."[12]

Ricardo drove Mary to Cortina D'Ampezzo on December 16, and she began fixing up the Villa Aprile. She had fun planning meals and arranging the furniture, hoping Ernest would enjoy the views and the fire. She confided to her journal when she was alone in the evenings, "the only pleasure is knowing he is coming soon. Otherwise, I'm quite empty. How quickly four years is, quick for this—he has become the most important part of me."[13] Mary was becoming more emotionally dependent upon Ernest, just as he was falling hopelessly in love with an eighteen-year-old girl.

Ernest and Adriana spent more time with each other, and Adriana said, "Ernest became young." He invited the young people to Torcello and they ate at Locanda Cipriani. In Venice, he reserved tables for them on the terrace of the Hotel Gritti, and sometimes he and Adriana went for long walks through the alleys of Venice. One evening, Ernest performed a corrida. He cleared the dining table, took the tablecloth, and told Mary, who had returned from Cortina, that she was the bull. In the middle of the room, he began fighting the beast. "Aha, Toro, Aha, Toro," the audience shouted, clapping their hands. Adriana said Ernest seemed like a real torero, his face becoming severe and intense. Then he smoothed his brow with his hand, took a carnation from a nearby table, and offered Mary the flower saying, "Bravo Toro." [14]

When Mary and Ernest moved to Cortina and were alone again, they read during lunch and felt relaxed and free. Mary worried Ernest might find it dull, but she believed it was good for him to take a break, and they stayed up late talking. They passed a peaceful Christmas at Villa Aprile.

Life published Malcolm Cowley's "Portrait of Mr. Papa" on January 10. The piece is a fawning account of Hemingway's adventures in World War II based on his reports for *Collier's*. Cowley presents a kindly description of his marriages and previous work and a sketch of his life at the Finca surrounded by his adoring children and many cats. Photographs show Ernest as a seven-year-old-boy-fisherman sporting a straw hat, an eight-year-old posing with his family, a wounded soldier in a wheelchair in World War I, and a heavily bearded man in flight gear preparing to board a bomber in World War II. In another, Papa wears boxing gloves, resting on the ropes of a boxing ring, with the caption explaining that he used the ring to get in shape for war tasks. There are photographs of Ernest and each of his four wives and a full-page photo of the famous author eating breakfast in his bedroom under Juan Gris's painting the *Guitar Player*, surrounded by some of his favorite cats.

Cowley's portrait helped shape Ernest's public image as a hypermasculine figure with a sensitive, artistic side. Everything about Ernest was grand and admirable. He was built like a boxer; his head was big and leonine; his memory was accurate; he listened to people thoroughly. He lived on a patriarchal scale, surrounded by his family, friends, and retainers. The living room of the Finca was sixty feet long, its walls lined with the heads of the beasts Hemingway had shot in Africa. His expenses were high, but so were his earnings, most of which came from Hollywood. There was a separate house at the Finca for his three sons, who worshipped their father and visited him at every opportunity. Ernest's friends included wealthy sportsmen, West Point generals, priests, prizefighters, jockeys, matadors, and movie stars. Most of his friends had achieved excellence in some activity that engaged Ernest's passionate interest. They had in common physical or moral courage, combined with the know-how to be dependable in a crisis. Ernest wrote in the mornings and went fishing in the afternoons. [15]

The portrait was so grand it embarrassed Ernest, and he told Hotch, "I had a nice private life before, with a lot of undeclared nonpublished pride, and now I feel like somebody had shit in it and wiped themselves on slick paper and left it there." [16] Cowley later explained to Robert Coates, "Ernest was kind, generous, thoughtful, brave, and he was also (till about 1940) cowardly, and he was also envious, spiteful, and on occasion mean as cat piss." Cowley had not mentioned this in the *Life* profile because he had let himself "get too damned involved with him, something a critic shouldn't do." [17] He referred to the fact that Ernest had offered him a loan, and had agreed to the interview so Cowley's family could get a vacation and allow Cowley to pay for his son's university education. Cowley's correspondence with Ernest during the period is sycophantic, and Cowley felt guilty about subordinating himself and abandoning his critical perch.

Cowley scarcely mentioned Mary in the lengthy piece. "Mrs. Papa—also known as 'Kittner' and 'Miss Mary'—runs the household efficiently and makes out the income tax returns." Cowley claimed she was the daughter of "a prosperous lumberman" (which amused her father when he read it), had attended (but not graduated from) Northwestern University, and after three reporting jobs, had landed at *Time* where she met Ernest. The cursory description of Mary's contribution to the partnership couldn't have pleased her. She must have been unhappy about the photos of Ernest with each of his four wives—she was so obviously just the latest.

Lucy and Alan Moorehead arrived in Cortina for a visit on the evening of January 17 and Mary met them in front of the Hotel Posta with a sleigh. They returned to the Villa Aprile to have dinner with Ernest, who was returning from Venice. Alan Moorehead remembered Ernest's arrival and noted wryly, "he came in from shooting ducks, 'a walking myth of himself,' cartridge belts and strings of teal and mallard festooning his shoulder."[18] They spoke after dinner, and in their quiet conversation Alan found a serious man who talked about writing, "with the humility and doubt of a writer who reads for five hours or so every day, and who writes and re-writes for as long as his brain will work, knowing that it is only a miracle that he will ever achieve a phrase, even a word, that will correspond to the vision in his mind."[19] In this short account, Moorehead sketched an endearing portrait of Ernest as a sincere and sensitive artist, features missed entirely by Cowley.

Mary enjoyed having Lucy and Alan's company, and she hiked and skied with them in the valley bordering the Villa. Three days later, as they were skiing fresh tracks in a foot of snow, Mary fell head over heels and cracked her right ankle. The local doctor, who was familiar with ski injuries, applied a cast and she stayed in bed until the following Monday when the Mooreheads left. The cast remained on for twenty-five days, causing Mary to hobble around the villa in a black felt shoe with rubber sole made by her doctor. Once able to walk on the slippery tiled kitchen floor, she began to cook as a diversion. Her life became tranquil, and she spent long mornings in bed and an hour outside in the sun at noon. [20]

In mid-February, Ernest came down with a miserable flu and spent ten days in his bed. When the illness abated, he resumed working on a short story set in Torcello about a dying man hunting ducks on the marshes which would grow into his next novel, *Across the River and Into the Trees*. They returned to their old room at the Gritti Palace Hotel on March 17. Mary was pleased to see the clean white silk curtains, pressed sheets, and soft pillows. Ernest was content to be close to Harry's Bar and the prospect of outings with Adriana. Mary noticed Ernest and Adriana "were busily launching a flirtation." Still, she said little about it, believing an affair with the young woman was unlikely because she thought Adriana would not fall in love with the much older Ernest. [21]

Adriana remembered Mary was smiling and affectionate, yet watchful. In the beginning, Adriana did not suspect Mary worried about her. However, one day Mary told Adriana she was "perplexed" about the interest Ernest showed in her and wondered "which attitude she would have to take." Adriana believed at a certain point, Mary "understood that I was not seeking secondhand fame and that my affection for Papa would not transform itself into love." [22] Ernest's infatuation with Adriana hurt Mary, and she worried his wholehearted and naïve pursuit of the young woman would lead to embarrassment all around. "Ernest was weaving a mesh which might entangle and pain him," Mary wrote. "But I was sure that no cautionary phrases of mine could arrest the process. I held my tongue." [23]

They returned to Cortina, finding the town emptied of winter tourists. Heather bloomed on the green hillsides and crocuses burst from the grass around Villa Aprile. Mary's ankle had healed and she could ramble through the valley and walk to town. The stream ran cold along the valley floor, the sheepdogs barked, and sheep moved through the green pastures. Ernest complained about his left eye, which was painful in bright light, and in a few days he had developed a severe infection with dried mucus crusting over his eyelids. A painful rash appeared on his face, and he came down with a fever which worsened despite injections of penicillin. Ernest was "very miserable, eating almost nothing, his eye constantly sticking together with mucous, and the light badly hurt him." [24]

The local doctor worried Ernest might be suffering from erysipelas, a potentially fatal and penicillin-resistant precursor to flesh-eating disease. He advised Ernest to visit a Catholic clinic in Padova. There, the specialist gave Ernest antibiotic shots every three hours, took him off his blood pressure pills, and ordered him to stop drinking alcohol of any kind, as the recurrence of erysipelas is linked to alcoholism. Ernest recovered but was gloomy as he couldn't read, drink, or eat exciting food. The hovering nuns did nothing to improve his mood, and Mary tried to console him by reading articles from *Holiday* and even Stevenson's *Treasure Island*. However, Ernest was melancholic and found no joy in her efforts to distract him. Two weeks later, they returned to Cortina to prepare for their voyage home to Cuba on the *Jagiello*.

By the time they boarded their favorite ship, Ernest had made a full recovery, and they enjoyed their passage back to Havana on the comfortable *Jagiello*. Mary read André Gide's diaries and they took time for lovemaking. They stayed in bed until late in the morning and talked happily about their friends. Free from the pressure of other people, they lost their self-consciousness and lived in effortless harmony with each other. They made "small loving jokes, speculations on girl and boy love, which Ernest was brimming with those days. The Kinsey people would not have believed us."[25] In her draft memoir, Mary described their sexual life. "Papa's theory on lovemaking, that it is the boy's pleasure to make the girl come, and to keep himself still and durable, even at the expense of coming himself. He enjoys my abandon, but no more than I do." Ernest "taught me many new delights. I have taught him some. Also, we have learned together, and we have elaborated and improved. Now I seem both to get stirred more easily and thoroughly and to get tired more easily, in a mere hour."[26]

The journey was over too soon, and Mary noted in her journal, "this had been the best vacation of my life."[27] Friends hanging off the railings of *Pilar* greeted them as they cruised into Havana Harbor on the afternoon of May 25. The blue Buick and Mary's boxes of Venetian glass, china, linens, and books made it to the Finca. René had prepared the house, and they were happy to be home. The pets greeted them, and Blackie was delirious with joy.

TWENTY-ONE

Ernest Taunts Me with This

May 1949–March 1950

Ernest shared his story about duck hunting in the Veneto with Mary. After reading it, she urged him to go beyond the duck blinds sunk into the marshes and make the story about Venice, too. Ernest took her advice, and the project energized him. He rose each morning with fresh ideas and wrote until he became tired but not exhausted and knew where he would head the next day.

The finished tower looked magnificent, rising high above the house and providing a beautiful view of the green countryside, with Havana and the sea in the distance. Mary helped Ernest move his things up to the bright room, featuring a writing table and the bookcases she had designed and Pablo had crafted. The eaves of the roof extended to prevent the sun's hot rays from penetrating the interior. Well-placed windows allowed a cooling breeze to circulate, and Ernest was happy with the new space. Mary knew the noises coming from the cooks and gardeners would not interrupt him, and she would no longer have to tiptoe around the house. The tower's bottom floor became "the cat-house," where their thirty or forty cats were safe and comfortable at night. The cats' original bedroom was in the main house, and Mary's nose had long been affronted, particularly during northerly winds. [1]

A few days later, Ernest came to Mary in the kitchen, holding his typewriter at his side. "It's lovely up there," he said, "it's calm and beautiful, and thank you." But it's "too lonely, and I miss the sounds of the house—René sweeping the matting." [2] Ernest resumed working in his bedroom, standing before his typewriter set on a bookshelf. He never used the tower for serious writing again, though he went there to escape annoying visitors, read over drafts, and nap.

Mary had a vision for what the Finca should become, and she began supervising renovations and repairs. She replaced crumbling red tiles on the terrace and converted a guest room and sitting room into an extensive library lined with bookcases. Slowly she transformed the Finca into the comfortable, but not ostentatious, home it remains today.[3]

◆

In August, Mary and Ernest took *Pilar* to their favorite anchorage at Paraíso[*] and Mary swam ashore, realizing that only four years earlier, starfish had frightened her, let alone the stingrays that cruised below. Mary confided to her journal that when Ernest was good, he could be endearingly so—he had offered to rip in half and share with her the last tissue in a box. That such a small act of generosity was worthy of note may suggest kindness did not prevail.

Jean-Paul Sartre came for a visit with his girlfriend Dolorès Vanetti on August 27. Mary wondered what the woman found attractive about the diminutive intellectual whose smelly pipe had ground down his discolored teeth. She did not find Sartre charming or the woman interesting, and she marveled at their mutual attraction. Vanetti, who was shorter than Sartre, with a beautiful oval face, had been an actress in Montparnasse before moving to New York in 1940. She was bicultural, speaking perfect English and French and bridging the gap between France and America. Sartre later told Beauvoir, "Dolorès gave me America."[4] Dolorès and Sartre had fallen in love, and they planned to marry. Dolorès was thirty-seven, four years younger than Mary, who seems to have slightly misread the scene in her memoir. "Sartre's girl was so freshly abloom and attentive, and Sartre's looming intellect so masked by his slow-moving eyes and square contours of face that I wondered what forces had created their mutual attraction and concluded that the girl must be more profound with him privately then she was with us and he somehow more beguiling."[5] Mary had looked forward to the dinner as a chance to get an inside view of the world of existentialism and an update on the latest

[*] Ernest nicknamed a cove in Mayo Medano de Casiguas as "Paraiso." It is on the north side of Cuba, not far from Levisa. *How It Was*, 204.

philosophical controversies sweeping Paris. To her disappointment, Ernest and Sartre "passed by the topic lightly, Sartre saying only that the term was invented by his disciples, who pressed it upon him." Instead, they discussed the nuts and bolts of publishing problems, "like a couple of hardware salesman. I couldn't have been more disgusted—and disappointed."[6] They compared the deals they had with their publishers and spoke of ways to increase the percentage of royalties they received.

During dessert, Sartre made "a small, poetic speech, which sounded unrehearsed," about his incapacity to find satisfaction in nature—it was a loss to his spirit.[7] He wished he could open himself to the wild and find contentment in fishing, and hunting birds and animals, as Ernest had done. Mary was relieved Ernest did not invite him to come fishing on *Pilar*. By the time dinner ended, it was so late that Juan was off duty, and Mary made up beds in the little house and arranged for their breakfasts. In the morning, Juan drove them to Havana to collect their luggage and catch their plane. Mary noted in her diary they drank five bottles of wine at dinner.[8] The relationship between Sartre and Vanetti broke down the next summer, and Sartre returned to Beauvoir.

Ed Hotchner and his wife, Geraldine (Gerry), who was four months pregnant, arrived the day Sartre left, and Ernest invited them to stay in the guest house at the Finca. Though Ernest had deposited the advance, he had made no progress on the "Future of Literature" article for *Cosmopolitan*. Hotch felt it would be improper to inquire too vigorously, and a few days later Ernest proposed substituting two short stories for the article, as his forte was fiction, not think pieces. He pointed out stories were more valuable, and Hotch's editor eventually increased the payment to twenty-five thousand dollars.[9]

Hotch and Gerry had fun with the Hemingways, and in his thank you letter, Hotch wrote about how fond he and Gerry were of Mary. He apologized they had been "pains in the ass as fishermen" for, given Gerry's pregnancy, Ernest had to pilot *Pilar* with more care than he otherwise could have done.

In early September, Mary flew to Chicago to visit her parents. After noting her arrival, "laden with wahoo steaks," the literary journalist Fanny Butcher marveled at Mary's "indestructible beauty, even after going through the depressing weeks of 'knitting' a broken ankle."[10] Ernest began writing to her daily, saying how much he missed her and telling her to buy a mink coat with the three checks he enclosed. A mink would "protect her against the chills of the canals, and the snobberies of Venice."[11] Mary described her mink shopping expedition to Ernest, reporting that she and her cousin Bea went to several stores. While natural mink was more expensive than the farmed variety, she believed natural mink was far superior. Given the generous checks Ernest sent, Mary opted for wild pelts. She told him it was "the real thing" and "I know you're going to love it. And when you see it among the class minks in New York and the non-class minks, I'm sure you're going to see we have got value for your dough."[12]

She told Ernest about having her hair done. "Then the oil and the shampoo, and my hair came out glossy, truly glossy, and as soft as yours. Going to get another before I come home, just to show you —everybody around the shop saying what lovely hair." The massage woman was also flattering and said, "it's a pleasure to work on you, Mrs. Hemingway, you have such a lovely little body." She "guessed that I was 34 to 36 years old."[13]

◆

Ernest worked hard on the story about duck hunting in the Veneto. It now featured a fifty-year-old impotent American army officer, Colonel Cantwell, who was in love with an eighteen-year-old countess, Renata. Ernest gave Adriana's face to Renata. "She had pale, almost olive-colored skin, a profile that could break your, or anyone else's heart, and her dark hair, of an alive texture, hung down over her shoulders."[14] Ernest told Mary, Hotch, Charlie Scribner, and Buck Lanham the book was coming along very well. He updated them in every letter on the number of words he wrote each day. Ernest believed it would be his finest book, and he told Charlie Scribner it would sell so well he should "start chopping down trees for the paper now. If it isn't good, you can hang me by the neck until dead."[15]

◆

Mary returned to the Finca on October 6 carrying gifts for Ernest and showing off her mink. The fur helped Ernest smooth over things with Mary. As he told Hotch, "a man should know how to get out of the doghouse, or else he should turn in his suit. The other thing that makes things better is that I love Miss Mary truly. She knows this, and it helps her to forgive me when I'm in the wrong."[16] A few days later, Ernest found himself back in the doghouse when photos taken by Roberto Herrera surfaced. They showed the Floridita's new bar girl, Xenophobia, modeling three dresses against the backdrop of the Finca during Mary's absence. Ernest told Hotch he had "thought of a pretty quick answer but could not make it stick."[17] One evening, Ernest was drunk, and Mary wrote him a note on a small file card, "Mr. Hemingway, you are drunk. When you are drunk, you are a bore, and now is the time to stop." Ernest scrawled on the bottom of the page, "I love you. EH."[18]

Mary noted that Ernest was in the final phase of his novel, and she had typed the latest copy of the manuscript. She was unhappy about the middle and later parts. Though she felt disloyal even thinking it, she found the conversations between Colonel Cantwell and Renata "banal beyond reason and their obsession with food, and the ploy of the emeralds, a mysterious lapse of judgment."[19] Mary kept her mouth shut, for she did not want to undermine Ernest's self-confidence, and she hoped someone at Scribner's would help edit those passages. However, since Max Perkins's death, no one at Scribner's had the standing with Ernest to challenge his prose.

A month later, on November 16, Mary and Ernest flew to New York and checked into the Sherry-Netherland Hotel. They spent several days partying with friends before boarding the *Île de France* for their trip to Le Havre. Lillian Ross attached herself to their entourage for several days as she interviewed Ernest for a profile she was writing for the *New Yorker*. Mary met Alfred Rice, Ernest's new lawyer, for the first time, and confided to her diary, "he seems intelligent, capable and loving, also industrious. He's really working hard on our income tax."[20]

◆

Mary and Ernest sailed to France accompanied by Jigee Viertel, the long-lashed shapely actress and wife of the young novelist and screenwriter Peter Viertel, whom they had met in Sun Valley. Viertel had expected to travel with his wife and the Hemingways, but at the last moment, he received a lucrative offer to write a proposal for a screenplay. Ernest promised Viertel he would look after Jigee.

Much to Mary's chagrin, Ernest's idea of looking after Jigee involved spending hours with her in their stateroom. Dressed in his red silk emperor's robe, which Mary had a seamstress make for him in Cortina, Ernest pontificated about life to the adoring Jigee. She listened with devoted attention as Ernest repeated philosophies and catchphrases Mary had long ago found tedious. Jigee listened like

Blackie did, Mary commented in her diary. Ernest overused "truly" in solemn tones, called Jigee "daughter" too often and disingenuously, and littered his chat with lazy phrases such as "when the chips are down" and "how do you like it now gentlemen?" He taught the abstemious Jigee to drink, beginning with whiskey sours and graduating her to harder cocktails, conditioning her to alcohol, for which she would develop a lifelong addiction.

Ernest was drinking excessively, and he became argumentative with Mary—she blamed his exhaustion from working on the novel. She found relief exercising, receiving massages in the ship's spa, and talking with her journalist friend from London, Sammy Boal. When they arrived in Paris, Mary was happy to take up residence in her old room at the Ritz, chambre 86, which was unchanged. Even the table on which she had typed dispatches was still there, and Ernest worked at it revising the novel. Hotch arrived from New York carrying the most recent consolidation of the novel, which he was editing for serialization in *Cosmopolitan*. The article on the future of literature for which Hotch had first advanced funds had morphed into a short story and then into a novel. [21] Ernest asked Jigee to read it in his presence. He watched her for signs of appreciation, and when she told him it made her feel like crying, he accepted that as a genuine compliment. [22]

After Peter Viertel arrived in Paris, he couldn't help but notice Ernest's obsession with his wife and he soon learned that thanks to Ernest's influence, Jigee was becoming a lush. Jigee told him Ernest had a crush on her, but she insisted their relationship had remained platonic for he was in love with the Italian countess Adriana, who figured in the novel. Despite Ernest's ravings about Adriana, Jigee suspected the relationship was "merely an aging man's rather pathetic fixation." [23] Ernest continued to favor Jigee over Mary at lunches and outings to such a degree Peter became suspicious, and after one evening, he asked Jigee if she found Ernest attractive. Jigee ridiculed Peter for asking. Even if she weren't in love with Peter, "Ernest's protruding stomach, unkempt odor, and the rash on his face would have put her off. He was generous and paternally protective, but impossible to take seriously as a suitor." [24]

Ernest worked on the draft manuscript in the mornings, and in the afternoons they went for elegant lunches before the races at Auteuil. Hotch and Ernest were serious about the horses and sought tips from Ernest's friend, Georges, the chief of the Ritz's Big Bar. Thanks to Georges's advice, they had two spectacular successes at the track. Their most magnificent horse, Bataclan II, paid 27 to 1. After

Ernest paid Georges a handsome tip, he divided a mountain of franc notes into three large piles on the bed in chambre 86. He gave one pile each to Hotch and Mary and kept one for himself. Mary bought an elegant sable coat with her share of the winnings.[25] On December 10, Ernest finished the manuscript, and they celebrated at Auteuil, flush with their Bataclan jackpots.

On December 24, Ernest's entourage packed into a chauffeur-driven Packard for a journey to the Riviera and Venice. Ernest took the seat next to their favorite driver, George Malibat, while Jigee and Mary sat in the back and Peter and Hotch arranged themselves in the jump seat. Over the next four days, they visited Bourgogne villages, walked on the Pont d'Avignon, and examined the fortified town of Aigues-Mortes. They passed through the Van Gogh countryside around Arles and the Cézanne scenery around Aix-en-Provence.

Peter Viertel later wrote that he chafed under "the overbearing leadership" of Ernest and wanted to be alone with his wife.[26] They spent an evening in Aix-en-Provence, sitting at Les Deux Garçons on Cours Mirabeau drinking champagne and watching life go by under the plane trees and past the fountains. Mary and Ernest stayed at the Hôtel Roi René not far from Cours Mirabeau. The next morning, they drove to Nice, and after quick farewells at the bar, Hotch and Peter and Jigee left for Paris. Writing in her journal, Mary said she had become fond of Jigee. She changed her mind days later when Ernest told her of Jigee's efforts to entice him to move with her to California, where they could have a ranch and raise horses.[27] At about the same time, Jigee told Peter of Ernest's desire to marry her and have a daughter.[28] It's not clear who was pursuing whom, but Ernest's efforts to charm younger women were unpleasant for Mary, and she thought again about leaving him.

George drove them to Venice, and at the Hotel Gritti they found the grand maestro looking older but still beaming. A welcoming fire greeted them in their rooms overlooking the Grand Canal and the singing gondoliers. The next evening, they went to Harry's Bar and met Giuseppe Cipriani, whose eldest daughter brought a bunch of roses for Mary. He showed them his plans for expanding the Locanda at Torcello by adding servants' quarters, a fresh bar, and a covered, unwalled dining space in the garden, which is now glassed in. Adriana and her boyfriend Tony from Milano joined them for dinner. Mary wore a black dress and gold earrings and showed off a new gold box she had purchased that afternoon. Later, they went to see a pianist at Ciros, the current hot place in Venice. They sang along and Ernest performed his bullfighter dance with Tony and Mary playing the bulls. It was snowing hard when they left Ciros and came back to the Gritti. Adriana and Mary gave a bottle of wine to the gondoliers to help warm them. After taking some photos, they returned to the room, ordered more champagne, and sang more songs. In the morning, there was a foot of snow on the marble balustrade outside the window and Mary wrote, "Venice is more beautiful than ever."[29]

Over the next few days, while Mary visited her favorite sites in Venice, Ernest went to find Adriana. He told her that before he met her, he could no longer write, but extra energy had passed through her and entered him. Adriana recalled Ernest saying, "You made it possible for me to write again, and I will be grateful to you always. I could finish my book, and I gave the protagonist your face."[30] On January 9, Hotch brought a typed copy of the manuscript to Venice for Ernest's review. A week later, he carried it back to New York so *Cosmopolitan* could serialize it.

Accompanied by their now almost-constant companion Adriana and one of her girlfriends, Ernest and Mary moved to the Hotel Posta, at the center of Cortina D'Ampezzo's ski activity. Even the manicurist who came to do Mary's nails expressed disapproval of Adriana's interest in Ernest. Mary knew Ernest was smitten and would be hurt, but she decided not to say anything, "sure that no cautionary phrases could arrest the process. I held my tongue, even when Ernest quoted to me in awe such commonplace young-woman ambitions as Adriana's wish to do good deeds for her family."[31] Ernest's gullibility astounded Mary, but because she knew they were not having a sexual affair, she put up with it.

◆

Cosmopolitan published the first installment of *Across the River and Into the Trees* in early February. The story concerns the last few days in the life of Richard Cantwell, a fifty-year-old American colonel stationed in Trieste who overmedicates his fatal heart condition. He spends part of his leave in Torcello hunting for ducks and then moves to Venice to enjoy the city he has long adored. He meets with Renata, the eighteen-year-old Italian countess of his dreams. Cantwell is a veteran of the First World War who served in Fossalta di Piave, where he received a wound just as Ernest had. Cantwell later fought in the Second World War with the 4th Division in Normandy, then in the Battle of Huertgen Forest and the Battle of the Bulge. Of course, Ernest had been embedded as a journalist with the 4th Division in these very places. Demoted from brigadier general for following faulty orders which caused his men's deaths, Cantwell is haunted by his mistakes. The impotent colonel seeks escape in the arms of Renata under a blanket in a gondola. We know he will soon die.

One early reader was Martha Gellhorn, who was then seeing Bill Walton and wrote to him about the book. She was "revolted" because Ernest kept injecting himself into his novels, building up a dream version of himself. "Now he is a fifty-year-old Colonel of Infantry with high blood pressure, a great education, and a passion for duck hunting." Martha observed, "the women get younger and younger; so that now the woman is an olive haired Italian of nineteen. And I feel quite sick; I cannot describe this to you. Shivering sick." Martha watched Ernest, "adoring his image, with such care and such tolerance and such accuracy in detail, and such abject bottom-licking narcissism. I weep for the eight years I spent with him, worshipping his image with him."[32] There is no evidence Ernest ever saw this withering review; Walton must have decided not to share Martha's reaction.

During February, Ernest and Mary moved back and forth between Venice and Cortina. Their room at the Hotel Posta was too small for Ernest to work in, and on February 18, he left Cortina to take Adriana home as her mother had commanded. Mary stayed behind to enjoy the excellent skiing with her instructor, Zardini, on the white powder slopes of the Dolomites under bright blue skies. A week later, while carving a right turn, Mary cracked her left ankle. She suffered so much pain that she became nauseous, and they had to carry her down the hill on a sled. Doctors applied a cast improperly and two weeks later the bone had to be re-broken and re-set.

Mary returned to Venice and the Gritti, finding the suite in disarray and Ernest still enthralled with Adriana. He told Mary he wanted to invite Adriana and her mother, Dora, to visit them at the Finca to reunite them with their brother and son, Gianfranco, who was working in Cuba. Mary thought the idea was ridiculous and doubted Dora would accept the invitation, but she agreed to convey the offer for the sake of propriety. Mary invited Dora to lunch at Harry's Bar, and when Dora arrived, she pretended not to have met Mary before. Ernest excused himself and went to talk with his friends at the bar. This left Mary to chat over lunch about weather, food, and fashion. Dora's English was excellent but careful, and she remained reserved. During the conversation, Dora asked obliquely how long ago

Mary had married Ernest, and she seemed relieved to learn they had not married in the Catholic church. Mary supposed Adriana was Dora's one remaining jewel, and the mother wanted to restore the family's social standing and wealth through a strategic marriage of her daughter.

Mary extolled the virtues of Cuba and presented the invitation. It surprised her that Dora seemed to have expected the offer, and far from dismissing it, she asked for time to consider the idea. Mary did not like Dora and said as much in her memoir, a fact Adriana later relied upon as justification for writing her own account of her relationship with Ernest. Mary and Ernest left Venice on March 9 to drive to Paris. When they stopped for lunch, they talked about his infatuation with Adriana. Mary told Ernest her faith in him was "unshakeable." She said he had "a wise head, quick to correct mistakes." He replied, "But my heart is not subject to discipline . . . it's a target of opportunity." And Mary said, "My poor big kitten with a fractured heart. I wish I could help you."[33] Mary explained, "I was not feeling ironic. He was trying to be honest, and I felt sorry for him. I did not define 'helping' as turning him over to a budding Venetian girl."[34]

They reached Paris on March 13 and checked into Marlene Dietrich's old suite at the Ritz. Ernest spent the next few days going through accumulated mail, nursing a bronchial condition, placing bets through Georges in the bar, and dining in their room. Mary went exploring in the galleries around Place Vendôme and Montparnasse. Much to Ernest's delight and Mary's unease, Adriana arrived with a girlfriend-chaperone and they dined together at a chic restaurant in rue Royale. Ernest praised the sketches Adriana had drawn for the cover of *Across the River.* Adriana had not yet read the book, but she knew it was about a woman from Venice. She had sketched a leaning tower above three hills over an arched bridge through which a gondola was passing.[35] Under duress from Ernest, Charlie Scribner would later select Adriana's piece from among several other submissions. When he first saw the sketch, Charlie did not know Ernest's muse was the artist or guess a woman had drawn it. Ernest relied upon these facts as objective evidence of Adriana's brilliance. Mary acidly observed that Ernest considered Adriana to be "the girl wonder of the art world."[36]

Mary and Ernest set sail for New York aboard the *Île de France* on March 22. The weather was awful, and under a gray sky the gray sea pounded the ship, causing it to pitch and roll. The weather was conducive to staying inside and reading, drinking, and chatting with the barmen rather than strolling around the spray-drenched decks. Ernest loosened up and told Mary stories about his time as a reporter for the *Kansas City Star* when he covered the railway station, city hospital, and police station.

They arrived in New York five days later and checked into the Sherry-Netherland Hotel, where they partied with Hotch, Lillian Ross, and many others. The phone was often ringing, and they enjoyed "a merry-go-round of people, projects, problems, pretensions, pleasantries, and pleasures," all of which prevented them from spending much time together.[37] Patrick came from Harvard to seek Ernest's approval to marry Henrietta Broyles of Baltimore, and Winston Guest came to talk about fishing off Florida. Marlene Dietrich visited for dinner and delivered a diatribe against *Stromboli*, a film Ingrid Bergman had recently made in Italy, which became controversial in America because of her affair with the director Roberto Rossellini.

Mary visited her doctor for an examination to determine whether she could have the baby she and Ernest both wanted. The results were mixed. Mary was healthy, but the fallopian tube that remained after the ectopic pregnancy was blocked, and without intricate surgery she could not hope to become pregnant. Even if she chose surgery, her doctor could not guarantee success, and Mary was sad, in part because she knew how disappointed Ernest would be. Mary returned to their suite but did not interrupt the party to deliver her depressing news. Several days later, she told Ernest and later described the incident in *How It Was*. Though Ernest's face drained of color, he assured her he did not want her to risk surgery. "That's our lousy luck, my kitten," Ernest said, "but we'll share it. It will be our lousy, dark secret which we will keep together. No. You won't have that 'maybe' operation."[38] Mary felt "a failed member of the human race, being unable to contribute a creature to it."[39] In her memoir, Mary departed from the truth and said Ernest never again referred to her "incapacity."[40] She revealed the truth in a letter to Charlie and Vera Scribner. "I don't know if I ever told you, but last spring in New York, after thorough examinations, I discovered definitely that my one remaining reproductive tube is congested, and I can't have a baby." Mary said, "Ernest taunts me with this. And it may be one of the basic reasons for his behavior."[41]

Rose Marie Burwell suggests, though she cannot point to direct evidence of it, that Ernest blamed Mary's condition on a venereal disease that had run its course before Mary met Ernest. [42] There is a fragment of a letter in Norberto Fuentes's book which Burwell relies upon to support her view. Ernest wrote in a passage seeming to point to Mary, "I think most sterile women were clapped early and just didn't notice it." [43] Patrick Hemingway told me his brother Greg, who was then a medical doctor, said Mary's ectopic pregnancy was caused by gonorrhea. [44] Mary believed the basic reason for Ernest's taunting and abusive behavior was that she could not have a baby.

Ernest had other reasons to be unhappy which contributed to his anger. The terrible critical reception of *Across the River* disturbed him and led to his growing realization that he would never consummate his relationship with Adriana. Ernest's portrayal of her as Renata disgusted and alienated Adriana, her family, and her friends.

TWENTY-TWO

It Lays Me Open,
Raw, and Bleeding

March 1950–January 1951

O
n March 27, 1950, Mary and Ernest went for dinner to the historic Bar 21 with the *New Yorker*'s editor-in-chief, Harold Ross, and his wife. Irwin Shaw wandered over to their table to chat. He smiled at Mary and she lit up, delighted to see him, but Ernest exploded. Ernest "had always felt a competitive edginess toward Shaw, and *The Young Lions* had pushed him to fury."[1] The *New York Times* had declared it "the best war novel written by an American,"[2] and *Kirkus Review* said it was "the outstanding novel to have come out of the war."[3] Shaw was basking in his success. In contrast, Ernest's attempt at a wartime novel was out in serialized form, but *Across the River and Into the Trees* was failing with the critics. In the inevitable competition between the writers, Ernest had little to show. He must have decided a good offense was the best defense, and he attacked Shaw, using "scarifying" language, and embarrassing Mary so acutely, "I could not remember his phrases."[4] Mary admired Shaw for maintaining his composure instead of "bleeding from every pore."[5] Ernest excoriated him for basing characters in the novel on his "bloody, unfortunate brother" Leicester, on Mary, and himself. He had warned Shaw to stay away from him and was furious he had crossed the line.[6]

This was a somewhat hypocritical attack coming from an author who, in his own fiction, had filleted his friends to create characters. Oddly, Ernest pretended anger on behalf of Leicester, whom he loathed. Years earlier, Ernest had shared his contempt for Leicester with Buck Lanham. "I was always ashamed of my chickenshit kid brother who is no more like a soldier than a yak is like a race-horse, and I had to apologize for same, so you wouldn't think he was from the same stable."[7] In a similar vein, Ernest wrote to Peter Viertel complaining that Shaw's book made Leicester out to be "a jerk." "He is a jerk," Ernest wrote, "but he is still my brother."[8]

Shaw portrays Mary in the novel as the fiery but capable female war correspondent Louise M'Kimber, who has "a deft, tricky way with men."[9] Despite Ernest's protests, Mary embraced the idea she had been so crucial in Shaw's life, he immortalized her in the best novel coming out of the war. The real problem may have been that Ernest hated Shaw's portrayal of himself as Ahearn, "a short, fat correspondent for *Collier's*" who has "a very serious round face, mottled heavily with much drinking."[10] Ahearn is self-important, pretentious, often drunk, and he injects himself into every story. His breath is "as solid as a brewery wall, . . . 'Pass the whiskey, please,' he said . . ." Shaw had lampooned Ernest's character and style and it was too much for Ernest to abide. He was jealous of his younger, successful rival who enjoyed the acclaim of the critics and the affection and admiration of his wife.

Ernest's behavior appalled Mary. In her diary, she recorded, "it installed a cold, impenetrable ridge of acrimony between us."[11] The next morning, Ernest wrote a note to her. "Please let us not fight about what I said to Irwin Shaw . . . I thought what he wrote about my poor bloody unfortunate brother, you, and me was quite despicable . . . I had warned him to keep away from me."[12] Despite Shaw's "despicable" portrayal of himself, he said he understood Shaw was an old friend of hers, and she could see him if she wished. The incident added another layer of misunderstanding and regret. After this incident, Shaw wrote to his friend Peter Viertel, "Papa doesn't like anyone to invade what he considers his literary terrain, war." Viertel concluded the episode widened the rift between the two men.[13]

◆

Toward the end of April, Mary's cousin Bea came for a visit bearing gifts for the Finca. She hit it off with Ernest because she could talk baseball, and Mary loved having a woman visit. Bea fit in, and apart from two sightseeing trips into Havana, Mary and Bea stayed home and visited at the pool and in the garden while Ernest worked. Two weeks after Bea's arrival, Mary and Gregorio took her out on *Pilar* for an hour of fishing in the Gulf Stream to give her a taste of Cuban adventure. Bea was thrilled when Mary caught a small dolphin, saying, "your catching a fish was just like Babe Ruth hitting a home run."[14] They brought the boat around to the Club Nautico in Havana harbor and tied up, waiting for Ernest, who was to join them on board for lunch. Not only was he an hour late, but when he did arrive he was slightly drunk from several hours of downing frozen daiquiris. Roberto Herrera accompanied him along with "Havana's youngest, prettiest whore, whom he had named Xenophobia."[15] This was the same woman who had posed for the photos taken at the Finca a month earlier. Mary could not blame the young woman who stayed to share their food, but she was furious with Ernest. He had left them waiting for an hour in the scorching sun and embarrassed her in front of her cousin.[16] Bea said the visit of Xenophobia amused her, as she'd "never seen a designated whore before."[17] This was the last straw for Mary, and she told Ernest she would leave him. Two days later, she set out her reasons in a long letter.[18]

Mary wrote that, in 1944, Ernest was, "a straight and honorable and brave man, magically endearing to me. . . . Although I was suspicious of your over-drinking, you said so often that your chief desire was to be good and adult, I believed you and in you." He told her he loved to write and was never happier than when he was doing so. She had assumed that if he were working, he would be a companionable and considerate husband, "as well as gay and charming and sturdy in spirit, which you are when you are not drunk."[19] Mary had expected to contribute her loyalty and devotion to his projects, family, and household, do whatever jobs he entrusted to her, and show good balance and tenderness toward him. Everything had looked promising in 1944. However, by May 1950, Mary felt they had both been failures. She had lost Ernest's interest, devotion, and respect. "Your principal failure is that you have been careless and increasingly unthinking of my feelings . . . Undisciplined in your daily living. Both privately and in public, you've insulted me and my dignity as a human being."[20]

If he had shown genuine remorse, she might have believed they could make things better. But for a long time, his only reaction to the possibility he was mistaken "is a petulant irritability, protecting your steel-bound ego, that your rectitude or infallibility should be questioned." They should admit the marriage was a failure. "Therefore, let us end it. And if we have not succeeded in conducting it gracefully,

let us, please, try to finish it gracefully and without further violence." She told
Ernest she would leave as soon as she could move out.[21] He could "imagine that
it is not at all easy for me to move out, to give up the only home I have and the life
I love, and the fresh air and *Pilar* and the garden and the house." She hoped "that
will help you to be graceful about it."[22] After reading the letter, Ernest came to
Mary's room. He declared he understood her and asked her to "[s]tick with me,
kitten. I hope you will decide to stick with me."[23] Once again, Mary relented and
became busy with projects improving the Finca.

◆

A week later, the *New Yorker* published Lillian Ross's piece, "How Do You Like
it Now Gentlemen?"[24] Mary had known that when Ross visited them in New
York, Ernest was on the brink of exhaustion from his hard work on the novel and
he needed to relax. She had private reservations about Ross, which she recorded
in her draft memoir. "Lillian speaks slowly, tries to be just. Always diligent, she
appears to have much more interest in being a good writer than I ever had but is
not much better as a reporter."[25] Mary was not pleased with the result.

Ross wrote that Ernest unwound by drinking excessively, dropping his articles,
and speaking what Ross called "Indian talk." Jack Hemingway explained that his
father felt so relaxed with Ross, "he let down his guard and behaved in a manner
that was usually reserved for family and close friends, using a sort of play-talk
which varied with seasons and from year to year." However, "Lillian had an ear
like a tape recorder, and what came out on paper was so literally accurate it sounded
completely phony." In Jack's view, "the profile made him look ridiculous."[26]

Ross followed Ernest and Mary for three days.[27] Ernest drank champagne,
spoke enthusiastically, and punctuated his speech with the meaningless question,
"what do you think of it now, gentlemen?" Ernest later told Thomas Bledsoe, an
editor at Rinehart, he had seen the profile in proof. Though he was horrified, he
did not think Ross wrote the piece with malice. He knew it was as harmful to
him as Cowley's *Life* piece, but as he had just finished writing a book, he didn't
give a damn. "There was no harm intended and much received. But I am still fond
of Lillian."[28] Ernest complained, "My work is criticized from the standpoint of
these friends' impressions of me rather than the work itself."[29] The literary critic
Irving Howe opined, "Nothing more cruel has happened to an American writer

than the Lillian Ross interview . . . a smear of vanity and petulance that only a journalistic Delilah would have put into print." [30]

❖

Mary loved *Pilar* and believed the boat had a personality when she had the wheel. One morning they headed out into the stream, and Mary went up top to relieve Gregorio. She was alone on the bridge and so spooked by the towering waves, she felt "uneasy in her guts." *Pilar* seemed so small and defenseless against the ocean's power. Mary breathed in and sang "Onward Christian Soldiers" as loud as she could into the wind, and her anxiety disappeared. She took the wheel the next day to relieve Gregorio, and singing into the wind again, felt less anxious and was not afraid. [31]

On Saturday, July 1, 1950, they set out to do some fishing near Escondido. Gregorio, Ernest, and Mary were on *Pilar*, and Roberto followed in the *Tin Kid*. Ernest, who had been drinking all morning, was climbing to the bridge when Gregorio made a sudden turn to avoid a reef. A wave hit *Pilar* broadside, causing the boat to lurch to starboard. Ernest fell backwards over the railing, hitting his head on a metal hook and cutting open his scalp close to an artery. Gregorio called for iodine. In the fifteen seconds it took Mary to retrieve it, blood flowed fast down Ernest's neck and shoulders and spread over his chest, stomach, legs, and arms. Mary held a wad of toilet paper against his head, but she could not see where or how large the wound was. Gregorio anchored *Pilar*, Roberto came aboard and made a bandage, and the bleeding slowed. Mary checked Ernest's pupils and found they were normal. He rested and dozed on the way back to Havana, and they took a taxi to the Finca. José Luis came out, cleaned the wound, and put in three stitches of silk thread while Ernest sipped a strong gin and tonic as an anesthetic. José Luis feared Ernest had suffered another major concussion. [32]

❖

On September 7, while Mary was traveling to visit her mother, Scribner's published *Across the River and Into the Trees* to a scathing reception. An anonymous review in *Time* sneeringly subtitled "On the Ropes" focused on Ernest's use of a boxing metaphor to describe his prowess as a writer. "The book never wins a round—fans could only hope that the champ had an off day." [33]

The hero, Colonel Cantwell, was startlingly parallel to Hemingway himself, but "he gives his admirers almost nothing to cheer about." His story was a parody of the famed Hemingway style, "the love scenes are rather embarrassing than beautiful, the language of love forced and artificial. With his truculence, his defensive toughness, his juvenile arrogance, Hemingway's hero becomes a bore who forfeits the reader's sympathy." Mary read the *Time* review on the train coming to Chicago and wrote a letter to her "dearest sweetheart." She supposed the writer must be someone Ernest had brushed with, for no mere reader of books for a living could be so venomous. The *Newsweek* review somewhat consoled her. Then, for more consolation "and for loneliness too," she reread the book. "And darling, it is awfully good. Every single time, it lays me open, raw, and bleeding. It came too close to the aching heart of everything. For readers who don't feel, that won't matter. For the feeling ones, I hope they are also courageous. Because if not, they won't be able to endure it."[34]

Knowing her views about the banality of the dialogue between Renata and Cantwell, the weakness of the talk of food, and the plotting around the emeralds, one can only marvel at Mary's loyalty in this letter. She knew Ernest was hurting and did her best to show her support for him. "My husband needed friendship, sympathy, and if I could summon it, compassion, more than at any other time I'd known him."[35] After she saw more ferocious reviews, Mary exaggerated her praise for his style at some personal cost. Adriana had become linked to Ernest, not only as the inspiration for Renata but as the creator of the cover art. It was almost too much to bear. The book's dedication, "To Mary with love," was now, at the very least, ironic. Mary would have had to have been a saint not to have experienced a scintilla of schadenfreude at the scathing reviews.

Most of the twenty-two reviews the book received were negative or even hostile.[36] The most favorable review, by novelist John O'Hara, went so far in its praise of the author, Ernest felt embarrassed by it. O'Hara called Ernest "the most important author living today, the outstanding author since the death of Shakespeare."[37] Ernest wrote to Buck about O'Hara's review: "He started off saying I was the best writer since Shakespeare which will make me plenty of friends, I imagine."[38]

During October, Ernest was in a sour mood. At 4:45 A.M. on the morning of October 3, Mary wrote to Ernest that she, at last, understood he had been trying to get rid of her over the previous six months. Instead of saying so directly, he had "shot insults and hurts and cuts and accusations on me, all the accusations untrue completely, in your Gentleman's way of getting rid of me." She told him she was ready to go even though she didn't want to leave, "because I love you as I used to know you. But I shall be happy to leave your ugliness and injustice and brutality." She asked that they work out a plan so "without further hyperbole or nastiness, you can get rid of me, and you will be happy and free of me, and I will, at least, not be further brutalized." Mary had wasted five important years with him, trying to make the fine, splendid life he had promised. "You have had your sweethearts and your whores, and you have written a fine book." Mary had accomplished nothing, losing his love, faith, fidelity, and even the ordinary courtesy a man gives a woman. "I feel sorry for you with your overweening egoism, which excludes truth."[39] This time Ernest did not come and repent, and relations between them deteriorated. Looking through his carbons, Mary saw Ernest had described her to Charlie Scribner as "difficult," and she defended herself.[40]

Mary wrote to Charlie to tell him and Vera why she was planning to leave Ernest. It would not be easy for her since she had no other home and no money, but she spelled out why she had to go. Ernest had "destroyed what I used to think was an inexhaustible supply of devotion to him. He has been truculent, brutal, abusive, and extremely childish. It is more than a year since he has actually hit me."[41] Even so, he bullied her relentlessly. His "favorite and frequent means of protesting any word, glance, gesture, or food he doesn't like is to put his full, freshly served plate on the floor." Recently, he "dumped the entire platter of bread and crackers on top of my plate." Ernest had also been verbally abusive, and in the last few months, "he has called me and repeated the names, rolling them around juicily on his tongue: whore, bitch, liar, moron. On several occasions and with fervor, I have called him a shit."[42] Moreover, Ernest taunted her for her inability to bear a child, and she thought that was one of the basic reasons for his behavior. Mary didn't want to bore Charlie with her efforts to analyze Ernest's behavior but "it looks like the disintegration of a personality to me." She closed, asking Charlie to let her know if he heard of any job she might be able to do in New York. She asked him not to bother answering her letter because Ernest opened her mail before she saw it.

A few days later, Ernest returned from a fishing trip filled with daiquiris but still unhappy. He called Mary "a scavenger and camp follower."[43] She could not remember what it was she had done to provoke this reaction. The next week, Ernest told Mary she had the face of Torquemada, the grand inquisitor of the Spanish Inquisition, suggesting she looked like a torturer.[44] Completely surprised by this cruel comment, she retired to the shade of the lychee tree by the pool, where she wept and considered her options. She wondered how long she could take these insults and whether she had any pride at all and wished she had a big brother who could take care of the situation. If she left Ernest because of her wounded pride, no one would care. Mary concluded her pride was a luxury she could not afford, for she had worked at other places where the boss had "punctured, flattened and waltzed all over her pride." She could take it. There was no point hitting him or killing him because she needed him, and she loved him, and when he was good, he was entrancing.[45]

Mary decided she would try not reacting to Ernest's fluctuating tempers. He expected her to break into a slobbering mess, but she would resist his inanities. Too much of what they had together was good, and she would not allow it to fall apart. In the last two years, Mary had decided to leave Ernest three times. Still, each time she changed her mind and stayed, sometimes after he apologized or begged her forgiveness, but sometimes because after calculating the benefits and costs, she determined it was better to hang on to the arrangement.

◆

On Friday, October 28, Adriana and Dora arrived in Cuba. Ernest insisted on taking out *Pilar* to meet their boat, the *Luciano Manara*, and as it entered the port of Havana, he gave a siren of welcome. *Pilar* circled the ship twice, and Adriana saw Gianfranco, Mary, and Ernest on the bridge waving three handkerchiefs against the blue sky. Ernest bellowed through the megaphone, "Cuba greets you. We'll see each other at the port." They went to Club Nautico to eat a lunch of crab and then drove to the Finca. Adriana wore a becoming cotton lavender dress and Dora dressed in widow's gray. They were enchanted with the little house, which Mary had prepared for their visit from flower arrangements to thermoses of iced water, fluffed pillows, and tight bedsheets. By dinner time, Gianfranco arrived with their luggage.

Over the next days they toured Havana, and Ernest showed Adriana and Dora all his favorite places. Adriana moved her pencils and drawing paper up to the workroom in the tower and sketched local scenes, later laughing with Ernest about their business, "White Tower Inc." Gianfranco, who was trying to make a go of banana farming in Cuba, took her to Havana to meet his friends. Adriana often climbed to the top floor of the tower where Mary was suntanning to solicit her comments about dresses she planned to wear to town. Dora and Adriana accompanied Mary on shopping expeditions she made into Havana. Mary was remarkably hospitable to the Ivancich family, given Ernest's infatuation with Adriana, and one wonders how many women would have put up with such an interruption in their lives.

Despite his pleasure with his house guests, Ernest was constantly unhappy with Mary and attacked her for a range of unexpected failings, often in front of the guests, hoping perhaps to goad her into leaving. She recorded the abuse in her journal but left it out of her memoir. He called her dark dress "your hangman's suit, your executioner's suit," and said she "sabotaged" a film by wearing it. He "removed his letters from my desk and also stole mine—put them he says in the bank."[46] He warned Mary "to straighten up and fly right."[47] Ernest objected to Mary helping Gianfranco fill out a visa application, picked up her typewriter, and threw it onto the stone floor while José Luis and Gianfranco watched.[48] Ernest took offense at something Mary said and threw his red wine in her face, staining the white wall behind her forever. "Dora and all the others saw it."[49] He shot out the lamp near the front terrace, causing Adriana and Dora to depend on a flashlight to find their way to the little house.[50] On October 21, Ernest asked Mary about a small bruise on her arm, and she told him truthfully it was because Gianfranco had gripped her arm on the way home. Ernest maintained she was "displaying [her] badge of shame from fighting with [her] lover." Throughout, Gianfranco maintained an embarrassed silence, perhaps because Ernest had announced he would "shoot off Gianfranco's arm."[51] Adriana and Dora pretended not to have seen or heard anything.[52]

Finally, Mary had enough, and she summoned Ernest to her room for a meeting, breaking the rule about not interrupting him while he was working. As Ernest stood submissively next to her desk, Mary told him in a controlled voice she understood his feelings for Adriana and sympathized with him (holding back words like "fool" and "juvenile"). Mary said she loved him and their life together at the Finca, and she was not going to be provoked by his cruel behavior into leaving him. "No matter what you say or do—short of killing me—I'm going to stay here and run your house and the Finca."[53] If he wanted her to go, he would have to come to her in the morning, when he was sober, and tell her "truthfully and straight" he wished her to leave. Ernest never did ask her to leave, and Mary admitted to her journal, "where I am cowardly, is in my fear of breaking away from this life and making a new one on my own."[54] In the meantime, Mary managed Ernest like the lout he was, calling attention to his bad behavior and demanding apologies and adult conduct. She was not afraid of him and knew he was a bully—but a weak one.

On New Year's Eve, Adriana went to Havana with Juan Verano, a young man from a good family, for a night of dancing. Ernest was put off Adriana was out partying with her boyfriend, and he called Mary a slut and threw a beautiful ashtray she had bought in Venice out the door onto the red-tiled terrace, where it shattered. Mary unloaded on him, saying he was acting "like a pimply adolescent and a boor," and asked what he was trying to achieve.[55] She did not receive an answer.

◆

On the sea voyage to Havana two months earlier, Adriana and Dora's ship stopped over in Tenerife. Adriana gasped when she saw her artwork on the cover of *Across the River and Into the Trees* in a bookstore window.[56] She didn't buy a copy, however, knowing Ernest would give her one. When Ernest did present her with a book, it was inscribed, "For Adriana who inspired everything that is good in this book and nothing that is not. With love, Mister Papa." Despite the flattering inscription, she didn't bother reading the book until after Christmas. Once she did, Adriana told Ernest the dialogue was uninteresting. She asked, "How could Renata—no, any girl with that education and traditional family, and so young—slip away to amorous encounters and swallow one martini after another as if they were cherries."[57] Renata was full of contradictions; she was not real.

Ernest defended himself, saying Adriana was too different from Renata to understand, "but I assure you that such girls do exist. And Renata is not only one woman but four different women, whom I have actually known."[58] Adriana could not understand why Ernest gave her features to the promiscuous Renata, for Adriana was a virtuous young woman, almost certainly still a virgin. The sexual fantasy Ernest constructed in the book with the impotent Colonel Cantwell using his shot-up hand to massage the clitoris of the willing Renata under a blanket in a gondola, bringing her to climax three times in a row, was assumed by some to mirror his actual relationship with Adriana, and would cause her no end of pain. Adriana told Bernice Kert her first husband called her "a whore for her relationship with that pig Hemingway."[59]

TWENTY-THREE

People Are Dying
That Never Died Before

January 1951–March 1952

L ife at the Finca became a social whirl after the Ivanciches arrived. Ernest
endured activities he had rejected with Mary to show hospitality to Adriana.
They heard Arthur Rubinstein play Chopin, visited nightclubs where they danced
late into the night, and attended a circus in Havana over Christmas. They visited the Floridita many evenings to drink Papa Doblés, sing, and play the guitar,
and took three-day long fishing trips aboard *Pilar*. Never before or after was life at
the Finca so vibrant. The festivities culminated in a large party of some eighty guests
at the Finca. They invited Adriana's new Cuban friends and Ernest's and Mary's
Cuban, British, and American ones. Adriana and Gianfranco helped in the
days of preparation leading to the gala, making posters and decorations. On the night
of the party, double rows of candles sparkled in the grass leading to the pool area.
The band from the Floridita wandered the grounds playing maracas and guitars while
bartenders filled guests' glasses with champagne, daiquiris, whiskey, and rum.[1]

Waiters from the Floridita served a buffet dinner in the house, and guests sat
on cushions before low tables and footstools about the edges of the rooms. Mary
had converted the library to a dance hall where young people swayed to the band.
Ernest sent for more whiskey from the village after the guests drained thirty
bottles of French champagne. He hated large gatherings and stayed out of the
action, nursing his drinks and his resentment so as not to disappoint Adriana.

Ernest preferred smaller groups where he was the center of attention and could dispense anecdotes and dominate the room by the sheer force of his personality. Mary saw him standing to the side watching Adriana with her boyfriends. She wondered how long Ernest's attraction for Adriana would last, even if she were to step out of the picture and present Adriana to him.[2] How long until he found the social demands of the youthful Italian countess mindless and irritating?

Mary went all out for Christmas that year, roasting a turkey which sent a delicious aroma throughout the Finca while the guests sat around Ernest as he distributed Santa Claus gifts. Gianfranco was touched by his yellow blanket, sweater, and shirt, and Adriana screamed gaily over her gifts of perfume and a typewriter.[3] Greg joined the celebrations, surprised to find his father was in love with the nineteen-year-old Adriana whose mother chaperoned her attentively. Greg commented, "well, she was dull and had a hook-nosed mother in constant attendance."[4] Despite this, "Papa was ecstatic just to have her nearby. Not to touch, not to kiss, not to make love with." Greg watched his father and Adriana chatting, sometimes in English, sometimes in Italian, and could tell he was in love. The girl was "flattered by his attention, or perhaps bored and just being polite or amused, as only young girls can be amused with an infatuated old man, but certainly not in love with him." Greg observed Adriana was "very sweet and considerate and never betraying her inner emotions. Never hurting him. That's the way I like to remember Papa."[5]

The next evening, they ate tiny sandwiches in the living room. Mary and Gianfranco played a Bartok Symphony and she found it to be "excellent terrible music, strong and moving."[6] They stood the entire time by the record player, and afterward they talked about Gianfranco's philosophy of life and what kind of wife he needed. In the beginning, he was weeping at the music and his happiness at the day, but later he grew calm and Dora came and took him off to bed.[7] When Ernest wasn't furious with him, he was avuncular toward Gianfranco. Walton remembered Gianfranco "fitted in very gracefully with their life. And he was a companion to Mary that she needed. One that Ernest approved of. They could go off on a shopping trip, or anything and Ernest thought it was dandy."[8] Mary had a soft spot for him, and Rose Marie Burwell told Walton she believed Mary had an affair with Gianfranco.[9] While there are signs of affection in their correspondence, Mary makes no such admission in her memoir or journals. Valerie Hemingway told me she does not believe Mary and Gianfranco had an affair.

After the holidays, Ernest resumed writing a story about an old Cuban fisherman and his struggle to land a giant marlin. From the very beginning, the work went well, and he wrote as he had when he was twenty-five years old and composing *The Sun Also Rises*. It took him nine weeks to write the first draft of the novel, and he finished what would become *The Old Man and the Sea* in eight weeks. [10] Ernest believed his love for Adriana inspired his burst of creativity, and he told her, "now I will write another book for you, and it will be my most beautiful book. It will speak of an old man and the sea." [11] He visited her in the workroom in the white tower and read passages to her.

Ernest gave daily drafts to Mary, which she typed and reread each evening from the beginning in the silent house after the guests had retired for the night. Ernest watched as she read to discern the impact his words were having. When he saw goosebumps on her arms, he knew his prose was finding its mark. Ernest wrote to Hotch, "Mary read it all one night, and in the morning, she said she forgave me for anything I'd ever done and showed me the real goose flesh on her arms." That was not all: "Adriana read it and rated it the same. So, have been granted a sort of general amnesty as a writer. I hope I'm not fool enough to think something is wonderful because people under my own roof like it." [12] Mary found the writing reminded her of "Bach fugues and Picasso line drawings without clutter or frills." [13] In a piece for *Flair*, Mary marveled at Ernest's ability to work despite the uproar enveloping the Finca from animals and visitors. While some might call it chaos, "We call it freedom. It is a manner of living about as formal and regulated as the wag of a dog's tail, and Ernest seems to thrive in it." [14]

In Mary's memoir, the Ivanciches decided to leave the Finca in early February to visit the museums, churches, and theaters of New York before resuming their return journey to Venice. In truth, the departure was more dramatic. Someone sent Dora a copy of an article in *Samedi-Soir*, a French gossip tabloid, which linked Adriana to Renata. The piece dismissed claims of Hemingway's affair with Adriana but did so in such provocative detail that the allegations were spread even more broadly. From Adriana's point of view, it presented everything in a different, false light. Dora feared the scandalous consequences of the allegations and decided to take Adriana home to preserve the family's reputation. The scandal engulfed the Finca, with Dora becoming loathsome, Ernest regretful he had not foreseen this result, Gianfranco paralyzed, and Mary resisting the temptation to tell Ernest, "I told you so." She had advised Ernest to model Renata on a blue-eyed redhead from Trieste—not Adriana. Adriana was too inexperienced to apprehend the threat to her reputation.

Mary flew with Adriana, Dora, and Adriana's boyfriend Juan to Key West. Otto Bruce had arranged a car for the journey up the keys to Miami, then to New Orleans. When planning the trip they assumed Ernest would be with them, but Dora would not hear of it given the whiff of scandal. Pauline and Otto Bruce met them at the Key West airport, and they went for coffee with Pauline at her house and set off in the car before noon. Pauline shot Mary her famous raised eyebrow as the Italian guests were leaving, an eyebrow which seemed to ask, "so this is what all the fuss has been about?"

Mary found it tedious traveling with the disorganized group. They fumbled with suitcases and lacked curiosity about the birds, fish, and places they passed. She wished she were traveling with her well-prepared and inquisitive husband instead. The first night, they stayed in rooms on the fifteenth floor of a hotel overlooking Key Biscayne, and Mary reported to Ernest that Adriana was ecstatic about the view. They walked out for an Italian dinner, and the Ivanciches became excited to be in the United States. The next day, they reached New Orleans and had tea and sugar cookies made by Mary's mother, who was amusing and gay. Mary was proud of her and told Ernest, "I hope I never become shit enough to be ashamed of my origins, which basically are okay as anybody's." [15]

Ernest wrote, telling Mary he missed her power to cheer him up and watching her reading the book so he could gauge his progress. "Am in the toughest part of the story to write. He has the fish now and is on the way in and, the first shark has shown up. Christ, how I miss you being here to read it." [16] Ernest swore, "Have been a good boy all the time. No whores, fights violence, nor intemperance. I love my sweet Kittner." [17] Ernest depended on Mary's intelligent reading of his work to see if his words were effective. He discussed the plot with her and invited her suggestions.

Mary had put up with the Ivanciches for four months, and she was thoroughly sick of them. They caught a train for New York at Jacksonville, leaving Mary and

Juan to drive back to Key West for a flight to Havana. Mary felt glad to be back home and to find Ernest hard at work on the book.

Adriana wrote a letter of thanks to Mary from New York. "My heart is still with my dear Finca . . . and I realize only now how much I am attached to my second family." After thanking Mary for being so kind to her and her mother during their visit, she closed by saying that she was "fond" of Mary.[18] The letter doesn't read as if written by a scheming homewrecker planning to steal Mary's husband. Nor does Adriana's correspondence with Ernest suggest it was ever her plan. Adriana confirmed as much in an interview that coincided with the publication of *The White Tower*, Adriana's account of her relationship with Ernest. "Ours was a great love, not an adventure, not sex; I'm not erotic—I'm romantic." Far from acting out the sexual fantasy Ernest had imagined between Cantwell and Renata, Adriana said she and Ernest never indulged in anything more than occasional kisses—which they decided were "mistakes." "Never" did Ernest "do the slightest thing that might oblige me to be defensive." And though Ernest once came close to proposing marriage to Adriana, he realized she would say no. She would not have entertained the proposal, for "he was too old . . . He was married. It was unthinkable."[19]

Meanwhile, Ernest was missing Adriana, and he worried about the impact the scandal would have upon her and her attitude toward him. He wrote to her, "You are not the girl in the book, and you are not responsible for her sins or mistakes." He offered to hold off publication of the book in Italy if she wished. "But daughter, it would've been the same if I'd never written a book about the Veneto." Ernest claimed, "people would have noticed that we went together, and we were always happy and never said serious things. People are very jealous of those that are happy."[20] This seems a sad effort to avoid responsibility for what he had done. No one would have vilified Adriana's character had Ernest not given Renata her face and features and fulfilled Cantwell's (and possibly Ernest's) sexual fantasies at her expense.

❖

Charlie and Vera Scribner came for a visit to the Finca, and Ernest gave Charlie a draft of the story about the old man and the marlin and watched with anticipation as he read it. "I was very happy you liked what you read of the book, but I would've thought you a certifiable fool if you had not," Ernest said. "There is never any doubt when something is right. But it makes you very happy to have someone you like and respect say so. I had been getting good opinions only from my family."[21]

Mary typed the drafts each evening, and she became anxious about the fate of the old man. She loved him and feared he would die after his fight with the sharks. She said to Ernest, "You know I don't pretend to know about writing. You're the house writer, Lamb. But it seems too easy to kill him off. Too facile. And nothing in this book so far reads facile or tricky." Ernest replied, "I'm glad you like him so much." And Mary observed, "I'll bet everybody would be happier if you let him live."[22] A few days later, Mary smiled when she read the novel's ending: the old man slept in his shack, dreaming of lions while the young boy watched over him. Mary repeated her claim to have saved Santiago's life in various interviews.[23]

◆

In early August, Mary's mother wrote to say her father was ill. He had abandoned the drugs prescribed to manage his prostate cancer and was relying instead on readings of Christian Science tracts. Mary went for a visit and found him uncomfortable and distrustful of his doctors. Ernest told Mary not to worry or allow her parents to worry about expenses. He said she should stay until things settled down and ensure her father remained in the hospital as long as necessary. Mary spent the month visiting her father and staying with her mother. On August 28, Thomas was released from the hospital. His doctor advised Mary that though the carcinoma was spreading, hormonal treatments somewhat controlled it. Ernest wrote a frank letter of advice to his father-in-law, urging him to take the medicines prescribed by his "conscientious and reputable doctor to avoid, if possible, an absolute and miserable end to your life." Ernest pointed out there were no miraculous cures at eighty and "no man should be too proud to accept the aid of science . . . We must all die, and it is better to die with the minimum of discomfort and true pain."[24] Ernest's letter had the desired effect on Thomas, and he promised he would take the tablets as long as his doctor prescribed them. In a revealing comment to Ernest, he said, "I realize that there is about the same percentage of fanatics associated with the Christian Science movement as with practically all other religions."[25]

◆

While Mary was away, Bill Walton kept Ernest company at the Finca. He loved being with Ernest, and they often sat around the dinner table with Ernest's Cuban friends, "laughing at everybody's jokes, and just sobbing with amusement, with their heads on the table."[26] Their consumption of alcohol was massive and far beyond Walton's limits. It started just after siesta when René prepared a marvelous punch and continued through dinner when Walton knocked back wine like water and got jolly. Nobody competed with Ernest or crossed him, and he was seldom unpleasant.[27]

Ernest asked Walton to read the manuscript of *The Old Man and the Sea*, and he later said, "I loved it. I really loved it. And not to have heard a word about it, it was very powerful. Wonderful."[28] "Its simplicity and its great artistic skill actually were very apparent right away."[29] By this time, Walton had become recognized as a visual artist in New York, and he painted a cover for *The Old Man and the Sea* of a fisherman in the main plaza of Cojímar. When he showed it to Ernest, "he took one look and said, 'I have other plans.' He later used a terrible drawing by Adriana instead—a very undistinguished drawing." According to Walton, Ernest selected Adriana's sketch because he was besotted with her. He put it succinctly but crudely: "She wasn't in love with him. This was not an affair. He never laid her."[30]

Ernest received a cable from his sister, Sunny, on June 28, advising him their mother had just died in a nursing home in Memphis. Walton was with him the night he got the cable, and Ernest was so pleased he lit bonfires. Walton recalled, "he detested her. He hated her guts. He was irrational, completely."[31] On the evening he received news of her death, Ernest said, "Thank God that old bag is dead! For Christ's sake! She drove my father to suicide. She's driven me half crazy."[32]

After settling her parents, Mary passed through Key West on her way home to the Finca. She visited Pauline, who had returned from the Mayo Clinic where she'd undergone a battery of tests to diagnose the cause of her headaches and high blood pressure. Pauline made light of her condition and spoke happily of the trip she was about to take to visit her sister Jinny in San Francisco. Mary returned to the Finca and sank into her life with Ernest, the dogs and cats, her garden, and *Pilar*.

A few weeks later, Pauline died suddenly in Los Angeles. Mary described her friend's death in her memoir, using anodyne phrases that concealed the unpleasant reality of Ernest's involvement. We now know that nineteen-year-old Greg phoned

Pauline from Los Angeles and told her the police had arrested him and he needed her help. She sent a cable to Ernest, warning him of the trouble and informing him she was on her way to Los Angeles to find out what was wrong. It turned out that Greg "had gone into the women's restroom of a movie theatre in drag and had been caught—for the first time—and arrested."[33] Greg urged his mother not to bring his father into the matter, but Pauline phoned Ernest at the Finca from Jinny's house. What began as a calm conversation escalated into a shouting onslaught by Ernest, who accused Pauline of having been a permissive mother and the cause of all Greg's problems. What shocked and outraged Ernest most was that Greg was in drag when he was arrested.[34]

Jinny saw Pauline shouting into the phone and sobbing helplessly. After the call ended, Pauline went to bed in tears, and several hours later she awoke, screaming in pain.[35] They rushed her to St. Vincent Hospital where she died of shock on the operating table. Her blood pressure had escalated rapidly and dropped suddenly. Jinny notified Greg his mother had died of a heart attack, and she cabled Ernest with the same story. Pauline was fifty-five.[36] The news of Pauline's death horrified Mary because she had heard Ernest screaming at her over the phone, and she had protested Ernest's brutal behavior. Mary confided to her journal that Ernest and one of his friends, Alto, "talked like vultures" about Pauline's estate and, "I told him so." She recalled, "Ernest followed me to my bathroom, and he spit in my face." The next day he gave her two hundred dollars, which she "cravenly accepted."[37] Mary omitted this incident from her memoir. In *How It Was*, she lamented the loss of Pauline but didn't mention Ernest's extreme abuse and subsequent effort to buy her forgiveness. Instead, she hid the incident and said, "Pauline, with her knowing eyes, was a high-spirited sharp-minded woman, an accidental friend to me, both generous and loving. I would miss her for a long time."[38]

On the day of Pauline's death, Ernest wrote to Charlie Scribner, "the wave of remembering has finally risen so that it has broken over the jetty that I built to protect the open roadstead of my heart." Now, he had "the full sorrow of Pauline's death with all the harbor scum of what caused it. I loved her very much for many years and the hell with her faults."[39] Jinny buried Pauline in an unmarked grave in Hollywood Memorial Park. Despite the generous inheritances she left to her sons Patrick and Greg, they felt so estranged from her they saw no reason to honor her with a headstone.

Soon after Pauline died, Ernest revised what would become the Bimini story in *Islands in the Stream*. He killed the characters based on Pauline and their two sons in a car accident.[40] A telegram announces, "Your sons David and Andrew killed with their mother in motor accident near Biarritz attending to everything pending your arrival deepest sympathy." Thomas Hudson and his friend, Eddy, speculate that the youngest "conceited" son, Andrew, had been driving.

In real life, Ernest blamed Greg for Pauline's death, and he punished Greg by revising his will. In the event Ernest and Mary were to die together, he directed that Mary's parents were to receive one hundred and seventy-five dollars per month. The rest of his estate, worth well over one million dollars, was to be paid in equal shares to Jack and Patrick. He dictated, "I hereby bequest to my son Gregory Hemingway the sum of One ($1.00) Dollar."[41] Through the insulting and unequal bequest of one dollar, he disowned Greg.

Valerie Hemingway told me Ernest and Greg "never conceded or patched up their quarrel. When Greg needed money over the next ten years, he would ask his father for it, remaining fairly conciliatory until the money arrived and then continuing the feud."[42] They never had a civil relationship after Pauline's death. Patrick told me that Pauline's death "wasn't anybody's fault, but the way it happened, made it look as though it was the result of emotional stress. I think everybody was trying to blame everybody else."[43] Valerie wrote to me, "just one thing that is neither here nor there: Greg died in prison on October 1, 2001, at sixty-nine years, fifty years to the day after the incident I wrote you about [Pauline's death]. Sadly, he did not have his mother to bail him out."[44]

◈

Mary developed a severe crick in her neck, so painful she couldn't turn her head, and her contracting muscles caused difficulty breathing. The pain dogged her for five or six days, during which Ernest had to help with household duties that he detested. Mary recorded in her journal, "he has also been unkind—screaming when I complained, as I certainly have done, 'we all know you hurt worse than anyone.'"[45] Ernest charged they were not making good enough use of the vegetables in the garden. Mary protested; if he felt that way, it would be easy enough for him to pick some carrots, onions, beets, or Swiss chard. "He made a speech about what a coward I have been about this stiff neck! Later he came into my room and repeated it, Coward-Coward-gloatingly."[46] Mary belittled his bloated self-importance, which prevented him from helping around the house.

Ernest rushed off, and Mary fell back on her pillow sobbing, ending another domestic crisis in the home of the great writer. Mary reflected in her journal, "it may be perfectly true that I am a coward—though a better word about the non-breathing would be 'complainer.' Where I am cowardly is in my fear of breaking away from him and this life and making a new one on my own."[47] Mary had considered leaving often enough; she must have thought about her options. As a forty-four-year-old former journalist, her career prospects were not bright. She had given up her job with *Time,* where she had filled a niche as a foreign correspondent knowledgeable about the war in Europe. Even if she could find a similar job, her wages would be low, and her standard of living would decline significantly. Financially, it made sense to hang on to Ernest. Bill Walton remarked, Mary "put up with really brutal treatment in different periods." She "wanted to be Mrs. Ernest Hemingway." And she stuck it out: "She made it."[48] Walton enjoyed independent wealth, and he didn't fully understand Mary's predicament. Mary was a resolute, if not stubborn person, and she was not going to be pushed into poverty by the tempestuous fits of the man she loved. She would wait for the storms to pass.

After Mary's neck relaxed, they cruised on *Pilar* to their favorite anchorage near Paraíso, where the fishing was excellent, and domestic bliss returned. While they bobbed at anchor, Ernest made super dry martinis and they listened to Strauss waltzes on the radio. Gregorio fried a grouper in butter in the galley, and the delicious smell wafted on the gentle breeze. After dinner, darkness came, and Mary fell into a deep sleep. When she woke, Ernest was looking at her and told her she was a pretty kitten, and all the wrinkles had disappeared from her face. She said Ernest looked fit and tanned, and they embraced.[49]

A few months after Pauline's funeral, Greg and his wife Jane brought their daughter Lorian to visit Ernest and Mary at the Finca. Ernest was pleased to meet Greg's wife for the first time, and Greg thought the visit was going well. One afternoon, Greg and Ernest chatted about Greg's future and the recent past. He told Ernest the trouble in Los Angeles wasn't so bad. Ernest replied, "No? Well, it killed mother." The remark devastated Greg, and for many years he believed it must be true.[50] At the end of the month, Ernest wrote to Charlie Scribner and instructed him to stop paying one hundred dollars a month to Greg and make no further payments.[51]

◆

After Mary typed the last version of *The Old Man and the Sea*, Ernest came up for air. He examined their finances and decided they must begin an austerity program. Mary stopped buying expensive beef and they drank bottles of claret they had long stored in the cellar. Ernest proclaimed they could live cheaper on *Pilar*, and they embarked on a cruise down the coast, eating fish they caught along the way. When they returned to Cojímar a few days later, Juan met them with grave news. Clara Paz, who had worked for some time as Mary's maid, had died by suicide. Tough old Gregorio burst into tears, and they drove to the Finca to find out what had happened, but there was no easy explanation. It seemed Clara had grown tired of her life and ended it by swallowing a bottle of Ernest's Seconal tablets. Her death clouded the Finca in gloom and sadness. Mary and Ernest escaped on *Pilar* and cruised along the shore to Paraíso. The water was twenty shades of blue, and Mary wrote they were "caught in the web of endearments to our senses, from which no one wished to break away."[52] They had become interlocking parts of a single entity, "the big cogwheel and the smaller cogwheel . . . with no need for asserting togetherness . . . Maybe we were androgynous."[53]

Mary and Gregorio went ashore in the *Tin Kid* on February 16 to get supplies from the nearby village of La Mulata. She phoned René to find out what was new at the Finca. He reported a telegram had arrived the day they left home saying Charlie Scribner had died of a heart attack. Mary carried this sad news back to Ernest aboard *Pilar*, and two days later, he wrote to Vera Scribner, telling her they were both stunned and sick about it. Ernest told her he had loved Charlie. "Now, my dear and good friend is gone, and there is no one to confide in nor trust nor make rough jokes with, and I feel so terribly about Charlie being gone that I can't write anymore."[54] Mary wrote to her parents, "dear Charlie, was a true gentleman of the old school, and he was always particularly lovely to me. We shall both miss him very much."[55] Mary grieved Charlie's loss because he understood how difficult her life with Ernest could be and empathized.

In the last three years, Ernest had lost the two men who cared most for his writing and understood him best. Without Charlie Scribner and Max Perkins

in his corner, Ernest felt alone and exposed. Young Charles Scribner IV left the
navy to take over the firm, and he established a good working relationship with
Ernest. "I had to set the tone of relations, neither acting standoffish nor polishing
the apple," Scribner recalled. Hemingway "loved professionalism, whether in a
writer or bullfighter. He admired people who had a trade and stuck to it. That
decided me: I would be a professional publisher."[56]

◆

Ernest's friends from Hollywood, Leland and Slim Hayward, visited the Finca
for two days of fishing aboard *Pilar*, partying at the Floridita, and dining at home.
Ernest gave Leland a copy of the manuscript of *The Old Man and the Sea* to read
overnight, and the next morning Leland had firm ideas for the piece. He felt the
story was brilliant, and Ernest should publish it, not just as a standalone book,
but in its entirety in a large circulation magazine like *Life* or *Look*. Leland was
an accomplished Hollywood producer, and Ernest was so taken with his idea he
allowed him to take away a copy of the manuscript.

◆

A month later, on March 22, fifty-one-year-old General Fulgencio Batista seized
power in Cuba. He suspended the Constitution and promised his government
would stay in power only long enough to establish public peace. He asked the
cooperation "of all the people of Cuba in undertaking this task of peace and
cordiality."[57] The US government recognized Batista's regime on March 27,
and officials and company representatives visited promising investments and
continued US economic support. Soon Batista canceled elections, dissolved
Congress, imposed censorship, and installed a military dictatorship for three years.
Then, through fraudulent elections in 1955, the regime perpetuated its power for
another four-year term.

On the day of the coup, Juan drove Mary and Ernest into Havana along the
road crowded with army trucks carrying sleepy soldiers. There were no guns in
sight, and because they could not think of any reason the dictatorship would harm
the Finca, they went onboard *Pilar*, lifted anchor, and cruised toward Paraíso.
They caught red snapper, grouper, yellowtail, and mackerel to stock the freezers

at the Finca. Stormbound for six days, they could not return to the Finca until late March. When they finally got home, they found a letter from their friend Marjorie Cooper. Dick had drowned while bird shooting on a lake on their estate, and they had buried him in the rose garden near their home. Ernest remarked, "people are dying that never died before."[58]

TWENTY-FOUR

Every Real Work of Art Exhales Symbols and Allegories

April 1952–August 1952

E rnest's optimism revived when he received a telegram from Scribner's welcoming *The Old Man and the Sea* and a proposal from *Life* to publish the entire piece in a single issue of the magazine. The Book-of-the-Month Club was also interested, and Jonathan Cape in London wanted to publish the book at the same time as Scribner's. Ernest was delighted to receive a letter from Adriana enclosing an impressionistic watercolor of a Cuban village for the dust cover. He told her that Wallace Meyer, a quiet scholarly man who was now his contact at Scribner's, had selected the sketches of old Anselmo and the bay and the blue gulf behind. "It is really splendid. Just what I would have wanted if I had brains enough to ask for it. Gianfranco and Mary both thought it was wonderful too." He told her he was proud of her and he loved her very much, "with all mistakes."[1]

In April, Ernest's old friend from the Spanish Civil War, Herbert Matthews, now an eminent foreign correspondent for the *New York Times*, came for a visit. He was in Havana covering the Batista coup and shared Mary's skepticism about Batista's promise to end martial law and restore Cubans' voting rights. Mary and Ernest tried to stay out of local politics but appreciated their friend's hardheaded analysis and were prepared to believe the worst about Batista. Ernest wrote to Buck that Batista's coup was well planned and executed, but there was an "undercurrent of people being spooked. Last administration was unbelievably corrupt, and the people are glad they are out. But they would've preferred to see them thrown out by a constitutional process in a regular election."[2]

On September 1, *Life* printed *The Old Man and the Sea*. This marked the first time the magazine had ever published the entire text of a book, and it sold over five and a half million copies within forty-eight hours. Ernest became the first author in history to enjoy the prospect of five million people reading his latest book within a few days of each other. Scribner's advance sales exceeded fifty thousand books and settled down to sales of three thousand a week. Ernest was jubilant at the statistics but even more moved by the reviews. Everyone seemed to love the book, and he began receiving hundreds of letters of congratulation. *The Old Man and the Sea* was a literary phenomenon.

Bernard Berenson wrote a letter of praise, and in his reply, Ernest revealed a secret: "there isn't any symbolism. The sea is the sea. The old man is an old man. The boy is a boy, and the fish is a fish. The shark are all sharks, no better and no worse. All the symbolism that people say is shit. What goes beyond is what you see beyond when you know. A writer should know too much."[3] In a later review of "the little masterpiece," Berenson observed, "no real artist symbolizes or allegorizes—and Hemingway is a real artist—but every real work of art exhales symbols and allegories. So does this short but not small masterpiece."[4]

The success of *Old Man* buoyed Ernest's spirits. Letters of congratulation came from famous friends and everyday GIs, police officers, sportsmen, and teachers. Charles Scribner Jr. recalled, "The enormous success of *The Old Man and the Sea* did not change Hemingway except for a certain glow he ever after felt about it." The sale to *Life* "made a great deal of money for Hemingway when he needed it badly," and when the book became a contemporary high school classic, Ernest "moved from the slough of low earning into the class of high-income writers."[5]

Mary proposed they take a trip to celebrate to Paris, or at least to New York. Ernest didn't want to put up with the publicity or the scrutiny of journalists which would greet him if he were to travel. He still felt burned by the Lillian Ross and Malcolm Cowley pieces. Ernest believed a book should stand on its own feet; journalistic interest in its author would be a distraction and would achieve nothing positive. He preferred to go fishing to allow himself to calm down. However, he thought Mary should go to New York City for a week to take in the latest plays and revel in the book's success. She didn't want to travel without him, but he insisted, and when their friends the Samuelses offered to have Mary stay with them in their apartment overlooking Central Park, she agreed. Mary flew north on September 25, and two days later wrote Ernest that she missed him and wished he could be with her to enjoy the perfect autumn weather. She loved being back in America, with endless hot water, fresh milk, splendid telephone service, excellent shopping, and luxury.

On Thanksgiving Day in 1952, Mary wrote a note to her "big kitten," listing the things which made her thankful. "In spite of stresses and strains, both kittens are healthy, in their heads and in their beat-up tough, strong bodies." She was grateful for their temperate, amiable climate, the beautiful world outside their doors, and the fact that "my big kitten does not feel it necessary to have constantly younger and more beautiful wives." She was thankful "[m]y big kitten has been so good, and considerate, and kind and generous, imposing his own wise restraints, for so long."[6] The positive reception of *Old Man* made living with Ernest much easier than it had been only months before.

◆

Patrick and his wife, Henny, were traveling in East Africa, and Patrick's letters described the countryside, wildlife, peaceable people, and the hospitality of Ernest's favorite professional big game hunter, Philip Percival. The letters made Mary and Ernest long for a trip to Africa where they could be alone and free from press attention. They made plans for a trip the next fall before the big rains. *Look* and *Life* both proposed sending photographers to accompany them on their safari. Ernest resisted because he wanted to get away from work and the inevitable publicity that would follow press reports. He wanted a private vacation, and that meant not having to stage hunting expeditions for photographers.

Leland Hayward came to discuss making a film version of *Old Man*. He wanted Peter Viertel to write the screenplay and Spencer Tracy to play the old man. Over drinks at the Floridita, Leland pushed Ernest to participate by fishing for the old man's giant marlin off the Cuban coast so that they could film the struggle between man and beast. Ernest succumbed to Leland's blandishments and complained to Mary on the drive home to the Finca they would have difficulty getting to Africa before the big rains.

One of Ernest's comrades from the Spanish Civil War visited and told him their friends imprisoned in Spain were now free. Ernest had vowed he would not visit

Spain so long as Franco was in power but learning about his friends tempted him to visit the places and people he had known in the thirties. He had regaled Mary with stories of his adventures in Spain, and the place intrigued her. She could use the language skills she had acquired in Cuba and she supported traveling to Pamplona and Madrid to watch the bullfights.

Mary and Ernest hosted a lunch for Leland Hayward and Spencer Tracy. Ernest had been skeptical about casting Tracy as Santiago but found that he liked the man. He introduced Tracy to Anselmo, the grandfather of fishermen in Cojímar, who shared many features with the old man in his story. Anselmo's philosophy and fishing techniques impressed Tracy, and Ernest watched as the actor absorbed the old man's personality. Ernest later complained to René that Tracy, who refused to get in shape for the role, "looked more like an old, rich, overweight actor than an old starving fisherman."[7]

On Mary's forty-fifth birthday, Ernest gave her "a sweet and loving birthday note with a check big enough to buy a clock or watch."[8] He wrote, "Happy Birthday and all my love to my dearest lovely Kitten, and many happy returns of all our trips. You are so lovely and so beautiful and so kind and good and talented, and I love you so much. Papa." Mary confided to her journal, "this has been the best year, in harmony and good friendship, between Papa and me."[9]

On May 4, Ernest and Mary went fishing on *Pilar*, and they sat at anchor sipping martinis and listening to the radio from Miami for the weather report. The six o'clock news came on, and they heard Ernest had won the Pulitzer Prize for literature for *The Old Man and the Sea*. They celebrated with a dinner of oxtail soup and an extra slice of cheese. Mary woke up in the middle of the night and sat on the stern, looking at the southern constellations, sipping an ice-cold beer, and having a smoke. The prize was a testament to their successful partnership. Despite Ernest's mercurial temperament, she knew he depended on her for emotional stability and sober judgment. He had once said she was as necessary to him as a compass, and she knew it was true. Even though he was sometimes reluctant to admit it, she was essential to his creative process. She knew she had been right about urging him to allow Santiago to live. Without her advice, the old man might have died like Robert Jordan or Colonel Cantwell, and the story would have dismayed, rather than inspired, its readers. She had a feel for these things, and she had steered him gently but wisely. Mary was so close to Ernest, she felt she knew his mind, and she told an interviewer, "When you live close, you can't help but know the thought processes and the judgments, especially about literary stuff." [10] Mary was not simply the manager of Ernest's house, or a chef and hostess for his guests, or the typist of his manuscripts. They had an intellectual affinity, and Ernest sought her judgment about whether he'd got it right.

They returned to the Finca a few days later. Bill Lowe, an editor of *Look* tasked with persuading Ernest to allow a photographer to accompany them on their African safari, visited. Lowe proposed a very attractive financial package. *Look* would pay fifteen thousand dollars for a picture story about the safari, with captions written by Ernest, and a further ten thousand dollars for a story of 3,500 words. When Ernest learned they proposed to use an experienced wildlife photographer, his objections fell away. Mary could not believe their good fortune—the money would cover their expenses and allow them to purchase first-class equipment.

Mary and Ernest went to Abercrombie's in New York to ensure they shipped the proper shotguns, rifles, and ammunition. They planned to have custom boots made by Ernest's favorite boot maker in Madrid and bush jackets and pants crafted by an Indian overnight tailor in Nairobi. On June 23, they sailed on the French Line's new passenger ship, the *SS Flandre*. A week later, they docked at Le Havre and were greeted by Gianfranco and his friend Adamo, their new chauffeur. In Paris, they received warm greetings at the Ritz Hotel from reception clerks, baggage men, barmen, and waiters who hailed them like old friends. They sat with Gianfranco at their favorite table in the dining room and enjoyed exquisite wines with a spectacular meal of smoked salmon followed by veal. Mary felt elated to be back in Paris.

For two days, they wandered the streets, taking in the culture Mary had missed in Cuba. Mary spoiled herself, eating delicious croissants with café crème at breakfast, veal with more cream at lunch, and magret with frites at dinner, always accompanied by excellent wines thanks to *Look*'s generous travel expenses.

Adamo drove them to Saint-Jean-de-Luz, the French resort town Mary had visited with Noel just before the war. They met Peter Viertel, who by now had separated from Jigee and was worried Ernest would say something cruel. [11] One reason Viertel had left Jigee was that he could not tolerate her drinking, for he was an abstainer himself. Perhaps recognizing his role in Jigee's descent into alcoholism, Ernest did not mention her but tried to persuade Viertel to write the screenplay for *Old Man*. Viertel recalled, "I wasn't eager to get involved in a screenplay of a book whose magic was contained in the prose rather than its action, and I said so guardedly." [12] Although Viertel loved the book, he could not see how to dramatize Santiago sitting in his small boat waiting for a fish and then fighting the marlin and sharks for days.

Mary went for a long walk along the seafront and through the winding streets and could not help but be nostalgic for the simpler days when she had vacationed in the town with Noel. Not that she wished to reunite with him, for Ernest had become much more settled and easier to live with since the favorable reviews of *Old Man*. The Lancia and its passengers left Saint-Jean-de-Luz the next day and headed south. They reached the French frontier at the Bidasoa River and crossed the bridge into the Basque town of Irun. Ernest had worried how the officials of the Franco regime might receive him, for they had once declared him a *persona non grata* for his anti-fascist activities. The immigration officer who met them held out his hand for their passports. When he saw Ernest's name, he asked if he was a relation, and after looking again at the photo and then at Ernest, he stood up and shook Ernest's hand and welcomed him back to Spain.

Adamo drove the powerful Lancia along the same roads Ernest had traveled thirty years earlier and described in *The Sun Also Rises*. They passed through the beech forests surrounding San Sebastian and climbed the winding road high into the Pyrenees of Navarre before descending through fertile farmland toward the "plateau of Pamplona rising out of the plain." [13] Well-kept vineyards and orchards bordered the road until they reached the suburbs of anonymous high-rises that had sprung up since Ernest's last visit. They reached Pamplona's central square, Plaza del Castillo, just after noon, and Ernest was happy to be back in the familiar neighborhood, the setting for his first novel. They could not find rooms in Pamplona because the city was crowded with tourists hoping to live the adventures Ernest had described in *The Sun Also Rises*. Instead, they found a new hotel in the nearby village of Lecumberri, away from the constant noise of the festival.

They lunched at the outdoor tables of the Café Iruña and drank refreshing beer. Mary visited the tiled interior of the café and noted the octagonal columns holding up the high, gold-painted ceiling hung with chandeliers made of curly-cued bronze. The room looked more like a palace than a café. After quenching their thirst with the sharp beer, they ate exquisite tapas and cheese with crusty bread and drank local Tempranillo. Excitement was building among young men wearing red kerchiefs tied around their necks, roving in bands with their arms over the shoulders of their fellows and drinking from botas. A staggering party was beginning, and after lunch, Gianfranco disappeared into the crowds. Ernest suggested they ought to check into their hotel, and Adamo drove Mary and Ernest to Lecumberri, where they had a refreshing nap.[14]

The next morning was July 7, the beginning of the festival of San Fermin, and they rose early and drove toward the rising sun in the pink-hued sky. At Plaza del Castillo, crowded with tourists and excited country people, they drained cups of strong coffee and tied red kerchiefs around their necks, paying homage to the beheading of San Fermin, the first bishop of Pamplona. They met Ernest's old friend Juanito Quintana, the foremost authority on bullfighting in Spain.

At seven o'clock each morning of the festival, the *encierro* began with the release of the fighting bulls from the corral at the edge of town. The frenzied bulls charged up the slippery, cobble-stoned streets to the bullring at the Plaza de Toros, chasing a crowd of young men before them. On the first morning, one man fell and was gored. Gianfranco had planned to run with the bulls, but he drank too much wine and fell asleep outside a bar, awakening only to the boom of the cannon announcing the *encierro*.[15] Ernest and Mary watched as over a hundred young men in white shirts with red kerchiefs tied around their necks ran into the bullring just ahead of the seven bulls due to fight that day. Ernest had warned everyone to be careful of pickpockets, but he was the one to fall victim. He was sheepish when he realized one of the skilled thieves had stolen the fine new wallet Mary had bought for him in New York.

After the *encierro*, they returned to the Iruña to drink, eat, and chat with friends until the bullfights later in the day. Mary noted the bulls were handsome, noble beasts, with enchanting faces; "they had no expression of menace or of a wish to destroy anything." Instead, they looked "eager, excited, confused but wanting to learn this new game into which they had been thrust."[16] Ernest explained in *Death in the Afternoon*, "Bullfighting is based on the fact that it is the first meeting between the wild animal and a dismounted man. This is the fundamental premise of modern bullfighting—that the bull has never been in the ring before."[17] An experienced bull is a killer. "After his first charge or so, he will stand quite still and will only charge if he is certain of getting the man or boy who was tempting him with a cape."[18]

Mary had no qualms about the bullfighting, having overcome her youthful queasiness about injured animals, and seemed to enjoy every part of the experience. On the second day, they watched Antonio Ordóñez, the son of Niño de la Palma, the bullfighter in *The Sun Also Rises*. Mary found he was "so skillful, valiant and melodic that he lifted the afternoon from sport to poetry."[19] He hypnotized the bulls, and they died as he slipped the blade between their strong shoulders. She reflected, "the bulls have had a fine, free life with no chores and burdens their full four years, and thinking how lucky they are to have it finished in excitement in no more than fifteen minutes, I am not upset by the killing of them."[20] Over the remaining days of the festival, they journeyed between Lecumberri and Pamplona and grew familiar with the scenery of Navarre: valleys of gold and green and red, changing colors with the sun, and Lombardy poplars standing to attention along the roads and against the sky. What a pity Van Gogh had never painted Navarre, Mary thought.[21]

In Pamplona, they established their headquarters at Kutz's café in a corner of the Plaza del Castillo, and friends dropped by to drink and laugh. They praised *Old Man* and their enthusiasm lifted Ernest's mood. The Wertenbakers came from Ciboure, the Taylors from New York, and Ernest's English friend Rupert Bellville was a constant presence. Peter Viertel dropped by, but he found the afternoons "tedious with much sitting around in the bars and cafés on the main square." As a non-drinker, he was "a fish out of water in Pamplona."[22] Mary recalled they moved as a mob, lunching in riotous confusion, watching the pipe bands playing and dancing, and buying trinkets from the shops.

One afternoon, a matador dedicated his first bull to Ernest, and though Ernest enjoyed the honor, it proved to be a poor bull. Later, they watched with fascination as Antonio Ordóñez entered the ring and performed his magic, exhausting a strong bull with forty close passes and then kneeling on the ground facing the standing animal for what seemed like a minute. When the bull made its last charge, Antonio killed it gracefully, and the crowd erupted in shouts of "violent approval."[23]

The next morning Gianfranco ran with the bulls, and they saw him scamper into the bullring. He was pleased with himself and celebrated late into the night with a newfound friend. When Mary was away from the bullfighting, she gathered folk songs celebrating the festival and sang with the troubadours. She had a low, expressive voice like Edith Piaf's, and the guitarists were happy to accompany her.

After the festival ended, they set out for Madrid, and Mary admired the scenery along the way. Ernest spotted a rare hoopoe bird with its distinctive crown of feathers and black-and-white striped back and wings. He associated the hoopoe with his first visit to Spain and was excited to see several more of them probing for nectar in flowers at a roadside inn where they stopped for lunch. In the afternoon, they drove through the forest around the Río Eresma where Ernest had set *For Whom the Bell Tolls*. He pointed out the high, barren hilltop where the calvary attacked El Sordo.

For days they wandered Madrid, the city Ernest believed to be one of the finest in the world. He showed Mary his special places, but she found Madrid compared weakly to London, New York, or Paris. Ernest's favorite beer was served at the Cervecería Alemana in the Plaza Santa Ana, and it became their rendezvous point. He had a special table in the window overlooking the square, and he sat there for hours meeting his old friends from bullfighting who passed through the restaurant. [24]

To mark Ernest's fifty-fourth birthday, Mary found two gold-and-jade medallions and had a jeweler convert them into cufflinks. She also found a wallet to replace the one pickpocketed in Pamplona. They celebrated alone with a quiet lunch. Every morning they spent an hour touring the Prado, for that was as much art as they could absorb at one time. Ernest found a hoopoe bird in the left panel of Hieronymus Bosch's tryptic of the "Garden of Eden."

Just as they were about to leave Madrid for the fiesta at Valencia, they learned the chic French ship they had booked to take them to Mombasa had canceled its sailing due to a smallpox outbreak. The only available boat was of the inferior British Union-Castle line, and they could only reserve a windowless cabin. It was to sail on August 6, a week earlier than they had planned to leave.

They took the Lancia to Paris, and the next day Charlie Ritz treated them to a sumptuous lunch at one of his favorite restaurants. On August 4, they drove to Marseille, and two days later boarded their lavender-hulled ship with forty-six pieces of luggage. They had a tearful farewell drink with Adamo in the ship's bar. Over the next two weeks, they churned east through the Mediterranean and then southward. Mary studied Swahili and typed up her notes from Spain. Ernest made friends with the other passengers and read. His only complaint: the beer was warm.

The ship met the outer edges of a monsoon as it steamed through the Indian Ocean, and wind off the starboard bow caused the decks to heave and fall. Everyone felt queasy despite the captain's admonition it should remind them of a rocking cradle. On August 21, they reached Mombasa, and Ernest's friend, Philip Percival, welcomed them. Two of his men loaded their luggage into an enormous hunting car and drove them to the Manor Hotel. They enjoyed a fine curry dinner, and afterward, pleased to be back on solid land, they fell asleep in large beds enclosed in mosquito nets.

TWENTY-FIVE

Safety Off, Hold Steady, Squeeze

August 1952–December 1953

B ritain colonized Kenya to exploit its rich farmland and local labor, expecting British farmers would grow highly profitable crops like tea and coffee for export. Many of the original white settlers were "the sons of aristocratic families," and in the beginning, it was "a world of 5,000-acre farms."[1] Later, immigrants from Britain, often returning soldiers from the world wars, were recruited to take up tracts of fertile farmland seized from the local populations, who were moved to reserves. "Like all colonial governments, Kenya's was illegitimate, as it derived its power not from democratic consensus but from a host of repressive laws that forced the local population to obey, using taxation, pass laws, imprisonment, legal floggings, and terror."[2] The Kenyan government became more oppressive as it tried to maintain control over the increasingly restive African population. The Kikuyu people were the main victims of the displacement. They responded by forming a resistance organization opposing the British colonial objectives and seeking the expulsion of whites from Kenya. The colonial administrators sought support from the Kamba (also referred to as the Wakamba[3]) people and recruited them to join the colonial army and take jobs in the colonial administration. Kamba chiefs were put on the British payroll, and the King's African Rifles were formed from Kamba warriors. Meanwhile, the white settlers, who were likened to the land-owners of the south of colonial America, played a large role in Kenyan politics, pushing the colonial administration to take harsh measures against the Kikuyu.[4]

By the time the Hemingways came ashore in Mombasa in late August 1953, the British colony was in crisis. Over the last year, almost daily stories in the *New York Times* described the increasingly fierce guerrilla war between the members of the Kikuyu tribe who had taken the Mau Mau oath and Africans who cooperated with the colonial regime, white settlers, and British Army units. The Kenyan Legislative Council had passed emergency laws strengthening the government's hand, "fighting the Mau Mau, a secret society terrorizing thousands of natives and threatening to drive all whites from Kenya."[5] The emergency laws restricted the movement of black Africans, controlled the press and publishing, required registration of societies of ten or more members, eased the use of confessions to the police in court trials, and increased penalties for sedition.[6]

The British colonial secretary came to Kenya to survey events. He reported the Mau Mau had become so bold, "it carried out its attacks in broad daylight frequently with the use of hired assassins," making use of stolen firearms, gelignite, and dynamite. The Mau Mau leaders were attempting "to usurp the functions of the legal government and to destroy all authority with the people except its own."

The leader of the Kenya African Union, British educated Jomo "Burning Spear" Kenyatta, was arrested and charged with masterminding the Mau Mau terrorism.[7] He was put on trial before a magistrate who had been bribed by British authorities to return a guilty verdict after hearing evidence from witnesses who had also been bribed.[8] Kenyatta's appeal of his seven-year sentence was denied.[9]

Meanwhile, there were reports of Mau Mau atrocities exacted against fellow Kikuyu who failed to uphold the oath and, occasionally, against white settlers. "Mau Mau, armed with long native knives, hacked to death a Kikuyu schoolteacher in his home today and seriously injured a native clergyman of the African Anglican church."[10] A month later, "at least 150 men, women and children of the Kikuyu tribe were killed by their Mau Mau fellow tribesmen in a three-and-one-half hour massacre in the uplands area near Nairobi." The official view was "that the attack was directed against all loyal Kikuyu in the district, mainly the African employees of the government in the area and the home guard. There is little doubt this was the motive."[11]

The authorities responded with mass arrests. Police and troops detained 6,000 Kikuyu in just two days in March of 1953.[12] British troops and the native police, "fearing a mass Easter Sunday attack by Mau Mau killers, rounded up seven thousand more natives in predawn raids." All the prisoners were released after questioning, "except for about three hundred who were held for intense screening."[13] Two weeks later, hundreds of European and African police and troops evicted thousands of African families, "driving goats, chickens, and livestock ahead of them from two shanty villages known to be hotbeds of the anti-white Mau Mau cult." A senior police official said, "today's raid—one of the biggest of the emergency had unearthed more thugs per head of population than any other single operation of a similar nature."[14] The response of the colonial authorities became more and more vicious, and there was routine police torture of suspects, white settler vigilantism, forced labor, and removals of Kikuyu to concentration camps.[15]

Political opposition to the oppressive Kenyan colonial regime grew in the British Parliament. Labour members forced an emergency debate, and the former colonial secretary declared, "there seems to be every danger that we are rapidly reaching the stage in Kenya of what amounts to Civil War."[16] The British Liberal Party, at its annual assembly, passed a resolution deploring "mass punishment in Kenya and other practices contrary to the basic conceptions of British justice."[17] As if to highlight the outrages, on the day the Hemingways arrived in Mombasa, the Kenyan government announced it had awarded seventy dollars to a tribal policeman for shooting and killing his own brother, said to be a member of the Mau Mau.[18]

Aboard ship, Mary heard stories from a police officer's wife about the trouble brewing underground among the Kikuyu. According to her, one of the government's problems was the weakness of the governors, who were either "stupid, or weak and indecisive."[19] Mary and Ernest were guests of the British Colonial Government and the Kenyan game department, which "hoped that good publicity would encourage the safari tours (both shooting and camera) that Kenya needed." Officials wanted the visit to "overshadow the horror stories of Mau Mau atrocities that appeared regularly in newspapers and magazines around the world." The department believed, "Hemingway's name on the cover of a popular magazine [*Look*] had enormous power to draw serious, monied readers eager to follow in his footsteps."[20] Patrick Hemingway told me the Mau Mau rebellion was an important part of the background to the safari. "My father was the guest of the British Colonial regime, not the Mau Mau. The regime did everything it could to accommodate my dad because it was a very big deal to have Ernest Hemingway visiting Africa and diverting attention away from the Mau Mau rebellion."[21]

Ernest used his *Look* article to support the colonial authorities and minimize the impact or legitimacy of the Mau Mau cause. Despite the horrific political context in which their safari adventure played out, Mary made not a single reference to the Mau Mau in her memoir, though she did make several revealing comments in her African journal.

◆

Percival drove Mary and Ernest inland in his comfortable hunting car, which was large enough to hold all their gear. They traveled upward for two days onto Kenya's high central plateau. Mary was astounded by the herds of wild animals stretching across the yellow plains. The car climbed the red road through the green coastal hills until they found themselves in a thorn scrub desert. They drove on until they reached a high plateau where rains had failed for two years. Twenty years earlier, when Ernest had known the plateau, it had been a green or orange-brown land. Now it was gray to red, with dust that caked everything and followed cars or trucks moving along the road. Ernest acted as Mary's travel guide, pointing out geographic features and describing the animals' habits.[22]

Next to Percival's farm at a hillside camp, the crew had already set up a village of tents around blazing campfires. Percival, wearing a wide-brimmed felt hat, his blue eyes shining from the reflected flames, introduced them to the twenty-two safari servants who would accompany them. They were all members of the Kamba tribe, and they were excited at the prospect of a hunt guided by Bwana (Boss) Percival, the doyen of Kenya's professional big game hunters. He had guided Teddy Roosevelt in 1909, and in the years since had hunted with the Duke of Windsor, the Duke of Gloucester, and many American and European big-game hunters. He had also guided Ernest and Pauline on their safari twenty years earlier. Percival, now aged sixty-eight, had agreed to come out of retirement from cattle and horse ranching to guide Ernest and Mary in the fall and winter of 1953 and 1954. Everyone expected a splendid adventure. To start things off on the right foot, Ernest had the men unload a case of liquor. Then they shared dry martinis—without ice—with the white members of the hunting party.[23]

Percival was a quintessential white settler who had obtained his ranch of nine thousand acres from the colonial regime.[24] He was fiercely loyal to the white settler movement, despised the Kikuyu, and had no empathy for their condition as displaced people or their efforts to gain some form of political recognition. In her journal, Mary reported Percival saying of the Kikuyu, "the bastards. I'd shoot them all, the lot."[25] Percival wanted "to eliminate" the Kikuyu. He agreed with a district commissioner, who said, "Before any palliative measures are introduced, Mau Mau must be crushed." Detention camps were constructed to hold the Kikuyu "for punitive rather than rehabilitative purposes."[26] Percival did not think much of the Masai people either, telling Mary, "they'll die off—they're useless."[27] Percival detested the Kikuyu and Masai, but he tolerated the loyal Kamba serving under his second-in-command, Keiti, a Kamba hunter who had been with him since the First World War.[28]

Mary liked Keiti right off because he always looked amused and was gracious and gentle. He never raised his voice, and the crew worked as a capable team under his soft-spoken commands. They were members of his family, and they each had assigned tasks and special skills. Keiti was something of feudal overlord, and one reason he enjoyed loyalty and obedience was that he had the power to dismiss the members of the safari crew, condemning them to poverty.[29] It was the custom to call them "boys," but Mary found the term condescending, and she and Ernest made a point of learning their names. N'bebia was the chief cook, M'kao, the chief skinner and tracker, and M'windi their personal servant. They grew loyal to these men and had confidence in them. Ernest conferred a particular honor upon M'windi when he gave him a large roll of Kenyan banknotes for safekeeping. M'windi accepted the gesture of trust. Ernest's gun boy, N'gui, was the same height as Mary, both too short to see over the tall grasses. When Ernest learned he was the son of M'cola, with whom he had hunted twenty years earlier, he treated him like a nephew.

The *Look* celebrity photographer, Earl Theisen, joined them. Far from being a meddlesome interloper, "Ty" was an affable companion with stories to tell about his assignments. A serious craftsman, he wanted to get on with the job of taking photos of Ernest in action. They also met Denis Zaphiro, a young, good-looking game warden of the Kajiado District they were visiting who had a military background, having served in the Sudan defense force. Zaphiro was a "conservation-minded ranger" who had "just secured permission to open the southern game reserve to hunters."[30] He welcomed the Hemingways on behalf of the game department in Nairobi and eventually persuaded his superiors to appoint Ernest an honorary game warden. Ernest adopted Denis as a son, and Mary developed a long and affectionate friendship with him. Denis was fresh and optimistic and traveled with a police-dog puppy named Kibo. Mary loved the affectionate puppy who was curious about everything. She wrote in her journal, Kibo was a "self-propelled set of teeth which any day [might] chew down the camp. He even has a taste for tent poles."[31]

Mayito Menocal, one of their Cuban friends, also joined the safari party. In the first few days, they sighted-in their rifles by target shooting, and Mary's inconsistency with the gun concerned Ernest. She had outstanding days and bad ones and could miss a target for no apparent reason. Given her goal to shoot a lion, her bad luck as a shooter worried the entire camp. The big cats were dangerous, and a missed shot at close range could have disastrous consequences for members of the hunting party. Ernest and Percival drilled Mary often, coaching her on tracking, sneaking up on game, and aiming for a spot just behind the shoulder. Mary went out on shoots to hunt meat for the camp and improve her accuracy.

One morning they spotted two lions feasting on a gazelle the crew had left as bait. Ernest hurried around a tree and fired. They could hear "the whack" of a bullet hitting bone, but the lion didn't fall or roar. The party crept to the site, but the lion had disappeared, leaving a blood trail into the bush. This was the most dangerous phase of a hunt, for a wounded lion could be a killing machine. Ernest told Mary to stay in the car while the men tracked the animal through the thick bush. They found the wounded lion in about half an hour, finished him off with two shots, and brought his corpse back to the lorry where Mary sat nursing her rifle. The young male, weighing about four hundred pounds, had been in his prime "with long forearm muscles, hard leg muscles, thick bones, and strong paws." Mary thought he had "such pretty ears."[32] M'kao skinned the lion, and Ernest cut out some tenderloin from beside the spine. He gave a piece to Mary, and she "thought the clean pink flesh delicious, steak tartare without the capers."[33] Denis told them the flesh would make them sick, and Percival declined a taste. Mary noted that in Kenya some unexplained taboo kept people from eating lion, but she and Ernest felt no such constraint, and they had N'bebia marinate the tenderloin in sherry before he grilled it. They ate it with tomato and garlic sauce as if it were Italian veal.

Ernest shot a zebra for camp food, and close to the body, they found a newborn Grant's gazelle abandoned by its mother. Concerned the baby would die, they took him back to camp, and Ty made a nipple of cotton-batten and gauze and coaxed him to drink tinned milk. They called him "Baa," for that was the sound he made in the night. He soon became the center of attention, and Mary worried about him. One morning Kibo rushed up to Baa, baring his teeth and growling, but the little gazelle butted the puppy, who soon learned to keep a respectful distance. They bought a baby's bottle and nipple from a small Indian store in the local village of Laitokitok, and Baa came three times a day for his tinned milk mixed with water. Baa began sleeping in their tent, and he slept in a box that Mary carried on the seat of the hunting car when they left the camp. She worried what would become of the infant gazelle because he smelled of humans, and his herd would not accept him. If they released him, a jackal, hyena, or leopard would soon eat him.

◆

The Hemingways filled their days with a pleasant routine: hot tea in the morning while they dressed, driving in the hunting car looking for beasts, and returning to the mess tent for breakfast or lunch. After taking a siesta in camp, they explored again in the late afternoon and returned to the campfire at dusk for cocktails and dinner. Mary was learning to identify trees, birds, and insects and pick out the best animal in a herd. She was learning Swahili and something of the geography and history of Kenya. They seemed blissfully unaware of the colonial government's determined efforts to eradicate the Mau Mau just over the mountains.

Ernest was more like the man she had fallen in love with, and Mary found him an endearing companion. He committed himself to the hunt, became respectful of the safari team, learned who was more and who less reliable, and dealt with the inevitable crises. Gone was the quick temper which spilled over into nasty remarks and even physical abuse. He continued to drink significant quantities of gin, but the careful habits of Percival and Zaphiro, who never let themselves drink so much they could not take charge in an emergency, helped to subdue his drinking. It was amazing what a difference the positive reception of *Old Man* had made to Ernest's sense of well-being and how his relationship with Mary prospered. They retreated to their tent and played sexual games on the narrow cot under the mosquito netting. Mary recalled, "we made up games and secret names and joyous jokes, as only lucky people who are friends do."[34] She hoped the warmth and affection would continue, and the five months in Kenya were some of the happiest of their relationship. Thinking back to those days, Mary wrote, "we wanted to hear the Lions speaking in the evenings and the fun of trying to fit ourselves into a single narrow camp cot. Some parts of us stuck out, but we were pleased with this maneuver."[35]

Despite almost constant practice, Mary continued to be an unreliable shooter—sometimes she could drop an animal with a single shot, but often her bullets kicked up dust around her target. One day, Mary, Ernest, and Zaphiro went out in the hunting car to find meat for the camp. They found a herd of eland, and Zaphiro pointed out the one to shoot only seventy yards away. Mary aimed, shot, and missed. She tried again and missed, "perhaps singeing the hair of his knees." They drove on, found a second herd, got out of the car, and walked closer. Mary missed again. "So, it goes," she confided to her journal. "It is lonely being the only incompetent here." She felt the "grey misery of missing beasts" and wondered why she was having so much trouble.[36] After lunch, they rested, and Mary fell into a deep sleep. She dreamed of Irwin Shaw and his wife, Marian, whom she had never met, and their baby boy.[37]

The next day, they were cruising in the Jeep, when they saw a class of half a dozen Thomson's gazelles (Tommy bucks), and Ernest told Mary to shoot one with his Springfield. Mary got a buck in her sights and noticed there was no shaking in her forearm this time. She shot and dropped him, but it was a bad shot, not in the shoulder. They walked up to the wounded animal, and Mary finished him off, shooting him just below his ear. As Mary recalled, "I felt ashamed and sorry but pleased, too, that I finally shot something instead of forever missing. Felt more a working part of the safari than a useless baggage."[38] That afternoon, during her nap, she dreamed she met a warthog dressed in a black morning coat, and black porkpie hat, on the steps of a Gothic church. He was making elaborate German philosophical speeches in a guttural tone. People told Mary to shoot him just below his ear, and she kept shooting, though with no effect, as he lifted his paws to his ear and brushed away the shots like they were flies. Mary woke up before he finished his speech about "the ambiance of immortality."[39] Her anthropomorphic dreams continued, increasing the pressure on her to avoid hitting the animals, who came to her with human personalities and speeches at night.

Two days later, Mary, Zaphiro, and Ernest came upon a herd of zebras, and Zaphiro told Mary to shoot one for dinner. She aimed with the Springfield and missed him. They followed the zebras to a flat, pleasant country until they were well within range. Mary missed, again and again, even when they were so close she could've hit them with a well-aimed stone. She confided to her journal, "I've tried to think and assess and analyze, and I do not understand at all why I shoot so badly. My eyes see, my hands do not shake. I see him clearly in the sites. And I miss. It is on the verge of being comic."[40]

◆

Mary knew Baa could not continue living with them, although he was becoming affectionate and nibbled her arms and legs and her chin after drinking his bottles of sweetened milk. He enjoyed being held and stroked but hated having his face washed. He feared the spear-carrying Masai, but not the domestic camp boys. One afternoon they returned from a hunt and found Baa's leash broken and no sign of the little gazelle. Mary walked for hours along paths close to the camp calling his name but to no avail. "Night fell and no Baa and, my spirits entombed, I decided we'd seen the last of him." Mary, Ernest, and Percival were subdued, sitting around the fire having a drink before dinner, when Baa appeared out of the grasses, walked daintily toward Mary, and nibbled on her chin. There was "a thundershower of affection around."[41] Mary knew they had to find a home for Baa, and Mrs. Laurie Aitkin from a nearby town said she would be pleased to take care of him. Mary worried he would not do well, but she had no better options, and she confided to her journal, "I feel terrible, awful, about having left him there—my only child."[42] Perhaps Mary's emotional attachment to the helpless Baa was all the stronger because she could not give birth to her own child.

◆

A delegation of Masai came to complain that a large lion was killing their cattle. Percival decided to help, and they jumped into the hunting car. Mary checked her ammunition, for she knew since Ernest had already shot his lion, they would give her the honor of the first shot. After they drove eastward for several miles, Percival stopped the car and said they would track the lion on foot. The sun was high in the cloudless sky, and Mary felt sweat running down her face and dripping down her back. The rim of her felt hat became soaked with sweat as she tried to keep up with the fast-moving trackers. After about an hour, they halted at a thicket of thorn trees. Percival touched her arm and pointed. It took a full thirty seconds for Mary to spot the lion, twenty yards away, camouflaged in the trees. She was "breathless and sweating, burning with excitement, and hope, and expectation." She aimed at his shoulder because she wanted to spare his face. "Safety off, hold steady; squeeze," she chanted inside her head. [43] Holding her breath, she squeezed the trigger, and her round spit up dirt about a yard in front of the lion, which stood up, turned around, and retreated into the forest. This was a serious mistake, and no one laughed. The team had worked hard to give Mary a chance, and their disappointment showed. In the first few minutes, she was not ashamed to have missed but exhilarated to have seen the large lion.

Everyone treated her with kindness and spoke words of quiet encouragement, but despite their gentle manners, Mary felt shame. She knew she had let down the team, and there was only one way to regain their respect. She woke up that night dreaming of the lion, who spoke to her in an Oxford accent. Mary was damp with sweat and frightened she would miss again.

Mary, Ernest, and Mayito were climbing a hill when Mayito, who was just ahead of Mary, shot to the right. Ernest fired in the same direction, and Mary's gun boy grinned, for twenty paces away was a dead leopard. This delighted Ty Theisen because he could finally photograph Ernest with a dead dangerous beast. Theisen arranged a scene, with a nonchalant Ernest holding his rifle and smiling into the distance, while the dead leopard crouched next to Ernest, looking like he was about to pounce. Ty took several photographs despite Mary's protest that it may not have been Ernest's bullet that brought down the leopard. She thought Mayito deserved credit for the kill and was appalled Ernest posed for the photographs as if he had shot the leopard himself. Mary told him his attitude was morally repugnant, and they bickered about the issue for a month, one of the few arguments they had in Kenya. Ernest maintained he would shoot a leopard himself, and that would solve the problem.

Mary's attitude toward the killing was ambivalent. She wanted to enjoy the respect of the men in the hunting party, and to prove herself, she needed to shoot well. Pauline had killed a lion on her safari with Ernest twenty years earlier, and Mary felt she must measure up to Pauline's achievement. She did her best to shoot well and kill game to provide meat for the camp, and she celebrated with the others when they killed magnificent beasts. However, she also felt bad about killing the animals.

In early October, she and Ernest were sightseeing when Ernest's gun-bearer pointed out a handsome male greater kudu with two pretty does on a hill half a mile away. Ernest told Mary to take the shot, and she slammed a cartridge into the chamber of her Mannlicher. They started fast through the yellow grass and scrambled over red lava rock, keeping cover between them and the animals on the hill ahead, finally coming upon an anthill which was just the right size for Mary to use as a support for her shot. She aimed, held her breath, and fired. The kudus disappeared. Mary and Ernest scrambled up the hill to the place where the magnificent creatures had stood, and twenty yards into the bush, they found the handsome young male lying dead from a shot that had punctured his jugular vein. Mary wrote, "He was very pretty and very neat when I first saw him, his eyes still bright, a tiny trickle of blood coming from the small hole and from his mouth. Too young and too handsome and too full of life with his pretty does to die by a lucky shot from a stranger."[44] Ernest paced the shot and figured Mary had made the kill from 240 yards. All the gun boys, Mayito, and Ty complimented her, and the entire safari crew produced a jamboree, singing, beating on tin pans, and shaking her hand when she returned to camp. Mary confessed, "I felt bad, privately. I had shot badly and missed animals time after time, I decided, because privately I couldn't bear to kill them."[45]

Mary knew it was difficult to raise Grant's gazelles in captivity because they develop digestive problems. About a month after she left Baa with Mrs. Atkin, she learned he had died. Mary berated herself, "I should never have left him there, seeing how little there was for him to nibble, seeing the cement enclosure where she proposed to keep him. I was weak to leave him there." She should have made "the bold, quick, rude decision to keep him with me, for we did understand each other, and I think his trust in me would've prevented the digestive upset." She realized, "no amount of sorrow and shame can suffice to excuse my stupidity and weakness about him. Lord, how I wish I could get him back to us."[46] Mary felt almost inconsolable grief and guilt at the fate of the only fur baby in Africa she had adopted. The other animals did not enjoy her protection, though she sought to justify killing them because they were guilty of crimes against the villagers, or they were necessary for food, or because they were injured. The fact they appeared to her in dreams wearing porkpie hats and speaking about philosophy in Oxford accents showed the depth of her inner conflict.

◆

Ernest's appointment as an honorary game warden came through on November 3, 1953, and he was given "full authority to act" under the Kenyan Wild Animals Protection Ordinance of 1951.[47] He was to protect people from marauding animals (which involved killing dangerous beasts), prevent poaching, and monitor the movement of Mau Mau in the neighborhood. Ernest had become an agent of the colonial administration, and he took his duties seriously. He told Harvey Breit, "Got made an Honorary Game Warden and due to the emergency [Mau Mau rebellion] been acting game ranger here. It is a first-class life. Problems all day and night."[48] According to a "Top Secret directive," issued on December 23, 1953, under the code name "Operation Long Stop," Kenyan police "swept and screened the Laitokitok area and detained thirty-seven Mau Mau suspects." In order to "nip in the bud any further spread of subversive activity," a series of arrests were planned following simultaneous raids. "Game Wardens were part of the plan, and Laitokitok was considered a likely point of entry."[49] Two days later, Mary reported in her journal, "the police have been raiding Kikuyu on the other side of the mountain. We met them on the road to town this morning, the officer stopping us to interrogate us briskly but cheerfully."[50]

In early January, Mary reported, "Fifteen Mau Mau have escaped from Machakos jail and may be around here tonight. It would be too bad, especially this year, to be carved up in bed by a race fanatic, but Keiti doesn't think they'll come this way."[51] Mary was concerned about the stories of Mau Mau actions against Europeans, and Ernest took the warning seriously. Ernest posted one of his trusted safari crew members, "Arap Menah in one of the Kamba shambas and [Ernest] went to see if the Mau Mau had showed." Ernest thought, "the escaped boys had first got caught from being drunk, and they'd head for drink." They would probably go to Laitokitok, "since all Wakamba know that there are these shambas here—and have been here since thirty years ago." Ernest went to Laitokitok, "to check the bars but bought something in each place so as not to look like a policeman." Ernest was armed, and luckily for him and the Mau Mau escapees, he did not find them.[52] By this time, Ernest had adopted his role as an officer of the colonial administration. He sided with the Kamba "who were completely loyal to the British." Patrick Hemingway told me his father failed to express any empathy for the Kikuyu.[53]

The Masai complained about a large black-maned lion killing their cattle, and Percival decided Mary should shoot him. They set bait close to the lion's lair, chaining dead zebras to a tree so the lionesses could not drag the game back home. They hoped this would draw the male himself for a free meal. Late on the afternoon of December 5, the lion came for dinner. As they pulled up in the hunting car near the bait, the lion stood thirty yards in front of them. Ernest jumped out and ran to the left. Mary found his hip in her sights, held her breath, and squeezed the trigger. Almost at the same time, Ernest and Zaphiro both shot. They told Mary she had fired first. [54]

They found the lion dead 350 yards away. The safari truck drove up, full of people singing, yelling, and beating on tin pans. There were handshakes and back-slaps all around, and the boys sang a song of triumph about the small Memsa'ab killing the huge, frightening creature. Mary loved the attention, but she was embarrassed because she wasn't sure her shot had hit the lion. Percival said he had not seen such a celebration in twenty years. After dinner, the safari boys danced around the fire and celebrated the Memsa'ab slaying the Simba. [55]

The next day when they skinned the lion, they found Mary's bullet had broken his leg and Zaphiro's heavier round had severed his spine. He was nine feet long and weighed 384 pounds. Mary and Ernest ate the lion's tenderloin, marinated in sherry and grilled. The meat was tender and delicious. In the days following the long campaign and thrill of the hunt, Mary felt subdued, empty, and purposeless. A few nights later, she woke up weeping in the night, finally understanding she could not lay any claim to the lion. She felt foolish, for she realized Zaphiro had shot him and then tricked her into thinking her round hit him first. Mary felt heartbroken and frustrated she couldn't shoot well enough, and after such "a long, sincere, serious, purposeful pursuit, it should have finished in such a farce." [56] She said so at lunch, and Zaphiro somewhat harshly replied they had handed her a lion on a platter. Mary confessed to her journal Zaphiro deserved credit for the lion, but she left this out of her published memoir. In *How It Was*, Mary claimed the lion as her kill, just as Ernest took credit for Mayito's leopard in the *Look* article about the safari.

Mary and Ernest met a young pilot, Roy Marsh, who flew charter flights out of Nairobi in small aircraft. He introduced them to a new adventure, brief flights from the base camp to observe herds of wild animals only minutes away. On December 12, he took them on a flight over the Kimana swamp and to the Chyulu hills. They saw sixteen different rhinos, six herds of eland, three vast herds of oryx and zebra, and a big herd of buffalo. They buzzed Masai villages and Laitokitok and came home. Mary found it the most exciting hour they had spent in Africa apart from her lion hunt. [57]

Mary accompanied Marsh to Nairobi so she could do some Christmas shopping. Five days later, she returned to the camp and found Ernest had shaved his head "to the scalp, like a Masai girl's, shiny and showing all the scars." [58] He had dyed some of his clothes, including his blue and white shirt, two suede jackets, and a khaki shirt into various shades of Masai rusty pink ocher. [59] While Mary had busied herself making Christmas preparations in Nairobi, Ernest had occupied himself hunting and partying with the safari staff and the nearby Kamba. He had shot a leopard after a dangerous hunt and organized a celebration back at the camp. He gave a beer to each of the safari boys, a practice frowned upon by most professional hunters because they believed the Africans could not hold their liquor. After a campfire, he went to bed for a nap, but a wild party woke him. Someone had invited the local Kamba girls to join the bash. Ernest took the girls to Laitokitok and bought them dresses for Christmas, and he asked them back to the camp for dinner, but no dinner was served. Instead, he invited his favorite, Debba, and two of her friends into the Hemingway's tent. As Mary reported in her journal, "the celebration there was so energetic that they broke my bed." [60]

While Mary was away, Ernest killed a hyena with a spear and she was glad she had not seen it. Ernest wrote to Harvey Breit he had shaved his head because his Kamba fiancé, Debba, liked to feel all the holes and welts in his head. [61] While Ernest made a fuss about Debba and called her his fiancé, Bill Walton thought Ernest was fantasizing. Like his romance with Adriana, "This was just one of his phony sort of male menopause romances. It was all in his head. I think the same thing is true of all that Shamba talk in Kenya about having a brown mistress down in the Shamba." [62] Patrick Hemingway, who was present for much of the safari, told me Debba "was largely a fictional creation. My father went native because he wanted to have a better understanding of African culture. He wanted to try hunting with spears." [63]

◆

Despite the excitement in camp during Mary's absence, Ernest celebrated her return, and they slept "tightly interlocked most of the night in Papa's cot."[64] Carl Eby writes the "vague or unconscious" erotic fantasies Ernest had during the 1920s and 1930s seem "to have been acted out by him in actual practice in the late 1940s and throughout the 1950s."[65] He began bringing his fantasies to life when he found a willing partner in Mary, and she helped him realize his fantasy of "a woman sodomizing a man."[66] There is an account of such a night in Mary's African journal, which she made public in her memoir. The fact she included it in her autobiography is significant because she could have left it out, as she did with so many other things. It seems reasonable to conclude she wanted readers to know she was the sexually dominant partner in her relationship with Ernest.

On December 19, 1953, Ernest took Mary's journal and made his own entry. He wrote a mock interview with "Papa" by a reporter from "a Recondite magazine." Ernest denied his wife was a lesbian but said she was a boy. His favorite nocturnal sport was "sodomy," and his wife participated in the sport.[67] Next, Ernest wrote, "a new names department," in which he gave Mary the name Peter and called himself Catherine.[68] After listing the variations of the names they used in their sexual games, he wrote, "Signing off happy about last night and every night."[69]

The next day, Ernest again took over Mary's journal and wrote a lengthy entry praising Mary and describing their sexual life. He said he had laid off hunting, to devote the day to rest, and to cutting and bleaching Mary's hair, "to look especially beautiful for all visiting guests."[70] While Mary's hair was naturally blonde, she made a present to him of having her hair "platinum-blonde as she was at Torcello," where they "made love at least every morning, noon, and night."[71] Mary's short, platinum-blonde hair not only turned on Ernest but, according to Carl Eby, it was a fetish essential for his sexual satisfaction.

Ernest wrote that loving Mary had been a complicated and wonderful thing for over nine years, "(sometimes fights and mutual wickedness (my fault) and sometimes hers, but always made up and always made presents to each other)." He described Mary as a "Prince of Devils," with "wonderful breasts that rise like the Chuly Chuly hills, and if you are not prepared to take and hold these hills, you would be well-advised not to touch them even by accident." She "has the loveliest place I have ever known, and almost any place you touch her, it can kill both you and her." Ernest described their sex. "She always wanted to be a boy and thinks like a boy without ever losing any femininity . . ." She "loves me to be her girl, which I love to be, not being absolutely stupid and also loving to be her girl since I have other jobs in the daytime." "In return," Mary "makes me awards, and at night we do every sort of thing which pleases her, and which pleases me." Mary "has never had one lesbian impulse but has always wanted to be a boy." Ernest confessed, "Since I have never cared for any man and dislike any tactile contact with men except the normal Spanish abrazo, I love feeling the embrace of Mary, which came to me as something quite new and outside all tribal law." He wrote, "On the night of December 19, we worked out these things, and I've never been happier."[72] Ernest had shaved his head to become a Kamba girl, and this girl surrendered to Peter (Mary).

In her letters to Ernest and throughout the African journal, Mary dropped hints about her sexual relationship with him, which tracked Ernest's fantasies. She said, "they made up secret names"[73] and "we cut and bleached and washed my head, gay and happy"[74] and "before lunch, Papa bleached my hair."[75] Ernest defined "buggery" as "sodomy when practiced by those who are not gentlemen,"[76] and they retreated "to the bedroom for a nap which turned out to be a love-feast, love-fest, love fiesta." Having finished dinner, they went to "bed immediately afterward and a bigger, happier, lovelier love-fest-feast."[77] She wrote to Ernest telling him she got her hair "cut and washed and think you and Mr. S. might like it. XXXXX to you both."[78] In her journal, Mary wrote, "We've had big business with my hair which we've bleached again, and Papa cut very short then I cut across the front in idiot imitation of the local Kamba girls."[79]

In another letter, Mary thanked Ernest "for being my friend, and my brother, and my husband, and my kitten, and my girl, and my boy."[80] Signing off another letter, she wrote, "Dearest, much love from half a woman or half a boy-Mary."[81] These are the very words Catherine speaks in the original manuscript of *The Garden of Eden*: "It isn't everybody who has someone that's half boy and half girl."[82]

TWENTY-SIX

A Plague Began
to Descend Upon Us

December 1953–March 1954

I n *The Garden of Eden*, Ernest seems to draw from his lived experience with
Mary, elaborating upon what he wrote in her journal. It is not a purely imagined
work. As Richard Fantina noted, Hemingway often spoke of the need to write
from experience. "You need an awful lot of past performances," he wrote in *Green
Hills of Africa*. "It's very hard to get anything true on anything you haven't seen
yourself."[1] Ernest experienced with Mary the same gender reversal his characters enacted in the novel. Together, they broke through the socially constructed
confines of gender.

In the novel, David calls Catherine his "devil" for introducing him to androgyny.
He "felt the weight and the strangeness inside," suggesting that Catherine sodomized him. David changed into Catherine's girl, and he let her "take" him. David
became Catherine, and she became Peter, just as Ernest became Catherine and
Mary became Peter.

> He lay there and felt something and then her hand holding him and
> searching lower and he helped her with his hands and then lay back
> in the dark and did not think at all and only felt the weight and the
> strangeness inside and she said,
> "Now you can't tell who is who, can you?"

"No."

"You are changing," she said. "Oh, you are. You are. Yes, you are, and you're my girl, Catherine. Will you change and be my girl and let me take you?"

"You're Catherine."

"No. I'm Peter. You are my wonderful Catherine. You're my beautiful, lovely Catherine. You were so good to change. Oh, thank you, Catherine, so much. Please understand. Please know and understand. I'm going to make love to you forever."[2]

These well-known passages have received the attention of scholars seeking to reconcile them with Hemingway's hypermasculine persona. Rose Marie Burwell interprets the passages to mean Catherine had anally penetrated David with her finger. Burwell argues Hemingway was exploring his own "ambivalent attitude towards androgyny as both a catalyst and a threat to the writer."[3] In her view, true androgyny would mean a balance between maleness and femaleness, which would give the writer access to the full range of emotional and behavioral features of men and women. This would function as a catalyst, releasing creative energy and allowing David to authentically portray both men and women.[4]

Eby also argues, "Catherine's searching hand . . . does indeed sodomize David," and he says it brought about "something still more unusual and profound: a transvestic hallucination."[5] Hemingway revealed his lifelong fetishistic desire to be sodomized by a phallic woman to create a transvestic hallucination that turned him, if only for a flash of time, into a woman. Fantina writes Hemingway gave "full rein to his submissive and masochistic sensibility, a part of his character totally absent in his public persona."[6] Given the negative public image attached to reversing traditional gender roles of domination and submission, "many male masochists (including Hemingway) and their lovers have not often historically revealed this element of their relationships."[7] Fantina argues Hemingway did not intend to publish the confessional paragraphs in Mary's journal. If Fantina is right about Hemingway's intentions, it is remarkable Mary revealed his secret.

In *True at First Light*, Hemingway invokes the same fantasy elements. He writes about the African safari and Mary's return from Nairobi after her Christmas shopping trip. Mary "smelled very good, and her hair was silver gold, cropped close."[8] Mary joined Ernest in his bed, "and I put the other Africa away somewhere, and we made our own Africa again. It was another Africa from where I had been, and at first, I felt the red spilling up my chest, and then I accepted it, and I did not think at all and felt only what I felt, and Mary felt lovely in bed. And then we made love again, and then after we had made love once more, quiet and dark and unspeaking and unthinking and then like a shower of meteors on a cold night, we went to sleep." [9]

The sexual practices described in Mary's African journal found their way into both *True at First Light* and *The Garden of Eden*. Carlos Baker hinted at this in his biography. "In the *Garden of Eden*, Ernest was trying to embody certain secret phases of his sexual life with Mary." [10] Back on the safari, Mary and Ernest sat around the fire, reflecting on their sexual activities. Ernest proclaimed, "This week has been the happiest in my life." [11] If Ernest had written nothing about their gender fluidity in Mary's African journal, no one would be the wiser. However, having raised the topic, Ernest invites us to consider the implications of these activities in his relationship with Mary. She was the woman with whom he realized his deepest sexual fantasies, and this may explain why he could not give up Mary. Each time she threatened to leave him, he prostrated himself, caved to her demands, bought her gifts, and promised to mend his ways. He needed her to achieve sexual equilibrium and to guide him like a compass. No one else could do it like Mary, and they both knew it.

What happened to Ernest when he became Catherine, Mary's girl, and stopped thinking and let her "sodomize" him? For Eby, he became a woman for a flash; for Burwell, the androgynous experience increased his capacity to understand and describe the female point of view; for Moddelmog, it allowed him to break free from social and marital norms; and for Fantina, it showed his "belief in female superiority, at least in sexual relations." [12] This recognition of female superiority did not carry forward to the social sphere. Mary punished and rewarded him, making the Pulitzer Prize winner and world-famous author submit to her. Ernest maintained the pretense of male hegemony during the day, but at night Mary dominated him. Did Mary feel power over Ernest? At a minimum, she must've felt confident about her role in their relationship. She decided not to hide the truth of their union, and in her memoir, she outed Ernest by revealing their secret. Mary's African journal confirms and celebrates their experiments with gender shifting.

Ernest continued dying his clothes Masai orange-pink and perfecting his spear throwing. His embrace of Masai customs allowed him to escape the confines of western culture and explore his identity free from the strictures of western morality or sexual mores. By "going Native" or experimenting with "primitivism," he tried to reinvent himself as someone other than an iconic white American male writer trapped by the expectations of his celebrity. As Suzanne del Gizzo observes, Ernest was "seeking liberation from the sexual restrictions of western culture."[13]

◆

On Christmas Day, Ernest invited people from the surrounding tribes to the camp, including Debba and her mother. They chanted songs and ate a lunch of cold birds and salad. Mary sang "Holy Night" to add a touch of non-African Christmas at the campfire and excused herself for a nap. Later that evening, the Masai and Kamba leaders and Ernest delivered lengthy and solemn speeches, and the safari scouts put on their own dance. Mary was relieved the merriment did not go on as long as usual, and they sat down for a quiet dinner of Tommy chops.[14] Ernest announced Mary's special Christmas present was a January air safari with himself and Roy Marsh across the Serengeti Plain and Lake Victoria and down the Congo River to Stanleyville.

On New Year's Day, Mary wrote her resolutions in her journal. She wanted to shoot well, restrain her appetite for food and drink, see, hear, smell, and learn more sharply, and become more womanly and more wifely. With Ernest back on track, despite his adoption of Masai grooming and clothing, she no longer thought of leaving him, and she wanted to make their life together happier.[15] Sitting by the fire, Mary and Ernest talked about the marvelous time they had enjoyed in Africa and how much they had learned. Ernest said, "We were smart kittens to come to Africa."[16] He showered Mary with compliments: "my kitten-brother is the bravest, loveliest, most understanding, and best kitten in and out of bed, and more fun to talk with on any subject and with sounder opinions, and the best and finest ideals of anyone that I've ever known, ever in my life."[17] Mary recorded his words in her journal so she could look at them if she ever felt low.

Roy Marsh brought mail from Nairobi, including a copy of the *Look* magazine issue with the safari story. Mary thought Ernest's prose and captions read well, but the "feeble" unflattering photos of herself disappointed her. There were several action shots of Ernest: aiming his rifle, watching a Masai warrior with a spear, seated with Mayito's leopard, boxing with a safari boy, stalking game, chatting at the fireside with Percival, and aiming a rifle at a cigarette Ty Thiessen held in his hand. The photos of Mary were not glamorous but focused on her feeding Baa with a bottle and standing next to Ernest, looking at Mount Kilimanjaro in the distance. A caption Ernest composed did not help—"Mary kept a diary and a newborn Grant Gazelle." He was the great hunter, and she was a camp follower.

The article met the expectations of the Kenyan government. Ernest minimized the danger from the Mau Mau and emphasized the pleasure and safety of hunting game with a white hunter. Despite "the war on upcountry where it was necessary to bear arms," there was no need for a visitor to bring a pistol to Nairobi. Ernest reported, "the war which is being fought each day is a long, complicated and ugly story, and we know something of it . . . you may be sure it will continue for a long time." Then he sold the package: "But know truly that no one coming to Africa who is interested in the kingdom of the animals need worry about it personally" unless they traveled to certain areas. He assured readers a foreigner was safer in Nairobi than in New York, Memphis, Jacksonville, or Brooklyn. Ernest stoked the publicity machine and distracted readers from the ugly reality of British repression. He described Philip Percival as "the finest man that I know." Given the blatantly racist views Percival freely expressed and his support for eradicating the Kikuyu, Ernest's lack of insight is disturbing. Patrick Hemingway told me that while his father was usually a liberal and ought to have been more sympathetic to the aspirations of the Kikuyu people, his judgment failed in the safari piece. And while Patrick was fond of Philip Percival, who mentored him in the business of big-game hunting, Patrick later realized his views about the Africans were dangerously old-fashioned. Patrick shared a comment Percival made after an African policeman visited their camp: "They used to be better before we gave them boots."[18]

Elkins observed, "in 1954 for the British colonizers to agree to a hastening of colonial retreat from Kenya was unthinkable." The colonial government's main concern was "to retain power and reaffirm its dominance in the face of Mau Mau, rather than to prepare the colony for some kind of immediate multiracial, liberal democracy."[19] Ernest was clearly on the wrong side of history in his *Look* piece. As Fantina noted, "in his role as Great White Hunter, Hemingway viewed Africa as a playground to which he had a perfect right. The empathy he so often displays deserts him here.[20]

The safari adventure was ending, and Ernest and Mary traveled to New Stanley, where they spent four days at the Hotel Nairobi eating and drinking too much. On January 21, they met Roy Marsh with his blue and silver Cessna and flew out of Nairobi in the early afternoon. The plane flew west across the Serengeti, and they saw thousands of beasts in mixed herds. They flew across the lake after refueling, climbing higher and higher, clearing one mountain ridge after another. Roy seemed happy skimming their tops, but Mary worried they might hit the next crest. They landed at dusk at the Bukavu airport and traveled by Jeep to a hotel where their enormous room overlooked Lake Kivu.

Next, they flew to the Lake Victoria Hotel in Entebbe and toured the local market. On Saturday, January 25, 1954, they left Entebbe and cruised west, passing over thatched-roof villages of fishermen, and saw men, women, and children working in dugout canoes. Mary wrote, "The huts were round and wearing pretty straw hats."[21] They reached the Murchison Falls and circled once while Mary took black-and-white photos, then again while she took color photos. She had one color frame left when Roy suddenly dove to avoid a flock of ibises. The plane's tail hit a telegraph wire, which sliced through the rudder. Roy struggled to get the Cessna under control, but the plane kept losing altitude. They angled away from the hillside, close to the waterfall. Roy skimmed over the hills and said, "we have to set down. Sorry, we're coming down now. Get ready, get ready, get ready."[22]

Mary heard ripping, metal-tearing noises as they crashed to a stop among low trees and bushes. She turned in her seat, covering her face with her arm to protect against the breaking windscreen, but the Plexiglas held. Her only feeling during the last minute was "Shit! at being soon dead or broken."[23] They got out of the plane fast, but it didn't catch fire. Mary went through the cabin contents and found that her cameras still worked. Ernest and Roy studied a map, discovering it was about forty miles to the nearest village. The thought of walking miles through the forest in her soft-soled blue shoes daunted Mary. Her heart was pounding fast, she felt a sharp pain in her left chest, and Roy suggested she lie down.

Ernest and Roy tried to straighten the wireless antenna, and Roy sent international distress Mayday messages reporting on their position. There was no reply. They heard animal noises in the bush but couldn't see more than a few yards in any direction. Ernest decided it would be safer to move up the hill away from the river, and they picked up some gear and moved upwards. Ernest carried a box of bottles and tinned food, and Mary her camera equipment. Halfway up, they stopped to open one of their precious bottles of beer. Mary dropped it, and they lost half of its contents because she couldn't bend down fast enough to retrieve it. They made camp on a patch of sand. Ernest listened to Mary's heart, tried to take her pulse but couldn't find it, and advised her to lie down on the hard sand and put her raincoat under her head.

Mary could not help gather firewood or grasses for beds because her heart pounded with the slightest movement. Roy walked back to the plane several times to transmit Mayday messages on the radio. For dinner, they ate pieces of corned beef with the remains of sandwiches. Meanwhile, none of the Mayday messages were received. A scheduled BOAC flight cruising near the Murchison Falls reported the wreckage and no sign of survivors. The world's newspapers began reporting the deaths of the Hemingways and their pilot.

Roy and Ernest gathered wood, and they built a fire. Mary fell into a fitful sleep on a bed of grass, waking at about 5 A.M., cold and aching, and saw Roy and Ernest looking for more firewood. She sipped water, smoked a cigarette, and went back to sleep. When she woke up, Ernest gave her cheese and two small bananas for breakfast. He was in obvious pain from the damage to his right arm and shoulder. He told her that while scouting for firewood, he had seen a boat coming up the river. A few moments later, when it came into view, they waved their raincoats but received no sign of recognition. The boat docked at a landing below them, tempting Mary to run down the hill, but elephants were between them and the river.

A small group of Africans moved up the hill, and Mary signaled to them. Though they were skeptical about the story of the plane crash, they escorted Mary back to the boat. She learned Ian McAdam, a surgeon from Kampala, had privately chartered the boat with his wife and son and her parents, who were celebrating their fiftieth wedding anniversary. Mary explained their predicament, but the Indian captain of the boat was reluctant to take on more passengers. Roy arrived with Dr. McAdam, who had gone walking to the top of the falls, and they soon persuaded the captain to accommodate the plane crash survivors—after they had paid. They sent some boys up the hill to get Ernest.

After Mary showered, Mrs. McAdam offered her talcum powder, and Dr. McAdam examined her, diagnosing two cracked ribs. Ernest did not want the doctor to examine him. Mary napped during much of the cruise downriver, and they arrived in Butiaba in the late afternoon. It turned out John Huston had used the boat, *The Murchison*, when he filmed *The African Queen* on the same river.

A biplane came overhead, circled several times, and landed on the airfield which had been used to bring in supplies for the filming of *The African Queen*. Mary, Roy, and Ernest caught a ride to the plowed-up airstrip to catch a flight to Entebbe. The pilot of the old De Havilland Rapide, Reggie Cartwright, cruised the runway in a police truck and assured them they could take off. Mary wrote, "I was too tired to try to persuade them we could wait and also didn't want to appear a coward."[24] They boarded the aircraft, and Cartwright started the engine. As the plane rolled along, it bumped over the old furrows, lifted, set down, lifted off, set down, and hopped the length of the field until there was a wrenching crash. Mary saw flames outside her window before she could get her seatbelt undone. She tried to open the door, but it had jammed. Roy called her forward. He had broken a window, and she pushed him through it headfirst and scrambled out after him. The window was far too small for Ernest, and he tried to free the jammed door. His arm and shoulder were inoperative from the earlier crash, so he used his head as a battering ram and popped the door loose. Mary and Roy walked away from the plane. When Mary looked back, she saw Ernest standing on the wing. Cartwright also got out, and soon the entire plane was burning inside and out. They listened for exploding bottles of gin.

Two hundred local people who had gathered at the starting point set up a cheering section, and they came running and yelling, "Mungu mkono"—"in the hand of God."[25] Later, there was a big welcome party at the Railway Hotel, and Dr. McAdam bought a round of drinks. Several pilots explained how they had hunted for the first downed aircraft all day, saying they had not heard Roy's Mayday transmissions. Dr. McAdam looked at Ernest's head and said, without examining him, in a stunning example of medical negligence, "Nothing to it, Old boy, let's pour some gin on it."[26] They went to bed, and Mary had a fitful sleep because of her pain. When she woke in the middle of the night, she screamed from the pain in her knee and woke Ernest. No one had offered to clean his head wounds, and cerebral fluid soaked his pillow. In the morning, an African doctor came and cleaned them up, putting bandages above Ernest's left ear where the scalp was oozing, disinfecting the wounds on his legs, and bandaging Mary's knee.

Roy organized a car and driver to take Mary and Ernest to Entebbe. The press was waiting, and Ernest, "his head swathed in bandages, and carrying a bunch of bananas and a bottle of gin," quipped, "My luck, she is running very good."[27]

Ernest made a careful statement about the crashes of the Rapide and the Cessna, saying that the Cessna crashed when "Mr. Marsh dived at low altitude to avoid hitting a flying flock of ibises—black and white jungle birds big enough to smash the canopy of the plane."[28] Ernest downplayed the seriousness of the crashes with humor, contributing to his reputation as a masculine hero. Given the severity of his injuries, his bravado was impressive. The next morning Mary stayed in bed, but Ernest busied himself opening masses of cables from around the world. Patrick arrived on a flight from Dar es Salaam at noon, carrying a welcome wad of cash. Patrick told me after he heard about the crash, he thought they might be "discombobulated because they lost everything, so I hired a pilot and flew to Entebbe and brought cash because I thought that might be useful." He found, "they had had a terrible time, and it completely altered the relationship because my dad, I don't know what it was, but there was something wrong." Patrick said, "the physical injuries affected him, but I think it was more of a moral crisis. He felt disappointed in himself. Roy Marsh rescued Mary while he fended for himself. You know it wasn't particularly grace under pressure."[29] Patrick observed his father changed completely after the crashes.[30]

Though brave and uncomplaining, Ernest was suffering, but neither he nor Mary understood the extent of his internal injuries. Weeks later, in Venice, they discovered he had sustained two cracked and impacted discs in his spine, ruptures of his liver and one kidney, paralysis of his sphincter, dislocation of his right arm and shoulder, and a fractured skull.

Roy returned with a new Cessna to fly them to Nairobi, and Ernest flew with him to show faith in his ability as a pilot. Terrified, Mary could not bring herself to board the plane. She held off until the next day when she took a scheduled flight to Nairobi with Patrick on East African Airways. Denis Zaphiro met them at the airport in Nairobi, and they partied into the night.

They set up camp at the new Stanley Hotel in Nairobi, and Ernest read telegrams of congratulation from around the world. A doctor examined Ernest and recommended x-rays, which he refused. The doctor felt Ernest's liver and ordered an immediate halt to his alcohol intake, total rest, and no visitors. The first telegram to arrive in Nairobi touched Mary, for it was from Noel Monks wishing them both well. Obituaries came from newspapers around the world, and Ernest read them with great interest while Mary protested his ghoulish egotism. *Look* magazine sent a stenographer so Ernest could dictate a story about the recent plane crashes.

Ernest was in serious difficulty. He kept bright red urine samples in glasses in the bathroom; the wound on his leg was healing slowly; his hearing was bad in his burned ear; he could not see well, and his new glasses were uncomfortable on his badly bruised nose.[31] Still, he refused medical treatment from the local doctors. Mary busied herself organizing new passports, health certificates, making banking arrangements, and buying food for evening snacks in their room since Ernest did not want to go to restaurants. The dictation sessions became shorter, and Ernest wrote and read less often. He stayed on for a week in Nairobi before joining their long-planned fishing holiday on the Indian Ocean at Shimoni, south of Mombasa. Mary went ahead with Patrick and Henny and set up their beach house.

When Mary and Patrick picked up Ernest, his lack of enthusiasm and silence during the drive back concerned her. Once he arrived at the beach house in Shimoni, he began conversing with whoever was around—repeating old jokes, retelling stories, and expounding his homemade philosophies. But he went fishing only once. He made the veranda his command post and sat there while the others went fishing. He wrote to Bernard Berenson and Harvey Breit, thanking them for their cables of congratulations and updating them on the state of his injuries. He told Berenson his concussion was very strong, and he had been studying it: "Double vision; hearing comes and goes, your capacity for scenting (smelling something) can become acute beyond belief."[32] Ernest told Breit, "Have established some communication between the right hand and the head so can write you by hand. Wrote a lovely letter to [Adriana in] Venice and then found when I read it before mailing, it was about half in Wakamba."[33]

The Percivals left to return home, and, after sad goodbyes, in Mary's words, "a plague began to descend upon us, an evil miasma, a foul-smelling deafening raucous bird of destruction and disaster enfolding us."[34] Ernest became impossible. He smashed the dugout canoe of a neighbor with a piece of driftwood, breaking a paddle and a seat. Mary sent apologies and a payment. On March 3, Ernest convened a conference to determine what bait they had before a fishing trip. Patrick replied they had "squid more or less in order." Ernest yelled he did not permit "more or less in order." He launched a terribly unfair attack on Patrick, and Henny's eyes filled with tears. At the end of Ernest's speech, Patrick declared, "we're leaving." He immediately left the table and began packing their Land Rover. Patrick told me the "whole atmosphere of the trip was ruined by the crashes. I left because I felt I wasn't doing any good there. That was the last time I saw my father."[35]

Two days later, Zaphiro and Mary came in from fishing and found Ernest sitting on the veranda, "a mass of raw, burnt, burned-smelling, flesh."[36] According to Mary, he had tried to help extinguish a bushfire and had fallen into the flames. His legs, stomach, chest, and chin were burned like a hamburger. Mary applied burn-relieving medication and bandaged those parts which could be bandaged. Zaphiro helped as much as he could, especially in the morale-boosting department. Patrick tells a very different story. "Papa's behavior was really strange after the second crash. He actually rolled in the fire, proving that fire didn't mean anything to him. He didn't trip; he did it deliberately." Patrick told me "he rolled in the fire. For all intents and purposes, when he was there at the coast and Shimoni, he behaved as if he were crazy. Take that from someone who knows what it's like to be crazy."[37]

It was time to leave Africa, and with the help of Zaphiro and some of the safari crew, Mary managed to get Ernest and their luggage aboard *The Africa*, a beautiful white cruise ship based in Trieste. The ship's doctor visited their stateroom three times a day with whatever pain relievers he had on board. The medication was ineffective, and Ernest assuaged his jangled nerves by abusing Mary. Though she felt sorry for his predicament, she could not tolerate his cruelty, and she escaped after breakfast to the decks, the swimming pool, the air-conditioned public rooms, and the bars. All the happiness of the previous months vanished. Ernest wrote a long letter to Hotch describing his injuries. He also complained about Mary, saying he had never seen her be kind except to the servants, and he had never seen her in a good temper in the morning. "I guess being an only child known within the family as 'love of God' is not the best training for a barracks life." She had been lovely for four months on the safari and most of the time was quite brave and indulgent. "She will sort out okay. But I married a woman one-half Kraut, and one-half Irish, and that makes a merciless cross, but a lovely woman."[38]

TWENTY-SEVEN

The Swedish Thing

March 1954–February 1955

D istraught at the news reports of the Hemingways' deaths, Adriana felt her heart had turned to stone. She wrote to Mary, "You can't imagine how many things one gets to think, on the death of someone one loves. I saw you, gay and smiling, picking up flowers at the Finca, and riding with us in the car, and visiting your parents." Now she knew Mary was alive, Adriana wanted to tell her "how much and truly I love you, Mary . . . The kiss I send you is strong like a stone, big like the ocean, and true like my love for you."[1] This is not the letter one would expect from the lover of one's husband and is more evidence Adriana did not have an adulterous relationship with Ernest.

Ernest wrote to Adriana, claiming, "I love you more than being alive, more than the moon and the sky, and for as long as I live . . . Both times I died, I had only one thought: I would not wish it in order not to make any sorrow to Adriana." Perhaps the concussion caused Ernest to misstate wildly Mary's feelings about his love for Adriana. He told Adriana her beautiful letter touched Mary, and she had always thought of Ernest's love for Adriana as a "cosa sagrada" (a sacred thing). "It was just something that struck me like lightning at the crossroads in Latisana in the rain."[2] In fact, Mary thought he was a silly old man besotted with a teenager, and she had long waited for his infatuation to burn out.

Adriana wrote using more measured tones than Ernest: "I felt guilty of not having told you many times and with more energy that I love you and that you are a companion, a friend, a father."[3]

Mary and Ernest were both exhausted when they arrived in Venice on March 23, and they went to bed soon after they checked into the Gritti Palace Hotel. Federico Kechler arranged for Ernest to see several specialists to diagnose the extent of his injuries and prescribe more effective painkillers. Ernest was still miserable, but as Mary recalled, he "decided that I should have a break from my job as bumbling nurse and whipping boy for his frayed nerves."[4] Ernest organized a Paris holiday for Mary from his bedside. She felt somewhat guilty about leaving her battered husband to recover on his own, but she knew Ernest was desperate to see Adriana. While she didn't mind, she had no interest in watching Ernest fawn over his young imaginary lover. Before Mary left, she and Ernest had a farewell lunch at Harry's Bar. On their walk to the restaurant, Ernest noticed an antique necklace in a shop window. Mary loved the piece, and he bought it for her. Employing his practiced technique, Ernest made amends for his boorish behavior.

Mary checked in at the Ritz in Paris, and the staff fussed over her and inquired after Ernest. She did her best to buoy Ernest's spirits by writing to him about how the staff loved him and how they'd been sad when they heard about the plane crashes but never believed that he was dead. Not much was happening in Paris over Holy Week, and Mary decided she would have more fun celebrating Easter in London. She checked into the Dorchester and visited with Joy Milne from her Chelsea days, and Jacqui Kennish, who had worked with her at *Time*, and spent a long weekend with Alan and Lucy Moorehead. Mary continued to write affectionate letters to Ernest, describing how anxious friends had been at the news of the plane crashes.

On her return to Paris, Mary had tea with Pamela Churchill at her flat near the Seine, dined at Maxim's one evening, and met Ernest's old friend Rupert Belleville, a former test pilot, to begin the drive to meet Ernest in Madrid. Rupert was an aggressive driver, and Mary could not help but tell him to slow down. He cheerfully ignored her pleas and raced along the motorways and through the countryside, careening around corners and overtaking trucks up steep hills. Mary finally resigned herself to his risky driving and tried to relax. After a few days, she found she enjoyed whizzing around trucks and buses into oncoming traffic, "as if on a roller-coaster gone berserk."[5]

Rupert was a charming companion, knowledgeable about bullfighting and the customs of Spain, and he distracted Mary with constantly changing scenery and activities. Despite the daily gaiety, Mary worried about Ernest and looked forward to meeting him. When she next saw her husband, seated under the glittering dome of the dining room at the Palace Hotel in Madrid, Mary's delight turned to distress. New wrinkles lined his face, and he did not look or act as if he were much improved. Though he had visited with Adriana during Mary's absence, he was depressed. Adriana had been shocked to see Ernest's withered face, the papery skin on his hands, and his lack of energy. He told her he had fought for six days to stay alive to see her, and he broke down in tears, telling her, "now you can say you saw Hemingway crying."[6]

Ernest had told Mary his internal injuries were healing, but when she saw him in Madrid, he described the grueling ordeal he had suffered undergoing medical treatments in Venice. He waited on cold tables for x-rays, had his bladder bruised by a careless doctor, and put up with a general lack of concern about his high blood pressure, which was now 180 over 120.

Ed Hotchner visited Ernest at the Gritti Palace on May 2, six weeks after the crashes. He found him reading through a pile of his own obituaries. Hotch had last seen Ernest just before the African trip, and Ernest's altered appearance shocked him. He had aged significantly in the last five months. Most of his hair had burned off, and what the fire left had turned white. His singed beard was also white, and "he appeared to have diminished somewhat; I don't mean physically diminished, but some of the aura of indomitableness seemed to have gone out of him."[7]

On June 6, Mary and Ernest boarded the *Francesco Morosini* at Genoa to begin their voyage to Havana. They took separate cabins because Ernest could not sleep and spent half the night reading. Mary found the ocean crossing one of the dullest she had made, and it didn't help that Ernest was in a foul mood much of the time. One evening, he nagged at her in the ship's dining room about his missing pocketknife. She couldn't remember in which of their many bags she had packed the knife. Before the startled diners, Ernest yelled, "You are a thief." Mortified, she resisted the temptation to explain to the others she had mislaid his knife. Mary was so disturbed by Ernest's unfairness, she wrote him a long letter, pleading with him to remember how he used to understand justice.[8]

After thirteen months of traveling in Europe and Africa, they finally arrived home, but before she could settle in, Mary received alarming news that her father was in severe pain. He had again refused to take the medication prescribed to relieve his prostate cancer. She packed, took a plane to New Orleans, and caught a bus to Gulfport. Mary's father was in the hospital and doctors had inserted a drainage system to deal with the fluids accumulating because he refused penicillin. A tube from his abdomen connected to a rubber sack which had to be emptied often. Mary spelled off her mother so she could get some sleep. She wrote to Ernest describing the scene and her father's "saint-like acceptance of the ministrations." Ernest empathized, suggesting her father should stay in the hospital regardless of the cost. "He's going to die, and he should die with some dignity and some regard for other people."[9] Mary found a nursing home that could accommodate her parents, but the rates were higher than she expected. Ernest told her to proceed and stay as long as her parents needed her. He advised Mary to drink as much gin as she required to get through the nightmare, for she could sweat out the alcohol afterward.

Ernest wrote to Mary of their time in Africa. "Kittner, we had such a lovely time in Africa, and you remember the noises of the beasts in the night and how we would sleep in the tiny cot quite comfortably and really love each other."[10] It relieved Mary to hear Ernest was in a better frame of mind. She appreciated his generosity toward her parents, especially since he had never bothered much with his own mother when she was ailing. Feelings of guilt assailed Mary about her parents' condition, for she knew her visit heartened them. Her father's appetite improved, his pain declined, and he was cheerful in his daughter's presence. Adeline made Mary feel she had neglected them. Although Mary felt defensive because she had not tried to accommodate them at the Finca, the fact was they did not understand Spanish and could not have communicated with the people who would have surrounded them. Their presence would have imposed a terrible strain on her relationship with Ernest. He was difficult enough to manage on his own, and she had made a rational decision to keep her parents in long-term care facilities. With a heavy heart, Mary donated her father's book collection to the local library and sold or gave away their furniture.

Mary traveled back to Cuba, and Ernest met her at the airport bearing a cold daiquiri. The next day was Ernest's fifty-fifth birthday, and she accompanied him into Havana early in the morning so that he could accept Cuba's highest award for civilians, the Order of Carlos Manuel de Céspedes. Ernest did not want to support the Batista government and declined an invitation to attend a ceremony at the presidential palace. Instead, they made the presentation in a low-key ceremony at the Havana yacht club. Ernest replied to the undersecretary of state's speech by underlining his admiration for the Cuban *pueblo*, the ordinary people. A boisterous lunch followed at the Floridita. Mary told her parents Ernest deserved the medal after all he had done for Cuba.[11]

A few nights later, Mary attended a party given by the British ambassador. She discussed their African safari with Edward "Ted" Scott, a New Zealander who was a columnist for the *Havana Post*, the local English-language newspaper. Mary mentioned they had eaten the tenderloins of the lions they had killed and said the meat was delicious. This shocked the reporter, who told her it was a barbaric thing to do. She rebuffed his verbal assault, calling Scott "a stupid British colonial." A few days later, Scott criticized Mary in his column, saying he could take this insult from a woman but "he would never stand still for it if it had come from her husband."[12] Ernest became irritated, but Mary told him to ignore it. In a few days, Scott attacked again, this time blaming Ernest for Mary's offensive behavior and challenging Ernest to defend his honor with a sword. Given his injuries, Ernest could not accept the challenge, and he wrote a cutting letter instead. Scott persisted and sent a radiologist-friend, Dr. Pedro Sanchez Pessino, to present Ernest with a formal challenge to a duel. Ernest refused to apologize and said Scott was not a suitable opponent for a duel. He wrote, "aside from other considerations, my obligation at this time is to regain my health . . . If any friends of Mr. Scott consider that to be an act of cowardice, they are at liberty to think so."[13]

News of the dispute reached the desk of J. Edgar Hoover, Director of the FBI. The legal attaché in Havana reported Pessino had challenged Hemingway to a duel. In his letter rejecting Pessino's challenge, Hemingway "gave as his reasons the fact that he is in ill health and has a lot of writing to do. Hemingway further stated that he felt sure that a court of honor would not consider this cowardice on his part."[14]

◆

Life returned to normal at the Finca, and Ernest improved to the point he could resume fishing on *Pilar*. He wrote in the mornings, standing at the bookcase, and worked on his memories of Africa. Ava Gardner came to Havana with Luis Miguel, and they went fishing with Ernest and Mary on *Pilar* and came to lunch at the Finca, following which, according to René, Ava swam nude in the pool.[15] Mary told her mother the lunch was fancy, for she had prepared fresh lobster soup, a peppery hot Indian curry with turkey, and ice cream with lingonberries. Mary enjoyed working in her kitchen at the Finca and she became a serious cook, filling her journal with recipes or serving ideas from restaurants they visited. She later told an interviewer, "I am a great cook. I cook Creole, Cuban style, Spanish, French, Italian, and American. I learned Chinese cooking in Cuba because Ernest liked Chinese food."[16]

◆

The head of the Kenyan game department sent an account for the fees the Hemingways owed for hunting in Kimana swamp, a detail they had neglected to deal with after the plane crashes. The bill for killing fifty-one animals was $58.57. Mary worried, as she wrote the check, the Kenyans undervalued the animals' lives.

◆

Eight months after the crashes, Ernest was still having trouble concentrating, and he told Bernard Berenson he was working "at about one half the capacity I should have, but everything is better all the time."[17] Malcolm Cowley, reflecting on the period, wrote that Ernest "began to lose his sense of reality. Why? We aren't ever going to know. It may have been drinking too much, it may have been early senility," but he was "pretty sure that the process was helped along by his getting knocked on the head so much, in one accident after another; he was punchy like an old fighter. The airplane accident in Africa proved to be the final blow."[18]

Buck Lanham told Carlos Baker that Ernest's decline began with the plane crashes. In his letters to Buck over the years, Ernest reported his medical condition, giving his weight, blood pressure ranges, and cholesterol readings. Buck had a fair understanding of Ernest's evolving medical condition. Buck told Baker, "in no circumstances should he be judged by the last two years when his great body was disintegrating, and the first tendrils of the fog of death were wrapping about his magnificent mind. All the aberrances of that time should be understood and forgiven. Much of Ernest Hemingway died in Africa in the two plane crashes."[19]

Mary was sleeping in on the morning of October 28, 1954, when Ernest, who had been working since dawn, came to her bedroom and tapped her arm. As she woke up, he told her the United Press had phoned and told him he had won "the Swedish thing."

"Hells bells. You mean the prize, the Nobel Prize?" Mary asked as she clung to him, hugging and kissing. Ernest smiled sheepishly.[20]

Mary realized they would have visitors, and she dressed and went to see René about organizing a reception. Mary reported to her parents, "The house was bursting with reporters, photographers, film photographers, television people . . . good friends, mere acquaintances, hangers-on, and strangers who guessed it would be a good place to come for free drinks."[21] About a dozen people came for lunch, and Ernest spent hours talking to journalists. In the afternoon, he gave a brief speech in Spanish, proclaiming good-naturedly he was a man without politics; he liked the fighting cocks, the Philharmonic orchestra, and the ordinary people of Cuba. He said he wanted to give the Nobel medal to "Our Señora the Virgen de Cobre," the revered figure of "Our Lady of Charity" found in the Basilica of El Cobre. The small statue is one of the island's most treasured figures, representing hope and salvation in the face of misfortune. After this solemn announcement, Ernest joked the prize money had not yet arrived, so there was no point in breaking into his house. He told the local press he doubted he could travel to Stockholm to accept the prize in person because of the injuries he had suffered in the plane crashes.

The day was long and grueling, and in the late afternoon, Mary slipped away to the silence of the pool and swam thirty laps. Refreshed, she found Ernest sitting in his chair, reading telegrams, and sipping gin with coconut water. Mary performed Gershwin's song, "Somebody Loves Me, I wonder Who?" gliding around the room until she settled in Ernest's lap. Ernest worried he had been corny in his telephone interview with Harvey Breit of the *New York Times*. Mary had listened to his replies, and she reassured him it was "perfectly good, straight stuff."

The next day, the Swedish consul in Havana and his wife, accompanied by two Swedish journalists who had flown in from New York, came for a simple ceremony in the Finca library. The consul conveyed the news: Ernest was the forty-seventh winner of the Nobel Prize for Literature. They stayed for martinis and a lunch lasting until 6 P.M. During the rest of the week, Ernest and Mary responded to the letters of congratulation from friends around the world. Despite their hard work, they could not answer even half the messages. The flow of well-wishers and tourists was never-ending. Visitors routinely ignored a sign on the gate of the Finca announcing only invited guests were welcome. They felt exposed and unhappy with their loss of privacy and escaped in Mary's yellow convertible, driving to a fishing village where Gregorio met them and took them to *Pilar*, anchored in Paraíso. In the coming days, Mary fished with Gregorio around the coral heads toward Levisa Island. It delighted her to be on the water in their favorite anchorage where life followed a simple rhythm of fishing and swimming, exploring beaches, and eating Gregorio's delectable dishes. One day, Ernest went with Gregorio to the nearby town of La Mulata and returned with supplies, mail, and magazines, including a copy of *Time* with Ernest on the cover. The story was pleasant and accurate, and Ernest seemed to relax. Mary told her parents Ernest was resting, escaping from people, "and becoming more tranquil every day—and of course, I love this life. No problems except wind and weather . . . Paradise."[22]

On the evening of December 11, they listened to radio reports of the Nobel Prize ceremony in Stockholm. Despite the poor reception, they heard the US ambassador read Ernest's brief speech. "No writer who knows the great writers who did not receive the prize can accept it other than with humility . . . [The writer] should always strive for something that has never been done or that others have tried and failed. Then sometimes, with great luck, he will succeed."[23]

In mid-January, Mary was happy to plant roses, nasturtiums, African tulips and tend her flourishing vegetable garden. She also typed her African journal. Ernest was back at work on his African story, and they spent two happy weeks. On January 30, a phone call from the nursing home informed Mary her father had collapsed with "a cerebral accident." Mary instructed the staff to take him to the hospital and asked them to provide all necessary care. She wrote to her mother, telling her, "whatever things or services, large or small, you or Papa may want, please don't hesitate to get them . . . You know that Ernest wants Papa to have the best possible attention and care and expects to pay for it."[24]

Mary tried to buy a ticket to fly to New Orleans but couldn't get a flight for two days. When she finally reached the hospital, she found her father had regained the use of his right arm, but he was not lucid. The next day, Mary told Ernest her father was becoming more coherent, "still a living organism, breath moving in and out . . . A faint, sad resemblance to my father."[25] By telephone, Ernest advised Mary to keep her sanity by treating the event as if she were a reporter covering a story.

She found this constructive advice, especially since her mother called upon her to read Christian Science tracts to her ailing father, who could not understand them.

Once her father stabilized, Mary flew back to Havana. A few days later, the nursing home called to inform Mary her father was fading fast. He passed away before she could get to New Orleans. Mary traveled to Gulfport, and the following day attended a twenty-minute service with her mother in the undertaker's chapel. All her muscles were shaking, but she couldn't express her genuine feelings to her mother, who spoke only in Christian Science platitudes. When she was alone, she remembered how much she loved her father. "For years and years, I thought my father was the handsomest, best-dressed, best-educated, and most intelligent man in the whole world."[26] From their days spent together canoeing and camping when she was a young girl, he had given her "the assurance that men and women can be friends without antagonism based on sex."[27] He was an innocent who believed, perhaps naïvely, that humanity could improve, and he was hopeful, optimistic, and enterprising. It relieved Mary he was free from his painful cancer, but she missed him terribly.

ABOVE LEFT: Mary's mother, Adeline Beehler, enjoyed attending fancy dress balls when she worked in a state senator's office in the 1880s. Later she became a Christian Scientist and believed in reading religious tracts to ill persons rather than seeking active medical treatment. Unfortunately, her beliefs resulted in Tom enduring needless pain when he developed prostate cancer. ABOVE RIGHT: Mary's father, Thomas (Tom) Welsh, was a college-educated lumberman who could recite *Hamlet* by heart. In 1889 he wore his first tailor-made suit for this photo. BELOW: Tom Welsh used the steamboat *Northland* to pull log booms across Leech Lake, and the boat ferried passengers on excursions across the lake on weekends. Mary spent her childhood summers aboard the *Northland* with her father. In the evenings, when it was moored, the boat became an island of high culture in the backwoods of Minnesota. Mozart sonatas and Chopin piano concertos floated through the windows from the wind-up gramophone in the salon, while Thomas and Mary sat in wicker chairs and read from the ship's library. *All three images from* How It Was.

TOP: Paul Bunyan and his blue ox, Babe, stand in the center of Mary's hometown of Bemidji, Minnesota, signifying the importance of the lumber industry. Mary escaped from the land of the lumberjacks to pursue her dream of becoming a journalist. *Photo courtesy of the author.* CENTER: The Welsh residence in Bemidji, where Mary spent her childhood, is now converted to apartments. *Photo courtesy of the author.* BELOW: The Canadian millionaire and friend of Churchill, Lord Beaverbrook, pursued Mary romantically and gave her a job as a reporter at his London *Daily Express*, the most widely circulated newspaper in the English language. *Photo from Alamy Stock.*

Mary and her second husband,
Noel Monks, photographed
in their war correspondents'
uniforms. Noel reported for
the British Army, and Mary
was the only woman accredited
with the Royal Air Force at
the beginning of the war. *Photo
from* How It Was.

Mary was one of the first women
reporting on foreign affairs for
Time-Life, and here she wears her
US Army war correspondent's
uniform. *Photo from the Ernest
Hemingway Photograph Collection, John F.
Kennedy Presidential Library and Museum.*

Mary described wartime London as "a Garden of Eden" for single women. "There was a serpent hanging from every tree and street lamp, offering tempting gifts and companionship, which could push away loneliness, and warm, if temporary, affections." *Photo from the Ernest Hemingway Photograph Collection, John F. Kennedy Presidential Library and Museum.*

Mary working at the *Time* offices in London in front of a bomb-damaged window. The war came close, and like many of her friends, Mary narrowly escaped death or injury. *Photo from* How It Was.

ABOVE LEFT: Mary dated the American novelist Irwin Shaw for months, reviewing his short stories and appreciating his technique. She described him to her friend Bill Walton as "the best lay in Europe." *Photo from the Library of Congress, copyright Alfredo Valente.* ABOVE RIGHT: Ernest Hemingway was wearing a massive beard in this photo for his US Army identity card. This is how he appeared when he first met Mary. Ernest believed the beard had protected his skin against cancer from the searing sun of Cuba. *Photo from the Ernest Hemingway Photograph Collection, John F. Kennedy Presidential Library and Museum.* RIGHT AND BELOW: Captain Mary Welsh Monk's US Army identity card was issued on May 9, 1944. Standing at five feet three inches and weighing one hundred twenty pounds, Mary was likely one of the most petite captains in the army. She met Ernest seventeen days after this photo was taken. *Photo from* How It Was.

ABOVE LEFT: Ernest Hemingway after he shaved off his massive beard. Mary liked the face which emerged. *Photo from the Ernest Hemingway Photograph Collection, John F. Kennedy Presidential Library and Museum.* ABOVE RIGHT: Mary reports on the training exercises of the Local Home Guard in the west of England. *Photo from* How It Was. BELOW: Ernest Hemingway with Col. Buck Lanham in the Huertgen forest. Ernest wrote incessantly to Mary of the danger he faced each day. He sought to prove his manliness through his writing—despite his impotence. Mary eventually succumbed to his insistent pleading. *Photo from the Ernest Hemingway Photograph Collection, John F. Kennedy Presidential Library and Museum.*

TOP: Mary and Ernest on their wedding day in Havana on March 14, 1946. *Photo from the Ernest Hemingway Photograph Collection, John F. Kennedy Presidential Library and Museum.* CENTER: Ernest piloting *Pilar* and Mary following in the *Tin Kid* past the Morro Castle guarding Havana's harbor. Mary became a skilled and fearless boater in Cuba. *Photo from the Ernest Hemingway Photograph Collection, John F. Kennedy Presidential Library and Museum; copyright Roberto Herrero Sotolongo.* BOTTOM: Mary and Pauline, Ernest's second wife, in San Francisco in November 1947. Pauline showed Mary a swell time, according to Patrick Hemingway, Pauline's son, who was also present for the visit. Mary and Pauline developed a close friendship as graduates of the same alma mater—marriage to Ernest. *Photo from the Ernest Hemingway Photograph Collection, John F. Kennedy Presidential Library and Museum.*

ABOVE: Mary and Ernest stand before the front door of their estate, the Finca Vigia. The Cuban government has carefully preserved the estate as a museum to Ernest Hemingway. *Photo from the Ernest Hemingway Photograph Collection, John F. Kennedy Presidential Library and Museum.* BELOW: The dining room at the Finca with a replica of Miró's *The Farm* on the sideboard. Everything is just as it was when the Hemingways lived there. *Photo courtesy of the author.*

TOP: The tower that Mary designed and built for Ernest at the Finca in 1949. She thought he could work there, free from the domestic noises of the house, but Ernest missed the sound of René sweeping, and he returned to work in his bedroom, standing before a bookcase. *Photo courtesy of the author.* CENTER: The view of Havana and the sea in the distance from the tower. *Photo courtesy of the author.* BOTTOM: Mary and Ernest relax on *Pilar* after fishing. Mary became a competent fisher with Ernest's encouragement, and he appreciated the fact that, unlike his third wife, Martha Gellhorn, Mary loved being at sea on *Pilar*. *Photo from the Ernest Hemingway Photograph Collection, John F. Kennedy Presidential Library and Museum.*

Ernest and Mary carry puppies in Jai-Alai baskets. They had no children, but they raised many cats and dogs to whom they gave their love and affection. *Photo from the Ernest Hemingway Photograph Collection, John F. Kennedy Presidential Library and Museum.*

ABOVE: Mary and Ernest on *Pilar*'s flybridge. Mary loved the boat, thought it had a unique personality, and she sang into the wind when she was at the controls by herself. *Photo from the Ernest Hemingway Photograph Collection, John F. Kennedy Presidential Library and Museum.* LEFT: Mary's calming influence upon Ernest at Sun Valley. Mary knew Ernest better than anyone, and he was psychologically dependent upon her. According to his psychiatrist, Ernest depended on Mary but denied it for fear he would appear weak. *Photo from the Ernest Hemingway Photograph Collection, John F. Kennedy Presidential Library and Museum.*

TOP: Mary and Ernest lounging on *Pilar*. *Photo from the Ernest Hemingway Photograph Collection, John F. Kennedy Presidential Library and Museum.* CENTER: Mary and Ernest in Cortina, December 1948. Mary loved skiing in the Dolomites. *Photo from the Ernest Hemingway Photograph Collection, John F. Kennedy Presidential Library and Museum.* BOTTTOM: Ernest and Mary in the bar of the S.S. *Flandre* on yet another transatlantic crossing. *Photo from the Ernest Hemingway Photograph Collection, John F. Kennedy Presidential Library and Museum; copyright Jacques Lucas.*

Mary, Ernest, and Adriana in Venice. Mary put up with Ernest's infatuation with the teenaged countess, but as we shall see, it was not easy for her. *Photo from the Ernest Hemingway Photograph Collection, John F. Kennedy Presidential Library and Museum.*

TOP: Locanda Cipriani on Torcello, the famous inn visited by royalty and movie stars over the years, stands in the evening at the end of a canal. CENTER: The Santa Fosca suite at the Locanda Cipriani, where Mary and Ernest stayed in November 1948, is unchanged to this day. Ernest wrote about making love to Mary before the beech logs burning in the fireplace and said he had "the loveliest time Papa ever knew." BOTTOM: The obelisk marks the place on the bank of the Piave River where an exploding Austrian mortar shell wounded Ernest Hemingway in June 1918. Ernest visited the site and buried a ten thousand lira note in the soil where he nearly died. *All three images courtesy of the author.*

Mary and Ernest relaxing by the pool at the Finca. The pool was cooled with iced water and made life bearable in the hot and humid climate. *Photo from the Ernest Hemingway Photograph Collection, John F. Kennedy Presidential Library and Museum; copyright Louis Hamburg.*

Adriana and Gianfranco Ivancich beside the pool at the Finca, November 1951. *Photo from the Ernest Hemingway Photograph Collection, John F. Kennedy Presidential Library and Museum; copyright Manzana.*

Mary and one of their cats wait for Ernest to get off the phone. *Photo from the Ernest Hemingway Photograph Collection, John F. Kennedy Presidential Library and Museum.*

Mary and Ernest examine the horns of an antelope he has just shot on their African safari in November 1953. *Photo from the Ernest Hemingway Photograph Collection, John F. Kennedy Presidential Library and Museum.*

Mary feeds Baa from a baby bottle in October 1953. Mary loved the tiny gazelle they adopted in Kenya and felt anguish and guilt when she learned of his death. *Photo from the Ernest Hemingway Photograph Collection, John F. Kennedy Presidential Library and Museum.*

Fidel Castro and Ernest after Fidel won Ernest's silver medal for catching the largest marlin in the annual Ernest Hemingway fishing contest in May 1960. This was the only time the two men met. *Photo from* How It Was.

Mary and Gianfranco at the Floridita in Havana. Mary sang like Edith Piaf with a vibrating alto voice, and she often performed her renditions of folk melodies for the amusement of Ernest and their friends. *Photo from* How It Was.

Ernest is immortalized in a bronze statue standing at his favorite place at the bar of the Floridita. The bar is often crowded with patrons ordering Ernest's favorite drink, Papa Doblès, while a wandering mariachi group performs local music. *Photo courtesy of the author.*

Yousuf Karsh's informal portrait of Mary and Ernest in front of the Finca, 1957. Karsh and his wife visited the Finca to capture the great writer in an iconic portrait. *Photo from* How It Was.

ABOVE: Wearing her hair platinum blonde for Ernest's delight, Mary feeds him an olive.
BELOW: Mary at the Finca's dining room table with Miró's *The Farm* behind her. *Both photos from the Ernest Hemingway Photograph Collection, John F. Kennedy Presidential Library and Museum.*

ABOVE LEFT: The Hemingway house located outside of Ketchum, Idaho. Ernest shot himself in the vestibule. ABOVE RIGHT: The view of the Big Wood River from the Hemingway house with the Sawtooth Mountains in the background. BELOW LEFT: The Christiania Restaurant in Ketchum where Ernest ate his last meal. Ernest thought FBI agents were trailing him, and Mary tried to persuade him they were merely traveling salesmen and ordered a bottle of Chateauneuf de Pâpes to divert him. BELOW RIGHT: Ernest and Mary's corner table at the Christiania Restaurant. *All four photos courtesy of the author.*

ABOVE LEFT: Bill Walton briefs JFK in the oval office, possibly concerning Mary's travel to Cuba to retrieve Ernest's manuscripts, correspondence, and art. *Photo from the Ernest Hemingway Photograph Collection, John F. Kennedy Presidential Library and Museum.* ABOVE RIGHT: Fredrick March, Mary, JFK, Jackie Kennedy, and Mrs. George Marshall at the White House dinner for Nobel Laureates on April 29, 1962. *Photo from the Ernest Hemingway Photograph Collection, John F. Kennedy Presidential Library and Museum.* BELOW: The statue dedicated to Ernest's memory outside the Bullring in Pamplona, Spain. Mary and Bill Walton attended the ceremony on July 6, 1968, and Walton described the piece as "very primitive art." *Photo courtesy of the author.*

Mary chatting with Fidel Castro in Havana in July 1977. Mary told reporters that Fidel "is just the sort of man I like." *Photo from the Ernest Hemingway Photograph Collection, John F. Kennedy Presidential Library and Museum.*

Connie Ernst Bessie and Mary at Mary's seventieth birthday party at Peter and Susan Buckley's apartment on April 5, 1978. *Photo courtesy of Susan Buckley.*

Mary reading *The Old Man and the Sea* outside the Ketchum house on a sunny day. Mary typed and read the manuscript each day from the beginning while Ernest was writing it, and she suggested that Ernest let the old man live instead of allowing him to die. *Photo from the Ernest Hemingway Photograph Collection, John F. Kennedy Presidential Library and Museum.*

ABOVE: Mary's grave is between Ernest's identical slab and the small stone marking the grave of their old hunting buddy Taylor "Beartracks" Williams. The trees Mary planted after Ernest's death are now forty feet tall, and their roots penetrate the earth. In the distance, the jagged teeth of the Sawtooth Mountains witness the brevity of human existence. BELOW: *Pilar*'s final resting place on the grounds of the Finca. Mary wanted to sink the vessel at sea, but the Cuban authorities had other plans for the iconic boat. *Both images courtesy of the author.*

LEFT: Valerie Hemingway and I in front of her house in Bozeman, Montana, September 8, 2019. We were on our way to Ted Turner's Montana Grill for a dinner of buffalo accompanied by Decoy merlot and more talk about Mary and Ernest.

BELOW: H. R. "Stoney" Stoneback and I in front of Stoney's house near Poughkeepsie, New York, June 16, 2017. Stoney and I had talked almost all through the night about Mary and Ernest. *Both images courtesy of the author.*

ABOVE: Bonifacio Brass and I in front of the Locanda Cipriani, October 17, 2016. Bonifacio was a gracious host and shared family stories of Ernest and Mary. BELOW: The memorial erected by the fishermen of Cojímar in memory of Ernest Hemingway. *Both images courtesy of the author.*

TWENTY-EIGHT

She Knows How to be Lazy as a Cat

March 1955–September 1956

N ow Mary had to deal with her mother. Adeline was lonely and dissatisfied with everything: her accommodation, her food, her neighbors, and the behavior of the staff at the nursing home. She wanted to move to Chicago, but it was impractical. Mary persuaded her to remain in Gulfport where she had friends who visited her almost every day to chat about Christian Science or read aloud from religious tracts. Mary knew her mother was depressed, but there was little she could do about it. Surrounded by the Christian Science practitioners, Mary wrote to Ernest that she missed "his sharp, rich fine head—and our jokes and your lovely built-in shit detector and your perpetual motion pomposity-repeller, and especially your piety protector—you don't like pious people, and neither do I."[1] She was finding it harder to put up with the "fanaticism, the prejudice, the repetition in which they take such comfort, and the really remarkable non-sequiturs." Two days later, in preparation for her trip home, she wrote, "Got my hair cut and washed, and think you and Mr. S. might like it. Bless you, both, enormous blessings— x xxxx xo to you both and ooo."[2]

Soon after Mary's return to Cuba, Ernest's eldest son Jack visited the Finca. He was struggling to make a living and support his young family, which now included two daughters, Muffet and Margot (who later renamed herself Margaux when she learned she had been conceived under the influence of that magnificent wine). Jack wanted the advice of his father about his career prospects and hoped to get a loan. His father's appearance worried him, for he did not look well and was overweight. The Nobel Prize had brought him little satisfaction, and Ernest complained it had reduced his privacy.

Jack found his father's mood as much changed as his appearance. He was less gentle and warm, more often "plaintive, occasionally truculent, often so with Mary, and with an underlying bitterness."[3] After lunch one day, Jack asked to have a private conversation with his father, and Mary left to nap. Jack could finally bring up the real reason for his journey to Cuba, and he complained, "I just can't seem to make a decent living. Not enough to support my family."[4] He told Ernest he should never have left the army because it was so hard outside. Ernest was unsympathetic and told him if he kept changing jobs, he would find himself unemployable. This remark hurt because Jack was thirty-three years old and had already faced business failure—he broke down weeping and said he sometimes wondered whether it was worth going on living. Ernest replied, "The one thing you must promise me you will never do, and I will promise you the same, is that neither one of us will ever shoot himself like grandfather. Promise me, and then I'll promise you."[5] They exchanged promises.

Ernest agreed to provide some financial help, but not before he clarified he had significant financial problems of his own. However, Ernest said Jack needn't worry about his long-term future because he had provided for him in his will. Since Patrick and Greg had already inherited substantial sums from their mother, Pauline, Jack would receive half of Ernest's estate, and Pat and Greg would share the balance. Ernest did not mention Mary, and Jack presumed his father thought they would die together.

◆

Two weeks later, Leland Hayward and Peter Viertel came to make the final arrangements for the film version of *The Old Man and the Sea*. Peter recalled Mary "looked somewhat worn, the skin on her face prematurely wrinkled from exposure to the strong sun."[6] Ernest took Leland and Peter fishing on *Pilar*, and they caught three marlins. A photo showed the three of them posing with their catches. Peter kept the photo on the mantel in his study, and when he looked at it, he noticed Ernest looked twenty years older than his age. "His eyes already have the detached look that people acquire as they near the end of their lives," and "his gray hair and his stooped posture are that of a much older man."[7]

Peter had finally agreed to write the screenplay, and he stayed in the guest house at the Finca for two weeks to familiarize himself with the setting. Mary acted as his interpreter on visits to Cojímar to interview fishermen and get a feel for the place. Ernest booked a room for Peter above La Terraza bar in Cojímar. A dense cloud of mosquitos made sleep impossible, and when he rose at 5 A.M., he watched "the spectacle of the dozen or so men carrying lanterns down the dusty road" to their boats.[8] The scene made its way into the eventual movie.

❖

Mary's mother now became determined to move to Minneapolis, so much so that the nursing home proprietors began encouraging Mary to move her. Ernest agreed with the plan, and to Mary's relief, Bill Walton wrote asking to come for a visit during the time she would be away. "Dearest Welshie, I see light ahead and have a deep burning hope that I'll be able to see you two, to eat mangoes, go swimming, paint some bamboo, and talk endlessly. I miss your talk more than anything. Answer quick and true."

In Gulfport, Mary soon became overwhelmed with her mother, who had great faith in what Mary considered gibberish. Mary described her frustration to Ernest, "But the C. S. nonsense. Mother prates, 'infinite mind directs each day, all we should note, do and say.' Mumble-jumble God of the Congo couldn't do better. I wonder how Mrs. Eddy didn't get them started worshipping testicles or trees." Mary mused, "The Romans, arranging chicken entrails for divination were a cut above Mrs. Hale, divining the cause of mother's constipation. 'It's a thought of resistance,' she said, 'we must work on that.'"[9]

Mary longed to be home. "Ah Lamb, I'll be happy to get back to you and away from this never-never land. I just hope my good manners will prevail, and I'll be able to finish it out without blasphemy or violence." She gave most of Adeline's old things to her "vulture friends," bought clothing suitable for the northern climate, and traveled with her by train to Minneapolis. She took her to the home of Mrs. Kerr, a Christian Scientist, who ran a small boardinghouse. Mary's mother seemed pleased with the new arrangements, and Mary prepared to return to Cuba. She wrote to Ernest, "I washed my hair in Gulfport today and, with my suntan still holding on skin, I think you would like it—lighter—it looks to me—than you ever saw, and sort of rippling—and quite long." [10]

◆

Filming of the fishing scenes for *The Old Man and the Sea* began off Cojímar on September 1. Four old skiffs of the type Santiago had used left the harbor, followed by *Pilar*, with Ernest at the helm, carrying camera operators and assistants. Another boat carried four camera crew. For the next two weeks, the fishermen tried to catch a marlin large enough to portray Santiago's giant fish. The weather was rainy and often the sky was too dark to permit good photography. Despite these conditions, each morning Mary picked up twenty-seven pre-made lunches at La Terraza and delivered them in the *Tin Kid* to the six boats twelve to sixteen miles offshore. Despite the efforts of the fishermen of Cojímar, they caught only two small marlins. Ernest had wasted his time, but he complimented Mary on her hard work in supporting the effort.

◆

Over the years, Ernest changed his will depending on who was in or out of favor. Two wills, including the last one, were holographs handwritten by him. The others were careful legal documents prepared by his lawyers Maurice Speiser or Alfred Rice. Ernest handwrote his last will and testament, borrowing from some legal examples. [11] On September 17, 1955, Ernest signed the will, witnessed by his old sparring partner from New York City, George Brown, the Finca's majordomo, René Villarreal, and Mary's maid, Lola Richards. Before Ernest wrote his last will, he asked Mary if she would look after the kids, who were, by then, men. She assured him she would do whatever she could and forgot about it. [12]

Ernest gave all his property, "real, personal, literary or mixed, absolutely," to Mary and appointed her executrix of his estate, including his literary estate. Concerned about his literary reputation, Ernest trusted Mary to shape his legacy. As to his children, Ernest wrote, "I have intentionally omitted to provide for my children now living or for any that may be born after this will has been executed as I have complete confidence in my beloved wife Mary to provide for them according to written instructions I have given her."

Ernest's will signaled a vote of confidence in Mary because she was the only person he trusted to manage his estate and protect his literary reputation. He had changed his mind about who would be his literary executor—in the previous will, he had appointed Alfred Rice to the position, but in the new will, Mary became executrix. For a man as concerned about legacy as Ernest, this was an enduring declaration that Mary was the most reliable and trustworthy person in his life. Ernest gave the handwritten will to Charlie Scribner Jr., not Alfred Rice, to hold until his death. Scribner was pleased to be asked because he and Ernest had had some misunderstanding and "I was happy to learn that I had not forfeited his trust." When Charlie visited Ernest at his New York apartment, Ernest asked, "'Have you any place you can lock something up in your office?' I said, 'Sure. I can put it in a filing cabinet and lock the cabinet.'" [13]

Ernest said, "'I want you to take this valise down to Scribner's and put it in that filing cabinet of yours.' I said I would, and he went on: 'Now, don't lose it, my will is in there.'" Charlie assured Ernest he would not lose it and added "a childish remark: 'If I lose it, I'll shoot myself.' To which he made a typical Hemingway rejoinder: 'That wouldn't do me any good.'" Charlie practically chained the valise to his wrist and took it by taxi back to his office. A couple of mornings later, Ernest came to Charlie's office and asked to see something in the valise. Charlie gave Ernest the valise, and he rummaged through his belongings. Charlie recalled, "I knew perfectly well he just wanted to make sure I hadn't lost his valuables. Everything was in order, so he came back in, filled with joyful reassurance—or at least good cheer." [14]

Greg returned home to the States in October 1955. His African experiment had ended badly because he had invested half of his inheritance from his mother in a coffee farm but didn't have the skill or patience to make it profitable. He also had an affair with the daughter of a local plantation owner and ended his marriage. His wife Jane took their daughter Lorian and returned to Arkansas. Greg followed, hoping to make amends and visit his daughter, but he became depressed, drank too much, and was arrested for disturbing the peace. Jane ended the marriage. [15]

Ernest worked on his story about Africa, writing three to four hundred words a day. [16] As he got deeper into the mood of the piece, he asked Mary to pierce his ears with a sterilized needle so that he could wear gold earrings in sympathy with his Kamba friends. The idea appalled Mary, and she persuaded him to drop it. She wrote a stern letter, arguing it was socially unacceptable for men to wear earrings, his doing so would find its way into print, and it would harm his reputation. "I know that you are impassioned about Africa and the Africans, writing about them, and delivered by the mystery and excitement of becoming one of them. And you know that I love the fun of make-believe as much as you do." However, Mary warned, "the attempt to convert fantasy into actuality can only result, I think, in distortion and failure." [17] She urged him to find some other way of proving his brotherhood with the tribesmen. Ernest took her advice, and Mary managed Ernest's public persona. She probably didn't agree with the social convention but knew Ernest would pay with his reputation if he breached it.

The Batista government wanted to latch onto Ernest's burgeoning international reputation and insisted on presenting him with another medal, the Order of San Cristóbal. The presentation took place on a chilly evening before glaring television lights at the Sports Palace in Havana. Ernest complained he had to wait for two hours under the television lights, and he sweated through his clothes. He changed his shirt and coat in an unheated dressing room and "ended up catching a bad cold on the right kidney which had ruptured in the air crash." He knew it was bad when his right foot "swelled like a football, and the pressure brought blood out at the base of the toenails." [18]

Mary had traveled to Key West to supervise repairs to Pauline's house so they could rent it, and she negotiated with realtors and decided on renters. [19] On her return to the Finca, with her hair rinsed pale gold, she found Ernest in bed suffering from nephritis. He was confined to his bed throughout Christmas, and he read from piles of newspapers and magazines. Mary noted his convalescence from the plane crashes was taking much longer than his usually resilient body required. Forty-seven-year-old Mary's health was not good either, as she suffered from anemia. She managed the books, gathered receipts for deductions, and prepared the tax information for all the Hemingway enterprises. She fatigued often, felt weak, and had trouble concentrating. Her doctor gave her a series of blood transfusions which brought some relief, and she felt more optimistic.

Filming of *The Old Man and the Sea* resumed in the spring of 1956, and a team of producers, photographers, and supporting staff invaded the Finca. The film footage of the fishing efforts the previous September was poor, and Ernest persuaded Leland Hayward they might have better luck finding a giant marlin off Cabo Blanco, Peru. Ernest and Mary traveled with the crew and for the next month they patrolled the Humboldt current, trying to lure a photogenic marlin to jump from the sea. The fish Ernest caught were large, but they didn't fight the way the marlin of Cuba did. Still, Ernest felt the weight of the fish in the soles of his feet, his forearms, and back. When a fish was dead tired, Gregorio harpooned it, "to try for the camera shot you needed in the picture. It was steady, punishing work each day." The "seas ran like onrushing hills with snow blowing off the tops," and it was too rough for movie photography.[20] They failed to get usable footage, and the film's budget would not permit further attempts to do so.

◆

Mary received complaints about her mother, who was suffering from dementia and behaving like "a capricious, naughty child," using the telephone and disturbing the Kerr household at night. Mrs. Kerr thought it might be necessary to put Adeline in a public institution. Mary empathized but hoped her mother's behavior would improve so she would not have to move or require a night nurse, which would "put my mother's living expenses higher than my husband's and mine." Neither Mary nor her husband wanted to put her mother into a public institution unless it was unavoidable. "Poor old lady, it is hard to believe that she would behave like this if she really understood how much distress and worry she is causing to other people, particularly to you and me."[21]

◆

Look magazine proposed sending Ty Thiessen to do a follow-up story on how Ernest and Mary were getting along three months after the plane crashes. Ernest was reluctant to have further interruptions but Ty was a pleasant companion, and *Look* offered to pay five thousand dollars for a brief article, including the captions for the photographs. The money would help pay for the trip to Spain they were planning for the fall. Ty's photos show Ernest and Mary as a happy couple, lounging and playing with their cats. In one, Ernest chats with Mary and she nuzzles his neck. Others show Ernest standing before his bookcase at his typewriter or reading in his chair (flanked by a low table bearing bottles of liquor). Still others show him at the helm of *Pilar*, fishing off the stern, posing with a giant marlin, and talking with Spencer Tracy. The images convey the cozy, creative ambiance of the Finca, close to the adventure of the sea and his beloved *Pilar*. In his captions, Ernest described the Finca as the place where he could work best, uninterrupted unless bothered by visitors.

In his essay, Ernest celebrated Mary. Remembering she'd once said, "the first thing her husband needed in a wife was that she be durable," he wrote Mary was not only durable but also "brave, charming, witty, exciting to look at, a pleasure to be with, and a good wife." He praised her for being "an excellent fisherwoman, a fair wing shot, a strong swimmer, a really good cook, a good judge of wine, an excellent gardener, an amateur astronomer, a student of art, political economy, Swahili, French and Italian, and she can run a boat or household in Spanish." He added, she could also sing well, with, "an accurate and true voice." When she was away, the Finca was, "as empty as the emptiest bottle."[22] These words of praise made up for Ernest's earlier piece in *Look* which failed to recognize Mary's contribution to his life and the African safari.

Mary typed the new article and told Ernest he had gone too far in his praise, but privately her husband's words must have pleased her and exonerated him. Ernest portrayed their marriage as a healthy and productive partnership. He wrote, "She does not suffer fools gladly. She does not suffer them at all. She has great energy, and she can stay the distance, but she also knows how to be as lazy as a cat."[23]

TWENTY-NINE

If You Have a Message, Call the Western Union

September 1956–September 1958

Mary and Ernest set sail from New York on their favorite ocean liner, the *Île-de-France*, on September 1, 1956. They arrived in Paris six days later after a voyage spent reading, working out in the ship's gym, and resting. The autumn weather was warm and dry, and Mary hoped the change in climate would hasten her recovery from persistent anemia. She heard distant church bells and the September weather was "blissful with the light shimmering pale gold in the plane trees."[1] They saw a collection of seldom-seen Impressionist paintings at a special exhibition at the Musée de l'Orangerie, and Mary went back twice to take it in. In the city she had long adored, she began feeling healthier.

After ten days wandering the streets, betting on the horses at Auteuil, and visiting galleries, they left Paris for Spain. Mario Casamassima, a "dark, devilish-looking friend of Gianfranco's," drove them in the Lancia.[2] Mario "gives you the confidence a racing driver does and still scares the shit out of you in the traffic, which is very congested."[3] They crossed the Spanish border on September 21, and the next day, they walked through the crowds to the Plaza de Toros in Pamplona.

Antonio Ordóñez gave a master class in bullfighting, and another matador, Giron, dedicated his second bull to Ernest. He worked the beast with patience. By the end, Mary was exhausted, and they retreated to their hotel. Her respite was brief, and for the next several days, they took in the Feria and then drove to

Madrid where they found lodging at El Escorial in a lovely hotel overlooking a monastery. They enjoyed out-of-season rates and excellent food and wine. Each day they went to bullfights, and afterward celebrated with friends who had come from London, Rome, and Paris, often eating and drinking late into the night. The frenetic pace played havoc with Mary's anemia, and she withdrew to their room. Ernest was drinking too much, and his blood pressure soared to 210 over 105. Mary insisted he visit his trusted friend from the civil war days, Dr. Juan Manuel Madinavieta, the only doctor who had said Ernest would recover from the African crashes. After examining him, Madinavieta ordered Ernest to reduce his alcohol intake and stop sexual intercourse.

Ernest told Hotch he had flunked all the medical tests, and Madinavieta had put him on a strict food diet. "Only one glass of wine per meal and five ounces of whiskey per day, and no, repeat, no screwing."[4] He told Buck Madinavieta had used a fluoroscope to diagnose inflammation of the aorta and had also found cirrhosis of the liver. "The non-drinking is a pain in the ass as I am used to drinking for more than forty years and used it to forget the writing as soon as I stopped until the next day."[5]

Mary came down with a violent cold on top of her anemia, and she and Ernest were miserable together, not straying far from their sitting room. She recovered, and thanks to his strict discipline, Ernest brought his blood pressure down to a normal range within three weeks. For the next few months, Ernest struggled to reduce his intake of alcohol. Mary advised Bernard Berenson the doctors had "completely deleted strong drink from [Ernest's] diversions, which causes wear and woe to the nervous system."[6] She might have added that Ernest's trial with abstinence caused her misery, too.

◆

On October 1, Greg was drafted into the army at Fort Bragg. He hoped to become a paratrooper, but his military career ended a few days into basic training when doctors diagnosed him as "schizoid-paranoiac."[7] Greg went to Miami to await his discharge papers and took work unloading trucks. He wrote to Ernest, announcing he planned to take a summer course at Harvard to get into medical school. Greg asked his father for a loan so he could travel to Africa to sell the plantation. Despite his misgivings, Ernest covered the expenses for the trip.

Ernest shared his disappointment in his son with Buck: Greg was "just as nasty before he was crazy." He explained, "nearly all the get in Pauline's family are either born strange or have what they then called nervous breakdowns at adolescence."[8] Both Pauline's sons, Patrick and Greg, suffered so-called "nervous breakdowns" or more serious mental health issues, and both underwent electroconvulsive therapy.

◆

Mary and Ernest drove to Paris where they took two rooms at the Ritz facing away from Place Vendôme and overlooking the hotel's small garden. When the porters brought the Hemingway's luggage to their room, one of them reminded Ernest he had, thirty years before, left two suitcases at the Ritz for safekeeping. Ernest reclaimed the cases and found they held blue and yellow notebooks, handwritten in pencil, and pages of typed stories and sketches. Mary watched as Ernest sat on the floor, absorbed in the writings from his early days in Paris. He remarked it was just as challenging to write in those days as now.[9] The notebooks would inspire him to write the series of Paris reminiscences which became *A Moveable Feast*.

◆

Sad news came from Cuba. Blackie had died, and the report of their loyal friend's death deepened their malaise. Despite the attractions of Paris, gloom descended. Ernest's diet of no more than five ounces of meat a day with some vegetables but no fats or eggs and minimal quantities of wine depressed him. What could be more disheartening than a cholesterol-reducing diet in Paris, a city celebrated for its culinary delights? Ernest shared his frustration in a letter to Archie MacLeish. "Me, I'd trade all the honors of this world for two good bottles of claret a day and to have my Black Dog back again young and well and not buried down at the pool alongside the tennis court."[10]

Friends urged Mary and Ernest to travel to London, but Ernest had never liked the place and he wanted to linger in Paris. He bid Mary bon voyage on the night train, and she spent a week visiting friends and finding the perfect gift for Ernest—a small silver flask. On her return to Paris, she had Cartier's engrave it with a facsimile of his signature. The flask delighted Ernest when he opened his gifts on Christmas morning because it brought back the happy memories of his drinking days and suggested his wife would not object to the odd swig.

The Hemingways left Paris on January 22. Their crossing aboard the *Île-de-France* was rough, causing passengers to stay away from the bars and dining rooms, thus enhancing Ernest's and Mary's privacy. Ernest reduced his alcohol intake and got his blood pressure down to 140 over 80, the best it had been in months. He had trouble trying to reduce his drinking because he depended on his lifelong habit to relax and take his mind off the ever-present work. When the ship reached New York, Ernest persuaded his old friend George Brown to come aboard and sail with him to Cuba. Mary disembarked, took the train to Minneapolis, and a friend drove her to the clinic where her mother was staying. Mary had not seen her mother for eighteen months. At first, Adeline treated Mary as a stranger, then she unloaded her burden of complaints. Lost in a fog of senility, Adeline was miserable, and though Mary stayed for a week, there was little she could do to lighten her mother's mood despite eating with her, reading to her, and chatting with her good-naturedly. Nothing seemed to work, and as Mary prepared to leave, Adeline left her with the stinging rebuke, "you don't care anything about me."[11]

When they returned to the Finca, Ernest busied himself going through the notebooks he had rescued from the Ritz. Machakos, their new black dog, named after the district in Kenya where Percival's farm was located, was enthusiastic, but he didn't have Blackie's long history and had not yet learned the ways of his master. Ernest maintained discipline, drinking only a glass or two of wine a day, but Mary was not under orders to abstain and she enjoyed gin and coconut water. Though Mary told herself she was drinking to keep Ernest company, she was drinking for reasons of her own—and she was drinking more. In mid-March, *Pilar* underwent routine repairs and they took her out on a test run. The fishing went well and they caught four dolphins. However, the decent fishing lasted only until May, and they caught half the marlin of past years. Other fishermen noticed the change too but had no explanation. Ironically, they had invited Denis Zaphiro to come and experience fishing the Gulf Stream for four months.

In mid-August, a squad of Batista's soldiers, under the command of a young sergeant, entered the grounds of the Finca at 4 A.M. Machakos barked at the intruders and woke Ernest. The sergeant told Ernest they were looking for a member of the Castro revolutionary forces, but Ernest protested, and the patrol left without searching. The next morning, they found Machakos dead near the kitchen steps. Someone had struck the dog on the head with a rifle butt. Ernest went to the local military post to demand an explanation, but the sergeant in charge denied he or his men had killed the dog.[12] Ernest was furious, but all he could do was fume. Mary wept as they buried Machakos, close to where he'd fallen defending the Finca.

Jack, his wife Byra Louise (Puck), and their two pretty daughters moved to Havana so Jack could take a job as a salesman with Merrill Lynch. He didn't get along well with the local manager and later described the eighteen-month stay in Cuba as "nightmarish."[13] Since Jack's paycheck didn't cover their rent, Ernest helped with expenses, and they found a small apartment in Havana overlooking the ocean near the mouth of the Almendares River.[14] In the entire time Jack's family lived in Cuba, Ernest came to see them only once, but he refused to leave the car and go up to their apartment. Puck had made a special effort to have their home ready for Ernest's visit, and his strange behavior hurt. "We felt very much estranged, and I never felt that Papa was his old self," Jack recalled. Weeks later, Jack suffered an attack of acute hepatitis, and he was confined indoors. Mary helped by looking after the children, and she began liking them very much. She concluded, "people grow to love living creatures from taking care of them. It is not necessarily love first impelling the care."[15] Mary had to care for cats, dogs, and Ernest, but she never experienced the love of a mother for her child.

Besides helping with the children, Mary was busy looking after the gardens of the Finca. Ernest, oblivious to his son's problems and a first-class shirker of domestic responsibilities, continued to work at his typewriter on top of his bookcase. Mary "sweated through four or five changes of shirts and shorts doing house, garden and kitchen chores." She reflected, "males of our species make the best music, pictures, sculpture, dams, ships, corporations, books partly perhaps because they never questioned the superior importance of their endeavors over the mechanics of living, the cleaning, grooming, feeding." Whenever she posed such questions to Ernest, he, "seldom one to juggle philosophical theses," responded, "If you have a message, call the Western Union."[16]

Given the terrible fishing, the extreme heat, and the fact Ernest was not much fun on his strict, non-drinking regime, Mary suggested taking Denis Zaphiro to New York City. Sugar Ray Robinson was to box with Carmen Basilio, and this provided the ideal excuse. They stayed at the Westbury Hotel, and Toots Shor picked them up in an enormous black Cadillac and took them to the fight. They sat so close to the ring that they could hear the sweaty fighters smacking each other. Bursts of sweat erupted into the air after each punch. Over the next few days, Ernest visited Charlie Scribner Jr. and Alfred Rice, and had dinner and drinks with Marlene Dietrich. Mary noted that Marlene tidied up, leaving the kitchen in their little suite sparkling clean, and she regaled Ernest with stories of her grandchild. Charlie Scribner Jr. remembered Ernest's visit because "he was failing visibly. He seemed almost frail; his arms weren't the old burly limbs. He was tentative in his movements and uncommonly shy."[17]

They returned to the Finca, all of them a few pounds heavier but refreshed after escaping the heat of Cuba. It was soon time for Zaphiro to return to Kenya, and Mary regretted they had failed to find him a suitable woman. Zaphiro laughed off her concern; the Finca seemed empty after his departure.

◆

In mid-October, Ernest went to Miami to meet Greg after his discharge from the hospital. They drove to Key West to check on Pauline's house, where Greg had spent his childhood. The electroconvulsive therapy had not worked, and Greg entered the hospital in Miami for another series of treatments on December 2. This was the last time Ernest and Greg saw each other. Greg remained in the hospital until the end of January, and Ernest continued to cover the mounting costs.[18]

◆

The celebrity photographer Yousuf Karsh wanted to photograph Ernest, and he enlisted the support of the Canadian ambassador to Cuba, Harry A. Scott. Karsh told Scott, "an important gap will be left unfilled if Hemingway's portrait does not appear" in the book he was assembling about the "greatest personalities of our time."[19] Scott urged Ernest to sit for the photographer, and he wrote to Mary later that same month, hoping they could "find Ernesto in the right mood one of these months." In early 1957, Karsh and his wife, Solange, visited the Finca and made portraits of Ernest. Karsh sent proofs of the photos and wrote, "I found photographing Ernest Hemingway to be a most stimulating and rewarding experience; Solange still speaks nostalgically of her delightful visit in the garden with Miss Mary and of the calm chat she had with you both."[20] For some reason, the letter and proofs did not arrive, and Mary assumed the worst after hearing Karsh had sold a photo and published a story in the *London Daily Express*. She had also received a cable from the US magazine *Parade* saying they had bought a cover picture of Hemingway by Karsh. Mary wrote to the new Canadian ambassador, Hector Allard, complaining about Karsh's unethical behavior. "Mr. Hemingway would never have consented to pose for unauthorized pictures if he had imagined they were to be peddled about to any buyer; but since Mr. Karsh came here under the auspices of the Canadian Embassy, we did not question his integrity."[21] The ambassador replied the next day, saying he was, "somewhat startled to read your letter concerning Mr. Karsh," and telling her, "I find it difficult to believe that Mr. Karsh would've sold a picture of Mr. Hemingway to anyone without first having had a selection made by Mr. Hemingway himself." Allard had received advance notice that there was a parcel containing proofs on the way from Karsh.[22] The tempest blew over when the proofs were received in good order two weeks later. Mary wrote to Karsh and his wife, telling them what "pleasure, delight, reassurance, comfort, and happiness it gave us both to see the beautiful photographs and then to have your charming letter." She asked them to excuse her for having grown nervous and explained they had had bad experiences with her old employer, the *Daily Express*, "a newspaper which is frequently uncomplimentary and untruthful." Mary said, "we are delighted with the photographs, all of them, so much so that we cannot yet take advantage of your offer to send one for framing."[23]

In October, Karsh sent a copy of his iconic photograph of Ernest via the Canadian ambassador. He said, "this particular photograph I feel to be that which best portrays Hemingway, the creative artist, and I hope the choice which I've taken the liberty of making will also have your approval. Please accept it with my affectionate high regards."[24] Karsh also sent along a wonderful photograph of Ernest and Mary posing beside the ceiba tree on the front steps of the Finca. Ernest holds her left wrist and drapes his hand over her right shoulder. Mary is smiling happily, and Ernest looks pleased. This photo, which Mary described as "one of Yousuf Karsh's few informal photographs," appears on the jacket of Mary's memoir.[25]

As 1957 drew to a close, Mary wrote about the three things they should be thankful for: the regeneration of Ernest's liver and kidneys, his lowered blood cholesterol, and the decline of her anemia. She balanced the good with the bad: the unhappiness of her mother, Greg's mental illness, Jack's problems with finances, the death of Machakos, and the bombings and shootings in Cuba. She wrote that, on balance, the good outweighed the bad.[26]

On New Year's Eve, Mary was making a lime pie when the phone rang. The Western Union operator read a cable: her mother had died after an illness lasting twenty-four hours. The news overwhelmed Mary with sadness and regret. She arranged a Christian Science funeral service at the "Temple" in Prescott, Wisconsin, and flew to Minneapolis the following evening. She arrived in Prescott at 5 A.M. the morning of the funeral exhausted and frayed. Adeline lay in an open casket in her favorite red dress surrounded by flowers. Though the morticians had rouged her cheeks and combed her hair, Mary noted, "no artistry could erase the look of permanent distress on her features."[27] Some of Adeline's friends came down from Minneapolis to pay their respects, and Mary chatted with them and accepted their well-intentioned, Christian-Science-inspired commiserations.

Mary felt a mixture of sorrow and relief. Her mother had succumbed to senility and died lonely and miserable, and not even her Christian Science faith seemed to bring much comfort in her last year. None of the platitudes of that faith helped with Mary's grief, for she believed none of it. On the train to Chicago, Mary began feeling thankful her vigil was over. She knew her mother had never approved of her life choices, and she had wanted Mary to return home to Bemidji to give her the gift of grandchildren. Realizing there was now an end to her mother's condescending judgment brought some comfort. She would miss her mother's sweetness, though even that had disappeared in the fog of her dementia.

◆

During these months, Castro's underground army carried out brutal killings, and Batista's forces engaged in grisly retaliation. Batista's soldiers arrested some young men in San Francisco de Paula, imprisoned and tortured them, and left them dead in ditches, their terrible wounds a warning to others. Batista imposed news censorship, and it was difficult to know what was happening. Rumors replaced journalism, and Mary and Ernest relied upon René and their Cuban friends for updates. The atrocities were appalling. Mutilated men were found hanging head down in wells. Soldiers beat and tortured women, threw live phosphorus bombs into busloads of passengers, and burned cane fields. It was an orgy of violence, and everyone became suspicious of everyone else. When Mary went to Havana, she felt the tension in the streets and noticed the few pedestrians glancing at each other furtively. Even the high-end women's shops were almost empty. Castro's Revolutionary Council initiated a plan to liquidate informers and began propagandizing for a general strike. Batista responded by encouraging workers to shoot anyone who advocated a strike.

In mid-March, Ernest proposed a fishing trip on *Pilar*, and they headed out of Cojímar. When they were well into the Gulf Stream, Gregorio deployed the outriggers and baited the hooks, just as if they were going on a routine spring fishing trip. Ernest drove *Pilar* further offshore than usual. When they were about ten miles out, he asked Mary to take over the helm and maintain a heading, taking them further out to sea. Down below, Gregorio opened drawers, tore apart bunks, and removed from their hiding places an assortment of pistols, machine guns, heavy rifles, grenades, and ammunition. He and Ernest threw the weapons overboard, and it took about an hour to complete the task. It stunned Mary to see the arsenal, hidden since the days when *Pilar* worked for the American Navy hunting for German submarines. Ernest had decided the weapons, if discovered, would cause even more deaths in the ongoing revolution, and he wanted no part of it. He told Mary to keep their mission secret, and she had no difficulty agreeing. Indeed, it would still be a secret if Mary hadn't written about the incident in her memoir.[28]

Over the Easter weekend, the Revolutionary Council called for a general strike, but it didn't materialize and the traffic kept moving. On April 5, Mary celebrated her fiftieth birthday, and Ernest presented her with homemade gifts and a large check. Mary's face had become deeply lined from her constant exposure to the hot sun of Cuba, Idaho, and Africa, and when she smiled with appreciation, furrows appeared in her cheeks and spread from the corners of her eyes almost to her ears. She was proud of her wrinkles, which were hard-earned in the outdoors. In the afternoon, they shot at bottles set on the steps of the abandoned cowshed.

The general strike had not started by April 7, and no one knew when it would. None of the Finca staff, or anyone they knew in the village, wanted the strike or the violence. On the morning of April 10, they heard the police sergeant from the station down the road from the Finca, the one whom they believed had killed Machakos, was himself murdered, along with several others, during the night. Despite the unsettling guerrilla warfare, Ernest and Mary were doing rather well apart from her stubborn anemia. Ernest's blood pressure was in a healthy range, and he was working on his reminiscences of life in Paris. In the afternoons they both swam laps in the pool, trying to make a mile before pre-dinner drinks, and Mary reckoned she swam twenty miles in twenty days.

When Ernest's Paris sketches reached three hundred pages, each one typed by Mary in triple space, he worked again on the manuscript for *The Garden of Eden* which he had started ten years earlier. He had not asked Mary to read it each evening, as he had done with other books, and when she typed the piece, she found it very long, "repetitious, and sometimes supercilious." She also thought it contained some spots of "excellent narrative."[29] Mary didn't say in her memoir how she felt about Ernest describing their gender-changing games. Still, she must have approved since she published those parts of her African journal in which Ernest described those very nocturnal activities.

THIRTY

I Wished for a Room of My Own

October 1958–July 1959

Mary went to Havana to see Spencer Tracy's film *Bad Day at Black Rock*, and she was captivated by the scenes of vast plains, purple mountains, and cottonwoods bending in the wind. She longed to return to the American west and told Ernest about the film. A few days later, Ernest suggested they travel to Ketchum in the fall, and he arranged a trip west with Toby and Betty Bruce in their comfortable station wagon. They left Chicago on October 4, with Toby driving and Ernest providing commentary from the front passenger seat during the four-day journey. As they drove west, they snacked on fruit and sandwiches and celebrated cocktail hours, sipping rum on ice, Scotch with lime, and dry martinis. Near Yellowstone, they encountered black bears, and Ernest entertained everyone by speaking to the animals. At dusk on the fourth day, they reached the home of Pappy and Tillie Arnold in Ketchum. After joyful embraces from their friends, they enjoyed a fried chicken dinner, complete with botas of red wine. Tillie thought Ernest looked old despite the fact he was only fifty-nine. "The white beard was part of it, as was his thinning white hair that he had combed forward to hide his baldness. And it was not only his looks. He acted old in some of his mannerisms, and he acted old when he walked."[1]

Mary and Ernest rented a log cabin across a vacant lot from the Christiania restaurant, and in the coming days they hunted for mallards. On one outing, Ernest attempted to vault over a fence, but he landed awkwardly and sprained his heel. When they got back to their cabin, Pappy phoned the Sun Valley Hospital, and a new member of the staff, Dr. George Saviers, came and bandaged Ernest's foot. Saviers had instant credibility with Ernest because he had served with the US Navy during the war. He soon became Ernest's doctor in Ketchum, and the two men became friends who hunted together. Saviers remembered, "when I knew him, he was fairly healthy, and he was a kind, generous, nice gentle person. He was never this macho guy that you read about. He was just a nice fellow."[2]

When Saviers was a student at the University of California, he had been an enormous Hemingway fan, and he read all his books. He owned first editions, and when Ernest came to his home for dinner, Ernest delighted in writing comments in them. One evening, when they talked about writing, Ernest wrote next to the short story, "The Big Two-Hearted River," "George . . . this was as good as I could do then, or maybe always." Saviers recalled, "Ernest considered himself to be the best writer in the world. He always knew he was going to be a great writer, and he knew other people were wrong for not recognizing it."[3]

With Mary's encouragement, Ernest bought four adjoining lots with a magnificent view across the street from Pappy Arnold's place. Mary sketched a perfect house, with large windows and doors facing southwest to collect the winter sunshine, but much to her regret Ernest was in no hurry to build, and they put off the project.

On New Year's Day, reports from Cuba said Batista had fled from Havana, and Fidel Castro and his allies were in control of the capital city. News services began calling Ernest for his reaction, and he read a prepared statement. "I believe in the historical necessity for the Cuban revolution, and I believe in its long-term aims. I do not wish to discuss personalities or day-to-day problems."[4] When the *New York Times* phoned, Ernest departed from his statement and said he was "delighted" with the revolution. Mary overheard his comment and thought he had gone too far because he had no way of knowing whether the new regime might commit excesses. Castro might have been lining up opponents before firing squads, or Castro's enemies might take revenge against their friends, such as Gregorio. Ernest resisted her advice to phone in a correction, arguing that nobody would care what he said, but Mary lectured him on the power of words, and he relented. Ernest phoned the reporter and substituted the phrase "hopeful" for "delighted."[5] Mary was more experienced than Ernest with straight journalism, and she gave him solid advice about maintaining a neutral position in public.

They spent the next couple of months shooting and partying with their friends. Mary noted they had one of the happiest days of 1959, when they went magpie shooting with Chuck and Flo Atkinson at the Silver Creek Rod and Gun Club. Besides their weapons and ammunition, they brought along four and a half gallons of wine, a huge salad, and roast duck. Mary downed two fast birds, and Ernest commented her shooting was like a razor blade cutting. She recorded the rare compliment.

Ernest worked most mornings on the lengthening *Garden of Eden* manuscript, but his work was interrupted on February 18 when their old friend Taylor "Beartracks" Williams died of a ruptured stomach. Mary wrote to Charlie Sweeney about Taylor, who had come to the Finca each spring to fish the Gulf Stream with them. The people who said it was all for the best, since Taylor was failing, appalled her. People said such things, she supposed, to ensure they didn't have "to come to grips with any strong, uncomfortable grief."[6] For her and Ernest, Taylor's death was a body blow.

Mary missed Hotch and wrote an affectionate letter inviting him to join them in Ketchum. She described their log cabin with a gigantic fireplace and said he could have his choice of rooms upstairs. This followed an earlier letter in which Mary said, "It has been really unbearable, waking up and thinking, 'no Hotch today'—I miss you, sweetheart, and I'm sure Papa does too."[7] Hotch took the bait and came to stay for a week.

◆

Mary and Ernest left Ketchum on March 16 in a rented Chevrolet Impala with Hotch chauffeuring. They stopped at a motel in Phoenix and watched the second half of Hotch's TV adaptation of *For Whom the Bell Tolls*. Mary liked Jason Robards and Maria Schell's performances, but Ernest was disappointed because the drama failed to show the corruption and evil on both sides of the conflict. Hotch drove them to Tucson, and they visited Ernest's old friend from his Paris days, the artist Waldo Peirce, who greeted them warmly. Bearded and as large as Ernest, he charmed Mary with little jokes, friendly words, and simple modesty about his impressive work. Waldo showed them several of his pieces, two of which contained small portraits of Ernest. In one, Ernest sat at the bar of the crowded Silver Slipper Nightclub in Key West while sailors danced with local ladies to the band's wild tunes. In another, Waldo pointed out something to Ernest while they were watching an *encierro* in Pamplona. Waldo was fifteen years older than

Ernest, and their gentle banter revealed a genuine affection for each other which had lasted a lifetime. Waldo had had four wives himself and he embraced Mary, who found him enchanting. He later sent her his canvas of monks sweeping the Pamplona Cathedral floor in ballet movements, and she treasured the piece for the rest of her life.

They dropped off Hotch in New Orleans, and Ernest drove them east along the coast road past gardens filled with fuchsias and azaleas in full bloom. They reached Key West on March 28, and the next afternoon flew to Havana. Juan greeted them at the airport and took them to the Floridita for a brief reunion with their bartender friends. Then, Juan drove them home, and they hugged René on the front steps of the Finca beneath the ceiba tree.

Ernest had decided in Ketchum that he wanted to update his book about bull-fighting, *Death in the Afternoon*. He had arranged with his friend Bill Davis to stay at his house near Málaga. Mary had never met the Davises and was skeptical about moving into the home of strangers, but since Ernest had already accepted Bill's invitation he downplayed her concern about being at the mercy of their hosts' living habits.

They stayed at the Finca for the rest of March and the first two weeks of April, during which friends brought them stories about the Castro revolution. Most people hoped for the best, but Mary noticed signs the economy was slowing. When she went to Havana, she saw private construction projects had stopped, suggesting a lack of confidence by investors in the new government. The police acted with courtesy, and they saw no signs of corruption in the young administration. Mary wrote to her friend Allan Stewart in the state department, declaring her support for the Castro government. Washington only dimly perceived some facts about the US-Cuba relationship. Airplanes based in Florida were daily invading Cuban airspace to ignite sugarcane fields and buzz Castro's home in Cojímar. Mary said it was "morally inexcusable" for the US to permit these attacks and suggested the government should establish a system to inspect chartered aircraft. She proposed that President Eisenhower should visit Cuba, where he would receive a warm welcome from the people. "A friendly gesture now could do much to dissipate the Cuban government's irritations and feelings of inferiority." Mary urged removing the causes of annoyance in the relationship between the two countries. She told him, "the Castro regime continues to be the most popular, wholeheartedly and seriously supported government this island has ever had."[8] Mary was seriously out of step with the thinking in Washington about Cuba.

◆

The Hemingways left New York on April 22, aboard an American cruise ship, the SS *Constitution*, destined for the Port of Algeciras on the Bay of Gibraltar. When they docked, Bill Davis, "a tall, grave-faced, balding man," was waiting for them.[9] He transferred their luggage into a pink Ford sedan he had rented for their visit. His wife had sent turkey sandwiches, and they ate them and sipped wine as they drove to the Davises' house, La Consula. The old Spanish mansion's carved oak front doors opened to white walls hung with brightly painted Jackson Pollocks, Goya prints, and old maps. Vases filled with fresh flowers surrounded the simple furniture. Much to Mary's relief, Annie Davis turned out to be a generous hostess—an American who had lived abroad so long, she seemed European.

They drove to Madrid on May 14 to celebrate San Isidro's fiesta, and for the next eleven days, they attended bullfights, festive luncheons, and dinner parties that lasted until 2 A.M. They partied with Spain's leading bullfighters, including Antonio Ordóñez, his wife Carmen, Juan Belmonte, Luis Miguel Dominguin, and their entourages. Despite her exhaustion, Mary managed two peaceful mornings at the Prado Museum, where she visited her favorite paintings by Bruegel, Hieronymus Bosch, Titian, Tintoretto, and Veronese.

◆

Bill Davis had heard Ernest liked to work standing up, and he furnished a tall, sloped writing table. Ernest used it whenever they weren't traveling, and he was making progress on an introduction to a new collection of his short stories. When Mary typed the piece, it dismayed her because it was "tendentious, truculent, and smug."[10] She wrote a brief note to Ernest laying out her concerns and suggesting revisions. Mary asked him to remove "the qualifying phrase about Ava [Gardner]—'as she was then'—unnecessarily hurtful and spiteful sounding."[11] She advised he should edit a little more: "You talk arrogant and naughty, 'They could drop dead. It wouldn't make any difference.'" Ernest's friends would know that he was just letting off steam and was not "arrogant or dirty or malicious." But people who didn't know him might think ill of him. She added a handwritten note, "Anyone who feels assured he can make no mistakes is riding for a fall." Mary signed the note with an uppercase, "I LOVE YOU," and a tiny red kitten face, with black eyes and whiskers. She wrapped her stiff suggestions in loving—and defensive—gestures. Ernest took her advice on two points but didn't invite her to discuss her ideas. She had supposed he would speak to her, but he simply asked her to retype the revised piece. Later, Charles Scribner Jr. agreed with Mary's revisions and cautioned Ernest against coming across as condescending. Mary feared Ernest was becoming pompous and boastful.

Bill and Ernest left in the pink sedan on June 25 to watch a series of Antonio's bullfights. Mary wasn't feeling well, so she didn't mind staying behind, but she cared that Ernest hadn't asked her to accompany him. She thought it was the first time he had not invited her along.[12] Mary worked on a story about Antonio for *Sports Illustrated* and she got to know Annie better. Mary found they had very different personalities. Annie was gentle, passive, unpunctual, and sophisticated, while Mary considered herself to be "aggressive, impatient, and unsympathetic to feminine niceties. I wished I could escape." Indeed, Mary declared in her memoir, "I wished for a room of my own for which I would not be beholden to anyone."[13] This was an obvious allusion to the theme of Virginia Woolf's essay, "A Room of One's Own," which Mary had read.[14] Woolf argued, "Women have had less intellectual freedom than the sons of Athenian slaves. Women . . . have not had a dog's chance of writing poetry. That is why I have laid so much stress on money and a room of one's own."[15] Woolf claimed all of the leading male poets had money from inheritances or college positions, which were closed to women, and women had long been discouraged from writing or pursuing intellectually demanding careers by the patriarchal demands that they bear children and devote themselves to domestic chores. Woolf had been liberated from this cycle. Her aunt fell off her horse and died, leaving young Virginia with five hundred pounds a year forever. Woolf noted, "it is remarkable, what a change of temper a fixed income will bring about. No force in the world can take from me my five hundred pounds. Food, house, and clothing are mine forever." She noted, "not merely do effort and labor cease, but also hatred and bitterness. I need not hate any man; he cannot hurt me. I need not flatter any man; he has nothing to give me."[16] As Woolf famously stated, "A woman must have money and a room of her own if she is to write fiction."[17]

Woolf's views influenced Mary, who was increasingly dissatisfied with her financial dependence upon Ernest and questioning the traditional female role she was playing, subordinating her life energy in service of her husband's art.

Mary wanted to have enough money to be financially independent, to do as she pleased, perhaps to take up a different sort of writing. As the idea was jelling, she considered the freedom she might gain by moving away from Ernest and establishing her own life in New York. She must also have considered the advantage of staying and inheriting Ernest's estate, just as Woolf had done. Pragmatic Mary considered her options, mindful of the life debt she owed Ernest for saving her in the little hospital in Casper.

Mary decided to host a joint celebration of Ernest's sixtieth and Carmen's thirtieth birthdays at La Consula on July 21, 1959. Carmen invited her own guests, including Peter Buckley, who had fallen out with Ernest in Madrid earlier that summer. Peter was an old friend of Carmen's husband, and Antonio had invited Peter to his room as he dressed for a corrida. When Ernest found Peter in Antonio's room, he exploded in anger, excoriating Peter for having presumed on Ernest's relationship with Antonio despite the long friendship between Peter and the matador. Carmen ignored Ernest's petulance and invited Peter to her birthday. Meanwhile, Mary wrote and posted thirty invitations and was delighted when the first acceptance came from the ambassador to West Germany, David Bruce, and his wife.

Annie and Mary drove to Madrid on July 2 to rendezvous with their husbands. Ernest was annoyed when Mary withdrew from the daily three to four hour lunches and dinners with his entourage to work on her story about Antonio. The lengthy meals were becoming tedious for Mary, and she tired of seeing Ernest perform his role as a jolly raconteur and man about town. He played to the crowd, seemed to adore the attention, and ignored her.

A young Irish woman, Valerie Danby-Smith, joined Ernest's circle, and Mary suspected her motives, writing she had come "purportedly to interview Ernest for the Irish press."[18] Valerie was nineteen, a year older than Adriana had been when she met Ernest, but she later wrote that Mary had nothing to worry about: "I was not in awe of him. I enjoyed all Pamplona had to offer, his insight into bullfighting gripped me, and my Irish background gave me great stamina for enjoying the long hours of drinking, storytelling, and merrymaking. My only agenda was to enjoy the moment."[19] Mary "was cordial and happily accepted me." Though Mary was not as refined as Valerie's mother, "she had enormous spunk, was fun to be around and swore like a man, which was a new experience for me."[20]

The entourage moved on to Pamplona and swelled to include the photographer Peter Buckley, Dr. George Saviers and his wife Pat from Sun Valley, Ed Hotchner, and Juanito Quintana. They pulled three or four tables together at Las Pochólas restaurant on the central square and Ernest presided over the ensemble, signing autographs for anyone who came along. Valerie recalled that when Ernest was in public he surrounded himself with friends who acted as a buffer against the public who thrust themselves upon him demanding autographs and photographs. "I thought he was enormously forbearing and patient, not showing his annoyance at the intrusions."[21] They lived hard, dining and drinking until 2 A.M., falling into bed and waking up at 5:30 A.M., bathing and dressing and turning up at the Choko Bar for a stiff coffee, taking their places in the bullring and waiting for the bulls chasing the young men through the streets to enter the stadium. They followed this punishing schedule each day of the Feria. Mary became fed up with the whole bullfighting scene.

One afternoon, they drove to the Village of Aoiz for a picnic and swimming along the Irati River. The American girls wore bikinis and there was bantering and attraction between them and Hotch and Antonio. When Mary scrambled over some stones to enter the water, she slipped and broke the third toe of her right foot in two places. Ernest said he was sorry she had broken her toe but not sympathetic. "Papa was downright cruel to Mary, and he did not know how Mary could put up with it," Saviers said of the episode.[22] Valerie thought Ernest's annoyance arose from the fact that Mary was drawing attention away from him. Ernest "behaved as if Mary did it just to annoy him. He told her if this is too much for you, you can do something else."[23] Valerie found "Ernest was cruel and unsympathetic to Mary when she broke her toe."[24]

Mary noted a change in Ernest. He was drinking an astonishing amount and getting less than three hours of sleep a night. He headed off in the early morning and walked around central Pamplona, chatting and drinking for hours at his entourage's table in the Plaza del Castillo. Mary was "repelled by the dirty tables, the sour smell of spilled wine, the stupid chit-chat with strangers who moved in for autographs and free drinks, and Ernest's endlessly repeated aphorisms."[25] She could not tolerate the relentless partying every night, and she escaped to their rooms to read and eat fruit.

◆

Mary returned to La Consula to finish preparations for the birthday party which Ernest now called "a little country fiesta." Dozens of hidden spotlights shone up into the tall trees around the house. Strings of plain white lights were threaded in the vines and shrubs around the house and pool. Mary hired a burro for guests to ride and imported a target-shooting booth with swinging ping-pong balls to challenge the partygoers. She brought in six cases of dry pink wine, four cases of champagne from Paris, and many bottles of Scotch, gin, and vodka. The cooks prepared fifty pounds of Chinese sweet-sour turkey featuring vegetables from London and a sauce made by Mary and large casseroles of Basque-style cod-fish stew with shrimp and red peppers. She brought in a fireworks expert from Valencia, Flamenco dancers from Málaga, and musicians from Torremolinos. She paid for most of the party with money she had earned from *Sports Illustrated*. In her mind, the dazzling celebration of Ernest's birthday and his achievements would also salute the successes of their partnership.

The guests arrived two days in advance and stayed at a new hotel on a local beach where Ernest greeted and entertained them at lunches and dinners. General Buck Lanham arrived from Washington and endeared himself to Mary, as he was the only guest to congratulate her on the decorations. Buck later wrote to Mary expressing his admiration for her as a hostess and a decorator: "the imagination that went into the decor really knocked me from between my horns. No wonder Ernesto is so damned proud of you. No wonder the two of you have battled it out and stuck together all of these years."[26] Valerie had heard Ernest's stories about Buck's bravery and military prowess. When Bill Davis introduced her to Buck she was surprised because Buck was balding, "mild-mannered, and diminutive, with a soft, husky voice. He treated Ernest with a deference that amounted to awe."[27] She got to know Buck in the coming days, and he was no longer the brave soldier Ernest had portrayed, but a short man timorous about his economic prospects.

Gianfranco Ivancich and his wife drove from Venice in a new Lancia Ernest had purchased with his Italian royalties. Ed Hotchner, Peter and Connie Buckley, Harris Williams, Ricardo Sicré, the Maharaja of Jaipur, his wife and son, and a variety of Ernest's old friends came from Madrid. Ernest also invited two American girls sightseeing in Europe and Valerie Danby-Smith, who had become his "secretary to the cuadrilla" for the summer. In all, thirty-four guests came. Ernest was happy to see George Saviers because he had collected samples of his urine in bottles and jars in his room for analysis. Saviers diagnosed a kidney infection, which had been irritated by his over-drinking in Pamplona.

THIRTY-ONE

Smashed Like an Eggshell

July 1959–January 7, 1960

Ambassador David Bruce gave a warm toast to Ernest and spoke to the beauty and bravery of Carmen. Ernest led a conga line around the grounds, the Flamenco dancers performed with energy, and the cook danced on the big wooden table to enthusiastic applause. After opening his mound of presents and displaying each one, Ernest shot cigarettes from the lips of Antonio and the Maharaja of Jaipur. The party's climax came during the half hour fireworks display when sparks set off a fire at the top of a royal palm near the house. The fire department arrived, doused the blaze, and stayed for drinks. Ernest wore the fire chief's metal hat for the rest of the evening. The party began at 10 P.M. and celebrations continued through breakfast the next morning and on into the day.

Buck complimented Mary, "was there ever a party like that one—a marathon party—a party that broke all records?"[1] Years later, after he had soured on Ernest, Buck panned the event to Carlos Baker, calling it "a damn dull party from beginning to the end."[2] Hotch got into "a bitch of a fight with a little character from North Africa" and "[t]he fair Valerie was constantly at Ernesto's side or heel." The day before, at a luncheon, Buck had such a serious quarrel with Ernest, "I never forgave him for what he did to me. I couldn't, and I can't even now that he is dead."[3] When Buck was returning to his chair, he passed by Ernest who was seated at the head of the table and put his hand on Ernest's shoulder, and brushed against Ernest's head, disturbing his hair. "As I sat down, he exploded. I told him that I hadn't touched him, and I said it in a complete rage." Ernest, sarcastically, ripped into the fact Buck was a general, and the remark so angered Buck he wanted to leave the party and Spain that instant. Ernest later gave a tearful apology, explaining he was bald, and combed his hair forward, and he thought Buck had tried to expose his secret. Buck then realized why Ernest wore an eyeshade, even at night and in the pool. It had never occurred to him "Ernest was cursed with such staggering vanity."[4]

Buck reported another incident illustrating Ernest's fragile ego. Buck brought an advance copy of the 22nd Regiment's history as a gift for Ernest. Buck had written "an extravagant statement about Ernest's role" in front of the book, expecting Ernest would say it was overblown and untrue. However, Ernest read it, and wept, and then passed the book around so everyone could see what Buck had written. Buck assured Baker that Ernest had "never contributed to the formulation of any plan for the 22nd combat team" or provided any intelligence.[5]

George Saviers found Ernest was a different person in Spain from the pleasant man he had known in Idaho. In Pamplona and Málaga, Ernest drank around the clock. Saviers told Tillie Arnold, "he was loud, he pontificated as an expert on everything, and he told stories about himself that were obvious lies."[6] Saviers was a recovering alcoholic himself, and he attributed the change in Ernest's personality to excessive drinking.

◆

Buck informed Baker that Ernest seldom went to his seat at the bullfights but draped himself over the rail close to the matador and his team. "It also made him conspicuous to the crowd . . . this was the big man on campus bit."[7] One day, a cop gestured for Ernest to take his seat. He resisted, but the policeman seized his arm, and Ernest turned and walked to his place. Ernest later said, "he would kill the bastard, and so on," but that was the last time he stood with the matadors. "Thereafter, he took his seat meekly like the rest of us."[8] Buck also reported Mary and Ernest argued, and Mary hit Ernest with her fist, slicing an arch over Ernest's eye with her ring. He was proud of the battle scar. As Buck departed for the States, Ernest gave him "a bone-crushing abrazo, and the tears started down his face." Buck's eyes stung, too. He was "morally certain" he would never see Ernest again.[9]

◆

Ernest planned to use the trip to Spain to update the appendix to his book *Death in the Afternoon*. Given the success of *The Old Man and the Sea*, *Life*'s editors wanted to publish his manuscript before it came out in hardcover. Ernest agreed to the arrangement, though he had not a single word on paper, and he now felt obliged to follow the rest of the summer's program of bullfights.

In the beginning, Mary didn't speak to Valerie at all, "or if she spoke to me it was something sarcastic, like 'Oh I hope you're having a lovely day,' but you could tell she meant, she hoped I was having a lousy day." [10] Eventually, Mary accepted Valerie and treated her more like "a pupil than a hireling." [11] Valerie came to admire Mary's "spunk, independence, and outspokenness." While she noted tensions between Mary and Ernest, she also observed an understanding and caring that had grown over the years of their marriage. [12] Despite accounts to the contrary, Valerie told me Ernest never tried to seduce her. "We were grand friends, like equals; we had a rapport. He could confide in me, let off steam or whatever, knowing it would go no further." [13]

As summer ended, Mary worried she had become "inaudible" to Ernest, who seemed preoccupied with the endless series of bullfights and overdrinking. She excused herself from a trip to Logroño to watch Antonio in favor of two days of shopping in Madrid. Bill, Annie, and Ernest joined Mary a few days later in Madrid and they traveled to Alicante to sleep after seeing Antonio in yet another corrida. As they were going to bed, Mary asked Ernest for a glass of water. He exploded in anger, accusing her of not buying Listerine for him in Madrid (in fact, she had). Ernest called her demand for water excessive and said she was just like his mother who had driven his father to suicide. He didn't stop railing until 4 A.M. [14]

Back at La Consula, Mary noted she had also become "invisible" to Ernest. He was so inconsiderate, Mary decided she had had enough. Ernest's announcement that he had invited Antonio and Carmen to visit them in Cuba and Idaho provided Mary with an excuse to leave Spain. She would return to Cuba to put the Finca in working order. She had serious doubts about going forward in her marriage, but she "loved Ernest in spite of himself" and "would not allow hurt or pique to propel me into hasty, hysterical action." [15] On October 4, Ernest saw Mary off at Orly on her first flight on a jet plane. Valerie noted "a cloud of gloom remained" after Mary's departure, as Ernest pondered her obstinacy while conceding he may have been the cause. [16]

Ernest implored Valerie to come to the Finca the following January, but she had her own plans and didn't want to visit "the old man, world-weary, eyes half-closed." Ernest whispered that if she didn't come, "he would have no reason to go on." He had never been more serious about suicide. "Life without me by his side, he told me, was nada."[17] Valerie was angry but then realized she would lose nothing by promising she would see what she could arrange. Ernest became jaunty again and acted as if they had decided Valerie would come to Cuba. This led Ernest to fantasize with Valerie about the life they would have together after Mary divorced him. Perhaps they would have the daughter he wanted. Valerie humored Ernest, who was "as old as the hills to me. I was a teenager; I had no interest in marriage."[18]

Despite his longing for a younger woman, Ernest worried about the reunion he would face at the Finca with the wife he loved and needed. He decided to buy Mary an expensive gift to smooth the waters. When they passed through Paris, Ernest took Valerie, Annie, and Bill shopping at Cartier. Mary had hinted that she required diamond earrings to begin reconciliation, but Ernest found earrings were too expensive. He purchased a diamond pin instead, worrying whether it would be an acceptable peace offering.

Mary wrote "a situation report" to Ernest describing her efforts to order furniture and accessories for the Topping house in Ketchum. She told him she was working on a letter about their relations but was having difficulty—she was "too clogged up with emotion and loneliness and heartbreak." In summary, "all evidence, as I see it, shows that you have no further use for me in your life." Though Ernest had shown many women affection over the summer, he had shown her none. He had grown into the custom of giving orders. "I will not submit for the rest of my life to being ordered about if I can stay out of prison camps." He had become hostile, and she didn't want to be with him. Ernest had not even thanked her for the birthday party which everyone thought was spectacular. Mary planned to earn her living as a journalist or freelance writer.[19] Ernest responded with a cable thanking her for the work she had done, disagreeing with her conclusions, but saying he respected her views and telling her he still loved her. Mary doubted him.

Mary told Ernest she would start a new life for herself and take a small flat in New York: "The reason I must move out of your life is that I cannot, physically or in my nerves or in my reason, stand up to the neglect you have showed me, combined with your frequent barrages of disparagement, cruel and unjust abuse and criticism."[20]

Mary's determination to separate from Ernest was hindered by her loyalty to the lifestyle they had shared for sixteen years, and her responsibility for both the Finca and the newly purchased house in Ketchum. She intended to put both houses in order before she moved to New York. Mary looked forward to an independent life and becoming engaged in the world beyond Ernest. Bill Walton intrigued her with the idea of helping with the presidential campaign of John F. Kennedy. Walton believed her "political thinking was parallel" with his and admitted his "first step toward Kennedy was motivated only by a burning desire to prevent Nixon from ever becoming president of my country." Walton saw no one "except Kennedy who had the slightest chance of beating slippery Dick." He had known Kennedy for a long time, casually, but when he began working with him, he "found his ideas close to mine and his mind a fascinating and complex one. Any doubts I had have been resolved as the campaign develops." Walton declared, "Here is a guy of great integrity and of the capacity that even he can only dimly perceive."[21] Mary became enthusiastic about the prospect of meeting some kindred souls and stopping Nixon.

◆

When Ernest returned from the extended visit to Spain on November 3, 1959, he was interviewed at the airport by Prensa Latina, Cuba's official state news agency. Contrary to his custom, and perhaps because Mary was not there to stop him, he made several comments on the local political situation. These comments were recorded in an FBI memo dated November 6, 1959, from the American embassy in Havana to the department of state in Washington, DC. Hemingway's opinion of the revolutionary government was unchanged since January: "he supported it and all its acts completely, and thought it was the best thing that had ever happened to Cuba." Hemingway said he had not believed any of the information published abroad against Cuba. The FBI quoted the Prensa Latina report: "He sympathized with the Cuban government and all our difficulties. Hemingway emphasized the our and was asked about it. He said he hoped Cubans would regard him not as a Yanqui (his word), but as another Cuban." Following that comment, Hemingway "kissed a Cuban flag which was nearby. He refused to repeat the gesture for photographers, saying he 'had kissed the flag with sincerity,' implying that publicity would cheapen the act." Hemingway said he knew nothing about any recent note from the American government to the Cuban government on relations between the two countries. "He said that he had come from New York, where they 'knew nothing about Cuba or the world. There all they talk about is Van Doren and the scandal of the TV quiz shows.'"[22]

A section of the memo marked "Official Use Only" was partially redacted, but read, "Comment: Hemingway's remarks have been strongly played by Prensa Latina and given wide publicity locally. It is unfortunate that blank of his position and blank Redaction."[23] While it is not clear what the rest of the comment was, it seems reasonable to conclude the FBI kept an eye on what influential Americans, and Hemingway in particular, said about the Cuban government.

By the time Ernest arrived with Carmen and Antonio, Mary had brought the Finca up to standard and even arranged bouquets in the guesthouse for Carmen. Ernest's peace offering of the diamond pin failed to change Mary's mind about him, and she didn't want to act as hostess for Antonio and Carmen. Ernest complained to Hotch when Mary didn't thank him for the pin. She told him he should have known she didn't want a pin, and if he bought one anyway, it was his own fault.[24] Mary and Lola left Cuba and flew to Chicago to shop for the Ketchum, Idaho, house. Then they took the train to Ketchum and worked hard setting up the place. A few days later, Ernest arrived in Ketchum with Antonio, Carmen, and Roberto Herrera, who had helped Antonio with the driving. They planned to go hunting the next day, but one of Antonio's sisters in Mexico phoned to say she was about to leave her husband and she needed her brother by her side. This upset the plans, and Ernest spent two days helping with visas, allowing Antonio and Carmen to leave for Mexico. Ernest returned to work on the Paris sketches, and Mary continued to improve the house. She planned to finish the work on the house and leave for New York. Ernest didn't like the idea and tried to persuade her to stay.

In late November, fate intervened. Ernest and Mary went duck hunting with George Saviers in a frozen swamp. While walking about twenty paces behind George and Ernest, Mary tripped on a stick. She kept her loaded shotgun pointed into the air and landed on her elbow, "smashing it like an eggshell." They returned to the car and began the drive to the Sun Valley Hospital. Mary groaned from the unbearable pain, and Ernest told her to keep it quiet. After surgery, the doctors decided Mary should stay in the hospital for a night or two so she could summon help when the pain became too intense. Though she had broken both her ankles and cracked her ribs before, Mary found the pain from the shattered elbow was of a different magnitude. It was so bad she couldn't even read for two days. Ernest was annoyed she stayed in the hospital.

Though Ernest attempted to show sympathy, Mary felt he treated her as if she had deliberately broken her elbow to interrupt his work on the Paris sketches. He grumbled about having to do the shopping, although he was the only one who could drive. Ernest also complained about her one-armed cooking. He said he was being asked to do a servant's work when Mary asked him to help her take off her pants one evening. "Tonight, helping me undress, you spoke of doing 'maids work'—I will arrange that you won't have to do this anymore," Mary said, in a handwritten note composed at 12:02 A.M. [25] Ernest confronted her, saying, "You can only go to bed happy if you have made the fight and made somebody miserable so they can't sleep all night." Mary strongly denied this and replied, "Look, Lamb—if you want to get rid of me, please just say so, calmly and without all the insinuations and assaults and cruelties. Just say so." But, she asked, "Please, let us not go on with the nightly false accusations and hurts. I love you—yes, I do." She drew a small kitten face. [26]

Mary wished she could move to New York, but her broken elbow made that impossible. Close to Christmas, the doctors had to re-break her elbow and the pain was as intense as on the first break. George Saviers gave her morphine tablets but warned her to take as few as possible. Mary was an obedient patient, endured the pain, and returned the bottle half-full.

Pappy and Tillie Arnold invited them for a roast beef dinner early in the new year. Since Ernest didn't like driving at night, Pappy picked them up. Heavy snow was falling outside the Arnold's picture window, creating a beautiful winter scene. Ernest noticed the lights were on at the bank down the street, and he said FBI agents were checking their accounts because they wanted to get something on him. Tillie tried to reassure him it was just the usual cleaning women, but Ernest protested. Once the bank lights went out, he worried there was so much snow they couldn't get home. Tillie recalled, "You have to appreciate that this was not Papa talking. This was a different man who was gelatin inside, a terribly insecure man, a depressed man with irrational fears." [27] Pappy put chains on his tires to allay Ernest's fears, and they made it home without difficulty.

The skies were a brilliant blue for the next few days and Ernest's mood seemed to lighten. However, he grew restless and said he wanted to return to Cuba to work standing before his bookcase in the Finca. On January 17, they left Ketchum to catch the train in Shoshone and traveled to Cuba. Mary's painful elbow had shattered her dream of settling in New York on her own.

THIRTY-TWO

Lots of Problems but
We Will Solve Them All

January 1960–September 25, 1960

M ary was back among her flowers at the Finca and Ernest began working harder than usual. José Luis Herrera recommended exercise and massage for Mary's healing elbow, and Ernest spent half an hour each day massaging her arm with an electric vibrator. Since Mary could not use her typewriter, Ernest suggested they invite Valerie to the Finca to help with the *Life* piece. Mary thought it would be good for Ernest to enjoy Valerie's gentle wit, and she arrived at the end of January and took up residence in the Little House. Valerie understood that Mary had agreed in October to her coming to Havana, not in January.[1]

Valerie recalled Mary was unfriendly at first, but as time passed and Valerie kept to her work, it became clear she was not interested in Ernest. Mary's distrust waned, and they laughed and joked with each other. They took trips to the market in Havana and Valerie helped in the garden. Mary bought bright fabrics at the market and designed flamboyant suits and dresses for Valerie to wear at the Finca. Valerie also became closer to Ernest. They went fishing on *Pilar* without Mary, who feared the possibility of re-injuring her elbow, and they went for walks, and Ernest occasionally embraced her in bear hugs. Valerie "grew to treasure our moments together, to cherish the harmony, tranquility and intensely private life" they lived at the Finca, away from the celebrity-hunters of Spain.[2]

Valerie described the serene atmosphere of the Finca as "a Garden of Eden." She remembered, "Mary could be jolly and fun, and she had this enthusiasm about things. To me, it was somewhat ridiculous because I grew up with a garden, and we ate things from our garden." Mary would say, "look how beautiful this lettuce is, this radish is. She would come in and show Ernest. Look at these beautiful vegetables, Lamb. Look at what we have to eat." Mary "had this way of making things grand because there was not a lot going on in Cuba, and they were really curtailing their intake. They were on these diets, so every piece of food had to have some significance." Ernest "would enthuse over it. I used to think it was idiotic, but it was pleasantly idiotic. She was like that about the fruits and the thirteen types of mangoes. She was ecstatic about the mangoes in their life."[3] Ernest "loved the animals, the people, he loved the Finca; it was his real home. Mary was a very homey person; she ran the servants well and ran the household." Ernest's life "went smoothly; he wasn't good on the domestic front, he hated repairs."[4]

Valerie recalled that Ernest was "very particular in what he drank, and he would do without if the offering was inferior."[5] In Cuba, they drank very little, "two drinks before dinner, a rum or whiskey. Mary drank gin and tonic. We drank wine with dinner and occasionally, whiskey after. And wine at lunch. On the boat, we had rum and beer." Ernest "didn't drink cheap wine, he liked good wines. He knew the name and what was going to pair with it. He was careful. Alcoholics don't do that in my experience, they drink everything and anything—whatever is there. They mix-and-match." Valerie said, "Ernest never got drunk, I never once saw him drunk."[6]

Valerie observed Ernest wrote standing up because he had a metal kneecap and sitting down was painful. The knee had never been replaced, and since it was metal, it conducted heat and cold and caused him pain. "He didn't take painkillers but used alcohol."[7]

The American ambassador to Cuba, Phil Bonsall, was a regular dinner guest at the Finca, and over the months, he had become more pessimistic about the relations between the two governments. Eventually, Bonsall gave Ernest a blunt warning: The US was about to end diplomatic relations with Cuba, and the famous American writer ought to leave Cuba or risk becoming an embarrassment. Ernest's continuing presence in Cuba might be seen as tacit support of the Castro regime, and Bonsall reported some might even suggest Hemingway was a traitor. These words weighed heavily on Ernest and Mary's mood and became even more poignant when the US recalled Phil Bonsall as ambassador.[8]

◆

Ernest usually accorded Mary first reading rights of his work, but he had not shown her anything of the *Life* piece. One day when he was massaging her arm she asked him how it was coming, and he complained he was having a hellish time getting it all down. He gave Mary a sheaf of papers to review, and his work bewildered her. Some passages about the scenery in Spain were graceful, and he captured the exuberance of the crowds, but the bullfighting scenes were repetitive. When Mary returned the manuscript, she suggested he remove some recurring scenes but he said they all belonged, and far from being mere gestures, they were artful displays of courage. He never asked her to review the manuscript again.[9] Mary had identified many of the passages Hotch would later remove.

During the next few months they stayed home, reading and walking, but occasionally, venturing to the Floridita for an evening of drinking and singing. The revolution made necessities scarce, drove away tourists, and reduced the flow of visitors to the Finca. Ernest worked on his bullfighting story, and they did little entertaining.

◆

Anastas Mikoyan was the number two man in the Soviet Union and a close ally of Premier Nikita Khrushchev. Mikoyan visited Cuba to meet with Fidel Castro on sensitive business. The diplomat was also a Hemingway fan, and he paid an impromptu visit to the Finca, with an enthusiastic entourage, including his son Sergo. Mary improvised to feed the hungry, vodka-swilling Soviets who stayed for hours. Mikoyan made a lengthy speech and presented Ernest with a braille version of *The Old Man and the Sea* and a nested egg doll.[10] He said Ernest was read and much admired in Russia, and Ernest's books were selling so well, the USSR owed Ernest $250,000 in royalties. He offered to arrange payment at ten thousand dollars a year, but Ernest declined the offer, saying, "I shall be happy to collect my royalties when you do the same for other American writers."[11]

Soon after Mikoyan's visit, Mary wrote to Buck, telling him the Soviet leader was "mighty astute" and giving him an update on the Cuban revolution. "Don't let the US Press kid you, that like other Cuban revolutions, this is just a change of army and palace guard. It's not."[12] The Cuban people were solidly behind this one. She reported her arm was recovering, and Ernest was working "like a steam turbine on his bullfight piece." He was swimming half a mile a day in the pool.

◆

At the end of May, Ernest entered *Pilar* in the annual Hemingway Marlin-Fishing Tournament. Fidel Castro and some of his friends appropriated one of the American-owned boats and entered the competition. Mary and the others watched Fidel's boat through binoculars, and, on the first day, they saw him catch two marlins, both according to the big-game fishing rules. The next day, he caught a third marlin, and the combined weight of his three fish won first prize—Ernest's silver trophy. Ernest presented the award to Castro on the dock that evening. It was the only time they met, and they chatted about fishing. Ernest told Mary in the car on the way home that Castro said he'd read *For Whom the Bell Tolls* and had used its ideas about guerrilla warfare in his battles in the Sierra Maestra.

◆

Two weeks later, Ernest asked Valerie to stay behind at the Finca while Mary went to the Havana markets. Valerie assumed he had some extra work for her to do, but he wanted to make a small speech. Ernest told Valerie her presence in Cuba had saved him from suicide, but his eyesight and general health were deteriorating, and he was finished. Though he loved her, they could no longer have a future together, and he wanted to release her. This surprised Valerie, for she had never imagined a future as Ernest's consort. Valerie promised she would be a good and faithful friend, but Ernest wanted more. He wanted her to know his plan to kill himself, to know it was inevitable, but to keep it a secret from Mary. Valerie knew there was no point in arguing with him, and "our eyes met, and I silently assented."[13] Fixed with the knowledge of Ernest's plan, Valerie wondered about her responsibility to intervene. And if she should intervene, how could she do it? She wavered between trying to save Ernest and fleeing from the madhouse the Finca had become for her. Despite her private torment, Valerie pretended cheerfulness.

◆

The political climate in Cuba became uncomfortable. Castro proclaimed Americans who had never exploited the Cuban people were safe. Still, bearded soldiers were moving into the homes of wealthy Americans, Cubans, and Spaniards and appropriating whatever they wished. When Juan took Mary shopping in her yellow convertible, the people in the village were friendly, and their old friends in Havana were glad to see her. However, signs were appearing on walls saying: "CUBA SÍ! YANQUI NO!"(Cuba Yes! Yankee No!) The warnings were ominous.

Ernest's manuscript grew to one hundred and twenty thousand words by the end of May, and he couldn't cut down the story to the agreed number of ten thousand words. To add to his difficulty, Antonio and Luis Miguel planned to resume their *mano a mano* bullfighting contest in the summer, and Ernest felt he couldn't write a conclusion without knowing the outcome. He asked Hotch to come to Cuba to help him edit the piece. On June 27, Ernest and Juan met Hotch at the airport and they drove to the Finca. Mary served a lunch of cold fruit soup and bonito in the dining room. Ernest ate very little and drank water from his wineglass. He rubbed his eyes and pressed them with his fingers.[14]

After lunch, Ernest gave Hotch the manuscript of almost seven hundred pages, and he took it to the office in the tower to read. Hotch worked through the afternoon, evening, and next morning despite the extreme heat and handed Ernest a list of eight proposed cuts from the first one hundred pages. Hotch went back to work and met with Ernest the next morning. Ernest gave him a set of notes rejecting each of the proposed cuts. Hotch thought Ernest's reasons made little sense, and many seemed petulant. It surprised him, for he had often worked with Ernest on his manuscripts and never had Ernest made notes. Hotch realized Ernest was under tremendous pressure, and he didn't press his recommendations but kept working on the manuscript.[15]

On the fourth day, Ernest accepted a cut of three pages. Then, he agreed to more cuts until they had extracted sixty thousand words by the end of the ninth day.[16] Ernest complained his eyes were too sore to allow him to continue, and Hotch took the manuscript to the editors of *Life* in New York to make further cuts. Ernest told Hotch he was beat-up because everything he had was in Cuba, and he would soon lose it all. The conflict between the US and Castro would soon force him to give up his home, library, boat, and place he loved.

◆

For the last seven months, Mary had been considering how to remove herself from Ernest's life. However, she put the idea on hold because Ernest was facing so many problems and he had resumed addressing her as "My dear Kittner."[17] Once again, Mary put aside her plans because she felt sorry for Ernest and knew he needed her. Even after Ernest entrusted his manuscript to Hotch, he felt anxious. He decided he had to return to Spain to make a final assessment about the *mano a mano* contest. Mary chose not to accompany him, and traveled to New York instead. Hotch found her a modest, half-furnished townhouse at 1 East Sixty-Second Street.

Ernest, Mary, and Valerie boarded a ferry from Havana to Key West on July 25, intending to return the following autumn or winter. Toby Bruce met them, helped with the luggage, and got them to the airport for a flight to New York.

When Mary arrived in New York, she liked the townhouse and began making it comfortable. The cooler temperature was agreeable, and she started seeing her old friends. Her life as a single person was promising.

Ernest left by jet aircraft for Madrid on August 4 and sent a cable saying he was staying at the Suecia Hotel. On August 8, Mary received a message from Hotch saying the press had reported Ernest collapsed in the bullring at Málaga and was very ill. Mary made plans to fly to Madrid and tried to confirm the press reports.[18] After an agonizing wait and many efforts to reach Ernest and other Spanish friends by cable, she received news that Ernest had denied the press reports. In her brisk style, Mary confessed to Ernest she "blubbered. Val danced around the room. Stopped blubbering, called travel man, canceled flight, Got good, big drink—Val too." Mary reported, "We couldn't unwind quickly. Val wanted to go to the Stork Club to celebrate. I much too tired."[19]

Valerie went to Paris to stay with friends. After she had been there only a few days, Ernest asked her to come to Madrid to help him select photographs for his *Life* story. The man Valerie met on her arrival was a diminished figure, who had lost weight, lacked energy, and seemed anxious and distracted. His eyes no longer sparkled. He looked over his shoulder, fearing people were eavesdropping on their conversations, and he worried his portrayal of Luis Miguel in the *Life* piece would upset him. They joined Bill Davis, who was no longer easy-going and happy around Ernest but guarded and wary. In Madrid, they dined in the same restaurant every night, and Ernest always ordered the same meal.[20] Over the next month they followed the corridas, with Davis driving them from place to place in Ernest's Lancia. Ernest seemed tense, and he was silent during the drives. He took Valerie aside and told her Davis was trying to kill them in a car accident. Valerie protested but said she would keep a careful watch.[21]

◆

Mary phoned René each week to check on conditions at the Finca. He told her thieves had broken into the garden shed and stolen gardening tools, and the carpenter had quit for lack of money to buy materials. All the Hemingways' mail arriving at the post office was being opened and resealed, and René advised Mary against making a trip to Cuba.[22]

Ernest wrote to Mary complaining he couldn't sleep due to cramps, nightmares, and loneliness. The bullfighting business was corrupt and now seemed unimportant. He feared "a complete physical and nervous crack-up from deadly overwork."[23] Mary assumed Ernest was overtired and would recover after he finished the *Life* piece. The first installment of "The Dangerous Summer" was well-received, and Mary cabled Ernest about the enthusiastic reception. Ernest replied he thought the piece was not bad, but the horrible face on the cover (his own photo) made him sick. He could not stand the comparison between this mere journalism and *The Old Man and the Sea*. Mary wrote back the next day wishing she could take him on a refreshing holiday to Paraíso so they could sleep like kittens on *Pilar*. Ernest wished Mary was there "to help me out and keep from cracking up. Feel terrible, and am just going to lie quiet now and try to rest."[24]

Mary urged Ernest to stop working so hard and get some rest. She reported news of their friends in New York City. Bill Walton was in great form "and working like a dog, heading the whole NY effort" for Kennedy's presidential campaign. Mary thought she would help out in the Spanish-speaking parts of the city. One night she went with Walton to a meeting at the Biltmore Hotel and heard "Young Bob Kennedy" give "a ten-minute speech—a miracle of non-palaver and non-crap."[25]

Mary was enjoying her "bachelor-girlhood life," as she called it.[26] Alfred Rice found tickets for a Royal Ballet performance of "Sleeping Beauty" starring Margot Fonteyn, and Mary enjoyed "a perfectly marvelous evening."[27] She went with Val's friend to see Jean Genet's "The Balcony" in Greenwich Village, and she enjoyed "the evil wit."[28] A day later, the editor of *The Paris Review*, George Plimpton, took her to observe a United Nations Security Council session, followed by an amusing dinner. Mary treated Bill Walton to a home-cooked Chinese dinner of sweet and sour shrimp, and he gave her "various tidbits of inside dope on politics, and foreign policy," so sensitive she did not want to write about them in her letter to Ernest.[29] The columnist Earl Wilson invited her to go nightclubbing, and she planned a trip to Chicago to visit her cousin Bea. Mary's days and evenings were filled with friends and pleasant activities, contrasting starkly with Ernest's increasing anxiety.

◈

Ernest didn't want to see anyone in case his *Life* piece had offended them. At night, insomnia plagued him, and he asked Valerie to sit by his side until he fell asleep. Despite Valerie's efforts to divert him, Ernest continued to be obsessed with thoughts of his suicide. Hotch arrived on October 2 to discuss an offer by Twentieth Century Fox to make a movie based on the Nick Adams stories. His flight was delayed and Ernest assumed the airline was covering up an air crash at sea.[30] Ernest soon told Hotch that Davis was trying to crack up the car and kill him, and he warned Hotch to take taxis rather than ride with him. Ernest was nervous and fatigued, down on everyone, constantly talked about his kidneys the way he used to talk about his eyes, and was impossible to manage. Davis said it was imperative to get him back to the States.[31]

Over the next few days, Ernest continued his strange behavior. He grabbed a waiter by the sleeve and shouted at him in English. The owner came, and Ernest shouted at him, too. That afternoon, Ernest went to bed and stayed there for four days, each day postponing his scheduled flight to New York. Ernest worried he wouldn't be allowed to carry excess baggage and would lose his large collection of bullfighting photos. Hotch weighed Ernest's luggage, checked with the airline, and secured a letter from the Madrid office manager permitting his extra luggage.[32] When the departure time arrived, Valerie, Bill, Annie, and Hotch saw him off.

Valerie hugged him, hoping her strength could somehow transfer to Ernest, but she couldn't bring herself to look into his eyes. Later she needed to be alone to grieve because "in my heart of hearts, I had already made my farewell. For me, Ernest was already dead."[33]

◆

Years later, looking back, Mary admitted she did not recognize the warning signs of Ernest's decline. He had always recovered before, and she believed he would do so again. Ernest seemed to justify her hopes when he wrote an optimistic letter on September 23 describing his visit to the Prado Museum and saying he would return in early October. "Lots of problems, but we will solve them all."[34]

THIRTY-THREE

A Vegetable Life

October 8, 1960–April 24, 1961

M ary and George Brown met Ernest at Idlewild (soon to be renamed John F. Kennedy) airport when he returned from Spain on October 8, 1960. Ernest had combed his hair forward, in the style of a Roman Emperor, to cover his bald spot. His haggard face showed the flight had been an ordeal. After greeting Mary with a hug, he reached into the pocket of his old tweed jacket, retrieved his silver flask, and took a hearty swig. Mary found the scene theatrical and not at all charming, and she didn't know what to expect next from her volatile husband. Leaving him was still on her mind. After they got home to the New York apartment, he was silent and preoccupied with problems he did not wish to discuss. Ernest was afraid to leave the apartment to walk in Central Park, saying, "someone was waiting out there."[1] Mary lost patience and told him to quit acting like a fugitive—he withdrew and retreated into himself.

Two days later, they traveled by train to Shoshone and George Saviers met them with his car for the drive to Ketchum. After they loaded the luggage, Ernest sat in the front passenger seat. He saw two men wearing overcoats come out of a restaurant and claimed they were tailing him. Saviers assured him they were traveling salesmen. Ernest complained about his high blood pressure and a recurring kidney infection on the drive to Ketchum, and Saviers promised he would arrange tests. The car filled with Ernest's nervous tension and Saviers worried whether he had the skills to deal with his shaken patient because, as he often told people, he was a simple country doctor.

They arrived home late on October 22, and the following day, Ernest began working at his pulpit desk in front of the window overlooking the valley of the Big Wood River. His mood improved as he remembered more of his life in Paris and worked on the sketches that would appear in *A Moveable Feast*.

A windstorm blew down a tall cottonwood tree across the river, creating a natural bridge onto their land, and Ernest worried someone might walk over it to enter their property. Mary assured him they were surrounded by friends, and there was no one to fear. While he was parking his car in Ketchum, Ernest nicked the vehicle parked next to his. He took down the license number and contacted the owners of the other vehicle. Even though they thought the scratch was minor, Ernest fretted the sheriff would come after him. He also worried they couldn't afford to continue living in the Ketchum house because the taxes were too high, and Mary tried to dispel his concerns. She contacted his New York bank and listened on an extension phone while a manager explained there was a healthy balance in Ernest's accounts. Ernest did not believe the manager.[2] Mary reacted the way most people would to Ernest's delusions. She told him his fears were groundless and tried to find rational explanations, but his worries did not fade.

Ed Hotchner came for a brief visit. He arrived by train in Shoshone a few minutes early and waited for Ernest in their favorite bar. Soon Ernest entered and told Hotch they had to leave right away in Duke MacMullan's car because the FBI was tailing them. He told Hotch they had bugged his car and George Saviers's car and tapped his phone at home. When they drove into Ketchum, Ernest saw two men working in the bank after hours, and he told Hotch they were auditors going over his accounts. Hotch could not persuade him otherwise. Over the next few days, many of Ernest's friends told Hotch they were worried about Ernest because he had changed. He acted depressed, refused to go hunting, complained about old friends, and looked terrible.[3]

Ernest didn't allow Hotch to talk to Mary alone, and they had to arrange a meeting in the back of a grocery store. Mary told Hotch she was worried about Ernest's behavior. She showed him a letter Ernest had written to his bank the day before. The salutation and first sentence were fine, but the words turned into gibberish. Mary told Hotch that Ernest's ability to work had deteriorated to the point that he spent hours standing at his desk leafing through the pages of the Paris sketches.[4] Hotch suggested to Mary that he consult a psychiatrist in New York, Dr. James Cattell, on Papa's behalf. Mary agreed, hoping he might find help.

Hotch first talked to Dr. Saviers, who was at his wits' end about how to treat Ernest and was supportive of the idea of using Ernest's high blood pressure as an excuse for sending him to a hospital where he might also receive psychiatric help.

Tillie Arnold saw Ernest walking every day, and when she chatted with him, he told her he hoped the exercise would stimulate his mind, help him write better, lower his blood pressure, and reduce his desire for alcohol. A few days later, she saw him again. Tillie and Lloyd were about to go on a trip to California, and she said a tearful goodbye to Ernest. He buried himself in her arms and sobbed, and she knew he was trying to tell her goodbye for good. "When I got into the car, I was crying, and, as I told Lloyd what happened, I also said that something dreadful was going to happen, that something was about to break in Papa."[5]

Saviers suggested that Ernest should go to a better-equipped hospital for a proper diagnosis of his fluctuating blood pressure. Ernest rejected the Menninger Clinic in Topeka because he thought everyone would think he had lost his marbles if he went there. Saviers and Hotch found him a place at St. Mary's Hospital in Rochester, Minnesota, where the nearby Mayo Clinic specialists practiced. The ostensible reason for Ernest's visit was to treat his high blood pressure; the true purpose was for him to see a psychiatrist. To preserve his privacy, they booked Ernest into the hospital as George Saviers. Dr. Hugh Butt was to treat his hypertension and Dr. Howard Rome, the chief psychiatrist at the Mayo Clinic, would care for his mental issues. George Saviers remembered, "I would say that he went voluntarily in the sense that he knew he was going to get his blood pressure down, but he realized that his life wasn't worth living."[6]

Mary's life was frustrating and lonely while Ernest was in St. Mary's. She stayed at the Kahler Hotel in Rochester, registered as Mrs. George Saviers. The hotel was filled with patients and family members visiting the Mayo Clinic. When the weather wasn't too cold throughout December, instead of taking a cab, Mary walked an hour to the hospital and visited with Ernest. After a few hours with him, she walked back to the hotel and had dinner by herself in the hotel restaurant. She kept a lonely vigil and worried whether he would recover.

As his paranoia blossomed on December 4, Ernest wrote a letter on the back of a Mayo Clinic diet form clearing Mary of involvement in any illegal activities. "My wife Mary, at no time, believed or considered that I had ever committed any illegal act of any kind. She had no guilty knowledge of any of my finances nor relations with anyone." He declared, "she was neither an accomplice nor in any sense a fugitive and only followed the advice of a doctor friend she trusted."[7]

Whenever Mary was in New York while Ernest remained a patient at the Mayo Clinic, she invited Valerie to the flat and gave her updates on Ernest's condition. Mary shared her hope that the electroshock therapy would defeat his depression and renew his desire to live. Valerie didn't disclose to Mary that Ernest had told her in Spain he intended to kill himself. Mary tried to persuade Valerie to come out to Ketchum in the summer, hoping her visit would cheer Ernest. Valerie recalled, "Mary wanted me to commit to come and spend the summer with them. I didn't want to do that, but I didn't say yes or no because there wasn't any point. I thought it was hypothetical."[8] Valerie was working for *Newsweek* magazine in New York, and she was not sure she wanted to take up with the Hemingways again, for they had parted on good terms, and she thought she should leave it that way. Valerie told Mary she would think about her invitation.[9]

Ernest's delusions of persecution did not end after psychotherapy, and Dr. Rome took Ernest off his hypertension medication to see if that might reduce his depressive state. Next he prescribed electroshock therapy, considered "the fail-safe cure for depression (usually at a 90% cure rate in the 1950s and 1960s)."[10] In 1961, the procedure involved putting the patient on an intravenous flow of amobarbital until they fell asleep. Then, "a blood pressure cuff tightened around one ankle, and another intravenous infusion of succinylcholine paralyzed his muscles. A rubber bite-guard was placed in his mouth, and a conductive gel was rubbed in circles over his temples." Next, "a rubber strap was placed around his head, holding two metal electrodes, one over each temple, in place." Finally, "the ECT machine was set at a high enough current level to induce a seizure. Though Hemingway was paralyzed, direct current through the temporal muscles would cause his jaw to clinch, but the bite-guard prevented any injury."[11] When Ernest woke some forty-five minutes later, his mouth was dry and his vision blurred. His head "felt clouded. He wanted to get up, he wanted to speak, but his body wouldn't do what his brain wanted it to do. . . . His head felt heavy, his body was numb and not moving, the noise came in waves."[12] Ernest would've been in a state of amnesia and confusion, which generally clears but, in his case, cleared more slowly and never fully, and he believed the ECT treatments destroyed his memory.[13] The procedures continued through December, and it is thought Ernest received fifteen treatments.[14]

On those days when he was not receiving electroshock treatments, Ernest was allowed to roam through the hospital and the town of Rochester, and he visited Dr. Butt's house to sit in the sunroom or use his library. Butt and Ernest became such good friends, the doctor invited the Hemingways to his home for Christmas dinner with his wife and four daughters. The Butts served one of the best wines from their cellar and a Yule log cake.[15] After the meal, Mary and Ernest sang Italian and French folksongs to entertain the Butt family.[16]

The night before, on Christmas Eve, 1960, Mary sat in her room at the Kahler Hotel and wrote a long and revealing journal entry, one she kept out of her memoir. She had just left Ernest at St. Mary's Hospital and wrote, after twenty-four days and nine electric shock treatments, "he seemed to me today to be almost as disturbed and disjointed mentally as he was when we came here."[17] She noted he had improved in some areas, for example, he no longer insisted an FBI agent hid behind the door to his bathroom with a tape recorder.

Ernest complained he felt terrible, but only when the nurses were out of the room and out of hearing. Despite his banker's assurances, he believed the Ketchum house would be seized for non-payment of taxes. He felt guilty about using George Saviers's name to throw off the press and believed the FBI would investigate and arrest him for using an assumed name. Mary confessed it was difficult to sustain her composure for over four or five hours at a stretch. "I dread going back to the gloom and phony disaster . . . tomorrow." She knew, "he had to be pampered with all his illusions but didn't understand why the pampering causes me such distress. . . . It is possible that I am distressed because I feel I too may begin to confuse illusion with reality."[18] People who agreed with Ernest had always surrounded him, flattered him, and done his chores, packing, valeting, and chauffeuring. "What I am most repelled by now," she wrote, "is the idea of spending the rest of my life in a high degree of pampering, agreeing, chore-doing, all of it with the target of preserving this one creature, and for him cutting off sunshine, gaiety, delicacy, love, affection, friends and all the big bright world."[19] She left these dark thoughts out of her memoir.

Mary finished the note to herself at 12:15 A.M. on Christmas Day, frightened she might lose her grip on reality and get dragged into Ernest's delusional world. She resented the energy it took to indulge Ernest, and the thought of spending the rest of her life preserving him revolted her. Mary did not want to sacrifice her life for his. He charmed the nurses, "who competed with each other to do him extra favors, finding tempting tidbits in the kitchen or amusing reading."[20] Mary didn't understand why Dr. Rome couldn't see through it.

Mary had had enough, but she couldn't see a way out for herself. There was no one else to take care of Ernest because his sons were preoccupied with their own problems or absent. Jack was having financial problems, Greg, mental issues, and Patrick, in whom Mary and Ernest both had the most confidence, was far away in Africa. Bill Walton thought Mary realized Ernest would not live as long as actuarial tables might suggest, and her best course forward was to survive him as his widow.[21]

The Mayo Clinic doctors hosted a lunch with Ernest as the guest of honor on January 8. Afterward, Dr. Butt took him trapshooting at an abandoned quarry where Ernest hit twenty-seven clay pigeons one after the other.[22] A couple of days later, the United Press International revealed Ernest was under the care of doctors from the Mayo Clinic for an ailment "reported to be not serious."[23] The *New York Times* reported the famed novelist was being treated for hypertension and his condition was satisfactory.[24]

On January 13, 1961, the FBI special agent in charge of Minneapolis sent a memo for the personal attention of J. Edgar Hoover, the director of the FBI, concerning Ernest Hemingway.[25] The memo reported Hemingway had been a patient at the Mayo Clinic and was presently at St. Mary's Hospital. He had been at the clinic for several weeks "and is seriously ill, both physically and mentally, and at one time the doctors were considering giving him electro-shock therapy treatments." A representative of the Mayo Clinic (likely Dr. Rome) reported that to eliminate publicity and contacts by newsmen, Mr. Hemingway was advised to register under the alias George Saviers. "Mr. Hemingway is now worried about his registering under an assumed name and is concerned about an FBI investigation." The Mayo Clinic representative advised this worry was interfering with the treatment of Mr. Hemingway and "desired authorization to tell Hemingway that the FBI was not concerned with his registering under an assumed name."[26] The FBI officer advised the representative "there was no objection" to so informing Hemingway.

On the face of the memo, the FBI accommodated Ernest's doctor's request for assurance that there was no investigation underway concerning his use of George Saviers's name. Hemingway biographer Jeffrey Meyers makes much of this memo: "The FBI had, in fact, tracked Hemingway to the walls of the Mayo Clinic and discussed his case with his psychiatrist. The agents were following him, he knew it, and was more realistic than his wife and friend (Hotch)." Meyers concludes, "Dr. Rome's contact with the FBI gave substance to Hemingway's fear 'that one of the interns was a Fed in disguise.'"[27] Meyers's allegations twist the plain meaning of the memo. There is no evidence in the memo the FBI "followed Ernest" to the Mayo Clinic or that one of the interns was "a Fed in disguise."

President Kennedy invited Ernest to attend his inauguration. The recognition pleased Ernest, but he composed a letter of regret in which he blamed his inability to participate on his treatment for hypertension. Mary found the letter "a bit too fulsome for my taste."[28] On January 20, Mary and Ernest watched the inauguration on television in St. Mary's Hospital, and Ernest became so cheerful, Dr. Rome pronounced him cured. Ernest wrote to President Kennedy after the event, "Watching the inauguration from Rochester there was the happiness and the hope and the pride and how beautiful Mrs. Kennedy was and then how deeply moving the inaugural address was." He concluded, "It is a good thing to have a brave man as our President in times as tough as these are for our country and the world."[29]

Ernest was released from St. Mary's Hospital on January 22, and Dr. Rome wrote a letter setting out his diagnosis.[30] "The depression, agitation, and tension" Ernest had suffered resulted from an untoward reaction to his blood pressure medication. Rome wrote, "Serpasil provokes this type of untoward response in a significant number of patients." These symptoms were "accelerated by the use of Ritalin" prescribed to offset the depression. Rome found, "the pharmacological action of these agents fulminated the condition we first witnessed." Rome noted that Dr. Butt agreed Ernest should stop taking the blood pressure medication, and he recommended Ernest continue taking Lithium until he returned to a normal tenor of life. He prescribed Seconal to ensure a good night's sleep. The psychiatrist concluded his letter on an optimistic note. "It is my judgment that you have fully recovered from this experience, and I see no reason to anticipate anything further on this score."[31] Dr. Butt's discharge letter to Ernest agreed with Dr. Rome's findings but suggested his enlarged liver might indicate he had "a very rare disease called hemochromatosis. However, I do not feel that this should be investigated further at this time."[32] According to both Rome and Butt, a drug reaction had caused Ernest's depressive condition, and they both believed "you have made a very good recovery."[33] Dr. Butt added a handwritten postscript: "at the present time, I see no reason why you cannot drink wine but not to exceed a liter a day, and I would hope less."[34]

After Ernest returned home, the tension increased so fast, Mary feared she was on the verge of a breakdown herself. She walked with Ernest every day along the highway in five-mile segments to cheer him up and make sure he got enough exercise. Ernest told Tillie Arnold he walked to relieve his frustration that he couldn't write after his release from the Mayo Clinic. He continued to work on the Paris sketches, and some days he stood at his desk shuffling papers but writing nothing.

The White House asked Ernest to contribute a few sentences to a book being prepared as a gift for President Kennedy. Mary went to town, bought the specified paper, and cut several sheets to the required size. Ernest sat at a desk in the living room and worked for hours, but he could not complete the task. Mary went out walking to give him some space. When she returned, he was still trying to find the right words. This went on for a week and Ernest became despondent, "with almost a smell of desperation oozing out of him," before he completed the job.[35] Tillie and Lloyd Arnold saw Ernest almost every day and observed he was becoming more withdrawn. Tillie remembered, "often, when we would be around him, he would wander off and stare out the window, his mind miles away. I could see him aging almost before my eyes. In short, he was deteriorating rapidly."[36]

George Saviers thought Ernest suffered from depression most of his life. "I think he thought about suicide all his life," and he talked of suicide even when he was a kid. "I think when he had so much difficulty in writing, compared with the old days, when he was young and could turn out short stories in a few weeks, it added to his depression."[37] Saviers recalled Ernest was trying to get *A Moveable Feast* together, and it was tough because he wasn't well. His depression was getting more serious. Saviers went to see Ernest at about noon each day to check his blood pressure and talk to him. One day, Ernest was sitting on a lounge chair in the front room. "And boy, he was in a deep depression, and he said, 'George, it just won't come anymore.'"[38] Tears ran down his cheeks. Saviers remembered, "I used to talk with him about other people in other professions, telling him that professors retire, and executives retire, but he paid no attention to me. When he couldn't write, he just didn't have the will to go on."[39]

During March, Ernest became more and more silent, his eyes vacant.[40] One bitterly cold day, Tillie picked up Ernest when she saw him walking on the road. He began complaining about the incurable disease he had. She remembered a previous conversation in which Ernest had stated that suffering from an incurable disease would justify a person in taking their own life. She asked him if he was trying to tell her something and if he was referring to their earlier conversation. He said, "Yes, daughter, I am. There is no other way out for me. I am not going back to Rochester, where they will lock me up. I can't live like that. I am not going." Tillie looked him in the eye and said, "Papa, I don't blame you."[41] Tillie never told Mary about their conversation and doubted she would have forgiven her for agreeing with Ernest.

◆

Don Anderson had met Ernest and Mary in 1947 through their mutual friend Taylor "Beartracks" Williams. Don was a guide and assistant sports director at the Sun Valley Resort. He was a big quiet man with close-cut, graying hair. Ernest called him "the kid" and they had hunted birds for hundreds of hours together, enjoying each other's company. Anderson believed Ernest was "remarkably unsure and anxious about his writing . . . and that he was aggressively competitive with a terrific drive and a real perfectionist in whatever he undertook." When he "stalled out in writing, he could be as surly as a bear in the spring."[42] Anderson saw signs of Ernest's sharp mental decline after his return from the Mayo Clinic when he became suspicious of even close friends and had delusions of persecution. The electroshock treatments hadn't worked, and Ernest was indecisive, suffered from memory loss, became a recluse, and stayed at home. Don thought Ernest realized he was going over the hill mentally, and "all of his thoughts during the spring were concerned with how to commit suicide."[43]

Ernest kept to himself at home, becoming talkative at night when he berated Mary for her failure to accept his delusions about their precarious financial state. He complained she was spending too much on groceries and she was not doing enough to deal with their tax crisis. Mary never defended herself because that seemed to disturb him even more. She complained they were leading "a vegetable life with our spirits half atrophied."[44] One morning, in early April 1961, just after her fifty-third birthday, Mary awoke after a poor sleep caused in part by Ernest's hectoring the night before. As she described in a letter to the Bruces, "I fell down the stairs, cut a big gash in my head—but no concussion—sprained a foot . . . lucky I didn't break my neck."[45] Now she had to shuffle about with a cane.

On April 21, Mary limped down the stairs and found Ernest dressed in his red emperor's robe, standing next to the gun rack, holding his favorite shotgun—two shells rested on the windowsill. Mary began talking to him about the importance of life, fishing off the Yucatan Peninsula, and subletting a flat in Paris, hoping to divert him until the visit of George Saviers, who was coming at noon to check his blood pressure. She told Ernest how great his work was, praised his courage in Africa, and reminded him of their dream to return there. She spoke to him calmly and didn't try taking the gun from him, fearing "he could blast my head off at this short distance."[46] He had written a note which he crumpled into his pocket and later destroyed. Ernest remained sullen and stared into the distance, saying nothing. After fifty minutes of tension, Saviers arrived, entered the house, and grasped what was happening. He talked in a calm voice to Ernest and persuaded him to hand over the gun. Then Saviers phoned his colleague Dr. John Moritz, who soon arrived and the two of them took Ernest to the Sun Valley Hospital, where they sedated him.

Dr. Saviers decided Ernest had to return to the Mayo Clinic. He asked Don Anderson to take Ernest home to pick up some clothes for his upcoming stay in Rochester. Don's girlfriend, Joan Higgins, a pretty girl in her late twenties who was also one of Ernest's nurses, went with them. They arrived at the back door of the Hemingways' house, and Joan walked Ernest to the door. Ernest said they didn't have to bother coming in, and he wouldn't take long. Don replied that Dr. Saviers had detailed them to stay with him all times.[47] Ernest raced through the kitchen, to the gun rack in the living room, "picked up a shotgun, slipped two shells in, closed it, and pointed the weapon to his throat. Don seized the gun, trying to wrestle it away from Ernest who held it in a vice-like grip."[48] Don felt for the unlocking lever, opened the gun, and told Joan to take out the shells. She picked out one shell and then the other. As the rounds rolled away on the floor, Ernest quit fighting. Don pushed him onto the couch and tried to talk him down, telling Ernest, "he must think of his family and continue with the treatments. Ernest sat with glazed eyes, sullen, without speaking."[49] Having heard the scuffling, Mary came downstairs and tried to calm Ernest. She called Dr. Saviers, and he came and gave Ernest a sedative.

They drove Ernest back to the hospital and put him to bed after locking away his clothes to make an escape more difficult. The Nobel Laureate had become a fearful, desperate old man.

THIRTY-FOUR
Good Night, My Kitten

April 25, 1961–July 2, 1961

T he next morning, a Piper Comanche piloted by Lawrence Johnson left Hailey Airport on the sixteen-hundred-mile flight to Rochester. George Saviers sat beside the pilot, and Ernest and Don Anderson sat in the back seats. Saviers later described the trip "as a nightmare."[1] Ernest remained sullen and silent, despite the sunny morning. The Hailey Airport sits in a valley surrounded by sharp mountain peaks arranged like teeth in a giant stone saw. The plane flew high over the Big Wood River, above clusters of sagebrush and green Lodgepole pines, clinging to life in the harsh landscape, between the sand-colored ridges of the Sawtooth Mountains.

Johnson landed the plane in Rapid City to refuel and have a magneto replaced. While the repairs were being made, Ernest led Don on a tour of the repair hangars and parking lot. Don stuck close as Ernest searched through mechanics' toolboxes and the glove compartments of parked cars, muttering that mechanics often kept a spare gun in their toolboxes.[2] When told the Comanche was ready to fly again, Ernest saw a DC3 taxiing to park, and "he began to walk towards its still whirling propellers." The pilot cut the engine at the last moment when Ernest and Don were no more than thirty feet away. "Don had not laid a hand on him but guessed at Ernest's purpose."[3] The Piper Comanche took off and reached the Rochester airport later that afternoon. George Saviers recalled Ernest tried to open the airplane door to jump out while they were airborne.[4]

Dr. Butt and two orderlies from the Mayo Clinic met them at the Rochester airport. Happy to see Dr. Butt, Ernest willingly entered the limousine after saying a wistful goodbye to his friends. In their first interview, Ernest candidly told Dr. Rome there were many ways to kill himself, such as using light cords or coat hangers. Rome told Ernest he could not work with him if he were continuing to threaten suicide, and he put Ernest on his honor not to attempt it. Ernest promised and shook hands with Rome.[5]

After Ernest left, Mary sat down to type "a hard-to write letter" to Ernest's favorite sister, Ursula (Ura), in Honolulu. Mary said it was her duty to tell Ura, "Papa has been suffering from some form of paranoia characterized by acute depression, anxieties, hallucinations, etc., and in the last week by suicidal intentions."[6] She described the events of the last months, including a detailed account of Ernest's latest attempt to shoot himself, and told Ura she had written to Jack and Patrick and Alfred Rice, "about the whole business. Otherwise, I'm trying to keep it as quiet as possible. (Papa, of course, does not know I am writing any of these letters.)" Mary confessed, "my nerves and emotions are torn to shreds. I'd love to have any advice or suggestions for Papa's well-being you might send."

The next day, Mary wrote to, "My dearest lamb," telling him George Saviers had phoned to say they had arrived safely in Rochester after "a rough and tough" flight. She described the silver-blue river and her sighting of a black-throated gray warbler.[7] Over the next month, Mary wrote to Ernest every few days telling him how much she missed him, sending him "buckets full of kisses" and "mountain streams of kisses," describing the wildlife and fine views from their home, forwarding friends' best wishes, and answering his questions about their finances and bank accounts. Though she missed him, she hoped he would "stay there until it is absolutely positive that you are wholly recovered." They didn't want a repetition of the last three months and, "PLEASE LAMB, DON'T CON THEM into sending you home until they are sure you are ready for it."[8]

Mary read a *Time* account of the Bay of Pigs fiasco and told Ernest, "the ignorance and stupidity in Washington is really frightening. But then I remember the ignorance and stupidity of the American High Command in London about France before June 1944." She remarked, "that time, at least it was possible to do a little something about it."[9] Ernest requested Mary to give him an analysis of his income stream, and Alfred Rice provided the numbers. Her report to Ernest shows he was well-off, and his concerns about their finances were exaggerated—if not delusional. *Life* had paid him $85,000 for "Death in the Afternoon" ($740,000 in 2020), and Twentieth Century Fox would pay him $67,500 in January ($585,000 in 2020). In addition to the income from these special projects, his average annual recurring income was over $100,000, consisting of $45,000 from foreign royalties, $40,000 from Scribner's, $13,500 from bank dividends, and $5,000 from Jonathan Cape. After deductions for projects Rice managed, Ernest's taxable net income was $88,000, and his after-tax annual income was $58,000. This was his "continuing, steady income not augmented by sales of special properties such as movie and TV."[10] The annual sum would be equivalent in purchasing power to $500,000 in 2020. No reasonable person would say Ernest was impoverished.

Mary traveled to Rochester in early June and visited Ernest at St. Mary's Hospital. As she described "in a situation report" to Jack and Patrick, "Papa showed only intense hostility to me—I'd railroaded him there, making them destroy his memory, would be happy only keeping him as a fixture in a madhouse, would steal his money, etc."[11] The next day, Mary spent eleven harmonious hours with Ernest. He showed her the letters he had received from friends, and they made a list of the paintings they had in Cuba and chores she was to do for him in New York. She spent seven hours with him the following day. He made plans for getting out of the hospital and grew angry because Mary did not support going to the Feria in Pamplona on July 6. On Dr. Rome's advice, Mary sent cables to Antonio Ordóñez and Bill Davis announcing the plan to visit them in Europe so Ernest could look forward to the trip.

Mary noted to his sons, "What gave me concern was that Papa's feelings of insecurity did not seem to have been mitigated at all up to that point."[12] He still insisted he could not return to Ketchum because he would go to jail for non-payment of taxes. Ernest thought Alfred Rice was lying when he said he had arranged a deferment of taxes for one year. Further, he believed the statements from his bank showing sufficient funds to meet current expenses were mistaken.[13] Dr. Rome explained Ernest's feelings of impoverishment came from the idea he was "impoverished in his head—that he no longer has what it takes to write."[14] Ernest assured Mary he no longer had any suicidal intentions, but when they were alone he said he could do it at night when she was asleep.[15] Mary plainly told the boys about the ongoing threat of suicide.

She told them that Dr. Cattell had recommended Mary look at the Hartford Institute of Living and consider moving Ernest there. It was expensive, but she could finance Ernest's stay there if they could persuade him to go, and if she could get the boys to agree it was the best place for him. After having reported all these developments to Patrick and Jack, Mary asked them for help. "I cannot possibly assume by myself the responsibility for making the decision about trying to move Papa to Hartford." Since Ernest did not believe he needed treatment, he would think Mary a traitor to him if he knew she was investigating the Hartford option. "Therefore, any recommendations must come from Dr. Rome and Dr. Hugh Butt, who is his medical doctor at Rochester and in whom he has confidence."[16]

Mary intended to visit Hartford and see the place for herself and told Jack she would phone him when she returned. If they moved Papa across the country from Rochester to Hartford, she planned to ask Jack to drive Papa because he would not suspect Jack's motives. She was also keeping their friends Lee Samuels and George Saviers informed about the situation so they could form an opinion about the entire business together and decide what course of action was best. Mary asked Jack to send a copy of the letter to his Aunt Ursula in Hawaii. In his memoir, Jack said of this careful, factual, and balanced letter from Mary, ". . . we received a panic-stricken letter from Mary in which she revealed part of the situation with Papa and expressed the hope that I would agree with her decision to take him for treatment to the Mayo [sic] clinic."[17] Jack's summary of his correspondence with Mary wholly misstates the information in Mary's letter and ignores her efforts to keep him and Patrick up to date. Jack phoned Mary to give his, "complete support for whatever action she deemed appropriate." Then he forgot about the problem: "That is, after all, one of the greatest benefits of fishing."[18]

Jack's memoir was published the year Mary died, so he could say what he liked without fear of contradiction. Jack's reaction was disingenuous because no fair person would find Mary's focused, competent, reporting letter "hysterical." Indeed, it is doubtful Mary was ever hysterical about anything. Having lived through the Blitz as a wartime reporter, she was level-headed under pressure, and she described the facts, including the risk of suicide, and sought advice from the boys. When Jack gave Mary his approval for whatever she thought best and then went fishing, he lost the right to complain. Jack simply failed to repay Ernest and Mary for the efforts they had made when he was badly wounded and captured in Germany. The estrangement between father and son had become so fixed that Jack could not bring himself to take an active interest in his father's condition.

In early June, at Dr. Cattell's suggestion, Mary visited the Hartford Institute of Living, which had a larger acreage that Ernest would find comforting during an extended convalescence. Mary wrote to Dr. Rome seeking his advice about "whether the advantages of Hartford's facilities for rehabilitation outweigh the quite probable disadvantages of Papa leaving his friends in Rochester, especially you, for new places, new faces, etc., which might make him feel insecure again."[19] Rome replied that Ernest should not be moved.

Ed Hotchner came to see Ernest at St. Mary's Hospital in early June during a respite in the course of electroconvulsive therapy. The treatment was to resume after Hotch's visit. As Hotch entered the compact room, he saw Ernest facing the window, standing at a raised hospital table. He was wearing his red silk emperor's robe cinched with his "Gott Mit Uns" belt, a pair of old moccasins, and, over his eyes, a stained tennis visor.[20] After a brief pause, Ernest recognized Hotch, wrapped his arms around him, and pounded his back in a Spanish abrazo. Ernest was gaunt, and his beard was scraggly. Hotch sat on the only chair and Ernest sat on his bed and they talked. At first, Ernest seemed on firm ground, but then he repeated his old fears that his room and the telephone outside his door were bugged, and he complained of his poverty, imagined taxes, and inadequate clothing. He repeated "his accusations against his banker, his lawyer, his doctor in Ketchum, all the fiduciary people in his life."[21] It was clear the electroshock therapy had not worked. Hotch let Ernest talk himself out and tried to cheer him up with thoughts of spring, but Ernest would not be diverted, saying, "Hotch, if I can't exist on my own terms, then existence is impossible. Do you understand? But that is how I've lived, and that is how I *must* live—or not live."[22]

In the second week of June, Ernest received a note from George Saviers telling him his son Fritz was not well. Ernest and the nine-year-old boy were friends. The previous Christmas, Ernest had given Fritz a warthog skin from Africa, which the boy hung on his bedroom wall.[23] Fritz was in the hospital with viral heart disease, which would take his life five years later. Ernest wrote a letter to Fritz on June 15, 1961. He sounded like himself and did not speak down to the boy. Instead, he treated Fritz as a pal, and his compassion seeped through, as he described the countryside they would both prefer to be visiting.

In the last week of June, Dr. Rome called Mary in New York and told her Ernest's sexual urges were reviving and that a conjugal visit would help him. Mary felt somewhat embarrassed but took the bus to Rochester, expecting they would meet in the privacy of her room at the Kahler Hotel. Instead, the visit took place behind the locked doors of the psychiatric ward. As they tried to comfort each other in his single bed, and Mary told him to think about their bed in Africa, "other inmates pushed through the door, hollow-eyed men looking for something we could not give them." Ernest seemed to accept them as part of his incarceration, but they "unnerved" Mary.[24] Neither of them found satisfaction, and in Mary's view, the visit did no good. She felt relief on escaping the locked ward and thought it was no place for Ernest either, but she couldn't think of an alternative for him.

Two days later, Dr. Rome asked Mary to come to his office for a meeting. To her astonishment, as she entered the room, she saw Ernest wearing street clothes and "a smile like a Cheshire cat."[25] Dr. Rome declared Ernest was ready to go home. Mary knew Ernest harbored the same illusions and anxieties he'd clung to upon admission, but since the office was so small, she couldn't raise her doubts without making Ernest think she was a traitor. Dr. Rome assured her the chances of Ernest taking his own life were minimal, and he would not release a vulnerable patient. He later told her, "I truly felt that the risks were negligible and that he and his future was worth all of them and more besides."[26] The psychiatrist charged with Ernest's care believed he was fit to return to normal life. Mary could do little but accept the diagnosis and hope Dr. Rome was right. She wanted to believe Ernest was better and would improve when released from the hospital setting. While Ernest stayed in the hospital for two nights, Mary planned the trip home.

Mary knew Dr. Rome cared for Ernest, and he would not have made his recommendation if he felt his celebrity patient was still at risk of suicide. On the other hand, she knew how manipulative Ernest could be and worried he had conned Rome into believing his thoughts of suicide had disappeared with the depression. In the memoir Mary wrote fifteen years later, she said, "I knew that Ernest was not cured, that he entertained the same delusions and fears with which he had entered the clinic, and I realized in despair, that he had charmed and deceived Dr. Rome to the conclusion that he was sane."[27]

Mary phoned their old friend George Brown and asked if he could fly to Rochester and drive them home to Ketchum. She rented a two-door Buick and they began the drive west on June 26, with Ernest sitting in the front passenger seat. Mary brought along some wine so they could picnic on the way, but Ernest worried state troopers might pick them up for carrying alcoholic beverages. He also worried about where they would sleep each night. Never before had he fretted about such things. Mary poured the wine into a ditch and called ahead to make reservations. Once or twice she even went into a phone booth and dropped coins in the slots to convince Ernest she had made a call. They often stopped as early as 2:30 in the afternoon to make sure they had lodgings.[28]

Five days later, on the afternoon of June 30, they arrived in Ketchum, and Ernest seemed glad to be home. Mary showed George to the cinderblock guest house ten yards from the principal house and made dinner from food she'd left in the freezer. The next morning brought a bright day, and Ernest took George walking in the hills behind the house. Then, they drove to see George Saviers at the hospital. Young Fritz had been delighted to receive Ernest's letter, and he and his father came out to the house for a visit. They were to catch a train out of Shoshone at midnight to take Fritz back to the University of Colorado Hospital in Denver. According to Saviers, Ernest and Fritz talked about baseball and fishing, and "Ernest put on a great show."[29] Later in the afternoon, Chuck Atkinson, Ernest's longtime friend and proprietor of the local grocery store, came over for a chat outside in the warm sunshine of the first day of July.

That evening, Ernest took Mary and George to dinner at the Christiania Lodge Restaurant. As they were being seated in their favorite corner booth at the back of the restaurant, Ernest noticed two men at a small table. He asked the waitress who they were, and she said they were visiting salesmen. "Not on a Saturday night; they'd be home," Ernest said. "They're FBI."[30] Alarmed that Ernest's old fears had resurfaced, Mary tried to divert him, pointing out the men were showing no interest in them, and she ordered a bottle of his favorite wine, a Chateauneuf du Pape. Ernest continued to watch the men as he drank the wine and ate his rare New York steak.

After dinner, George Brown, who did not drink wine, drove them home. As she was undressing, Mary sang their old love song from Torcello, "Tutti mi chiamano bionda. Ma bionda io non sono." From his room, just down the hall, Ernest joined her in the next phrase, "Porto capelli neri." She cuddled into her big sweet-smelling bed where Ernest was always welcome. "'Good night, my lamb,' I called. 'Sleep well.' 'Good night, my kitten,' he said. His voice sounded warm and friendly."[31]

The next morning, Mary woke up at about six for a glass of water, and she noticed Ernest was already up. "He always went early to bed so we could get up early . . . And because of that, I wasn't surprised he was up already . . . I went back to sleep . . . I used to get up later than him, at seven."[32] When Mary woke later, she heard what sounded like two drawers pulled from a cabinet and dropped on the floor. She got up, noticed that Ernest had slept in his bed, and went downstairs. Mary found "a crumpled heap of bathrobe and blood, the shotgun lying in the disintegrated flesh, in the front vestibule of the sitting room."[33]

THIRTY-FIVE
The Sun Also Ariseth

July 2, 1961–July 4, 1961

M ary ran to get George from the guest house, phoned the Sun Valley Hospital, asked them to send a doctor, and contacted the sheriff. She phoned Chuck Atkinson, told him what had happened, and asked if she could come to their house. Before the doctor arrived, Mary phoned her friend, the nationally syndicated columnist Leonard Lyons.[1] "The ringing of the phone woke me," Lyons recalled. "'Ketchum, Idaho, calling,' said the operator. I heard Mary Hemingway's voice: 'Papa is dead.' Then she paused as if she knew of the late-night cobwebs in my head." They had "just returned from the Mayo Clinic, a leisurely five-day ride by car, and he felt well enough again Sunday to think of hunting again and was cleaning his gun. It went off, and he died." Mary asked Lyons "to notify the press because she would be busy making the funeral arrangements and trying to locate his kin. I followed her instructions and phoned the wire services."[2]

Dr. Scott Earle was called at home at 7:40 A.M. He was George Saviers's partner and his wife was a nurse who had looked after Ernest when he was in the Sun Valley Hospital. Minutes after receiving the call, Dr. Earle parked in the driveway of the Hemingway home, and Mary signaled him from a second-floor window. Mary met him at the kitchen door and introduced him to George Brown, who led him to the vestibule near the front door. According to Earle, Ernest's body slumped across the linoleum tiles in a large pool of blood. The body lay clothed in blue pajamas and a red silk robe. The knees were bent, and a double-barreled shotgun lay between them with its muzzle resting on the chest. Above the body, the ceiling was "speckled with yellowish-red fragments of blood, brain, and bone. The entire cranial vault had been blown off by a double blast from the shotgun." Dr. Earle reported, "the face below it was a bloodless caricature. The disc-shaped and empty skull was visible from the living room. The odor of death was strong in the place."[3]

Earle said, "it was clear what the victim had done."[4] The guns were locked in a basement room, and the keys to the room were on a windowsill in the kitchen. Ernest took the keys, walked downstairs, opened the locked room, selected his pigeon gun, a double-barreled Scott shotgun, and picked up two shells. He locked the room and returned upstairs to the front entry. He loaded the gun, "leaned forward, pressed the muzzle to his forehead just above the eyebrows, and tripped both triggers. The enormous explosion inside his head was the last thing he ever heard."[5] Dr. Earle completed his examination just as the town marshall, Les Jankow, arrived. Jankow was also a friend of the Hemingways and told the New York Times that residents had told him Mr. Hemingway "looked thinner and acted depressed."[6]

Chuck Atkinson came but could not bring himself to look at the body.[7] He drove Mary to the apartment he shared with his wife, Flo, above their store. Mary recalled that Flo gave her a tranquilizing pill and put her to bed. "For an hour, I shook, unable to control my muscles. Then in a flash of sanity, I wondered why I should be so destroyed by the sudden violence I had long but too vaguely anticipated." She thought it might "be shock at Ernest's deception," for he had fooled Dr. Rome, the staff at the Mayo Clinic, and herself, but she "dismissed the notion. He knew he could not confide in me."[8] An hour later, Chuck took Mary to the hospital, and they gave her a sedative to quiet her nerves. Mary expanded on her feelings in a draft of her memoir, which she omitted from the final version. "For weeks, I could not admit to myself, or anyone else, the stark reality of Ernest's blowing the top of his head off."[9]

When she regained her composure, Mary phoned Greg and Jack and sent a cable to Patrick in Africa. Dorice Taylor, the director of Sun Valley's "well-oiled, celebrity-fueled publicity machine," fielded telephone inquiries from reporters.[10] Dorice contacted Chuck Atkinson and suggested Mary should prepare a statement for the press. Then all the calls could be routed through the Sun Valley office and Dorice would answer them and give out the statement. Mary continued to cover up the suicide. She typed, "Mr. Hemingway accidentally killed himself while cleaning

a gun this morning at 7:30 A.M. No time has been set for the funeral service, which
will be private."[11] Chuck Atkinson delivered Mary's note to Dorice Taylor, and
"he hedged when Dorice asked if it was suicide."[12] Mary's version matched the
one she had instructed Leonard Lyons to use: the accident occurred while Ernest
was cleaning the gun. Dorice Taylor repeated the accidental death statement to
members of the public and the press phoning from New York to London to Italy.

Many of the townspeople and Ernest's friends downplayed the suicide angle in
the interviews they gave to reporters. Chuck Atkinson told the *Times* he had seen
Ernest the day before. "He seemed in good spirits. We didn't talk about anything
in particular."[13] Atkinson said, "Mary felt it was accidental, and I hope that's the
way it will go out."

A recent Idaho law required the chief law enforcement officer to investigate
every case of violent death and determine the cause.[14] The officials investigating
Ernest's death shaped their comments to fit in with the accident story. The *Idaho
State Journal* reported on July 3, "a group of law officials went to the literary giant's
country home today to talk with his wife, Mary. They issued their statement a few
minutes later. The ruling left officially open a determination of whether Hemingway's death was accidental, or otherwise."[15] The coroner, Ray McGoldrick, who
was also the local funeral home owner, had attended at the Hemingway home at
7:45 A.M. and took the body back to his mortuary. After visiting Mary, he said
to the press, "I can only say at this stage that the wound was self-inflicted. The
wound was in the head. I couldn't say it was accidental, and I couldn't say it was
suicide. There wasn't anybody there."[16] Deciding that no inquest was necessary
because there was no evidence of foul play, McGoldrick said the death certificate
would read, "Self-inflicted gunshot wounds in the head."[17] He recapped, "We
do not know whether it was an accident or suicide. Mrs. Hemingway thought
it was an accident."[18] Sheriff Frank Hewitt told the press after his preliminary
investigation, "the death looks like an accident."[19]

With help from Leonard Lyons, Dorice Taylor, Chuck Atkinson, the coroner,
and the sheriff, Mary controlled the narrative. All the national newspapers
reported on July 3 that Ernest had died from an accident—not suicide.[20] For
example, the *San Francisco Chronicle* printed Mary's statement about the accident
and reported Ernest had been "hospitalized at the Mayo Clinic for treatment
for hypertension (high blood pressure) and . . . a very old case of hepatitis."[21]
The *Chronicle* reported the author was in the hospital a year earlier for the same

condition, and Hemingway's physician at the Mayo Clinic had described his health as excellent. The *New York Times* reported Ernest shot himself by accident while cleaning the weapon.

Don Anderson later told Carlos Baker he heard about the shooting and drove to Hemingway's house. Given the series of suicide attempts, he never believed it was an accident. By the time he arrived they had removed Ernest's body and the room was being cleaned. He heard Sheriff Hewitt say, "he wouldn't mind having some of the brains that had been blown about so carelessly." The gun was still there, a double-barreled English shotgun made by Boss.* Don opened the gun and retrieved the empty shells. Ernest had fired both barrels. [22]

Lloyd Arnold was more devastated at the news than Tillie. When they visited Hemingway's house, Lloyd went to find the keys to the storage room, and he was surprised to see them lying on the windowsill where they usually sat. Lloyd was angry when he came out. He told Tillie, "Papa tried to kill himself twice in that house, and how could a wife, knowing that have even left the ammo in the same house, let alone have left the keys to where it was stored so he could easily find them." [23] Lloyd "smoldered for a long time after that, saying nothing but blaming Mary for Papa's death." [24] Tillie was not angry, for she felt death was a genuine relief for Papa, who did not want to live as "a mental cripple." She had already told Ernest, to his face, that she understood his decision. Tillie did not blame him for what he did. Valerie told me Lloyd Arnold went off his head and never recovered after Ernest's death. Valerie thought it was easy for Lloyd to blame Mary, but Ernest had decided to die by suicide: "If someone wants to do it, they do it anyway." [25]

Jack received a message he was to phone Mary, and when he did, she told him Papa had shot himself earlier that morning. Jack flew to Ketchum, and by the time he arrived, Mary had checked into the hospital and was under sedation. Jack remembered, "the press was starting to home in like wasps at a barbecue.

---

* Don Anderson and Dr. Scott Earle both reported to Carlos Baker, five years later, the death weapon was a shotgun made by Boss. They were evidently mistaken, for Sheriff Hewitt's notes, taken at the time, recorded the precise description of the gun, and Emmett Watson transcribed Hewitt's note in his story of the death. Calabi, Helsley, and Sanger surmise the "Boss legend" began with Ernest himself who had "a penchant for nicknames and calling one thing something else, and anyone unfamiliar with fine guns easily could be misled. Perhaps an admirer simply wanted such a famous life to have ended with a famous gun." Calabi, Helsley, and Sanger, *Hemingway's Guns: The Sporting Arms of Ernest Hemingway*, 153.

The phone never stopped ringing, and it was a madhouse."²⁶ Jack claimed he
was shocked to learn how long his father's health problems had been going on,
seeming to suggest Mary ought to have kept him better informed. Ernest had not
wanted to tell his sons about his mental issues and had told them he was having
problems with high blood pressure. Ernest, not Mary, instigated the program of
misinformation. Still, Jack knew from Mary's letters that his father was suicidal,
and he did nothing to inquire or assist. She could have used some family backup
at the hospital, but Jack was fishing and Patrick was in Africa.

When Mary returned home from the hospital, she continued to insist to
the press that Ernest had shot himself by accident. Mary phoned and asked
Valerie to come to Idaho for the funeral. Valerie felt "numbed rather than
stunned" by the news. She had been waiting eight months for Ernest to die by
suicide, and while she had hoped he might recover, she had resigned herself to
his fate: "I could not cry for Ernest. He was at peace. Demons would no longer
disturb his sleep."²⁷ Valerie did not want to attend the funeral, but Brendan
Behan insisted she should, saying it was her duty to pay respects to her friend.
Newsweek granted her time off but expected she would write a story in return.
Valerie knew this would lead to severe problems with Mary, who was still in
denial about the suicide. She decided to attend the funeral but not report on it for
Newsweek, even though she believed Mary, a reporter herself, would not have
resisted such a scoop.

Valerie checked in at the Christiania Lodge, owned by Chuck and Flo
Atkinson, and phoned Mary, who seemed unfriendly. Valerie guessed that Mary
had reconsidered and now feared Valerie would report for *Newsweek* that Ernest had
killed himself. Mary avoided Valerie for the week and excluded her from family
activities. The snub hurt.

Greg flew to Sun Valley for the funeral, seated next to his aunt Marcelline.
They did not talk much because Marcelline was busy taking notes for her forthcoming book on Ernest, whom she had not seen since the funeral for their father
twenty-eight years earlier. Greg appreciated Mary's hospitality and all she had
done, and his assessment was kinder than Jack's or Patrick's. "Mary had been
through hell the last two days, starting with discovering my father's body." Still,
she received them "lovingly" despite the time "some of us had been estranged
from Papa—and the feeling that we had abandoned him, leaving her to stand
alone as his final protector." He concluded, "the courage and the real class she

showed was the kind one later admired in Mrs. Kennedy, walking down broad
Pennsylvania Avenue on that Day of Drums."[28]

The three sons were together for the first time since the late forties when they
had spent the summer fishing in Idaho, Wyoming, and Montana. Jack was now
thirty-eight, Patrick was thirty-three, and Gregory was thirty. Although solemn
at first, they soon began laughing and joking as they had in the old days. Greg
stayed with Mary and Ernest's old friend, Clara Spiegel. She loaned him her station wagon, and while he was driving from Ketchum toward Sun Valley, he offered
a lift to a tall girl walking by the side of the road. She had a lovely complexion and
amber, green eyes that changed color as he talked to her. "I liked her right from
the start, and I finally fell in love with her, and we were married in 1966."[29] The
girl was Valerie Danby-Smith.

Patrick told me, "they kept me pretty much in the dark. I was completely
surprised by it. I had no idea what Papa was going through. The story about
hypertension was completely misleading." Patrick saw "the irony because it's something that happened to me when I was off my head years before, and it very much
foreshadowed what happened to him. He would've been very aware, knowing what
it was like, having looked after me. And suddenly, he was in the same position."[30]

President Kennedy issued a statement mourning the death of one of America's
most celebrated authors, "and one of the great citizens of the world."[31] Mary knew
Bill Walton had a hand in the president's message.

The funeral took place at the cemetery on the north side of Ketchum on
Wednesday, July 5, 1961. A chain-link fence enclosed the lawn, beyond which a
group of photographers and reporters stood watching. Guests were admitted to
the cemetery after they presented invitations.

The simple graveside service began at 10:30 A.M. and lasted twenty-four min-
utes. About fifty guests attended the funeral, including Ernest's three sisters, his
brother, Leicester, and nephew, "Little Uncle Ernie," Madelaine's son. It marked
Mary's first public appearance since Ernest's death the previous Sunday. She wore a
plain black jersey dress, a wide-brimmed black hat without a veil, and dark glasses.
She held Jack's arm as they walked to the chairs beside the grave accompanied by
Greg and Patrick. Father Robert Waldemann, the Roman Catholic pastor of Our
Lady of the Snows in Ketchum, said graveside prayers, but it was not a formal
Catholic service and there was no Mass or rosary. Father Waldemann told the
press the matter of accident or suicide had no bearing on the funeral. "We passed

no judgment on that and asked no questions," he said.[32] Patrick told me that after he arrived from Africa, he and Greg and George Brown met with Father Waldemann to plan the burial service, and the question of suicide did not arise in their discussion.[33]

Father Waldemann said there would be "a meditation on death," but no eulogy, and the only mention of Ernest's name—his first name—came when the priest said, "Oh Lord, grant to Thy servant Ernest, the remission of his sins. Eternal rest grant unto him, Oh Lord."[34] He said, "We are at times like this witnessing the actions of the meeting between what man has done and the prevailing hand of God. So, it is at times like this we do not evaluate the deeds of him who has gone before us. We leave them to the kind and merciful hand of God."[35]

Mary had requested Father Waldemann read from verses 3, 4, and 5 of the first chapter of Ecclesiastes. He read the third and fourth verses. Mary was upset he passed on to another thought and didn't read the fifth verse, which alluded to the title of Ernest's first great novel, *The Sun Also Rises*: "the sun also ariseth, and the sun goeth down, and hasteth to his place where he arose." She later told Leicester, she wanted to stand up right then and say, "Stop the ceremony."[36] According to Tillie Arnold, Mary was furious the priest had forgotten to read the passage. "The son of a bitch went on and on with the Hail Marys, and he didn't even mention the passage from Ecclesiastes. I suppose the only way I can hurt him is by not paying him."[37] She later calmed down and paid for the service.

Following the prayers, the coffin was lowered under a blanket of red roses beside the grave of Ernest's old friend, Taylor "Beartracks" Williams, with whom he had hunted and fished for twenty years. Mary said nothing about the funeral in *How It Was* except that it took place in Ketchum's peaceful, pretty cemetery. Valerie recalled, "devoid of feeling, I concentrated on the ceremony. I had said my goodbye to Ernest several months before and had mourned for him then. Now concealing a deep sadness, I felt hollow, empty, absolute nothingness."[38] Greg felt "profound relief when they lowered my father's body into the ground, and I realized that he was really dead, that I couldn't disappoint him, couldn't hurt him anymore."[39] Jack reflected, "the truth is, I think for years, any of us who were involved with him suffered some form of trauma."[40] Tillie Arnold looked over at Lloyd and knew he was thinking that even though he was sick, Papa should not be in that casket. He should be living and scheduled for a new treatment. Ernest's sister Madelaine ("Sunny") found the funeral a "nightmare," with radio and television men announcing guests' names and describing the service with stage whispers. She left, "still not knowing any details of Ernest's death."[41]

Many friends sided with Mary's explanation. "Everybody definitely knows it wasn't suicide," said Forrest "Duke" MacMullan, Ernest's old hunting buddy and a casino host at the Union Plaza Hotel in Las Vegas, who served as a pallbearer at his funeral.[42] MacMullan recalled, years earlier, he had sent off several of Ernest's guns for repairs. The trigger on the Scott shotgun was stiff, and he asked them to grind it down. "They honed it down too much. You could drop the gun, and it would go off. It's hard to say that it didn't go off accidentally, that he didn't jar the gun, and it just went off. It was a shotgun, but it fired like a rifle. Maybe he did have the intention or whatever, but I prefer to think it was an accident."[43]

◆

In the week following Ernest's death, the national newspapers reviewed his contributions to American life and literature. They published photographs of him carrying shotguns with Gary Cooper in Idaho, posing with a prong-horned antelope in the Sawtooth Mountains, on safari in Africa, attending bullfights in Spain, and posing with Mayito Menocal's dead leopard. After reviewing the press reaction, John Bittner concluded it was the most covered story in American literary history.[44] Speculation built about the cause of Ernest's death, and reporters were frustrated by the refusal of the coroner, Ray McGoldrick, to rule whether the death was an accident or a suicide.

Instead of deciding one way or the other, McGoldrick said, "People can make up their own minds."[45] The *New York Times* reported, "Despite reports that Mr. Hemingway had been killed while cleaning the shotgun, the coroner said there had been no cleaning paraphernalia in evidence where he had been shot to death."[46]

THIRTY-SIX

This in Some Incredible
Way Was an Accident

July 5, 1961–July 10, 1961

The *Seattle Post-Intelligencer* sent their reporter Emmett Watson to Ketchum after Ernest's death. When Watson arrived, he found reporters from *Life*, the *Chicago Tribune*, the *New York Times*, and local newspapers. The key question was whether the cause of death was suicide, and "The question was important because Hemingway wrote so much about it."[1] According to Watson, the reporters cooperated as a team and interviewed the residents, who said, "Oh, how we loved him," and "he was a nice man," and so on.[2]

The headline of the *Seattle Post-Intelligencer*, for July 7, the day after the funeral, proclaimed, "Emmett Watson Learns: Real Story of Death of Hemingway. Speculation Clarified on Fatal Shotgun Blast."[3] Watson copyrighted his story to assure attribution. "The manner of Hemingway's death has been the subject of international speculation. His immediate family, including his wife, Mary, and all of his close friends, have steadfastly maintained that the author's death was accidental." Watson revealed, "it was learned authoritatively today that Hemingway, who recently returned from the Mayo Clinic in failing health, placed the shotgun muzzle in his mouth and deliberately killed himself." Watson did not disclose his source. "Relatives, friends, and villagers carefully, even defiantly, avoid the hard fact of Hemingway's health . . . In their love of the man is the resolute belief that Hemingway left by accident . . ." Watson continued, "The *Post-Intelligencer* learned that the death weapon was a silver-inlaid double-barreled shotgun with a hammerless tandem trigger mechanism. Both barrels had been fired. The 12-gauge hunting gun was an Angelini and Bernardin, made by W.C. Scott and Sons, of London." Watson specified, "On the left barrel was inscribed '55 Victoria Street, London, Scott's Improved Bolt, Monte Carlo B.'"[4] He concluded, "Inquiry by the *Post-Intelligencer* along other channels disclosed that the author's death definitely was a suicide. Thus, ends speculation which may well have plagued Hemingway scholars for years to come."[5]

The story of how Watson discovered the suicide did not emerge until thirty-six years after Ernest's death. The account rests in the archives of the Ketchum Community Library in a transcript of an interview John Bittner conducted with Emmett Watson in 1997. Bittner, a professor of journalism and mass communication at the University of North Carolina, never disclosed the name of Watson's source, and he took the secret to his grave. To the best of my knowledge, this is the first time Watson's source is being revealed.

Watson told Bittner that he and a few of his fellow reporters went to Hailey to talk to Sheriff Hewitt. When they arrived, the sheriff was at lunch at his house across the street from the sheriff's office. They knocked on his door, and he told them he would be over in a little while. The reporters decided to do "a little con job on him." When he came over, they said, "Sheriff, we sure like the way you're handling this, you know with all the press here. It must be difficult. And it warmed the atmosphere up." So, we talked about it, and he said, "Well, you're pretty nice, so I'm gonna give you something."[6] He went out of the room and came back with a slip of paper identifying the shotgun as a Scott over-under. Watson used the precise description of the gun in his story.

Watson asked Sheriff Hewitt if one shot could've triggered the other. "And he looked at me kind of quizzically and finally said, 'Oh, no.' He put two fingers over-under in his mouth, and that was it. Blew his head off."[*] Thirty-six years later, when Bittner interviewed him, Watson was still reluctant to identify Sheriff Hewitt as his source. Watson said, "And then, Oh God, now don't get me in trouble. So, I never used his name. I obscured his name, of course. 'Cause see, at that time Mary Hemingway had not admitted anything." Watson recalled,

---

[*] Sheriff Hewitt's statement to Watson contradicted the statement he had made to the *New York Times* the day of the death, following his investigation and meeting with Mary. Then Hewitt said, "The death looks like an accident."

". . . the family was arriving and uh, so I went ahead and copyrighted the story. I didn't think it was too strong as I wrote it, but it was the first revelation that he had actually committed suicide."[7]

Mary had controlled the narrative until Sheriff Hewitt demonstrated Ernest putting the gun in his mouth and blowing off the top of his head. Without Hewitt's statement, Mary's version would have prevailed. We don't know if Mary figured out Hewitt was Watson's source. We do know Mary angrily attacked Sheriff Hewitt, later saying, "I am awfully sorry for my rudeness and discourtesy to you on the telephone a week or two after my husband's death." Mary did not say what had prompted her rudeness. "I apologize for my behavior that day and hope that eventually you will understand that I am not usually so ill-tempered or profane."[8] Had she learned Hewitt was the source for Watson's story and lashed out at him?

Sheriff Hewitt's version of the suicide was different from Dr. Earle's. Hewitt said the shotgun was placed in Ernest's mouth while Earle said it was placed on Ernest's forehead. At this distance it is not possible to determine conclusively which version is correct. However, Hewitt's statement was made to Watson at the time, within days of the death. Earle's statement to Baker was made some five years later and he may not have remembered the details of Ernest's death. Given the timing of the statements, I think Sheriff Hewitt's version is more likely correct, but it is impossible to be certain.

◆

The morning after the funeral, Alfred Rice met with Mary and Ernest's three sons in the living room of the Ketchum home. As Jack recalls, "the grey eminence of our lives laid the chill hand of our father's will upon us." Rice gave "a short summation to the effect that Papa had left everything to Mary and that no provision of any kind had been made for anyone else."[9]

Ernest left his entire estate to Mary, "real, personal literary or mixed, absolutely," making her a millionaire and appointing her executrix to manage the estate.[10] With Mary's approval, Rice proposed paying the royalties from the foreign sales of Ernest's works into a trust fund. He would distribute the money in four equal shares among Mary and the boys. Each quarter share of the fund, in 1961, was approximately ten thousand dollars (eighty-six thousand dollars in 2020). The

boys were appalled they were to receive so little compared to Mary. Patrick
Hemingway told me, "Charles Scribner Jr. and Alfred Rice had a plan to take
over the Hemingway property, and Mary was simply just part of that plan."[11]

In his memoir, Jack said he didn't see the will until years later when he had
his attorney make a copy from probate files.[12] However, in Alfred Rice's files are
copies of letters to each of the boys, dated one week after the funeral. In these
letters, Rice enclosed "a copy of Ernie's last will and testament," and he asked each
of them to execute a waiver and consent so he could probate the will. All three
boys complied with his request. While all three sons were shocked to be receiving
a limited income, Rice's news most devastated Jack. He had understood he would
receive half of his father's estate to make up for the generous inheritances the other
boys had received from their mother, Pauline. Jack was so surprised he couldn't
react, and it was not until months later that his mother Hadley and her husband
Paul Mowrer took legal action.

◆

For two days after the funeral, Mary remained in semi-seclusion at her home in
Ketchum. She changed the telephone number, and a deputy marshal guarded the
driveway. Barry Farrell[13] of *Time* magazine, who had also sat in on the interview
with Sheriff Hewitt, wrote to Mary on behalf of himself and Emmett Watson
requesting a meeting "to provide a true and corrective close to the story that has
surrounded you this past week."[14] They wanted to learn about "the nature and
degree of the illnesses of the past few years." Mary ended her isolation and met
with four reporters, including Watson and Farrell, in the living room of her
home.[15] Dressed simply, in blue slacks and a blouse, Mary told the reporters
Ernest's "spirits had been so good he could not have committed suicide, and she
said that he had planned to resume work this week on a manuscript kept in an
Idaho bank vault."[16] Mary explained that Ernest was working on a three-part
collection, and *The Old Man and the Sea* was the first of three parts. She said he
had never been eager to publish because it made his income tax go from 75% to
95%. The unpublished work was his bank account.[17] Mary changed her story
about "the accident." The adjustment was necessary because the coroner had said
there was no cleaning paraphernalia near Ernest's body. Now Mary said Ernest
was "merely looking at [the gun] when it discharged."[18]

Mary told the reporters, "everything that happened in the hours beforehand convinced her that Mr. Hemingway was not despondent. There had been a pleasant trip from the Mayo Clinic in Minnesota, then Saturday night dinner at their favorite Sun Valley Restaurant, and happy conversation before bedtime." [19] Mary told the reporters, "All this makes me feel quite certain that this in some incredible way was an accident." [20]

To the written question, "Can you tell us the nature and degree of Mr. Hemingway's recent illnesses?" Mary read from a statement she had typed: "It was hypertension (high blood pressure) that did not respond promptly to the usual treatment of that disease. If you want a further elucidation, you could ask Dr. George Saviers of the Sun Valley Hospital, his physician here, or Dr. Hubert of the Mayo Clinic, since I make no pretension of being a medical expert." [21] Mary maintained her composure until the end of the interview. "People didn't know what a quiet, gentle . . ." She could not continue and stepped quickly from the room.

Emmett Watson told Bittner volunteers from the town had cleaned the place, and there were no pellet holes in the vestibule ceiling, nor any signs anyone had been shot. Watson said Mary was adamant during the interview "that it was some kind of a horrible accident." [22] Dr. George Saviers later spoke to the reporters, and he confirmed the cover story he and Mary and Ernest had earlier concocted to mislead the press. Saviers did not mention Ernest's mental health and said he sent Ernest to the Mayo Clinic both times because his blood pressure rose, and they feared a heart attack. [23]

Mary had worked at the highest levels of *Time-Life* in London and New York, and she knew how to spin a story. She wanted to protect Ernest's privacy and his reputation. She sensed if the reading public knew Papa Hemingway had died by suicide, sales of his books would drop. The only sensible thing to do was lie. Mary maintained in public that Ernest's death was due to an accident for six years until Hotchner published *Papa Hemingway*, which described Ernest's mental decline.

Patrick recalled, "I still have a very hard time understanding the events of that day, but now I wonder more about the role of George Brown." Brown was "there to take care of my father if he tried anything physical. My father respected him, and we all did. It will always be an enigma what happened exactly." [24] Patrick said, "What I've been told about the incident is that he put the barrel inside his mouth against the roof of his mouth, and it would be difficult to say that was an accident." After years of reflection, Patrick told me, "the whole story is very strange and in the heart of it is George Brown. He was a very dear friend of our family, and I never thought at the time to really question him about it, but I just don't know what went on. I don't understand how Papa was discharged from the clinic and then allowed to get hold of a shotgun."[25] Indeed, Patrick wondered if the sons had a right to question Mary's actions since they had abandoned their father to her. "We left Mary with the clean-up operation, and the burden on her was impossible."[26]

Many of those close to Ernest knew he no longer wanted to live because he had lost the power to write. George Saviers saw him daily and concluded his inability to write deepened his depression, despite Saviers's efforts to persuade him to simply retire. Hotch tried to convince him there was life besides writing, and his creativity might come back if he rested. Valerie had urged him to forget about suicide and to live. Bill Walton knew Mary was making up the story of an accident and had expected Ernest's suicide.[27] Don Anderson knew Ernest intended suicide and never believed there was an accident. Ernest told Tillie Arnold he would kill himself because he could not live with his incurable disease locked up in a hospital. Ernest's brother, Leicester, said he died like a samurai warrior who realized his own body had attacked him.[28] Those who knew Ernest realized he had deteriorated and was desperately unhappy with his life. But all these observations were made after the fact, and none of the friends alerted Mary to their perception of the danger of imminent suicide. Valerie and Tillie both knew of Ernest's intentions but deliberately did not tell Mary. And Tillie did not tell her husband, Lloyd, who could have warned Mary about the keys on the windowsill. Saviers was one of the last people to see Ernest alive, and he didn't mention the guns or warn Mary. Neither did Chuck Atkinson, who saw Ernest just before Saviers. And Ernest's old friend, George Brown, who was staying in the guest house, didn't pick up on Ernest's plan or discuss cautionary measures with Mary. A number of people were anticipating Ernest's suicide, yet no one took active steps to prevent it.

Perhaps Ernest had decided to end his life at the first opportunity and complied with the regime in St. Mary's hospital to persuade Dr. Rome he was fit for release. After fooling the head of psychiatry at the Mayo Clinic, he fooled his friends and was dead within six days of his discharge. In *How It Was*, published fifteen years after Ernest's death, Mary recounted that, before she left Ketchum, "she had locked all the guns in a storeroom in the basement, leaving the keys among those on the kitchen windowsill." She had thought of "hiding the keys," but she "decided that no one had a right to deny a man access to his possessions." She also "assumed that Ernest would not remember the storeroom."[29]

When Mary left the Ketchum house in early June to travel to New York and visit Ernest in Rochester, she had no reason to expect Ernest's imminent release. In fact, she expected he might be transferred to Hartford, as Dr. Cattell had suggested. Even if she had known of Dr. Rome's plan to release Ernest, would she have more carefully considered what to do with the guns?

Dr. Rome believed Ernest was better, and he would return to a normal life once he could resume his work. Rome certainly did not warn Mary to keep guns away from Ernest or remove them from the house. Hiding the keys to the storeroom would not have prevented Ernest from breaking the lock or using a lamp cord or piece of glass or clothes hanger, as he had pointed out to Rome in their first conversation about suicide. Rome released Ernest because he thought he was no longer suicidal, and he would never have discharged Ernest expecting Mary could prevent him from killing himself. Psychiatric protocols today are very different, and "It is now standard to ensure that all guns are not 'locked up' but rather removed from the home of suicidal individuals. Prior to discharge, this must be arranged."[30] Had this protocol been followed in Ernest's case, the outcome may have been different. But how different and for how long?

Rose Marie Burwell wrote, "for Mary Hemingway, as for the heroine of a Victorian novel, death had done the work of the divorce court." Burwell had, "no doubt that—exhausted and without help from Hemingway's family—she saw, but could not bear to admit, that his suicide was the only release for either of them."[31] Burwell suggested to Bill Walton, in their 1993 interview, "Unconsciously, Mary wanted him to do it," and Walton replied, "Now that you have said it, I will say what I have never said before, but have known since Mary called me a few hours after Ernest's death: yes, she did."[32] It is possible to speculate about Mary's unconscious thoughts, including things she saw but could not admit to herself, as long as it is recognized these ideas lead nowhere. As a victim of suicide, Mary had to put up with speculation about her unconscious wishes, but none of this would have held up in a court of law where evidence must be capable of proof. This is not to deny the psychological insights of friends or critics but to corral them in the arena of posthumous guesswork. A different friend had a different view: Valerie

Hemingway believes that Mary was angry at Ernest and said, "I don't think she forgave him for killing himself."[33]

Another comment Mary made about Ernest's suicide in *How It Was* is interesting. "Years later, reconsidering, I wondered if we had not been crueler than kind in preventing his suicide then and there," after his second attempt when Don Anderson intervened.[34] Mary did not have a problem, in principle, with suicide and may even have been conscious of the likelihood that Ernest would take his own life. In retrospect, she wondered if making him suffer through the treatments was crueler than it would have been to let him go. She understood and accepted he no longer wanted to live, and she could accept his existential choice.

Mary's oddest statement in her memoir concerned her attempt to explain the story she made up about the accident. "Not consciously lying, I told the press that the shooting had been accidental. It was months before I could face the reality."[35] However, one of Mary's first acts was calling Leonard Lyons and asking him to spread the story that Ernest died accidentally when cleaning his gun. It is clear she was lying from the time she discovered Ernest's body, and she knew what she was doing. Then two days after the funeral, she set up a press conference in her home and lied to the reporters in her living room about "the pleasant trip" from the Mayo Clinic. The truth was, Ernest's paranoia was returning, and the last few days had been unpleasant because Ernest's old fears had resurfaced.

Mary must have been conscious she lied, but why did she do it? For several reasons, according to Valerie. Mary's story about the accidental discharge of the gun allowed for a Catholic service. While there was no formal Mass, at least a Catholic priest said the graveside prayers, which reinforced the message of accidental death rather than suicide. Mary wanted to keep the service as private as possible. She felt Ernest's mental issues were privileged personal information, and she feared if the press knew the cause of death was suicide, they would have been even more intrusive. She wanted to protect Ernest's reputation from those who would think of suicide as a coward's death, as Ernest had long maintained. Patrick believes Mary did her best to hide the truth to safeguard his father's reputation.[36] When she found herself in an almost unimaginable hell, Mary lied to avoid the stigma of suicide.

THIRTY-SEVEN

Picking up the Pieces

July 15, 1961–October 16, 1961

After Ernest's funeral, Mary felt empty and exhausted. Ever since the sedated afternoon in the home of Chuck and Flo Atkinson and her brief stay at the hospital, she'd been frenetically busy. She notified relatives and friends of Ernest's death, organized the funeral service, and arranged accommodations and meals for the visitors. Mary talked with close friends and helped to manage their surprise and grief. She tried to persuade the press Ernest died from an accident and had not died by suicide. She dealt with his sons who were surprised by his death and shocked by his will. Mary was a strong person and a capable organizer. "She was tough because she had to be," Valerie Hemingway told me. [1]

It must have seemed odd to Mary, in the way it does to those in grief, that people were going about their daily business and moving on with their lives despite her devastating loss, for it preoccupied her. Every free minute, her mind returned to the days and hours preceding Ernest's death, and she searched her memory for some detail to explain what had happened. Part of her wanted to believe her lie, that his death was accidental. No matter how hard she looked, the missing clue, if it existed, eluded her. It took some time for her to realize she would never know why he had chosen that morning to die. Ernest had killed himself. She had to accept it and admit to herself she had lied about how he had died.

In the 1960s, the public believed death by suicide was shameful and sinful. [2] While Americans are slightly more accepting of suicide today, the majority still disapprove of suicide except in one instance—where the person is suffering from an incurable disease.[3] Typically, the survivors of suicide experience guilt and shame. They wonder why it happened and why they didn't see it coming. They feel guilty about not doing what they might have done, and these haunting thoughts come daily. Often, survivors feel self-blame, as if they were responsible for the loved one's suicide.[4] Mary cycled through these feelings.

In the days after Ernest's death, despite her grief, Mary was also feeling a growing relief. The last few years with Ernest had been wretched for her; his physical and mental decline had been awful and frustrating to watch. His sense of humor had disappeared entirely, and he had become dissatisfied with everything, suspicious of old friends, even of her. Now, she glimpsed a future free from Ernest's madness. She no longer had to confront his delusions or create diversions. She noticed the silence and lightness and embraced them, and she resolved not to let Ernest's death ruin her life or her chance for future happiness.

❖

Mary was fifty-three and a wealthy woman, with Ernest's literary reputation to enhance and protect. There were manuscripts in vaults in Ketchum, Cuba, and Charlie Scribner's office, and correspondence, personal papers, and art in Key West and Cuba. She owned four properties to administer: the Finca, the Ketchum house, Pauline's house in Key West, and the New York apartment. When the estate settled, and after she paid taxes, funeral expenses, and legal fees, Mary received about two hundred thousand dollars in cash, four hundred and twenty thousand dollars in stocks and bonds, and approximately eight hundred thousand dollars' worth of miscellaneous property (eleven million six hundred thousand dollars in 2020). Ernest's stock portfolio contained blue-chip securities, which provided him with more income in the last five years of his life than his published works. Mary also received the valuable original manuscripts for *A Farewell to Arms, To Have and Have Not*, and Ernest's unpublished manuscripts. Over the last five years, Ernest had received one hundred and eighty thousand dollars in royalties.[5] This was a fortune for the former *Time* reporter whose life savings when she met Ernest amounted to five hundred dollars.

Two weeks after the funeral, Alfred Rice came to Ketchum with papers for Mary to sign. She appointed Rice to act in her name, "both individually and as executrix of the estate of Ernest M. Hemingway." She empowered him to grant licenses for works copyrighted in Ernest's name and receive payments from the licenses.[6] Rice gained financial control over the estate—an ironic result because Ernest had lost trust in Rice and talked about firing him. Indeed, Ernest had changed his will to remove the power of literary executor from Rice and given it to Mary instead. By executing the power of attorney, Mary delegated the authority back to Rice. Revenues flowed through Rice's hands, and he created a rule requiring Mary to get his approval for any purchases over one hundred and ninety-nine dollars. Ostensibly, this was to protect Mary from the many people who asked her for money—especially Ernest's sons. They implemented the rule immediately, and when Greg asked Mary for help to pay for the tuition, books, and equipment he needed for medical school, Mary referred him to Rice. Greg wrote to Rice asking for $1,297, and Rice sent a check.[7] A few months later, Mary sought Rice's permission to buy a green 1960 Pontiac for $2,400, and Rice approved the purchase a week later.[8]

One year older than Mary, Rice had graduated from Fordham University Law School, and he represented many writers. According to Valerie Hemingway, "He was essential to her [Mary], not sexually, but they were very close and couldn't have been closer. Rice told Mary not to fraternize with the boys but to keep control of everything." Rice warned Mary if more than one person had control of the money, it would be too difficult to make decisions, and Mary might lose control. According to Valerie, the arrangement was profitable for Rice: "Rice got 30% off the top: 10% as an agent, 10% for legal fees, and 10% as trustee."[9]

One reason for the closeness between Mary and Alfred Rice was that she had helped Rice and his wife to adopt their Cuban son, Felipe, in 1952. Mary found Felipe in an orphanage, recommended him to Rice, and helped Rice compose a letter to the head of the orphanage, Dr. Portela. Rice wrote to Mary that he and his wife would be "forever grateful to you for the time, effort and sincerity you have poured into this project."[10]

The correspondence between Mary and Rice reveals a closer than normal solicitor-client relationship. Mary often signed her letters to Rice, "with love" or "Love, Mary."[11] Rice signed a fee letter to Mary, "Love, Alfred Rice."[12] Mary often wished Rice could come fishing or hunting with her. "Duck season has opened, and I hope to get in a half day's hunting later this week. Wish you could do that too."[13] She wished he could share the natural scenes she enjoyed from her house in Ketchum. "Dear Alfred, I wish you could have been here the last four days—the aspens and the cottonwoods blazing gold and copper outside our windows, the sky totally uncluttered blue, the sun hot, the breeze cool."[14] She often expressed great confidence in Rice's judgment and sought his opinion on every aspect of the estate and her personal affairs.

◆

A few days after the funeral, Mary received a phone call from Dr. Carlos Olivares, the Cuban minister of foreign affairs. After expressing his personal condolences, and those of Prime Minister Fidel Castro, Olivares said the Cuban government wanted to acquire the Finca and preserve it as a monument to Ernest. He wanted to know with whom he should negotiate. Mary told him she was the sole heir to her husband's estate, and he must speak to her alone. Olivares asked if he could send a contract for her to sign, and his presumption shocked Mary, but she thought quickly and explained that when she and Ernest left the Finca, they had fully intended to return. The place was full of their papers and art, and Ernest had left several manuscripts in a safe deposit box at his bank in Havana. She asked if she could come to Cuba to retrieve their documents. Olivares said he would seek instructions and call her back the next day. Mary knew the Cuban government could confiscate the Finca and its contents, as it had done with other American-owned properties. Still, she hoped Ernest's reputation would make Castro more cautious—and generous.

The next day, Olivares phoned and invited Mary to Cuba to discuss converting the Finca into a museum honoring Ernest. He also proposed building a *casita* on the property where she could live and keep her possessions. Even if Mary had wanted to live on the grounds of her former home, given the fraught politics between the US and Cuba, her government would not permit her to live there. After she consulted Rice, they decided the best strategy would be to give the Finca as a gift to the Cuban people in exchange for the right to remove Ernest's manuscripts, some paintings, and her personal effects. It was a bold plan since the Cuban government could seize everything. Still, no one intimidated Mary, and she relished the challenge of dealing with Castro. Now she focused on planning the trip, and it gave her something positive to ponder.

Knowing she would need help, Mary phoned Valerie, apologized for her behavior during the week before the funeral, and asked forgiveness. Mary wondered if Valerie would come with her to Cuba to help sort through the possessions Mary and Ernest had collected over their life there together. The chance to get out of New York pleased Valerie, for she resented the constant inquiries from acquaintances probing for details about Ernest's death. She also had fond memories of the Finca and thought she should help Mary.

Realizing she needed special permission to make the trip, Mary thought of her friend Bill Walton, who was close to President Kennedy. She phoned "darling Willie" and told him of her invitation to Cuba. Since Walton knew the Finca well, he understood the scale of the problem. Within hours, Walton met with the president in the Oval Office and explained the situation. President Kennedy was empathetic, picked up the phone, called Abram Chayes, the general counsel for the state department, and told him to see Walton and do whatever he asked to help Mrs. Ernest Hemingway get to Cuba. The next day, Chayes allowed Mary to travel to Cuba with one assistant. [15]

Mary wrote to Hadley, telling her she was off to Havana the next day "to try to rescue Ernest's manuscripts and their personal letters before the 26th, the anniversary of Fidel's revolution, when, it is widely believed, he will announce the imminent confiscation of all private property." Mary shared her strategy: "The Cuban government called me announcing it wanted to make a monument/ Museum to Ernest at the Finca, and I hope to use that as a lever for bargaining with them." Mary planned, "to get their permission to take to the US our personal, private things. Making a Museum of the Finca seems better to me than outright confiscation, as they have done with almost all other American property there." [16]

Mary's swift action in dealing with the Finca stemmed from her sense of adventure, relief at escaping the Ketchum house, and mission to protect Ernest's legacy. She also had an overarching desire to protect her property. Mary had endured years of scrimping, and she had paid her dues as Ernest's wife. Now she had come into a relative fortune; she would not allow her assets to slip from her grasp. The expropriation of the Finca might be inevitable, but Mary planned to save as much of her estate as she could.

Mary and Valerie arrived in Cuba on July 23, just nineteen days after Ernest's funeral. Juan met them at the airport and drove them to the Finca in Mary's yellow convertible. René remembered Mary looked thin and sad when she arrived. They hugged and cried and struggled to regain their composure. [17] Mary found the Finca as she remembered it. Cocks crowed all day and night; bougainvillea blossoms were flourishing. African drum rhythms drifted up from San Francisco de Paula. The weather was hot, but the east breeze was cooling, and there was ice in the bucket next to Papa's chair. In the evenings, Havana sparkled in the distance. All that was missing was Ernest. In her familiar bed, Mary had trouble falling asleep.

Roberto Herrera, who had acted as a part-time secretary to Ernest over the years, visited the day after their arrival. He brought the key to the steel filing cabinet in the library, and when he opened it, he found an envelope with a typed message: "IMPORTANT. To Be Opened in Case of My Death, Ernest Hemingway, May 24, 1958."[18] He gave the envelope to Mary, and she examined it before slitting it open. Inside was a typed letter, signed by Ernest, to his executor: "It is my wish that none of the letters written by me during my lifetime shall be published. Accordingly, I hereby request and direct you not to publish or consent to the publication by others of any such letters."[19] Mary saw Ernest had dated the envelope four days after he wrote the letter, on May 20, 1958, suggesting he had taken some time to think about what he'd meant to say. She took the instructions conscientiously and mostly followed them in the years ahead. Twenty years later, she allowed Carlos Baker to publish a selection of Ernest's letters, but she forbade others from quoting from them.[20]

Months earlier, the Cuban government had ordered the opening of all safe deposit boxes in Cuban banks and confiscated their contents. Mary contacted her bank branch in Havana and learned the authorities had stored Ernest's manuscripts at the Banco Nacional de Cuba. Juan drove her there and she found them in good condition. The bank had wrapped each one and sealed it with red wax. After she signed a few papers, the bank turned over forty pounds of manuscripts, and Mary placed them in her locked luggage in her bedroom.[21]

Mary and Valerie began going through Ernest's papers, some of which went back as far as 1926 when he and Hadley lived in Paris. He was an obsessive collector of scraps of paper, and they filled almost every drawer in the house. René remembered, once they finished going through the library and the papers stored in the basement, Mary directed him to burn several boxes of old magazines, other junk, and a bundle of Ernest's letters. According to Valerie, Ernest had marked them, "To be burned in case of my death."[22] René built a fire behind the shed, and Mary watched as the first box burned. René remained by the fire until he reduced the remaining boxes of photographs, letters, and papers to ashes.[23] Mary was fond of René and concerned about what would happen to him once she handed the Finca over to the government. She asked him if he wanted to come to the States with her, but he was reluctant to leave his parents. René showed her a letter Ernest had written to him, and she wept as she read it. She handed it back to him and told him to keep it. Raul Villarreal told me his father and Mary kept in touch for the rest of her life, and his father often sent her flowers on Mother's Day.[24]

Mary saved the letters written to Ernest by other writers, including Ezra Pound, Scott Fitzgerald, John Dos Passos, James Joyce, and his editor, Max Perkins, and planned to return them to their author's estates. Significantly, she left behind much of her own correspondence from the period before she met Ernest. The Museo Hemingway has archived that correspondence and made copies available to the John F. Kennedy Presidential Library.

In the first week, Valerie and Mary got through most of the papers and found several of Ernest's forgotten manuscripts and reams of his notes. Then they worked with a representative of the Cuban ministry of foreign affairs to record the provenance of many of the objects she would hand over. These ranged from animal heads and Venetian glass pieces to first galley proofs Ernest had corrected by hand and their collection of seven thousand books. Finally, they went through thousands of photos.

In her negotiations with the Cuban authorities, Mary offered to give the Cuban people the whole Finca, including its contents, provided the Cuban government would allow her to take to the States Ernest's papers and a few personal photos and paintings. She was not sure Ernest would have approved of her plan, but since she could not sink the Finca at sea, which she planned to do with *Pilar*, Mary wanted to make the Finca the best research museum she could. Mary wanted to take the paintings by André Masson, Paul Klee, and Juan Gris. According to Valerie, Mary made up the story Ernest had given them to her over the years as birthday gifts or anniversary presents.[25] However, the council of culture refused to allow her to export any of the paintings. As Mary reported to Bill Walton, "It was the Cultural and Art type Commies, most of them with long experience in other countries, who nearly did me in down here."[26] They wanted to keep the paintings, and when Mary suggested they could get such pieces from the Hermitage, "they patted me sympathetically on the shoulder and said: 'You know how [they] got them?'" The officer underlined the fact that the Hermitage collection itself had been seized from private owners.

Mary left several unanswered messages with the office of the minister of foreign affairs. Then she contacted their former doctor, José Luis Herrera, who had been a childhood acquaintance of Castro and was now the chief of the army's medical section. Herrera phoned one of Castro's aides and said Mary needed help with a problem. Half an hour later, the aide called back to say the prime minister would visit the Finca the following day. Mary let the whole staff at the Finca know about the impending visit, and they lined up at the front door when Castro and his entourage arrived the following evening. Two soldiers took up positions next to the gate, and others fanned out through the Finca's grounds. Castro's stocky bodyguard came into sight first, looking about suspiciously and moving his hand to his holster when a cat howled. The Bay of Pigs invasion had failed only three months earlier, and he was taking no chances. No harm would come to the prime minister on his watch.

A moment later, thirty-five-year-old Fidel Castro got out of his jeep and walked confidently up the steps to the front door. Over six feet tall, lean, and well-muscled from regular workouts, he had the bearing of a commander of men. Fidel went straight to Mary, took her hands in his, and said how sad he was about the death of Ernesto, a man who had understood the aspirations of the Cuban people. He hoped to do the right thing to honor his memory. Mary found him charismatic—Fidel had Ernest's magnetism. Though the press never mentioned his private life, Mary believed the rumor he had several children by different women.

Mary thanked him for coming, in Spanish, knowing though Castro was reasonably fluent in English, he preferred not to speak the language of the enemy. Mary came up just above Castro's shoulder, and his hairy head towered above her. Her short curly hair was tinted blond, and her face was lined from the sun. Mary introduced the members of the household and said she hoped Castro could keep them on. Castro greeted the servants, and he paid particular attention to René, whom he knew had enjoyed Ernest's trust.

Mary invited him into the sitting room where Castro lowered himself into Ernest's chair. Mary mentioned it had been her husband's favorite, and Castro, chastened, rose to move to a different spot, but she insisted he take the seat of honor in her home. Sitting and smiling, Castro asked how he might be of service. Mary explained Ernesto gave her most of the paintings in the house. They were all precious to her, and she could not leave Cuba without them. Officials from the council of culture had denied her permission to remove them. Ernest's paintings, including several pictures of bullfights by Roberto Domingo, would remain at the Finca. Castro asked why she didn't stay in Cuba, and Mary explained she had much work to do on Ernesto's estate, and she could not do it in Cuba.[27] She wondered if she might show him the house and its valuable contents, all of which she planned to give to the Cuban people, on behalf of her husband. She hoped Ernesto's generosity would impress him, and he would see that removing a few paintings would not be noticeable.

Mary persisted in characterizing the transaction as a gift. Castro must have known this was a gambit since the Cuban government could confiscate the property, but he was gracious enough to go along with her approach. His reaction was not only out of respect for Ernest but doubtless because he realized it would not look right to evict a widow from her home to create a memorial to her late husband. As they toured the house, the mounted animal heads drew his eyes, and Castro wanted to know where Ernesto shot a lion and what sort of gun he had used to kill it. He was also curious about an elk with a massive rack of antlers, which Mary explained Ernest had shot in Wyoming—the largest ever taken up to that time. In Mary's room, he asked about the greater kudu head with magnificent curled horns. She boasted she had killed it with a single shot to its heart. Castro pointed to his chest, mimicking a shot entering his rib cage, and complimented her on the great shooting.[28]

After admiring the animal heads, Castro stood for a moment on the terrace, overlooking Havana in the distance. Then he strode to the tower and quickly climbed the stairs ahead of his bodyguard, heedless of the danger. Mary joined him in the tower, and he pulled out a cigar and looked at the twinkling lights of Havana.[29] He offered a cigar to Mary, but she took out a Camel, and the bodyguard held a match in his cupped hands, illuminating her face in the pitch darkness. Castro mused the tower would not be useful militarily because the enemy could approach under cover of the brush on the hills. He exhaled a cloud of smoke, studying the view, and stroking his beard.

Castro asked whether Ernesto enjoyed writing in the tower, and Mary told him he preferred to write in the house. He missed the domestic noises and cooking smells. Castro concluded Ernesto was a man like himself, who took a great interest in cooking and wine, and he chuckled when Mary told him Ernesto had a keener interest in eating than cooking. Ernesto did most of his writing standing at the typewriter in his room, but he read and did some editing in the tower. Castro turned back to the view and said wistfully he wished he was free to come and read in the tower. He seemed lost in thought. Then, Castro told Mary that Cuban law provided valuable fine art belonged to the government. He smiled and said he would have to break a little law to honor her request to take the paintings.[30] "I won't help, but I won't hinder you," he said. Mary thanked him, and they made their way back to the sitting room. Castro sat and had a cup of coffee. Mary learned later he would have preferred whiskey, which she would have gladly served him had she known because she would have loved a stiff drink herself.

Castro said he had admired Ernesto because he spoke for the little man. He said he had read *For Whom the Bell Tolls* many times during the three years he spent leading attacks from his base in the Sierra Maestra. Ernesto wrote about the tactics of irregular warfare.[31] Standing up to take his leave, he told Mary her husband had helped him with strategy and had given him the courage to persevere. Ernesto was a great man, and he would ensure the Finca was a museum worthy of his name. As they walked down the steps, he said they would keep the *casita* for her use whenever she visited, which he hoped would be often.

As she said goodbye, Mary had mixed emotions. She knew donating the house to the Cuban people was a fiction. Castro was taking her property, so his offer to keep the guest house for her use was small compensation. He had agreed she could take the paintings, and she had the manuscripts. He was a complex, thoughtful young man, and she understood why people were drawn to him. She felt the attraction herself and regretted her government considered him an enemy. Valerie recalled, "I thought Castro was an amazing fellow, and Mary did a brilliant job."[32]

Two days later, Castro's aide phoned with instructions to have her belongings in crates at a pier in Havana by eight the next morning. A shrimp boat the size of *Pilar* was about to return to Tampa with an empty hold because the boat's refrigeration equipment had failed, and spare parts were not available in Cuba. Mary satisfied herself the hold was dry and arranged for the captain to store her precious cargo in Tampa until she could pick it up.[33] She returned to the Finca to tackle a few more jobs. She met with Gregorio Fuentes and asked him to take *Pilar* into the Gulf Stream and sink her. Appalled at first, Gregorio agreed that would be an honorable end for the boat. The revolution had brought sport fishing to a halt in Cuba, and death duties in the US were too high to allow Mary to keep the boat in Key West. She told him to strip *Pilar* of its fishing gear and keep that for his use. However,

Mary's plan to sink the boat came undone. The Cuban government used *Pilar* as a workboat until they displayed her on the grounds of the Finca.[34]

Mary deposited three thousand dollars into her Havana bank account and wrote a check against it for each member of the household staff to thank them for their years of loyal service. In several cases, "the token of appreciation from Papa" was equivalent to a year's wages. It was now the end of August, and time to say goodbye to the place where she had lived for many years, and Mary wept as she hugged René and the rest of the staff. Juan drove her and Valerie to the airport, crowded with people hoping to buy a ticket to Miami. The airplane was packed with passengers and their belongings. After the plane struggled into the air, Mary worried she had not insured her cargo aboard the shrimp boat, but she had not wanted to draw attention to the value of the goods she was removing from Cuba. Mary felt in her pocket for the envelope of precious jewelry she was taking to Miami for a friend and felt pleased she had smuggled out these pieces.

When Mary and Valerie fetched the crates in Tampa, they found them dry and intact. Once home in Ketchum, Mary wrote to Bill Walton to thank him for all he had done, and she enclosed a copy of the document she had "invented" to give the Finca to the people of Cuba. Mary signed the paper, and Valerie and Roberto Herrera witnessed it. The single page recited that Ernest had been a friend of the Cuban people for twenty-five years, that he had never taken part in its politics, and had given his Nobel Prize medal to the Virgin del Cobre. Therefore, she believed he would be pleased to present his Cuban property to the people of Cuba, to be maintained in his memory as a place for education and research.[35] Mary also phoned Walton and told him what Castro had said. Walton went straight to the White House and briefed the president. Walton later said President Kennedy felt very good about Mary's donation of the Finca to the Cuban people rather than the Cuban government. Kennedy said, "That was brilliant! That's exactly what I hoped she would do, and I'm so proud of her for doing this."[36]

◆

On September 4, Mary wrote to Henry Ehrlich, the senior editor at *Look* magazine, declining his offer to write a piece about her trip to Cuba. She explained that she went as a guest of the Cuban government, and it would be discourteous to write her impressions, which some might consider unflattering. Also, she felt she did not have a good enough sense about what was happening in Cuba, although, she said, "I know more than the C.I.A." Finally, she did not want to be "hung out for saying some true things which American readers would interpret as being pro-commie."[37] Instead, she proposed a different article, and two weeks later, Mary's piece, "Papa—How He Used to Be," appeared in the magazine. It had been two months since Ernest's death, and Mary described Ernest's love for *Pilar* and fishing on "the great, deep blue river" of the Gulf Stream. Every day they left for a voyage of discovery. "We were proud and happy about our close, smooth teamwork. We felt not merely male and female, but friends and brothers. Papa was my only brother and the best friend I ever had."[38] The cheerful picture of their relationship shows Mary's determination to prevent the truth about Ernest's decline from blemishing his sterling reputation. *Look* paid her five thousand dollars for the piece.

◆

When they returned to Ketchum, Mary and Valerie got their driver's licenses. According to Valerie, "the Sheriff just gave us the licenses, and we didn't have to take a test. They thought everyone could drive." The Pontiac Mary bought was pale green, and Mary bought them matching pale green leather jackets and pale green pants, and they drove places together. Valerie recalled they had fights when one was driving and telling the other to slow down, that they were going too fast. She remembered going off the road because she didn't know how the steering wheel worked.*

◆

For months after Ernest's death, Mary longed for him to be with her. She was "starved for the smell of his chest where my nose always nuzzled" and she longed to touch his smooth skin.[39] She missed his pats, hugs, kisses, daily endearments,

---

* Valerie's driving has improved. When I visited her at her home in Bozeman, Montana, she drove me in her thirteen-year-old Subaru Forester up a winding mountain road to Bridger Mountain ski chalet for a "picnic" lunch with friends and neighbors she had lived with in Bridger Canyon twenty-one years ago. She told me the story of the matching outfits, and she pushed her car like a rally driver, but I never once felt nervous.

and flattery, but also his discipline and counseling. The worry there was something else she could have done to help him at the end haunted Mary, and she replayed scenes from his last few days over and over in her mind, hoping to discover a clue. Valerie Hemingway recalled that after Ernest's death, Mary was much more independent. She was relieved and not strained but she wondered why Ernest did it.[40]

◆

Patrick Hemingway told me recently, "Mary was a person I was fond of, and whom I tried in every way to help. She was flawed like we all are. I think she had a terrible time because she undertook to ride a horse, and that horse was too much for her."[41]

THIRTY-EIGHT

A "Vastly Different Outcome"

October 1961–January 1963

I n late October, Mary wrote to Ernest's psychiatrist, Dr. Howard Rome, asking if there was anything they could have done to save him. She received a lengthy reply from Rome on November 1. His letter is important because he carefully sets out his understanding of Ernest's condition, given the prevailing psychiatric standards, and he accepts responsibility. Rome wanted Mary to know the question of suicide permeated all their discussions since the day Ernest was admitted. Rome had to explain to him that he was confined to a closed psychiatric unit because he was sick and could not see things objectively.[1]

From their initial talks, Rome concluded Ernest had the typical features "of an agitated depression," including "loss of self-esteem, ideas of worthlessness, a searing sense of guilt at not having done better by you, by his family, by his friends, by the myriad people who had relied upon him." Rome prescribed electroshock treatments to treat the depression, and while they were grueling and caused a feeling of loss of control and confusion, Rome noted that Ernest improved and his melancholy lightened. Their discussions changed, from suicide to the familiar theme that he could not trust his lawyers and financial advisors. They talked about Ernest's plans for the future, and the relative merits of living in Idaho, Europe, or Africa. Rome became convinced the risk of Ernest killing himself was minimal. "It was this that prompted me to say to you I felt I had to trust him, that if he were ever to get back to work which was life for him, he had to get to it in his way, free of doctors, nurses and all the encumbrances which were a perpetual reminder of sickness."[2]

Ernest never pushed Rome to release him from the hospital, and Rome felt he "was not gulled" into doing so. "The advice I gave you [that Ernest was ready to go home], good or bad, was entirely my responsibility." Mary believed Ernest had skillfully manipulated Rome, and next to this paragraph, she wrote in red pencil, "Papa too smart." Rome told Mary that he could not see what more she might have done. "He often said that he knew he was a difficult person to live with and that you had somehow gained the knack." Ernest was "especially proud of the fact that you shared with him what he frequently referred to as that thing in his head—tapping his forefinger against his temple." Ernest had become dependent on Mary and was unhappy about it: "dependent and yet constantly struggling against an admission of it for fear that it would betray some weakness."

Rome decided to discharge Ernest from the hospital so he could go home and write. Rome said, "if I had to do it over again today with the information I had, I would do it again as I did then." He stated, "I truly felt that the risks were negligible and that he and his future was worth all of them and more besides. I could not, and cannot, see Papa having his life measured out with coffee spoons."

Rome empathized with Mary's anguish but stuck by his decision. "I think I can appreciate what this has meant to you, the whole ghastly, horrible realization of its finality. And all the endless echoes of why, why, why, why?" He realized the answers "were totally unsatisfying," and he observed, "this kind of violent end for a man who we knew to possess the essence of gentleness is an unacceptable paradox."

It took two full weeks for Mary to respond to Rome. She thought, if she had been "brighter and stronger and managed to exhibit more vitality and more hope and especially more love towards Papa," she might have persuaded him "life on a somewhat reduced scale could still be full and fruitful enough to be worth sustaining." Her failure to achieve this was a defeat. She also thought Ernest "knew with one part of his brain that the earthquakes in it which . . . started that horrible summer in Spain, had created a rift which could not be bridged . . . by any sort of treatment."[3] With the "sounder part of his brain, he realized that [his] fears were not reasonable, but this realization did not help him expunge them or control them, and so he decided not to endure them any longer."[4]

Mary told Rome she didn't know how close to the truth her assumptions were and realized it would be "easy to make up a story which would allow me the smug and comfortable conclusion that I did all possible to help him. I don't want that."

However, it would be equally irrational "to manufacture a great big black guilt complex for me to carry around and show off to people."[5]

We see from this exchange that Mary knew and accepted Ernest had died by suicide. She did not pretend there had been an accident. Mary also remained skeptical about Rome's decision to release Ernest. She continued to believe Ernest had outsmarted him because, less than six days after Rome discharged Ernest, he was dead. Mary's refusal to admit publicly Ernest had killed himself was not self-deception or a delusion brought on by grief. It stemmed from her fear that it would blemish Ernest's reputation and hers by association.

◈

After Ernest's death, there were various efforts to explain his depression and death, ranging from hereditary hemochromatosis (the "Celtic Curse") to chronic traumatic encephalopathy, also known as "dementia pugilistica." Dr. Andrew Farah, a forensic psychiatrist, recently published *Hemingway's Brain*, a study he describes as "a forensic psychiatric examination of his very brain cells—the stressors, traumas, chemical insults, and biological changes—that killed a world-famous literary genius."[6] Farah's book is welcome as an authoritative account of how today's psychiatrists would have diagnosed and treated a patient presenting Ernest's symptoms. Of course, it is a hypothetical work because Farah could not examine the patient nor obtain access to his medical files. He certainly could not examine Ernest's actual brain cells or tissue. Instead, he relies upon the work of biographers, the memoirs of family and friends, and personal correspondence to provide a narrative of neurological and psychiatric illnesses, which progressed over the years. This produces an interesting narrative, but it is obviously no substitute for examining the living patient or the actual medical records.

Farah disposes of the idea Ernest suffered from hemochromatosis. On Ernest's first discharge from the Mayo Clinic, Dr. Butt had advised him, "you might possibly have a very rare liver disease called hemochromatosis," but he did not believe it should be further investigated.[7] Farah observes, "liver biopsies, particularly in 1960, carried a risk of hemorrhage, possibly a fatal risk and one that outweighed curiosity."[8] Ernest's doctors likely rejected the diagnosis based on serum tests, or "because he lacked many of the hallmark clinical findings and because his clinical picture so obviously suggested something else . . . dementia with associated depression and psychosis."[9] Farah contends the Mayo doctors failed to diagnose the presence of dementia. The depression, paranoid delusions, and suicidal impulses were "all symptoms of an over-arching illness—'dementia, mixed etiology.'"[10] Dr. Rome prescribed electroconvulsive therapy because he believed Ernest's "cognitive issues, memory deficits, disinhibition, paranoia, and personality changes were all secondary to the depression."[11] According to Farah, Ernest "received the state-of-the-art therapy while at Mayo, but for the wrong diagnosis."[12]

Ernest had suffered nine major concussions, including two wave blast injuries, and "these repeated concussive blows did cumulative damage so that by the time he was fifty, his very brain cells were irreparably changed, and their premature decline now programmed into his genetics."[13] Individuals who suffer multiple concussions "can progress from post concussive symptoms to a form of progressive brain degeneration. . . . 'chronic traumatic encephalopathy' or C.T.E."[14] Farah concluded, Hemingway's case was "a textbook example" of CTE which combined with his heavy drinking, untreated diabetes, and hypertension "propelled the pathology" to a "permanent dementia."[15]

Had Ernest presented himself for diagnosis today, he would have undergone an MRI scan of his brain, which would likely have shown the exaggerated shrinkage or loss of brain volume common in dementia. A PET scan would likely have shown accumulations of dead cells in his brain lobes. Farah hypothesizes, "no doubt, his PET scan would have some abnormalities, but this test is the most challenging to predict because of his several concussions. . . . What limited data we have from boxers and NFL players shows that multiple areas are affected, frontal and cerebellar areas in particular."[16] Equipped with such findings, which were not available to the Mayo doctors who examined Ernest, Farah would have treated Ernest's dementia "aggressively."[17] He would have prescribed a detoxification program, possibly substituting Valium for alcohol; a course of "reality-based" psychotherapy focusing on Ernest's health; physical exercise; playing soft music while he was sleeping; and a variety of drugs including vitamin B, a potent antioxidant, omega-three fatty acids or "fish oil," calcium found in the drug Namenda, drugs which may improve memory including Aricept and Exelon, and the antipsychotic drugs iloperidone at bedtime or lurasidone to reduce his delusions.[18] Farah concluded, "results with this type of aggressive therapy have been generally positive. If such a plan had been fully implemented, Hemingway's future would've been vastly different—but for his time, his diagnosis, and the options available, his outcome was inevitable."[19]

Even accepting the validity of Farah's hypothetical diagnosis, the key to the regime proposed by Farah would be compliance by the patient. Ernest would have had to quit drinking, perhaps taking Valium to achieve relaxation. I can't imagine Valium replacing wine for long in the Hemingway household. While the absence of electroconvulsive treatments would have been welcome, the program of reality-based psychotherapy would have tested the treating psychiatrist against Ernest's cagey persona and litany of worries. The exercise, music while sleeping, and vitamins might have improved his rest and mood. The memory-enhancing drugs might have worked to some degree, and the antipsychotics might have reduced his delusions, but what about the side effects of drowsiness, nausea, dizziness, weight gain, diarrhea, face/muscle twitching, and dullness, which patients on these drugs commonly experience? How long would Ernest have continued taking the antipsychotics or complying with the treatment regime? Could Mary have kept Ernest away from wine, ensured he took his meds, played music for him at night, and managed to buoy his spirits? Her life would have become unbearable. The diagnosis itself is depressing, and I doubt Ernest would have been placated to learn his symptoms were caused by dementia, which was actively diminishing the very brain he relied upon to write. I can understand the delight of contemporary forensic psychiatrists in their advanced diagnostic machinery and cornucopia of vitamins and drugs, but it seems rash to predict, "Ernest's future would have been vastly different." "Isn't it pretty to think so," as Jake Barnes said, but I doubt Ernest would have conscientiously taken his drugs daily for years. It is painful to imagine him padding about the Ketchum house in his moccasins, older than his years, calmed by Valium, delusion-free, but drowsy, flat, dull, and still succumbing to dementia. Would Mary have stayed with him, or would she have committed him to a long-term care facility? How confident can we be the outcome would have been "vastly different?" When Hotch met with Ernest and tried to persuade him life was worth living, Ernest responded, "but what have they given me to keep me going? I'm sixty-one years old, and I'm empty." He said, "the books and stories I promised myself to write will never be written." He asked, "What does a man of my age care about? Being healthy. Working good at his calling. Eating and drinking with the people he cares about. Good sex, traveling to the places he loves. I'm denied all of 'em." He continued, "Why should I stick around? How do I pay the goddamn taxes if I can't write the stuff that pays for them?" Hotch could not think of an answer but told Ernest he had to get over "the craziness."[20] How would Dr. Farah answer Ernest's questions since reality therapy requires him to be truthful about the diagnosis? Predicting a "vastly different" outcome in a patient one has never even examined seems the very definition of hubris. When Ernest assessed his life, he made an existential choice.

Farah's speculation about Hemingway's brain appears to run contrary to the ethical principles the American Psychiatric Association (APA) has had in place since 1973 when they developed the so-called "Goldwater rule." Members of the APA must "refrain from publicly issuing professional medical opinions about individuals that they have not personally evaluated in a professional setting or context." The APA ethical standards "require review of medical and psychiatric history and records and a complete examination of mental status."[21] Doing less "undermines the credibility and integrity of the profession and the physician-patient relationship." Oddly, Farah does not mention this ethical obligation or explain how the claims in his book do not contravene the profession's ethical standards. I inquired of the APA whether "the Goldwater rule applies to expressing psychiatric opinions about a famous dead person the psychiatrist has never met, and whose medical records the psychiatrist has not seen?" The communications officer for the APA told me the general counsel's office said in response to my questions: "I'm not aware of anything directly answering that question, but I believe the Goldwater Rule would apply to prohibit, for example, the diagnosing of a deceased public figure that one has not examined."[22]

◆

Within months of Ernest's funeral, two paperback biographies were already circulating, one written by "a cheap stinker named Kurt Singer." Mary sent Alfred Rice a copy of Singer's book, *Hemingway: Life and Death of a Giant*. She called it "a quick, clever, and chronological misrepresentation of Ernest's life," and she asked Rice to get his libel experts to review the book. Although she did not want to be "a suing widow," she found the book "outrageous."[23]

To combat the incessant rumor mill, Mary appointed Carlos Baker, the Woodrow Wilson Professor of Literature at Princeton University, to be Ernest's official biographer. Paul Mowrer was Mary's first choice. Mary appointed Baker only after Mowrer refused to undertake the biography, and Baker agreed to consult her on a wide range of subjects.

Charlie Scribner Jr. and Harry Brague advised Mary that Carlos Baker "would be by far the best person" to do the biography because Baker had made a lifetime study of Ernest's work and had completed much of the research. "He is also reliable in matters of personal judgment, and . . . I would trust him not to write anything that would betray a confidence."[24] Mary asked Alfred Rice for his opinion concerning Baker as a biographer, wondering whether "it would be possible for us to insert some phrase showing that I would have veto rights on the use of material?" Or, might she get "some authority over his manuscript whenever it is finished?"[25]

Unconvinced Baker was the best choice, Mary wrote to Hadley and her husband Paul Mowrer, proposing Paul as Ernest's official biographer. If he wrote the book, "it would be far superior to one by Carlos Baker."[26] Mowrer might seem a curious choice, for he had married Hadley six years after her divorce from Ernest. As we have seen, Mary knew Mowrer because he had been her boss at the *Chicago Daily News*, and she respected him as a writer. Mowrer knew Ernest in his formative years in Paris and was familiar with his later efforts. Mary conceded it might be unfair to judge Professor Baker's style from the one book she had read and from the two letters he wrote to her. Still, a book written by Mowrer, a Pulitzer Prize winner, "would be better written than one by Baker."[27] She also complained about Baker's style to Harry Brague: "It would seem curious to me to read about Ernest in the rather pretentious, professorial language which Mr. Baker sometimes employs. (For heaven's sake, please don't mention this to him.)"[28]

It's hard to imagine a writer closer to Ernest and his personal history than Mowrer, because he could simply check with his wife to gather information on the Paris years. Mary told Alfred Rice, "The fact he is married to Hadley . . . would make no just, or unjust, difference to the work. Hadley and Ernest have always remained friends."[29]

Unaware Mary had asked Mowrer to do the job, Baker wrote to Mary saying he had spoken to Brague that morning and become worried Mary did not consider him to be the right biographer because, "We have never met; I might turn out to be dull, dry, academic, even a stinker."[30] Baker said whoever did the job must enjoy Scribner's, and Mary Hemingway's, confidence. The task should take five years and would include a worldwide search for material. Elderly witnesses to Ernest's life would not be around long to offer their views, and the job must begin at once.

"In approaching people, the biographer has to say he has Mary Hemingway's blessing." Baker put the proposal squarely to Mary: "Will you agree to my going ahead? If you prefer to postpone a final decision until after we meet, I will wait." In the meantime, he wanted to search for letters and people, "and a provisional green light from you would help." [31]

Two days later, Mary informed Alfred Rice that Paul Mowrer had given her "an absolute no" to becoming Ernest's biographer. At seventy-four years of age, Mowrer felt too old to finish the job. Now that Mowrer had ruled himself out, Mary didn't want to offend Baker by putting off a decision. She would appoint him if he accepted Mary's "right to be consulted and to give advice," and she asked Rice to compose a letter of agreement detailing her rights, including vetoes. Six days later, Mary wrote the words Baker longed to read, "Yes, let's not delay any longer getting you started as Ernest's official biographer." She told Harry Brague to publish an announcement and assured Baker her delay in firing the starting signal did not arise from her mistrust of him or doubt in his ability. [32] She knew "he was not a stinker," but she had trouble relinquishing control over Ernest's work and reputation. "It makes me feel very much alone, perhaps like giving some stranger permission to marry your child." [33] We don't know if Baker ever learned he was the second choice.

Mary asked Baker to give her consultation rights, "to fill in odd corners of your knowledge of Ernest, which even extensive research might leave dim." He should consult her about their life "at the Finca and on *Pilar* and at Paraíso . . . and the two African safaris." Baker should talk to Mary about "fishing, and hunting out here, of how he regarded illnesses and accidents." And she wanted Baker to consult her about Ernest's women. One of the "dreadful little paperback biographies suggested he spent every night in a different bed. It was not so in the years I knew him." [34] In return, Mary promised Baker she would not insist Ernest "must be promoted to sainthood, with not even a misdemeanor reported." She remained confident, "even with all misdemeanors, mistakes, and other evidence of evil fully reported, Ernest in the round will look good." [35] Mary offered to help by writing whatever letters he might need and providing a list of people to interview.

Baker replied a week later, "I have neither been able to stop shaking at the idea of such responsibility nor really settle down to write you a decent reply." He accepted her conditions and promised to ask her many questions over the coming years. Baker would consult her, "ad nauseam and about everything from safaris

to fishing and hunting to illnesses and accidents to women." He would not sensa-
tionalize but tell the truth. He agreed, "Ernest in the round is going to look good.
So, on that score, I hope there will be no problems between us."[36]

As he worked on the biography, Baker made good on his agreement to consult Mary, and she provided him with generous access to Ernest's papers. Once
appointed, he approached his task with high energy, and after fulfilling other
commitments, he devoted himself full-time to the project. He enlisted his wife,
Dorothy, to deal with Mary. Baker's letters are businesslike, but Dorothy wrote
friendly letters of thanks for dinners Mary hosted, commending her culinary skills
and chatting about her own family. Dorothy tried to soften her husband's brusque
manner, writing, "I've just read the long letter Carlos wrote to you, and I don't
think he really conveyed to you how grateful we both are for your kindness. He's
so preoccupied that I'm afraid he seems curt and over-businesslike."[37]

Briefing Baker on Ernest's friends, Mary said that Ed Hotchner presented
himself in the press, "as the sole friend . . . and interpreter of Papa." Though
Hotch enjoyed excellent times with Ernest, Baker should not consider him "an
authority, and he should not exaggerate his importance in Papa's life." Buck
Lanham remained, "a longer, closer, and truer friend."[38]

◆

Mary traveled to Key West in 1962 to sort through the documents and personal
effects Ernest left behind when he moved to Cuba in 1939. He had stored them
in boxes in Sloppy Joe's Bar and for three weeks, Mary arrived each morning in
the barn-sized bar, "and tied on her working clothes—a long white butcher smock
which she put on backward to protect her blue slacks and shirt from the dust."
Then she filled cartons with letters and books for Valerie to sort in New York.[39]

While in Key West, Mary met with Agnes Stanfield (née Von Kurowsky),
Ernest's love interest during the First World War. Agnes was the nurse Ernest met
while hospitalized in Milan and she inspired the character of Catherine Barkley
in *Farewell to Arms*. Mary returned the letters Agnes had written to Ernest and
interviewed Agnes on behalf of Carlos Baker. He had provided Mary with a list
of questions for the sixty-nine-year-old Agnes, and Mary wrote a full account of
the interview for Baker, attaching photos of Agnes and Ernest. Mary described
Agnes as "a crisp, unsentimental woman who was no doubt the same way as a

young, pretty girl," and from what Agnes said, Mary doubted she had ever loved Ernest. Agnes did not tell Ernest "of her private decision not to marry him until after he was back home in Chicago" because Ernest "had such a tempestuous nature . . . I was afraid to tell him."[40] Ernest had told Mary, when Agnes refused to marry him, "I thought I couldn't stand it—I wanted to die."[41] This was invaluable material for Baker's biography.

◆

Mary teased Baker about his stodgy, pretentious personality.[42] She had recently visited Toots Shor's restaurant, the haunt of celebrities from Frank Sinatra to Joe DiMaggio to Ernest and seen several old friends. Mary told Carlos he would "have to leave the groves of academe and make acquaintance with the dives" to get an insight into Ernest's life, and she thought Toots's place would be an excellent start. She invited him to lunch there. Baker defended himself, for he did not plan "a compendium of anecdotes and crawling from bar to bar is about as rewarding as hiding behind the trees in the groves of academe." He defended his careful approach to drinking: "I find it helps me to remember better when I come away and write it down."[43] Baker remained a sober professor.

Baker asked persistent and sometimes awkward questions of Mary. She told Hadley, "I find it difficult to answer questions which sometimes seem to me to be so personal and private that I wouldn't wish to discuss them with anyone, much less a comparative stranger."[44] Baker probed about Ernest's afflictions of his liver, kidneys, hepatitis, and partial loss of memory. "My information is that these should be added to the list of high blood pressure and mental depression. Is this information wrong?" Recognizing he taxed Mary's patience, he asked her to "[f]orgive my trespasses."[45] When he gave Mary another set of questions, he hoped the project "is not becoming anathema to you."[46] Baker wanted Mary to write "amplifications" of sensitive events. He wanted to learn about her tubal pregnancy, the Adriana Ivancich affair, and Mary's life before meeting Ernest, including their courtship in London. He asked about the beginning and development and ultimate diagnosis of Ernest's last illness. Baker wanted her reaction to the view that Ernest recognized a decline in his writing powers after the war. He wanted her to react to the belief that anyone who criticized Ernest's writing became "*ipso facto* a jerk in his eyes."

He asked for her candid estimate of Ernest's faults as a person and husband. These intrusive questions made Mary defensive.

In answer to Baker's questions, Mary asserted Ernest never considered his writing powers had declined. "When he was writing *Across the River,* he used to say, 'We'll show them who's the champ.'" Ernest never thought it wasn't an excellent book. "He was happy every day he wrote the *Old Man and the Sea.* And he was happy when he was writing the Paris book."

Baker asked Mary to send him the filing cases of materials Valerie had arranged and promised to cover the shipping charges and give "a guarantee of safe storage in my hideout in the library." [47] Mary sent Baker a box of files containing correspondence from Ernest to others, but underlined her concern the letters not be published: "Sending you all these documents is really a big compliment to you from me—it means I trust you won't pilfer." [48] Mary's note wounded Baker. "According to my vocabulary, pilfering is petty stealing, and according to my code of personal behavior, it is not done." He cared not to possess physical objects, but he needed the information they contained, and he was grateful to receive the files. Baker called them "a biographer's dream." [49]

The Bakers spent a week with Mary at her home in Ketchum in August, and she arranged interviews with several of Ernest's friends, including George Saviers, Chuck Atkinson, and Tillie Arnold. Mary told the prudish Baker that Ernest had always loved Tillie, and Tillie confirmed she loved Papa too. Tillie remembered saying to Baker, "'I want to tell you one thing. We never went to bed together,'" and Baker's "mouth flew open like that! And he stopped dead still." [50]

Meanwhile, Mary entertained the Bakers, cooking elaborate meals and organizing interviews. Dorothy sent thanks for Mary's hospitality and for introducing Carlos to her friends. "It was good to feel the real friendship and admiration that everyone felt for you and Ernest. We feel it now too and are happy that we saw it and that we had the opportunity to see you at home in beautiful Idaho." [51] Carlos thanked Mary for "the gourmet cooking and the vintage wines and the numerous phone calls setting up interviews." The visit made a great impression, and he couldn't thank Mary enough. He hoped that his book would be better for the exercise. [52] The Bakers sent Mary a juicer as a thank you gift.

In 1963, Mary resolved to be "less friendly with alcohol, prettier, neater, compacter, quieter, more amusing, wiser, more knowledgeable and more self-contained."[53] For the last eighteen months, she had worked tirelessly to protect Ernest's legacy and her estate. As Bill Walton remarked, Mary "enjoyed being Ernest's widow." She "had a lot of fun" and "it was a happy time for her."[54] In a similar vein, Rose Marie Burwell commented, Mary knew "it was much easier to be the keeper of a national monument than the wife of an extremely difficult man."[55] As much as Mary enjoyed making decisions about the estate, she delighted in presenting her business card, which announced, "Mrs. Ernest Hemingway," as did her personal letterhead. With exclusive control over Ernest's literary legacy, Mary became a serious player in American literature.

THIRTY-NINE

You Are Rated as
Politically Unreliable

December 1961–July 1962

O ne of Ernest's most valuable possessions was Joan Miró's painting *The Farm*, which Ernest loaned to the Museum of Modern Art in February 1960. It had become the artist's most famous work and was insured for two million dollars (eight million dollars in 2020). Miró began the piece as part of his therapy while recovering from a nervous breakdown on his family's farm at Montroig del Camp in Catalonia and finished it in Paris in the winter of 1922. It is a detailed study of the farmhouse, a woman doing laundry at a well, a tree filled with individually rendered leaves, and on the ground, independent blades of grass, portraits of lizards, ants, goats, and dogs. Miró said, "I wanted to put everything I loved about the country into that canvas—from a huge tree to a tiny little snail." He worked seven or eight hours a day on *The Farm*. "I suffered terribly, horribly, like a condemned man. I wiped out a lot, and I started getting rid of all those foreign influences and getting in touch with Catalonia."[1]

Hemingway and Miró became friends in Paris and despite their differences in size, the diminutive painter sparred with the gigantic author. More often, Miró acted as a timekeeper for matches between Hemingway and Morley Callaghan at the American Club. Miró, who spoke not a word of English, was short and wore black suits with starched white shirts topped off with a bowler hat.[2]

Given his precarious financial circumstances, Miró tried to sell *The Farm*, but the Paris dealers found it too avant-garde. Finally, in the spring of 1925, the

Galerie Pierre offered it to Ernest's friend, Evan Shipman, at a nominal price. When Shipman told Ernest of his good luck, Ernest's face fell, for he had seen the painting a year earlier and wanted it. Shipman agreed to toss a coin with Ernest to settle the question. Even though Shipman won, he agreed to sell the piece.[3] Miró recalled Ernest "became so crazy about [The Farm] that he wanted to buy it."[4] John Dos Passos remembered Ernest "had the same shrewd eye for painting as Gertrude Stein. . . . He brought the picture home to the sawmill in triumph," for Hadley's thirty-fourth birthday, and they hung it over their bed.[5]

When Ernest divorced Hadley, she kept the painting, and it hung in the home she shared with Paul Mowrer. A few years later, Ernest asked to borrow the piece. He hung it in Pauline's house in Key West and later at the Finca next to the dining room table. Ernest loved The Farm: "it has in it all that you feel about Spain when you are there and all that you feel when you are away and cannot go there. No one else has been able to paint these two very opposing things."[6] When Ernest loaned The Farm to the Museum of Modern Art in 1960, the painting arrived in terrible shape. In sixteen years hanging next to the Finca's dining table, Miró's brilliant colors faded, the paint cracked, mildew covered the surface, water stains and candle wax showed, and in several places termites ate away the canvas, leaving only the paint. Miró came to see the painting, "and he kept saying it has a skin disease. He was so upset."[7] Ernest agreed to pay for the restoration, though he tried to blame the MoMA for the damage. The painting was beautifully restored.

❖

Ernest's will stunned Jack because he had believed he would receive half of his father's estate, and he was too numb to react quickly. Hadley and Paul Mowrer believed Ernest's will inflicted a great injustice upon Jack, and they acted on his behalf, requesting that Mary acknowledge Hadley's ownership of Miró's The Farm.[8] Hadley had loaned the painting to Ernest for five years, but she had not kept the letter he sent asking to borrow the painting and acknowledging her ownership. Mowrer wrote he hoped he did not upset Mary by bringing up the Miró. He assured her there would be no family trouble over the painting. Hadley did not want possession of it, for they had no appropriate place to hang it. Neither did Jack. Paul "merely thought that, if the rumors of its present valuation are justified, it might place an undue strain on your estate tax if there was a failure to recognize that the painting belongs to Hadley." In his view, the best place for it would be a museum if she wished to donate it, "in which case, as I understand it, there would be no tax, I rather think Hadley and Jack would be willing to go along."[9]

Since no one had ever mentioned to Mary the picture did not belong to Ernest, she felt deceived—less by Ernest, who would have told her it belonged to Hadley than by Hadley, Paul, and Jack. She told Rice if she needed the painting as capital and sold it to contribute to her support, she would do so. She didn't believe Hadley owned *The Farm*, which had hung in her and Ernest's home in Cuba for sixteen years, with no question of its ownership ever arising.

Mary interpreted Mowrer's letter as an attempt to gain ownership of the painting. She told Rice the letter was "bloody outrageous" and the concern over putting "undue strain" on her estate tax "was sheer comedy." She didn't think there was any hurry about settling the issue, and she had no intention, unless compelled by law, to hand over the painting to either Hadley or Jack. Mary wanted to leave it where it was in the Museum of Modern Art, with a plaque saying it was in memory of Ernest. Mary pointed out that Hadley and Ernest's marriage lasted, at the most, for five years, and he had given her the rights to *The Sun Also Rises*. "If he did, in fact, give Hadley the Miró, and she then asked for it back, it seems likely to me he felt she had enough with the rights to the book."[10] Fourteen months after Ernest's death, the Mowrers notified the museum they were suing Mary for the painting, and there were rumors that the Mowrers would sell the piece on the open market. Alfred Rice sought assurance that the museum recognized Mary's ownership, but the museum replied it could not return the painting until they resolved the question of ownership.[11]

Valerie Hemingway told me that when she was going through Ernest's papers, she found a carbon copy of a letter from Ernest to Hadley, dated sometime in 1934, asking to borrow the Miró painting and a positive response from Hadley. Valerie gave the letters to Mary, and she doesn't know what Mary did with them. Assuming the letters would have established Hadley's claim to the painting, it is troubling that they seem to have disappeared.[12] Mary felt sufficiently vulnerable about the court action that she made an ex-gratia payment of twenty-five thousand dollars to Jack to resolve the issue, and the Mowrers withdrew the suit.[13] The painting was returned to Mary in January 1964, and she displayed it in the dining room of her penthouse.

Leonard Lyons continued to follow Mary as a celebrity worthy of comment, and in his column on March 7, 1962, he noted, "There have been and will be rumors about Mrs. Ernest Hemingway's possible interest in other men." Lyons reported Mary's response: "No. I'm out of the race permanently. I will marry them only from afar. Papa molded me to fit him only—in his philosophy and in his rare way of life. There can never be another. I am permanently retired."

◆

Early in 1962, Bill Walton phoned with news of an invitation. President Kennedy was planning a dinner in April for Nobel Prize winners, and Mary would be invited. The president wanted the actor Frederic March to read something by Ernest, and they were thinking about an excerpt from "The Killers." Walton thought Mary might prefer something else. He said it should be a grand evening and regretted he would not be there himself because he'd never won a Nobel Prize. Mary asked if she could stay with Walton at his home in Washington so they could catch up, and he agreed at once. Mary wondered what to wear and how she could compete with Jackie, and Walton assured her she would have fun trying. She decided she would have a dress made—something elegant and suitable for an evening at the White House with the president. She also started thinking about what she would say to him and realized this would be a precious opportunity to let him know what she felt about Cuba. Mary remained upset about the Bay of Pigs invasion launched a year earlier on April 17, 1961, and the continuing anti-Castro policy of the American government. She would take advantage of the occasion to speak, and perhaps change his mind.

◆

Mary could not have known how unwelcome her views on Cuba would be to the president, especially concerning the Bay of Pigs disaster. Indeed, until the release of recent documents, it was not known that the fiasco resulted because Kennedy failed to understand the nature of the operation when he launched it. He blamed his lapse on poor briefings from his advisors, and, in particular, the CIA. [14] Mary would not have known that the plan called for thirteen hundred Cuban exiles, trained by American advisors as anti-Castro resistance fighters, to land at night

on the beaches of the Bay of Pigs. They were to establish and hold a beachhead
for up to a month, their example provoking a popular uprising among the Cuban
people, leading to efforts to overthrow the Castro government. The uprising would
create a pretext for landing a provisional government, recruited in Florida, and the
provisional government would invite US support—American forces would invade
Cuba backing the new government. The US would provide covert support
to the operation and maintain plausible deniability of American involvement.

The key to the plan was a preemptive strike to destroy Castro's air force on the
ground by aircraft ostensibly launched by Cuban rebel pilots from airfields in Cuba.
Cuban-exile pilots, recruited and trained in Nicaragua, were to fly sixteen aircraft
painted and marked to resemble those operated by Castro's air force. The day before
the strike, April 19, 1961, Kennedy reduced the number of planes to eight. The first
strike destroyed five of Castro's planes, but at least seven were still airworthy. Kennedy
canceled a series of strikes designed to destroy the remaining aircraft. His refusal to
allow the airstrikes meant Castro maintained air supremacy, a fatal defect for any
invasion plan, as had been well-learned in World War II.

The Cuban-exile troops landed overnight at the Bay of Pigs, but they ran into
trouble. Coral reefs blocked access to the beaches and prevented landing craft
carrying troops and equipment from reaching the shore. In the following days,
Castro's army, assisted by his air force, destroyed the invasion force and sank two
ships carrying supplies. America abandoned the Cuban-exile fighters, and they
died or became captives as they ran out of food and ammunition.

Kennedy knew that one command from him launching planes or bombard-
ments from naval guns could ensure the survival of the Cuban exile-brigade.[15]
He resisted advice to start an attack, fearing Khrushchev would use the American
invasion of Cuba as a provocation justifying the Russian occupation of Berlin.
Without air cover, the invasion failed, and Kennedy owned the decision. The
operation was a humiliating failure, and Kennedy "spent much of Wednesday
afternoon in the private residence of the White House with his wife. At one
point, he went into her room and lay on her bed, close to tears. Jacqueline tried to
comfort him." Kennedy also called his father several times that afternoon. "The
proud family patriarch found the effort of buoying Jack's morale exasperating.
He lost his patience and snapped at his son, 'Oh, hell, if that's the way you feel,
give the job to Lyndon.'"[16] Mary would not have known about many of the plan's
features or Kennedy's anguish. She suspected the US had backed the invasion, and

she opposed American military action against the Castro government because she believed diplomatic relations should be established instead.

◆

By late April, Mary had a tailored black chiffon dress. It was expensive, but a woman had to be presentable. She thought it demure, with sleeves and big pink silk roses drifting across the bottom of the full-length skirt. It had to be full-length—it was for the White House. She thought Ernest would approve the "[m]erry widow touch."[17]

Meanwhile, Mary traveled between Ketchum and the little flat in New York, where she worked on finding and listing all receipts and expenditures for the last two years so Alfred Rice could determine the inheritance tax. Mary visited Rice at his office and, taking a break from tax issues, she selected a few pages from "the Sea book" and provided them to Frederic March to consider for his reading at the White House dinner. She wrote to Kennedy's secretary, Letitia Baldrige, and explained, though the selection was not festive, March thought it would work, and she hoped Miss Baldridge agreed. Mary said, "I have slightly deleted and slightly disguised most of the profanity of the book but should appreciate hearing . . . whether it was sufficiently cleaned up for the present purpose."[18]

Mary arrived at Bill Walton's redbrick house in Georgetown after lunch on a bright spring day, and he was delighted to see her. He was divorced and living as an eligible bachelor, and he showed Mary his latest paintings hanging on the walls of his home filled with family furniture and antiques he had collected.[19] Mary and Walton were so close, even after months of separation, the distance soon vanished. They talked with ease to each other, touching upon every subject, even hurtful ones, for Mary had been his confessor and confidant since their days in London. She told Walton she had decided against having Frederic March read "The Killers" and instead had substituted a few pages from a book about the sea.[20] She had written an introduction and read it to Walton for his reaction, just as she might have read a paragraph to him for his comments in the old days. He loved it. After a dinner prepared by Walton's housekeeper and a few gin and tonics accompanied by intimate conversation with a man who knew her well, Mary retired to her bedroom and fell into a deep sleep.

The next morning, she met with two of the directors of the Library of Congress who were lobbying to have her donate Ernest's papers and manuscripts. She was also getting pressure from the president of Columbia University, and Carlos Baker persisted in his efforts to persuade her to donate to Princeton. The directors took Mary on a tour of the library and showed her where they stored the papers of George Washington, deep in the basement. She didn't like the feel of the place. Then they showed her the reading room, which had "dinky little desks" where scholars could study the library holdings. She was polite and told the chairman she would give the request careful consideration. Privately, Mary "hated the idea of Ernest being stuck down in the ground in those dark corridors with so, so, so many other people."[21]

Mary broke free by mid-afternoon and rushed back to Walton's house to prepare for the evening. She tried on the black chiffon dress again and looked in the mirror, thinking she had never owned a more beautiful dress. She had colored her hair platinum blonde, the way Ernest loved it, and she wished he were there to smile and tell her how beautiful she was. Mary did her face and still had time for a quick gin and tonic with Walton, who had come home early to admire his guest. He was effusive in his praise.

The president greeted Mary, telling her he had admired Ernest and was sorry for her loss and America's loss. He looked forward to chatting with her at dinner. She moved on to meet the first lady. Jacqueline was wearing a sea-foam-green chiffon gown which draped over one shoulder and she had her hair puffed in a page-boy style. She was radiant and looked younger than her thirty-three years. Jacqueline told Mary they were pleased she had come and that Jack had wanted Ernest to be at the inauguration.

The guests assembled for photographs, and the president asked Mary to sit next to him. Hundreds of flashbulbs fired, and Mary could see bulky television cameras recording the event. President Kennedy whispered in her ear, telling her how delighted he was she had accepted his invitation and had selected a new work by Ernest for Frederic March to read. His eyes twinkling, he asked if she had to clean up the language. Mary caught herself smiling at the suggestion, knowing he must have heard how many swear words she had altered. He introduced her to the widow of General George Marshall, and Mary told her how much she had admired her husband, but she could not help thinking Mrs. Marshall's clothing was frumpy. She wore a mink stole and black lace bonnet and seemed harmless, if not a little bewildered.

Mary was delighted to find herself sitting on the president's left at dinner. Seated on her left was Dr. Carl Anderson, a Nobel Laureate in physics from California. Mrs. Marshall sat on the president's right. The room filled with light-hearted chatter as guests introduced themselves and old friends reacquainted themselves. The president rose to propose a toast, joking that some had called the event "the Presidents Easter Egghead roll." He said, "I think this is the most extraordinary collection of talent, of human knowledge, that has ever gathered together at the White House, with the possible exception of when Thomas Jefferson dined alone."[22]

The audience laughed good-naturedly at the president's remark, and as he sat down, Mary complimented him on his gentle humor. While she still had his attention, Mary told him about the interview she had conducted with his father before the war, when he was the American ambassador to the United Kingdom. She drew him in and then launched into her mini lecture on Cuba. "After preliminary niceties, I suggested to our host that the US Government's position toward Cuba was stupid, unrealistic, and worse, ineffective, especially—*sotto voce*—since the Bay of Pigs fiasco."[23] Anyone who had hunted in Cuba knew the Bay of Pigs was no place to launch an invasion since the ground was too swampy to support armored vehicles.

Mary pressed her argument but sensed the president was tired of her subject as he turned to engage Mrs. Marshall. "President Kennedy was looking irked and impatient."[24] She chatted with Dr. Anderson and asked him what the effect would be on America's intellectual future if a bomb were to hit the room in which so many Nobel Prize winners sat. Anderson smiled and told her there would be a minor effect since most of the people in the room were older. The younger generation was doing the exciting science busily working in their labs, not eating at a lavish banquet.

The president reached for the salt, and Mary took advantage of the opportunity to reengage. She offered to parachute into Cuba, telling him the Cubans liked her husband, and she knew Fidel.

"Have you read Katherine Anne Porter's *Ship of Fools*?" the president asked.

"No. I'm sorry to be so persistent, but I would be happy to talk to Fidel . . ."

"You are rated as politically unreliable," said the president.[25]

Dinner ended, and Frederic March took the stage. The Oscar-winning actor and longtime supporter of the Democratic Party read for thirty minutes. For ten minutes, he read an excerpt from Sinclair Lewis's *Main Street* and passages from the 1947 speech of the late secretary of state, George Marshall, given when he inaugurated the Marshall plan. Then March spent twenty minutes reading excerpts from the unpublished work by Ernest Hemingway. March read Mary's introduction, which summarized the opening of *Islands in the Stream*, [26] and then he used distinct voices and accents for each of the characters. After the readings, the president rose to lead the audience in applause, and as the lights glowed again, he led Mrs. Hemingway and Mrs. Marshall to join him on stage. In his concluding comments, President Kennedy said, "I regard this as the most distinguished and significant dinner that we've had in the White House since I've been here and, I think, in many, many years." [27]

Writing the following Sunday in the *Washington Post*, Richard L. Cole said, "it was as though a deftly civilized couple had invited the brainiest folks they could think of to dine and be entertained." He wrote, "it remained a party in which everyone was openly delighted to see everyone else." [28]

Mary enjoyed herself and wrote to Clara Spiegel that the evening went off "gracefully," and the audience was most attentive to Frederic March's reading. Of her conversation with Kennedy, she said, "We had a fine time yakking—he is a well-honed wit." Photos taken before dinner show Mary sitting next to the president for a posed shot with all the guests. Her hands in long white gloves rest in her lap, and the roses on her black dress stand out. She has diverted President Kennedy, and he looks at her with his full attention, as she is caught in mid-sentence. Mary told Clara there was so much TV and newsreel coverage, people began stopping her in the street and asking her questions. When Mary was shopping, a woman approached her in a dressing room, saying, "You're a famous person," to which Mary replied, "No, my husband was, not me." The stranger persisted, "Oh, yes, you are, and we love you." [29]

The Robert Kennedys drove Mary home to Walton's house, where she had another drink and told Walton how pleased she was with the evening. Walton recalled, as far as he knew, everything had gone well. A day or two later, the president telephoned Walton and asked, "Is your friend, Mrs. Hemingway, still there?" Walton told him Mary had left.

"I don't know what you see in the woman," Kennedy said, "what a dog!"

Walton asked what he meant, and the president said, "I have never had such foreign-policy conversations in my life! She was telling me how to run the State

Department and how to handle Castro, and I've never had so much uninterrupted advice in my life."[30] She never "even smiled or cracked a joke."[31] Kennedy described the conversation and said he turned, as soon as he could, to get away from Mary, to talk to Mrs. Marshall. "If I hadn't had Mrs. Marshall, I would have had a terrible night. After Mrs. Hemingway had been haranguing me, I turned to Mrs. Marshall and told her what I'd been getting on my left."[32] She said, "Oh, Mr. President, I'm so happy to get out of my briar patch and come here for dinner. You don't have to worry about me at all."[33]

Mary "could be a crashing bore when she was on a high horse like this," Walton later said.[34] Mary's criticism of the Bay of Pigs operation tore a bandage off an open wound. Her suggestions about negotiating with Castro must have seemed absurd to the president because he had already approved Operation Mongoose, a CIA plan to remove Castro from office, and he was aware of a Mafia plan to assassinate him.[35] Unknown to Mary, the time for reconciliation was long past, and Kennedy's reaction was to call her "a dog"—or might Kennedy have said, "bitch," after which Walton cleaned up the statement. Walton never told Mary about the president's comment.[36] The simple fact was Kennedy had botched the Cuban operation, and the last thing he wanted was to hear criticism from a knowledgeable, articulate, strong woman (who had herself negotiated with Castro) about how he should have handled his job.

The president's comment about Mary being "rated as politically unreliable" was odd, given that Mary had worked on Kennedy's campaign and was an old friend of the president's close friend and advisor Bill Walton. It also seems strange the president would have chosen to have a politically unreliable person sit next to him at dinner. Presumably the president was relying upon an official briefing and not joking. From the records publicly available, it may be the interview Ernest gave at the airport to the Prensa Latina, the official state news agency of Cuba, several years earlier, on November 3, 1959, that gave rise to the rating.[37]

◆

Mary wrote to Patrick about her plans to come to Africa with her friend Clara Spiegel. She wanted to take photos because the color slides she had taken on her previous trip to Africa had all molded away in Cuba, and someday she might want to write about the trip and would need recent photos. Mary told Clara,

"Denis Zaphiro, a thirty-something British Game Warden from Kenya," had put aside June for them, so they could have him with them wherever they went. Zaphiro and Patrick got along well with each other, "and I can't imagine your not liking him—maybe even falling very hard for him. Excitement beginning to simmer—loads of love."[38]

By the time Mary arrived in Nairobi, the state of emergency had been rescinded, the war against the Kikuyu was over, steps were being taken toward Kenyan independence, and within a year Jomo "Burning Spear" Kenyatta would become Kenya's first prime minister.

◆

Patrick picked up Mary and they drove to Arusha, where Clara joined them. On June 1, 1962, they left for the Serengeti Plain and the bordering Maswa Reserve where Patrick had a permit allowing him to take a client for one lion. Over the next month, Mary remembered why she and Ernest had so loved Africa, and she missed him. His absence caused an enormous hole in her picture of Africa, but she saw the scenery around the edges.

Clara was lucky and took a handsome black-maned male lion, "a hunter's dream," with two shots after only three days of hunting. In her *Life* story, Mary described how, after spotting the male only forty yards away, Patrick whispered to Clara, "Shoot him if you like." Meanwhile, Mary photographed the lionesses standing too close to the truck. After "what seemed like an hour, Clara shot one shot. The lion bounced into the light . . . fell, got up, bounced another five yards, and went down on his back with his great paws clawing the empty air."[39] As they walked toward the prone cat, Patrick told Clara to give it a throat shot for insurance. "No such thing as a dead lion," he said.

While she had not wanted to hunt or kill any animals on this trip, Mary helped track a child-killing leopard. Mary claimed the big cat had "carried a baby in its jaws up a tree and devoured the baby's head while the frantic mother screamed helpless below."[40] Mary thought this justified her joining the hunt. After shooting two gazelles and hanging them for bait, Patrick and Mary hid in the tall grass, waiting for the guilty leopard to come for dinner. They maintained their vigil for five evenings until a leopard appeared and began tearing at one of the hanging gazelles. Mary aimed for its spine between its shoulders, squeezed the trigger of

Clara's .270 Winchester, and the leopard fell back to the ground, dead. He was a handsome young male, but it was impossible to tell if he was the leopard that had killed the child. Mary hoped he was so that she could justify his death. She wrote the caption attached to the *Life* photo of her grasping the loose neck skin of the gorgeous dead leopard: "This beauty smelled sweet, like our cats at home in Cuba."[41] Patrick told me Mary was a very difficult client. Among other things, "she shot a leopard but made up all sorts of funny stories about the leopard killing children. That was absolute nonsense."[42]

The month long safari was filled with adventures, and Mary had plenty to write about for her *Life* story. After Clara shot her lion, they relaxed in the luxury of safari living, enjoying "the natural sounds of rivers, winds, birds, animals, and insects to distract or attract us." They knew each day would be different and hold at least one surprise for them. On the anniversary of Ernest's death, Mary chartered a small plane and flew with Clara through the clouds to salute, in Ernest's honor, the summit of Mount Kilimanjaro, "which rose like a frosted cupcake on a platter."[43] As the tiny plane circled the majestic mountain's summit, Mary sensed an ending to her year of looking backward.

FORTY

A Moveable Feast

November 1956–2015

Ernest began reminiscing about his early days in Paris when the Ritz baggage men brought two trunks to his room in November 1956. He wrote to his friend, Lee Samuels, about the discovery: "I found stuff here that has been in storage for thirty years . . . Some is pretty exciting to see again."[1] The trunks contained blue and yellow notebooks, which stimulated Ernest to think about his adventures in Paris,[2] and Ernest's memoir of his life as a struggling writer in the twenties became one of his most beloved works. The story of how the book came into being shows Mary boldly shaping Ernest's literary legacy. Scribner's published *A Moveable Feast* in 1964.

When Mary and Ernest returned to Cuba in February 1957, Ernest began working on "the Paris sketches." Mary typed drafts, corrected spelling and punctuation, and consulted about phrases needing reorganization. "By December, he'd written the opening chapter and the Gertrude Stein and Ford Madox Ford chapters."[3] Mary was disappointed the stories were not autobiographical but were about others. Ernest replied he was writing "biography by *remate*." Mary explained, "*Remate* idiomatically is used to mean a two-wall shot in [the Basque sport called] *Jai alai* by reflection."[4] An image of Ernest would appear from the effects of his actions upon others and their reactions to him.[5] In addition, Carlos Baker noted, "many clues to his personal character were meant to emerge either in conversation or in response to scenes and events in which he was observer, participant, or both."

Suzanne del Gizzo argues Hemingway did not simply intend to use reflections or rebounds. He meant to include the idea of "a kill shot," and he used his memoir to even the score with his contemporaries. This explains his cruel treatment of erstwhile friends, such as F. Scott Fitzgerald, Gertrude Stein, and Ford Madox Ford. He was making an unanswerable kill shot in his assessment of them.[6] Ernest worked on the sketches during the spring and summer and took the work with him to Idaho when he and Mary went there for fall shooting. He took some chapters to Spain in the spring of 1959. After Mary finished typing the manuscript at La Consula in Málaga, she criticized the book's ending before their host, Bill Davis. Ernest wrote to Davis that Mary's criticism "touted me off."[7]

Ernest put aside the Paris book when he began writing about the rivalry between the two great matadors, Antonio Ordóñez and Louis-Miguel Dominguin. By the time *Life* published an abridgment of the bullfighting book, Ernest had become appalled by the injustices in the business of bullfighting. He put *Dangerous Summer* on hold, wrote more sketches about his first years in Paris, and revised and polished his work. Mary thought he intended to write two books about the Paris years, one covering his time with Hadley and the other with Pauline.

On April 1, 1960, Ernest wrote to Charles Scribner Jr. telling him he had "better scratch the [Paris] book from the fall list." He was sorry not to have it ready, but he had been working hard on the bullfighting book, "and it is stupid to work yourself to death."[8]

Ernest tried to finish the Paris book before and after his treatments at the Mayo Clinic. After checking out of St. Mary's Hospital in February 1961, he wrote to Harry Brague, his editor at Scribner's, to report on his progress in Ketchum. "Have material arranged as chapters—they come to 18—and am working on the last one—No 19— also working on title. This is very difficult." Ernest had tried to strengthen the manuscript "by ruthless elimination of much I wrote (Not the parts you saw—none of that). But anything should be judged by the man who writes it by the quality of the material he can eliminate. All the truth and magic in, but we need a better title than *The Paris Stories*."[9]

During this phase, Ernest had incredible difficulty focusing. Without Hotch's help, he had been unable to edit down his extended essay about bullfighting to the ten thousand words required by *Life*. Later, Ernest could hardly compose a few sentences to commemorate President Kennedy's election. And he wept before Georges Saviers because he couldn't finish the Paris sketches. Given his deteriorating mental state, he couldn't compose a preface or decide how to end the book.

In "The Making of the Book: A Chronicle and a Memoir," which appeared in the *New York Times,* coincident with the book's publication, Mary described her work on *A Moveable Feast.* [10] After Ernest's death, she found the typescript in a blue box in Ernest's room at their home in Ketchum. It comprised "his dated draft of his preface and a list of titles. . . . Making a list of titles and choosing one were the last chores Ernest performed for a book. He must have considered the book finished except for the editing, which even the most meticulous manuscripts require." [11]

Mary asked Malcolm Cowley to read the typescript, and he urged her to publish it. She went over the manuscript and gave it the same "hard-headed editing" as she used to do in Cuba. Mary explained, "I put in or removed commas and checked the spelling." Sometimes, she "cut out repetitious words or phrases which I felt sure were accidental rather than intentional or for phonetic or poetic effect." [12] On July 27, 1963, Mary sent Harry Brague the Paris book "as revised by Papa from the first draft he left with you and lightly, slightly edited by me. This is the only corrected copy. He had titled some chapters, and I've tentatively titled the rest." [13] Mary told Brague, "the preface I made up from notes [Ernest] left about the book." She offered to show Brague the original notes, "if you would like to verify my impression of his original intentions for the preface." [14] Mary let him decide whether to publish the "Note" she had written. Later, with Brague's help, she made "a few further cuts and switched around two chapters for continuity's sake." However, she insisted, "no one added any word to the book." [15] Later, Mary flew to Paris and retraced Ernest's steps to ensure the accuracy of his memory. She found only two misspellings of street names. [16]

In *How It Was,* Mary explained her reaction when she first reviewed the manuscript Ernest had left behind. "With the exception of a couple of chapters, about which he had worried, and which I felt not sufficiently germane to the tenor of the book, I thought it read well." Harry Brague at Scribner's thought so, too. "We worked together checking Ernest's last draft, making a few further cuts, and switching about some of the chapters for continuity's sake." [17]

According to Charles Scribner Jr., the manuscript required editing, "and we worked with Mary on the text because at times he repeated himself over and over. In the one about the pilot fish (the marriage breakdown), for example, Harry

Brague and I knew that the intolerable redundancy ought to be cut, and we cut." Without the edits, "it would not have been publishable—or if published, readers would have found those passages a discredit to his memory."[18]

Hotch met with Harry Brague several times while the book was in galleys, and Mary called Hotch about the title. Scribner's planned to call it "Paris Sketches," but Hotch remembered Ernest referring to Paris as "a moveable feast" and suggested using that as the title. Mary and Scribner's asked Hotch to capture what Ernest had said, and they printed his words on the title page of the book. "If you are lucky enough to have lived in Paris as a young man, then wherever you go for the rest of your life, it stays with you for Paris is a moveable feast. —Ernest Hemingway to a friend, 1950."

A Moveable Feast appeared in *Life* on April 10, 1964, and on May 5, Scribner's published the hardcover edition. A month later, Carlos Baker wrote to congratulate Mary on the success of *A Moveable Feast*. "Dorothy and I have both read it and think it is a great book." They had seen Mary on the *TODAY* Show, where she was fine, but everything else was "like a commercial sandwich." The important thing is "the book stands there as the real living Monument, and you were wise to choose it as the first."[19] Baker continued to delight in the public's reception of the book as it climbed to become a best seller. "Glad to see the *Feast* at the top of the list. Hope it stays up fifty-two weeks at least."[20] *Feast* was on the *New York Times* best seller list for non-fiction for twenty-nine weeks.

Hadley thanked Mary for the complimentary copy, which she found "very, very beautiful." She was "extremely moved by it all—the memories roused and the strong appreciation of Ernest's great sensitivity—making the suffering and the happiness equally intense." Hadley was "moved greatly, of course, by being 'told about' in such affectionate and appreciative turns—more than I have ever deserved, but it warms the heart all the same."[21] They had settled the lawsuit over Miró's *Farm* a year earlier, and Hadley and Mary had restored their relationship. On behalf of herself and Paul Mowrer, Hadley said, "We both send our love and hope that you are well."[22] Ernest's favorite sister, Ura, also "loved" the book. "It sounded just the way he talked—and also, I think you were a very generous gal to publish it—making Hadley so very proud."[23]

Years after the publication, scholars questioned Mary's claim to have published Hemingway's finished work. On August 4, 1975, Mary wrote to Gerry Brenner, then a professor of English at the University of Montana. She responded to his questions about Ernest's titles for *A Moveable Feast* and how she and Harry Brague had rearranged the chapters. She wrote, "it seems to me an excess of delving into minutiae."[24] After the release of Ernest's papers and manuscripts in 1979, Brenner spent time at the Kennedy Library reviewing the drafts of *A Moveable Feast*. Three years later, he published an essay calling into question Mary's assertion in her "Note" that Ernest "finished the book, in the spring of 1960 in Cuba." Brenner contended that Mary and Harry Brague "altered, cut and added significant material."[25] He alleged that the substantial changes raised an ethical question as to the claim of the book's authenticity. Brenner argued that Scribner's ought to issue a disclaimer or publish an accurate edition of the book that Ernest Hemingway, not his widow, had prepared for publication.

Brenner couldn't find a draft of the Preface and claimed Mary must have pulled it together from other materials. She did this, as she had pointed out to Harry Brague in the letter referred to above. Brenner objected to the line in the Preface, "if the reader prefers, this book may be regarded as fiction." He could find no such declaration in the drafts. Furthermore, Brenner contended, "the finished typescript," composed, completed, and corrected by Hemingway, had one less chapter than the published version, which contained a new tenth chapter.

Brenner noted Mary put the chapter about Ernest and Hadley's marriage's breakup at the end, rather than leaving it as chapter sixteen. While he agreed this ordering provided a satisfactory climax to the book, he argued it toned down Hemingway's regrets about taking part in the affair with Pauline. "Mary Hemingway seems intent upon striking from the record any impression that Hemingway suffered either guilt or remorse for his conduct."[26]

Professor Jacqueline Tavernier-Courbin expanded upon Brenner's analysis. She undertook a detailed comparison of the published version of *Feast*, with the last typescript Hemingway had seen and corrected. After a meticulous study of the documents, she concluded, "one might well say that the book published is not really the book Hemingway had written or wanted published."[27] The Preface and the last chapter were as much Mary's as Ernest's. Tavernier-Courbin identified some 413 changes between the published version and the last typescript Hemingway saw. She declared the last chapter of Mary's version "has been much rewritten, and much material has been deleted, especially descriptions of Hemingway's uncertainty at the time he loved both Hadley and Pauline, of his lying and pretending, and of his remorse."[28] Hemingway was not sure how to deal with his guilt in the duplicity leading to the breakdown of his marriage with Hadley. This is the intolerable redundancy Scribner had identified earlier.

Patrick Hemingway "thought the original edition was just terrible about my mother."[29] His nephew, Seán (Greg and Valerie Hemingway's son), undertook "a Restored Edition" of *A Moveable Feast*, which Scribner published in 2009. The *Restored Edition* left out the Preface and Mary's "Note," re-ordered the chapters, and added ten "Additional Paris Sketches" and "Fragments" containing alternative introductions drafted by Ernest. Seán moved the marriage breakdown from the last chapter to a less prominent place in one of the additional sketches, "The Pilot Fish and the Rich."

Professor Robert Trogdon converted Mary's and Seán's versions to Word files and compared them using a collation program.[30] He found 373 substantive differences between the versions. The changes he found resemble very closely the alterations found by Professor Tavernier-Courbin.[31] In the *Restored Edition*, Seán reversed almost all the edits Tavernier-Courbin attributed to Mary and Harry Brague, and the *Restored Edition* appears to depend heavily on Tavernier-Courbin's painstaking work. However, Seán told me that after reading Tavernier-Courbin's book, he put it aside, and he "did not cite it more extensively because I worked primarily with the original manuscripts."[32] Thus, it seems that two scholars (Jacqueline Tavernier-Courbin and Seán Hemingway) working independently on the same materials twenty years apart from each other came up with virtually identical results. Tavernier-Courbin's were in the list of changes in her Chapter 8 and Seán's in the actual changes to the *Restored Edition*. That is why virtually all the 373 changes Seán made and Trogdon identified appear in Tavernier-Courbin's Chapter 8.

Seán is a scholar in classical art and is the curator in charge of the department of Greek and Roman art at the Metropolitan Museum of Art. He has written, "As a classicist, perhaps I am more accustomed to fragments of literature from the Greek lyric poets" and, in his view, "there is poetry in some of the fragments of Hemingway's writing that are included from manuscripts for the book."[33] He recognizes that "the fragments from *A Moveable Feast* are kernels of writing by Hemingway that never came to fruition. Still, they are evocative to read."[34] Seán says that classics "involves looking at fragments of manuscripts to draw conclusions."[35] This scholarly approach perhaps helps to explain why parts of the *Restored Edition* read more like the report of an archeological dig than literature. Seán assembled a collection of fragments he found in the manuscripts, and his version seems less finished than Mary's.

Ernest certainly did not work like Seán. The master writer edited himself ruthlessly, eliminating much of what he wrote and claiming the merit of a work was to be judged by the quality of the material he removed. Seán reassembled the pieces as if reconstructing a classical work from shards. The problem is there was no classical work to emulate because Ernest could not finish the book.

Seán believes that he has added back passages that "paint his grandmother in a more sympathetic light."[36] This invites us to consider whether Seán's treatment of the marriage breakdown portrayed Pauline more sympathetically than Mary's version. Seán added passages that Scribner, Brague, and Mary thought were redundant. These passages describe Pauline as a cunning, calculating, manipulative woman set on stealing Ernest from Hadley. They show Ernest in love with and torn between two women and too weak to prevent the breakdown of his marriage. It begins "when the unmarried one decides to marry. The wife does not know about it and trusts the husband. . . ."[37] The new one says, "you cannot really love her if you love your wife too." Then, "you lie to all around, and all you know is that you truly love two women."[38] Later, "you break all promises," and the "one who was relentless wins. But finally, it is the one who loses that wins, and that is the luckiest thing that ever happened for me."[39] Now, "you love them both . . ." and "everything is split inside of you, and you love two people instead of one."[40] Then, "she began to move steadily and relentlessly toward marriage; never breaking her friendship with your wife, always preserving an appearance of complete innocence."[41]

Ernest is filled with remorse at his betrayal of Hadley and describes his "remorse" four times in two pages. The "new and strange girl. . . made only one grave mistake. She undervalued the power of remorse."[42] Ernest said, "the black remorse came and hatred of the sin and no contrition, and only a terrible remorse."[43] He said it was "a terrible thing" for the girl to have deceived her friend, "but it was my fault and blindness that this did not repel me. Having become involved in it and being in love, I accepted all the blame for myself and lived with the remorse."[44] Finally, "the remorse was never away day or night," until his wife had married a far finer man than him, and she was happy.[45]

By inserting these passages, Seán repeated Ernest's allegations about Pauline's relentless campaign to seduce him and undermine the marriage; Ernest's confessions of lying and betraying Hadley's trust; and Ernest's expression of his "remorse," four times in two pages. The word "remorse" does not appear in Mary's concise version of the breakup. It seems Ernest was unable to choose which phrases to capture the breakdown of the marriage crisply. Mary agreed with Charles Scribner Jr. that Ernest had "repeated himself over and over" with "intolerable redundancy."

In the last chapter in Mary's version, an unmarried woman (Pauline is not named) becomes the temporary best friend of another young woman (Hadley) married to Ernest. The unmarried woman (Pauline) goes "to live with the husband and wife and then unknowingly, innocently and unrelentingly sets out to marry the husband."[46] At first, "it is stimulating and fun, and it goes on that way for a while." Then, "you lie and hate it, and it destroys you and every day is dangerous, but you live day to day as if in a war."[47] After Ernest returns to Paris from New York, he stays with "the girl [Pauline] I was in love with" in Paris. "When I saw my wife [Hadley] again standing by the tracks as the train came in by the piled logs at the station, I wished I had died before I ever loved anyone but her."[48]

Mary knew how Ernest felt about the breakdown of his marriage with Hadley; Seán did not. Drawing on that understanding, Mary edited the manuscript using Ernest's more direct language in summarizing the events leading to the rupture. Her version leaves out nothing essential, and the emotional damage to all the parties is plain, but Mary did not repeat over and over the claims of Pauline's treachery or dwell on Ernest's remorse. Mary sanitized the breakdown perhaps because she believed that Ernest had beat up Pauline, making her responsible for the marriage disaster, and repeatedly expressing his regret at his relationship with her. Mary had intervened on behalf of women before. In Spain, she had urged Ernest to alter his language in the new introduction to his short stories because he had gratuitously insulted Ava Gardner. And Mary urged him to base Renata in *Across the River* upon an imaginary blue-eyed redhead from Trieste rather than Adriana. She foresaw that giving Renata Adriana's features would result in a world of trouble for Adriana and Ernest. When she cut passages from *A Moveable Feast*, it was as though she was saying, "Enough, you've blamed Pauline enough. Quit repeating your allegations of treachery." By doing so, Mary limited his allusion to the misogynist trope of the other woman.

The irony of Seán's edition is that he restored these allegations against Pauline. Far from sympathetically portraying his grandmother, he repeated Ernest's disparaging assertions about Pauline's betrayal of Hadley and underlined Ernest's remorse at his complicity in the scheme. Mary's version was more discreet about the breakdown. Pauline had been Mary's friend, which may be why Mary's edition was kinder to Pauline than Seán's.

Following the publication of the *Restored Edition*, Motoko Rich described the book as a "heart-wrenching depiction of marital betrayal."[49] Patrick Hemingway told Rich that the new edition reminded readers his father was happy with Pauline. "He's more human and less self-justifying." Patrick did not blame Mary for her editing and said, "I think she did an excellent job, given the circumstances of the time."

Valerie Hemingway typed drafts of the sketches and believes Ernest intended to publish the Paris book, which she could not say about some of the other posthumous books.[50] She prefers the original version because she was involved in it.[51] "I typed chapters of it in Cuba. When we parted in October 1960, he was fairly satisfied with the book and intent upon its publication."[52]

The *Restored Edition* has encountered its share of criticism. Steve Paul commented that the fragments of Ernest's efforts to create an introduction ought to have stayed in their folders at the JFK library. "In the context of his end-of-life tailspin, the section struck me as profoundly sad and unnecessary."[53] It is hard to believe that Ernest would have permitted publication of these thought fragments as if they were shards of pottery to be displayed and interpreted.

Seán Hemingway conceded that his version is in some ways less finished than Mary's and that her version will remain in print.[54] Gerry Brenner commented that the *Restored Edition* might interest scholars, but "I couldn't imagine why ordinary readers would find this sufficiently enticing . . . to really want to buy this new edition."[55] The son of the publisher Charlie Scribner told Steve Paul the *Restored Edition* was an instance of repackaging "like New Coke versus Old Coke" and was "about commerce and not about literature."[56]

Ernest signed off neither version, so both are inauthentic in that sense, and it is difficult to credit Seán's contention that "my grandfather would be happier with the text presented in the *Restored Edition*."[57] How could Seán possibly know? The question is which editor had a better sense of what Ernest was trying to achieve. Mary defended her unique qualifications to edit Ernest's work. "When you live close, you can't help but know the thought processes and the judgments, especially about literary stuff. What I did (to finish the book) was climb inside his head and stay there."[58] Thomas Lipscomb took a kindly view of Mary's efforts, noting she had worked with Charles Scribner Jr., Harry Brague, Ed Hotchner, and Carlos Baker to put together the manuscript for publication. "They had a lot of information, often confusing, direct from Hemingway about his intentions, his fears, and his concerns. They had no other agenda than to do what they could to carry out his wishes. In *A Moveable Feast*, they succeeded admirably in publishing the work that, at least those who knew Hemingway, overwhelmingly supported as reflecting his thought and writing at the time."[59]

Mary knew all the people involved in the marriage story, and she worked with a close team of Ernest's friends and associates on the editing effort. Their goal was to give expression to Ernest's wishes for the book. Seán didn't know anyone involved, and he performed a somewhat mechanical revision. Patrick had sensed there might be more about his mother in the manuscripts, and Seán found and inserted the passages. I side with those who find Mary's version more polished.

When Mary and Scribner published the 1964 edition, they presented it as Ernest's work and did not disclose the entire editorial process. At the time, Mary maintained in public that Ernest's death had been accidental, and she didn't reveal that Ernest was incapable of concluding the work himself and that she had to finish it. However, Ernest had recently accepted Hotch's significant edit of *Dangerous Summer*, and he had agreed with Mary's suggested edits in the past. Thus, she had good reason to believe he would have agreed with the version edited by Hotch, Brague, Scribner, and herself. Still, we will never know which version Ernest would have preferred. Unfortunately, the 1964 edition is now more challenging to find than the *Restored Edition*. Ironically, the version prepared by a classicist will render the earlier edition a relic of former times.

Mary's version succeeded with the public and became one of Ernest's best-loved books. In 2015, the French version, *Paris est une fête*, which by this point was Seán's version, rocketed to the top of the bestseller lists in Paris because Parisians bought thousands of copies as an "emblem of cultural defiance" against terrorist attacks on restaurants and nightclubs.[60]

FORTY-ONE

Defending Papa's Reputation

February 1964–August 1966

Mary was the subject of several celebrity interviews in 1964. The interviewers described her petite, almost boyish stature, her short blond hair, and piercing blue eyes. "Mary Hemingway is one of those women who cannot be captured on film or quickly sketched, she is far more attractive than either the photographs or sketches of her." Mary's "white-flecked, blonde hair is cut short, and in her pierced ears, she wore gold, looped earrings." She has "a very youthful figure and moves quickly. When she smiles, her face crinkles up in happy lines."[1]

They described her penthouse in a new building with an oblique view of the Metropolitan Opera. She filled it with souvenirs of her life with Ernest. Karsh's portrait of Ernest dominated the room from a bookcase of first editions of his work. Mary loved her suite, with its sunny rooftop vista, and said, "I'm in my bubble, and I love it, sky, wind, stuff like that." Her typewriter rested on a big desk at the end of the living room. Beneath her hideaway, Mary complained, the city was dirty: "It stinks beyond measure." Overcrowded New York did not allow "enough space or time for proper reflection," and she compared it to other places. "The housekeeping is frightfully bad compared to London or Paris."[2] In Paris, "even on the left bank, and in the West End of London, the gutters are clean, but not here."[3]

Mary described her busy life. She sorted Ernest's papers and corresponded with translators and foreign publishers of Ernest's works. She spoke to women's clubs around the nation and made occasional television appearances.[4] Mary continued to promote *A Moveable Feast*, bragging about the number of copies sold and weeks spent on the bestseller list.

Often asked whether she would remarry, Mary always replied she would not. Ernest had molded her, and she could never find another man as impressive, and no one would want to put up with a wife preoccupied with a previous husband.[5] Columnists probed for details of Ernest's death, and Mary held to her terrible accident story. They often sought news about her plans to publish further works, and Mary alluded to the short stories and two novels she found in the forty pounds of manuscripts retrieved from Cuba. Mrs. Ernest Hemingway was a minor celebrity, and she did not shun the press attention.

◆

In 1963, the Cuban government issued a commemorative stamp featuring Ernest's face and a scene of Santiago standing in his small skiff and spearing a giant marlin. The scene is labeled *El Viejo y el Mar* (The Old Man and the Sea). Mary worried the stamp might hurt Ernest's reputation if journalists or some communist publication used it to suggest Ernest had supported the Cuban government or had close ties to Castro. She sought the help of her old friend Quentin Reynolds to resolve the issue. Reynolds had been a member of the staff of *Collier's Magazine*, "and one of the outstanding correspondents of World War II."[6] It was said Reynolds's broadcasts from London during the Blitz had so abused Hitler and so praised British courage "that an English poll placed him second in popularity only to his good friend, Winston Churchill."[7] Reynolds was also friends with FDR, and had addressed the 1944 Democratic National Convention in Chicago. He was well placed to intervene with another friend, J. Edgar Hoover, the director of the FBI.

On January 6, 1964, Reynolds wrote a letter to "Edgar" on behalf of Mary and Greg Hemingway. He raised the issue of the Cuban commemorative stamp featuring Ernest's face. Reynolds described Ernest's relationship with Cuba, saying, "I knew Hemingway very well and knew him as a non-political guy. He owned a house in Cuba, and like most Americans and residents there, he hated Batista and, like millions, welcomed anyone who could oust the dictator." Hemingway "didn't know Castro well; Mary says he met Castro at a fishing party and talked to him for five minutes—He never met him again." Reynolds hated to bother Hoover with something, "so trivial but of course it isn't trivial to Mary or her

step-son. Mary just wanted someone in authority to know the facts in case some
jerk columnist or some communist publication gets hold of it and uses it to help
Castro." He gave Mary's New York address, in case "you want one of your boys
to talk to Mary." In a postscript, Reynolds asked to get back the envelope bearing
the stamp if the FBI didn't need it. [8]

In Hoover's handwriting at the bottom of the letter is the following note:
"Return it. See that appropriate notation is made in our files. Knowing Hemingway
as I did, I doubt he had any communist leanings. He was a rough, tough guy and
always for the underdog." [9] The handwritten note is signed with the initial "H"
for Hoover. The notation shows the director of the FBI believed Ernest had no
communist leanings. This does not mean the FBI didn't keep tabs on the famous
author, but the most powerful man in the organization believed he was simply a
tough guy supportive of the underdog, not a communist.

In his reply, "Edgar" thanked "Quent" for the letter and stated, "I can certainly
understand Mary Hemingway's concern as well as your own. You may be certain
this will be made a matter of official record." Hoover returned the envelope bearing
the canceled stamps. [10]

◈

Mary campaigned for the Democrats in 1964, and she hosted "a Citizens for
Johnson" tea at the Christiania restaurant in Ketchum attended by over one hundred guests. Bouquets of red, white, and blue flowers decorated the tables. Senator
Frank Church phoned Mary from Washington, DC, on an amplified phone, and
the guests heard the senator stressing the election's importance. Two weeks later,
Mary wrote a letter to the editor of the *Statesman* attacking Barry Goldwater
and supporting Lyndon Johnson. [11] "In my opinion, Goldwater, no matter how
personally charming, must be regarded as a maverick, both by cattlemen and all
the rest of us." He had won the presidential nomination, but he had "usurped the
Republican brand." Mary argued, "we cannot allow our country to be led, or even
influenced, by a maverick. Johnson is the thinking man's president." She became
a charter member of "Conservationists for Johnson" to promote LBJ's candidacy.

On October 27, Mary signed a joint letter in the *New York Times* supporting
Robert Kennedy for a Senate seat. She joined two hundred and forty-five writers,
artists, composers, and members of the performing arts in declaring Kennedy had

"a better chance of becoming a great United States Senator" than his opponent, Kenneth Keating. Mary's candidates both did well. Lyndon Johnson won the largest share of the popular vote of any presidential candidate in recent history, and Robert Kennedy defeated the incumbent by a wide margin.

◆

In their last collaboration, Mary and Ed Hotchner published an hour-long recording of Ernest reading from several of his works.[12] They cut the record from four hours of tape owned by Hotch, described as "a close friend of the author and adapter of many of his works to dramatic form." Ernest performed the readings over a tape recorder between 1948 and 1961. The record started with Ernest reading his acceptance speech of the Nobel Prize for Literature in 1954.

Mary recounted that Ernest's voice was young, and when he was sixty, he still sounded like he was twenty-five. The record featured two love poems by Ernest which he wrote to Mary in 1944, two years before they married. Mary told Harry Gilroy of the *New York Times* she worried some would "think it immodest of me to have given the poems for publication." In justifying her decision, she claimed the poems were a departure from much of Ernest's writing. "I thought people would be interested to see this side of his work." He entitled the poems "To Mary in London" and "Second Poem to Mary." She told Gilroy that Ernest was "with Col. Lanham in the battle of Huertgen Forest when he began the second poem." He finished it during a brief leave at the Ritz Hotel in Paris.[13] The critics panned both poems, and Mary would not have known that Buck had already criticized Ernest's poems to Carlos Baker. In his "chronology," Buck recalled a morning when Ernest came into his trailer and told him, "I have written a hell of a 'pome' this morning while taking a crap." Ernest reached into his pocket and handed Buck a crumpled sheet of paper, on which his "pome" was written in pencil. As he read it, Buck was convinced "this was a gag," but when he looked at Ernest "with laughter in my throat," he "suddenly realized that this was no joke at all; that he was in deadly earnest." Buck believed that if he had laughed, it would have done something serious to their friendship. He read the "thing through twice in order to allow [himself] an opportunity to devise a suitable comment. I finally looked up and said that's quite a pome." Buck did not doubt Ernest's sincerity or the violence of his emotion. "I am unable to regard 'First Poem for Mary' as a poem or as poetry," Buck said, "but as a capsule statement of what one man felt who had lived with this horror, it will stand despite its defects." [14]

At the end of July, Mary presented a copy of the recording "The Voice of Ernest Hemingway" to the Community Library of Ketchum in Sun Valley. [15] While she was in Ketchum, Mary arranged a birthday party in Ernest's honor, and at the last moment, she eliminated speechmaking from the program, believing Ernest would have preferred drinking and listening to music with his friends.

◆

Ed Hotchner's attempt to publish his memoir, *Papa Hemingway*, brought about a dramatic rupture in his friendship with Mary. To gauge the damage, it is helpful to remember how close they once were. Hotch told an interviewer Ernest seemed like a father to him. Hotch didn't have a friendly relationship with his own father, "and there was an easy transference because [Ernest's] attitude toward me was father to son. He taught me about wines and foods and what oysters were good, and almost everything I came to prize later came from Ernest." [16] A reviewer of Hotch's final book about Ernest, *Hemingway in Love*, called Hotch Ernest's "fourth son," and the idea is not ridiculous. [17]

Ernest seldom saw his own sons through the last ten years of his life. Patrick lived in Africa and never saw Ernest again after their argument in Shimoni in 1954, though they carried on a warm correspondence. Greg had been persona non grata with Ernest since 1951 when Ernest removed him from his will, and Ernest had not seen Greg since October 1956 when he took his son to Key West to visit their old family home. Jack seldom visited, and his persistent financial troubles strained his relationship with his father.

In his last decade, Ernest spent far more time with Hotch than with his three sons. Sometimes accompanied by Geraldine (Gerry), his Canadian-born wife, Hotch stayed at the Finca and he fished on *Pilar*. He traveled with the Hemingways in France, Spain, Italy, Ketchum, and New York. Hotch kept in touch through the mail and over the phone. He produced and promoted Ernest's short stories for radio and television, and Hotch's efforts earned a significant amount of money for Ernest. [18] While Jack and Greg drained Ernest's treasury, Hotch contributed to it. Ernest never trusted his sons to touch his writing, but he relied upon Hotch to do almost everything. Hotch reviewed and commented upon

Ernest's work, spoke with editors and television producers on Ernest's behalf, and negotiated contracts. Hotch dramatized pieces for broadcast, and he edited the *Life* piece "The Dangerous Summer."

Ernest and Mary corresponded with Hotch and Gerry, and the salutations on Mary's letters to Hotch smack of fondness: "My Sweet Ed," "Honey Hotch," "Hotch Darling."[19] Mary wrote friendly letters to the young couple and expressed compassion on the death of their infant son. The lives of Ernest and Mary intertwined with those of Hotch and Gerry. Hotch came to play an important role listening to Ernest and Mary complaining about each other and arranging an apartment for Mary in New York; he helped her to find work to support herself when she planned to leave Ernest; and he helped her when Ernest deteriorated. Mary trusted Hotch to interview psychiatrists and confided in him during the time of Ernest's hospitalizations.

◆

On Thursday evening, June 3, 1965, Mary held a small party in her penthouse. She overheard Hotch telling the *Times*'s Harry Gilroy that he was completing a book about his years with Ernest. This news surprised and concerned Mary because she opposed any version of Ernest's life except the authorized biography Carlos Baker was writing and the book she was writing herself.

Her concern turned to livid anger when she read the galley proofs of Hotch's memoir six months later. Hotch told the full story of Ernest's demise. The next day, she wrote to Bennett Cerf, the president of Random House and the publisher of *Papa Hemingway*. "Not since my husband shot himself in July 1961 have I suffered the traumatic shock which has engulfed me since yesterday when I read AE Hotchner's book purporting to be a true account of his association with Ernest and me."[20] Mary said the book was "a job of treachery" and "a shameless penetration into my private life, and the usurpation of it for money." She accused Hotch of misquoting her and Ernest and asserted her conversations with Hotch, while Ernest was ill, were confidential and should remain so.

Mary contended that Hotch fictionalized his accounts of events during Ernest's illness or based them on areas of her private life, which were her private property. She had never "granted him the right to invade my privacy for his personal profit," and Hotch's dedication of the book to Mary was an effort to persuade the public the book was authentic and "obviate" her objections to it. Mary urged Cerf to forgo publication of the book. Three weeks later, Cerf replied. He had been distressed to receive her letter, and he did not want her to think he had been ignoring it. He had asked his lawyer to speak to hers "immediately to see what might be done to make you feel better about the publication. We think this is a very important book, and I hope you know that it certainly is not our intention to offend you in any way."[21] Next to this phrase on the original letter, Mary scrawled in red pencil, "hypocritical."

The next day, Mary's attorneys wrote to Random House, alleging the galley proofs showed that Hotch had infringed the property rights of Ernest Hemingway. Mrs. Hemingway had succeeded to these rights, and Mary's lawyers warned they would seek an injunction to prevent publication.[22] Mary responded to Cerf on Christmas Day, claiming she was "bewildered" Cerf thought the book "important." Never had she known Random House to approve a manuscript "which is inaccurate, fictitious, muck-raking yellow journalism, and so far beneath your company's usual standards." She found his intention not to offend her low comedy, "unless you believe that people enjoy having their private lives misrepresented and exploited in print."[23]

Early in the new year, Hotch wrote to Mary, expressing his frustration: despite his having agreed to almost all the changes she wanted, she had taken legal action to stop publication. "As an old-time lawyer, I am very aware of what this kind of public, newspaper reported controversy can do to the parties involved—you as well as me."[24] He suggested they meet to talk about why she opposed the book, cautioning, "lawsuits are two-edged swords—they cut both ways—although plaintiffs commonly think the attack is all theirs." This proved wise advice, even though it was self-serving.

The next day, Gerry Hotchner wrote to Mary. Gerry was a graduate of the Columbia School of Journalism and the daughter of a Canadian lawyer.[25] She was "bewildered" by the letter Mary sent to Bennett Cerf, and she denounced Mary's ingratitude for Hotch's "extraordinary tact and good friendship," for he revealed "only those aspects of your marriage to Ernest, which were favorable." Gerry rebuked Mary for minimizing Hotch's role in Ernest's treatment because they had talked daily. Gerry had been there when Mary's desperate calls came in from Ketchum and Rochester, and she was there for the chatty calls from Ernest and the heartbreaking letters from Mary. Gerry had admired Mary's courage in carrying the brunt of the load herself, but she had seen Hotch stand by her and rush to Ketchum and rush to Rochester. "I was there when Hotch put everything to one side for his friend." Gerry protested, Mary was "trying to throttle another man's voice! What an irreparable loss when the dead are dead and cannot speak!"[26]

In the next few days, Mary discussed settling the court action with Hotch. She offered to withdraw the lawsuit if he removed the last three chapters dealing with Ernest's breakdown and ultimate suicide.[27] In these chapters, Hotch described virtually all of Ernest's delusions and fears: he was going blind, he was poor, the tax authorities would remove them from the Ketchum house. Ernest could not cut down the *Life* story of "The Dangerous Summer," he feared Miguel would be blackmailed from the *Life* photos, he thought Bill Davis was trying to kill him in a car accident. Hotch recorded Ernest's irrational attack on a waiter and restaurant owner, his worries about excessive luggage, and his fear that he was being followed and bugged by FBI agents. Hotch also reported on Ernest's refusal to hunt with old friends or to allow Mary to speak with him. He reported on Ernest's attempts at suicide, Ernest's committal to the Mayo Clinic, Hotch's visits with him there, and his discussions with psychiatrists on Ernest's behalf. He recalled his inability to persuade Ernest to take life easy and Ernest's ultimate suicide. Hotch had appropriated the story of Ernest's decline and death in the last three chapters of his book, and he refused Mary's demand to remove them.

Mary hardened her position and prepared for court.[28] She felt that Hotch was using private information about Ernest's condition to profit, and she believed she had a duty to protect Ernest's privacy. They argued the case before Justice Harry B. Frank of the New York State Supreme Court, on January 28, 1966. During the hearing, Hotch argued, "Mary wanted to hide from the public, and perhaps herself, the truth of Ernest's death." He called Mary's complaints "dismal whining, compounded from conjecture, frustration, and pique, none of them actionable in equity."[29] A few weeks later, Justice Frank issued an eight-page judgment, dismissing Mary's claim.[30]

When Mary's attorneys applied for an injunction to stop publication of the book, they argued four points. First, Ernest's comments and expressions were his property under common law copyright. Second, by using Ernest's comments, Hotch took Ernest's property, and Hotch's book would unfairly compete with other literary works written by Ernest. Third, the book used material Hotch gathered when he held a position of trust and confidence to Ernest. Finally, the references to Mary violated her right to privacy under Section 51 of the New York Civil Rights Law.

Justice Frank dismissed the last three claims peremptorily. He found there was no evidence of unfair competition or breach of fiduciary duty. "The allegations directed to such claims are so vague and conclusory as to be almost meaningless."[31] He dismissed Mary's claim of invasion of privacy. She was the wife and widow of a man "of celebrated prominence." Ernest had received "both the Nobel and Pulitzer prizes during his lifetime." As a "newsworthy personality" and a "figure of public interest," Mary was "without the protection of the statute."[32]

Justice Frank then decided that Ernest had no common law copyright in the conversations with Hotch. When they spoke to each other, they both contributed, and they were both architects of the conversations. The contents did not come only from Ernest's intellectual effort, and therefore, the common law of copyright did not protect them.[33] Hotch's writing gave meaning to the conversation, and without Hotch's creativity, the talks would have remained "a disoriented conglomeration of unconnected expressions."[34] Justice Frank decided there would be a disproportionate burden upon Hotch if he granted the injunction because Mary had been silent over the three years she knew Hotchner was working on the book.

Mary's lawyers made a major blunder. They based their claim on Exhibit 1, the galley proofs of Hotch's book. These contained several "verbatim quotations, comments, opinions, and words expressed by Mr. Hemingway," including some "originating in letters and tape recordings."[35] Hotchner had removed them from the publication-ready manuscript he presented to the court. Justice Frank found the publication-ready draft was relevant. This meant Mary's lawyers attacked the wrong version of the book.[36] The error is obvious and fatal to the plaintiff's case, and I can't imagine how Mary's lawyers overlooked the point as they prepared for the injunction application.

Despite losing the case, Mary tried to prevent Hotch's book from being serialized. She wrote to Matthew J. Culligan, the chairman of Curtis Publishing, urging him not to publish installments of the book in the *Saturday Evening Post*. Mary warned, "in the interest of civil rights, I intend to carry this fight as far as law permits," and this would be detrimental to the public image of the Curtis Publishing Company.[37] A few days later, Mary urged John Mason Brown of the Book-of-the-Month Club not to publish Hotch's book.[38] Mary complained, "the contents of the book were stolen without Ernest's or my knowledge or consent."[39]

Despite Mary's protests, on March 12, 1966, the *Saturday Evening Post* began serializing Hotch's account of his relationship with Ernest.[40] Having failed to prevent publication, Mary's next move was to affect reviews of the book. She simply refused to accept that Hotch could get away with exploiting Ernest's demise and death. It turned out she was wrong in law, but perhaps not morally, as many reviewers commented. She received a letter from Harvard Professor John Kenneth Galbraith, who advised her he was reviewing Hotch's book for the *Herald Tribune*. He said, "I gather you are strongly adverse. Could you give me a word or two of backgrounded guidance on your antipathy? I will be an example of discretion to the most secretive."[41] Mary provided her criticisms of Hotchner's work, and Galbraith's review raised the question of Hotch's integrity in recording Ernest.[42] A close friend would have told him the recorders were running. After Galbraith's review appeared, the idea that Hotch had betrayed Ernest's trust surfaced in other reviews.

In the *New York Post*, Pete Hamill questioned how Hotch could claim to be Ernest's friend and yet write such demeaning passages about him. "Hotchner, who professes to admire Hemingway greatly as a writer, seems to embrace this dummy with an uncritical mind." Hamill wished for "a better fate for great writers other than falling into the hands of the wrong friends."[43]

Notwithstanding the controversy, or perhaps because of it, the book did well, spending twenty-five weeks on the *New York Times* best seller list for non-fiction. *Look* magazine paid forty thousand dollars for excerpts, and the Book-of-the-Month Club made *Papa Hemingway* one of its selections.[44]

Viewing from this distance, it is hard to be critical of Hotch's book. There were a few errors, and he did disguise the names of certain characters, but for the most part the book tells a true story, as can be seen from reviewing correspondence and documents of the time. One can understand Mary felt betrayed by Hotch for disclosing information she considered private and for revealing she had lied about Ernest's decline and the manner of his death for five years. If Hotch had not written the book, or if Mary had succeeded in her lawsuit, we might not know much about the story of Ernest's mental health and eventual suicide. It would be hypocritical of a biographer to argue the truth should have been buried along with Ernest. It is possible to admire Mary's tenacity but still be glad she lost her injunction application.

As Hotchner's work appeared in serial form and galleys went out to reviewers, Mary honed a counterattack. Her essay, "That Magnificent Man and His Converter Machine," appeared in June 1966, shortly before his book came out. Here she found a brutal metaphor to illustrate what he had done. Hotch had created "a people converter," as deadly as any designed by the Nazis, to destroy members of the human species. He fed people, some alive and some dead, including Mary, into the machine and pushed the button that started it turning. After three years, two unique products emerged, a string of soiled people and wads of beautiful green money. Ernest would have read Hotch's book with "abiding and controlled fury."

Mary argued Hotch "does not have the moral right to use Ernest's words, which compose about two-thirds of his book." Despite the court setbacks, she hoped to prove Ernest's words were his literary property. In the meantime, Mary applauded the sales of Hotch's book because once justice prevailed, the book's earnings would come back to her as damages. She would split the money between a trust fund to educate a talented child and the legal defense fund of the NAACP.

A small metal plaque embellished the door of Mary's penthouse: "The Pilar. Mary Hemingway." The plate was from a fishing reel Ernest had made for Mary. The living room had tropical wooden bead drapes, and a large zebra skin covered the floor. Spanish tiles of jungle beasts circled the little yellow Franklin stove which served as a fireplace and a porcelain tiger curled on the raised hearth. There were the paintings *The Guitar Player* by Juan Gris and Joan Miró's *The Farm*. Waldo Peirce's 1929 portrait of the thirty-year-old Ernest, *Alias Kid Balzac*, hung over Mary's bed. Mary had told Peirce she thought, "it is really he. I like him with his hair black, gray, or white, with or without his beard." [45]

In the hallway from the living room to her bedroom, photos of Mary were displayed. She was on *Pilar*, in the Floridita with Ernest, at Villa Aprile in Cortina D'Ampezzo, in London during the Blitz, fishing off Peru, watching a bullfight in Pamplona, and duck hunting in Ketchum. Mary's black-maned lion with a bullet hole in its rump was arranged on the opposite wall of the hallway. A pale blue typewriter rested on Mary's desk which looked over the skyscrapers. Her leopard hung on the study wall, and Ernest's leopard rested over the back of a lounge chair.

Aline Mosby, the celebrity reporter who became the first female foreign correspondent to report from the Soviet Union, visited Mary in May 1966.[46] Mosby was a first-class journalist, and she crafted a fine portrait of Mary. "Her voice deep, a little rough, sensual. Her figure tiny in the fashionably short blue dress but strong and womanly. Her white hair short, the blue eyes warm and direct." Mary stood on the zebra carpet defending Ernest, and she attacked Hotch's bestseller as "a phony, sensational book" with "vast inaccuracies." Mary said, "it smells to high heaven."

Mary told Aline that she spent hours answering letters from persons seeking information for articles about Ernest. She feared their writings would be wrong if she did not do this. She checked Carlos Baker's work, and whenever she found an error, it drove her wild. Mary had a million words in diaries covering her seventeen years of marriage with Ernest, and she had pounded out forty thousand words of her memoir on the pale blue typewriter.

Mary admitted to being a reluctant New Yorker. After she gave the Finca to the Cuban people she had moved to New York, but she kept the home in Idaho, which she visited every summer and fall. "New York is a stinking place to live," she told Aline. She would have stayed in Idaho, but she couldn't deal with editors by long-distance telephone. "They'd rather take you to a fifty-dollar lunch in New York than spend five dollars on the telephone to Idaho."

Mary mused, "I've lots of friends in New York, but I don't go out to dinner and have fun." She worked at night, "when the phone stops ringing."[47] Mary's loneliness seeped through Aline's interview. She could not get away from Ernest and lived surrounded by mementos of her years with him. Mary buried herself in Ernest's papers and defended his reputation.

❖

On Ernest's birthday, his sisters Ura and Sunny came to stay with Mary in Ketchum, and they dedicated a memorial to him in Sun Valley. In mid-August, Mary received a supportive letter from Malcolm Cowley, saying, "I was revolted by Hotchner's job on Ernest." Cowley told her he would do a piece in *Esquire*, "about some of the twerps attacking Ernest's literary reputation. They can't forgive Ernest for having lived a glamorous life, and when they speak of it, they reveal a spiteful envy."[48]

❖

Throughout 1966, Mary labored under tremendous, truly soul-shaking pressure. For five years, she had maintained in public that Ernest had died by accident. Hotch's book made it impossible to hold the line. Soon after Judge Frank's decision, the serialized version of *Papa Hemingway* revealed Ernest's breakdown and suicide. Mary received letters from readers appalled to learn the truth about Ernest—some were disgusted, others were more inclined to sympathize. But everyone knew Mary had lied. She came clean in an interview with Oriana Fallaci published in *Look* magazine in late August.

FORTY-TWO

No, He Shot Himself.
Shot Himself. Just That.

March 1966–September 1968

Oriana Fallaci, "the most extraordinary journalist Italy has ever produced," met Mary in March 1966, over drinks with friends.[1] Though Fallaci was twenty-one years younger than Mary, they were both petite women who had survived in wartime journalism, and they hit it off. They spoke about literature, and after the ice broke, Mary showed Fallaci her penthouse, which Fallaci described as "the shelter of a woman who looks at the future coldly because her life is still in the past."[2] Mary must have decided Fallaci could help her because she invited her back to her penthouse the next day for an interview. Weighing on Mary's mind was Judge Frank's decision dismissing her injunction application two weeks earlier and the beginning of the serialization of Hotch's book by the *Saturday Evening Post*, on March 12, 1966. I suspect Mary wanted to get out her version of the story and explain why she had lied about the cause of Ernest's death. If the injunction had been granted and Hotch's book was held up by the courts, I doubt Mary would have given the interview to Fallaci. As it happened, Mary chose Fallaci for the most intimate conversation she ever held with a member of the press. Fallaci wrote, "sincerely, I don't understand why she accepted this interview."[3] Though Mary responded to Fallaci's probing questions, Mary was still trying to control the narrative of Ernest's death and to portray herself as a victim of both Ernest's suicide and Hotch's book.

Fallaci sketched a portrait of Mary: "She is small and slim and nervous, and most of the time, she wears slacks. So, from a distance, you would say she is a boy, not a woman in her early 50s." Her face "is sharp, as pointed as the beak of a stork, and has the mysterious beauty of things seasoned by storms; its lines engraved by the wind, the sun, a tragic dawn of five years ago." Mary's eyes are firm, "without illusions. Her lips are hard, with no lipstick. Her movements are sudden, sometimes masculine." They talked for three hours, and Fallaci recorded their conversation, interrupting Mary as little as possible, though with skill when she did so. Mary sat on the floor while Ernest observed them from Karsh's portrait.

Mary told Fallaci she hated the filthy noisy city, and her real home was still in Cuba. She felt loyal to the house in Ketchum. "The fact that he killed himself there doesn't make me dislike it."[4] Fallaci interrupted, saying that to her knowledge, this was the first time Mary admitted Ernest's suicide. "Until now, and against all evidence, you've always maintained his death was accidental."[5] Mary responded, "no, he shot himself. Shot himself. Just that. And nothing else. For a long time, I refused to admit it even to myself, it's true." She didn't know "what happened in my subconscious, I mean, I've never discussed it with a psychiatrist, but I suppose it had something to do with self-defense." Perhaps, "admitting the truth would've snapped my nerves, split open my brain. But I soon realized it was stupid to go on pretending and believing in an accident. Absolutely stupid."[6]

Ernest's sister Ura once said, "if Ernest thought this was the best thing to do, then he was right to do it." It was difficult for Mary to agree because she missed him so much. Yet she wouldn't want to see him "alive but sick, insecure, and unhappy. . . . What for? Only to have him with me. How selfish it would be. Yes, if Ernest thought that was the right thing to do, I must accept it."[7]

Mary told Fallaci Ernest had been "sick and desperate, and we cannot judge the behavior of a sick and desperate man." His kind of loneliness was "much worse than my present one. Writers are lonely persons, even when they love and are loved."[8] When he went to the Mayo Clinic in the fall of 1961, his blood pressure was very high, "but his real problem was a serious, very serious breakdown. He was so depressed. I cannot even say when he started to feel so depressed." Though Ernest had serious health problems, Mary did not believe anyone should tell the public about them. "A writer doesn't belong to the public, only his writing does." That is why she was against Hotch's book. "No one should be authorized to tell the dissolution of a man, even less to tell it for money or sensationalism. It should make part of the civil rights of the human dignity, to prohibit, to write about others' intimate life." She had made this right to privacy the core of her legal campaign. Mary told Fallaci, "It is my duty to defend the dignity of my husband as I can, . . . it's a matter of principle."[9]

Look published the Fallaci interview on August 22, 1966, and the next day, every major newspaper in the United States quoted the interview under headlines such as, "Hemingway's Death Suicide, Wife Concedes."[10] No longer would Mary maintain that Ernest died by accident. We know Mary had long ago admitted the truth to herself, possibly as soon as her phone call to Leonard Lyons with the concocted story of an accident or the press conference in her home, but certainly by the time she corresponded with Dr. Rome about what more could have been done to save Ernest. With the Fallaci interview, Mary adjusted her public position. Now she rationalized that admitting the truth "would've snapped my nerves, split open my brain."[11]

The Fallaci interview followed the unsuccessful injunction application and the beginning of the serialization of Hotch's book. Mary selected the most empathetic interviewer she could find to launch her revised story, excoriate Hotch, and justify her decision to maintain a lie about Ernest's death in public for five years.

❖

Ernest's favorite sister, Ursula (Ura), a well-known artist in Honolulu, died on October 30, 1966. Mary thought Ura was the sensible sister and had enjoyed visiting with her and consulting her on estate business.[12] She suffered from cancer and depression, and her death at sixty-three came from an overdose of drugs. Police recorded her death as "an apparent suicide."[13] In homage to her brother, Ursula had earlier established the Ernest Hemingway Memorial Award for Creative Writing at the University of Hawaii.

❖

Justice Schweitzer of the New York Supreme Court granted Hotch's application for judgment in the injunction application matters. The judge criticized Mary's lawyers for mixing the galley proofs with the published manuscript. He rejected their claim that sixty-five percent of *Papa Hemingway* was "literary matter created and expressed by Ernest Hemingway."[14] On April 13, 1967, Mary's lawyers appealed Justice Schweitzer's decision to the New York Supreme Court Appellate Division, and they argued the case during October 1967. Chief Judge Fuld dismissed Mary's appeal on behalf of the unanimous court of seven judges. It is striking that of the nine judges who heard Mary's case, not one found in favor of any of her arguments.

The affidavit Hotchner filed to support his defense is a masterpiece of legal writing. Though Hotchner trained as a lawyer, he had not liked law practice, but it is clear he understood, far better than Mary, the case's legal dimensions. A summary of the affidavit evidence shows why the court reached its decision and preferred Hotch's evidence to Mary's. Hotch swore his book was a memoir of his close relationship with Ernest, and it was factual and based only on what he saw and heard; he had made extensive notes of his conversations with Ernest and of the adventures they had together, and Hotch had a natural talent for remembering conversations; he had honed this skill while interviewing people for the three hundred magazine articles he'd written, and he relied only upon his notes and memory. There were no quotations from Ernest's letters or the wire recordings, and the conversations were not verbatim but Hotch's version of them.

When Hotch used Ernest's conversations in articles about their adventures, Ernest never objected, and, in fact, Ernest liked them. Hotch attached four such pieces. Several works published by others relied upon accounts of Ernest's conversations, but Mary had attacked none of those articles. This was the first time Mary claimed conversation as literary property, and Hotch complained Mary's real motive was "to suppress my book." She did not want competition from any book which included conversations with Ernest because she planned to write her own book featuring her conversations with him.

Mary alleged Hotch based sixty-five percent of his book on Ernest's literary utterances which Hotch had taken from letters, notes, tape, and wire recordings. Mary claimed she was entitled to damages because the original galleys were published when Hotch distributed them to sixteen publishers.

Chief Judge Fuld made a crucial finding of fact: Hotchner had published several articles in which he quoted Ernest's conversations. These included pieces for *This Week Magazine*, which consisted mainly of Hotch's versions of conversations with Ernest. Examples were "Hemingway's Fifty Cats" (1952), "All Star Bullfight" (August 8, 1954), "The Most Fascinating Man I Know" (February 13, 1955), and "Hemingway Talks to American Youth" (October 18, 1959). Ernest had not objected to these publications, so even if literary property existed in conversation, none could be claimed here because Ernest had approved Hotch's use of the notes and recordings. Ernest knew Hotch was accumulating the material, and in these circumstances, "authority to publish must be implied." There was "no reservation of any common law copyright."[15] Since Ernest approved Hotch's writing about him, Mary could not say that Hotch had unfairly competed with Ernest. Further, there was no proof Hotch breached a confidential relationship when he used Ernest's conversations.

The Chief Judge agreed with Judge Frank that the Civil Rights Law did not protect Mary's privacy. Mary was a newsworthy public figure. The judges decided overwhelmingly in Hotch's favor, and the court's findings of fact demolished Mary's claims. Put simply, the judges believed Hotch, not Mary. Bear in mind, by the time the case got to the Court of Appeal, Mary had already publicly admitted Ernest had died by suicide in her interview with Oriana Fallaci. Perhaps the court felt Mary was trying to punish Hotch for telling the truth.

One can't help but wonder about the quality of the legal advice Mary received, because any lawyer could see her case was difficult. Her attorneys' focus on the original galley proofs, instead of the published work, doomed the case to failure, for Hotch had removed the offensive passages from the book to be published. The costs of the litigation must have been enormous, and it was a complete waste of money.

◆

The mayor of Pamplona invited Mary to dedicate a sculpture of Ernest outside the Plaza de Toros. Mary asked Bill Walton to fly over for the ceremony. She met him in London and they spent two days at Claridge's, then traveled to Paris for a few days. They drifted down to Biarritz, where they rented a car for the drive to Pamplona and reminisced about London and Paris during the war and talked about everything since. Walton remembered they had "a marvelous time" because Mary was "in control of all her senses and very funny." They had a picnic on the Irati River, near where Mary had broken her toe nine years earlier. With cooked chickens bought in the market and "loads of wine put in the stream to chill, we had a riotous picnic. I never had more fun, and Mary was at her best."[16]

In the mornings, they gulped down strong black coffee, tied red kerchiefs around their necks, and hurried in the crowd to the bullring. Seated in the stands, they watched the boys, chased by the bulls, racing into the Plaza de Toros. In the evenings, they ate and drank at the restaurants on the central square. Mary recalled that they "danced half the night in the streets, drank wine from a dozen friendly botas, and yelled olés at the bullfights."[17]

Mary and Walton were honored guests at the dedication of Ernest's statue just outside the bullring's main gates. The bust is loosely based on Yousuf Karsh's portrait of Ernest wearing a turtleneck sweater. The plaque reads, "For Ernest Hemingway, Nobel Literature Prize Laureate, a friend of this town and admirer of its fiestas, which he was able to describe and spread." The statue comprises an enormous granite turtleneck sweater, topped by a crudely carved bronze head. By this time Walton had become a well-established artist in New York and had chaired President Kennedy's Fine Arts Commission charged with reviewing architectural designs for Washington, DC. He described the statue as "very primitive art. It's just awful. And from one hundred paces, you can see how bad it is."[18] Walton had significant experience judging public art, and it is easy to concur with his assessment.

◆

Adriana wrote to Mary, telling her she was in desperate financial straits. Adriana had married a German nobleman, Count Rudolph von Rex, had two sons with him, and was now a countess living north of Milan. They needed money for renovations, and Adriana asked Mary if she could publish the correspondence between her and Ernest to raise some funds. Valerie Hemingway recalled Mary talking to her about Adriana's predicament. Valerie knew Mary wasn't really seeking her opinion but asking her to concur with Mary's view that she couldn't allow Adriana to proceed because Ernest had forbidden the publication of his letters.[19]

Mary wrote to Adriana, offering to find an American buyer for the letters if she wanted to sell them but forbidding her to publish them.[20] In 1966, Adriana auctioned the letters through Christie's, the London art dealer. Literary experts had estimated they were worth between twenty and thirty thousand dollars,[21] but the sale fetched only seventeen thousand dollars.[22]

In 1974, Hotchner found himself defending his friendship with Hemingway again after a leading Spanish journalist penned his impressions of Hemingway in Spain and Cuba in the late fifties. Doubleday translated and published his work as *Hemingway in Spain*. The author, Luis Castillo-Puche, never met Hotch. Nevertheless, he described him as a manipulator, toady, hypocrite, crass opportunist, two-faced, obsequious servant, and exploiter of Ernest's reputation. The author quoted Ernest as saying he didn't trust Hotch.[23] In fact, Doubleday watered-down this excerpt. In the original translation, Castillo-Puche quoted Ernest saying Hotch was "dirty, and a terrible ass-licker. There's something phony about him. I wouldn't sleep in the same room with him."[24] Not surprisingly, Hotch, who had portrayed himself as Ernest's trusted and stalwart companion, found these words offensive. He sued in libel, seeking $1.5 million in damages, and the case was tried before a jury in April 1976. The author, Castillo-Puche, was not present, so the publisher, Doubleday, became the sole defendant. Doubleday called Mary as a witness for the defense. She hadn't seen Hotch in years, but she had not forgiven him and avenged herself, testifying the descriptions of Hotch were "generally accurate."[25] They were "simple, friendly banter, meaning nothing."[26] The trial judge offended Mary when he wondered, "Why the life of this rich libertine and destroyer of wildlife should be of such great and continuing public interest a decade following his suicide we cannot and need not say."[27]

The jury awarded Hotch one dollar for each of the two counts of libel as compensatory damages and $125,000 as punitive damages. Doubleday appealed the ruling and succeeded. Though the Appellate Court agreed that the words were defamatory, since Hotch was a public figure, there had to be proof the publisher made the defamatory statements knowing they were untrue. The court ruled there was no evidence Doubleday knew or even suspected that the statements made by the author were false.[28] Thus, Hotch was defamed, but he had no remedy. Mary may have celebrated with a large gin and tonic, swirling her ice cubes, and laughing as she looked over the skyline.

FORTY-THREE

Who the Hell is
He Writing About?

July 1966–February 1975

M ary planned to visit Cuba with the Bakers in the summer of 1966, but
Carlos canceled the trip. He called it off "because of the State Department's
damnable procrastination" with travel permission, and the fact his daughter was
pregnant and soon due.[1] Baker never did travel to Cuba to experience firsthand
the atmosphere of Havana and the Finca. Peter Buckley, who remained close to
Mary after Ernest's death, knew Baker from Princeton when Buckley had been a
student there. Buckley offered to take Baker to Spain to introduce him to the world
of bullfighting. When Baker refused to journey to Spain or Cuba, Mary and Peter
were appalled, as they felt Baker must see the places to understand Ernest better.
H. R. Stoneback has described Baker as an "armchair biographer." Still, Baker
continued making progress on the biography and asked Mary to write a piece about
her marriage to Ernest in Havana. She described the wedding and participated in
a lengthy telephone conversation, answering more of Baker's questions.

Mary proposed changes to words or phrases, and more fundamentally, took
issue with Baker's account of certain events and stipulated he remove episodes
she found unacceptable. Mary insisted he scrap references to Ernest's program of
"self-aggrandizement" and her dream in Casper before her pregnancy ended. She
asked him to remove an allusion to her anger with Louella Parsons, the Hollywood
gossip columnist, and an entire paragraph relating to the hunt for Mary's lion

in Kenya in 1953. Mary didn't like Baker's description of the African plane crashes, and he rewrote the passages, basing them on her diary. He sent her the rewritten paragraphs. "If you still have any objections to the new version, I will rewrite again."

◆

When he began the project, Baker reported to Mary that A. E. Hotchner was being "a little standoffish."[2] In contrast, General Buck Lanham cooperated happily, and he became a willing collaborator. The link between Baker and Lanham blossomed into a close friendship, with Baker paying Lanham the ultimate compliment. He dedicated *Ernest Hemingway: A Life Story* "to my friend Buck Lanham and my wife Dorothy Baker, who fought it out by my side during the seven-year siege."[3] In his interviews, conversations, and lengthy correspondence with Baker, Lanham transformed from a loyal friend of Ernest Hemingway into a spiteful critic. At the outset, Buck prepared for Baker a forty-eight-page, single-spaced typescript, setting out a chronology of anecdotes of Ernest's World War II adventures in Buck's company. Baker was grateful to receive the chronology, and he relied upon it.

In the largely laudatory chronology, Buck praised Ernest's "great physical power and great sureness [which] gave him the air of an 18th-century pirate."[4] He possessed "a marvelous instinct for terrain and a built-in battle sense."[5] Ernest behaved, "Like a fighter. Like a great cat. Easy. Relaxed. Absorbed. Intent. Watchful. Missing nothing."[6] He proved "a natural humorist given the proper circumstances and the proper friends."[7] Ernest's "coolness throughout this grisly time moved him so high in my category of brave men I still have no words for just what I felt and still feel."[8] Ernest was "a big-hearted man. He always wanted to do something for his friends."[9] When "EH gave his friendship, he gave it without reservation."[10] Buck idolized Ernest in his chronology. "I was spell-bound by this magnificent human being—simple, gentle, direct, unaffected. No man before or since has ever struck so swiftly and so deeply into my mind and affections."[11] Buck said, "EH, and I were locked into a species of brotherhood that both of us knew would last as long as we lasted. It did."[12] Ernest "was one of the most compassionate, sensitive, gentle people I've ever known of either sex." The long years after the war strengthened Buck's feelings. "He was a great writer, but under the hard-boiled pose he affected for the world, he was a still greater human being."[13]

When Buck first met Baker in late 1961, he celebrated his relationship with Ernest, but Buck's feelings for Ernest changed during his friendship with the professor. Buck was shocked by the revelations in Baker's emerging chapters. He discovered Ernest was not the raconteur and hale companion he remembered, and from the distance of twenty years, Buck reconsidered his earlier impressions of Ernest's character and behavior. In August 1965, after reading Baker's draft covering the years 1944 to 1945, Buck said the account "has shaken me in a number of departments."[14] Ernest "certainly wrote a lot of crap to Mary in those days. I cannot understand this chest-beating. Why of all people did he feel he had to inflate himself in this way?" Ernest's "reputation was secure in every way. It is a sad thing."[15] Buck called the chapter "vital" because it showed Ernest's character: "You and I both rationalize EH's monstrous untruths in terms of the creative ferment, etc." Given Ernest's inflated language, Buck found it necessary to issue a warning to Baker: "At no time from beginning to the end of our wartime association did he ever make a military suggestion of any sort."[16] He suggested Baker should prefer David Bruce's account of the events at Rambouillet over Ernest's. Further, Buck made it "absolutely clear" Ernest was not present for the assault on the Siegfried Line, despite Ernest's efforts to create that impression.

After reading Baker's draft chapter, Buck was "no longer sure about anything. I suppose I simply refused to see what was there to be seen because I had such a deep affection for him." Buck said, "The revelations from your research saddened me more than I can tell you. Some of them almost made me physically ill." Buck concluded, "no matter how you cut it, Carlos, I am a simple, naïve sonofabitch, and I shall die one. I simply cannot believe that people are obviously what people obviously are."[17] Buck's change of heart was stunning. "I can at least thank God for one thing as I survey the wreckage of this latest ruin: I have not written anything about EH for publication. Now I am just about certain that I never shall. I would gag on it."[18]

In early December 1966, Buck reviewed several more of Baker's chapters. Buck told Carlos his account of Ernest's marriage to Hadley hit him with the "wallop of a sledgehammer." Here, "still in the bud," were qualities which would come to "full flower." Some would have "the odor of skunk cabbage and others the heady fragrance of a field-grown carnation."[19]

Carlos and Buck and their wives socialized. When the talk turned to Ernest, Buck's wife, Pete, poured forth her contempt for Ernest. Baker must have been grateful to receive the inside account. He valued Buck's encouragement and contributions to the story, and their friendship deepened. Buck transferred his allegiance from the dead author to the living scholar. His views about Ernest grew closer to those of Pete, who wrote Baker two letters seething with her dislike of Ernest. Pete described the two weeks she and Buck had visited Ernest in Cuba in 1946, by the end of which she and Ernest had grown to dislike each other thoroughly. Two days before they left Pete consumed too much wine at dinner. She confronted Ernest about his theories on coexistence with Russia, saying, "it sounds like straight appeasement to me." Ernest leaped to his feet, his face "fire red and eyes blazing and prepared to hurl his wineglass straight into my face." Pete considered that "unpardonable from a host at his own dinner table and—just-in-time—he did too, apparently, for he held onto his glass." Despite apologies, Ernest never forgave the remark and never asked Pete to join them again. "All this is to explain why I subconsciously find it difficult to be objective about the man." [20]

Pete was positive Ernest hated all women, except his current favorite—who was then Mary—because he never said a kind word about any woman. He hated Martha and his mother because they had the courage to stand up to him and defy him. When I told Valerie Hemingway about Pete's comment, she protested that Mary stood up to Ernest. "Mary stood up to him all the time." [21] After reading *A Moveable Feast*, Pete told Baker that she found it the saddest book she had ever read. "Here is a man soon to kill himself, leaving as his legacy an apology for his whole life." [22]

Two years later, Pete wrote to Baker permitting him to use anything she had said and correcting his draft. She didn't feel "outrage or shocked amazement" about Ernest's behavior. Instead, she felt "distaste with his frankness" and his "completely pleased with himself air." Pete said, "When all of your friends and biographers finish writing about him, ascribing to him various traits, emotions, etc. I shall still be left convinced that Ernest Hemingway was a heel, the garden variety type." [23] Pete realized Carlos must be careful what he wrote about Mary, but she thought Ernest was abominable to her, "and she really had to eat dirt to hold on to her position all those years." [24] In closing, Pete asked Carlos to "come down and hoist a few with us. I'm really quite a little treasure trove as far as Ernest is concerned—you really have only heard half." [25]

Pete's letters to Baker tapped into a deep well of anger toward Ernest, and her fury may have stemmed from the fact that Ernest had counseled Buck about leaving her. Buck had written to Ernest, telling him he was considering taking a job with the foreign service to get away from Pete, but he wasn't sure how it would affect his pension or housing allowance. In his reply to Buck's "very unquieting letter," Ernest said, everything appeared to be "up fucked." Buck's domestic life had become "completely impossible," and he advised Buck on the relative merits of a contested divorce or having Pete committed to a mental hospital. [26]

Ernest cautioned the problem with the foreign service option was Buck's "vulnerability to a local divorce," and he advised him to find out about the law of property settlement. He asked Buck how much property he could afford to lose and how much Pete could get from a court. "Surely what you are obligated to pay must be more or less what she can get unless you have her committed. If she is committed, who pays? You or the government?" [27] Ernest suggested that having Pete committed might be a way to remove her rights to the matrimonial property.

Ernest warned Buck not to give up all the dough it took to make a home because he "would have to make it on a minuscule basis and with someone who'll take that." Or he would make do with a single room or a bachelor's quarters. When Ernest had seen Buck in the war, he seemed "busy, beat up, and happy," and when he saw him at the Finca, he appeared "happy and relaxed and only unhappy with the unreasonableness of the woman . . . when he was unhappy and morally disgusted." [28] The foreign posting didn't look like a permanent solution, but if Buck decided on a divorce, it might make sense to do it in Cuba rather than Reno because Buck could stay at the Finca until the job was done. Ernest's stark analysis of the options caused Buck to reconsider and stick with Pete. We don't know if Pete read Ernest's letter or learned of his advice, but if she did sense Ernest's involvement in her own marriage, her spiteful attacks on Ernest and Mary in her letters to Baker may be explained. While Ernest was alive, Pete's letters to Mary and Ernest were affectionate, without the slightest trace of the venom that poured forth in her letters to Baker. And both Mary and Ernest always expressed best wishes to Pete in their letters to Buck, sympathizing with her poor health and the problems she had caring for her aging parents.

◆

Baker's book was published in 1969, and it received a mixed reception. No one doubted his efforts over seven years. He had researched the correspondence between Ernest and others, combed through his papers and manuscripts, and interviewed many people. Arnold Gingrich, the publisher of *Esquire Magazine*, where many of Ernest's writings between 1933 to 1943 first appeared, found the book was "unflinchingly interesting," and it was "hard to think of a better biographer" than Baker, "living or dead."[29] Geoffrey Wolff of the *Washington Post* wrote, "it is difficult to imagine that this job could have been done better than Carlos Baker has done it." Wolff found the biography "a surpassing achievement, evenhanded, generous, persuasive."[30]

Others were concerned Baker failed to bring Ernest to life. Irving Howe found the work "excessively factual." He called Baker "the Great Dispatcher" among recent literary biographers. "All those Americans who enjoy pouring over time-tables will find in him a sympathetic spirit." Baker "failed to provide a convincing portrait of the man." He focused on hunting, fishing, bullfighting, and drinking. Baker didn't show Hemingway's inner, spiritual, or intellectual life. He spent only a sentence on Turgenev, an outstanding mentor, while he gave many sentences to marlins, lions, and bulls.[31]

Mary acknowledged the comprehensive nature of the work but maintained Baker had missed the real man. She told Judith Martin of her disappointment with the book. "Ernest took himself not at all seriously. We had no heroes at the Finca and no hotshots. He loved being cheerful." Ernest's spontaneous wit didn't come through in Baker's book. "I don't think he is the kind of man who would have understood Ernest."[32] Mary complained to the journalist William Stimson that Baker's account got most of the facts correct but captured nothing of Ernest's spirit. "How could he? They never went hunting or drinking or even chatted together. Mr. Baker is a very great scholar, but no one can describe a person he has never met."[33] Therefore, "the tenor of his book—and I'm speaking of just the tenor—would be perhaps a little bit warmer."[34]

After reading many of the interviews and much of the correspondence Baker relied upon in writing the last third of his book, I find two things stand out. Mary constrained the biographer, and Baker relied heavily upon the opinions of Buck Lanham. Baker shaped the story of Ernest during the years Mary knew him according to her instructions, following her orders in describing incidents and removing or altering passages at her direction. Baker did not quote from any of Ernest's letters, he downplayed difficulties in the Hemingway marriage, and he did not use much of the material he gathered about Ernest's death. He skimmed

over the story of Ernest's disintegrating personality and treatment at the Mayo
Clinic and didn't say much about Ernest's relationship with his sons, perhaps
because Mary withheld that correspondence from him.

Baker's account of Ernest in World War II depended on Buck Lanham's
chronology, and Buck's changing perception of Ernest colored the narrative
and affected the tone of the book. A feedback loop developed as Buck became disil-
lusioned about Ernest through Baker's research, and then Baker became discouraged
by Buck's descriptions of Ernest's behavior. Buck was Baker's most important
witness for the war years, and many, if not most, of the stories Buck shared
with Baker expressed disapproval of Ernest. There were three general points of
censure: Ernest fabricated, exaggerated, and even lied about his role in military
actions; he treated friends and colleagues poorly; and he displayed slovenly habits
and unforgivable rudeness and crudity. Baker accepted all these stories uncriti-
cally, and he added to them the disparaging comments made by Buck's wife
Pete without questioning her motives. Between them, the Lanhams diminished
Ernest's reputation.

According to Buck, Ernest lied about military actions in his pieces for *Collier's*. He invented a story about Buck leading an attack with his .45 on a German
position,[35] and he said he was an eyewitness for the attack on the Siegfried
Line when he wasn't even present.[36] Baker wrote, "None of his dispatches
was completely accurate. He seemed to be far more concerned with the feel
of things than with the facts. As a lifelong purveyor of fiction, he could not
resist the temptation to fictionalize."[37] Ernest told Buck he loved combat and
enjoyed killing the enemy, but Buck told Baker it was made up. Baker wrote,
"His conscience never bothered him about the killing, whether done by others
or, as he liked to hint, by himself."[38]

Buck advised Baker to trust the account of Colonel David Bruce about the
action at Rambouillet.[39] Baker wrote Ernest "was trying to impress his new love
Mary Welsh with the splendor of his exploits, nurturing the germs of truth in his
private laboratory until they grew far larger-than-life size."[40] Baker concluded,
with Buck's tacit support, Ernest perjured himself in the inspector general's
investigation.[41]

Ernest told Buck that Colonel David Bruce promised to recommend him for a
Distinguished Service Cross (the second-highest military award) for his conduct
at Rambouillet. Buck told Baker he doubted Bruce had promised Ernest a DSC

because that honor was for service members for extreme gallantry and risk of life in combat, not for civilians. [42]

Ernest informed Buck he had immortalized the 22nd Regiment in his short stories about the war. Baker remarked snidely, "Although Lanham read them through with understandable interest, he did not find them impressive enough to suggest immortality." [43] Ernest told Buck that Colonel Cantwell in *Across the River and Into the Trees* was a composite of Buck, Charlie Sweeney, and himself, and Baker used the story as an insight into Ernest's thinking about the novel. [44]

Buck told Baker about Ernest's poor treatment of his friends and his former wife Martha Gellhorn. He described Ernest's conduct when he came to Rodenbourg following the Battle of the Bulge, including a full account of Ernest's arguments with Martha and his "program of harassment" of her. [45] Buck described Ernest's "backbiting" criticism of Bill Walton's writing style. After a going-away party for Walton, Ernest said, Walton's *Life* piece on the Huertgen campaign was "like giving your dog a copy of Aeschylus and supposing he would read it instead of chewing it up." [46]

Buck told Baker about Ernest's slovenly habits, unforgivable rudeness, and his crudity. When Buck visited Ernest and Mary at the Ritz in Paris, he presented Ernest with German machine pistols. Buck described Ernest's "adolescent trick" of spraying Noel Monks's photo with bullets as it rested in a toilet bowl. Baker used this story. [47] Baker interviewed Buck about his visit with Ernest at Gardiner's Island when Buck "found Ernest acting primitively." To Buck's astonishment, "Hemingway had made no move to change his clothes. He was wearing skin-tight denim levis, a shirt which was missing several buttons, no necktie, and felt bedroom slippers. He also omitted to shave." [48] Baker used Buck's account of the visit and transformed Buck's observations into more general criticism of Ernest's character. Baker wrote that Buck "observed somewhat sourly" Ernest reverted to "primitivism." He spoke in "a choppy, pseudo-Indian style, as if verbal primitivism could somehow shield him from the incursion of urban civilization." [49]

When Ernest telephoned Buck with the news he'd won the Nobel Prize for Literature, Buck extended his heartfelt congratulations. Ernest complained, "I should have had the damn thing long ago," and "I'm thinking of telling them to shove it." Buck told Ernest he couldn't do that and reported the story to Baker, who used it. [50]

The vignettes provided by Buck and used by Baker all cast doubt on Ernest's character, and they colored the picture of Ernest which emerged in Baker's biography. Buck didn't have to share the stories which deprecated Ernest. Some "friends," especially those who, as Buck bragged, had locked themselves into "a species of brotherhood that both of us knew would last as long as we lasted," might have been more forgiving and discreet.[51] In many passages, Baker channeled Buck's criticism of Ernest but portrayed Buck as a heroic figure. The West Point general formed a gentleman's club with the Princeton professor, and they deplored Ernest's bad manners and poor behavior. Buck provided evidence for Baker's criticism of Ernest's tendency to brag, lie, exaggerate, and fictionalize, and his letters to Baker tarnish, rather than polish, Ernest's character. Absent is the idolizing apparent in Buck's chronology.

When Jack Hemingway first read Baker's book, he reacted, "Who the Hell is he writing about? It sure isn't anyone I know!"[52] Jack concluded, "Papa made a mistake in believing that Buck Lanham was, indeed, his best friend. I think it becomes clear as one reads Baker that Buck changed his view of my father with the passage of time." This was "a large factor in coloring Baker's overall representation of my father." Buck's friendship was not as reliable as it had seemed, and Jack thought Pete Lanham "wore down Buck's resistance after a time." Jack sensed this without the benefit of Buck's chronology and the letters we have reviewed. "The tragedy is that Papa thought he had actually joined Buck Lanham's club, something you could never really do without a service academy ring."[53] The documents support Jack's claims. Patrick told me his nickname for Carlos Baker was "Careless" Baker because of the number of mistakes he made. Patrick considered Baker "a creature of Charles Scribner Jr.," and when he met Baker at Princeton, under a picture of Woodrow Wilson, Baker "referred to Papa's short story called 'Today is Friday' as tasteless. Baker was a Christian prude." Patrick believes Buck's attitude toward his father changed dramatically after the birthday party in Spain "when Buck saw another, disturbing side of my father."[54]

Rose Marie Burwell remarked, "I think that it fed Lanham's vanity to have a famous professor of English wanting him to write something that would go into the Hemingway biography."[55] After Buck reflected on Baker's research and reviewed his own memories, he stopped being Ernest's obsequious fan and friend for life. Instead, he became best friends with Carlos Baker and shared his scornful criticism of Ernest with the biographer. Baker rewarded Buck by dedicating his book to him. It is a sad story.

FORTY-FOUR

I Never Especially
Liked the Killing

July 1970–August 1974

A fter President Kennedy's assassination, his family decided to make the John
Fitzgerald Kennedy Presidential Library and Museum the only official
national memorial to the president. Jacqueline Kennedy's old friend Bill Walton
chaired a commission of world-famous architects to advise the family on how to
choose an architect and build the library, and Jacqueline reviewed every detail,
often with Walton. Ultimately, she and Bobby Kennedy appointed the Chinese
architect I. M. Pei, who was respected in the profession but not well-known to
the public. With Walton's advice, the family decided to broaden the collection
to include the writings of distinguished citizens who, though not connected with
Kennedy's administration, had lived through the Kennedy years.[1] When Mary
heard about this idea, she embraced it. At a party which Jacqueline Kennedy's secretary happened to be attending, Mary assumed her bold Mrs. Ernest Hemingway
persona to ask if the Kennedy family might be interested in Ernest's papers.
Within a few days, Jacqueline contacted Mary to embrace the idea.[2]

Years earlier, Ernest told Mary that he had considered leaving his papers to
the New York Public Library because he wanted them to be available to students.
He lost interest in the idea when he learned the library planned to break up his
collection.[3] After Ernest's death, the presidents of Columbia, Princeton, Yale,
and Harvard vied to acquire the papers of the Nobel Laureate. Since Ernest had

not advanced beyond Oak Park High, Mary saw no particular reason to give his papers to a university, and she'd already rejected the dark underground corridors of the Library of Congress.

Mary discussed the competing offers with Alfred Rice and Bill Walton.[4] Walton would hear her out and urge her to stay with the Kennedy Library: "the man you owe these papers to is right in Boston."[5] He believed Mary owed the documents to President Kennedy. "He had gotten the papers back for her and, by gosh, the place they ought to be was the Kennedy library. I finally convinced her of this, and she did follow through on it."[6]

Mary invited Walton to her apartment for a drink one evening in 1972. An antelope head stared from one wall and a lion skin hung from another in the small museum of artifacts Mary and Ernest had collected around the world. There were photos of famous friends, hunters, soldiers, writers, and family members. Miró's *The Farm* still dominated the room, and the fine Juan Gris painting of a guitarist decorated one wall. Books, including rare first editions, lined shelves and were stacked on the floor. "As we settled down with our vodkas, Mary looked around the room. 'I've decided to give it all to the Kennedy library. All except the Miró. That goes to the National Gallery in Washington. Do you approve? Alfred does.'"[7] So did Walton.

Several months before his death, President Kennedy had selected a site near Harvard University for his library. When the Kennedys had trouble getting planning approval in Cambridge, they found a new location next to the University of Massachusetts on the waterfront at Columbia Point with views of Boston's skyline and the Harbor Islands. I. M. Pei unveiled plans for the John F. Kennedy Library in May 1973, and a groundbreaking ceremony took place four years later. The building was completed and dedicated in October 1979, and in the meantime, the library housed its collection at the Federal Archives and Records Center in Waltham, Massachusetts.

Mary began sending papers to Waltham in 1972. Two feet of miscellaneous and fragmentary manuscripts arrived first, and papers continued to arrive until 1980. The documents came from Mary's New York apartment, her home in Ketchum, Harvard's Houghton Library, and Carlos Baker's collection in Princeton. Most arrived from Mary's bank vault and warehouse storage in New York. As the archivist Jo August recalled, "The papers arrived in boxes, trunks, filing cabinets, and shopping bags. For the most part, they were not organized, and the first task was gross sorting by type: manuscripts, correspondence, photographs, publications, and others."[8]

Aside from the published work and letters, there remained a quantity of unpublished materials, including one long work of fiction and some short stories. Mary would retain those until she decided, in consultation with Scribner's, what further, if anything, should be published. She withheld the photographs she recovered from Cuba until she decided what she wanted to use in her memoir.[9] The Hemingway Collection would have its own room at the Kennedy Library, and Jo August consulted Mary about the furnishings for it, suggesting they could make a scaled model of the library at the Finca if Mary could remember it well enough. Mary described the large room with twelve-foot ceilings, French doors overlooking a valley full of royal palms, and beyond the valley, the city of Havana, and the sea. She remembered the large tables and wide sofas where one could lie down and read.[10] The site planner adopted Mary's ideas. The atmosphere was to be "relaxed, gracious, and reflective of the Hemingway style," and furnishings were to include "his animal heads, paintings, and books by and about the writer." There would be "as much sea, harbor, and sky as possible."[11]

In February 1974, Mary offered to donate her own papers, her "stuff," as she called it, to the Kennedy Library, and Jo August suggested they put her materials in the Ernest Hemingway collection.[12] Later that year, Mary clarified her instructions on the unpublished manuscripts. She directed, "no permissions will be given to quote them at all—in whole or in part." Serious students might be permitted to see them on condition they did not attempt to paraphrase more than a couple of paragraphs.[13] A few years later, Mary reversed herself and decided, "nobody should have access to any of the unpublished work until Charlie and I have finished our work with the papers."[14] Mary drew a firm line, prohibiting access to unpublished manuscripts, because she worried someone might steal Ernest's work.

When the library opened the Hemingway papers to researchers early in 1975, the collection featured over 15,000 pages of manuscripts of Ernest's published novels and collections of short stories, and over 3,000 photographs. Archival work progressed to the still-photograph collection, the short stories, magazine and newspaper articles, poetry, and the incoming and outgoing correspondence. In December 1975, Senator Ted Kennedy wrote Mary, "Your donation of papers has made a distinguished contribution to the fulfillment of our expectations for the library, and I want to express my personal thanks for your kindness and generosity."[15]

Once Ernest's documents had been sent to the library, Mary considered every application to use the research materials. Jo August wrote many letters describing the various research proposals and seeking Mary's approval. Eventually, they settled upon a standard form, and August approved the routine applications. August consulted Mary often, and she usually approved the requests by researchers. Their requests amount to a Who's Who of Hemingway scholarship: the young Mike Reynolds, Gerry Brenner, Bernice Kert, Linda Wagner, Peter Buckley, among others.[16] During this period, Mary and Charlie Scribner continued trying to decide what they might publish next. Mary continued sending boxes of material from Ketchum to the delight of Jo August as each new "parcel of goodies" arrived. The galleys of *The Sun Also Rises* received in 1975 "made her day and the entire weekend."[17] Over the years, Mary became fond of Jo, and she took her out for lunches, plays, and dinners when Jo visited New York.

◆

On Ernest's birthday in 1970, Mary and Jack attended the dedication of the Ernest Hemingway School in Ketchum. Jack acted as emcee before the group of forty people and introduced the assistant superintendent, who dedicated the building to the memory of the famous writer, whose "dedication to perfection in his craft may serve as a guide to the students who will learn here."[18] Mary presented a statue of an African impala. She had designed the sculpture for Ernest's memorial, but friends warned it might attract souvenir hunters.[19] The impala stood in a stone wall surrounded by ferns. Mary said the animal signified creatures whose absolute survival is menaced today, and she challenged the audience to support conservation endeavors.

Mary had become a conservationist. The killing on safari in Africa had upset her, and in Idaho the only reason she hunted was to spend time with Ernest. She appreciated shooting well and the fellowship of the hunt, but she never relished the killing. That fall, Mary went duck hunting on the land surrounding the southeast edge of Lake Manitoba in Canada, and she penned a piece about the trip for *Rod and Gun*, raising her concerns about conservation. She opened by recounting the story of the hunt. After they moved their gear to a skiff, their skillful guide motored them to his favorite place deep in the marshes, and he set out their decoys. Mary wondered why she remained, turning colder by the minute, when she made donations to conservation groups? Why did she hope to murder ducks? "Need of food cannot excuse me . . . I do not enjoy killing birds." But then she rationalized, how else could she observe "fifteen or twenty miles of lake and marsh in changing light and wind?" She struggled to appease her conscience with the notion that about two hundred thousand waterfowl crossed the Delta in one morning's migration. Just as she lit up a cigarette, she heard the whir of wings behind her. She flipped off the safety on her shotgun as four mallards flew overhead. "I picked the lead bird and down he tumbled, rump over lovely head, into the reeds." The guide retrieved two mallard drakes, "neatly dead, but not as beautiful as they were flying above us, busy with their lives, ten minutes earlier."[20]

Mary considered herself an ardent conservationist, despite occasional hunting trips. When she showed the reporter Helen Markel through her apartment and came upon the black-maned lion tacked to the wall, Mary said, "I never especially liked the killing." But she loved the time before—"the mornings, the smells, the birds, walking close in the pale dawn." Mary told Markel, "My lion didn't bother my conscience. He was old, had a bad toothache, and was molesting the cattle. I got him with a single, clean shot after stalking him for ten days." This story was as big a lie as Ernest ever told because Mary knew Denis Zaphiro's shot killed the lion she now claimed. "Of all our vacations, the Safari was the happiest."[21]

Journalist Judith Martin watched Mary make soup with ducks she had shot herself. Mary remarked, "when you see them rise out of the water, they are beautiful. If you shoot them, you must use every grain." Mary called herself "an ecologist" and told Martin the dreadful tale of the leopard hanging on the wall in the study. "Once it had been alive and lethal. At the time, I didn't mind killing him. I believed he was the one who killed a child shortly before in the same area." Mary claimed to have changed over the years. "I couldn't shoot them any longer. I'm a conservationist."[22] Mary told journalist Martha Robinette she regretted killing a lesser kudu in 1953. His mounted head peered into her living room. "I've been sorry ever since. He was having such a pleasant time with his two girlfriends."[23] Mary told Robinette, "This country should declare a ten-year moratorium on hunting all birds and animals or any other molestation of wildlife. We should give wildlife a chance to recoup its existence."[24]

In 1970, Scribner's published *Islands in the Stream* and credited Mary and Charles Scribner Jr. with having edited the work. Mary was particularly pleased with the accuracy of the maps reproduced in the opening pages of the volume, and she also took credit for the fact "Thomas Hudson does not die because I asked Ernest not to kill him, to give the guy a chance." She told the *New York Times*, "I felt Hudson as a character is a charming and sweet guy, and Ernest agreed. He was wounded, but there was a chance that he would receive medical attention and be saved." When asked why Hemingway wanted Hudson to die in the first place, Mary responded, "because it was a nice and simple way to finish the book." She had intervened once before when Ernest was going to have Santiago die in *The Old Man and the Sea*. She had said, "no, he is too nice a man, please let him live."[25] Mary said *Islands in the Stream* was not rewritten. "We worked from parts of it which were in original handwriting and pencil that we put into type." Ernest had made "a few marginal notations. Mainly, we cut out redundancies of one sort or another . . . the public is not missing anything I am sure which Ernest would've wanted them to have seen." She said she decided to publish the novel because "it seemed to me the best and most complete of the many unpublished manuscripts Ernest left behind."[26]

Carlos Baker "was a dominant force" in editing the book but, "at his own request," his role was not acknowledged until Charlie Scribner Jr. published *In the Company of Writers* in 1990.[27] Scribner acknowledged, "the laboring oar in publishing *Islands* was wielded by Carlos Baker," and twenty years later, it was still on his conscience that Baker's role in editing the manuscript was never formally recognized.[28] According to Rose Marie Burwell's analysis of the manuscript, Baker ignored "complex musings on the problems of gender and creativity," and he left out "two long episodes about Hudson's concern with cross-dressing and creativity in his youth."[29]

Mary enjoyed good health, though she sometimes suffered from stomach ulcers, and in 1974 she developed an excruciating case of shingles. "I've had shingles—herpes zoster—since July," she told one correspondent, "with much pain, interruption of my work, and only now am slowly beginning to clear my desk."[30] Her lack of vanity charmed journalists like Judith Martin, who observed, "Mrs. Hemingway is a small, handsome woman with bright, laughing eyes." Mary told Martin, "All my friends have their faces lifted, but it's five grand, and I'd rather give it to charity." She was comfortable with her face. "Anytime I think of spending that much on myself, I think I could give it to the legal defense fund of the NAACP. So, I'll go around with the same old wrinkles this year, anyway."[31]

◆

One of the highlights of Mary's social life in New York was her friendship with Peter Buckley, who had been a childhood friend of Jack Hemingway. Peter's mother, Elinor, was a close friend of Hadley, and the two boys knew one another in Paris. Peter served as a counterintelligence agent in Europe during World War II. After the war, he returned to the States, graduated from Princeton, and then returned to France to complete a Ph.D. in philosophy at the Sorbonne. A year or so later, Peter abandoned philosophy and traveled to Spain to follow the bullfights. He became a filmmaker, writer, and photographer, eventually publishing a portfolio of his impressive work in *Bullfight*, considered a classic book on the subject. While he was in Spain in 1950, twenty-five-year-old Peter befriended the eighteen-year-old matador Antonio Ordóñez. When Ernest later met Antonio, he took possession of him, and he resented the relationship between Peter and Antonio. That led to the incident described earlier when one afternoon in Madrid, Antonio honored Peter by inviting him to his room while he dressed for a corrida. When Ernest discovered Peter in Antonio's room, he reamed out Peter as an intruder, screaming at him viciously.[32]

Mary understood how cruel Ernest could be, for she had seen him do the same thing to Irwin Shaw when he thought Shaw was trespassing on Ernest's subject—the war. Mary maintained a close friendship with Peter, and after Ernest died, Peter often attended parties in her penthouse and escorted her to social events in New York. Peter was present to assist with translation when Joan Miró, who could not speak more than a few words of English, visited Mary's penthouse to view *The Farm*. In 1971, Mary invited Peter to a special showing of *Blue Water White Death*, a documentary about sharks. Peter invited along his friend, the youthful Susan Washburn. Susan recalls Mary had expected that Peter would be

Mary's escort. Consequently, Mary was not welcoming and rather rudely asked whether Peter had cleared Susan with the hosts and whether there were enough seats at the dinner table. After Mary realized Peter was in love with Susan, Mary accepted her, and they became friends. Though, as Susan points out, "Mary was always more interested in Peter than me, and generally more interested in men than women."[33]

Susan and Peter saw Mary often and accompanied her to openings and galas. Mary organized glamorous outings which were always delightful because she included amazing people from the worlds of literature, politics, and journalism. She took them to the Audubon Dinner, and the spring galas for the MoMA and the National History Museum, sometimes with Bill Walton. Mary was treated like a celebrity wherever she went. Susan recounts in her charming memoir, *Eating with Peter*, that when Antonio Ordóñez and his family came to town, Mary and the Buckleys dressed up and went to fancy restaurants with the exalted matador surrounded by his entourage. Mary lived extravagantly and loved entertaining famous guests at parties in her penthouse. She invited luminaries such as Senator Frank Church, the playwright Moss Hart, and the writer Albert Murray, and journalists like Harry Gilmore of the *Times*. Bill Walton was a frequent guest, and Mary was flirtatious with him. Susan remembers listening to Mary in her penthouse kitchen, telling Susan that she was fasting to keep her weight down, "But of course I had some gin," she noted. Susan told me, "We all knew that her drinking was getting worse."[34]

Mary attended Susan and Peter's wedding in 1973. It was a small affair featuring a horse-drawn carriage for the drive from the church to the newlyweds' home for a reception of close friends and family. Susan vividly recalls they were cutting the cake when Mary said, "I have to go now because I have to get back to my manuscript."[35] Susan and Peter later realized the memoir gave Mary a raison d'être and provided some structure in her life, a structure that would collapse when the book was done.

One Saturday afternoon, Peter visited Mary at her penthouse and mentioned an idea he had for a book about Ernest. Mary leaped up and pulled out a drawer full of photographs and papers and put them in Peter's lap, saying, "here you can have all this and good luck." Then she gave him bags of photographs of Ernest and asked him to send them to Jo August at the Kennedy Library when he finished with them. Peter selected from among the ten thousand photos Mary owned, beginning with Ernest's first photo as an infant to one of the last shots of him standing in the woods in Ketchum. In *Ernest*, the extraordinary photographs of Ernest's life accompany Peter's almost painfully personal essay describing Ernest's life from the perspective of one who knew him and his family.[36]

Susan and Peter hosted a dinner for Mary's seventieth birthday, and her old friends Connie Bessie and Bill Walton joined in the celebration. Susan snapped a cheerful photo of Mary smiling toward the camera with her right arm around the shoulders of Connie Bessie, who is holding a cigarette in her right hand and hugging Mary's waist with her left. Connie smiles at her old friend.

While she worked on *How It Was*, Mary drank a fair amount of gin, but she began drinking more when she finished the project. After the memoir was published and the promotional tour ended, Mary's life seemed to lose purpose. She had friends but she wasn't that close to them. And she had no children or grandchildren to dote upon or divert her. As Mary aged and her alcoholism developed, her friends dropped off, but Peter remained loyal. He and Susan often picked up Mary and took to her a little lunch place, Old Denmark, a few blocks from her penthouse. Or they invited Mary and her nurse to their home for lunch or tea, and sometimes Mary came for dinner. Peter talked to her on the phone once a week. "By then she wasn't fun anymore, but we knew she needed to know that we still cared."[37]

FORTY-FIVE

Have Success in Something Instead of Talking About Equality!

February 1975

D uring the sixties and seventies, Mary continued writing articles for popular magazines and worked long hours on her memoir. She didn't need the money but she maintained the lifelong discipline of writing—she felt better when she was pounding out copy on her blue typewriter. Mary told Wood Simpson she wanted to write "some far-out things, really kind of crazy, fiction," and described a novel about a woman living in a New York triplex with five simultaneous husbands. Each husband had a meaningful career but shared part of his life with the common wife. A sociologist interviewed the husbands and the wife and asked how it was possible to do this. The woman explained, "Friend, it's a simple matter of ignoring that old-fashioned primal thing of jealousy."[1] Wood Simpson said the tale sounded "confused," but Mary replied it was entirely reasonable. She told him *Der Stern* had published a draft five or six years earlier, but the story scared American editors.

In Mary's papers is the start of a novel entitled, "Polyandry May Come to Stay," which follows the storyline Mary described to Simpson. "To the much-wedded wife, polyandry is a greater challenge than the mere job of looking after one man only and his get." It was not "for the rosebud bride of twenty," but it might appeal to a "woman with a decent education, broad interests, and good health." Her children by her first husband are already self-sufficient. It is for the woman who can "manage comfortably for each and all of her husbands." One "indubitable reward" is the wife has "neither the time nor the inclination" for those "undignified, gelatinous little extramarital affairs . . . into which many women wander."[2] She described the different husbands' personalities and their interactions with each other and with their common wife.

Mary sent a copy of *Polyandry May Come to Stay* to David Karr, a writer at Metro-Goldwyn-Mayer Inc., and he responded with encouraging words. "When we discussed this last week, I thought it had the potential for a musical comedy. I feel that even more strongly now that I have read it." He told her, "what we would need now is some conflict and a climax. In effect, what we have here is a darned good idea and first-rate plan for a first act and, perhaps, part or all of a second act. Do you have any ideas for a third act?"[3] Karr met with Mary on a visit to New York a few weeks later.

Polyandry had long intrigued Mary. In wartime London, she had sometimes turned to the topic to tease and provoke dinner companions. In her draft memoir, she recalled a dinner hosted by the US ambassador to Poland, Anthony Biddle. "Of course," Mary said airily, "we all know that any good, sound woman needs at least five husbands to make a full life." A man across the table asked, "for herself, or for whom?" Mary responded, "for herself and also her husbands, and of course for the children." A man from the Foreign Office a few chairs away snorted, "what tiresome nonsense." But Mary noticed people were getting involved in the common discussion. "What sort of man could this possibly be?" a Norwegian guest asked. Mary responded, "sensible men, who face the facts, see for themselves that they can't give the time and attention to their careers, and also be satisfactory husbands and fathers." A man across the table protested it was "impossible," for "no self-respecting man would share his wife with somebody else." Mary replied, "that's merely a western custom. In the Arab countries, lots of wives share one husband."[4]

In her draft novel, Mary came back to the topic. The heroine, slim-hipped and seductive Helen, divides her time between her five husbands: Thomas, a partner in a large and prosperous law firm takes natural history expeditions; Albert, a successful businessman enjoys the intricacies of making money and tying trout flies more than he likes using them; Edgar, a scientist in his thirties with inherited wealth, plays handball and collects antique jewelry; Rupert edits a magazine devoted to music, ballet, books, and theater; and the youngest, Peter, is a successful director of TV shows and the father of Helen's three-year-old daughter. They all love Helen's Cantonese dishes whenever she favors them with a meal. The multiple husbands share some of Ernest's qualities, but not one is a depressed novelist. Mary had exhausted that type and imagined different personalities and preoccupations. The model she explores is a complete break with conventional mores. The partners in her novel eschew romantic conceptions of love in favor of pragmatic arrangements. Perhaps it is the model Mary herself experimented with in London during the war. She was the one sought after, she maintained several simultaneous love affairs, and she never seemed to feel sad about failed romances. After her wartime affairs and three marriages, she explored the idea of relationships with interesting husbands who associated with each other in a family without pettiness or jealousy. Like Mary's gender blending experiments with Ernest, her curiosity about polyandry shows her lively imagination and willingness to break through socially constructed expectations for gender behavior.

❖

Mary made tremendous strides in the male-dominated field of wartime journalism, becoming one of the exceptional women who wrote about the war. She managed on her own, navigating among husbands and boyfriends until she decided to throw in her lot with Ernest. She was often asked whether she regretted sacrificing her career in journalism to support Ernest's writing. She gave many interviews on the topic, and the views here are not aberrations.

Mary told Robert Morley, "The fact is, the whole subject of women and women's rights, and particularly their yelling about their rights, is a bore to me. I think we are second-class citizens because of biology!"[5] She declared to Oriana Fallaci, "Women are second-class citizens and not only biologically. A female's first duty is to bear children and raise them: with the exception of a few freshwater fish, all animals follow this basic rule."[6] Mary admitted she rarely liked women. She wanted to shout, "Go and do something, have success in something instead of talking about equality!" Mary told Fallaci, "I didn't want to be Ernest's equal; I wanted him to be the master, to be stronger and cleverer than I, to remember constantly how big he was and how small I was." Asked whether she regretted giving up her writing career to marry Ernest, Mary punched the air with her cigarette-holding fist. "Women take their careers too seriously. Don't they know it's a great privilege to give their men affection, support, admiration? These things are more important than any woman's career."[7]

American women, Mary contended, were "too cocky." She told Robert Morley, "They're supposed to be subservient to men, but they aren't. They don't pay enough attention to the kitchen . . . and they are much too bossy." She pursued the point, "They don't wait upon men. They don't flatter men enough. They think their own problems are more important than their men's problems, which is untrue." As to second-class status, "You could have a mighty fine time as a second-class citizen if you handle yourself right." Mary concluded, "I have an inkling that the keywords here are affection, support, admiration. I don't think it's demeaning, but a great privilege to give your man those things."

Wood Simpson asked Mary whether she had sacrificed her career for Ernest's sake. Mary said she had enjoyed the best assignments when she was in journalism. It was fun, and she met quite a few famous people. "Women's Lib wasn't invented then, and I felt liberated anyway. I guess maybe I was terribly lucky, but I really felt in all those years very little discrimination against me because I was a female." When she worked on the *Chicago Daily News*, if she got a really hot story, "the fellows of the city room would say, that's because you are female." They said, "You were able to lure the information out of them." But if she lost a story, they'd say, "'there, you see, a female can't do it.' Well, poop! I never took it seriously."

Moving to Cuba brought a significant change. She found herself in a new country with a different language. It was unlike anything she had ever known, and she had "to rely on a single fellow for my food, rent, my clothing and housing and everything else." She took a chance: "What the hell. It wasn't very difficult because I thought that this was one of the most interesting creatures in the whole world." He proved to be "interesting and fascinating and complicated and charming."[8] Once she had made up her mind to stay in Cuba and marry Ernest, she felt no regrets.[9]

In these interviews, Mary perpetuated the myth of her happy subservience to Ernest's art. This was a deliberately constructed narrative to promote Ernest's reputation as a creative genius and her as the reliable partner, helper, and brother. She was not a mere handmaiden to his art but a contributor. "We were happy about our close, smooth teamwork. We felt not merely male and female, but friends and brothers. Papa was my only brother and the best friend I ever had."[10] Mary continued to advance this picture of their relationship in the articles she wrote exalting her life with Ernest. It was a public relations exercise. We know Mary's life with Ernest was not captured in these marketing pieces. She not only had second thoughts, but she tried to leave Ernest several times. Mary regretted her loss of independence and resented having to ask Ernest for money. She performed valuable services managing the sizable domestic establishment, keeping track of expenses, preparing tax accounts, editing his work, and making critical suggestions for revisions (to allow Santiago and Thomas Hudson to live, for example). Mary believed she deserved to be paid for her services—not forced to beg for money as some poor relation. She wanted a room of her own, free from Ernest's fluctuating moods. In her letters to Ernest, when she was angry and frustrated with him, she regretted her career sacrifice given his failure to show respect and appreciation for her contributions.

Mary told Fallaci that throughout the years of their marriage, she wrote for magazines as an escape from the daily routine of housekeeping. "Ernest approved; he liked my writing." Without Ernest, she was "totally lonely." She had longed for a child and was sorry she had not brought a miniature Ernest into the world. The failed pregnancy in Casper was "the greatest loss of my life, except the death of Ernest."[11] Mary believed she was exceptional; through hard work and determination, she had bypassed gender barriers, and she had succeeded in her field. Then she married the most successful writer of her time. She achieved financial independence, in the same way as Virginia Woolf, through inheritance. Her greatest disappointment in life was not having a child. She did not want to talk about equality because she did not perceive the systemic barriers to women's achievement. That work remained for second-wave feminism. Perhaps Mary would have been more empathetic if, like Betty Friedan, she had a couple of children and found the role of mother in a suburban setting strangely unsatisfying. She, too, might have said, "I want something more than my husband and my children and my home." Mary might have gained insight into the poverty of the "feminine mystique" which she seemed to embrace.[12]

FORTY-SIX

Ernest's Gift Was Joy

1951–1977

In a short bio prepared in 1966, Mary said she "dropped out" from Northwestern University in 1931 to take a job with a florist journal.[1] Behind Mary's self-confidence, Bill Walton detected slight insecurity concerning her educational achievements. Mary, like Ernest, "always felt a little nervous about not having gone to university."[2] This nervousness revealed itself in the relationship between the Hemingways and the academic community. When Mary became literary executrix, she carried forward Ernest's point of view. Mary's stringent control of the literary estate was rarely mean-spirited, and she helped many of the scholars interested in Ernest's writing. But like Ernest, Mary was suspicious of academic scholars. Susan Buckley recalls that Mary was always scathing about the scholarly treatises concerning Ernest. She would point to a bookcase full of them and she and Peter Buckley "would bemoan their pretension about a man whom they didn't know."[3]

Ernest had said, "The writing published in books is what I stand on, and I would like people to leave my private life the hell alone."[4] When scholars dug into Ernest's family, they invaded his privacy, and Ernest told Charles Fenton he did not want to be "tailed, investigated, queried about, by any amateur detective no matter how scholarly or straight."[5] Ernest objected to scholars' attempts to identify his fictional characters with him. As he told Thomas Bledsoe, "a critic has a right to write anything he wishes about your work, no matter how wrong he may be." Even so, "a critic has no right to write about your private life while you are alive . . ." and Ernest warned Bledsoe, "Public psychoanalyzing of living writers is . . . an invasion of privacy."[6]

One of the first scholars to raise Ernest's ire was Philip Young, a United States artillery officer in Europe from 1942 to 1946 who had long admired Ernest's writing. On his return to civilian life, Young wrote a Ph.D. thesis on Ernest's work and Rinehart and Company offered to publish it, if he cleaned it up "to get the Ph.D. out of it."[7] After Young had revised the manuscript in 1951, Rinehart hired Malcolm Cowley to review it, and Cowley sent an interim report to Young telling him that he "was brilliantly on the right track." Young's thesis was that the injuries and shell shock Ernest suffered when he was wounded at Fossalta di Piave in 1918 became the central experience in Ernest's writing. Cowley enthusiastically agreed with this point.

Further, Young argued, Nick Adams was a projection of Ernest's personal experiences, and he identified links between Ernest's fictional heroes and Ernest's life. Cowley warned Young "to be careful in your language when extracting biography from stories," and then he gave Young some background information about Ernest.[8] "It must not be quoted and must not be used except as background for your own judgments." He shared details about Ernest's wounding and supported Young's idea that Ernest was a frightened man for twenty years who conquered his fear by walking into danger. Had Ernest ever seen this letter, he could reasonably have considered it a betrayal by Cowley.

Having disclosed personal information to Young about Ernest, Cowley wrote to Ernest a couple of weeks later. He told Ernest he had agreed to report on Young's book for Rinehart, and he was glad he had done so because he wanted to make the book as good as possible. Cowley said Young showed "a deplorable tendency to confuse you as author with the various heroes of novels and stories." Cowley believed Young would make the changes he had suggested, and if he did so, "it still won't be a book you like, but it will make sense and help your permanent reputation as a writer."[9] Reviewing Cowley's letters, we see that he was trying to curry favor with both sides.

Ernest understood from Cowley's letter that Young was writing a book trying "to prove I was all of my characters."[10] He decided to stop the book by withholding permission to quote from his works and threatening legal action. After months of correspondence between Ernest and Rinehart and Young, Ernest relented with conditions.[11] He agreed to let Young quote from his books, "If you give me your word that the book is not biography disguised as criticism, and . . . not a psycho-analytical study of a living writer."[12]

Young published his short book, *Ernest Hemingway*, a few months later. His principal claim is that the Nick Adams stories provide the key to understanding Ernest because they contain autobiographical elements. As Young analyzes the stories and novels, he draws links back to events in Ernest's life. Nick Adams becomes the quintessential Hemingway hero, and Young claims every one of Ernest's heroes experienced "the exact equivalent of Nick's childhood, adolescence, and young manhood." The experiences which "shaped Nick Adams shaped Lt. Henry, Jake Barnes, Colonel Cantwell, and several other heroes. They all had Nick's childhood, Nick's adolescence, and Nick's young manhood."[13] To balance Nick's deficiencies, Ernest developed a set of "code heroes." These men embraced principles of "honor, courage, and endurance." The ultimate code hero was Santiago, from *The Old Man and the Sea*, who "behaves perfectly—honorably, with great courage and endurance—while losing to the sharks, the giant fish he has caught." The code hero inevitably loses to forces beyond his control, but what is important "is how you conduct yourself while you are being destroyed."[14] Young reads Santiago's struggle as an "allegory" of Ernest's effort to fight his way back to the top as a writer. Ernest did not agree "he was all his characters." He told Bledsoe he was not Jake Barnes, and he was not Francis Macomber. Ernest opposed "the public psychoanalyzing of living people," and he disagreed with Young's "trauma theory of literature."[15] When asked how he liked Young's book, Ernest replied, "How would you like it if someone said that everything you've done in your life was because of some physical injuries?"[16] Before the book was published, Malcolm Cowley wrote to Ernest. "I wish to God I hadn't ever seen the Philip Young manuscript." He confessed, "Undertaking to read and report on it last spring, then telling you about it, has got me into the damndest Hippocratic, hypocritic and hypercritical situation I never imagined."[17] After the mix-up, Ernest never again spoke to Cowley.

While Mary supported Ernest's opposition to Philip Young's book, years later, during her fight against Hotchner, she changed her mind about Young. He took Mary's side in her defense of Ernest by writing a stinging rebuke of Hotchner's *Papa Hemingway* ("On Dismembering Hemingway"), and Mary came to trust Young.[18]

When Young lunched with Mary in New York, she wondered if he would be too bored to visit the vault where she stored Ernest's published and unpublished manuscripts. "I said I didn't think I'd be too bored."[19] When they entered the bank vault, Young viewed "a treasure trove of manuscripts." He said, "I stuck my fingers in and just rifled around." Young volunteered to compile a bibliography with his colleague, Charles W. Mann, and Mary agreed.[20] They worked on the project Mondays and Tuesdays and took four months to complete the job. Among the precious materials, Young found five letters Ernest had written to him concerning his book. He described them as "obscene beyond belief," but Ernest had never mailed them. Charles Mann recalled, "Mary helped us by taking us to lunch and getting us plastered." She cooked them a marvelous meal when they finished the work, and Mary expressed disappointment the project was completed, and no discoveries remained. Once they published the bibliography, the authors became academic celebrities.[21]

◆

In a fiery exchange, Mary corresponded with Professor Gerry Brenner in 1975. The volleys began with Brenner's request for information concerning *A Moveable Feast*. Brenner wanted to see a list of titles for the book and know how Mary and Harry Brague rearranged the chapters. Mary proclaimed this "an excess of delving into minutiae." Mary also challenged Brenner's view that *Across the River* imitated Dante's *Divine Comedy*. It was "imagination or charlatanism, to assume or aver that. Come off it, please." Mary noted Ernest wrote most of the first draft in the winter they lived in Cortina D'Ampezzo from 1948 to 1949. They brought thirty to forty books with them—none of them Dante. Ernest did not read or discuss "Dante with me or anyone else. He never discussed what he was writing with anyone in the seventeen years I knew him."[22]

As for Brenner's thesis that Ernest gained his knowledge of literary traditions from Aristotle's *Poetics*, Mary recoiled. Maybe they owned the book in Cuba, but she doubted Ernest relied upon it. Ernest never discussed the art or science of writing, and Mary "never heard him discuss the mechanics of his trade." He considered the subject "much too pretentious." Not that Ernest was "an antiintellectual, he was simply anti-chicken shit." Mary concluded, "If this busts up your fancy theories, I'm sorry. But I deplore people's imputing to Ernest a variety of false pretensions he did not have or practice."

Gerry Brenner replied to Mary's letter, thanking her for responding to his questions. He realized his thesis might hang on "fragile or intangible or rotted thread." Still, he was not "pig-headed enough to stick to a thesis, whether it fits or not."[23] Changing the subject, Brenner suggested *Green Hills of Africa* showed more concern with the aesthetics than the violence of hunting. Though the book portrayed Ernest as a trophy hunter, he tried to capture antelope heads with exotic horns "to arrest a moment of beauty, the result of which is an art object." Did they display the heads "to give prominence to an event?" Brenner's imagination marveled at the "combination of those graceful, feminine heads and the purity of one of those horns. I should ask whether the heads of deer, elk, also adorn that living room at the Finca?"

Mary agreed with Brenner's first point. *Green Hills* did concern the aesthetics rather than the violence of hunting, but she recalled only three heads in their living room. As for Brenner's imagined vision, she said the heads could not be feminine since, in most antelope species, only the males carry horns. She did not understand what he meant by "special prominence," and dashing another thesis, she wrote, "We hung the heads where they seemed most appropriate."[24]

Mary wrote to Brenner on November 21, 1975, "astonished" he expected her to answer questions regarding "Jack's marriage and Ernest's relationship with his sons." She told him the details of family life were of no consequence, and he would be mistaken to impute any feelings of guilt on Ernest's part toward Gregory, "who was then, and continues to be, a very complicated and difficult person." In closing, Mary scolded Brenner, "Please don't tell me to address [these] questions in my memoirs. You may not be aware of it, but you're extremely presumptuous."[25]

Brenner asked Martha Gellhorn the same questions about Ernest's familiarity with the classics. Her answers corroborated Mary's opinion. Gellhorn said, "Your idea about Ernest is very amusing, and I'm sure would have pleased him greatly. The idea he relied upon Aristotle's *Poetics* would really have thrilled him." She added, "He was not a scholarly man, you know . . . and I take a small bet he never read Aristotle's *Poetics*." More likely, art has a way of resembling other art. "Again, finding a similarity between the *Bell* and *Paradise Lost* is enchanting but dotty. No reason to think Ernest read Milton any more than Donne." Martha told Brenner, Ernest "made himself, a really self-made artist." She said, "He didn't like talking about books. Just said they were great, good, lousy, etc. He also didn't like me as a literary critic. I hurt his feelings early on in the *Bell* by failing to be approving." Ernest, "hurt and furious, sought better audiences like his hunting and fishing chums." She described "a very funny sweet scene in Cuba." Ernest read aloud, "from the *Bell* to a bunch of grown-up well-off semi-literate pigeon shooting and fishing pals, they sitting on the floor spellbound." In closing, Martha said, though Ernest "was secretive in lots of ways . . . I doubt whether he was hiding anything . . . except his own lack of formal education."[26]

In October 1976, Mary made a presentation on *How It Was* to a symposium called "Hemingway: A Revaluation" at the University of Alabama. Three scholars from Texas A&M University interviewed her the following year when she visited their campus, and she recounted the symposium. "I listened with due respect to these elegant gentlemen with all those strings of letters behind their names and heard the longest profusion of drivel and misinterpretation." If they earned their living "by telling people what Ernest meant or why he wrote something," Mary supposed, "it certainly is easier than digging ditches or selling shoes."[27] But it did not raise her estimate of "what goes on in these groves of academe." Mary told them about Ernest's response to critics who identified the sharks as evil and Santiago as a Christ figure in *The Old Man and the Sea*. He said, "I wrote it as a story. If that's the way they want to interpret it, I can't help it." She said they often laughed over the criticism.[28]

Mary's frustration with traditional scholars is illustrated in a fascinating story which the celebrated Hemingway scholar, Professor H. R. Stoneback, told me over coffee in the kitchen of his magnificent home close to Poughkeepsie, New York.[29] Stoney had also attended the 1976 Hemingway conference in Alabama, which marked the reawakening of serious Hemingway scholarship. Lined up on the stage were all "the old guys who had poisoned the wells of Hemingway criticism in the 1950s." Stoney met Mary over a drink. They became social friends, and they talked about the world, not about Ernest. Thirty-five-year-old Stoney found Mary an interesting older lady, who was not only attractive but alive with insightful comments. They went back inside to hear the old guard of professors, all white-haired men in their sixties. Mary leaned over and said, "Stoney, save me from these assholes."

Stoney knew his friend Jerry Jeff Walker was giving a concert on campus that evening. Walker's fame had surpassed Bob Dylan's, who was almost forgotten at this time. Walker's song called "Stoney," a long ballad or story-song about H. R. Stoneback, was then his second biggest hit, right after "Mr. Bojangles." Mary and Stoney arrived at the concert, and since Stoney knew Walker's security people and stagehands, he took Mary backstage. Walker was on stage doing an acoustic number. He had just finished singing "Stoney." The real Stoney walked out, and Walker yelled, "Stoney, what are you doing here, man?" People in the audience thought it was practiced, but it wasn't.

Stoney said, "Hey man, I just dropped by to introduce you to Mary Hemingway."

Walker said, "Yeah, Stoney, Mary Hemingway, tell me another story."

Stoney said, "No, man, it is Mary Hemingway," and he introduced them. It was a great moment, and the audience roared its approval.

Mary and Stoney met each other in a natural way, which underlined her frustration with the things written and said about Ernest. Stoney's relationship with Mary developed over the years, and he visited her penthouse apartment on Madison Avenue in the East 60s. Their talk sometimes turned to Ernest, and Mary appreciated Stoney was not trying to enunciate grand theories of interpretation. Instead, he focused on the circumstances and places in which Ernest found spiritual inspiration.

Stoneback's intuitive and deep-seated appreciation for the spiritual dimension of Hemingway's work affected Mary, and she reposed confidence in him. Stoney tells the story of driving Mary home through Central Park, accompanied by pouring rain and "the slapping backbeat of the windshield wipers." He had raised the subject of Hemingway as one of "the great souls" of the century who had a great love of Chartres and an extraordinary devotion to Our Lady.

"Mary simply said: 'Yes. He was a strange old man.' 'Like Santiago,' I said, 'maybe not so religious in the usual sense but very devout?' Again, Mary said: 'Yes.'"

After they parked close to her apartment, Mary turned to Stoney and said: "No one, no one I ever knew or even heard about, brought more joy to other people. In spite of anything else I've ever said or written or anyone else has ever said or written, that is true. Ernest's gift was joy, he carried it in every room with him, he gave it freely."

Stoney knew this was an important insight and wrote it down. He wondered if Hemingway, "like some Saints and Mystics we have perhaps heard or read about, [was] one of the great joy givers? A refreshing and most satisfactory view, I think, necessary and exact, and closer to the true man and writer than anything else said or written about him." [30] What is so significant about Mary's revelation and Stoney's appreciation of it is it underlined the significant deficit Mary found in Baker's biography—his failure to capture the joy Ernest shared with others.

After their first meeting at the Alabama Hemingway Conference, the friendship of Mary and Stoney flourished in the later seventies and early eighties. Stoney introduced Mary at visiting speaker appearances, and he recalled, "Mary was a superb speaker." Together they attended cultural events in Manhattan, especially at The Lotos Club, located in a former Vanderbilt family mansion, one of the finest examples of French Renaissance architecture in America, just around the corner from Mary's penthouse apartment. The Lotos Club is one of the oldest and most distinguished private clubs devoted to literature and the arts in the United States. Early members included Mark Twain, and the overall roster of membership for 150 years reads like an American hall of fame of leaders in the academic, artistic, business, cultural, literary, and political fields. Thus, it is a matter of some note that in 1977, Mary Hemingway became the first female member in the long history of The Lotos Club. And in 1978 Mary co-sponsored (along with the leading poet-novelist-critic Robert Penn Warren) Stoney's Lotos membership.

FORTY-SEVEN

How It Was

From an early age, Mary wrote compulsively. She worked hard to perfect her style, and in time, she became a first-class journalist. For years Mary described her daily life, using notebooks or scraps of paper to capture her thoughts. Often she typed, but sometimes she wrote by hand in her distinctive but highly readable style. She avoided flourishes and used printed capital letters standing alone, with a cursive link for the small letters. She collected lists of words, noting their etymology, and folksongs, and recipes. Boxes at the JFK Library are filled with letters, diaries, journals, articles, and a draft novel.

Mary dutifully sent Sunday letters to her parents for years as she kept in touch and enlightened them about world affairs. The worldly wise daughter shared her thoughts about the war and her role as a female journalist, describing the development of socialism in Britain and extolling her love for Noel. She wrote affectionate letters to Noel until their relationship wore itself out, and she gave a sanitized account of the breakdown. During the war, Mary kept exacting notes about bombing missions, interceptor speeds, aircraft production, weapon development, ammunition supplies, miles of roads constructed, and bomb damage. Fluent in the wartime acronyms of the armed forces, Mary became proficient in military speech. She defended her plan to marry Ernest in letters to her parents, and for years wrote to Ernest, expressing her love, anger, or frustration with him.

Mary kept meticulous records of their expenses, noting each purchase. Her role as a manager required her to organize documents for tax reporting, and she corresponded with Alfred Rice. When she and Ernest traveled, she recorded every detail, rationalizing her notetaking as creating a record for Ernest's writing. Since Ernest seldom relied on Mary's notes, instead counting on his vivid, if flawed, memory for conversations and places, I suspect Mary planned to write her own account. She needed to write to capture not only her physical environment but her impressions and thoughts. Mary trusted her hard-won skill as a writer and confidently assumed her story would interest many people.

Often she began her notes describing natural surroundings, including the countryside they traveled through, the miles driven, the weather, the names of towns, places, and people. She reported facts, and her accounts were more likely to be accurate than Ernest's. Mary had developed a journalist's eye for neutral, objective fact-finding, while Ernest had honed a storyteller's flair, shading and shaping facts for dramatic effect.

After she met Ernest, Mary's notes and diary pages offered an outlet for complaints about him and reflections on their relationship. His bullying and irrational behavior caused her anguish, and she asked probing questions about her love for him, trying to understand why she put up with his abuse and whether it was worth it. She wondered if she possessed the courage to leave him. Not only was Ernest the most compelling man she had ever met, but he was also the most difficult, and her private notes contain pages of introspection. Far from living in denial, Mary obsessed over her relationship with Ernest. She loved him for his creativity, manliness, and joie de vivre, and he made her happy but sometimes sad. Mary did her best to create an environment in which he could be creative, and she recorded it all in her careful notes. She also made him pay for his insensitivity and occasional cruelty.

Mary told Wood Simpson in 1975 that she was not trying to duplicate or replace Baker's biography. She shared with Simpson what seems to have been her real purpose in writing the memoir. She wanted to show the world Ernest adored her: "I have a great deal of documentation of the fact Ernest approved of me, and I thought he was, as I said, the most enchanting creature on earth." Mary said, "It was simple as that. He was also . . . formidable sometimes, a tough guy, a tough man to handle." But she had managed, and she wanted the world to know that they loved each other.

Mary told Simpson that the most challenging part to write was Ernest shooting himself. She had tried to keep events in perspective, but she found it difficult,

"because even at this late time, there is still a possibility of getting too emotional."
She explained, "I just didn't want to get hysterical and stupid, and I tried not to. It
was a tremendous trauma for me, though." She tried to be a good journalist. "In
a thing like one's husband killing himself, one must attempt to be, rather than
'little me, hysterical,' objective and as straight and simple and truthful as possible.
And that's the way I wrote it."[1]

Mary submitted chapters of her draft memoir to Scribner's, and they suggested
revisions. Charlie Scribner Jr. recalled he was ready to publish Mary's book. "She
sent in several chapters, which I edited with the help of some of my colleagues.
We edited them heavily, too heavily. We didn't touch her material but made suggestions in the interest of fluency, organization, liveliness." Scribner admitted, "it
was the kind of editing . . . properly decried as 'creeping creativity.'" He conceded,
"It was my fault. Mary went through the roof. She 'fired' me, saying, 'you can
publish Hemingway, but you can't publish me.'"[2] Scribner noted that their relations remained good for other publishing purposes. As Bill Walton remembered,
Mary "went up in flames," and the relationship with Scribner's concerning her
memoir broke down. She told Walton and Scribner's, "I have a very acceptable,
good, straightforward, sensible prose, and I write my own books."[3]

Mary took her manuscript to Robert Gottlieb at Alfred A. Knopf Inc., and
after he read the first half, she sent him the rest on May 19, 1975. Gottlieb
remembers liking Mary: "she was peppy, hard-working, she meant well I think,
she was self-absorbed, but all writers are self-absorbed." She was not an analytical
person, but she shot from the hip. Gottlieb told me that he had never really cared
about Ernest Hemingway's writing, and he never particularly liked what he knew
of him. "I didn't have anything against Hemingway; I just never wanted to be in
his presence." Gottlieb, certainly, was not interested in promoting any particular
view or version of Hemingway's life, and while it was amusing to know Mary, it
didn't go further than that. They had a good working relationship, but they didn't
become close friends. Gottlieb "seemed to recall thinking at the time that Mary
was a big drinker."[4]

Walton recalled Mary "was so vain . . . she wouldn't allow any rewriting whatsoever," and he suggested Gottlieb published Mary's manuscript as it was written.
Walton told Megan Desnoyers that Gottlieb did so because "they wanted her, just
her name. They didn't want someone else to get it."[5] Gottlieb takes exception to
Walton's remarks, calling them "bitchy and preposterous," for why would he care

if someone else published the book if he didn't think it was very good. He believed his job as a publisher was to get books to the people who would enjoy them, and he thought there were "enough people interested in Hemingway to want to know what his final wife made of him." Gottlieb resented Walton's imputation that he published Mary's book to prevent someone else from getting it. At this remove of fifty years, Gottlieb doesn't recall whether he knew Mary was planning to publish with Scribner's, but it "wouldn't have bothered [him] in the least, for many of the successful books he edited and published had been rejected by other publishers."[6]

As to the suggestion that Mary's book was published without any changes, while Gottlieb doesn't remember the precise editing process for this book (one of eight hundred to one thousand he edited during his career), he knows what kind of reader he is, and he is, "a very hands-on editor, on both a large scale and on the sentence-to-sentence scale." It is inconceivable to him that he didn't have editorial thoughts about Mary's book because he has editorial ideas about everything he reads. There is no reason why he would have excepted Mary "from my standard procedure, which is to say this part is absolutely wonderful and just in the right proportion, there's too much of this, and I would like more of that." This is what he did with Bill Clinton, Katharine Graham, Lauren Bacall, and all the famous people he edited. "It is inconceivable I did not have editorial views and that I did not share them in some perhaps sugarcoated way because we were always tactful with our writers." Mary may have made it clear it was her version or nothing, and he may have been willing to publish it more or less as it was, but he still would have given it a thorough review and made suggestions. As Mary lived in New York during this time, he probably gave his editorial input in face-to-face meetings, which explains why there is little editing advice in the correspondence between him and Mary.[7] Susan Buckley recalls Peter and Mary discussing the possible move to Knopf and Mary saying that Gottlieb was prepared to publish the manuscript "without the heavy-handed editing advocated by Scribner's that would have substantially changed the piece."[8]

Knopf introduced *How It Was* in its catalog for 1976, describing the book as "the richest, most intimate and alive portrait of Ernest Hemingway we will ever have . . . written by the vibrant, spirited woman who was married to him for 15 years and who gives us now the whole story of her life." The story of their life together made for "a book whose concreteness, immediacy and feeling make us know—make us understand—how it was."[9] Knopf launched *How It Was* with a grueling cross-country tour. On September 22, Mary was the guest of honor at a dinner at The Lotos Club in New York City, and later that week, she gave media interviews. Mary flew to Texas for sessions in Houston and Dallas. She addressed the Wellesley Club Book and Author luncheon, then flew back across the country for events in Washington, Boston, Chicago, Alabama, Pittsburgh, New York, Nashville, Los Angeles, San Francisco, and finally, Philadelphia. The tour was simultaneously exhilarating and exhausting. She appeared on local television and radio programs and before women's clubs, literary societies, and university audiences.

For these events, Mary perfected a stump speech. The *Chicago Tribune's* celebrated society editor, Eleanor Page, covered Mary's presentation to the Chicago Women's Athletic Club in October 1977. Page's account shows the gusto Mary put into these performances. She began with a tease about a forthcoming book by Ernest and then filled her "chat" with vignettes about writers she had met during her travels. She described Clare Boothe Luce, who padded her oval dining room walls with pink satin, and Carl Sandburg, who became angry at Mary for suggesting that he, a Swede, sing an Irish ditty to newspaper reporters. She told of meeting George Bernard Shaw, who, when she complimented him on his costume, replied, "the surfaces of objects seldom proclaim the contents." J. B. Priestley advised her when she read radio reports to America, "Just sound sincere—no matter the lie you are telling." After she interviewed him in his home, H. G. Wells stuck out his face saying, "I exact an exit permit." Mary pecked his cheek.

Mary described her life with Ernest as "voluptuous—not as rich Americans live in Barbados, but in the sense of time. We had time to do what we enjoyed—swim naked, listen to the trees and birds—and to me, that is voluptuous." On safari, they ate loin of lion, which tasted "delicate like veal but with a firmer texture," and onboard *Pilar*, they hung marlin to age, like beef. Soon after he met her, Ernest said, "I want to marry you—you remind me of a Mayfly." Mary told the assembled ladies, "I thought it had something to do with fishing." Mary sang for her appreciative audience, and, as Page reported, "Mary may be touted as another Edith Piaf, some of the audience decided after hearing her sing two songs. (Mary has Piaf's petite figure, low, sexy voice, and earthy wistfulness.)" [10] One song told of a handsome soldier who hid under the bed when the fighting started, and the other was the one she'd sung with Ernest the night before he died. She did not mention that sad fact to the ladies.

How It Was received mixed reviews. The popular press welcomed the book, and reviewers complimented its author. Ballantine's brought out a paperback edition arrayed with blurbs from positive reviews. The book was, "As honest and revealing as anything Hemingway ever wrote!"[11] Mary's "Life was lived at a magnum pulse . . . A gift to us from the much-loved woman who always knew she was alive. They'll be reading it for generations."[12] "A rare, and quite possibly, a great achievement!"[13] "The most authentic memoir about Ernest Hemingway so far published."[14] "A glorious book . . . A vital portrait of Ernest Hemingway emerges . . . Filled with priceless glimpses of Hemingway as only she knew him."[15] Carlos Baker wrote a friendly, if verbose, review. "Long, lively, highly informative, packed to the brim, even running over, with the names and characteristics of people and places, speedily paced and well written, her narrative hums along like a well-tuned engine."[16] Jan Herman judged, "composed from diaries she kept with diligence during their fifteen-year marriage, the book is an enormous feat of reporting, easily read, superbly detailed and, most of all, candid."[17]

Others remained skeptical. E. R. Hagemann complained Mary's book was "either boring or dull, except in snatches here and there." Hagemann found it almost impossible to believe Mary Welsh lived with Ernest Hemingway for sixteen years, "and in the end comes up with so little of him." She presented "too many menus, too many diary entries, too many trivial events . . . and missed, deliberately or accidentally, opportunities to portray Ernest Hemingway, one of the masters of our literature." Hagemann said, "We care not a whit about her, yet she doesn't seem to understand or care. She must tell us of her parents, their illnesses, to the end."[18] Christopher Lehmann-Haupt complained "her autobiography is like an almost interminable list of names, animals, activities, and events; shapeless in form and tone; almost manic." In its "determination to keep moving, keep drinking, keep eating, keep socializing . . ." it does "not pause to weigh the relative value of the increments of life, not stop to reflect and define. It can be infuriating."[19]

Bernice Kert believed the criticism, though fair enough, hurt Mary, despite her toughness. "As a journalist, she had insisted that facts must speak for themselves. But she loaded the pages with unnecessary details and then zealously guarded them against the efforts of an editor."[20] Kert found exasperating "Mary's extreme reluctance to pause for reflection or examine her feelings." Rose Marie Burwell called *How It Was* "a chirpy unreliable memoir."[21] She sensed from the book "a pervasive superficiality, and I thought she wasn't capable of deeper feeling."[22] Bill

Walton found the book "horrible" because it contained "marvelous material. But she never had the right insight." He told Megan Desnoyers, "journalism does not necessarily make good books."[23] Valerie Hemingway found the book, "dull. It was like a journal. I was disappointed because the time I spent with the Hemingways was so exciting, so filled with joie de vivre and Mary's account seemed matter of fact."[24] Valerie said, when Mary wrote the book, "her memory was faulty. The part that dealt with what I knew was riddled with errors, intentional or not. It would've been simple for her to ask me various things since we saw each other a couple of times a week." Valerie concluded, "for whatever reason, she invented instead. She was already drinking heavily, and her judgment was impaired."[25]

After dinner at Mary's apartment one evening, Robert Gottlieb scribbled a note. "Just to thank you for last night, Angel of Mercy—for delicious Chinese chicken and for taking my friend in and for generally existing! Much love from your dreamboat—who to himself is more like an all-too-real old scow!"[26] Gottlieb describes the note as "jokey, but there was nothing underneath." Though he could not recall the evening, he thought the friend he brought was likely his now-wife of fifty years, the actress, Maria Tucci. When he checked with his wife, she could not recall ever having met Mary or being in her home, "and her memory is highly acute . . . We'll never know" which friend he brought to dinner.[27] Mary thought so highly of Gottlieb and his team that she acknowledged their contribution following the title page of her book, "Hail to RAG and his tribe."

In June 1977, Mary became agitated copies of her book were not available in book shops in Portland, Akron, Denver, or five bookstores in New York City. She asked Gottlieb, "are your salesman lame, blind, and halt?" She signed off, "You are a beautiful editor and my dreamboat. But you are a lousy salesman. Hardly necessary to clarify, but I am pissed off."[28] Mary's riposte tends to confirm Gottlieb's recollection she submitted to his editorial pencil. He replied the next day, "You are an angel of a woman and a good writer. But you will not grasp the realities of the book business. Here they are." Gottlieb lectured that the laws of economics required booksellers to return books still unsold after the first several months of a book's life. That explained why particular bookshops no longer stocked *How It Was*. Knopf sent out forty-six thousand copies of the book, and fifteen thousand copies returned for a net sale of thirty-one thousand copies. "Un-piss-off yourself, Mary. You are truly wrong about this and making me crazy into the bargain. Yours despairingly, Bob."[29] Mary replied five days later, thanking Gottlieb for his "prompt, kind, and instructive reply." She apologized for being "churlish as well as ignorant."[30] Reminded of the sales numbers, Gottlieb says, "looking back today, thirty-one thousand copies of a book like Mary's was an extremely good, pleasant result."

Two weeks later, Gottlieb replied, "all books are returnable like this; one-third is not in the least remarkable! Which is why publishers go gray (or are about to). So, you don't even have the distinction of having done worse than anyone else."[31] When Mary returned from a trip to Cuba the following year, Gottlieb wondered, "Shouldn't you be offering a piece on it to a mag? Maybe I should have been your agent, not just your editor!" Next, he sent the good news that the book's paperback rights had been sold to Futura in England. "The advance isn't large—one thousand pounds—but in English standards, that isn't so bad, and the important thing is that a good firm will bring it out and make it available to that many more people." Gottlieb remarked, "So I'm pleased and hope you are!"[32] Mary replied, saying it was "dandy" the paperback rights had been sold to Futura, "a very conscientious outfit."[33]

Mary never intended to analyze Ernest's writing method or create a nuanced portrait of him. Instead, as a gritty reporter who had learned her trade in wartime, Mary set about telling the story of her life, including her relationship with Ernest, from her point of view. The title of her memoir, *How It Was*, suggests the author will reveal the truth about how things transpired. Comparing Mary's autobiography with her correspondence, diaries, and journals shows she constructed a particular version of life with Ernest. She wanted the world to understand the celebrated author loved her, and, despite their difficulties, she loved him in return. Mary presented the facts in a journalistic style, but she left out inconvenient facts.

I have pointed out discrepancies between Mary's memoir and her correspondence and journal entries. She failed to mention her love for Noel Monks and the painful demise of their relationship. She left out his letters. Mary downplayed the importance of her connection with Irwin Shaw and her desire to marry him instead of Ernest, and she did not mention Ernest's impotence or her agreement to give him six months to recover. She lied about who killed her lion, omitted the Kikuyu fight for independence, ignored Philip Percival's extreme racism, passed over Ernest's role as a game warden in pursuing the Mau Mau, and left out her anthropomorphic dreams in Africa. She failed to include the story of Ernest driving drunk and causing the car accident in Cuba. Mary omitted details of Ernest's physical and verbal abuse. She left out Ernest's brutality before and after Pauline's death, and her craven acceptance of two-hundred and fifty dollars to makeup. Mary left out her letters to Ernest threatening to leave him and explaining her reasons for doing so. She failed to describe her despair at the prospect of spending the rest of her life caring for her depressed and delusional husband. Nor did she mention Dr. Rome's assessment of Ernest or discuss his treatment. She failed to acknowledge her role in creating the "accident narrative" of Ernest's death, which, but for Emmett Watson, Sheriff Hewitt, and Hotch, would likely have become the accepted story of Ernest's demise. Mary "lost" or destroyed Ernest's letter to Hadley, which proved Hadley's ownership of the Miró painting. She left out her effort to prevent Hotchner from publishing his account of Ernest's mental decline, and she omitted much about Ernest's will and the murky arrangements she and Alfred Rice made. Mary persuaded herself these critical and sometimes self-incriminating episodes were no one's business.

FORTY-EIGHT

It's a Beautiful Place of Bougainvillea and Poinsettia, but the Heart of it is Gone

May 1977–July 1977

On May 3, 1977, Metro-Goldwyn-Mayer's vice president, Richard Shepherd, announced MGM planned a film about the life of Ernest Hemingway at a press conference at the 21 Club in New York City. MGM had purchased the film rights to Mary's book to assist the scriptwriter, Waldo Salt, who had won an Oscar for his screenplay of *Midnight Cowboy*. They hoped to film some sequences in Cuba and said Mary and film officials would travel to Cuba in July to make arrangements. Shepherd stated the film was budgeted for "many, many, many millions of dollars—all put up by MGM." Production of the film was scheduled to begin in the fall of 1978.

Mary declined to say how much MGM paid for her book, and she did not expect to have much to do with the film. "I don't know anything about movie scripts. I know something about the subject but nothing about the technique." When asked what she thought about recent books concerning her husband, she answered with one word, "horseradish." Ending the interview, Mary moved to the bar in the 21 Club and asked, "Now, could I have a short snort?"[1]

In late June, the producer, Jay Weston, spoke about plans for the film. "We want to tell the Hemingway story, through the eyes of his former wives and his mistress. The mistress is the Lady Brett character, from *The Sun Also Rises*." Though there was no record of an actual affair, Weston asserted, "emotionally, she was his mistress." They hoped Faye Dunaway, Jane Fonda, and Diane Keaton would play his first three wives. "Shirley MacLaine has asked us if she can play Mary Hemingway." The screen story started with Ernest Hemingway at nineteen, when he was wounded as an ambulance driver in Italy. The film would unfold in "a nonconsecutive fashion through the Paris years, the Spanish Civil War, his time as a World War II correspondent when he liberated the Ritz wine cellars in Paris . . . Everything." Weston hoped Robert Redford would play Hemingway, though Steve McQueen also wanted the role. [2]

In July 1977, sixteen years after her last visit to retrieve Ernest's manuscripts, correspondence, and some of their art, Mary returned to Cuba. She was now sixty-nine years old but still filled with energy. Her visit lasted only five days, from Friday, July 8, to Wednesday, July 13. Though MGM had retained Mary as a consultant for the biographical movie, tentatively titled "Hemingway," Mary didn't presume they would make it a film about her life. "I don't mind. They paid me a bundle." [3] Weston, director Sidney Pollack, and screenwriter Waldo Salt accompanied Mary to Cuba and scouted scenes for the film. Pollack told reporters that Hemingway was a tough subject to tackle. "A great myth has grown up around him because of his preoccupation with macho and his childish behavior in public." For that reason, many people in the United States think they have outgrown him. "We are hoping that through Mary, we can get a feel for the more vulnerable side of Hemingway, for the private man." [4]

When asked who would play her on-screen, Mary replied, "Obviously, I hope they pick someone attractive, charming, witty, and delightful, natch. Who wants to be portrayed by an inarticulate lump?" [5] Mary visited the Finca and had a few minutes to wander through her old home, on her own, without the pack of reporters following her every move. The Cubans had maintained the place carefully and faithfully and had changed almost nothing. Ernest's reading glasses rested on his desk just as he left them, next to a stack of unopened mail. The tableware Mary found in Murano, and the ashtray she had bought in Paris, were in place, bearing the Hemingway crest Mary had designed. The Cubans had even arranged the bottles of liquor next to Ernest's chair. Mary had forebodings about returning to the Finca, but as she looked through her old things, she told reporters, "I didn't feel sad, why should I? I had a very good seventeen years there." [6] "Without Ernest, it is another place. It's a beautiful place of bougainvillea and poinsettia, but the heart of it is gone as far as I'm concerned."[7] Mary was amazed at how Havana had grown. When she left Cuba, the main thing one could see from the Finca was the National Assembly's dome, but now high-rises, workers' homes, and hospitals filled the view.

Mary met Fidel Castro at the presidential palace, and they talked for three hours. Castro's durability impressed her: "The first thing I said to Fidel was you haven't changed at all." He looked wonderful and in fine shape. "He doesn't have the stomach Ernest had, but otherwise looks so much like Ernest—the beard, the way his head sits on his shoulders, the height. Fidel is just the sort of man who appeals to me."[8] They chatted about Greece and Turkey's problems, about the lack of food south of the Sahara Desert, and world climate conditions. Mary asked Castro for forty books in the Finca library for the Ernest Hemingway Room in the John F. Kennedy Memorial Library in Boston. Weston recalled, "Castro exploded with mock indignation." He asked, "do you want me to be stood up against the wall and shot by the Cuban people?" He explained many thousands of visitors came each year, including sailors, tourists, small farmers, and fishermen. "I would be a traitor if I was to disturb this museum. You don't know what you're asking."[9] Castro suggested he could have reproductions of the books made for the Kennedy Library, but Mary insisted on the originals. Castro finally dropped the subject, saying he would take it under consideration. Then they started exchanging recipes.

Fidel told Mary how to make a delicious lobster dish. First, prepare a French "court bouillon," with fish heads, bones, and tails, and then cook the lobster in the bouillon. He guaranteed the dish would be much richer and tastier. In exchange, Mary told Fidel about her secret for ceviche. The trick was not to slice the lime until it was time to squeeze it. She told him not to put the lime juice in a jar ahead of time, for the action of the air had some negative chemical effect. "Just squeeze the juice on, and five minutes later, after you do, the fish is cooked."[10] Before she left, Mary sang an old revolutionary war hymn as a parting gesture.[11] Mary thoroughly enjoyed her meeting with Fidel and told reporters, "He is so alert, so smart, he keeps coming out with small witticisms. He was very gracious and said the Cubans would help in any way they could to make the film."[12]

Mary had a chance to talk with Gregorio Fuentes, who had been the master of *Pilar*. "He was older but good and strong." She had the joy of going fishing, and her hosts had the proper gear. Though they were out all day, they didn't get a bite, and Mary told reporters, "I waited for a Marlin to take to Fidel." On her final day in Havana, Mary posed for pictures with Fidel, and he took the occasion to praise Ernest's works. Fidel had read *For Whom the Bell Tolls* more than once and *The Old Man and the Sea* three times. He told again how invaluable *For Whom the Bell Tolls* had been in helping him plan guerrilla strategy in the Sierra Maestra. "We had to face an army and carry out a war like Hemingway wrote about in his book. It especially inspired me."[13] The *Minneapolis Star and Tribune* featured a photo of Mary "looking astonished at Fidel Castro's remarks" at the presidential palace.

Mary formed a positive impression of Cuba under Castro because unlike other communist countries she had visited, where the people felt restrained, the people seemed free in Cuba. "The Cubans were always cheerful, witty, and bright, no matter how little education they had, and as far as I can tell, the national character seems not to have changed."[14] Two days after her return to New York, Mary wrote to Castro. She told him her brief visit had been "joyous and enlightening." It pleased her to see "how very much your government has done for the betterment of the Cuban 'Pueblo,' how they retain their traditional sense of personal independence and good humor." She was pleased to see "how beautifully your administrators have maintained our old home." She thanked him for his many kindnesses and the most generous hospitality.

Mary sent along a copy of *Islands in the Stream*, for part of it was set in Cuba, and she explained to Castro why she had donated Ernest's papers to the JFK library. She knew relations between Kennedy and Castro had been fraught, but she thought it essential to justify her decision in terms he could understand. She wrote, "Ernest admired the late President Kennedy for saving the crew of his sunken boat in the war in the Pacific." That "was why I chose his library, rather than any of the others, as the repository of all of Ernest's manuscripts, letters, papers, and private books."[15]

Mary never saw Fidel, or Cuba, again.

FORTY-NINE

Life is Ruthless

September 1979–June 2019

V alerie remembered Mary's alcoholism became noticeable after the year she spent promoting her book. She enjoyed the months of being "toast of the town," and everyone she visited treated her well. She found the tour exhilarating, but when it ended, her life became less glamorous. Valerie commented, "Life is ruthless. You're the hero today, but next week someone else is the hero." This applied with a vengeance to Mary, who fell into a complete retreat after the attention ended. Valerie recalled Mary always drank a lot. She was a gin and tonic person, and she preferred that cocktail, or a martini, to the fine bottles of wine Ernest consumed. After the book tour, Mary sought respite from her loneliness and boredom in gin. [1]

Bernice Kert visited Mary when she was seventy-one years old at her home in Ketchum in September 1979. They relaxed together on the deck overlooking the Big Wood River on a hot afternoon. Small and frail, Mary carried her re-injured elbow in a sling, and her red-rimmed and watery eyes drew attention from her weathered skin. Mary's voice still sounded "musical, and she seemed faintly amused that anyone would travel so far to see her, especially since she remembered so little about the past." [2] As Kert persisted with her questions, it became clear that Mary's memory had severely deteriorated. Holding a cocktail glass with her good hand, she shrugged at Kert's questions and repeated, "Read my book. All you have to do is read the book. It's all there." [3]

Bill Walton recalled Mary's mental deterioration started in 1979, "when she turned into an old drunk." She lost control of her senses, and Walton stopped going to visit her, telling Alfred Rice, "Look, she doesn't even know me when I'm there. I'll tell her who I am. She says, 'Oh, hi.' And then she is gone completely, in fifteen seconds."[4] Walton told Rose Marie Burwell, "she was, as you know, a total alcoholic and a very irresponsible one." Walton worried about preserving "the big Miró painting of 'The Farm.'" He did "a lot of conniving to get it into the National Gallery for safety's sake."[5] Alfred Rice helped because he agreed the Miró should stay in the National Gallery. Walton and Rice feared "she was likely to set her bed on fire or something. The smoke would ruin that painting." The Miró never came back, and while Walton admitted "it was slightly illegal . . . it was in the interest of all. Ernest would have wanted it that way. She would have, too, in her right mind."[6]

Walton was eighty-four years old when he proudly recounted to Burwell how they saved the Miró and got the rest of the papers Mary had in her apartment to the Kennedy Library. He believed that the library treated Mary well. "They never closed in and kept asking for more. She sent them essentially everything." He told Burwell, "We are just lucky that she didn't lose them and everything because they were always just lying around her apartment." Burwell interrupted her 1993 interview with Walton to praise his actions in persuading and assisting Mary to keep the papers together and putting them in the Kennedy Library. They were "probably the most significant things that have been done for American literature in this century." She stated "there is no other author who had the influence on modern literature that Hemingway had, nor for whom we have the record of the composition and revision process which the Hemingway archives at the Kennedy have made available to scholars."[7] The Kennedy Library opened the Hemingway Room on July 18, 1980, and Jacqueline Kennedy Onassis attended the ceremony, with Patrick Hemingway representing the family.

Patrick remembers the opening ceremony very well. Alfred Rice asked him to attend because Mary was not competent to travel. "She became permanently alcoholic. I would say she was already started before Papa's death." Patrick and Clara Spiegel "made very hard attempts to intervene in her alcoholism. We did an intervention, but we just couldn't get her to quit. In her last days, she existed on two things, gin and milk. She suffered from alcoholic dementia."[8]

Valerie visited Mary in her penthouse and noticed there was little food in the refrigerator. Instead of groceries, Valerie found milk cartons, filled two-thirds with gin, and topped off with milk. "That's all she had. It sounds awful, but that's what she had before she went to St. Luke's."[9] Mary began hallucinating in 1981, and Alfred Rice feared she might be close to death. Rice asked Valerie to come to New York to sign Mary into St. Luke's Hospital because she had become Mary's closest living relative. Valerie visited Mary in the hospital during the days and spent the nights in Mary's apartment. On the third day, while Rice and Valerie discussed funeral plans, Mary started recovering. Mary begged Valerie to take her home to Montana, and Valerie seriously considered the idea and told me she would have welcomed Mary to her home. Still, she feared that Greg might poison her—his hostility to her had become that extreme.[10]

Rice arranged for Mary to receive twenty-four-hour nursing care in her penthouse, and Valerie visited her whenever she came back to New York. Mary continued to decline and began suffering from delusions. On one visit, Mary asked Valerie if she was twenty-one yet, and when she was planning to get married. At that point, Valerie was over forty, and Mary couldn't recognize or remember the photos of Valerie's children on her dressing table.[11] Mary spent her last years in the company of people employed to look after her. She retained sufficient funds to avoid the indignity of an institution, but she had no relatives or friends, and she fretted that her caregivers were stealing from her.

Mary died at the age of seventy-eight years on Wednesday, November 26, 1986, at St. Luke's Hospital in Manhattan. Death released her from an addled state, and her body was cremated, as she had instructed, and her ashes were interred in the Ketchum cemetery next to Ernest's grave at 11 A.M. on December 5. Valerie joined Jack, his wife Puck, and their daughter Muffet by the graveside. They greeted a few friends, including George Saviers and Clara Spiegel. Everyone attending, except Valerie, lived in Idaho.

As Mary had requested, there was no service, and there were no prayers or speeches before her ashes were deposited next to Ernest's grave. Valerie described the sad scene as the funeral director "placed a small pine-colored plastic box on an oblong piece of emerald Astroturf that covered the freshly dug grave. It could have been a cheap toolbox purchased at Kmart. The brief ceremony was over."[12] At a family lunch in a local coffee shop that followed, no one mentioned Mary. Her death could not have been lonelier or less lamented, and the driven, determined spirit that was Mary Welsh simply dissipated. Valerie said, "I admired certain aspects of her character, but I knew her far too well to be bowled over. Such is life!"[13]

Today, a large rectangular stone slab bearing Mary's name and dates rests between a similar slab for Ernest and a smaller stone for Taylor "Beartracks" Williams. Pilgrims have placed coins and pebbles on both slabs. On the morning of my last visit, a dead sparrow lay crumpled in the grass next to Mary's grave, and I remembered Mary sang the songs of the "Sparrow," Edith Piaf. The two sixteen-foot pines Mary planted at Ernest's burial are now forty or fifty feet tall. Their branches shade the graves, and their roots embrace the slabs and penetrate the earth.

Close to Mary and Ernest's graves are the burial places of some of the family and friends who figured in this story. Ernest's chums, George Saviers, and his son, Fritz, to whom Ernest wrote his last letter, share a stone decorated with a landing mallard. George Saviers had recalled, "the last thing Hemingway ever put down on paper was the letter to my son Fritz. It was a wonderful, wonderful letter, and you would never know that Ernest was seeking death."[14] "One of Nature's Noblemen," Jack Hemingway, his wife Puck, and daughter Margaux, also a victim of suicide, rest nearby. A granite headstone bearing the bold-chiseled words, "Dr. Gregory Hancock Hemingway," sits farther away. Tillie and Pappy Arnold "rest in loving memory" beneath a stone featuring entwining roses. Chuck and Flo Atkinson lie next to each other in separate graves marked by brass bas-relief mountain views, and in the distance, the jagged peaks of the Sawtooth Mountains bear silent witness to the brevity of human existence.

If someone had read a eulogy, it would have mentioned that Mary survived Ernest for twenty-five years. She retrieved his manuscripts from Cuba and edited and published one-third of his work after his death.[15] Mary defended Ernest's reputation by maintaining his death was an accident until Hotchner betrayed her by revealing the truth. She commissioned the authorized biography, supervised Baker's work, wrote her version of life with Ernest, and spoke of their relationship to audiences across America. Finally, Mary donated Ernest's papers to the Kennedy Library. Mary had devoted herself to Ernest's memory and endured loneliness instead of seeking a new relationship.

The next day, newspapers across the country carried syndicated articles about Mary's passing. They noted her long illness and confinement to her New York apartment, mentioned her career as a war correspondent, and highlighted her marriage to Ernest.[16] *Time* magazine reported that despite living in New York City, Mary retained ownership of the home north of the Warm Springs bridge in Ketchum. She said, "I love the house and its views—folded brown mountains, space, brilliant skies, and my river crooning over its stones. Ernest wouldn't have wanted me to sell it while it gives me so much pleasure. It enfolds me."[17]

Mary's death did not end the controversy over her management of Ernest's estate. Alfred Rice drafted her will, which left a painting, but no money, to each of Ernest's sons.[18] Mary willed one hundred thousand dollars each to four charities: The World Wildlife Fund Inc., the Audubon Society, the NAACP Legal Defense Fund, and the Hospital for Joint Diseases in New York City. She left her home in Ketchum, including its contents and land, and one hundred thousand dollars to the Nature Conservancy of Idaho to create a wildlife preserve. Mary honored her promise to Bill Walton and Jacqueline Kennedy Onassis and donated to the Kennedy Presidential library Ernest's portrait by Waldo Peirce, and custody of Ernest's manuscripts. She also gave the library all the remaining books and artworks in her New York penthouse.

Mary left gifts to some step-grandchildren. Jack's daughter, Margaux, received a 19th-century tea and coffee service, an antique Phoenician necklace, and other jewelry and silverware, but Mary did not mention her sister, Mariel. Mary gave another Hemingway granddaughter, Joanne, a silver candelabra, and Valerie's daughter, Vanessa, was to receive five pieces of jewelry, though one was missing. Valerie's son Seán received thirty thousand dollars to be distributed on his twenty-fifth birthday (which accrued to more than forty thousand dollars when he received it). Valerie's other children received nothing. Peter Buckley's daughter, Annabel, received a long pearl necklace.

Mary gave the Ernest Hemingway Foundation two hundred thousand dollars to establish the PEN/Hemingway annual prize for a previously unpublished fiction writer. The residue of Mary's estate was divided into equal shares among the American Museum of Natural History in New York, the United Negro College Fund, and the Meharry Medical College, a black medical school in Nashville.[19] A liberal to the end, Mary made donations to wildlife conservation groups and societies to defend and advance people of color. What is striking is that she left virtually nothing to Ernest's sons.

All the money came from Ernest's estate on his death or later earnings from his published works and posthumously published books. Mary never made enough money from her own writing to generate savings to distribute when she died. The estate she bequeathed came from property Ernest gave to her, and which increased in value after his death. We recall Ernest left his entire estate to Mary, and he named her literary executrix. He said concerning his sons, "I have intentionally omitted to provide for my children . . . as I have complete confidence in my beloved wife, Mary, to provide for them <u>according to written instructions I have given her</u>"[20] [my underlining]. Mary said in a draft of her memoir, "He [Ernest] had never given Alfred or me any instructions, written or spoken . . ."[21]

I was startled to find Ernest's written instructions to Mary in Alfred Rice's files in the New York Public Library archives. Ernest wrote the letter by hand, dated it the same day as his will, and referred to the will he had just written. I have transcribed the letter.[22]

> September 17, 1955
> Dearest Mary,
>
> I would like you to make a will leaving my estate, which you inherit <u>under the will I made today</u>, [my underlining] so that one half of the estate will go to Bumby (John H. N. Hemingway) and one quarter to Patrick. Please leave $1000 to Gigi (Gregory Hemingway). Both Patrick and Gregory have incomes and property of their own, and it is my considered intent that this is how they should share in the estate.
>
> I will write to you later how I wish the remainder of the estate to be disposed of and various legacies I wish to leave also about executors and trustees and letters about my literary properties.
>
> This is for basic guidance on what the children are to receive, <u>as I wrote today in the will</u> [my underlining]. Let us hope we do not have to have any wills operative for a long time.
>
> With much love,
> Your husband and partner,
> Ernest Hemingway

According to Mary's draft memoir, Alfred Rice never brought this letter to her attention. The letter did not form part of Ernest's will and was not legally binding. However, Ernest expressed his wish that Mary share his estate among his sons upon her death. Jack was to receive half, Patrick one quarter, and Greg one thousand dollars. If Mary had obeyed Ernest's directions, her will would have been very different. If the sons had learned of this letter, they might not have felt so angry with, or abandoned by, their father and they could have used their moral claim on the estate to monitor Mary's administration of it. Jack would have appreciated that his father had told him the truth about his will, Patrick might have considered the distribution fair, and Greg might have been furious at his unequal treatment. At least they would have known the truth. Alfred Rice caused years of misunderstanding by failing to show Ernest's letter of instructions to Mary.

As a measure of the boys' anguish, consider what Jack told Paul Hendrickson in a 1987 interview: "I believe that he never really intended to hurt us by leaving us out of his will. My own feeling is, there must have been another will. It's never been found, though." Jack said, "Look, if you have a parent like that, who all your life has told you, 'Bum, you'll never have to worry because I've made careful provision to take care of all you boys'—well, then it just doesn't seem possible he'd turn around like that."[23] Jack suspected there was another will, and he could not believe his father failed to fulfill his promise to take care of his sons.

I wished I could tell the boys about the letter of instructions I found to stop the hurt. I felt an ethical obligation to reach out to Patrick, the only surviving son, to let him know his father had not forgotten him or neglected to provide written instructions. After I read the letter to him, Patrick told me the letter was "not an unusual action for [his father] to take, especially being so harsh with Gregory. They had a very stormy relationship." Patrick said, "I'm pleased that he remembered me."[24] As to the role of Alfred Rice, Patrick described the lengthy litigation against the lawyer. "We sued in the New York courts, and they found in our favor, and we regained our rights."[25] "We managed to come out of it quite well at the end."[26]

After Ernest died, Charlie Scribner Jr.'s close personal friend and corporate attorney, Horace Manges, came to advise him what to do with Ernest's will, and they called Alfred Rice to open the will with them. Scribner remembered, "Out came the battered valise and the two lawyers searched through it. They finally saw what might be a will." Scribner was amused "that each man held on to a part of the paper in such a way that the other couldn't wrench it out of his hand. They had joint possession, and nobody present could do any sleight of hand." Alfred Rice, "got a clear look at it, heaved a sigh of relief, and said, 'He's left everything to Mary.'"[27] It seems likely Ernest gave his will to his publisher instead of his lawyer so Rice would not be aware that he had lost the role of literary executor.

When Rice had a chance to consider the will, it probably alarmed him because Mary, not he, would control the literary estate. Rice used his "loving" friendship with Mary to defeat Ernest's wishes, coaxing Mary to appoint him as her attorney, especially concerning her role as literary executrix. Rice took command over decisions to publish new books, re-issue titles, and serialize or dramatize works. Most importantly, he had control over the future income stream from the lucrative estate.

Valerie Hemingway explained to me why Greg was angry with Rice. Valerie had introduced Greg to Norman Mailer after they were married, and they attended a party at the Mailers' in 1969. There, they met Jerry Leiber, the songwriter who authored Elvis Presley's "Hound Dog," and Leiber told Greg the children of writers cannot be disinherited. Leiber referred to a United States Supreme Court decision about the rights of the widow and children of a songwriter to share in the renewal of copyright. [28] According to Valerie, "Greg didn't believe it until he had the best copyright lawyers in the States tell him it was so." [29] The law is quite clear. Under the Copyright Act then in force, before the original twenty-eight-year term for copyright expired, an application could be made to renew the copyright for a second twenty-eight-year term, by the author, if still living, or the widow or children of the author. [30] In the case Leiber mentioned, the court ruled, "on the death of the author, the widow and children of the author succeed to the right of renewal as a class, and are each entitled to share in the renewal term of the copyright." [31]

This meant the three sons were entitled to share with Mary in the royalties from the renewal term of the copyrighted material, notwithstanding Ernest's will which gave Mary all of his property. When Greg questioned Alfred Rice about the entitlement of himself and his brothers, Rice said they had waived their rights to a share in the renewals when they accepted quarter shares of the foreign rights. Greg reviewed the Foreign Rights Trust agreement and found it was silent as to renewal rights. The sons threatened legal action and negotiated a settlement with Rice, splitting the royalties from the renewal rights four ways and doubling the income each of them received. "Apart from being angry with his father for not leaving him anything in his will, Greg was fully aware that once Mary died, if nothing else, the three sons would inherit the copyrights bringing in a considerable income, so his daily prayer and wish was that Mary would die and soon." [32]

According to Valerie, "Mary was not a stupid person; she was complicit with Alfred in denying the sons their fair share." [33] After Mary died, the sons sued

Rice, but the case was not settled until after Rice's death when, according to Greg, the sons received more than a million dollars. Over the next several years, the sons received more than a million dollars each in royalties. Valerie wrote to me, "I think you can see from this why none of the sons were fond of Mary . . . all three felt that Mary had been less than fair with them."[34]

Greg told Valerie that Rice tried to sell as many rights for films or TV as he could before the books came into renewal so the boys would be shut out of any substantial income, other than regular royalties. "Mary made huge amounts of money, and she arranged for the paintings and papers and other items that would have been in her estate, to be donated, though not handed over in some cases till her death." That way she could "avail herself of the tax benefits in her lifetime."[35]

Mary's management of Ernest's estate shows her strength and determination, if not her generosity. Ernest's sons had all withdrawn from their father, leaving Mary alone to deal with his decline. She may have felt they didn't deserve anything given their abandonment of Ernest. Though she hid behind Alfred Rice, she was supportive of his efforts to manage her affairs.

Mary's love for Ernest was informed by a pragmatic assessment of her best interest. Some observers of their relationship said any self-respecting woman would have left Ernest and struck out on her own. Mary considered that option carefully but decided her best course was to endure Ernest's tempestuous outbreaks and focus on her underlying love for him. She told him, several times, she would leave if that is what he wanted and if he expressed his wishes to her in the morning when he was sober. She demanded a mature discussion and clear decision—she would not respond to drunken innuendo or cruel treatment—but Ernest never came forward. Mary owed him her life, their bond was more profound than a marriage vow, and they had a fulfilling sexual life, which allowed them both to satisfy their fantasies and discover gender fluidity. This was a significant factor in the longevity of their marriage and found expression in his writing. Ernest's psychiatrist observed Ernest was dependent on Mary, but he was unhappy about it: "dependent and yet constantly struggling against an admission of it for fear that it would betray some weakness." Dr. Rome wrote, "He wanted you to know . . . that he had a real need of you."

Ernest believed Mary was essential to his creative work, and she thought the sacrifice of her career was a valuable contribution to the artistic achievements of her husband. When Mary survived Ernest, she felt entitled to the estate she had helped to create. Her desire to control Ernest's legacy, and the works he had stored in bank vaults, was compensatory for the freedom she gave up in marrying him. If she could not control her life when she was with him, she could do it afterward. Like many widows, she idolized their relationship once he was gone.

The tough little girl who sang Irish ballads with her father in the wheelhouse of the *Northland* maneuvered her way into wartime journalism and became the first woman writing about foreign affairs for *Time-Life*. Mary survived the worst of the Blitz and thrived in London's chaotic, sex-charged atmosphere, dating generals, journalists, and novelists and sleeping with whom she pleased. When Ernest Hemingway came along, Mary was not intimidated by the world-famous writer, only the latest man to pursue her romantically. She eventually succumbed to Ernest's insistent overtures, believed he loved her, and married him. Despite his occasional cruelty, she knew he did not have the courage, when he was sober, to ask her to leave him. He needed her fine, clear intelligence to guide him like a compass. Mary loved him despite himself, and her underlying optimism and strength kept her sane during the downward spiral of his health and spirit. She survived his suicide and loved being Hemingway's widow, directing his literary legacy, and enjoying the celebrity it brought to her. Enduring occasional loneliness, she filled her days with writing, public speaking, friends, and glamorous social events.

For a woman born in 1908 in a tiny lumber town in Minnesota, Mary lived a surprisingly independent life on the world stage. She met and provoked her generation's leading politicians, military leaders, and writers with a lively, mocking sense of humor. Yet, a firm understanding of her own worth sustained Mary throughout her life, and she set her moral compass to pragmatic. Mary was brave and tough and pursued her interests passionately. Writing gave her life meaning, and when she finished her memoir and the exciting promotional tour that followed, she gave up her typewriter and surrendered to gin.

ACKNOWLEDGMENTS

I first read *A Moveable Feast* six years after it was published, when I was twenty-one years old and studying French in Aix-en-Provence. Ernest Hemingway's recollection of his days in Paris when he was a young man, trying to become a writer, inspired me with its freshness and immediacy. It spoke to me directly, perhaps because I too was writing in French cafés hoping the muse would visit. I became intrigued by Ernest, and wondered about the connection between his personal life and his literature.

I spent much of my career as a law professor and dean at the faculty of law at the University of Alberta, a chief federal negotiator resolving treaty claims with Indigenous people, and a labor arbitrator and mediator. I studied and wrote about the law but maintained an ongoing interest in Hemingway. I read the biographies and the books about his wives and attended conferences where I met Hemingway scholars.

I encountered Mary's memoir, *How it Was*, and she attracted me with her lively style and vivid story of her life with Ernest. I noted that critics dismissed Mary for lacking depth or self-awareness and merely living on the surface (Burwell) or being the lowest born of the four wives (Meyers). Some dismissed her for failing to analyze Ernest due to her lack of understanding or intellectual power (Desnoyers, Walton) and for being a mere "caretaker wife" (Dearborn). Martha Gellhorn went so far as to call her a "maggot of history." As I learned more about Mary, I began to think they wrote her off too quickly. I found she was of a good family, brave, disciplined, intelligent, an excellent writer, and aware of the inner and often bizarre workings of Ernest's mind. Mary seemed a deeper, more profound person than they said and an admirable woman who had succeeded as a journalist in a man's world in wartime. I became convinced the story I found through archival research and interviews with people who knew Mary deserved to be told, not just to correct the record, but to allow readers to meet and make up their minds about this strong woman.

The eminent Hemingway scholar, H.R. (Stoney) Stoneback, encouraged me from the start of the project. He read and critiqued chapters and wrote the

Preface, which illuminates Mary. Stoney welcomed me despite the fact I was not a Hemingway scholar; indeed, he said it was time for a fresh set of eyes, and he emboldened me to review Carlos Baker's classic work and revisit other relics. Over the years, Stoney extended a hand of friendship and invited me to a Hemingway Symposium hosted by Matt Nickel at Misericordia University and a fantastic musical evening at the Arts Club in New York. I stayed with Stoney in his Victorian mansion near Poughkeepsie, and we talked through the night about Ernest and Mary and our own lives. He asked me to present my work to the plenary session at the Sorbonne during the International Hemingway Conference, and he invited me to attend his retirement party at the Players Club in New York. Throughout, we have enjoyed a lively correspondence and traded stories about Aix-en-Provence, the city in France we both love. Without Stoney's encouragement, I would not have undertaken this project.

I first met Valerie Hemingway at the Oak Park Hemingway conference in 2016, and during the intervening years, I have met her many times at Hemingway events. She generously granted me interviews so I could ask her questions about Mary and Ernest. Valerie is one of the last living witnesses of their life together, and she knew Mary well until her death. She was initially reluctant to say very much as she had promised Ernest she would never write about his personal life. Nevertheless, Valerie told me many stories about her time with Ernest and Mary that went beyond the narrative of her fine book, *Running with the Bulls*. One of my favorite memories of Valerie is the day I spent with her at her home in Bozeman, Montana, when we talked about Mary over cups of Yorkshire Gold tea at her dining room table. Valerie kindly reviewed the manuscript, made many suggestions, and agreed that Mary deserves a biography. The book is better for her candid testimony.

Susan Buckley and I had Zoom meetings during the pandemic, and she told me invaluable stories about her experiences with Mary and her husband, Peter. Susan read the manuscript and made many helpful suggestions and provided photographs. It was a pleasure to chat with Susan and get below the surface of her excellent book, *Eating with Peter*.

Patrick Hemingway and his wife Carol granted two extended interviews, which turned into delightful conversations, and he spoke frankly about Mary and his father and mother and brothers. Patrick is now ninety-three, but he is lucid and engaging, and his voice lends authenticity and a fresh perspective whenever he speaks.

Robert Gottlieb edited Mary's *How It Was*. He generously shared his recollections of Mary, during that period in her life, in a lengthy phone interview and following correspondence. Bob kindly read my manuscript and offered wise advice, and best of all encouraged me to proceed.

Bonifacio Brass, the grandnephew of Giuseppe Cipriani, welcomed my wife and me to the wonderful Locanda Cipriani on Torcello and gave us the Santa Fosca suite for five nights. He has preserved it with the original furniture since the months Mary and Ernest lived there. Bonifacio and I had long chats about Mary and Ernest and our own lives, and he encouraged me to use several photographs of Mary.

Scott Donaldson offered his perspective on Mary in two extended telephone interviews, and he offered to read the manuscript, but his death intervened. Raul Villarreal enthusiastically supported the book and told me stories about his father and Mary. Still, our plan to get together for intense discussions in Cuba could not be realized due to his sudden death. Rest in peace, Raul and Scott.

Carol Sklenicka coached me through an advanced version of the manuscript, and she taught me much about the art of biography and writing. The book is far better for her careful reading. Carol's often humorous comments buoyed my spirits, and I have enjoyed getting to know her.

I joined Biographers International Organization (BIO) two years ago and have benefitted from Zoom discussions with a roundtable of fellow biographers every two weeks. I learned from the readings and writing of my BIO friends and their comments about their challenges. Hemingway biographer Steve Paul read a chapter of the manuscript and provided helpful comments and valuable alerts about events in Hemingway country. Carl Rollyson gave me good advice at critical moments about the strategy and mechanics of biography writing, and I have come to admire his boldness and vast experience.

Retired professor Jacqueline Tavernier answered many questions about her analysis of the 1964 edition of *A Moveable Feast*. Seán Hemingway read an early draft of the chapter about *A Moveable Feast* and provided clarifying observations. Professor Linda Patterson Miller, author of the superb essay "In Love with Papa," read the manuscript and made insightful comments. Kirk Curnutt responded promptly and wisely to questions about the status of the Mary Hemingway papers.

Gerry Loughran, a retired foreign correspondent, and writer of wonderful short stories, encouraged me in my post-legal writing endeavors and asked probing questions about emerging chapters. Gordon Lees, a celebrated surgeon, assured me it was plausible that Ernest saved Mary's life after her ectopic pregnancy.

Bernadette Rule read and edited early drafts, and she believed in the project and encouraged me. Dinah Forbes edited draft chapters and provided helpful suggestions. Joelene Heathcote critiqued an early draft and guided me toward biography. Michael McGovern, Jan and Preston Randall, and Sheila Greckol read and commented on draft chapters. As an excellent veteran writer, Heather Pringle provided advice and support when I needed it most. Beth Regan and Graham Peacock read the nearly completed manuscript, and their insights and ultimate approval were heartening. Finally, the Men of the Spirit Trail sustained me with their good humor and support as we hiked through the ancient forest every Sunday morning, rain, snow, or sun.

Stacey Chamberlain, reference archivist at the JFK Library, cheerfully helped identify sources and provided scanned copies of thousands of documents. Her colleague, Maryrose Grossman, video archivist at the library, helped find photographs and their provenance despite the constraints of the pandemic.

I am grateful to my agent, Sam Hiyate, who believed in the project from the beginning, stayed supportive during the long gestation, worked effectively to solicit offers, and advised me that enthusiasm in a publisher is more important than an advance.

Claiborne Hancock, Jessica Case, and the creative people at Pegasus Books deserve credit for making a beautiful product. Claiborne's literary sense and enthusiasm for the book excited me, and Jessica's artistic sense brought it together.

A project of this size takes years of concentrated work, and I am grateful to my wife, Kate Dykstra, for putting up with the disruption and planning the research trips to almost all the places Mary and Ernest lived and visited. Kate is a sophisticated reader, having spent hours with complex legal contracts, and she reviewed the manuscript carefully and made valuable suggestions.

I owe much to the many friends and colleagues who helped me along the winding path of discovery to Mary's story, and I am indebted to all of you. But, of course, the errors or shortcomings are my own.

—Timothy Christian, North Saanich, British Columbia

Bibliography

Addison, Paul. *The Road to 1945: British Politics and the Second World War.* London: Pimlico, 1994.

Arnold, Tillie, and William L. Smallwood. *The Idaho Hemingway.* Buhl, ID: Beacon Books, 1999.

Baker, Carlos. *Ernest Hemingway: A Life Story.* London: Collins, 1969.

———. *Hemingway: The Writer as Artist.* 4th ed., Repint, Princeton, NJ: Princeton University Press, 1990.

Beach, Sylvia. *Shakespeare and Company.* New ed. Lincoln: University of Nebraska Press, 1991.

Beauvoir, Simone de. *She Came to Stay.* New York: Norton, 1999.

Beauvoir, Simone de, Constance Borde, Sheila Malovany-Chevallier, and Judith Thurman. *The Second Sex.* New York: Vintage Books/Random House, 2011.

Beauvoir, Simone de, and Peter Green. *The Prime of Life. Translated by Peter Green.* Reprint, Harmondsworth: Penguin Books, 1973.

Beauvoir, Simone de, Sylvie Le Bon de Beauvoir, and Quintin Hoare. *Letters to Sartre.* New York: Arcade Pub, 2011.

Berg, A. Scott. *Max Perkins: Editor of Genius.* New York: Berkley Books, 2014.

Blume, Lesley M. M. *Everybody Behaves Badly: The True Story behind Hemingway's Masterpiece The Sun Also Rises.* Boston: Eamon Dolan/Houghton Mifflin Harcourt, 2016.

Brennen, Carlene. *Hemingway's Cats: An Illustrated Biography.* 1st ed. Sarasota, FL: Pineapple Press, 2005.

Brian, Denis. *The True Gen: An Intimate Portrait of Ernest Hemingway by Those Who Knew Him.* 1st ed. New York: Grove Press, 1988.

Broer, Lawrence R., and Gloria Holland, eds. *Hemingway and Women: Female Critics and the Female Voice.* Tuscaloosa: University of Alabama Press, 2002.

Bruce, David K. E., and Nelson D. Lankford. *OSS against the Reich: The World War II Diaries of Colonel David K.E. Bruce.* Kent, OH: Kent State University Press, 1991.

Burke, Carolyn. *Lee Miller: A Life.* New York: Knopf, 2005.

Burrill, William, and Ernest Hemingway. *Hemingway: The Toronto Years.* Toronto: Doubleday Canada, 1994.

Burwell, Rose Marie. *Hemingway: The Postwar Years and the Posthumous Novels.* Reprint, Cambridge Studies in American Literature and Culture 96. Cambridge: Cambridge University Press, 1999.

Calabi, Silvio, Roger Sanger, and Steve Helsley. *Hemingway's Guns: The Sporting Arms of Ernest Hemingway.* Camden, ME: Shooting Sportsman, 2010.

Callaghan, Morley. *That Summer in Paris: Memories of Tangled Friendships with Hemingway, Fitzgerald, and Some Others.* Toronto: Stoddart, 1992.

Capa, Robert. *Slightly Out Of Focus*. New York: Pickle Partners Publishing, 2015.

Cappel, Constance, and Ernest Hemingway. *Hemingway in Michigan*. Waitsfield, VT: Vermont Crossroads Press, 1977.

Cassius. *The Trial of Mussolini*. London: Victor Gollancz LTD, 1943.

Cato. *Guilty Men*. London: Victor Gollancz LTD, 1940.

Chamberlin, Brewster S. *The Hemingway Log: A Chronology of His Life and Times*. Lawrence: University Press of Kansas, 2015.

Cirino, Mark. *Reading Hemingway's Across the River and into the Trees: Glossary and Commentary*. Reading Hemingway Series. Kent, OH: Kent State University Press, 2016.

Cobb, Matthew. *11 Days in August: The Liberation of Paris in 1944*. London: Simon and Schuster, 2013.

Cohen-Solal, Annie. *Sartre: a life*. New York: New Press, 2005.

Colman, Penny. *Where the Action Was: Women War Correspondents in World War II*. 1st ed. New York: Crown Publishers, 2002.

Comley, Nancy R., and Robert Scholes. *Hemingway's Genders: Rereading the Hemingway Text*. 2nd. printing. New Haven: Yale University Press, 1994.

Cowley, Malcolm, and Hans Bak. *The Long Voyage: Selected Letters of Malcolm Cowley, 1915-1987*. Cambridge, Massachusetts: Harvard University Press, 2014.

Cumberledge, Geoffrey. *BBC War Report Six June 1944 to 5 May 1945*. London: Oxford University Press, 1946.

Curnutt, Kirk. *Reading Hemingway's To Have and Have Not: Glossary and Commentary*. Reading Hemingway Series. Kent, OH: Kent State University Press, 2017.

Dearborn, Mary V. *Ernest Hemingway: A Biography*. First edition. New York: Alfred A. Knopf, 2017.

Di Robilant, Andrea. *Autumn in Venice: Ernest Hemingway and His Last Muse*. First edition. New York: Alfred A. Knopf, 2018.

Dietrich, Marlene. *Marlene*. 1st ed. New York: Grove Press, 1989.

———. *Marlene Dietrich's ABC*. Revised edition, New York: Ungar, 1984.

Diliberto, Gioia. *Hadley*. New York: Ticknor & Fields, 1992.

———. *Paris without End: The True Story of Hemingway's First Wife*. 1st edition. New York: Harper Perennial, 2011.

Donaldson, Scott. *By Force of Will: The Life and Art of Ernest Hemingway*. New York: Penguin Books, 1978.

———. *Hemingway vs. Fitzgerald: The Rise and Fall of a Literary Friendship*. Woodstock, NY: Overlook Press, 2001.

Eby, Carl P. *Hemingway's Fetishism: Psychoanalysis and the Mirror of Manhood*. SUNY Series in Psychoanalysis and Culture. Albany: State University of New York Press, 1999.

Edel, Leon. *Literary Biography*. A Midland Book, MB- 69. Bloomington: Indiana University Press, 1973.

Elder, Robert K., Aaron Vetch, and Mark Cirino. *Hidden Hemingway: Inside the Ernest Hemingway Archives of Oak Park*. Kent, OH: Kent State University Press, 2016.

Elkins, Caroline. *Imperial Reckoning: The Untold Story of Britain's Gulag in Kenya*. New York: Henry Holt & Company, 2006.

Faber, David. *Munich: The 1938 Appeasement Crisis*. London: Simon & Schuster, Limited, 2009.

Fallaci, Oriana. *Limelighters*. London: Michael Joseph, 1967.

Fantina, Richard. *Ernest Hemingway: Machismo and Masochism.* Houndmills, Basingstoke, Hampshire; New York: Palgrave Macmillan, 2005.

Farah, Andrew. *Hemingway's Brain.* Columbia, SC: University of South Carolina Press, 2017.

Feldman, Andrew. *Ernesto: The Untold Story of Hemingway in Revolutionary Cuba.* Brooklyn: Melville House, 2019.

Fleming, Robert E., ed. *Hemingway and the Natural World.* Moscow, ID: University of Idaho Press, 1999.

Fuentes, Norberto, and Larry Alson. *Hemingway in Cuba.* 1st ed. Secaucus, NJ: L. Stuart, 1984.

Gellhorn, Martha. *The Face of War.* New York: Atlantic Monthly Press, 1988.

Gellhorn, Martha, and Caroline Moorehead. *Selected Letters of Martha Gellhorn,* New York: Henry Holt & Comapny, 2013.

Gilbert, Martin. *Finest Hour: Winston S. Churchill, 1939-1941.* London: Heinemann, 1984.

Giles, James Richard. *Irwin Shaw.* Twayne's United States Authors Series, 443. Boston: Twayne Publishers, 1983.

Gottlieb, Robert. *Avid Reader: A Life.* First edition. New York: Farrar, Straus and Giroux, 2016.

Griffin, Peter. *Less than a Treason: Hemingway in Paris.* New York: Oxford University Press, 1990.

Grimes, Larry E., and Bickford Sylvester, eds. *Hemingway, Cuba, and the Cuban Works.* Kent, OH: Kent State University Press, 2014.

Groth, John. *Studio: Europe.* New York: The Vanguard Press, 1945.

Hackett, Mary. *William "Bill" Walton: A Charmed Life.* Boston: Branden Books, 2013.

Halberstam, David. *The Powers That Be.* Urbana: University of Illinois Press, 2000.

Haldeman, Joe W. *The Hemingway Hoax.* 1st edition. New York: Morrow, 1990.

Hawkins, Ruth A. *Unbelievable Happiness and Final Sorrow: The Hemingway-Pfeiffer Marriage.* Fayetteville: University of Arkansas Press, 2012.

Heilbrun, Carolyn G. *Writing a Woman's Life.* New York: W.W. Norton & Co, 2008.

Hemingway, Ernest. *A Moveable Feast.* New York: Simon & Schuster, 2010.

———. *A Moveable Feast: The Restored Edition.* New York: Scribner, 2009.

———. *Across the River and into the Trees.* New York: Simon & Schuster, 1996.

———. *Death in the Afternoon.* Harmondsworth: Penguin Books, 1976.

———. *Ernest Hemingway's A Farewell To Arms.* New York: Scribner, 1995.

———. *Green Hills of Africa.* New York: Scribner, 2015.

———. *Islands in the Stream.* 1st Scribner trade paperback ed. New York: Scribner, 2004.

———. *Men without Women.* 1st Scribner Classic/Collier ed. New York: Collier Books, 1986.

———. *The Complete Short Stories of Ernest Hemingway.* Finca Vigía Ed. Scribner Paperback Fiction. New York: Simon & Schuster, 1998.

———. *The Fifth Column and Four Stories of the Spanish Civil War.* 1st Scribner Paperback Fiction ed. New York: Scribner Paperback Fiction, 1998.

———. *The Garden of Eden.* New York: Scribner Paperback Fiction, 1995.

———. *The Sun Also Rises.* 1st Scribner Classic/Collier ed. New York: Collier Books, 1986.

Hemingway, Ernest, and Carlos Baker. *Ernest Hemingway, Selected Letters, 1917-1961.* 1st Scribner/Macmillan Hudson River ed. New York: Macmillan, 1989.

Hemingway, Ernest, and Nicholas Gerogiannis. *Complete Poems.* Revised ed. Lincoln: University of Nebraska Press, 1992.

Hemingway, Ernest, and Patrick Hemingway. *True at First Light*. New York: Scribner, 1999.

Hemingway, Ernest, A. E. Hotchner, and Albert J. DeFazio. *Dear Papa, Dear Hotch: The Correspondence of Ernest Hemingway and A.E. Hotchner*. Columbia: University of Missouri Press, 2005.

Hemingway, Ernest, Robert W. Lewis, and Robert E. Fleming. *Under Kilimanjaro*. Kent, OH: Kent State University Press, 2005.

Hemingway, Ernest, and Larry W. Phillips. *Ernest Hemingway on Writing*. 1st Touchstone ed. New York: Simon & Schuster, 1999.

Hemingway, Ernest, Sandra Whipple Spanier, Robert W. Trogdon, and Albert J. DeFazio. *The Letters of Ernest Hemingway*. Cambridge Edition of the Letters of Ernest Hemingway. Cambridge: Cambridge University Press, 2011.

Hemingway, Ernest, and William White. *By-Line, Ernest Hemingway: Selected Articles and Dispatches of Four Decades*. 1st Touchtone ed. New York: Simon & Schuster, 1998.

Hemingway, Gregory H. *Papa: A Personal Memoir*. Boston: Houghton Mifflin, 1976.

Hemingway, Hilary, and Carlene Brennen. *Hemingway in Cuba*. New York: Rugged Land, 2005.

Hemingway, Jack. *Misadventures of a Fly Fisherman: My Life with and without Papa*. Dallas, TX: Taylor Pub. Co, 1986.

Hemingway, John Patrick. *Strange Tribe: A Family Memoir*. Guilford, CT: Lyons Press, 2007.

Hemingway, Leicester. *My Brother, Ernest Hemingway*. 4th ed. Sarasota, FL: Pineapple Press, 1996.

Hemingway, Mary Welsh. *How It Was*. 1st ed. New York: Knopf, 1976.

———. *How It Was*. New York: Ballantine Books, 1977.

Hemingway, Valerie. *Running with the Bulls: My Years with the Hemingways*. New York: Ballantine Books, 2004.

Hendrickson, Paul. *Hemingway's Boat: Everything He Loved in Life, and Lost, 1934-1961*. New York: Alfred A. Knopf, 2011.

Holland, James. *The Battle of Britain Five Months That Changed History, May-October 1940*. London: Corgi, 2011.

Hotchner, A. E. *Hemingway in Love: His Own Story: A Memoir*. 1st ed. New York: St. Martin's Press, 2015.

Hotchner, A. E. *Papa Hemingway: A Personal Memoir*. Hemingway centennial ed., 1st Carroll & Graf ed. New York: Carroll & Graf Publishers, 1999.

Hutchisson, James M. *Ernest Hemingway: A New Life*. University Park, PA: Pennsylvania State University Press, 2016.

Irujo Ametzaga, Xabier. *Gernika, 1937: The Market Day Massacre*. The Basque Series. Reno: University of Nevada Press, 2015.

Johnson, Paul. *Churchill*. New York: Penguin USA, Inc., 2009.

Jones, Mervyn. *Michael Foot*. London: Gollancz, 1994.

Justice, Hilary K. *The Bones of the Others: The Hemingway Text from the Lost Manuscripts to the Posthumous Novels*. Kent, OH: Kent State University Press, 2006.

Kale, Verna, and Ernest Hemingway. *Ernest Hemingway*. Critical Lives. London: Reaktion Books, 2016.

Kershaw, Alex. *Blood and Champagne: The Life and Times of Robert Capa*. 1st Da Capo Press ed. New York: Da Capo Press, 2004.

Kershaw, Ian. *Hitler*. Abridged ed. London: Penguin, 2010.

Kert, Bernice, and Ernest Hemingway. *The Hemingway Women*. Reissued with a new author's note. New York London: Norton, 1999.

Lynn, Kenneth Schuyler. *Hemingway*. 1st Harvard University Press paperback ed. Cambridge, MA: Harvard University Press, 1995.

MacDonald, Charles Brown. *Battle Of The Huertgen Forest*. New York: Pickle Partners Publishing, 2014.

Matthews, Herbert. *The Cuban Story a Personal Interpretation of the Cuban Revolution and Its Impact on the United States and Latin America*. New York: George Braziller, 1961.

Meyers, Jeffrey. *Hemingway: A Biography*. 1st Da Capo Press ed. New York: Da Capo Press, 1999.

Michie, Allan, and Walter Graebner, eds. *Their Finest Hour the War in the First Person*. London: George Allen and Unwin LTD, 1940.

Miller, Lee, and Anthony Penrose. *Lee Miller's War: Beyond D-Day*. Reduced format paperback ed. London: Thames & Hudson, 2014.

Miller, Madelaine Hemingway. *Ernie: Hemingway's Sister "Sunny" Remembers*. New York: Crown Publishers, 1975.

Miró, Joan, and Margit Rowell. *Joan Miró: Selected Writings and Interviews*. The Documents of Twentieth Century Art. Boston: G.K. Hall, 1986.

Moddelmog, Debra. *Reading Desire: In Pursuit of Ernest Hemingway*. Ithaca, NY: Cornell University Press, 1999.

Monks, Noel. *Eye Witness*. London: Shakespeare Head, 1956.

———. *Fighter Squadrons*. London: Angus and Robertson, 1941.

Moorehead, Caroline. *Gellhorn: A Twentieth-Century Life*, New York: Henry Holt & Company, 2004.

Morgan, Kay Summersby. *Past Forgetting: My Love Affair with Dwight D. Eisenhower*. London: Collins, 1977.

Morris, James McGrath. *The Ambulance Drivers: Hemingway, Dos Passos, and a Friendship Made and Lost in War*. Boston: Da Capo Press, 2017.

Mort, T. A. *Hemingway at War: Ernest Hemingway's Adventures as a World War II Correspondent*. New York: Pegasus Books, 2017.

Nickel, Matthew C. *Hemingway's Dark Night: Catholic Influences and Intertextualities in the Work of Ernest Hemingway*, Wickford, RI: New Street Communications, 2013.

Olson, Lynne. *Citizens of London: The Americans Who Stood with Britain in Its Darkest, Finest Hour*. 1st ed. New York: Random House, 2010.

Pérez, Louis A. *The Structure of Cuban History: Meanings and Purpose of the Past*. Chapel Hill: The University of North Carolina Press, 2013.

Pilat, Oliver. *Pegler: Angry Man of the Press*. Westport, CT: Greenwood Press, 1973.

Poitras, Jacques. *Beaverbrook: A Shattered Legacy*. Fredericton, NB: Goose Lane Editions, 2007.

Pyle, Ernie. *Here Is Your War*. New York: Pickle Partners Publishing, 2016.

Rasenberger, Jim. *The Brilliant Disaster: JFK, Castro, and America's Doomed Invasion of Cuba's Bay of Pigs*. 1st Scribner hardcover ed. New York: Scribner, 2011.

Reynolds, Michael. *Hemingway: The 1930s through the Final Years*. 1st ed. New York: W.W. Norton & Co, 2012.

Reynolds, Michael S. *Hemingway: The Final Years*. New York: W.W. Norton, 2000.

Richardson, John. *A Life of Picasso: The Triumphant Years, 1917–1932*. New York: Alfred A. Knopf, 2007.

Rollyson, Carl E. *A Private Life of Michael Foot*. Plymouth: University of Plymouth Press, 2015.

Rooney, Andrew A. *My War*. New York: PublicAffairs, 2000.

Ross, Lillian. *Portrait of Hemingway*. New York: Simon & Schuster, 2015.

Rowley, Hazel. *Tete-a-Tete: The Tumultuous Lives and Loves of Simone de Beauvoir and Jean-Paul Sartre*. New York: Harper Perennial, 2013.

Sanford, Marcelline Hemingway, and Ernest Hemingway. *At the Hemingways: With Fifty Years of Correspondence between Ernest and Marcelline Hemingway*. Centennial ed. Moscow, ID: University of Idaho Press, 1999.

Sartre, Jean-Paul, and Simone de Beauvoir. *Quiet Moments in a War: The Letters of Jean-Paul Sartre to Simone de Beauvoir, 1940–1963*. 1st American ed. New York: Scribner's, 1993.

Satz, Ronald N., and Laura Apfelbeck. *Chippewa Treaty Rights: The Reserved Rights of Wisconsin's Chippewa Indians in Historical Perspective*. Madison, WI: Wisconsin Academy of Sciences, Arts and Letters, 1994.

Scribner, Charles, III, and Charles Scribner. *In the Company of Writers: A Life in Publishing*. New York: Scribner, 2010.

Shaw, Irwin. *In the Company of Dolphins: A Memoir*. New York: Open Road Integrated Media, 2016.

———. *The Young Lions*. Reprinted, [d. Ausg.] 1949. London: Cape, 1974.

Shnayerson, Michael. *Irwin Shaw: A Biography*. New York: Putnam, 1989.

Smallwood, William L. *The Day Guernica Was Bombed: A Story Told by Witnesses and Survivors*. Gernika-Lumo, Bizkaia: Gernikako Bakearen Museoa Fundazioa Gernika-Lumoko Udala, 2012.

Smith, Jean Edward. *Eisenhower: In War and Peace*. Random House trade paperback ed. New York: Random House Trade Paperbacks, 2013.

———. *FDR*. New York: Random House, 2008.

Smith, Sally, and 3M Company. *Reflected Glory*. Place of publication not identified: Simon & Schuster, 2013.

Sorel, Nancy Caldwell. *The Women Who Wrote the War*. 1st ed. New York: Arcade, 1999.

Spilka, Mark. *Hemingway's Quarrel with Androgyny*. Bison Books. Lincoln, NE: University of Nebraska Press, 1995.

Stein, Gertrude. *The Autobiography of Alice B. Toklas*. London: Penguin, 2001.

Stoltzfus, Ben. *Hemingway and French Writers*. Kent, OH: Kent State University Press, 2012.

Stoneback, H. R. *Hemingway's Paris: Our Paris?* Wickford, RI: New Street Communications, 2010.

———. *Reading Hemingway's The Sun Also Rises: Glossary and Commentary*. Reading Hemingway Series. Kent, OH: Kent State University Press, 2007.

Sylvester, Bickford, Larry E. Grimes, and Peter L. Hays. *Reading Hemingway's The Old Man and the Sea: Glossary and Commentary*. Reading Hemingway Series 5. Kent, OH: Kent State University Press, 2018.

Tavernier-Courbin, Jacqueline. *Ernest Hemingway's A Moveable Feast: The Making of Myth*. Boston: Northeastern University Press, 1991.

Taylor, A. J. P. *Beaverbrook*. New York: Simon and Schuster, 1972.

Trogdon, Robert W. *The Lousy Racket: Hemingway, Scribners, and the Business of Literature*. Kent, OH: Kent State University Press, 2007.

Vaill, Amanda. *Hotel Florida: Truth, Love, and Death in the Spanish Civil War*. 1st ed. New York: Farrar, Straus and Giroux, 2014.

Vejdovsky, Boris, and Mariel Hemingway. *Hemingway: A Life in Pictures*. Richmond Hill, Ontario: Firefly Books, 2011.

Viertel, Peter. *Dangerous Friends: At Large with Hemingway and Huston in the Fifties*. 1st ed. New
    York: N.A. Talese, 1992.

Villarreal, René, and Raúl Villarreal. *Hemingway's Cuban Son: Reflections on the Writer by His Longtime
    Majordomo*. Kent, OH: Kent State University Press, 2009.

Wagner-Martin, Linda. *Hemingway's Wars: Public and Private Battles*. Columbia, MO: University
    of Missouri Press, 2017.

Wertenbaker, Lael Tucker. *Death of a Man*. Boston: Beacon Press, 1974.

Whiting, Charles. *Hemingway Goes to War*. Stroud: Sutton, 1999.

Wise, Richard E. *Hemingway in Wartime England: His Life & Times as a War Correspondent*. London:
    Janus Transatlantic, 2017.

Woolf, Virginia. *A Room of One's Own*. Los Angeles: Green Light, 2012.

Endnotes

Abbreviations found in the endnotes:
  MH: Mary Hemingway
  EH: Ernest Hemingway
  BL: Buck Lanham
  CB: Carlos Baker
  NM: Noel Monks
  PL: Pete Lanham
  AI: Adriana Ivancich
  AH: Ed Hotchner
  AR: Alfred Rice
  JFK: JFK Library, Boston
  MHPP: Mary Hemingway Personal Papers at the JFK
  WWPP: William Walton Personal Papers at the JFK
  EHMISC: Ernest Hemingway Miscellaneous at the JFK
  BKPP: Bernice Kert Personal Papers at the JFK
  EHPP: Ernest Hemingway Personal Papers at the JFK

PROLOGUE
1. Thomas Welsh to MH, August 7, 1947, JFK, MHPP-018-001.
2. The plausibility of Ernest's action was raised by a reader who also happened to be a nurse. I asked a professor of surgery and long-time practicing surgeon, Gordon M. Lees MD, FRCSC for his opinion. He said the fact that Ernest "had the assistant make the cut makes it more plausible, particularly with his experience in the war as an ambulance attendant and the things he would have seen. The veins are quite superficial so they wouldn't be that difficult to access." Dr. Lees sent photos showing the possible veins Ernest could have accessed. Gordon Lees to the author, June 2, 2021.

CHAPTER ONE
1. Marriage of Thomas and Adeline Welsh, JFK, MHPP-027-011.
2. Marriage of Thomas and Adeline Welsh, JFK, MHPP-027-011.
3. United States Census Bureau, 2019 Population Estimates, Census.gov.
4. Autobiography of Thomas Welsh, JFK, MHPP-034-001, iii.
5. Thomas Welsh to MH, March 31, 1958, JFK, MHHP-018-001.
6. *The Bemidji Pioneer,* January 14, 1915.
7. *The Bemidji Pioneer,* August 3, 1907.
8. Hemingway, Mary, "Red Indians Buffalo Bill's Ancient Enemies are Friendly and Few These Days," *The Bemidji Pioneer,* JFK, MHPP-024-003.

9. *The Bemidji Pioneer*, July 29, 1912.
10. Hemingway, Draft of *How It Was*, JFK, MHPP-003-008.
11. Hemingway, *How It Was*, 8.
12. Hemingway, *How It Was*, 8.
13. Hemingway, *How It Was*, 22.
14. *The Bemidji Pioneer*, August 3, 1907.
15. Hemingway, *How It Was*, 27.
16. Sandburg, "Chicago," Poetry Foundation 1914, poetryfoundation.org
17. *The Bemidji Pioneer*, September 14, 1922.
18. Herskovits's work advanced the cause of ethnic and racial equality in America. *Herskovits At the Heart of Blackness*, www.pbs.org.
19. W. F. Keckeisen, to "Whom it May Concern," Undated, JFK, MHPP-029-005.
20. Mary Hemingway, *Chicago Daily News*, undated, JFK, MHPP-012-024.
21. *Chicago Sun-Times*, July 16, 1961.
22. *Chicago Sun-Times*, July 16, 1961.
23. Hemingway, *My Brother, Ernest Hemingway*, 200.
24. Mary Hemingway, *Chicago Daily News*, undated, JFK, MHPP-012-24.
25. Max Aitken was born in 1879, one of ten children, to a Scottish-born Presbyterian minister and the daughter of a prosperous local farmer and merchant in the village of Maple, Ontario, Canada. From these humble origins, Aitken became an influential industrialist and was knighted in 1911 and made a peer in 1917, taking the title Lord Beaverbrook after a stream near his birthplace. Taylor, *Beaverbrook*.
26. Ruby Parson, "True Hollywood Touch to Mary Welsh's Story," *Fargo Daily Tribune*, December 6, 1942.
27. Ruby Parson, "True Hollywood Touch to Mary Welsh's Story," *Fargo Daily Tribune*, December 6, 1942.
28. Hemingway, *How It Was*, 45.
29. Valerie Hemingway to the author, May 18, 2021.
30. *Daily Express*, April 28, 1937.

CHAPTER TWO
1. Hemingway, *How It Was*, 53.
2. *Daily Express*, September 30, 1938.
3. *Daily Express*, September 30, 1938.
4. MH to Herbert Clark, September 22, 1938, JFK, *Ernest Hemingway Papers Collection, Museum Ernest Hemingway, Finca Vigia*.
5. Mary had for some time considered marrying Herbie Clark, but her parents opposed that relationship. Mary's father criticized Clark. "I was disappointed in his general appearance a little, but much more in what I thought was a lack of respect or consideration for your mother who, I am sure he knew detested both cigarettes and liquor and yet his special service to you appeared to be in serving you with both." Thomas Welsh to MH September 14, 1937, JFK, *Ernest Hemingway Papers Collection, Museum Ernest Hemingway, Finca Vigia*. Mary refuted her father's opinion in following letters, but she decided to marry Noel instead of Herbie.
6. Noel Monks to MH, undated, JFK, *Ernest Hemingway Papers Collection, Museum Ernest Hemingway, Finca Vigia*.
7. MH to her parents, April 9, 1939, JFK, MHPP-023-001.
8. Taylor, *Beaverbrook*, xiii.

9. *Daily Express,* March 2, 1939.
10. *Daily Express,* March 3, 1939.
11. *Daily Express,* June 28, 1939.
12. Monks, *Eye Witness,* 121.
13. Mary Hemingway, "A Gift of Love," *McCall's,* December 1968.
14. http://www.evesmag.com/hemingway.htm
15. Hemingway, *How It Was,* 65.

CHAPTER THREE
1. Hemingway, "England's Peoples War," 1964, JFK, MHPP-011-011.
2. *Time,* July 22, 1940.
3. *Time,* July 22, 1940.
4. *Time,* May 27, 1940.
5. Hemingway, *How It Was,*71.
6. *Time,* September 16, 1940.
7. *Time,* September 16, 1940.
8. Hemingway, *How It Was,* 68.
9. Hemingway, "England's Peoples War," 1964, JFK, MHPP-011-011.
10. *Time,* August 26, 1940.
11. *Time,* August 26, 1940.
12. *Time,* September 9, 1940.
13. Battle of Britain Historical Society, http://www.battle of britain1940.net/0040.html, 40.
14. Welsh, Mary, "Our House Was Bombed," in Michie and Graebner, *Their Finest Hour* (New York: Harcourt, Brace, and Company, 1941), 111.
15. Welsh, Mary, "Our House Was Bombed," in Michie and Graebner, *Their Finest Hour* (New York: Harcourt, Brace, and Company, 1941), 111.
16. *Daily Telegraph,* September 16, 1940.
17. *Time,* September 30, 1940.
18. Gilbert, *Finest Hour,* 785.
19. Hemingway, "England's Peoples War," 1964, JFK, MHPP-011-011.
20. *Chicago Sun-Times,* July 16, 1961.
21. *Time,* November 4, 1940.
22. *Time,* December 30, 1940.
23. Monks, *Eye Witness,* 131.
24. MH to her parents, April 21, 1943, JFK, MHPP-023-001.
25. Monks, *Fighter Squadron,* 60.
26. Monks, *Fighter Squadron,* 242.
27. Hemingway, "England's Peoples War," 1964, JFK, MHPP-011-011.
28. Cull, *Selling War: The British Propaganda Campaign Against America.*
29. Addison, *The Road to 1945; British Politics and the Second World War,* 108.
30. Hemingway, "England's Peoples War," 1964, JFK, MHPP-011-011.
31. *The Telegraph,* July 31, 2015.

CHAPTER FOUR
1. MH to her parents, February 21, 1943, JFK, MHPP-023-001.
2. Hemingway, Draft of *How It Was,* JFK, MHPP-003-007, 106.
3. MH to her parents, April 1, 1942, MHPP-023-001
4. Nancy Caldwell Sorel, *The Women Who Wrote the War.*

5.   *Life*, January 1942, JFK, MHPP-013-019.
6.   *Life*, January 1942, JFK, MHPP-013-019.
7.   Burridge, *British Labour and Hitler's War*, 726.
8.   Hemingway, Draft of *How It Was*, JFK, MHPP-003-007, 284.
9.   MH to her parents, May 23, 1942, JFK, MHPP-023-001.
10. Later that year he was placed in charge of information and censorship, which included responsibility for twelve radio stations. He wrote to his wife, Marjorie, bragging that his power to censor extended to "troop, mail and cables, civilian mail, radio, press, cables, telephone" and that he had "a total command of 1500 in an organization never contemplated in the Army." In 1944 he became director of the newly created psychological warfare division. He was to go on to lead the American efforts to de-Nazify Germany and to establish psychological warfare as a central component of the US Army Special Forces.
11. MH to her parents, May 23, 1942, JFK, MHPP-023-001.
12. MH to her parents, June 8, 1942, JFK, MHPP-023-001.
13. *Time*, August 3, 1942.
14. MH to her parents, August 16, 1942, JFK, MHPP-023-001.
15. An interest in art and painting took root during high school, sustaining him throughout his life. His family's prosperity meant freedom from want, which, coupled with free train travel and free accommodation at hotels, allowed him to broaden his horizons with trips to the art galleries and museums of Chicago. Hackett, *William "Bill" Walton, A Charmed Life*, 215.
16. Hackett, *William "Bill" Walton, A Charmed Life*, 215.
17. MH to her parents, August 16, 1942, JFK, MHPP-023-001.
18. Hemingway, Draft of *How It Was*, JFK, MHPP-003-007, 301.
19. *Time*, August 3, 1942.
20. *Fargo Daily Tribune*, December 6, 1942.
21. MH to her parents, December 3, 1944, JFK, MHPP-023-001.
22. MH to her parents, January 23, 1943, JFK, MHPP-023-001.
23. MH to her parents, January 23, 1943, JFK, MHPP-023-001.
24. MH to her parents, January 23, 1943, JFK, MHPP-023-001.
25. MH to her parents, April 21, 1943, JFK, MHPP-023-001.
26. Hemingway, Draft of *How It Was*, JFK, MHPP-003-007, 317.
27. MH to her parents, July 19, 1943, JFK, MHPP-023-001.
28. Monks, *Eye Witness*, 131.
29. Hemingway, Draft of *How It Was*, JFK, MHPP-003-006, 318.
30. Hemingway, *How It Was*, 105.
31. Over drinks one night, Wert told Mary he scandalized his family with his first book, *Boojum!*, which he wrote when he was twenty-seven. An autobiographical novel, it followed the tragi-comic escapades of a young bohemian. Wert's maiden aunt denounced him as a pornographer and a liar for dragging out family skeletons. His second novel, *Peter the Drunk*, did not mollify his family, and now he could never go home again. He told Mary the story as a colossal joke, laughing uproariously. Mary detected his sadness at his family's rejection. It did not help that he was separated from his son, who lived with his first wife in the States.
32. Hemingway, Draft of *How It Was*, JFK, MHPP-003-007, 302.
33. Wertenbaker, Lael, *Death of a Man*, 39.
34. Schnayerson, *Irwin Shaw, a Biography*, 131.
35. MH to Walton, May 11, 1945, JFK, WWPP-001-004.

ENDNOTES

449

CHAPTER FIVE

1. Hemingway, *How It Was*, 105.
2. Kert, *The Hemingway Women*, 403.
3. Burwell, Interview with William Walton, September 25 and 26, 1992, JFK, EHMISC-009-016, 146.
4. Schnayerson, *Irwin Shaw, a Biography*, 131.
5. *Time*, August 3, 1942.
6. Kert, *The Hemingway Women*, 403.
7. *Time*, August 3, 1942.
8. Smith, *Reflected Glory, The Life of Pamela Churchill Harriman*, Loc. 1530.
9. Smith, *Reflected Glory, The Life of Pamela Churchill Harriman*, Loc. 184.
10. Hemingway, Draft of *How It Was*, JFK, MHPP-003-007, 339.
11. Hemingway, Draft of *How It Was*, JFK, MHPP-003-007, 339.
12. According to Ernest, Mary wrote the speech General Eisenhower delivered on D-Day. Baker, *Selected Letters*, 863.
13. MH to her parents, May 23, 1942, JFK, MHPP-023-001.
14. Connie's offices were a couple of minutes away through Carlisle Street over to Wardour Street, where the radio station of the Office of War Information was buried deep beneath the street.
15. Morris Ernst was well known for his defense of freedom of speech in publishing. In one of his most famous cases, he had represented the relatively new and plucky publisher Random House in 1933 in its fight for the right to import copies of James Joyce's *Ulysses*. He persuaded the court to set aside a ban on the novel, arguing that it was a work of literary merit and, therefore, not obscene.
16. Jones, *Michael Foot*, 123.
17. Schnayerson, *Irwin Shaw, a Biography*, 103
18. Hemingway, Draft of *How It Was*, JFK, MHPP-003-007, 358.
19. Hemingway, Draft of *How It Was*, JFK, MHPP-003-007, 359.
20. Schnayerson, *Irwin Shaw, a Biography*, 131.
21. Schnayerson, *Irwin Shaw, a Biography*, 132.
22. Hemingway, Draft of *How It Was*, JFK, MHPP-003-007, 358.
23. MH to her parents, October 13, 1945, JFK, MHPP-023-001.
24. Hemingway, "Diary in London and Paris," February 29, 1944, JFK, BKPP-026-003.
25. MH to her parents, October 13, 1945, JFK, MHPP-023-001, 74.
26. MH to her parents, October 13, 1945, JFK, MHPP-023-001, 74.
27. Schnayerson, *Irwin Shaw, a Biography*, 132.
28. Shaw, *The Young Lions*, 365.
29. Shaw, *The Young Lions*, 32.
30. The White Tower is now the home of the House of Ho. The outside looks the same as photos of the place in Mary's day. Fittingly, a private members club is on the second floor. When I visited recently, the Polish waitress told me I could not go upstairs because a lunch club was meeting.
31. *Times of London*, November 10, 1943.
32. Hemingway, "England's Peoples War," 1964, JFK, MHPP-011-011.
33. Hemingway, Diary in London and Paris, May 22, 1944, JFK, BKPP-026-003.

CHAPTER SIX

1. *The Daily Mail*, May 20, 1944.
2. MG to Hortense Flexner, May 17, 1944, Moorehead, *Selected Letters of Martha Gellhorn*, 163-164.

3. MG to Hortense Flexner, May 17, 1944, Moorehead, *Selected Letters of Martha Gellhorn*, 163-164.
4. Ernest used these words to describe his creative drive to his psychiatrist, Dr. Howard Rome. HR to MH, November 1, 1961. JFK EHPP-Box OM12.
5. Hemingway, *My Brother, Ernest Hemingway*, 233.
6. Hemingway, *My Brother, Ernest Hemingway*, 200.
7. Hemingway, Draft of *How It Was*, JFK, MHPP-003-007, 371.
8. Hemingway, *How It Was*, 116.
9. Hemingway, *How It Was*, 117.
10. Schnayerson, *Irwin Shaw, a Biography*, 134.
11. Hemingway, *My Brother, Ernest Hemingway*, 233.
12. Hemingway, *How It Was*, 118.
13. Hemingway, *How It Was*, 118.
14. Thirty-three years later, in March 1977, Mary received a letter from Martha Gellhorn telling her that Hemingway had proposed to her after knowing her for just three weeks in Madrid. This at a time when he was still married to Pauline. Moorehead, *Selected Letters of Martha Gellhorn*, 425.

CHAPTER SEVEN

1. Hemingway, *How It Was*, 121.
2. Hemingway, *How It Was*, 121.
3. Hemingway, *My Brother, Ernest Hemingway*, 234.
4. Hackett, *William "Bill" Walton, A Charmed Life*, 49.
5. Bill Walton didn't see Hemingway again until a month later when he turned up at Cherbourg, bringing with him all of Walton's mail, a gesture which Walton thought was "terribly sweet." Hackett, *William "Bill" Walton, A Charmed Life*.
6. Hemingway, *My Brother, Ernest Hemingway*, 236.
7. Hemingway, *My Brother, Ernest Hemingway*, 237.
8. *Times of London*, May 26, 1944.
9. We see this in a photo taken of Ernest in St. George's Hospital.
10. Hemingway, *How It Was*, 123.
11. Hemingway, *How It Was*, 122.
12. Hemingway, Draft of *How It Was*, JFK, MHPP-003-007, 105.
13. MH to her parents, June 4, 1944, JFK, MHPP-023-001.
14. Hemingway, *How It Was*, 131.
15. Hemingway, Draft of *How It Was*, JFK, MHPP-003-007, 393.
16. Hemingway, *Byline Ernest Hemingway*, 343.
17. Capa, *Slightly Out of Focus*, 1811.
18. Capa, *Slightly Out of Focus*, 1852.
19. Wise, *Hemingway in Wartime England*, 108.
20. Hemingway, *Byline Ernest Hemingway*, 355.
21. *Time*, June 19, 1944.
22. Smith, *Reflected Glory, The Life of Pamela Churchill Harriman*, Loc. 2561.

CHAPTER EIGHT

1. Hemingway, *How It Was*, 125.
2. *Time*, August 14, 1944.
3. Hemingway, Draft of *How It Was*, JFK, MHPP-003-007, 398.

4. Hemingway, *Byline Ernest Hemingway*, 361.
5. MH to her parents, June 13, 1944, JFK, MHPP-023-001.
6. Hemingway, *How It Was*, 129.
7. Six years later, he kept his promise and dedicated *Across the River and Into the Trees* "To Mary with Love." Though Mary said in *How It Was* that it was his poorest book, she was privately encouraging to him as we shall see.
8. Mary described Ernest's impotence after the car accident twelve years later in a letter to her friends, Lou and Jr. Jennings. "Anyhow he heals quickly, thank heaven, and the problem quickly ceased to exist." MH to Lou and Jr. Jennings, December 29, 1957 JFK, MHPP-023-005, 32.
9. Meyers wrote that Mary "was praised in two intolerably sentimental poems (the worst things he ever wrote)." Meyers, *Hemingway: A Biography*, 394.
10. Hemingway, *How It Was*, 129.
11. MH to her parents, July 9, 1944, JFK, MHPP-023-001.
12. Burwell, Interview with William Walton, September 25, 26, 1992, JFK, EHMISC-009-016, 26.
13. *Time*, June 6, 1944. This story published in *Time*'s D-Day issue, was the only piece with a byline.
14. Hemingway, Draft of *How It Was*, JFK, MHPP-003-007, 384.
15. Hemingway, *How It Was*, 137.
16. Hemingway, *How It Was*, 132.
17. Hemingway, *How It Was*, 132.
18. Hemingway, *How It Was*, 140.
19. Hemingway, *How It Was*, 140.
20. Hemingway, Diary in London and Paris, July 17, 1944, JFK, BKPP-026-003.
21. Stoneback, H.R. "Hemingway's Happiest Summer-The Wildest Most Beautiful Time Ever; or the Liberation of France and Hemingway," *North Dakota Quarterly* vol. 64, no. 3 (1997), 191.
22. Walton loved receiving the letters from his mother and sister about his children. For weeks afterward, he read the letters whenever he wished to escape mentally from the war. Hackett, *William "Bill" Walton, A Charmed Life*, 67.
23. Hemingway, *How It Was*, 133.

CHAPTER NINE
1. Hemingway, Draft of *How It Was*, JFK, MHPP-003-007.
2. Miller, *Lee Miller's War*, 63.
3. *Time*, August 1944.
4. In the last stanza of "Soldier," Buck wrote *I see these things, still am I slave / When banners flaunt, and bugles blow, / Content to fill a soldier's grave / For reasons I shall never know.* Lanham, "Soldier," *Harpers Monthly Magazine*, August 1, 1933, 274.
   In "Empire Builders," Lanham regretted the lack of challenges for the peacetime soldier: *No savage continent remains to dare/ The eagle's brood, no sea to try their wings. / Their talons that gripped the hearts of kings/ Now curse on perches of a dark despair.* Buck's desire for action was to be more than satisfied in the coming weeks. Lanham, "Empire Builders, *Harpers Monthly Magazine*, December 1, 1932, 68.
5. Lanham, "Hemingway-Lanham Chronology 1944-45," JFK, BKPP-022-004 34.
6. EH to MH, July 31, 1944, Baker, *Selected Letters*, 558.
7. EH to MH, July 31, 1944, Baker, *Selected Letters*, 559.
8. EH to MH, July 31, 1944, Baker, *Selected Letters*, 560.

9.   EH to MH, July 31, 1944, Baker, *Selected Letters,* 558.
10. EH to MH, August 1, 1944, Baker, *Selected Letters,* 562.
11. EH to MH, August 1, 1944, Baker, *Selected Letters,* 562.
12. EH to MH, August 1, 1944, Baker, *Selected Letters,* 560, 562.
13. Lanham, "Hemingway-Lanham Chronology 1944-45," JFK, BKPP-022-004 118.
14. Lanham, "Hemingway-Lanham Chronology 1944-45," JFK, BKPP-022-004 34.
15. EH to MH, August 5, 1944, Baker, *Selected Letters,* 563.
16. EH to MH, April 14, 1945, Baker, *Selected Letters,* 584.
17. MH to EH, undated, 1944, Hemingway Collection of the Museum Ernest Hemingway of the Republic of Cuba in the Hemingway Collection of the John F. Kennedy Presidential Library and Museum.
18. MH to EH, undated, 1944, Hemingway Collection of the Museum Ernest Hemingway of the Republic of Cuba in the Hemingway Collection of the John F. Kennedy Presidential Library and Museum.
19. Lanham, "Hemingway-Lanham Chronology 1944-45," JFK, BKPP-022-004.
20. H.R Stoneback presents strong evidence Hemingway took up arms and fought with the Maquis. Stoneback, H.R. "Hemingway's Happiest Summer-The Wildest Most Beautiful Time Ever; or the Liberation of France and Hemingway," 202.
21. Bruce, *OSS Against the Reich,* Loc. 2932.
22. EH to MH, August 27, 1944, Baker, *Selected Letters,* 564.
23. EH to MH, August 27, 1944, Baker, *Selected Letters,* 564.
24. EH to MH, August 27, 1944, Baker, *Selected Letters,* 564.
25. Hemingway, *Byline Ernest Hemingway,* 369.
26. MH to EH, August 21, 1944, Hemingway Collection of the Museum Ernest Hemingway of the Republic of Cuba in the Hemingway Collection of the John F. Kennedy Presidential Library and Museum.
27. *Time,* August 28, 1944; Kershaw, *Hitler,* 866; Smith, *Eisenhower in War and Peace,* 533.
28. Smith, *Eisenhower in War and Peace,* 533.
29. Hemingway, *Byline Ernest Hemingway,* 374.
30. Hemingway, *Byline Ernest Hemingway,* 374.
31. Hemingway, *Byline Ernest Hemingway,* 381.
32. Bruce, *OSS Against the Reich,* Loc. 2944.
33. Bruce, *OSS Against the Reich,* Loc. 2949.
34. Bruce, *OSS Against the Reich,* Loc. 2949.

CHAPTER TEN
1.   Hemingway, *How It Was,* 136.
2.   Cobb, *Eleven Days in August,* Loc. 5728.
3.   Hemingway, *How It Was,* 137.
4.   Hemingway, *How It Was,* 144.
5.   Welsh, Mary, "Life Correspondents See The New Paris," in *Life,* September 11, 1944, 38.
6.   Welsh, Mary, "Life Correspondents See The New Paris," in *Life,* September 11, 1944, 38.
7.   de Beauvoir, *Prime of Life,* 597.
8.   *Time,* September 11, 1944.
9.   *Time,* September 4, 1944.
10. Hemingway, *How It Was,* 150.
11. The name of the shop had been painted over on Sylvia's instructions to confuse the Germans who were about to confiscate the shop's contents. They were unable to find the books which

had been hidden, but they did arrest and intern Sylvia for six months. Beach, *Shakespeare, and Company*, 216.

12. Sylvia later wrote: "We were impressed by his originality, his very personal style, his skillful workmanship, his tidiness, his storyteller's gift and sense of the dramatic, his power to create . . ." Beach, *Shakespeare and Company*, 81.

13. Sylvia intuited that Ernest was an unusually sensitive man. He had told her the story of his wounding in the First World War at Fossalta de Piave in Italy, and his baptism by a Roman Catholic priest when he was near death. Sylvia Beach remembered the young Hemingway as a "deeply religious man." Beach, *Shakespeare and Company*, 90.

14. Hemingway, *How It Was*, 147.

15. Hemingway, *How It Was*, 147.

16. Hemingway, *How It Was*, 148.

CHAPTER ELEVEN

1. Capa, Robert, *Slightly Out of Focus*, Loc. 2134.

2. MH to NM, August 30, 1944, JFK, MHPP-022-003.

3. NM to MH, September 2, 1944, JFK, MHPP-022-003.

4. When Mary later read Noel's autobiography, she was surprised to see no reference to her at all. He had erased her from his personal history, mentioning only his new wife and three daughters. (Monks, *Eyewitness*, 47.)

5. MH to EH, October 1, 1944, JFK, EHPP-IC14-005.

6. Hemingway, Draft of *How It Was*, JFK, MHPP-003-007, 468.

7. Schnayerson, Michael, *Irwin Shaw, a Biography*, 143.

8. There are different versions of how Hadley lost the valise and there is no consensus on where the valise was actually placed. It could have been placed in the luggage compartment (per Hutchisson, 62; Blume, 34; Griffin, 38), given to a porter (per Kert, 127; Lynn, 187; Baker, 103), or simply stolen from the train platform (per Chamberlin, 45). Ernest, himself, is not specific in *A Moveable Feast*, 62.

9. Hemingway, *How It Was*, 159.

10. MH to EH, October 1, 1944, JFK, EHPP-IC14-005.

11. Hemingway, Draft of *How It Was*, JFK, MHPP-003-007, 468.

12. Hemingway, Draft of *How It Was*, JFK, MHPP-003-007, 468.

13. EH to MH, September 11, 1944, Baker, Carlos, EHSL, 565.

14. EH to MH, September 11, 1944, Baker, Carlos, EHSL, 567.

15. MH to EH, September 13, 1944, JFK, MEHC-003-048.

16. EH to MH, September 11, 1944, Baker, Carlos, EHSL, 568.

17. EH to MH, September 11, 1944, Baker, Carlos, EHSL, 566.

18. EH to MH, September 11, 1944, Baker, Carlos, EHSL, 572.

19. MH to EH, September 15, 1944, JFK, MEHC-003-048.

20. *By-Line: Ernest Hemingway*, 396.

21. *By-Line: Ernest Hemingway*, 397.

22. BL to CB, August 23, 1965, JFK, BKPP-022-004.

23. MH to EH, September 20, 1944, JFK, MEHC-003-048-002.

24. MH to EH, September 20, 1944, JFK, MEHC-003-048-002.

25. MH to EH, September 20, 1944, JFK, MEHC-003-048-002.

26. MH to EH, September 20, 1944, JFK, MEHC-003-048-002.

27. MH to EH, September 20, 1944, JFK, MEHC-003-048-002.

28. EH to MH, September 13, 1944, Baker, Carlos, EHSL, 569.

29. Hemingway, *How It Was*, 158.

30. MH to EH, Undated, 1944, JFK, MEHC-003-048-002.

CHAPTER TWELVE

1. EH to MH, September 24, 1944, Hemingway, Mary, *HIW*, 156.

2. EH to MH, September 24, 1944, Hemingway, Mary, *HIW*, 157.

3. MH to EH, September 1944, JFK, MEHC-003-048.

4. Dietrich, Marlene, *Marlene*, 146.

5. Hemingway-Lanham Chronology, 1944–45.

6. Hemingway, *How It Was*, 170.

7. Hemingway, *How It Was*, 171.

8. Dietrich, Marlene, *Marlene*, 149.

9. Dietrich, Marlene, *Marlene*, 149.

10. Dietrich, Marlene, *Marlene*, 150.

11. Lanham, "Hemingway-Lanham Chronology 1944-45," JFK, BKPP-022-004.

12. JFK, EHPP-OM23-013.

13. Fuller, Robert, "Hemingway at Rambouillet," *The Hemingway Review*, vol. 33 no. 2 (Spring, 2014), 66.

14. Burwell, R.M., Interview with William Walton, September 25, 26, 1992, JFK, EHMISC-009-016, 50.

15. Baker, *Hemingway: A Life Story*, 429.

16. Hemingway, *Memories of a Fly Fisherman*, 175.

17. *Time*, November 6, 1944.

18. Burwell, R.M., Interview with William Walton, September 25, 26, 1992, JFK, EHMISC-009-016, 26.

19. Burwell, R.M., Interview with William Walton, September 25, 26, 1992, JFK, EHMISC-009-016, 26.

20. Burwell, R.M., Interview with William Walton, September 25, 26, 1992, JFK, EHMISC-009-016, 26.

CHAPTER THIRTEEN

1. MacDonald, *The Battle of the Huertgen Forest*, Loc. 3154.

2. MacDonald, *The Battle of the Huertgen Forest*, Loc. 3004.

3. Hemingway, *Across the River and Into the Trees*.

4. Walton, William, "The Battle for Huertgen Forest," *Life*, January 1, 1945.

5. Burwell, Interview with William Walton, September 25, 26, 1992, JFK, EHMISC-009-016, 47.

6. Lanham, "Hemingway-Lanham Chronology 1944-45," JFK, BKPP-022-004, 34.

7. Burwell, Interview with William Walton, September 25, 26, 1992, JFK, EHMISC-009-016, 44.

8. The letters are found in Norberto Fuentes's *Hemingway in Cuba*. The letters in Fuentes's book are now contained in the Museo Hemingway collection at the JFK Library.

9 EH to Hemingway Family, July 21, 1918, "The Letters of Ernest Hemingway, 1907–1922," in Baker, Carlos, EHSL, 12, 115–119.

10. EH to MH, November 11, 1944, Fuentes, *Hemingway in Cuba*, 346-347.

11. EH to MH, November 11, 1944, Fuentes, *Hemingway in Cuba*, 348.

12. EH to MH, November 11, 1944, Fuentes, *Hemingway in Cuba*, 348.

13. EH to MH, November 16, 1944, Fuentes, *Hemingway in Cuba*, 349.

14. EH to MH, November 16, 1944, Fuentes, *Hemingway in Cuba*, 350.
15. EH to MH, November 18, 1944, Fuentes, *Hemingway in Cuba*, 352.
16. EH to MH, November 19, 1944, Fuentes, *Hemingway in Cuba*, 353.
17. EH to MH, November 20, 1944, Fuentes, *Hemingway in Cuba*, 354.
18. EH to MH, November 21, 1944, Fuentes, *Hemingway in Cuba*, 357.
19. EH to MH, November 21, 1944, Fuentes, *Hemingway in Cuba*, 358.
20. EH to MH, November 22, 1944, Fuentes, *Hemingway in Cuba*, 360.
21. EH to MH, November 24, 1944, Fuentes, *Hemingway in Cuba*, 363.
22. EH to MH, November 25, 1944, Fuentes, *Hemingway in Cuba*, 364.
23. EH to MH, November 29, 1944, Fuentes, *Hemingway in Cuba*, 369.
24. MH to EH, November 14, 1944, JFK, EHPP-IC14-005, 8.
25. EH to MH, November 23, 1944, Fuentes, *Hemingway in Cuba*, 361.
26. William Walton, recorded interview by Meghan Floyd Desnoyers, October 5, 1993, 224, John F. Kennedy Library Oral History Program.
27. EH to MH, November 8, 1944, Fuentes, *Hemingway in Cuba*, 344.
28. Lanham, "Hemingway-Lanham Chronology 1944-45," JFK, BKPP-022-004, 22.
29. Lanham, "Hemingway-Lanham Chronology 1944-45," JFK, BKPP-022-004, 22.
30. Lanham, "Hemingway-Lanham Chronology 1944-45," JFK, BKPP-022-004 34.
31. Burwell, Interview with William Walton, September 25, 26, 1992, JFK, EHMISC-009-016 51.
32. MH to EH, November 15, 1944, JFK, MHPP-003-007.
33. Simone de Beauvoir, "The Art of Fiction No.35," interviewed by Charlotte Gobeil, *The Paris Review*, 1965.
34. Halberstam, David, *The Powers That Be*, 46-47.
35. Hemingway, *How It Was*, 177.
36. Hemingway, *My Brother, Ernest Hemingway*, 262.

CHAPTER FOURTEEN
1. MH to Connie Ernst, December 15, 1945, JFK, MHPP-023-004.
2. Mary's Journal, August 25, 1944, JFK, BKPP-026-003.
3. Mary's Journal, August 25, 1944, JFK, BKPP-026-003.
4. Mary's Journal, August 25, 1944, JFK, BKPP-026-003.
5. Olson, Lynne, *Citizens of London: How Britain was Rescued in its Darkest, Finest Hour*, Loc. 5049.
6. Summersby Morgan, *Past Forgetting: My Love Affair with Dwight D. Eisenhower*, 176, 213; Smith, *Eisenhower in War and Peace*, 386.
7. Olson, Lynne, *Citizens of London: How Britain was Rescued in its Darkest, Finest Hour*, Loc. 4791.
8. Summersby Morgan, *Past Forgetting: My Love Affair with Dwight D. Eisenhower*, 34.
9. Measured in today's currency, Ernest's gift would be worth $28,000. As Mary's life savings were $500 ($7,000), this was a fortune.
10. MH to EH, December 23, 1944, JFK, MHPP-023-006, 150.
11. Lanham, "Hemingway-Lanham Chronology 1944-45," JFK, BKPP-022-004 2.
12. EH to MH, December 27, 1944, Fuentes, *Hemingway in Cuba*, 375.
13. As quoted in Kert, *The Hemingway Women*, 416.
14. MH to her parents, January 15, 1945, JFK, MHPP-023-001.
15. MH to her parents, January 25, 1945, JFK, MHPP-023-001.
16. NM to MH, February 8, 1945, JFK, MHPP-022-003.
17. NM to MH, February 14, 1945, JFK, MHPP-022-003.

18. NM to MH, February 22, 1945, JFK, MHPP-022-003.
19. Lanham, "Hemingway-Lanham Chronology 1944-45," JFK, BKPP-022-004 2.
20. Hemingway, *How It Was*, 184.
21. Hemingway, *How It Was*, 184.
22. Hemingway, *How It Was*, 178.
23. MH to EH, November 14, 1944, JFK, EHPP-IC14-005.
24. MH to her parents, February 27, 1945, JFK, MHPP-023-001.

CHAPTER FIFTEEN
1. Hemingway, Patrick, "'Papa' Hemingway, as seen by a son," *Kansas City Star*, June 27, 1999.
2. Interview with Patrick Hemingway by Ginger Piotter, December 6, 1985, Ketchum Community Library, OH HEM 0177.
3. EH to MH, March 6, 1945, Baker, *Selected Letters*, 578.
4. Hemingway, Patrick, "'Papa' Hemingway, as seen by a son," *Kansas City Star*, June 27, 1999.
5. Interview with Patrick Hemingway by Ginger Piotter, December 6, 1985, Ketchum Community Library, OH HEM 0177.
6. Hemingway, Patrick, "'Papa' Hemingway, as seen by a son," *Kansas City Star*, June 27, 1999.
7. Patrick Hemingway, interviewed by the author, November 2, 2020.
8. NM to MH, March 13, 1945, JFK, MHPP-022-003.
9. MH to NM, Undated, 1945, JFK, MHPP-022-003.
10. EH to BL, April 2, 1945, Baker, *Selected Letters*, 579.
11. EH to MH, April 14, 1945, Baker, *Selected Letters*, 584.
12. Jones, *Michael Foot*, 124.
13. Transcript of MH Broadcast, JFK, MHPP-013-019 series 1.3.
14. EH to BL, April 14, 1945, Baker, *Selected Letters*, 585.
15. This vignette is found in the drafts of Mary's memoir, but she left it out of the final version. Hemingway, Draft of *How It Was*, JFK, MHPP-003-007.
16. EH to MH, April 9, 1945, Baker, *Selected Letters*, 581.
17. EH to MH, April 14, 1945, Baker, *Selected Letters*, 584.
18. EH to MH, April 16, 1945, Baker, *Selected Letters*, 587.
19. EH to MH, April 17, 1945, Baker, *Selected Letters*, 588.
20. Hemingway, *How It Was*, 191-192.
21. Martha Gellhorn to EH, May 28, 1945, Fuentes, *Hemingway in Cuba*, 376.
22. Hemingway, *How It Was*, 195.
23. Hemingway, *How It Was*, 195.
24. Hemingway, *How It Was*, 199.
25. Eby, *Hemingway's Fetishism*, Loc. 260.
26. MH Notes, October 13, 1945, JFK, MHPP-013-021 series 1.3.
27. Based on her reading of *How It Was*, Rose Marie Burwell concluded that Mary lacked analytical insight and that she lived in a state of denial. "Living on the surface was essential for Mary in sustaining the high level of denial which he had just chosen to exist in order to remain in the marriage . . ." Burwell, *The Postwar Years and the Posthumous Novels*, 157. Burwell apparently did not have access to Mary's journals, for reading them it is all too clear Mary realized what sort of arrangement she was entering, but she kept her private thoughts to her journal and did not publish them in her memoir.
28. Hemingway, "Cuban Journal," June 5, 1945, JFK, MHPP-014-002.
29. Hemingway, "Cuban Journal," June 7, 1945, JFK, MHPP-014-002.
30. Hemingway, "Cuban Journal," June 7, 1945, JFK, MHPP-014-002.

CHAPTER SIXTEEN

1. Hemingway, *Memories of a Fly Fisherman*, 200.
2. Hemingway, *How It Was*, 201.
3. Hemingway, *Memories of a Fly Fisherman*, 201.
4. Hemingway, *Papa, A Personal Memoir*, 18.
5. Hemingway, *Papa, A Personal Memoir*, 95.
6. Ginger Piotter, interview with Patrick Hemingway, December 6, 1985, Ketchum Community Library, OH HEM 0177.
7. Patrick Hemingway, interviewed by the author, October 30, 2020.
8. Patrick Hemingway, interviewed by the author, November 2, 2020.
9. Hemingway, *How It Was*, 202.
10. EH to Thomas Welsh, June 19, 1945, Baker, *Selected Letters*, 592.
11. Villarreal, *Hemingway's Cuban Son*, 56.
12. Villarreal, *Hemingway's Cuban Son*, 55-56.
13. Hemingway, "Cuban Journal," 1945, JFK, MHPP-014-002. Jack noticed when he saw Mary and his father in Paris that "Papa had entirely given up driving cars himself, probably as an aftereffect of the accident in Havana." Hemingway, *Memories of a Fly Fisherman*, 252.
14. Hemingway, "Cuban Journal," 1945, JFK, MHPP-014-002.
15. Hemingway, "Cuban Journal," 1945, JFK, MHPP-014-002.
16. Hemingway, *How It Was*, 210.
17. Hemingway, *Memories of a Fly Fisherman*, 202.
18. Hemingway, "Cuban Journal," 1945, JFK, MHPP-014-002.
19. Hemingway, "Cuban Journal," 1945, JFK, MHPP-014-002.
20. MH to Pam Churchill, July 4, 1945, JFK, MHPP-023-004.
21. BL to EH, October 9, 1945, JFK, BKPP-022-004.
22. Letter from Mrs. C.T. Lanham to Carlos Baker, May 10, 1966, JFK, BKPP-022-004.
23. Letter from Mrs. C.T. Lanham to Carlos Baker, June 1, 1964, JFK, BKPP-022-004.
24. Letter from Mrs. C.T. Lanham to Carlos Baker, May 10, 1966, JFK, BKPP-022-004.
25. Letter from Mrs. C.T. Lanham to Carlos Baker, May 10, 1966, JFK, BKPP-022-004.
26. EH to MH, September 1, 1945, Baker, *Selected Letters*, 595.
27. MH to her parents, October 13, 1945, JFK, MHPP-023-001.
28. Hemingway, *How It Was*, 222.
29. Rose Marie Burwell determined from reviewing the manuscripts that Ernest may have begun writing parts of what would become *The Garden of Eden* in the fall of 1945. Burwell, *The Postwar Years and the Posthumous Novels*, 95, 96.
30. Mary Hemingway's Journal, December 19, 1945, MHPP-013-021 series 1.3.
31. Martha Gellhorn to MH, July 25, 1946, JFK, MHPP-016-003.
32. Burwell, Interview with William Walton, September 25, 26, 1992, JFK, EHMISC-009-016.
33. Letter from Mrs. C.T. Lanham to Carlos Baker, June 1, 1964, JFK, BKPP-022-004.
34. MH to her parents, October 13, 1945, JFK, MHPP-023-001.
35. Michael Foot to MH, December 13, 1945, JFK, MHPP-016-003.
36. MH to Patrick Hemingway, November 11, 1945, JFK, MHPP-023-004.
37. Hemingway, Draft of *How It Was*, JFK, MHPP-003-007 604.
38. Undated, Hemingway Collection of the Museum Ernest Hemingway of the Republic of Cuba in the Hemingway Collection of the John F. Kennedy Presidential Library and Museum.
39. Mary Hemingway's Journal, December 19, 1945, MHPP-013-021 series 1.3.

40. Hemingway, *Papa, A Personal Memoir*, 96.

41. Hemingway, *How It Was*, 228-229.

42. Hemingway, Draft of *How It Was*, JFK, MHPP-003-007 614.

43. "Guide to Cuban Law and Legal Research," *International Journal of Legal Information*, vol. 45, no. 2 (2017), 201; Salas, Luis, T. "The Judicial System of Post-Revolutionary Cuba," *Nova Law Journal*, vol 8, 1983, 43; Beckford, *The Spanish Civil Code;* Evenson, Debra, "Women's Equality in Cuba: What Difference Does a Revolution Make," (1986) 4, *Law and Inequality: A Journal of Theory and Practice*, 295.

44. EH to Archibald MacLeish, May 5, 1943, JFK, Baker, *Selected Letters*, 545.

45. MH to her parents, March 8, 1946, JFK, MHHP-023-001.

46. Hemingway, Draft of *How It Was*, JFK, MHPP-003-014, 617.

47. Hemingway, *How It Was*, 230.

48. Hemingway, Draft of *How It Was*, JFK, MHPP-003-014, 617.

49. Hemingway, *How It Was*, 231; Hemingway, Draft of *How It Was*, JFK, MHPP-003-007.

50. Hemingway, Draft of *How It Was*, JFK, MHPP-003-014, 620.

51. Jones, *Michael Foot*, 124.

52. MH to Connie Ernst Bessie, March 27, 1945, JFK, MHPP-023-001.

53. Mary Hemingway's Journal, December 1945, JFK, MHPP-013-021.

54. MH to EH, undated, JFK, MHPP-023-004.

55. Dr. James Gough to MH, May 6, 1946, JFK, MHPP-016-003.

CHAPTER SEVENTEEN

1.   EH to BL, August 25, 1946, Baker, *Selected Letters*, 609.

2.   EH to Lillian Ross, July 2, 1948, Baker, *Selected Letters*, 645.

3.   Arnold, *The Idaho Hemingway*, 134.

4.   Hemingway, *Memories of a Fly Fisherman*, 226.

5.   Hemingway, *How It Was*, 247.

6.   Hemingway, *How It Was*, 246.

7.   Hemingway, *How It Was*, 246.

8.   Hemingway, *Ernie, Hemingway's Sister "Sunny" Remembers*, 133.

9.   Hemingway, *Papa, A Personal Memoir*, 98.

10. Hemingway, *Papa, A Personal Memoir*, 99.

11. "That night in Coconut Grove, I should have pressed Gigi for more details about this moment. Maybe a mind-fogged man wouldn't have had them. What I do know is he told me his father opened the door of the Finca's master bedroom and came in while he was putting on 'Marty's white nylons.' But almost as soon as he said this, Gigi's mind went to something else." Hendrickson, *Hemingway's Boat*, 515.

12. Hemingway, *Strange Tribe*, 113-4.

13. Greg suggested this led to his cross-dressing and eventual sexual reassignment surgery. Hendrickson, *Hemingway's Boat*, 505.

14. Patrick Hemingway, interviewed by the author, November 17, 2020.

15. Moorehead, *Selected Letters of Martha Gellhorn*, 124.

16. Fuentes, *Hemingway in Cuba*, 23.

17. Fuentes, *Hemingway in Cuba*, 24.

18. Villarreal, *Hemingway's Cuban Son*, 55.

19. Patrick Hemingway, interviewed by the author, November 2, 2020.

20. Patrick Hemingway, interviewed by the author, November 2, 2020.

21. EH to BL, May 24, 1947, JFK, BKPP-026-022.

22. Patrick Hemingway, interviewed by the author, November 2, 2020.
23. EH to CS, Baker, June 28, 1947, *Selected Letters*, 621-2.
24. Berg, *Max Perkins: Editor of Genius*, 97-98.
25. EH to CS, Baker, June 28, 1947, *Selected Letters*, 621-2.
26. Mary's Undated, Holograph Will, JFK, MHPP-030-012.
27. EH to CS, Baker, June 28, 1947, *Selected Letters*, 621-2.
28. EH to BL, May 24, 1947, JFK, BKPP-026-002.
29. Hemingway, *How It Was*, 366.

CHAPTER EIGHTEEN
1. Hemingway, *Memories of a Fly Fisherman*, 77.
2. Hemingway, *How It Was*, 262.
3. Arnold, *The Idaho Hemingway*, 151.
4. Patrick Hemingway, interviewed by the author, November 2, 2020.
5. Hemingway, *How It Was*, 266.
6. Hawkins, *Unbelievable Happiness and Final Sorrow*, 141.
7. Hawkins, *Unbelievable Happiness and Final Sorrow*, 188.
8. Hemingway, *Papa, A Personal Memoir*, 92.
9. Hemingway, *How It Was*, 213.
10. Hemingway, *How It Was*, 270.
11. Hemingway, Draft of *How It Was*, JFK, MHPP-004-003, 9.
12. EH to Marion Smith, May 31, 1948, Baker, *Selected Letters*, 635.
13. Cowley, Malcolm, *The Long Voyage*, 384.
14. Hemingway, *How It Was*, 641.
15. Thomas Welsh to MH, March 31, 1953, JFK, MHPP-018-001.
16. Hotchner, *Papa Hemingway*, 11.
17. EH to BL, August 25, 1948, JFK, BKPP-026-002.
18. EH to BL, August 25, 1948, JFK, BKPP-026-002.
19. EH to Lillian Ross, July 28, 1948, Baker, *Selected Letters*, 646.
20. EH to Sara Murphy, February 27, 1936, Baker, *Selected Letters*, 438.
21. EH to CS, October 29, 1947, Baker, *Selected Letters*, 629.
22. EH to CS, June 28, 1947, Baker, *Selected Letters*, 621.
23. EH to AR, December 15, 1948, Baker, *Selected Letters*, 654.

CHAPTER NINETEEN
1. Hemingway, Mary, "Italian Journal," JFK, MHPP-015-003.
2. Hemingway, Mary, "Italian Journal," JFK, MHPP-015-003, IJ 6.
3. Hemingway, Mary, "Italian Journal," JFK, MHPP-015-003, IJ 6.
4. Hemingway, Mary, "Italian Journal," JFK, MHPP-015-003, IJ 6.
5. Hemingway, Mary, "Italian Journal," JFK, MHPP 015-003.
6. Hemingway, Mary, "Italian Journal," JFK, MHPP 015-003.
7. Hemingway, Mary, "Italian Journal," JFK, MHPP 015-003.
8. Hemingway, *How It Was*, 281.
9. Hemingway, *How It Was*, 283.
10. Hemingway, "The First Italian Journey," JFK, MHPP-015-003.
11. The press account by Emmett Watson described the gun. "The Post-Intelligencer learned that the death weapon was a silver-inlaid double-barreled shotgun with a hammerless tandem trigger mechanism. Both barrels had been fired. The 12-gauge hunting gun was an

Angelini and Bernardin, made by W.C. Scott and Sons, of London." Watson described the gun in detail, "On the left barrel was inscribed '55 Victoria Street, London, Scott's Improved Bolt, Monte Carlo B.'" *Seattle Post-Intelligencer,* July 7, 1961. This issue is discussed below.

12. Hemingway, "The First Italian Journey," JFK, MHPP-015-003.
13. Hemingway, "The First Italian Journey," JFK, MHPP-015-003.
14. Hemingway, "The First Italian Journey," JFK, MHPP-015-003.
15. Hemingway, "The First Italian Journey," JFK, MHPP-015-003.
16. Hemingway, "The First Italian Journey," JFK, MHPP-015-003.
17. The current owner of Locanda Cipriani, Bonifacio Brass, the grandnephew of Giuseppe, maintains the Santa Fosca suite as it was in Hemingway's day. The same furniture decorates the room, and during our five-day stay there, it was easy to imagine Ernest and Mary sitting and reading in the comfortable chairs or standing on the balcony and looking out at the Basilica. Sitting there, sipping Amarone, and reading out loud the first chapters of *Across the River and Into the Trees*, perhaps imagined in that room, drew me into the landscape Ernest portrayed. Bonifacio told me his great aunt divulged to him that Mary brought down six empty bottles of Amarone each morning. The wine is so rich I can't imagine anyone could drink that much every evening.
18. Hemingway, Mary, "Italian Journal," JFK, MHPP 015-003.
19. Hemingway, Draft of *How It Was,* JFK, MHPP-004-006, 838.
20. Hemingway, *How It Was,* 466.

CHAPTER TWENTY
1. Moyal, Anne, *Alan Moorehead: A Rediscovery* (Canberra: National Library of Australia, 2005), 7-9.
2. Hemingway, *How It Was,* 288.
3. Moyal, Anne, *Alan Moorehead: A Rediscovery* (Canberra: National Library of Australia, 2005), 7-9.
4. Hemingway, *How It Was,* 291.
5. Hemingway, *How It Was,* 291.
6. Hemingway, *How It Was,* 291.
7. Hemingway, Mary, "Italian Journal," JFK, MHPP 015-003, 66.
8. Baker, *Selected Letters,* 654.
9. Hemingway, Mary, "Italian Journal," JFK, MHPP 015-003, 71.
10. Ivancich, Adriana, "I am Hemingway's Renata," translation by Mark Cirino. PMLA, vol. 129, no. 2 (March 2014): 257–66.
11. Ivancich, Adriana, "I am Hemingway's Renata," 257–66.
12. Ivancich, Adriana, "I am Hemingway's Renata," 257–66.
13. Hemingway, Mary, "Italian Journal," JFK, MHPP 015-003, 70.
14. Ivancich, Adriana, "I am Hemingway's Renata," 257–66.
15. *Life,* January 10, 1949, 86.
16. De Fazio, *Dear Papa, Dear Hotch, The Correspondence of Ernest Hemingway and A.E. Hotchner,* 25.
17. Cowley, Malcolm, *The Long Voyage,* 592.
18. Moyal, Anne, *Alan Moorehead: A Rediscovery,* 59.
19. Moyal, Anne, *Alan Moorehead: A Rediscovery,* 60.
20. Hemingway, Mary, "Italian Journal," JFK, MHPP 015-003, 77.
21. Hemingway, *How It Was,* 310.
22. Ivancich, Adriana, "I am Hemingway's Renata," 257–66.

23. Hemingway, *How It Was,* 320.
24. Hemingway, Draft of *How It Was,* JFK, MHPP-015-003, 90.
25. Hemingway, *How It Was,* 299.
26. Hemingway, Draft of *How It Was,* JFK, MHPP-004-006, 880.
27. Hemingway, *How It Was,* 300.

CHAPTER TWENTY-ONE
1. Hemingway, "Ernest's Homework," Book of the Month Club Bulletin, October 1970, MHPP-011-012.
2. Hemingway, "Ernest's Homework," Book of the Month Club Bulletin, October 1970, MHPP-011-012.
3. Hemingway, Draft of *How It Was,* JFK, MHPP-004-006, 838.
4. Annie Cohan-Solal, *Jean-Paul Sartre, A Life,* 238.
5. Hemingway, Draft of *How It Was,* JFK, MHPP-004-007, 17.
6. Tillman, Helen M., *Northwestern Alumni News,* November 1977.
7. Hemingway, Draft of *How It Was,* JFK, MHPP-004-007, 18.
8. Hemingway, Draft of *How It Was,* JFK, MHPP-003-007, 18.
9. Hotchner, *Papa Hemingway,* 19.
10. Fanny Butcher, "The Literary Spotlight," *Chicago Sunday Tribune,* October 16, 1949.
11. Hemingway, Draft of *How It Was,* JFK, MHPP-004-007, 58.
12. MH to EH, September 29, 1949, JFK, EHPP-IC14-006.
13. MH to EH, September 29, 1949, JFK, EHPP-IC14-006.
14. Hemingway, *Across the River and Into the Trees,* 101.
15. EH to CS, August 25-26, 1949, Baker, *Selected Letters,* 667.
16. De Fazio, *Dear Papa, Dear Hotch, The Correspondence of Ernest Hemingway and A.E. Hotchner,* 46.
17. De Fazio, *Dear Papa, Dear Hotch, The Correspondence of Ernest Hemingway and A.E. Hotchner,* 53.
18. EH, Miscellaneous Personal Notes, JFK, MHPP-030-015.
19. Hemingway, *How It Was,* 310.
20. Hemingway, Draft of *How It Was,* JFK, MHPP-003-003, 41.
21. Hotchner, *Hemingway in Love,* 62.
22. Viertel, Peter, *Dangerous Friends,* 85.
23. Viertel, Peter, *Dangerous Friends,* 84.
24. Viertel, Peter, *Dangerous Friends,* 85.
25. Hemingway, *How It Was,* 316.
26. Viertel, Peter, *Dangerous Friends,* 84.
27. Hemingway, *How It Was,* 318.
28. Viertel, Peter, *Dangerous Friends,* 84.
29. Hemingway, Mary, "Italian Journal," JFK, MHPP-014-005.
30. Ivancich, Adriana, "I am Hemingway's Renata," 260.
31. Hemingway, *How It Was,* 320.
32. Moorehead, *Selected Letters of Martha Gellhorn,* 204.
33. Hemingway, *How It Was,* 324.
34. Hemingway, *How It Was,* 324.
35. Mark Cirino suggested the "cover illustration features an unmistakably phallic white tower at an angle simulating an erect penis; at its base three tumescent hills sit above a tunnel that is being penetrated by a gondola." Ivancich, Adriana, "I am Hemingway's Renata," 260.
36. Hemingway, *How It Was,* 326.
37. Hemingway, *How It Was,* 328.

38. Hemingway, *How It Was*, 328.
39. Hemingway, *How It Was*, 329.
40. Hemingway, *How It Was*, 329.
41. MH to CS, October 12, 1950, JFK, BKPP-025-008.
42. Burwell, *The Postwar Years and the Posthumous Novels*, 50. Burwell wrote, "Mary's ectopic pregnancy in 1946, and what she describes as the occlusion of her remaining fallopian tube, diagnosed in 1949, were almost certainly the result of a pelvic inflammatory condition (of which venereal disease could be one cause)."
43. Fuentes, *Hemingway in Cuba*, 416.
44. Patrick Hemingway, interviewed by the author, November 17, 2020.

CHAPTER TWENTY-TWO

1. Schnayerson, *Irwin Shaw, a Biography*, 179.
2. Prescott, Orville, "Books of the Times," *New York Times*, January 1, 1945, 23.
3. *Kirkus Review*, October 1, 1948.
4. Hemingway, Draft of *How It Was*, JFK, MHPP-003-007.
5. Hemingway, *How It Was*, 329.
6. Shaw's biographer noted, "It was difficult to tell what he was most insulted by: the mocking portraits of himself and Leicester; the breezy acknowledgement in print that Shaw and Mary Welsh had had an affair (and that Louise M'Kimber had asked Michael Whiteacre to marry her); or perhaps worst of all, the sheer effrontery of this Brooklyn Tolstoy to presume he could write about the war at all, when clearly the war was Hemingway's exclusive purview." Schnayerson, *Irwin Shaw, a Biography*, 179.
7. BL to EH, June 9, 1945, Hemingway Collection of the Museum Ernest Hemingway of the Republic of Cuba in the Hemingway Collection of the John F. Kennedy Presidential Library and Museum.
8. Viertel, *Dangerous Friends*, 63.
9. Shaw, *The Young Lions*, 366.
10. Shaw, *The Young Lions*, 377.
11. Hemingway, *How It Was*, 329. In the draft of *How It Was*, Mary described it as "a cold impenetrable ridge of acrimony." Though she penciled out the words "cold impenetrable" and they were removed from the published version, the draft conveys her candid sentiment rather than her self-censored view of the incident. Hemingway, Draft of *How It Was*, JFK, MHPP-003-007.
12. Hemingway, *How It Was*, 329.
13. Viertel, *Dangerous Friends*, 63.
14. Beatrice Guck to MH, May 17, 1950, JFK, MHPP-016-004.
15. Hemingway, *How It Was*, 331.
16. In her letter of thanks, Bea said she had a wonderful time and praised the gentle lifestyle at the Finca. She sent "Love to you and your sweetheart," showing she bore no grudge at all.
17. Hemingway, *How It Was*, 331.
18. MH to EH, May 6, 1950, JFK, EHPP-IC14-006.
19. MH to EH, May 6, 1950, JFK, EHPP-IC14-006.
20. MH to EH, May 6, 1950, JFK, EHPP-IC14-006.
21. MH to EH, May 6, 1950, JFK, EHPP-IC14-006.
22. MH to EH, May 6, 1950, JFK, EHPP-IC14-006.
23. Hemingway, *How It Was*, 333.
24. Lillian Ross, "The Moods of Ernest Hemingway," *The New Yorker*, May 13, 1950.

25. Hemingway, Draft of *How It Was*, JFK, MHPP-004-003, 39.
26. Hemingway, *Memories of a Fly Fisherman*, 234.
27. Indeed, Edmund Wilson referred to her as "that girl Lillian Ross with built-in tape recorder." Elaine Woo, "Lillian Ross, Celebrated New Yorker Writer, Dies at 99," *Los Angeles Times*, September 20, 2017.
28. Baker, *Selected Letters*, 744.
29. Baker, *Selected Letters*, 745.
30. Howe, Irving, "Hemingway: the Conquest of Panic," *The New Republic*, July 24, 1961.
31. Mary Hemingway's Journal, JFK, MHPP-014-006, 11.
32. Mary Hemingway's Journal, JFK, MHPP-014-006, 13.
33. *Time*, September 11, 1950.
34. MH to EH, (undated), JFK, MHPP-023-004.
35. Hemingway, *How It Was*, 343.
36. Trogdon, *The Lousey Racket: Hemingway, Scribner's, and the Business of Literature*, Loc. 4708.
37. John O'Hara, "The Author's Name is Hemingway," *The New York Times Book Review*, September 10, 1950.
38. EH to BL, September 11, 1950, Baker, *Selected Letters*, 714.
39. MH to EH, October 3, 1959, JFK, EHPP-IC14-006.
40. MH to CS, October 12, 1950, JFK, BKPP-025-008.
41. MH to CS, October 12, 1950, JFK, BKPP-025-008.
42. MH to CS, October 12, 1950, JFK, BKPP-025-008.
43. Hemingway, Miscellaneous Journal Entries, October 15, 1951, JFK, MHPP-014-004.
44. Hemingway, Miscellaneous Journal Entries, October 18, 1951, JFK, MHPP-014-004.
45. Hemingway, *How It Was*, 349.
46. Hemingway, Miscellaneous Journal Entries, November 6, 1951, JFK, MHPP-014-004.
47. Hemingway, Miscellaneous Journal Entries, October 31, 1951, JFK, MHPP-014-004.
48. Hemingway, Miscellaneous Journal Entries, November 27, 1951, JFK, MHPP-014-004.
49. Hemingway, Miscellaneous Journal Entries, November 27, 1951, JFK, MHPP-014-004.
50. Hemingway, Miscellaneous Journal Entries, October 21, 1951, JFK, MHPP-014-004.
51. Hemingway, Miscellaneous Journal Entries, October 18, 1951, JFK, MHPP-014-004.
52. Mary Hemingway's Journal, JFK, MHPP-014-004, February 7, 1953.
53. Hemingway, *How It Was*, 354.
54. Mary Hemingway's Journal, JFK, MHPP-014-004. February 7, 1953.
55. Hemingway, *How It Was*, 355.
56. Ivancich, Adriana, "I am Hemingway's Renata," 56–261.
57. Ivancich, Adriana, "I am Hemingway's Renata," 57–263.
58. Ivancich, Adriana, "I am Hemingway's Renata," 58–263n.
59. Bernice Kert, Notes, JFK, BKPP-021-006.

CHAPTER TWENTY-THREE
1. Hemingway, *How It Was*, 356.
2. Hemingway, *How It Was*, 357.
3. Hemingway, Mary, Journal, December 26, 1951, MHPP-014-004, 28.
4. Hemingway, *Papa, A Personal Memoir*, 100.
5. Hemingway, *Papa, A Personal Memoir*, 112.
6. Hemingway, Mary, Journal, December 26, 1951, MHPP-014-004, 28.
7. Hemingway, Mary, Journal, December 26, 1951, MHPP-014-004, 29.
8. Burwell, Interview with William Walton, September 25, 26, 1992, JFK, EHMISC-009-016.

9. Burwell, Interview with William Walton, September 25, 26, 1992, JFK, EHMISC-009-016.

10. Rose Marie Burwell pointed out that there is no holograph of *The Old Man and the Sea* at the Kennedy Library, and "the virtually clean typescript, with word counts that go as high as 1805 per day, makes it clear that Hemingway was working with something he had done thoroughly before." Hemingway decided to remove "Old Man" from his larger manuscript, "The Sea Book" that he had been working on since 1934 and publish it separately. Burwell, *Hemingway: The Postwar Years and the Posthumous Novels*, 60.

11. Ivancich, Adriana, "I am Hemingway's Renata," 257–66, 260.

12. EH to AH, January 5, 1951, De Fazio, *Dear Papa, Dear Hotch, The Correspondence of Ernest Hemingway and A.E. Hotchner*, 111.

13. Hemingway, *How It Was*, 284.

14. Hemingway, Mary, "Life With Papa," *Flair*, January 1951.

15. MH to EH, February 11, 1951, JFK, EHPP-IC 14-006, 29.

16. Hemingway, *How It Was*, 360.

17. Hemingway, *How It Was*, 360.

18. Adriana Ivancich to MH, undated, 1951, JFK, MHPP-016-006.

19. DiRobilant, "Ernest Hemingway's Long-ago Crush on a Venetian Girl is Once Again the Talk of Italy," JFK, BKPP-021-006.

20. EH to Adriana Ivancich, March 18, 1951, JFK, BKPP-021-006.

21. Baker, *Selected Letters*, 720.

22. Hemingway, *How It Was*, 361.

23. In a conversation with David Stewart, Mary was asked: How much credit do you take for the ending of the story?
Mary replied: Well, I just thought Santiago was such a pleasant old man that he should be allowed to live. Ernest was going to let him die. I said, "Sweetie, I do feel it's mean; he's such a nice old man. And this is sort of a sleazy, easy thing to do—to just knock him off—to end your story. Don't do it." Ernest was sitting in his great big armchair, relaxed—this was in Cuba at our home—and said something profound such as, "Ummm." The next night as he was getting closer to the finish, I repeated, "It's a sleazy and much too simple way to finish the story." And he let Santiago live. And I was very pleased about that. But, in general, I made no effort to influence what he wrote and was not asked for advice. Really, I had no influence on his work whatsoever except in a couple of small incidents like this. "A Conversation With Mary Hemingway," David Stewart, Elizabeth Cowan, Gregory Cowan, and Mary Hemingway Source: *Cea Critic*, vol. 40, no. 1 (November 1977), 29-33. Published by The Johns Hopkins University Press.

24. Hemingway, *How It Was*, 364.

25. Hemingway, *How It Was*, 289.

26. William Walton, Recorded Interview by Meghan Floyd Desnoyers, October 5, 1993, 224, John F. Kennedy Library Oral History Program, 142.

27. Burwell, Interview with William Walton, September 25, 26, 1992, JFK, EHMISC-009-016.

28. William Walton, Recorded Interview by Meghan Floyd Desnoyers, October 5, 1993, 224, John F. Kennedy Library Oral History Program.

29. Burwell, Interview with William Walton, September 25, 26, 1992, JFK, EHMISC-009-016.

30. William Walton, Recorded Interview by Meghan Floyd Desnoyers, October 5, 1993, 224, John F. Kennedy Library Oral History Program, 223.

31. William Walton, Recorded Interview by Meghan Floyd Desnoyers, October 5, 1993, 224, John F. Kennedy Library Oral History Program, 70.

32. Burwell, Interview with William Walton, September 25, 26, 1992, JFK, EHMISC-009-016, 23.

33. Meyers, Jeffrey, "The Hemingways: an American Tragedy," VQR, Spring 1999, 274; see also Hendrickson, Paul, "Papa's Boys," *The Washington Post*, July 29, 1987.

34. Meyers, Jeffrey, "The Hemingways: an American Tragedy," VQR, Spring 1999, 274.

35. Hawkins, *Unbelievable Happiness and Final Sorrow*, 271.

36. Pauline's death certificate listed her cause of death as "hemorrhage into adrenal," and identified "antecedent causes" as "arteriosclerosis and hypertension." She died on October 1, 1951, at St. Vincent Hospital in Los Angeles. When Greg began medical school, he wrote St. Vincent Hospital and asked for an autopsy report. The report showed that Pauline had died of an unusual tumor of the adrenal gland (pheochromocytoma). The tumor was undetected in Pauline's case. These tumors may secrete unusually large amounts of adrenaline, which cause the blood pressure to increase to such high levels a rupture of an artery may result. Greg judged from the symptoms before Pauline's death that she had a variety of the tumor which could be triggered by emotional upset. Greg described his findings in a letter to his father in the summer of 1960. He told Ernest, "it was not my minor problems that had upset Mother but his brutal phone conversation with her eight hours before she died." Greg explained, "the tumor had become necrotic or rotten, and when it fired off that night, it sent her blood pressure skyrocketing; a medium-sized blood vessel, within or adjacent to the rotten area, had ruptured." He concluded, "then the tumor stopped discharging adrenaline, her blood pressure dropped from about 300 to 0, and she died of shock on the operating table." Hemingway, *Papa, A Personal Memoir*, 12. Apparently, Ernest was troubled by this letter, but he did not reply to it.

37. Hemingway, Mary, Journal, October 1951, JFK, MHPP-014-004, 32.

38. Hemingway, *How It Was*, 290.

39. EH to CS, October 2, 1951, Baker, *Selected Letters*, 737.

40. Burwell, Interview with William Walton, September 25, 26, 1992, JFK, EHMISC-009-016, 65.

41. Wills of Ernest Hemingway, JFK. October 27, 1951.

42. Valerie Hemingway to author, Ernest Hemingway, September 13, 2019.

43. Patrick Hemingway, interviewed by the author, November 2, 2020

44. Valerie Hemingway to author, Ernest Hemingway, second email note, September 13, 2019.

45. Hemingway, Mary, Journal, December 26, 1951, MHPP-014-004, 30.

46. Hemingway, Mary, Journal, December 26, 1951, MHPP-014-004, 30.

47. Hemingway, Mary, Journal, December 26, 1951, MHPP-014-004, 30.

48. William Walton, Recorded Interview by Meghan Floyd Desnoyers, October 5, 1993, 10, John F. Kennedy Library Oral History Program.

49. Hemingway, *How It Was*, 402.

50. Hemingway, *Papa, A Personal Memoir*, 8. Despite Greg's claim, there was one more meeting in Florida when Ernest took Greg to the hospital to undergo electroshock therapy.

51. EH to CS, February 25, 1952, Baker, *Selected Letters*, 756.

52. Hemingway, *How It Was*, 294.

53. Hemingway, *How It Was*, 294.

54. EH to Vera Scribner, February 18, 1952, Baker, *Selected Letters*, 749.

55. MH to her parents, March 3, 1952, JFK, MHPP-023-002.

56. Scribner, Charles, Jr. *In the Company of Writers: A Life in Publishing*. New York: Charles Scribner's Sons, 1990, 73.

57. *New York Times*, March 11, 1952.

58. Hemingway, *How It Was*, 366.

CHAPTER TWENTY-FOUR

1. EH to AI, May 31, 1952, Baker, *Selected Letters*, 762.
2. EH to BL, June 18, 1952, JFK, BKPP-026-002.
3. EH to Bernard Berenson, September 13, 1952, Baker, *Selected Letters*, 780.
4. Samuels, Bernard Berenson, *The Making of a Legend*, 518.
5. Scribner, Charles, Jr. *In the Company of Writers: A Life in Publishing* (New York: Charles Scribner's Sons, 1990), 74–75.
6. Hemingway, Journal 1952, JFK, MHPP–014–009.
7. Villarreal, *Hemingway's Cuban Son*, 119.
8. Hemingway, Journal 1952–1953, JFK, MHPP–014–009, 43.
9. Hemingway, Journal 1952–1953, JFK, MHPP–014–009, 45.
10. Sally Raleigh "Ms. Mary Works On," 1964, Clippings file, Articles About Mary, JFK, MHPP-024-002.
11. Viertel, Peter, *Dangerous Friends*, 182.
12. Viertel, Peter, *Dangerous Friends*, 183.
13. Hemingway, *The Sun Also Rises*, 90.
14. Hemingway, *How It Was*, 413.
15. Hemingway, *How It Was*, 414.
16. Hemingway, *How It Was*, 414.
17. Hemingway, *Death in the Afternoon*, 27.
18. Hemingway, *Death in the Afternoon*, 28.
19. Hemingway, *How It Was*, 415.
20. Hemingway, *How It Was*, 416.
21. Hemingway, *How It Was*, 417.
22. Viertel, Peter, *Dangerous Friends*, 186.
23. Hemingway, *How It Was*, 418.
24. Ernest's special table in the window of the Cervecería Alemana is today marked by a framed photo of Don Ernesto Hemingway on an adjacent wall. That photo was copied from the cover of Hotchner's *Papa Hemingway* and hung in Don Ernesto's honor at the invitation of the restaurant owner by the chairman of the Wellington Society of Madrid, Stephen Drake-Jones, at a ceremony attended by fifty people. On the day of the unveiling, they covered the photo with American and Spanish flags. Ramon, the son of Ernest's journalist friend, Peter Buckley, stood on a chair, pulled off the flags, and pumped his fist into the air, proclaiming, "Viva la Republic" and "Viva Hemingway." The crowd stood, raising their fists and roaring "Viva." Author's Interview with Stephen Drake-Jones, Cervecería Alemana, October 17, 2015.

CHAPTER TWENTY-FIVE

1. *New York Times* May 4, 1953.
2. Elkins, Caroline, *Imperial Reckoning: The Untold Story of Britain's Gulag in Kenya*, 83.
3. According to Carl Eby and Suzanne del Gizzo "Wakamba" is a Swahili word, while "Kamba" is the name in the Akamba language of the tribe itself. While Ernest and Mary use the terms interchangeably, I will use the word "Kamba." Del Gizzo, "Going Home: Hemingway, Primitivism, and Identity," 520, Note 2.
4. *New York Times*, May 4, 1952.
5. *New York Times*, September 7, 1952.
6. *New York Times*, October 2, 1952.
7. *New York Times*, October 22, 1952.

8. Elkins, Caroline, *Imperial Reckoning: The Untold Story of Britain's Gulag in Kenya*, 63.
9. *New York Times*, January 6, 1953.
10. *New York Times*, February 16, 1953.
11. *New York Times*, March 28, 1953.
12. *New York Times*, March 26, 1953.
13. *New York Times*, April 4, 1953.
14. *New York Times*, April 18, 1953.
15. Elkins, Caroline, *Imperial Reckoning: The Untold Story of Britain's Gulag in Kenya*, 392.
16. *New York Times*, April 1, 1953.
17. *New York Times*, April 12, 1953.
18. *New York Times*, August 20, 1953.
19. Hemingway, African Journal, JFK, MHPP-014-012, 15.
20. Based on Walton's report of a meeting with Denis Zaphiro, to Rose Marie Burwell. Burwell, *The Postwar Years and the Posthumous Novels*, 136.
21. Patrick Hemingway, interviewed by the author, November 17, 2020.
22. Hemingway, *How It Was*, 432.
23. Hemingway, *How It Was*, 433.
24. Hemingway, African Journal, JFK, MHPP-014-012, 136.
25. Hemingway, African Journal, JFK, MHPP-014-012, 30.
26. Elkins, Caroline, *Imperial Reckoning: The Untold Story of Britain's Gulag in Kenya*, 162.
27. Hemingway, African Journal, JFK, MHPP-014-012, 42.
28. Hemingway, African Journal, JFK, MHPP-014-012, 30.
29. Mary remarked in her journal, "These 15,000 acres, the life in them, and the communications with neighbors-all sons-in-law, etc.-is truly feudal." Hemingway, African Journal, JFK, MHPP-014-012, 30.
30. Burwell, *The Postwar Years and the Posthumous Novels*, 136.
31. Hemingway, African Journal, JFK, MHPP-014-012, 55.
32. Hemingway, African Journal, JFK, MHPP-014-012, 57.
33. Hemingway, *How It Was*, 470.
34. Hemingway, *How It Was*, 474.
35. *Look*, September 12, 1961, vol. 25, no. 19.
36. Hemingway, African Journal, JFK, MHPP-014-012, 62.
37. Hemingway, African Journal, JFK, MHPP-014-012, 60.
38. Hemingway, African Journal, JFK, MHPP-014-012, 66-67.
39. Hemingway, African Journal, JFK, MHPP-014-012, 67.
40. Hemingway, African Journal, JFK, MHPP-014-012, 69.
41. Hemingway, *How It Was*, 455.
42. Hemingway, African Journal, JFK, MHPP-014-012, 131.
43. Hemingway, African Journal, JFK, MHPP-014-012, 79.
44. Hemingway, African Journal, JFK, MHPP-014-012, 113.
45. Hemingway, *How It Was*, 484.
46. Hemingway, African Journal, JFK, MHPP-014-015, 175.
47. Carl Eby found and reproduced the certificate appointing Ernest as an honorary game warden. Eby, "'In the Year of the Maji-Maji': Settler Colonialism, the Nandi Resistance, and Race in the *Garden of Eden*," 25.
48. EH to Harvey Breit, January 3, 1954, Baker, *Selected Letters*, 825.
49. Eby, "'In the Year of the Maji-Maji': Settler Colonialism, the Nandi Resistance, and Race in the *Garden of Eden*," 26–27.

50. Hemingway, African Journal, December 25, 1953, JFK, MHPP-014-012, 217.

51. Hemingway, African Journal, January 9, 1954, JFK, MHPP-014-017, 236.

52. Hemingway, African Journal, January 10, 1954, JFK, MHPP-014-017, 236.

53. Eby, "'In the Year of the Maji-Maji': Settler Colonialism, the Nandi Resistance, and Race in the *Garden of Eden*," 26-27.

54. Hemingway, African Journal, December 6, 1954, JFK, MHPP-014-015, 189.

55. Hemingway, *How It Was*, 461.

56. Hemingway, African Journal, JFK, MHPP-014-012, 199.

57. Hemingway, African Journal, JFK, MHPP-014-012, 199.

58. Hemingway, *How It Was*, 464.

59. Hemingway, African Journal, JFK, MHPP-014-012, 200.

60. Hemingway, African Journal, JFK, MHPP-014-012, 202.

61. EH to Harvey Breit, January 3, 1954, Baker, *Selected Letters*, 827.

62. William Walton, Recorded Interview by Meghan Floyd Desnoyers, October 5, 1993, 224, John F. Kennedy Library Oral History Program, 9.

63. Patrick Hemingway, interviewed by the author, November 17, 2020.

64. Hemingway, African Journal, JFK, MHPP-014-012, 134.

65. Eby, Carl, "He felt the change so that it hurt him all the way through: sodomy and transvestic hallucination in Hemingway," *The Hemingway Review*, vol. 25, no. 1 (Fall 2005): 77. Fantina agrees, "But it is also fair to surmise that Hemingway's sex life with Mary, who he married in 1944, became more eventful than previously and developed certain areas more fully." Fantina, *Ernest Hemingway: Machismo and Masochism*, 117.

66. Eby, Carl, "He felt the change so that it hurt him all the way through": sodomy and transvestic hallucination in Hemingway," The Hemingway Review.25.1 (Fall 2005): p77. According to Eby, the sodomy was "a catalyst for his transvestic transformation." It is beyond the scope of this book to delve as deeply into Hemingway's psyche as Carl Eby has in *Hemingway's Fetishism: Psychoanalysis and the Mirror of Manhood*, or his "He felt the change so that it hurt him all the way through: sodomy and transvestic hallucination in Hemingway." I read Mary's African journal and Hemingway's *Garden of Eden* before I read Carl Eby and was intrigued by the parallels between the actual life Ernest described in the African Journal and the novels he wrote later. Carl Eby's rich analysis deepened my understanding.

67. Hemingway, *How It Was*, 466.

68. Under the heading, "New Names Department," Ernest listed: "Mary Peter Hemingway, Peter Mary Welsh-Hemingway, Pedro Maria Hemingway Welsh and HRH Mary Peter Welsh-Hemingway, HRH Mary Peter Welsh-Hemingway, Lady Mary Welsh-Hemingway, Ernest Welsh-Hemingway, Catherine Welsh, Catherine Ernest Hemingway, EK Hemingway-Welsh Ernest Catherine Inez Hemingway." JFK, MHPP-014-012, 205. Mary did not include the list of names in *How It Was*, but she referred to their game of making up secret names.

69. Hemingway, African Journal, JFK, MHPP-014-012, 205.

70. Hemingway, *How It Was*, 466.

71. Hemingway, African Journal, JFK, MHPP-014-012, 131.

72. Hemingway, African Journal, JFK, MHPP-014-012, 207.

73. Hemingway, *How It Was*, 443.

74. Hemingway, African Journal, JFK, MHPP-014-012, 207.

75. Hemingway, African Journal, JFK, MHPP-014-012, 187.

76. Hemingway, African Journal, JFK, MHPP-014-012, 148.

77. Hemingway, African Journal, JFK, MHPP-014-012, 148.

78. MH to EH, February 8, 1955, JFK, EHPP-IC14-008.

79. Hemingway, African Journal, January 3, 1954, JFK, MHPP-014-017.
80. MH to EH, February 18, (no year), Hemingway Collection of the Museum Ernest
     Hemingway of the Republic of Cuba in the Hemingway Collection of the John F. Kennedy
     Presidential Library and Museum.
81. Quoted in Eby, *Hemingway's Fetishism: Psychoanalysis and the Mirror of Manhood*, Loc. 3274.
82. Fantina, *Ernest Hemingway: Machismo and Masochism*, 128. The published version of
     The Garden of Eden was edited by Tom Jenks, working for Scribner's, in 1986. There is
     controversy about the passages and plots he left out, and scholars such as Burwell, Eby, and
     Moddelmog have found rich material in the original manuscript in the JFK Library.

CHAPTER TWENTY-SIX
1.   Fantina, *Ernest Hemingway: Machismo and Masochism*, 127.
2.   Hemingway, *The Garden of Eden*, 258.
3.   Burwell, *The Postwar Years and the Posthumous Novels*, 106.
4.   Burwell, *The Postwar Years and the Posthumous Novels*, 119.
5.   Eby, Carl, "He felt the change so that it hurt him all the way through: sodomy and transvestic
     hallucination in Hemingway," *The Hemingway Review*, vol. 25, no. 1 (Fall 2005): 77.
6.   Fantina, *Ernest Hemingway: Machismo and Masochism*, 127.
7.   Fantina, *Ernest Hemingway: Machismo and Masochism*, 7.
8.   Hemingway, *True at First Light*, 279.
9.   Hemingway, *True at First Light*, 282. Carl Eby examined the original manuscript at the
     JFK Library and found that the editor had substituted "red" for "old." Eby concluded "the
     very use of the word 'old' in these lines, however, calls attention to the familiarity of such
     an experience for Hemingway—a familiarity rooted in the very pattern which should
     now be so familiar to us: fetishized haircuts for both partners; ritualized 'unthinking';
     heterosexual sodomizing of the male; a merger and reversal of roles between lovers; and
     a magical, painful, physical transformation whereby the man—in this case Hemingway
     himself—momentarily becomes a woman 'Catherine Ernest Hemingway' if you will." Eby,
     Carl, "He felt the change so that it hurt him all the way through: sodomy and transvestic
     hallucination in Hemingway," *The Hemingway Review*, vol. 25, no. 1 (Fall 2005): 77.
10. Baker, *Hemingway: A Life Story*, 540.
11. Hemingway, African Journal, JFK, MHPP-014-017, 210.
12. Fantina, *Ernest Hemingway: Machismo and Masochism*, 8.
13. del Gizzo, "Going Home: Hemingway, Primitivism, and Identity," 518.
14. Hemingway, African Journal, JFK, MHPP-014-015, 216-217.
15. Hemingway, African Journal, JFK, MHPP-014-017, 226.
16. Hemingway, African Journal, JFK, MHPP-014-017, 228.
17. Hemingway, African Journal, JFK, MHPP-014-017, 229.
18. Patrick Hemingway, interviewed by the author, November 17, 2020.
19. Elkins, Caroline, *Imperial Reckoning: The Untold Story of Britain's Gulag in Kenya*, 163.
20. Fantina, *Ernest Hemingway: Machismo and Masochism*, 134.
21. Hemingway, African Journal, JFK, MHPP-014-017, 252.
22. Hemingway, African Journal, JFK, MHPP-014-017, 252.
23. Hemingway, African Journal, JFK, MHPP-014-017, 252.
24. Hemingway, African Journal, JFK, MHPP-014-017, 256.
25. Hemingway, African Journal, JFK, MHPP-014-017, 259.
26. Hemingway, African Journal, JFK, MHPP-014-017, 260.
27. *New York Times*, January 26, 1954.

28. *New York Times,* January 26, 1954.
29   Patrick Hemingway, interviewed by the author, November 2, 2020.
30   Patrick Hemingway, interviewed by the author, November 17, 2020.
31   Hemingway, *How It Was,* 628.
32. EH to BB, February 2, 1954, Baker, *Selected Letters,* 828.
33. EH to Harvey Breit, February 4, 1954, Baker, *Selected Letters,* 829.
34. Hemingway, *How It Was,* 390.
35   Patrick Hemingway, interviewed by the author, November 2, 2020.
36. Hemingway, *How It Was,* 494.
37   Patrick Hemingway, interviewed by the author, November 2, 2020.
38. EH to AEH, March 14, 1954, De Fazio, *Dear Papa, Dear Hotch, The Correspondence of Ernest Hemingway and A.E. Hotchner,* 158.

CHAPTER TWENTY-SEVEN
1.   AI to MH, (undated), 1954 "Venice, the day after your death." JFK, MHPP-016-006.
2.   EH to AI, February 13, 1954, JFK, BKPP-021-006, 50.
3.   AI to EH, January 25, 1954, JFK, BKPP-021-007.
4.   Hemingway, *How It Was,* 498.
5.   Hemingway, *How It Was,* 501.
6.   Which Adriana did, recounting the episode in her *Torre Bianca* at 324. Quoted in *Hemingway's Venetian Muse Adriana Ivancich,* 69.
7.   Hotchner, *Hemingway in Love,* 267. In an earlier letter, Ernest listed his injuries to Hotch: "rupture of kidneys, collapse of intestine, severe injuries liver, major concussion, severe burns legs, belly, left hand, head, lips, paralysis of sphincter, large blood clot left shin outside above ankle, dislocated right arm and shoulder." De Fazio, *Dear Papa, Dear Hotch, The Correspondence of Ernest Hemingway and A.E. Hotchner,* 160.
8   Hemingway, *How It Was,* 507.
9.   Hemingway, *How It Was,* 403.
10. Hemingway, *How It Was,* 404.
11. MH to her parents, July 23, 1954, JFK, MHPP-023-003, 29.
12. Legal Attaché, Havana, Cuba, to Director of the FBI, August 26, 1954, FBI Files on Ernest Hemingway, vault.fbi.gov.
13. Hemingway, *How It Was,* 407.
14. Legal Attaché, Havana, Cuba, to Director of the FBI, September 1, 1954, FBI Files on Ernest Hemingway, vault.fbi.gov.
15. Villarreal, *Hemingway's Cuban Son,* 98.
16. Enid Nemy, "Mary Hemingway: I'm Never Bored," *New York Times,* October 19, 1967.
17. EH to Bernard Berenson, September 24, 1954, Baker, *Selected Letters,* 837.
18. Malcolm Cowley to Robert Coates, November 27, 1966, Cowley, *The Long Voyage,* 592.
19   Lanham, "Hemingway-Lanham Chronology 1944-45," JFK, BKPP-022-004, 38.
20. Hemingway, *How It Was,* 518.
21. MH to her parents, October 31, 1954, JFK, MHPP-023-003, 41.
22. MH to her parents, December 17, 1954, JFK, MHPP-023-003, 44.
23. Hemingway, *How It Was,* 415.
24. MH to her parents, January 30, 1955, JFK, MHPP-023-003, 49.
25. Hemingway, *How It Was,* 417.
26. MH to CS, September 4, 1951, JFK, MHPP-023-004, 71.
27. Hemingway, *How It Was,* 418.

CHAPTER TWENTY-EIGHT
1. MH to EH, February 3, 1955, JFK, EHPP-IC14-008.
2. MH to EH, February 5, 1955, JFK, EHPP-IC14-008.
3. Hemingway, *Memories of a Fly Fisherman*, 283.
4. Hemingway, *Memories of a Fly Fisherman*, 284.
5. Hemingway, *Memories of a Fly Fisherman*, 285.
6. Viertel, Peter, *Dangerous Friends*, 251.
7. Viertel, Peter, *Dangerous Friends*, 254.
8. Viertel, Peter, *Dangerous Friends*, 256.
9. MH to EH, July 27, 1955, JFK, EHPP-IC14-008.
10. MH to EH, July 11, 1955, JFK, EHPP-IC14-008.
11. Ernest Hemingway's Will, dated September 17, 1955, JFK.
12. Hemingway, *How It Was*, 539.
13 Scribner, Charles, Jr. *In the Company of Writers: A Life in Publishing*, 76-77.
14 Scribner, Charles, Jr. *In the Company of Writers: A Life in Publishing*, 76-77.
15 Hemingway, *Strange Tribe*, 133.
16. EH to Wallace Meyer, December 5, 1955, Hemingway, *How It Was*, 852.
17. MH to EH, October 4, 1955, JFK, EHPP-IC14-008.
18. Hemingway, *How It Was*, 851.
19. MH to EH, October 4, 1955, JFK, EHPP-IC14-008.
20. Hemingway, "A Visit With Hemingway," *Look*, September 4, 1956, 26.
21. MH to Mrs. Kerr, May 19, 1956, JFK, MHPP-023-005.
22 Hemingway, "A Visit With Hemingway," *Look*, September 4, 1956, 26.
23. Hemingway, "A Visit With Hemingway," *Look*, September 4, 1956, 26.

CHAPTER TWENTY-NINE
1. Hemingway, *How It Was*, 553.
2. Hemingway, *How It Was*, 553.
3. EH to Harvey Breit, September 16, 1956, Baker, *Selected Letters*, 869.
4. Hotchner, *Papa Hemingway*, 189.
5. EH to BL, April 8, 1957, JFK, BKPP-026-002.
6. MH to BB, April 8, 1957, JFK, BKPP-026-002.
7. Hemingway, *Strange Tribe*, 130.
8. EH to BL, January 9, 1958, JFK, BKPP-026-002.
9. Hemingway, *How It Was*, 557.
10. EH to Archibald MacLeish, June 27, 1957, Baker, *Selected Letters*, 878.
11. Hemingway, *How It Was*, 443.
12. *The New York Times*, August 22, 1957.
13. Hemingway, *Memories of a Fly Fisherman*, 290.
14. Hemingway, *Memories of a Fly Fisherman*, 291.
15. Hemingway, *How It Was*, 563.
16. Hemingway, *How It Was*, 564.
17. Scribner, Charles, Jr. *In the Company of Writers: A Life in Publishing*, 75.
18 Hemingway, *Strange Tribe*, 138.
19. Yousef Karsh to Harry Scott, February 28, 1956, JFK, MHPP-022-009.
20. Yousef Karsh to MH and EH, May 15, 1957, JFK, MHPP-022-009.
21. MH to Hector Allard, June 4, 1957, JFK, MHPP-022-009.
22. Hector Allard to MH, June 4, 1957, JFK, MHPP-022-009.

23. MH to Yousef Karsh, June 20, 1957, JFK, MHPP-022-009.
24. Yousef Karsh to MH and EH, October 8, 1957, JFK, MHPP-022-009.
25. Hemingway, *How It Was,* 248.
26. Hemingway, *How It Was,* 565.
27. Hemingway, *How It Was,* 448.
28. Hemingway, *How It Was,* 569.
29. Hemingway, *How It Was,* 572.

CHAPTER THIRTY

1. Arnold, *The Idaho Hemingway,* 163.
2. Ginger Piotter, interview with George Saviers, Ketchum Community Library, January 19, 1990, OH SAV 0292.
3. Ginger Piotter, interview with George Saviers, Ketchum Community Library, January 19, 1990, OH SAV 0292. It is clear that George Saviers was much more forthcoming in his interview with Ms. Piotter than he was with Carlos Baker.
4. Hemingway, *How It Was,* 579.
5. Hemingway, *How It Was,* 579.
6. MH to Charlie Sweeney, March 3, 1959, JFK, MHPP-023-005.
7. MH to AH, JFK, August 26, 1958, JFK, MHPP-023-005.
8. MH to Allan Stewart, undated, 1958, JFK, MMHPP-023-005.
9. Hemingway, *How It Was,* 585.
10. Hemingway, *How It Was,* 593.
11. MH to EH, June 20, 1959, JFK, EHPP-IC14-008.
12. Hemingway, *How It Was,* 594.
13. Hemingway, *How It Was,* 594.
14. Hemingway, *How It Was,* 38.
15. Woolf, *A Room of One's Own,* 124.
16 Woolf, *A Room of One's Own,* 43-44.
17 Woolf, *A Room of One's Own,* 3.
18. Hemingway, *How It Was,* 470.
19. Hemingway, *Running with the Bulls,* 35.
20. Valerie Hemingway to the author, May 18, 2021.
21. Valerie Hemingway to the author, May 18, 2021.
22. Arnold, *The Idaho Hemingway,* 233.
23. Valerie Hemingway, interviewed by the author, September 8, 2019, Bozeman, Montana.
24. Valerie Hemingway to the author, May 18, 2021.
25. Hemingway, *How It Was,* 471.
26. BL to MH, August 10, 1959, JFK, MHPP-016-008.
27. Hemingway, *Running with the Bulls,* 39.

CHAPTER THIRTY-ONE

1. BL to MH, August 10, 1959, JFK, MHPP-016-008.
2. BL to CB, February 16, 1968, JFK, BKPP-025-008.
3. BL to CB, February 16, 1968, JFK, BKPP-025-008.
4. BL to CB, February 16, 1968, JFK, BKPP-025-008.
5. BL to CB, August 23, 1965, JFK, BKPP-022-004, 119.
6. Arnold, *The Idaho Hemingway,* 233.
7. BL to CB, February 18, 1968, JFK, BKPP-025-008.

8.   BL to CB, February 18, 1968, JFK, BKPP-025-008.
9.   BL to CB, February 18, 1968, JFK, BKPP-025-008.
10. Valerie Hemingway, interviewed by the author, September 8, 2019, Bozeman, Montana.
11. Hemingway, *Running with the Bulls*, 47.
12. Hemingway, *Running with the Bulls*, 56.
13. Valerie Hemingway, interviewed by the author, September 8, 2019, Bozeman, Montana. Jeffrey Meyers speculated that Valerie and Ernest were lovers. Meyers, *Hemingway*, 532. Farah repeats the allegation, Farah, *Hemingway's Brain*, 61.
14. Hemingway, *How It Was*, 600.
15. Hemingway, *How It Was*, 602.
16. Hemingway, *Running with the Bulls*, Loc. 1321.
17. Hemingway, *Running with the Bulls*, 106.
18. Valerie Hemingway to the author, May 18, 2021.
19. MH to EH, October 8, 1959, JFK, MHPP-023-005.
20. MH to EH, "The Personal Letter," 1959, JFK, MHPP-023-006.
21. Bill Walton to MH, undated, JFK, MHPP-017-010.
22. "FBI Files on Ernest Hemingway," November 3, 1959, vault.fbi.gov.
23. "FBI Files on Ernest Hemingway," November 3, 1959, vault.fbi.gov.
24. De Fazio, *Dear Papa, Dear Hotch, The Correspondence of Ernest Hemingway and A.E. Hotchner*, 273.
25. MH to EH, December 15, 1959, JFK, EHPP-IC14-008.
26. MH to EH, December 15, 1959, JFK, EHPP-IC14-008.
27. Arnold, *The Idaho Hemingway*, 212.

CHAPTER THIRTY-TWO
1.   Valerie Hemingway to the author, May 18, 2021.
2.   Hemingway, *Running with the Bulls*, 106.
3.   Valerie Hemingway, interviewed by the author, September 8, 2019, Bozeman, Montana.
4.   Valerie Hemingway, interviewed by the author, September 8, 2019, Bozeman, Montana.
5.   Valerie Hemingway to the author, May 18, 2021.
6.   Valerie Hemingway, interviewed by the author, September 8, 2019, Bozeman, Montana.
7.   Valerie Hemingway, interviewed by the author, September 8, 2019, Bozeman, Montana.
8.   Hemingway, *Running with the Bulls*, 128.
9.   Hemingway, *How It Was*, 611.
10. Hemingway, *How It Was*, 611.
11. Lyons, Leonard, "The Lyons Den," *New York Post*, March 21, 1962.
12. MH to BL, March 16, 1960, JFK BKPP-026-001.
13. Hemingway, *Running with the Bulls*, 129.
14. Hotchner, *Papa Hemingway*, 240.
15. Hotchner, *Papa Hemingway*, 241.
16. Hotchner, *Papa Hemingway*, 241.
17. Hemingway, *How It Was*, 485.
18. Mary sent a cable to Hotch: "Radio report from Stockholm broadcast here says Papa very ill stop please confirm or deny urgent to flat ready to fly or telephone stop." MHPP-0301-015.
19   MH to EH, August 12, 1960, JFK, EHPP-IC14-008.
20. Hemingway, *Running with the Bulls*, 129.
21. Hemingway, *Running with the Bulls*, 142.
22. MH to EH, August 19, 1960, JFK, EHPP-IC14-008.

23. Hemingway, *How It Was*, 489.
24. Hemingway, *How It Was*, 491.
25. MH to EH, August 26, 1960, JFK, EHPP-IC14-008.
26. MH to EH, August 6, 1960, JFK, EHPP-IC14-008.
27. MH to EH, September 18, 1960, JFK, EHPP-IC14-008.
28. MH to EH, August 20, 1960, JFK, EHPP-IC14-008.
29. MH to EH, September 25, 1960, JFK, EHPP-IC14-008.
30. Hotchner, *Papa Hemingway*, 252.
31. Hotchner, *Papa Hemingway*, 256.
32. Hotchner, *Papa Hemingway*, 259.
33. Hemingway, *Running with the Bulls*, 148.
34. Hemingway, *How It Was*, 491.

CHAPTER THIRTY-THREE
1. Hemingway, *How It Was*, 651.
2. Hemingway, *How It Was*, 652.
3. Hotchner, *Papa Hemingway*, Loc. 274.
4. Hotchner, *Papa Hemingway*, Loc. 274.
5. Arnold, *The Idaho Hemingway*, 221.
6. Ginger Piotter, interview with George Saviers, Ketchum Community Library, January 19, 1990, OH SAV 0292.
7. Letter from EH to "Whom it May Concern," December 4, 1960, Baker, *Selected Letters*, 909.
8. Valerie Hemingway, interviewed by the author, September 8, 2019, Bozeman, Montana.
9. Hemingway, *Running with the Bulls*, 164.
10. Farah, *Hemingway's Brain*, 102.
11. The procedure for ECT is described in Andrew Farah's *Hemingway's Brain*, 111. Farah believed that Ernest was misdiagnosed and that his overarching illness was "dementia, mixed etiology" (101). Therefore, the ECT was the wrong treatment. I will consider Farah's contribution to our understanding of Hemingway's condition from the perspective of medical science in 2020 later, but here I wish to convey the experience Ernest and Mary endured at the time.
12. Farah, *Hemingway's Brain*, 112.
13. Farah posited that "ECT did not erase his long–term memory, but the procedure itself was a biological stress that his brain could not handle, and that stress accelerated his dementia's progression." Farah, *Hemingway's Brain*, 111.
14. Farah, *Hemingway's Brain*, 110.
15. Farah disapproved of Ernest's continued use of alcohol. "Hemingway's doctors allowed him wine while hospitalized and drank with him at dinner parties, but alcohol had taken too much of a toll to be allowed to continue to flow freely." Farah, *Hemingway's Brain*, 155-56.
16. John Rosengren, "The Last Days of Hemingway at the Mayo Clinic," March 1, 2019, http://mspmag.com/arts-and-culture/.
17. MH Note, December 24, 1960, JFK, MHPP-028-007.
18. MH Note, December 24, 1960, JFK, MHPP-028-007.
19. MH Note, December 24, 1960, JFK, MHPP-028-007.
20. Hemingway, *How It Was*, 625.
21. Burwell, *The Postwar Years and the Posthumous Novels*, 182.
22. Baker, *Hemingway: A Life Story*, 557.
23. *The Times*, San Mateo, California, January 10, 1961.
24. *New York Times*, January 11, 1961, p.12.

25. "FBI Files on Ernest Hemingway," January 16, 1961, vault.fbi.gov.
26. "FBI Files on Ernest Hemingway," January 16, 1961, vault.fbi.gov.
27. According to Rose Marie Burwell the "biographer Michael Reynolds obtained the [FBI] file under the Freedom of Information Act and shared it with Jeffrey Meyers, who promptly published it in the New York Review of Books without acknowledging his source." Burwell, *The Postwar Years and the Posthumous Novels*, 199, Note 35. Meyers, Jeffrey, *Hemingway: A Biography*, 543.
28. Hemingway, *How It Was*, 626.
29. EH to President Kennedy, January 24, 1961, Baker, *Selected Letters*, 916.
30. It is interesting that Andrew Farah does not deal with Dr. Rome's letter or his diagnosis that a drug reaction was responsible for Ernest's condition.
31. Letter from Dr. Rome to EH, January 1961, JFK, EHPP, Box 0M12.
32. Hugh Butt to EH, January 19, 1961, JFK, EHPP, Box 0M12.
33. Hugh Butt to EH, January 19, 1961, JFK, EHPP, Box 0M12.
34. Hugh Butt to EH, January 19, 1961, JFK, EHPP, Box 0M12.
35. Hemingway, *How It Was*, 628.
36. Arnold, *The Idaho Hemingway*, 225.
37. Ginger Piotter, interview with George Saviers, Ketchum Community Library, January 19, 1990, OH SAV 0292. George Saviers was much more forthcoming in his interview with Ms. Piotter than he was with Carlos Baker.
38. Ginger Piotter, interview with George Saviers, Ketchum Community Library, January 19, 1990, OH SAV 0292.
39. Ginger Piotter, interview with George Saviers, Ketchum Community Library, January 19, 1990, OH SAV 0292.
40. Mary told H.R. Stoneback that she could always tell what sort of a day she was going to have with Papa by looking into his eyes. He had particularly expressive eyes, so she would have worried when they were vacant. Conversation with H.R. Stoneback, October 22, 2016, Dallas, Pennsylvania.
41. Arnold, *The Idaho Hemingway*, 227.
42. Carlos Baker, interview with Don Anderson, August 3, 1964, JFK, BKPP-026-001.
43. Carlos Baker, interview with Don Anderson, August 3, 1964, JFK, BKPP-026-001.
44. Hemingway, *How It Was*, 658.
45. MH to the Bruce's, April 7, 1961, JFK, MHPP-033-015.
46. Hemingway, *How It Was*, 630.
47. Carlos Baker, interview with Don Anderson, August 3, 1964, JFK, BKPP-026-001.
48. Carlos Baker, interview with Don Anderson, August 3, 1964, JFK, BKPP-026-001.
49. Carlos Baker, interview with Don Anderson, August 3, 1964, JFK, BKPP-026-001.

CHAPTER THIRTY-FOUR
1. Carlos Baker, interview with George Saviers, August 6, 1964, JFK, BKPP-026-001.
2. Carlos Baker, interview with Don Anderson, August 3, 1964, JFK, BKPP-026-001.
3. Carlos Baker, interview with Don Anderson, August 3, 1964, JFK, BKPP-026-001. George Saviers appeared to dispute that story and told Tilley Arnold that "he and Papa were standing together, just watching the airplane like any spectator would do, and he had no sense that Papa was ready to run into either of the rotating blades." Arnold, *The Idaho Hemingway*, 227. However, Georges Saviers told Carlos Baker that "it looked as if [Ernest] meant to walk into the propellers of a DC 3 while they were grounded at Rapid City. Carlos Baker, interview with George Saviers, August 6, 1964, JFK, BKPP-026-001.

4.   Carlos Baker, interview with George Saviers, August 6, 1964, JFK, BKPP-026-001.

5.   HR to MH, November 1, 1961, JFK, EHPP Box OM12.

6.   MH to Ursula Hemingway, April 25, 1961, JFK, EHPP-IC14-009.

7.   MH to EH, April 25, 1961, JFK, EHPP-IC14-009.

8.   MH to EH, May 1, 1961, JFK, EHPP-IC14-009.

9.   MH to EH, May 4, 1961, JFK, EHPP-IC14-009.

10. MH to EH, June 1, 1961, JFK, MHPP-023-006.

11. MH to Jack and Patrick Hemingway, June 2, 1961, JFK, MHPP-023-006.

12. MH to Jack and Patrick Hemingway, June 2, 1961, JFK, MHPP-023-006.

13. MH to Jack and Patrick Hemingway, June 2, 1961, JFK, MHPP-023-006.

14. MH to Jack and Patrick Hemingway, June 2, 1961, JFK, MHPP-023-006.

15. MH to Jack and Patrick Hemingway, June 2, 1961, JFK, MHPP-023-006.

16. MH to Jack and Patrick Hemingway, June 2, 1961, JFK, MHPP-023-006.

17. Hemingway, *Memories of a Fly Fisherman*, 295.

18. Hemingway, *Memories of a Fly Fisherman*, 295.

19. MH to Howard Rome, June 7, 1961, JFK, MHPP-023-006.

20. Hotchner, *Hemingway in Love*, 182.

21. Hotchner, *Hemingway in Love*, 196.

22. Hotchner, *Papa Hemingway*, 297.

23. Taylor, Dorice, "Fritz Saviers and Ernest Hemingway," Ketchum Community Library, RM 004-119. After Ernest died, Mary gave Fritz Ernest's automatic .22 Winchester, which he treasured.

24. Hemingway, *How It Was*, 613.

25. Hemingway, *How It Was*, 633.

26. HR to MH, November 1, 1961, JFK, EHPP Box OM12.

27. Hemingway, *How It Was*, 633.

28. Carlos Baker, interview with Mary Hemingway, August 3, 1964, JFK, BKPP-026-002.

29. Ginger Piotter, interview with George Saviers, Ketchum Community Library, January 19, 1990, OH SAV 0292.

30. Hemingway, *How It Was*, 665.

31. Hemingway, *How It Was*, 631.

32. Fallaci, Oriana, *Lamplighters* (London: Michael Joseph, 1967), 7.

33. Hemingway, *How It Was*, 636.

CHAPTER THIRTY-FIVE

1.   Ed Hotchner reported Mary's first act was to call the columnist Leonard Lyons. She told him Ernest had killed himself by blowing his head off with a shotgun. She wanted Lyons to convene a press conference and announce Ernest was cleaning his gun to prepare for a hunting trip when an accidental discharge shot him in the head. According to Lyons, as quoted by Hotchner, "Only after she had arranged all this with me did she phone Ernest's doctor and tell him what had happened." This story appears in the Preface to the 1999 edition of *Papa Hemingway*, published on the centenary of Ernest's birth, and after Mary had been dead for thirteen years (Hotch omitted it from the earlier editions). Mary told Carlos Baker that she called Leonard Lyons, but not until after she was at the Atkinsons and after phoning Jack and Gregory. Hotchner, *Papa Hemingway*, xviii; CB interview of MH, August 3, 1964, JFK, BKPP-026-002.

2.   Lyons, "Lyon's Den," *The Montgomery Advertiser*, July 9, 1961.

3.   Carlos Baker, Interview with Scott Earle, August 7, 1964, JFK, BKPP-026-002.

4.   Carlos Baker, Interview with Scott Earle, August 7, 1964, JFK, BKPP-026-002.

5.   Carlos Baker, interview with Scott Earle, August 7, 1964, JFK, BKPP-026-002.

6.   *New York Times*, July 3, 1961.

7.   Carlos Baker, interview with Scott Earle, August 7, 1964, JFK, BKPP-026-002.

8.   Hemingway, *How It Was*, 636.

9.   Hemingway, Draft of *How It Was*, JFK, MHPP-004-014, 1841.

10. Bittner, John R., "Dateline Sun Valley: The Press Coverage of the Death of Ernest Hemingway,"
     in *Hemingway and the Natural World* (Moscow, ID: University of Idaho Press, 1999).

11. *New York Times*, July 3, 1961.

12. Bittner, John R., "Dateline Sun Valley: The Press Coverage of the Death of Ernest
     Hemingway."

13. *New York Times*, July 3, 1961.

14. *New York Times*, July 3, 1961.

15. *Idaho State Journal*, July 3, 1961.

16. *New York Times*, July 3, 1961.

17. The death certificate filed on August 1, 1961, said that Hemingway died of a "self-inflicted
     gunshot wound in the head." The Blaine County Coroner Ray McGoldrick left blank the
     space that would have shown whether the death was an accident or a suicide. *New York
     Times*, August 2, 1961.

18. *New York Times*, July 3, 1961.

19. *New York Times*, July 3, 1961.

20. Bittner, John R., "Dateline Sun Valley: The Press Coverage of the Death of Ernest
     Hemingway."

21. *San Francisco Chronicle*, July 3, 1961.

22. Carlos Baker, interview with Don Anderson, August 3, 1964, JFK, BKPP-026-001.

23. Arnold, *The Idaho Hemingway*, 229.

24. Arnold, *The Idaho Hemingway*, 229.

25. Valerie Hemingway, interviewed by the author, September 8, 2019, Bozeman Montana.

26. Hemingway, *Memories of a Fly Fisherman*, 296.

27. Hemingway, *Running with the Bulls*, Loc 2683 of 4902.

28. Hemingway, *Papa, A Personal Memoir*, 116.

29. Hemingway, *Papa, A Personal Memoir*, 118.

30. Patrick Hemingway, interviewed by the author, November 2, 2020.

31. *New York Times*, July 3, 1961.

32. *New York Times*, July 5, 1961.

33. Patrick Hemingway, interviewed by the author, November 17, 2020.

34. *New York Times*, July 7, 1961.

35. *New York Times*, July 7, 1961.

36. Hemingway, *My Brother, Ernest Hemingway*, 17.

37. Arnold, *The Idaho Hemingway*, 4.

38. Hemingway, *Running with the Bulls*, 168.

39. Hemingway, *Papa, A Personal Memoir*, 118.

40. Hendrickson, Paul, "Papa's Boys; Hemingway's Older Sons, Scarred but Clinging to Tender
     Memories," *Washington Post*, July 30, 1987.

41. Hemingway, Madelaine, *Ernie*, 142.

42. AP story, "Friends discount suicide in Hemingway death," *The Times-News* (Twin Falls,
     Idaho), Tuesday, July 11, 1961.

43. Paul Perry and Jack E. Sheehan, "Forest 'Duke' MacMullan: A Friend to Papa," *Las Vegan*,
     May 1981.

44. Bittner, John R., "Dateline Sun Valley: The Press Coverage of the Death of Ernest Hemingway."
45. *San Francisco Chronicle,* July 4, 1961.
46. *New York Times,* July 4, 1961.

CHAPTER THIRTY-SIX

1.   John Robert Bittner, interview with Emmett Watson, August 15, 1997, Seattle, Ketchum Community Library, RHD MS 0735.
2.   John Robert Bittner, interview with Emmett Watson, August 15, 1997, Seattle, Ketchum Community Library, RHD MS 0735.
3.   *Seattle Post-Intelligencer,* July 7, 1961.
4.   Watson took down the description of the shotgun from the paper handed to him by Sheriff Hewitt. The sheriff presumably wrote the description from the weapon found at the scene. There is no suggestion that anyone changed the weapons after Ernest's death.
     Two other men identified the gun they saw at the scene as a Boss shotgun. Don Anderson told Carlos Baker Boss made the shotgun. Dr. Scott Earle also told Carlos Baker the weapon was a Boss.
     The sheriff's version is more likely true, for he took notes at the scene and seized the gun. Anderson and Earl mistakenly told Baker it was a Boss, but it was clearly a Scott.
5.   *Seattle Post-Intelligencer,* July 7, 1961.
6.   John Robert Bittner, Interview with Emmett Watson, August 15, 1997, Seattle, Ketchum Community Library, RHD MS 0735.
7.   John Robert Bittner, Interview with Emmett Watson, August 15, 1997, Seattle, Ketchum Community Library, RHD MS 0735.
8.   MH to Sheriff Frank Hewitt, September 7, 1961, JFK MHPP-023-006.
9.   Hemingway, *Memories of a Fly Fisherman,* 297.
10. Wills of Ernest Hemingway, JFK.
11. Patrick Hemingway, interviewed by the author, November 2, 2020.
12. Hemingway, *Memories of a Fly Fisherman,* 297.
13. Farrell's story in *Time* did not come out until the issue of July 14, 1961. He told the same story as Watson, without revealing Sheriff Hewitt as the source. "[Ernest] put the gun barrel in his mouth and pulled both triggers. The blast blew his whole head away except for his mouth, his chin, and part of his cheeks." "Mary Hemingway kept insisting that, somehow, her husband's death had been an accident. Plainly it could not have been. Moreover, Hemingway had been ill and depressed for a long time."
14. Barry Farrell to MH, undated, Ketchum Community Library.
15. In addition to Watson and Farrell, Mary met with representatives of United Press International and The Associated Press. *New York Times,* July 8, 1961.
16. *New York Times,* July 9, 1961.
17. *New York Times,* July 9, 1961.
18. *New York Times,* July 9, 1961.
19. *New York Times,* July 9, 1961.
20. *New York Times,* July 9, 1961.
21. *New York Times,* July 9, 1961.
22. John Robert Bittner, Interview with Emmett Watson, August 15, 1997, Seattle, Ketchum Community Library, RHD MS 0735.
23. *New York Times,* July 9, 1961.
24. Patrick Hemingway interviewed by the author November 17, 2020.
25. Patrick Hemingway, interviewed by the author, November 2, 2020.

26. Kert, *The Hemingway Women*, 503.
27. Burwell, Interview with William Walton, September 25, 26, 1992, JFK, EHMISC-009-016.
28. Hemingway, *My Brother, Ernest Hemingway*, 283.
29. Hemingway, *How It Was*, 635.
30. Farah, *Hemingway's Brain*, 160.
31. Burwell, *The Postwar Years and the Posthumous Novels*, Note 25, 230.
32. Burwell, *The Postwar Years and the Posthumous Novels*, Note 25, 230.
33. Valerie Hemingway, interviewed by the author, in Bozeman, Montana, September 8, 2019.
34. Hemingway, *How It Was*, 630.
35. Hemingway, *How It Was*, 637.
36. Patrick Hemingway, interviewed by the author, November 17, 2020.

CHAPTER THIRTY-SEVEN
1. Valerie Hemingway in conversation with the author in Oak Park, July 23, 2016.
2. Farberow, Norman L., "Shame and Guilt in Suicide and Survivors," in *Suicide Prevention: a Holistic Approach*, edited by D. De Leo, A. Schmidtke, & R. F. W. Diekstra (The Netherlands: Kluwer Academic Publishers, 1998), 157-161; O. Grad and A. Zavasnik, "Shame, the Unbearable Legacy of Suicide," in *Suicide Prevention: a Holistic Approach*, edited by D. De Leo, A. Schmidtke, & R. F. W. Diekstra (The Netherlands: Kluwer Academic Publishers, 1998), 163; Serani, Deborah, "Understanding the Survivors of Suicide," *Psychology Today*, November 2013.
3. Jacobs, Tom, "American's Attitudes Toward Suicide are Softening," *Pacific Standard*, September 23, 2018; Bryant, Clifton D., ed., *Handbook of Death and Dying, Vol. I: The Presence of Death* (Thousand Oaks, CA: SAGE Reference, 2003), 309-318.
4. Serani, Deborah, "Understanding the Survivors of Suicide," *Psychology Today*, November 2013; per McIntosh, John L., *Suicide Survivors: The Aftermath of Suicide and Suicidal Behavior* in Bryant, Clifton D., ed., *Handbook of Death and Dying, Vol. I: The Presence of Death* (Thousand Oaks, CA: SAGE Reference, 2003), 339–350.
"These three themes of suicide grief are (a) the greater struggle to find meaning in the loss of the loved one; (b) greater feelings of guilt, shame, responsibility, and blame; and (c) greater feelings of rejection, abandonment, and anger toward the deceased."
5. *New York Times*, February 22, 1964.
6. MH to AR, enclosing Power of Attorney, July 18, 1961, Hemingway Legal Files Collection, Manuscripts, and Archives Division. The New York Public Library. MssCol 18572.
7. Letter from Greg Hemingway to Alfred Rice, Hemingway Legal Files Collection, Manuscripts, and Archives Division. The New York Public Library. MssCol 18572.
8. MH to AR, September 1, 1961, and letter from Alfred Rice to Mary, September 6, 1961, Hemingway Legal Files Collection, Manuscripts, and Archives Division. The New York Public Library. MssCol 18572.
9. Valerie Hemingway, interviewed by the author, September 8, 2019, Bozeman, Montana.
10. AR to MH, November 15, 1952, JFK, MHPP-017-005.
11. MH to AR, April 27, 1962, Hemingway Legal Files Collection, Manuscripts, and Archives Division. The New York Public Library. MssCol 18572.
12. AR to MH, April 26, 1962, Hemingway Legal Files Collection, Manuscripts, and Archives Division. The New York Public Library. MssCol 18572.
13. MH to AR, October 17, 1961, Hemingway Legal Files Collection, Manuscripts, and Archives Division. The New York Public Library. MssCol 18572.

14. MH to AR, October 16, 1961, Hemingway Legal Files Collection, Manuscripts, and Archives Division. The New York Public Library. MssCol 18572.

15. Burwell, Interview with William Walton, September 25, 26, 1992, JFK, EHMISC-009-016.

16. MH to Hadley Mowrer, July 20, 1961, JFK, EHPP-IC14-011.

17. Villarreal, *Hemingway's Cuban Son*, 141.

18. The envelope and the typed letter it enclosed are in Alfred Rice's files.

19. Hemingway, *How It Was*, 153.

20. Hemingway, *How It Was*, 153.

21. Hemingway, *How It Was*, 640.

22. Hemingway, *Running with the Bulls*, 173.

23. Villarreal, *Hemingway's Cuban Son*, 142.

24. Raoul Villarreal, interviewed by the author, at Santa Fe College Conference, "Hemingway: Between Key West and Cuba," June 21, 2017.

25. Valerie Hemingway, interviewed by the author, September 8, 2019, Bozeman, Montana.

26. MH to BW, September 1961, JFK, WWPP-001-004.

27. Hemingway, *How It Was*, 642.

28. Hemingway, *Running with the Bulls*, 184.

29. Hemingway, *Running with the Bulls*, 184. Valerie's eyewitness account of Castro's visit is well-crafted and humorous.

30. Leonard Lyons reported a slightly different version of the story in his column in the *New York Post*, Tuesday, March 6, 1962.
    "When Castro visited the Finca, Mary showed him the thirteen paintings she wanted to take with her. It was against the law. 'Then we must break the law,' Castro conceded. He gave the necessary permissions."

31. In a televised interview, Castro said, "It is incredible how widespread Ernesto Hemingway's popularity is. He was very close to us."
    Castro credited Hemingway's novel *For Whom the Bell Tolls*, with giving him tips on guerrilla warfare when the revolutionaries were waging a successful battle against the dictator Batista during the late 1950s. "I can tell you, that of the works that helped me develop tactics for fighting against Batista's army, this novel by Hemingway was one of them." *The San Juan Star*, April, 27, 1977, MHPP–016–003.

32. Valerie Hemingway, interviewed by the author, September 8, 2019, Bozeman, Montana.

33. Valerie's account of the problems arranging for the shipment is far more detailed and amusing than Mary's. Hemingway, *Running with the Bulls*, 190.

34. Hemingway, *How It Was*, 644.
    Paul Hendrickson carefully considers the history of *Pilar* in *Hemingway's Boat: Everything He Loved in Life, And Lost, 1934-1961*. There are stories that the boat mounted at the Finca is a replica. Hendrickson concluded that "we can't know for certain" whether or not the mounted boat is authentic. Hendrickson also refers to a story that Hemingway left *Pilar* to Gregorio Fuentes in his will. As an examination of the will makes clear, this is not true. Neither is it true that Hemingway left written instructions to Mary to give the boat to Gregorio. I considered the letter of instructions above, and it deals with the proportions of Ernest's estate Mary is to give to the boys in her will. Hemingway does not mention *Pilar* or Gregorio.

35. The text of the document Mary "invented" reads as follows. "Whereas-my husband, Ernest Hemingway, was for 25 years a friend of the pueblo (people) of Cuba, and Whereas-he never took part in the politics of Cuba, and Whereas-he never sold any possession of his except his

written words, having given away cars, guns, books, and his Nobel Prize medal, which he gave to the Virgen del Cobre. Therefore, I believe that he would be pleased that his Cuban property, the Finca Vigia in San Francisco de Paula, Province de La Habana, be given to the people of Cuba. It will be a place of opportunity for wider education and research, maintained in his memory.

Therefore, with this document, as the legal heir of Ernest's estate and as executrix of his will, I give to the people of Cuba this property, in the hope that they may use it fruitfully to learn more and to enjoy more knowledge, as Ernest and I did.

Signed Mary Hemingway

Witness: Valerie Danby-Smith

Witness: Roberto Herrera Sotolongo," JFK, WWPP-001-004, 7.

36. Burwell, Interview with William Walton, September 25, 26, 1992, JFK, EHMISC-009-016.
37. MH to Henry Erlich, September 3, 1961, JFK, MHPP-023-006, 19.
38. Hemingway, "Papa—How He Used to Be," *Look*, JFK, MHPP-023-006, 20.
39. Hemingway, *How It Was*, 647.
40. Valerie Hemingway, interviewed by the author, September 8, 2019, Bozeman, Montana.
41. Patrick Hemingway, interviewed by the author, November 2, 2020.

CHAPTER THIRTY-EIGHT

1. HR to MH, November 1, 1961, JFK, EHPP-Box OM12.
2. HR to MH, November 1, 1961, JFK, EHPP-Box OM12.
3. MH to HR, November 15, 1961, JFK, MHPP-023-006, 54.
4. MH to HR, November 15, 1961, JFK, MHPP-023-006, 55.
5. MH to HR, November 15, 1961, JFK, MHPP-023-006, 55.
6. Farah, *Hemingway's Brain*, 2.
7. Hugh Butt to EH, January 19, 1961, JFK, EHPP Box OM12.
8. Farah, *Hemingway's Brain*, 100.
9. Farah, *Hemingway's Brain*, 101.
10. Farah, *Hemingway's Brain*, 101.
11. Farah, *Hemingway's Brain*, 102.
12. Farah, *Hemingway's Brain*, 153.
13. Farah, *Hemingway's Brain*, 27.
14. Farah, *Hemingway's Brain*, 39.
15. Farah, *Hemingway's Brain*, 40.
16. Farah, *Hemingway's Brain*, 154.
17. Farah, *Hemingway's Brain*, 155.
18. Farah, *Hemingway's Brain*, 156.
19. Farah, *Hemingway's Brain*, 160.
20. Hotchner, *Hemingway in Love*, Loc. 1389.
21. The American Psychiatric Association, Psychiatry.org.
22. Correspondence between the author and Ginnie Titterton, Acting Director, Corporate Communications and Public Affairs of the American Psychiatric Association, April 5-7, 2021.
23. MH to AR, October 16, 1961, NYPL, Hemingway Legal Files Collection, MssCol 18572.
24. Charles Scribner Jr. to MH, September 27, 1961, NYPL, Hemingway Legal Files Collection, MssCol 18572.
25. MH to AR, October 4, 1961, NYPL, Hemingway Legal Files Collection, MssCol 18572.
26. MH to Paul and Hadley Mowrer, October 12, 1961, JFK, MHPP-023-006.

27. MH to Paul and Hadley Mowrer, October 12, 1961, JFK, MHPP-023-006.

28. MH to Harry Sprague, October (undated), 1961, NYPL, Hemingway Legal Files Collection, MssCol 18572.

29. MH to AR, October 13, 1961, NYPL, Hemingway Legal Files Collection, MssCol 18572.

30. CB to MH, October 18, 1961, JFK, MHPP-015-007.

31. CB to MH, October 18, 1961, JFK, MHPP-015-007.

32. MH to CB, October 24, 1961, JFK, MHPP-015-007.

33. MH to CB, October 24, 1961, JFK, MHPP-015-007.

34. MH to CB, October 24, 1961, JFK, MHPP-015-007.

35. MH to CB, October 24, 1961, JFK, MHPP-015-007.

36. CB to MH, November 2, 1961, JFK, 015-007.

37. DB to MH, April 1, 1961, JFK, MHPP-015-007.

38. MH to CB, December 1, 1961, JFK, MHPP-015-007.

39. Wardlow, Jean, "Mary in Key West," *Miami Herald*, February 25, 1962.

40. MH to CB, December 1, 1962, JFK, MHPP-015-007.

41. MH to CB, October 22, 1967, JFK, MHPP-022-012.

42. MH to Hadley Richardson Mowrer, October 11, 1961, JFK, EHPP-IC14-011.

43. CB to MH, April 12, 1962, JFK, MHPP-015-007.

44. MH to Hadley Richardson Mowrer, April 27, 1962, JFK, EHPP-IC14-011.

45. CB to MH, April 18, 1962, JFK, MHPP-015-007.

46. CB to EH, April 24, 1962, JFK, MHPP-015-007.

47. CB to MH, October 15, 1962, JFK, MHPP-015-007.

48. MH to CB, October 19, 1962, JFK, MHHP-022-012.

49. CB to MH, October 31, 1962, JFK, MHPP-015-007.

50. John Bittner, interview with Tillie Arnold, September 26, 1996, Ketchum Community Library, RHD OH 0168.

51. DB to MH, August 22, 1964, JFK, MHPP-015-007.

52. CB to MH, August 22, 1964, JFK, MHPP-015-007.

53. MH Notes, JFK, MHPP-030-015.

54. William Walton, Recorded Interview by Meghan Floyd Desnoyers, October 5, 1993, 224, John F. Kennedy Library Oral History Program.

55. Burwell, *The Postwar Years and the Posthumous Novels*, 159.

CHAPTER THIRTY-NINE

1. Larios, Jordi, "*Noucentisme*'s 'arbitrary' nature in the Mont-roig landscapes of Joan Miró (1918–1922)," *Journal of Iberian and Latin American Studies*, vol. 20 , no. 3 (2014), 291–303.

2. Callaghan, *That Summer in Paris*, 169.

3. O'Rourke, "Evan Shipman and Hemingway's Farm," *Journal of Modern Literature*, vol. 21, no. 1 (Summer, 1997), 155–159.

4. Eakin, Hugh, "The Old Man and The Farm: The Long, Tumultuous Saga of Ernest Hemingway's Prized Miró Masterpiece," *Vanity Fair*, September 11, 2018.

5. John Dos Passos, *The Best Times: An Informal Memoir* (New York: Open Road Distribution, 1966), 210, 211.

6. O'Rourke, "Evan Shipman and Hemingway's Farm."

7. Eakin, Hugh, "The Old Man and The Farm: The Long, Tumultuous Saga of Ernest Hemingway's Prized Miró Masterpiece," *Vanity Fair*, September 11, 2018.

8. Hemingway, *Memories of a Fly Fisherman*, 299.

9. MH to AR, December 22, 1961, JFK, MHPP-023-006, 57.

10. MH to AR, December 22, 1961, JFK, MHPP-023-006, 57.

11. Eakin, Hugh, "The Old Man and The Farm: The Long, Tumultuous Saga of Ernest Hemingway's Prized Miró Masterpiece," *Vanity Fair*, September 11, 2018.

12. Valerie Hemingway, interviewed by the author at the Misericordia University Hemingway Symposium, Dallas, Pennsylvania, October 24, 2016.

13. Valerie Hemingway, interviewed by the author at the Misericordia University Hemingway Symposium, Dallas, Pennsylvania, October 24, 2016.

14. Rasenberger, *The Brilliant Disaster: JFK, Castro, and America's Doomed Invasion of Cuba's Bay of Pigs*, 354.

15. Rasenberger, *The Brilliant Disaster: JFK, Castro, and America's Doomed Invasion of Cuba's Bay of Pigs*, 303.

16. Rasenberger, *The Brilliant Disaster: JFK, Castro, and America's Doomed Invasion of Cuba's Bay of Pigs*, 303.

17. Helen Markel, "A Look Back, Look Ahead: Ernest Hemingway's Widow Talks About Her Life With Papa—and Without Him."

18. MH to Letitia Baldridge, JFK, MHPP-031-006, 1.

19. Hackett, *William "Bill" Walton, A Charmed Life*, 105.

20. Mary provided March with pages from what would become *Islands in the Stream*.

21. Jo August and William Johnson, interview with MH, June 21, 1973, JFK, EHMISC-009-015

22. *New York Times*, April 30, 1962.

23. Hemingway, *How It Was*, 651.

24. Hemingway, *How It Was*, 651.

25. Hemingway, *How It Was*, 680.

26. *New York Times*, April 30, 1962

27. *New York Herald Tribune*, April 30, 1962.

28. *Washington Post*, May 6, 1962.

29. MH to Clara Spiegel, May 5, 1962, JFK, MHPP-023-006, 68.

30. Burwell, Interview with William Walton, September 25, 26, 1992, JFK, EHMISC-009-016, 3.

31. William Walton, Recorded Interview by Meghan Floyd Desnoyers, October 5, 1993, 224, John F. Kennedy Library Oral History Program, 29.

32. William Walton, Recorded Interview by Meghan Floyd Desnoyers, October 5, 1993, 224, John F. Kennedy Library Oral History Program, 29.

33. Burwell, Interview with William Walton, September 25, 26, 1992, JFK, EHMISC-009-016, 3.

34. William Walton, Recorded Interview by Meghan Floyd Desnoyers, October 5, 1993, 224, John F. Kennedy Library Oral History Program, 30.

35. Rasenberger, *The Brilliant Disaster: JFK, Castro, and America's Doomed Invasion of Cuba's Bay of Pigs*, 352.

36. William Walton, Recorded Interview by Meghan Floyd Desnoyers, October 5, 1993, 224, John F. Kennedy Library Oral History Program, 29.

37. "FBI Files on Ernest Hemingway," November 3, 1959, vault.fbi.gov.

38. MH to Clara Spiegel, May 5, 1962, JFK, MHPP-023-006, 68.

39. Hemingway, Mary, "Safari," *Life*, April 19, 1963.

40. Hemingway, *How It Was*, 657.

41. Hemingway, Mary, "Safari," *Life*, April 19, 1963.

42. Patrick Hemingway, interviewed by the author, November 2, 2020.

43. Hemingway, *How It Was*, 658.

CHAPTER FORTY

1. Letter from Ernest Hemingway to Lee Samuels dated January 19, 1957, as quoted in Burwell, *Hemingway: The Postwar Years and the Posthumous Novels*, 139. Burwell's discovery of this letter disposed of the contention of Jacqueline Tavernier-Courbin that Mary invented the story about the discovery of the notebooks in the trunks. (Tavernier-Courbin, Jacqueline, "The Mystery of the Ritz Hotel Papers," *College Literature*, vol. 7, no. 3 (Fall 1980), 289.

2. Rose Marie Burwell says, "they were evocative rather than substantive in his creation of the text of *[A Moveable] Feast*." *The Postwar Years and the Posthumous Novels*, 151.

3. Hemingway, "The Making of the Book: a Chronicle and a Memoir," May 10, 1964, *New York Times*.

4. "Jai Alai" is a game played in Cuba which involves bouncing a ball at high speed off a wall with a curved handheld wicker basket. Hemingway, "The Making of the Book: a Chronicle and a Memoir," May 10, 1964, *New York Times*.

5. Philip Young explained, the concept of reflection allows the reader to see how "even when the focus, as so often, is on someone else there is an unflagging sense of presence of himself." Philip Young, *Ernest Hemingway: a Reconsideration* (1966), 78.

6. Del Gizzo writes that while Mary was correct to identify "*remate*" as a Jai alai term, she failed to recognize that "*remate* is used to refer to any type of 'kill shot,' a shot so forceful or perfectly placed that it cannot be returned." Suzanne Del Gizzo, "Redefining Remate: Hemingway's Professed Approach to Writing a Movable Feast," *The Hemingway Review*, vol. 28 (Spring 2009), 121.

7. As quoted in Burwell, *Hemingway: The Postwar Years and the Posthumous Novels*, 227.

8. EH to Charles Scribner Jr., April 1, 1960, Baker, *Ernest Hemingway: Selected Letters 1917-1961*, 901, 2.

9. EH to Harry Brague, February 6, 1961, Baker, *Ernest Hemingway: Selected Letters, 1917-1961*, 916.

10. Hemingway, "The Making of the Book: a Chronicle and a Memoir," May 10, 1964, *New York Times*.

11. Hemingway, "The Making of the Book: a Chronicle and a Memoir," May 10, 1964, *New York Times*.

12. Hemingway, "The Making of the Book: a Chronicle and a Memoir," May 10, 1964, *New York Times*.

13. As quoted in Burwell, *Hemingway: The Postwar Years and the Posthumous Novels*, 151.

14. As quoted in Burwell, *Hemingway: The Postwar Years and the Posthumous Novels*, 151.

15. Hemingway, "The Making of the Book: a Chronicle and a Memoir," May 10, 1964, *New York Times*.

16. Professor Tavernier-Courbin found many misspellings. Tavernier-Courbin, Jacqueline, *Ernest Hemingway's A Moveable Feast: The Making of Myth*.

17. Hemingway, *How It Was*, 659.

18. Scribner, Charles, Jr. *In the Company of Writers: A Life in Publishing* (New York: Charles Scribner's Sons, 1990), 79.

19. CB to MH, May 7, 1964, JFK, MHPP-015-007.

20. CB to MH, June 17, 1964, JFK, MHPP-015-007.

21. Hadley Richardson Mowrer to MH, April 1, 1964, JFK, MHPP-016-009.

22. Hadley Richardson Mowrer to MH, April 1, 1964, JFK, MHPP-016-009.

23. Ursula Jasper Jepson to MH, Undated, JFK, MHPP-015-007.

24. MH to Gerry Brenner, August 4, 1975, JFK, MHPP-023-006,

25. Brenner, "Are We Going to Hemingway's Feast?" *American Literature*, vol. 54, no. 4 (December 1982).

26. Brenner, "Are We Going to Hemingway's Feast?"

27. Jacqueline Tavernier-Courbin, *Ernest Hemingway's A Moveable Feast: The Making of Myth* (Lawrenceville, NJ: Northeastern University Press, 1991).

28. Jacqueline Tavernier-Courbin, *Ernest Hemingway's A Moveable Feast: The Making of Myth*.

29. Motoko Rich, "Moveable Feast is Recast by Hemingway Grandson," *New York Times*, June 27, 2009.

30. Trogdon, Robert W., "The Restored Edition: A Review and a Collation of Differences," *The Hemingway Review*, vol. 29, no. 1 (Fall 2009), 24.

31. Trogdon, Robert W., "The Restored Edition: A Review and a Collation of Differences."

32. Seán Hemingway to the author, September 7, 2021.

33. Hemingway, Seán, "How do you Like it Now, Gentlemen?: *Ernest Hemingway's A Moveable Feast: The Restored Edition*," Powell's Books, July 11, 2009.

34. Hemingway, Seán, "How do you Like it Now, Gentlemen?: *Ernest Hemingway's A Moveable Feast: The Restored Edition*," Powell's Books, July 11, 2009.

35. Miller, Farah, "Summer Reading Special: A Conversation with Seán Hemingway," https://www.oprah.com/omagazine/ernest-hemingways-grandson-sean-hemingway-on-a-moveable-feast/all.

36. Motoko Rich, "Moveable Feast is Recast by Hemingway Grandson," *New York Times*, June 27, 2009.

37. Hemingway, *A Moveable Feast: The Restored Edition*, 216.

38. Hemingway, *A Moveable Feast: The Restored Edition*, 216.

39. Hemingway, *A Moveable Feast: The Restored Edition*, 216.

40. Hemingway, *A Moveable Feast: The Restored Edition*, 217.

41. Hemingway, *A Moveable Feast: The Restored Edition*, 217.

42. Hemingway, *A Moveable Feast: The Restored Edition*, 218.

43. Hemingway, *A Moveable Feast: The Restored Edition*, 218.

44. Hemingway, *A Moveable Feast: The Restored Edition*, 219.

45. Hemingway, *A Moveable Feast: The Restored Edition*, 219.

46. Hemingway, *A Moveable Feast*, 209.

47. Hemingway, *A Moveable Feast*, 210.

48. Hemingway, *A Moveable Feast: The Restored Edition*, 210.

49. Motoko Rich, "Moveable Feast is Recast by Hemingway Grandson," *New York Times*, June 27, 2009.

50. Hemingway, *Running with the Bulls*, 213.

51. Valerie Hemingway to the author, May 18, 2021.

52. Valerie Hemingway to the author, May 18, 2021.

53. Paul, Steve, "New Coke vs. Old Coke: The Debate Over a Moveable Feast: The Restored Edition," *Hemingway Review*, vol. 29, 17.

54. Paul, Steve, "New Coke vs. Old Coke: The Debate Over a Moveable Feast: The Restored Edition."

55. Paul, Steve, "New Coke vs. Old Coke: The Debate Over a Moveable Feast: The Restored Edition."

56. Paul, Steve, "New Coke vs. Old Coke: The Debate Over a Moveable Feast: The Restored Edition."

57. Hemingway, Seán, "How do you Like it Now, Gentlemen?: Ernest Hemingway's A Moveable Feast: The Restored Edition," Powell's Books, July 11, 2009. www.powells.com /post/original-essays/how-do-you-like-it-now-gentlemen-ernest-hemingways-a-moveable -feast-the-restored-edition.

58. Sally Raleigh, "Miss Mary Works On," Clippings of articles about Mary Hemingway, MHPP-004-001.
59. Lipscomb, Thomas, May 25, 2011, *Huff Post*.
60. *The Guardian*, November 20, 2015.

CHAPTER FORTY-ONE
1. "Cuba and Central Park East Personality," by Connie Montgomery, February 20, 1964, Clippings of Articles about Mary Hemingway, JFK, MHPP-004-001.
2. "Mary Hemingway—her Sun also rises," by William Kennedy, Clippings of Articles about Mary Hemingway, JFK, MHPP-004-001.
3. "Cuba and Central Park East Personality," by Connie Montgomery, February 20, 1964, Clippings of articles about Mary Hemingway, JFK, MHPP-004-001.
4. "Mary Hemingway—her Sun also rises," by William Kennedy, Clippings of articles about Mary Hemingway, JFK, MHPP-004-001.
5. "A Look Back, Look Ahead: Ernest Hemingway's Widow Talks About Her Life With Papa—and Without Him," by Helen Markel, Clippings of articles about Mary Hemingway, JFK, MHPP-004-001.
6. Richard O'Connor, *Heywood Braun: A Biography*, 1975.
7. Oliver Pilat, *Pegler: Angry Man of the Press*, 1963.
8. Quentin Reynolds to J. Edgar Hoover, January 6, 1964, Vault.fbi.gov.
9. Quentin Reynolds to J. Edgar Hoover, January 6, 1964, Vault.fbi.gov.
10. J. Edgar Hoover to Quentin Reynolds, January 9, 1964, Vault.fbi.gov.
11. *The Statesman*, Saturday, October 18, 1964.
12. "Hemingway Tapes Cut into a Record: Caedmon to Issue Disk of Readings by the Author," by Richard F Shepard, Clippings of articles about Mary Hemingway, JFK, MHPP-004-001.
13. Harry Gilroy, "Mrs. Hemingway Releases Poems," *New York Times*, July 27, 1965.
14. Lanham, "Hemingway-Lanham Chronology 1944-45," JFK, BKPP-022-004, 38.
15. *The Hailey Times*, July 29, 1965.
16. "Fresh Air with Terry Gross," July 21, 1999: an interview with A.E. Hotchner National Public Radio (U.S) WHYY, Inc.
17. A. E. Hotchner, "Ernest Hemingway's love life is laid bare in book by fourth son," *The Guardian*, May 16, 2015.
18. Alfred Rice prepared a statement listing the revenues Ernest received from the dramatization and presentation of his stories on television and radio. "A series of four of his properties was televised, and he received $200,000. Other television properties included The Capital of the World; the Gambler, the Nun, and the Radio; Fifty Grand; For Whom the Bell Tolls; The Killers; The Battler; Now I Lay Me; The Three-Day Blow; The End of Something; The Light of the World, for the rights to all of which Ernest Hemingway received over $100,000." Hemingway Legal Files Collection, Manuscripts, and Archives Division. The New York Public Library. MssCol 18572.
19. Albert and Shirley Small Special Collections Library, The University of Virginia, Charlottesville.
20. Letter from Mary Hemingway to Bennett Cerf, December 10, 1965, MHPP-022-002.
21. Letter from Bennett Cerf to MH, December 22, 1965, MHPP-022-002.
22. Letter from Bergerman and Hourwich to Random House, December 23, 1965. MHPP-022-002.
23. Letter from MH to Bennett Cerf, December 25, 1965, MHPP-022-002.
24. Letter from Ed Hotchner to MH, January 10, 1966, MHHP-022-002.

25. *The Calgary Herald*, January 9, 1969.
26. Letter from Geraldine to Mary, January 11, 1966, MHPP-022-002.
27. "Fresh Air with Terry Gross," July 21, 1999, Interview with A.E. Hotchner, National Public Radio (US) WHYY, Inc.
28. Mary tried to disprove the claim Hotch made in his book, that he had met with Ernest while he was a patient at St. Mary's and that he had taken Ernest for a drive in the country. Mary doubted this happened and wrote to the administrator at St. Mary's Hospital, asking her to confirm that Ernest was not released from the secure facility in the company of Hotchner. The administrator replied that she believed Hotchner was incorrect. Letter from MH to the administrator at St. Mary's Hospital, January 11, 1966, and letter from the administrator to MH, January 18, 1966, MHPP-022-002. It is interesting that in his later telling of the tale in *Hemingway in Love*, Hotchner leaves out the story about taking Ernest for a drive in the country.
29. *Time*, February 11, 1966.
30. March 2, 1966. 49 Misc. 2d 726 (N.Y. Misc. 1966).
31. 49 Misc. 2d 726 (N.Y. Misc. 1966) 728.
32. 49 Misc. 2d 726 (N.Y. Misc. 1966) 729.
33. 49 Misc. 2d 726 (N.Y. Misc. 1966) 731.
34. 49 Misc. 2d 726 (N.Y. Misc. 1966) 731.
35. Argument advanced in Memorandum submitted by Mary's attorneys. MHPP-027-010.
36. Justice Frank held: "Plaintiff has submitted the original galley proofs of the book as an exhibit in support of her application and defendants account with a set of revised proofs in the form actually scheduled for publication. It is, of course, the latter version which is germane, and which will be referred to upon the instant disposition."
37. Letter from MH to Matthew Culligan, February 23, 1966, MHPP-022-002.
38. Letter from MH to John Mason Brown, February 26, 1966, MHPP-022-002.
39. Letter from MH to William A. Emerson Jr., February 28, 1966, MHPP-022-002.
40. *Saturday Evening Post*, March 12, 1966.
41. Letter from John Kenneth Galbraith to MH, February 24, 1966, MHPP-022-002.
42. Galbraith, John Kenneth, *Sunday Herald Tribune*, April 10, 1966.
43. Hamill, Pete, *New York Post*, March 10, 1966. MHPP-027-010.
44. *New York Times*, January 15, 1966.
45. Letter from MH to Waldo Peirce, April 16, 1966, JFK, MHPP-023-006
46. See Christian, Timothy, "Across the Seine from Notre Dame: Finding Aline Mosby," in *Brought to Light, More Stories of Forgotten Women*, ed. Bernadette Rule, Seraphim Editions, Niagara Falls, 2015.
47. Mosby, Aline, "A Character Out of Hemingway: Miss Mary Pulls no Punches," *Day*, May 29, 1966.
48. Malcolm Cowley to MH, August 14, 1966, JFK, MHPP-022-013.

CHAPTER FORTY-TWO
1. Popham, Peter, "Obituary: Journalist who relished controversy, whether in her interviews with world leaders or her attacks on Islam," *The Independent*, September 19, 2006.
2. Fallaci, *Lamplighters*, 2.
3. Fallaci, *Lamplighters*, 2.
4. Fallaci, *Lamplighters*, 4.
5. Fallaci, *Lamplighters*, 4.
6. Fallaci, *Lamplighters*, 5.
7. Fallaci, *Lamplighters*, 5.

8.   Fallaci, *Lamplighters,* 5.
9.   Fallaci, *Lamplighters,* 6.
10. *Chicago Tribune,* August 23, 1966, 39.
11. Fallaci, *Lamplighters,* 5.
12. Letter from Mary Hemingway to Alfred Rice, January 3, 1962, Hemingway Legal Files Collection, Manuscripts, and Archives Division. The New York Public Library. MssCol 18572.
13. *New York Times,* November 1, 1966, 3.
14. *Estate of Hemingway v. Random House* (N.Y.L.J., March 23, 1967), per Schweitzer, J. A57.
15. *Estate of Hemingway v. Random House,* 23 N.Y. 2d 341 (N.Y. 1968), 349.
16. William Walton, Recorded Interview by Meghan Floyd Desnoyers, March 30, 1993, John F. Kennedy Library Oral History Program.
17. Hemingway, *How It Was,* 665.
18. William Walton, Recorded Interview by Meghan Floyd Desnoyers, March 30, 1993, John F. Kennedy Library Oral History Program.
19. Valerie Hemingway, interviewed by the author, September 8, 2019, Bozeman, Montana.
20. *New York Times,* October 22, 1967.
21. *New York Times,* October 22, 1967.
22. Knigge, Jobst C., "Hemingway's Venetian Muse, Adrianna Ivancich," Humboldt University Berlin (Open Access) 2011, 76.
23. *Hotchner v. Castillo-Puche,* United States Court of Appeals, Second Circuit, 551 F.2d 910 (2d Cir. 1977), 915.
24. *Hotchner v. Castillo-Puche,* United States Court of Appeals, Second Circuit, 551 F.2d 910 (2d Cir. 1977), 915.
25. *New York Times,* April 30, 1976.
26. *New York Times,* April 30, 1976.
27. *New York Times,* August 3, 1976.
28. *Hotchner v. Castillo-Puche,* Per Lumbard, 911. https://casetext.com/case/hotchner v. Castillo-Puche.

CHAPTER FORTY-THREE
1.   CB to MH, May 21, 1966, JFK, MHPP-022-012.
2.   CB to MH, November 30, 1961, JFK, MHPP-015-007.
3.   Baker, *Hemingway: A Life Story,* i.
4.   Lanham, "Hemingway-Lanham Chronology 1944-45," JFK, BKPP-022-004.
5.   Lanham, "Hemingway-Lanham Chronology 1944-45," JFK, BKPP-022-004.
6.   Lanham, "Hemingway-Lanham Chronology 1944-45," JFK, BKPP-022-004.
7.   Lanham, "Hemingway-Lanham Chronology 1944-45," JFK, BKPP-022-004.
8.   Lanham, "Hemingway-Lanham Chronology 1944-45," JFK, BKPP-022-004.
9.   Lanham, "Hemingway-Lanham Chronology 1944-45," JFK, BKPP-022-004.
10. Lanham, "Hemingway-Lanham Chronology 1944-45," JFK, BKPP-022-004.
11. Lanham, "Hemingway-Lanham Chronology 1944-45," JFK, BKPP-022-004.
12. Lanham, "Hemingway-Lanham Chronology 1944-45," JFK, BKPP-022-004.
13. Lanham, "Hemingway-Lanham Chronology 1944-45," JFK, BKPP-022-004.
14. BL to CB, August 23, 1965, JFK, BKPP-022-004.
15. BL to CB, August 23, 1965, JFK, BKPP-022-004.
16. BL to CB, August 23, 1965, JFK, BKPP-022-004.
17. BL to CB, August 23, 1965, JFK, BKPP-022-004.
18. BL to CB, August 23, 1965, JFK, BKPP-022-004.

19. BL to CB, December 7, 1966, JFK, BKPP-022-004.
20. PL to CB, June 1, 1964, JFK, BKPP-022-004.
21. Valerie Hemingway, interviewed by the author, September 8, 2019, Bozeman, Montana.
22. PL to CB, June 1, 1964, JFK, BKPP-022-004.
23. PL to CB, May 10, 1966, JFK, BKPP-022-004.
24. PL to CB, May 10, 1966, JFK, BKPP-022-004.
25. PL to CB, May 10, 1966, JFK, BKPP-022-004.
26. Burwell, *The Postwar Years and the Posthumous Novels*, 30.
27. EH to BL, December 25, 1947, JFK, BKPP-026-002.
28. EH to BL, December 25, 1947, JFK, BKPP-026-002.
29. Book Week/*Chicago Sunday Times*, April 1969.
30. "Hemingway's Battered Life—The Bill Always Came," Geoffrey Wolff, *Washington Post*, April 1969.
31. Irving Howe, "The Wounds of all Generations," *Harpers*, May 7, 1969.
32. Martin, Judith, *Washington Post*, November 30, 1969.
33. Stimson, William, "An Interview With Mary Hemingway: Legend Still Lives in the Hills of Idaho," *Spokane Daily Chronicle*, October 16, 1974.
34. Simpson, Wood, "Interview with Wood Simpson," February 20, 1975, JFK, MHPP-024-009.
35. Baker, *Hemingway: A Life Story*, 426.
36. Baker, *Hemingway: A Life Story*, 427.
37. Baker, *Hemingway: A Life Story*, 407.
38. Baker, *Hemingway: A Life Story*, 408.
39. BL to CB, August 23, 1965, JFK, BKPP-022-004.
40. Baker, *Hemingway: A Life Story*, 405.
41. Baker, *Hemingway: A Life Story*, 429.
42. BL to CB, August 23, 1965, JFK, BKPP-022-004; used by Baker, *Hemingway: A Life Story*, 451.
43. Baker, *Hemingway: A Life Story*, 534.
44. Baker, *Hemingway: A Life Story*, 475.
45. Baker, *Hemingway: A Life Story*, 441.
46. Baker, *Hemingway: A Life Story*, 445.
47. Baker, *Hemingway: A Life Story*, 443.
48. Baker, Interview with Buck Lanham, JFK, BKPP-002-004.
49. Baker, *Hemingway: A Life Story*, 458.
50. Baker, *Hemingway: A Life Story*, 527.
51. Lanham, "Hemingway-Lanham Chronology 1944-45," JFK, BKPP-022-004, 22.
52. Hemingway, Jack, *Memories of a Fly Fisherman*, 320.
53. Hemingway, Jack, *Memories of a Fly Fisherman*, 320.
54. Patrick Hemingway, interviewed by the author, November 2, 2020.
55. Burwell, Interview with William Walton, September 25, 26, 1992, JFK, EHMISC-009-016, 44.

CHAPTER FORTY-FOUR
1. Walton, William, "A Sailor and a Fisherman," JFK, EHMISCS-008-023.
2. Jo August and William Johnson, interview with Mary Hemingway, June 21, 1973, JFK, EHMISC-009-015.
3. Jo August and William Johnson, interview with Mary Hemingway, June 21, 1973, JFK, EHMISC-009-015.

4.   Walton, William, "A Sailor and a Fisherman," JFK, EHMISCS-008-023.

5.   William Walton, Recorded Interview by Meghan Floyd Desnoyers, October 5, 1993, 224,
     John F. Kennedy Library Oral History Program.

6.   Burwell, Interview with William Walton, September 25, 26, 1992, JFK,
     EHMISC-009-016.

7.   Walton, William, "A Sailor and a Fisherman," JFK, EHMISCS-008-023.

8.   Jo August, "A Note on the Hemingway Collection," *College Literature*, vol. 7, no. 3 (Fall,
     1980), i-ii, iv-vi, 320. Published by The Johns Hopkins University Press Stable
     URL: https://www.jstor.org/stable/25111340.

9.   MH to William Johnson, January 6, 1973, JFK MHPP-017-001.

10. Jo August and William Johnson, interview with Mary Hemingway, June 21, 1973, JFK,
     EHMISC-009-015.

11. John Stewart to MH, July 20, 1976, JFK, MHPP-017-001.

12. Jo August to MH, February 12, 1974, JFK, MHPP-017-001.

13. MH to Jo August, November 11, 1974, JFK, MHPP-017-001.

14. MH to Jo August, February 5, 1978, JFK MHPP-017-001.

15. Edward Kennedy to MH, December 9, 1975, JFK, MHPP-016-006.

16. Mike Reynolds to MH, April 4, 1975, JFK, MHPP-017-001.

17. Jo August to MH, September 1975, JFK, MHPP-017-001.

18. *Wood River Journal,* Hailey, Idaho, July 23, 1970.

19. Judith Martin, *Washington Post,* November 30, 1969.

20. Hemingway, Mary, "The Hemingway Touch on the Delta Marsh," *Rod and Gun,* Fall
     1970.

21. Helen Markel, "Look Back, Look Ahead: Ernest Hemingway's Widow Talks about Her
     Life with Papa—and without Him," *Good Housekeeping,* February 1963, 32-37.

22. Judith Martin, *Washington Post,* November 30, 1969.

23. Martha Robinet, Articles about Mary Hemingway, JFK, MHPP-024-001.

24. Martha Robinet, Articles about Mary Hemingway, JFK, MHPP-024-001.

25. Henry Raymont, *New York Times,* September 12, 1970.

26. Henry Raymont, *New York Times,* September 12, 1970.

27. Burwell, *The Postwar Years and the Posthumous Novels,* 94.

28. Scribner, Charles, Jr. *In the Company of Writers: A Life in Publishing,* 80.

29. Burwell, *The Postwar Years and the Posthumous Novels,* 94. MH to Jo August, January 5, 1974,
     JFK, MHHP-017-001.

30. MH to Jo August, January 5, 1974, JFK, MHHP-017-001.

31. Mosby, Aline, "A Character Out of Hemingway: Miss Mary Pulls no Punches," *Day,*
     May 29, 1966.

32. Susan Buckley, interviewed by the author, January 18, 2021.

33. Susan Buckley, interviewed by the author, January 18, 2021.

34. Susan Buckley, interviewed by the author, January 18, 2021.

35. Susan Buckley, interviewed by the author, January 18, 2021.

36. Peter Buckley to MH, June 26, 1978, JFK MHPP.

37. Susan Buckley, interviewed by the author, January 18, 2021.

CHAPTER FORTY-FIVE

1.   Simpson, Wood, "Interview with Wood Simpson," February 20, 1975, JFK,
     MHPP-024-009.

2.   MH, "Polyandry May Come to Stay," JFK, MHPP-012-0022.

3. David Karr to MH, January 14, 1966, JFK, MHHP-023-006.
4. Hemingway, Draft of *How It Was*, JFK, MHPP-003-007, 298.
5. "A Redbook Dialogue: Mary Hemingway and Robert Morley," *Redbook Magazine*, November 1965.
6. Fallaci, *Lamplighters*, 2.
7. Vandervelde, Marjorie, "An Afternoon with Mary Hemingway," *Writer's Digest*, June 1972.
8. Interview with Wood Simpson, February 20, 1975, "Tropic Conversation."
9. Fallaci, *Lamplighters*, 14.
10. Hemingway, Mary, "Hemingway: A Personal Story By The Great Writer's Wife" in *Look*, September 12, 1961.
11. Fallaci, *Lamplighters*, 16.
12. Friedan, *The Feminine Mystique*, Loc. 475.

CHAPTER FORTY-SIX
1. MH to Miss Corse, July 5, 1966, JFK, MHPP-023-006.
2. William Walton, Recorded Interview by Meghan Floyd Desnoyers, October 5, 1993, 224, John F. Kennedy Library Oral History Program.
3. Susan Buckley to the author, April 7, 2021.
4. EH to Charles Fenton, June 18, 1952, Baker, *Selected Letters*, 767.
5. EH to Charles Fenton, June 18, 1952, Baker, *Selected Letters*, 767.
6. EH to Thomas Bledsoe, January 17, 1952, Baker, *Selected Letters*, 748.
7. Young, Philip, *Ernest Hemingway, A Reconsideration* (University Park and London: Pennsylvania State University Press, 1966), 7.
8. Malcolm Cowley to Philip Young, April 20, 1951, Cowley, Malcolm, *The Long Voyage*, 437.
9. Malcolm Cowley to EH, April 20, 1951, Cowley, Malcolm, *The Long Voyage*, 440.
10. Young was a professor at Pennsylvania State University.
11. Young told the whole story in considerable detail in the Foreword to his book, *Ernest Hemingway, A Reconsideration*.
12. Baker, *Selected Letters*, 760.
13. Young, Philip, *Ernest Hemingway, A Reconsideration*, 7.
14. Young, Philip, *Ernest Hemingway, A Reconsideration*, 13.
15. EH to Thomas Bledsoe, December 9, 1951.
16. Young, Philip, *Ernest Hemingway, A Reconsideration*, 26.
17. Malcolm Cowley to EH, January 28, 1952, Cowley, Malcolm, *The Long Voyage*, 494.
18. Young, Philip, "On Dismembering Hemingway," *Atlantic Monthly*, June 1966.
19. Judith Martin, *The Washington Post*, November 30, 1969.
20. Mann was professionally qualified to help as chief of special collections at the Pennsylvania State University Library.
21. Young, Philip, and Charles W. Mann, *The Hemingway Manuscripts: An Inventory* (Philadelphia: Pennsylvania State University Press, 1969).
22. MH to Gerry Brenner, August 4, 1975, JFK, MHPP-023-006.
23. Gerry Brenner to MH, September 12, 1975, JFK, MHPP-023-006.
24. MH to Gerry Brenner, October 5, 1975, JFK, MHPP-023-006.
25. MH to Gerry Brenner, November 21, 1975, JFK, MHPP-023-006.
26. Martha Gellhorn to Gerry Brenner, March 7, 1975, JFK, MHPP-023-006.
27. David Stewart, Elizabeth Cowan, Gregory Cowan, "A Conversation With Mary Hemingway," The Johns Hopkins University Press, 29–33, https://www.jstor.org/stable/44375785.

28. David Stewart, Elizabeth Cowan, Gregory Cowan, "A Conversation With Mary Hemingway," Cea Critic, vol. 40, no. 1 (November 1977), The Johns Hopkins University Press, 29–33, https://www.jstor.org/stable/44375785.

29. H. R. Stoneback, interviewed by the author, Poughkeepsie, NY, June 16, 2017.

30. Stoneback, H. R. "In the Nominal Country of the Bogus: Hemingway's Catholicism and the Biographies," *Hemingway, Essays of Reassessment*, edited by Frank Scafella (Oxford: Oxford University Press, 1991), 16.

CHAPTER FORTY-SEVEN

1. Interview with Wood Simpson, February 20, 1975, "Tropic Conversation."

2. Scribner, Charles, Jr., *In the Company of Writers: A Life in Publishing*, 83.

3. William Walton, Recorded Interview by Meghan Floyd Desnoyers, October 5, 1993, 224, John F. Kennedy Library Oral History Program.

4. Robert Gottlieb, interviewed by the author, August 20, 2020.

5. William Walton, Recorded Interview by Meghan Floyd Desnoyers, October 5, 1993, 224, John F. Kennedy Library Oral History Program.

6. Robert Gottlieb, interviewed by the author, August 20, 2020.

7. Robert Gottlieb, interviewed by the author, August 20, 2020.

8. Susan Buckley to the author, April 7, 2021.

9. "Knopf Catalogue for 1976," Alfred A. Knopf, Inc., 201 E. 50th St., New York, NY 1976.

10. Eleanor Page, "A Chat Offers the Adventures of a Hemingway," *Chicago Tribune*, October 8, 1977.

11. *Los Angeles Times*, Hemingway, *How It Was*.

12. *Boston Sunday Globe*, Hemingway, *How It Was*.

13. *Philadelphia Bulletin*, Hemingway, *How It Was*.

14. *Philadelphia Inquirer*, Hemingway, *How It Was*.

15. *Publishers Weekly*, Hemingway, *How It Was*.

16. Carlos Baker, "Mary Hemingway's Years with Ernest," *The Saturday Review*, October 2, 1976, 24-27.

17. *The Ithaca Journal*, December 27, 1976.

18. *The Courier-Journal*, Louisville Kentucky October 17, 1976.

19. *The Times Herald Record*, (Middletown, New York), September 28, 1976.

20. Kert, *The Hemingway Women*, 506.

21. Burwell, *The Postwar Years and the Posthumous Novels*, 200.

22. Burwell, Interview with William Walton, September 25, 26, 1992, JFK, EHMISC-009-016.

23. William Walton, Recorded Interview by Meghan Floyd Desnoyers, October 5, 1993, 224, John F. Kennedy Library Oral History Program.

24. Valerie Hemingway to the author, May 18, 2021.

25. Valerie Hemingway to the author, July 13, 2019.

26. Robert Gottlieb to MH, undated note, JFK, MHPP-016-007.

27. Robert Gottlieb to the author, August 27, 2020.

28. MH to Robert Gottlieb, June 25, 1977, JFK MHPP-016-007.

29. Robert Gottlieb to MH, June 28, 1977, JFK MHPP-016-007.

30. MH to Robert Gottlieb, July 3, 1977, JFK MHPP-016-007.

31. Robert Gottlieb to MH, July 17, 1977, JFK, MHPP-016-007.

32. Robert Gottlieb to MH, August 24, 1977, JFK, MHPP-016-007.

33. MH to Robert Gottlieb, August 31, 1977, JFK, MHPP-016-007.

CHAPTER FORTY-EIGHT

1. Stanley Johnson, "Hemingway's Life the Subject of Film," *The Burlington Free Press* (Burlington, Vermont), May 3, 1977.
2. Maggie Daly, "Mrs. Hemingway headed for Cuba," *Chicago Tribune*, June 26, 1977.
3. "Emile Hesse Keeps a Date with Mary Hemingway," *News-Gazette*, August 14, 1977.
4. Mary Murphy, "Homecoming in Havana: the Hemingway-Castro Connection," *New West*, August 15, 1977.
5. Laurel Gross, "Mary Hemingway Returns to Cuba for Film," July 27, 1977.
6. *New York Post*, July 19, 1977.
7. Earlene Tatro, *New York Associated Press*, July 20, 1977.
8. *New York Post*, July 19, 1977.
9. Maggie Daly, "Barbara Irritates Castro," *Chicago Tribune*, July 27, 1977.
10. "Mary Hemingway Visits Her Type of Man, Fishing for Castro," *Style*, July 20, 1977.
11. Mary Murphy, "Homecoming in Havana: the Hemingway-Castro Connection," *New West*, August 15, 1977.
12. *New York Post*, July 19, 1977.
13. Mary Murphy, "Homecoming in Havana: the Hemingway-Castro Connection," *New West*, August 15, 1977.
14. Mary Murphy, "Homecoming in Havana: the Hemingway-Castro Connection," *New West*, August 15, 1977.
15. Mary Hemingway to Fidel Castro July 15, 1977, JFK, MHPP-023-006.

CHAPTER FORTY-NINE

1. Valerie Hemingway, interviewed by the author, September 8, 2019, Bozeman, Montana.
2. Kert, *The Hemingway Women*, 507.
3. Kert, *The Hemingway Women*, 507.
4. William Walton, Recorded Interview by Meghan Floyd Desnoyers, October 5, 1993, 224, John F. Kennedy Library Oral History Program.
5. Burwell, Interview with William Walton, September 25, 26, 1992, JFK, EHMISC -009-016.
6. Burwell, Interview with William Walton, September 25, 26, 1992, JFK, EHMISC -009-016.
7. Burwell, Interview with William Walton, September 25, 26, 1992, JFK, EHMISC -009-016.
8. Patrick Hemingway, interviewed by the author, November 2, 2020.
9. Valerie Hemingway, interviewed by the author, September 8, 2019, Bozeman, Montana.
10. Valerie Hemingway, interviewed by the author, September 8, 2019, Bozeman, Montana.
11. Hemingway, *Running with the Bulls*, Loc. 4432.
12. Hemingway, *Running with the Bulls*, Loc. 43.
13. Valerie Hemingway to the author, July 13, 2019.
14. Ginger Piotter, interview with George Saviers, Ketchum Community Library, January 19, 1990, OH SAV 0292.
15. According to Desnoyers, Mary published one-third of Ernest's work posthumously. William Walton, Recorded interview by Meghan Floyd Desnoyers, October 5, 1993, 224, John F. Kennedy Library Oral History Program.
16. *Times-News*, Twin Falls, Idaho, November 28, 1986.
17. *Time*, December 4, 1986.
18. Valerie Hemingway to the author, September 12, 2019.

19. AP News, December 10, 1986.
20. Wills of Ernest Hemingway, JFK.
21. Hemingway, Draft of *How It Was,* JFK, MHPP-003-007.
22. EH to MH, September 17, 1955, NYPL, Hemingway Legal Files Collection, MssCol 18572.
23. Hendrickson, Paul, "PAPA's BOYS; Hemingway's Older Sons Scarred but Clinging to Tender Memories Series Number: 2/2," *The Washington Post,* July 30, 1987.
24. Patrick Hemingway, interviewed by the author, November 2, 2020.
25. Patrick Hemingway, interviewed by the author, November 2, 2020.
26. Patrick Hemingway, interviewed by the author, October 30, 2020.
27. Scribner, Charles, Jr., *In the Company of Writers: A Life in Publishing,* 76-77.
28. *De Silva v. Ballentine* 351 US 570.
29. Valerie Hemingway to the author, September 13, 2019.
30. CFR, 1938, s. 201.24(a): Application for the renewal of a subsisting copyright may be filed within one year prior to the expiration of the existing term by: (1) the author of the work if still living; (2) the widow, widower, or children of the author if the author is not living . . .
31. De Silva v. Ballentine 351 US 570 para. 19.
32. Valerie Hemingway to the author, September 13, 2019.
33. Valerie Hemingway to the author, September 13, 2019.
34. Valerie Hemingway to the author, September 13, 2019.
35. Valerie Hemingway to the author, September 12, 2019.

INDEX

A

academic community, 402–409

Across the River and Into the Trees (Hemingway): Adriana and, 163, 165, 175–176, 180, 181, 356; cover of, 175; inspiration for, 141–142, 143, 152, 386, 405; plot of, 161–162; publication of, 161; reaction to, 162, 165, 166, 170–171; writing of, 157, 158, 335

The Africa, 225

Africa, 192, 194, 198, 199–220, 224–225, 229, 346–348

The African Queen, 221, 222

airplane crashes, 220–225, 227, 231

Aitkin, Laurie, 207

alcoholism: of Ernest, 153, 159, 183, 244, 246, 263, 271; of Jigee, 159, 194; of Mary, 396, 423–425

Alfred A. Knopf, 412–414

Alias Kid Balzac (Peirce), 369

Allard, Hector, 249

Allard, Leola, 6, 8

The American Florist, 6

American Psychiatric Association (APA), 330

Anderson, Carl, 344

Anderson, Don, 287–289, 299, 309, 311

Anderson, Orvil, 101

Anderson, Robert "Andy," 50

Anderson, Sam, 34, 38

androgyny, 215–217

antipsychotics, 329

appeasement strategy, 14

Aquitania, 103

Aristotle, 405, 406

Arnold, Lloyd "Pappy," 120, 130, 253, 268, 286, 299, 426

Arnold, Tillie, 120–121, 130, 253, 263, 268, 281, 286–287, 299, 302, 309, 426

Asch, Nathan, 133

Atkin, Max, 7

Atkinson, Chuck, 255, 295, 296, 298, 300, 309, 312, 335, 426

Atkinson, Flo, 139, 255, 296, 300, 312, 426

August, Jo, 389–391

Australia, 25–26

B

Baby Blitz, 38

Bad Day at Black Rock, 253

Baker, Carlos, 343; on Hemingway's sex life, 217; on *How It Was*, 415; Lanhams and, 57, 58, 76, 86, 96, 231, 262, 380–387; on *A Moveable Feast*, 349, 352; as official biographer, 112, 317, 330–336, 370, 379–387; perjury claim of, 82; on suicide, 299; work on *Islands in the Stream* by, 393

Baker, Dorothy, 333, 335

Baldrige, Letitia, 342

Barnes, Jake, 329

Barton, R. O. "Tubby," 58, 59, 86

Basilio, Carmen, 247–248

Batista, Fulgencio, 188, 190, 240, 246, 250, 254, 360

Battle of Britain, 21

Battle of the Bulge, 95, 386

Bay of Pigs, 290, 340–342, 344, 346

Beach, Sylvia, 67

Beauvoir, Simone de, 65, 92–93, 156

Beaverbrook, Lord, 7, 8, 11, 18–19, 20, 34, 145

Beehler, Adeline. *See* Welsh, Adeline

Behan, Brendan, 300

Belleville, Rupert, 197, 227–228

Belmonte, Juan, 257

Berenson, Bernard, 191, 224, 231, 244

Bergman, Ingrid, 164

Bessie, Connie, 396

Bessie, Simon Michael, 118

Biarritz, France, 15–16

Biddle, Anthony, 398

birthday celebrations, 38, 127–128, 135, 193, 198, 251, 259–263, 265, 363, 396
Bittner, John, 303, 305, 308
Blackie (dog), 131–132, 137, 245
Bledsoe, Thomas, 169, 402, 404
Blitz, 21–23
Boal, Sammy, 159
Bonsall, Phil, 271
Book-of-the-Month Club, 367, 368
Boulton, Prudy, 52
Boyden, Sarah, 6
Braden, Maruja, 116
Bradley, Omar, 34, 38, 65
Brague, Harry, 331, 332, 350–353, 405
Breit, Harvey, 210, 212, 224
Brenner, Gerry, 352–353, 357, 391, 405–406
Brown, George, 101–102, 238, 246, 279, 294–296, 308–309
Brown, John Mason, 367
Brown, Mary, 279
Broyles, Henrietta, 164
Bruce, Betty, 253
Bruce, David, 60, 61, 62, 259, 385–386
Bruce, Otto, 180
Bruce, Toby, 129, 253, 275
Buckley, Annabel, 427
Buckley, Connie, 261
Buckley, Peter, 259, 261, 379, 391, 394–396, 402, 413
Buckley, Susan, 402, 413
bullfighting, 196–197, 243, 257, 258, 260, 263, 274, 276
Burwell, Rose Marie, 165, 178, 216, 217, 310, 336, 387, 415, 424
Butcher, Fanny, 156
Butt, Hugh, 281, 283–285, 289–290, 308, 327
buzz bombs, 51, 56, 61

C
Cairo Conference, 31
Callaghan, Morley, 337
Camus, Albert, 93
Cantore, Antonio, 140
Capa, Robert, 41, 46–47, 49, 56, 59, 70
Cape, Jonathan, 190
car accidents, 47–48, 59, 103, 111–112, 417
Cartwright, Reggie, 222

Casamassima, Mario, 243
Castillo-Puche, Luis, 378
Castro, Fidel, 250–251, 254, 256, 271–273, 315, 319–322, 341, 346, 360, 421–422
Cattell, James, 280, 291, 292, 310
Cerf, Bennett, 364–365
Chamberlain, Neville, 10, 11, 13, 18
Chayes, Abram, 316
Chiang Kai-shek, 31
Chicago, 6–8, 104, 110, 112, 125–126, 136, 156–158, 235, 267
"Chicago" (Sandburg), 5
Chicago Daily News, 6–7, 8, 57, 105, 331, 400
Chippewa tribe, 2, 3, 4
Christian Science, 2, 4, 125, 182, 234, 237, 250
Christmas celebrations, 22–23, 96–97, 116, 122, 131–132, 178, 218, 245–246, 283
chronic traumatic encephalopathy, 327, 328–329
Church, Frank, 395
Churchill, Pamela, 34, 50, 112, 227
Churchill, Randolph, 34
Churchill, Winston, 18, 19, 21, 24, 31, 34, 44
Cipriani, Giuseppe, 142, 160
Clark, Herbie, 11, 63–64
Cloud, Bob, 4
Coates, Robert, 150
Cole, Richard L., 345
Collier's Weekly, 40, 50, 52, 55, 61, 76
commemorative stamp, 360–361
concussions, 48, 59, 103, 125, 170, 224, 226, 231, 328
conservationist, Mary as, 391–392
Cook, Larry, 5–6, 66
Cooper, Dick, 117–118, 130, 189
Cooper, Gary, 130, 131, 134
Cooper, Marjorie, 130, 189
copyright law, 430
Cortina D'Ampezzo, 139–141, 149, 151–153, 161–162, 405
Cosmopolitan, 161
Cotton, Sam, 12
Cowley, Malcolm, 57, 133, 150–151, 191, 231, 351, 370, 403, 404
Cuba: Bay of Pigs invasion, 290, 340–342, 344, 346; Castro regime in, 315–322; commemorative stamp in, 360–361; coup

in, 188–191; Hemingways in, 100, 102–119, 122–124, 129–133, 153, 154–158, 167–169, 177–189, 229–237, 240, 246–252, 256, 266–267, 270–275; marriage and divorce laws in, 116–117; Mary's return to, 420–422; political climate in, 274; revolution in, 254, 256, 266–267, 272–273; US relations with, 267, 271, 274, 315, 340–342, 344, 422; violence in, 250–252. *See also* Finca Vigía (Lookout Farm)
Culligan, Matthew J., 367
Cunard, Emerald, 55
Curtis Publishing, 367
Czechoslovakia, 10–11

D

Daily Express, 7–12, 18, 145, 249
Danby-Smith, Valerie. *See* Hemingway, Valerie (Danby-Smith)
"The Dangerous Summer" (Hemingway), 276, 350, 364, 366
Dante, 405
Davis, Annie, 124, 257, 258, 259, 264
Davis, Bill, 124, 256–258, 261, 264, 276, 277, 291, 350
Davis, Floyd, 70
D-Day, 49–50, 56
Death in the Afternoon (Hemingway), 196, 256, 264
Debba, 212, 218
Debs, Eugene, 68
de Gaulle, Charles, 65
delusions: of Ernest, 280, 282, 283, 287, 291, 294, 313, 328, 329, 366; of Mary, 425
dementia pugilistica, 327–329
depression, of Hemingway, 282, 285, 286, 290, 294, 309, 325, 327, 328
Desnoyers, Megan, 412, 416
Dietrich, Marlene, 78–79, 81, 91–92, 97, 164, 248
Divine Comedy (Dante), 405
Domingo, Roberto, 320
Dominguin, Luis Miguel, 257, 350
Dorchester Hotel, 43–44, 227
Dorothea Dix, 49–50
Dos Passos, John, 318, 338
Doubleday, 378
Dunkirk, 15, 24

E

Earhart, Amelia, 8
Earle, Scott, 296–297, 299, 306
Eby, Carl, 213, 216, 217
ectopic pregnancy, of Mary, 40, 120, 164–165, 334
Ehrlich, Henry, 322
Eisenhower, Dwight, 28, 34, 44, 49, 61, 95, 256
electroshock therapy, 282, 283, 293, 325, 328, 329
Elkins, Caroline, 219
encierro, 196
England: World War II and, 15, 17–24, 30, 31, 33–45, 56–57, 97–98. *See also* London
Ernest (Buckley), 395–396
Ernest Hemingway (Young), 403–404
Ernest Hemingway: A Life Story (Baker), 380; Jack Hemingway's reaction to, 387; Lanhams and, 380–387; Mary's reaction to, 384–385; reception of, 383–384
Ernest Hemingway Foundation, 427
Ernest Hemingway Memorial Award for Creative Writing, 374
Ernest Hemingway School, 391
Ernst, Connie, 34–35, 37, 43–45, 101, 103, 118
Ernst, Morris, 34–35
existentialism, 92, 93, 155–156

F

Fallaci, Oriana, 371–374, 399, 401
Fantina, Richard, 215–217, 219
Farah, Andrew, 327–330
A Farewell to Arms (Hemingway), 130, 313, 333
The Farm (Miró), 337–339, 369, 389, 394, 418, 424
Farrell, Barry, 307
fascism, 9
FBI, 230, 266, 267, 268, 280, 283–285, 360–361
feminism, 399–401
Fenton, Charles, 402
Fields, Gracie, 14
Fighter Squadron (Monks), 23
financial issues, 75, 105, 119, 126, 187, 236, 258–259, 290–291, 313
Finca Vigía (Lookout Farm), 100, 102–103, 116, 153, 242, 276; Batista soldiers and,

246–247; Christmas at, 178; conversion to museum of, 315–316, 318, 321, 420–421; Cuban government and, 315–322; life at, 119, 121, 123–124, 136, 150, 154–155, 177–180; Mary as mistress of, 124, 131, 146, 155, 169, 175, 266, 267, 313; Mary's first impressions of, 106, 112; Mary's return to, 420–421; parties at, 177–178; raid on, 129–130, 132–133, 246–247; staff of, 123–124, 238; visitors to, 125–126, 156, 167–168, 173–174, 181–183, 186–188, 190–191, 230–231, 235–236, 267, 270–271; weapons at, 129–130, 132

"First Poem to Mary in London" (Hemingway), 53

Fitzgerald, Adeline, 6

Fitzgerald, F. Scott, 318, 350

Flanner, Janet, 70

Flexner, Hortense, 40

Foot, Michael, 27, 35, 38, 44, 103, 104, 115, 118

Ford, Ford Madox, 349, 350

Foreign Rights Trust agreement, 430

For Whom the Bell Tolls (Hemingway), 37–38, 40, 130, 198, 255, 273, 321, 422

France: German invasion of, 13–16; liberation of, 61–62; trips to, 135–137, 158–160, 163, 194–195, 227–228, 243, 245

Francesco Morosini, 228

Frank, Harry B., 366, 367, 372

Friedan, Betty, 401

Fuentes, Gregorio, 106, 134, 233, 321, 421–422

Fuentes, Norberto, 123–124, 165

funeral, of Hemingway, 300–303

G

Galbraith, John Kenneth, 368

Garay, Paco, 129–130

The Garden of Eden (Hemingway), 116, 130, 214–217, 252, 255

Gardner, Ava, 134, 230–231, 257, 356

Gellhorn, Martha, 40–41, 77, 96, 102, 105, 107, 110, 113–115, 123–124, 126, 131, 146, 162, 386, 406–407

gender reversals, 213–217, 252, 431

George VI, 23

Germany, 11–16; attack on England by, 18–24; invasion of France by, 14–16

"Get Yourself a Seeing-eyed Dog" (Hemingway), 145

Gilmore, Harry, 395

Gilot, Françoise, 68, 69

Gilroy, Harry, 362, 364

Gingrich, Arnold, 384

Gizzo, Suzanne del, 218, 350

Goldwater, Barry, 361

Goldwater rule, 330

Gorer, Gertrude, 47

Gorer, Peter, 47

Gottlieb, Robert, 412–413, 416–417

Gough, James A., 119

Graebner, Walter, 17, 33, 59

Great Depression, 6

Greene, Graham, 24

Green Hills of Africa (Hemingway), 215, 406

Gris, Juan, 318, 369

Guck, Beatrice, 104, 112, 157, 167–168, 277

Guck, Homer, 104

Guernica, 9

Guest, Winston, 164

H

Hagemann, E. R., 415

hair fetish, 107, 213

Hamill, Pete, 368

Hart, George, 20–21

Hart, Lillian, 20–21

Hart, Moss, 395

Hartford Institute of Living, 291–293, 310

Havana, 106, 117, 124, 133, 135, 174, 175, 247, 256, 288, 421

Hayward, Leland, 188, 192, 193, 236, 241

Hayward, Slim, 188

Hemingway, Byra Louise (Puck), 247, 425, 426

Hemingway, Ernest: academic community and, 402–409; Adriana and, 148–149, 151–153, 159–163, 165, 173–181, 183, 190, 226–228, 356, 377; affairs of, 152, 157–158, 171, 212; assessment of life by, 329–330; biographies of, 330–336, 364–369, 379–387, 411–418; Buck and, 380–383; car accidents, 47–48, 111–112; charisma of, 73; divorce from Martha by,

105, 115; drinking and drunkenness of, 94–95, 99, 104, 110–111, 153, 159, 183, 244, 246, 260, 263, 271; early relationship between Mary and, 52–57, 64–77; ego of, 94, 263; film about, 419–420; funeral of, 300–303, 311; as game warden, 210; gifts by, 73, 81, 96, 117, 133, 217, 265, 267; grave of, 425, 426; hair fetish of, 107, 213; Huertgen Forest battle and, 85–91; impotence of, 48, 54, 57, 59, 67, 72, 75, 97, 417; influence of, 424; injuries and illnesses of, 53, 59, 91–93, 96, 101–104, 111, 127, 140, 152–153, 170, 221–225, 228, 231, 240, 244, 252–254, 261, 308, 327–329, 334; legacy of, 316, 336, 431–432; letters and papers of, 317–318, 333, 335, 343, 377, 388–391, 404–405, 424, 426; letters to Mary by, 57–61, 74–78, 86–91, 96, 101, 105, 113; lost manuscripts of, 72–73, 90; manuscripts of, 317, 318; Marlene Dietrich and, 79, 81, 91–92, 97; marriage between Mary and, 134–136, 146–147, 153, 242, 400–401, 431–432; Mary's parents and, 121–122; memorials for, 391; mental decline of, 231, 236, 277–292, 308, 309, 313, 350–351, 366, 368, 373; in New York, 101; on Noel, 99; Normandy invasion and, 49–50; in Paris, 64–69, 70; party for, by Capa, 46–47; Pauline Pfeiffer and, 184; physical decline of, 236–237, 253, 273, 276–279, 313, 373; poems of, 362–363; political beliefs/comments of, 67–68, 266–267; post-mortem diagnosis of, 328–330; potential marriage between Mary and, 97, 100, 104, 113; press coverage of death of, 303–308; problems between Mary and, 80–81, 94–96, 99–100, 108, 112, 168–169, 172–175, 185–186, 225, 263–268; psychiatric treatment for, 281–285, 290–294, 309–310, 325–328; public image of, 150–151; questions over cause of death of, 304–308; recordings of, 362–363; relationship between Hotch and, 363–364; reputation of, 311, 323, 359–371, 387, 400, 426; return to Cuba by, 102–103, 105; saving of Mary's life by, xxi–xxii, 120; sexual relationship between Mary and, 97, 107, 134, 144, 153, 205, 213–218, 252,

431; Shaw and, 36, 166–167; sons of, 55, 110, 112, 121, 122, 245, 284, 300, 301, 306–307, 309, 314, 363, 406, 427–429; statue of, 376–377; suicide of, 295–301; talk of suicide by, 273, 277, 282, 286–287, 290, 291, 294; third marriage of, 40–41; as war correspondent, 40–41, 43, 50, 51–52, 57–62, 82, 432; in wartime London, 40, 43; wealth of, 71, 73, 75, 95–96, 191, 313, 427–428; wedding to Mary, 116–119; will of, 185, 236, 238–239, 306–307, 314, 338, 363, 418, 427–431; on women, 113, 382; writing style of, 90, 93; during WWI, 86–91; during WWII, 51–53, 57–62, 85–91, 96, 385–386

Hemingway, Grace, 107, 183

Hemingway, Gregory (Gigi), 183–187, 239, 302, 406; on Adriana, 178; on ectopic pregnancy, 165; Ernest and, 131, 185–187, 248, 363; Ernest's will and, 186–187, 236, 428–429; grave of, 426; Mary and, 116, 122–123, 300–301, 314, 425; mental health issues of, 244–245, 248, 284; Rice and, 430–431

Hemingway, Hadley. See Richardson, Hadley

Hemingway, Joanne, 427

Hemingway, John "Jack," 66, 67, 89, 105, 109, 116, 169, 426; Hemingway's death and, 299–300, 301, 302; Hemingway's will and, 307, 338, 428–429; Mary and, 111, 121, 292; reaction to official biography by, 387; relationship between father and, 236, 247, 363; visit to Finca by, 235–236; during WWII, 82–83

Hemingway, Leicester, 7, 41, 47, 93, 166–167, 301, 309

Hemingway, Marcelline, 107

Hemingway, Margaux, 235, 426, 427

Hemingway, Mariel, 427

Hemingway, Mary: academic community and, 402–409; accounts of Hemingway's death by, 306–308, 310–312, 325–327, 366; Adriana and, 179–181, 226; Baker and, 333–335, 379–380; during Blitz, 21–23; car accident of, 111–112; Castro and, 315, 319–321, 421–422; childhood of, 1–5; college education of, 5–6; as conservationist, 391–392; in Cuba, 105–119, 122–124,

129–130, 177–179; death of, 425, 426–427; diaries of, 3, 25, 36, 38, 49, 94, 112, 114, 116, 156, 158–159, 167, 380, 411; divorce from Noel by, 94, 98–99, 102, 110, 112; drinking/alcoholism of, 395, 396, 416, 423–425; early relationship between Ernest and, 52–55, 57, 64–69, 70–77; education of, 402; Ernest's sons and, 109–112, 115–116, 122–123, 132, 291–292, 300–301, 427–431; Ernest's suicide and, 296–301; Ernest's will and, 428–431; *The Farm* painting and, 338–339; first marriage of, 5–6, 66; first meetings between Ernest and, 41–45; funeral and, 301–302; German invasion of France and, 14–16; grave of, 426; Hemingway's decline and, 283–288, 290–295; infertility of, 164–165, 172; injuries and illnesses of, 127, 151–152, 162, 185–186, 220–222, 240, 243, 244, 252, 260, 267–268, 287, 393–394; interviews of, 359–360, 370–374, 399–401, 407; journalism career of, 5–19, 25–32, 73–74, 83, 97, 99–100, 107, 146, 399–401; in liberated Paris, 63–69, 78–81, 96–97; life after Hemingway's death for, 359–360, 369–370, 393–397, 426, 432; as literary executor, 239; loss of pregnancy by, xxi–xxii, 120, 401; marriage between Ernest and, 134–136, 146–147, 153, 242, 400–401, 431–432; marriage to Noel, 11, 25–26, 29–32, 43, 46, 48, 53–54, 70–71, 417; Martha Gellhorn and, 114–115; mental decline of, 423–425; in months after Ernest's death, 312–324; *A Moveable Feast* and, 349–358, 405; in New York, 191–192, 276–277, 359, 369–370, 394–396; on official biography, 384–385; *Papa Hemingway* book and, 363–371, 374–376; parents of, 1–5, 16, 29, 68, 104, 121–126, 132, 133, 228–229, 233–235, 241, 246, 250; Pauline Pfeiffer and, 125–128, 131, 132, 183–184; Peter Buckley and, 394–396; plan to leave Ernest by, 265–267, 275; politics of, 361–362; potential marriage between Ernest and, 100, 104, 113; pregnancy of, 119, 120, 164; problems between Ernest and, 80–81, 94–96, 99–100, 108, 112, 168–169,

172–175, 185–186, 225, 263–268; reaction of, to Hemingway's suicide, 310–313; relationships before Ernest by, 32–37, 54, 55; relationship with Irwin Shaw, 35–44, 53, 54, 72, 74, 83–84; return to Cuba by, 315–322, 420–422; return to North America by, 103–105; role of, as Hemingway's assistant, 114, 115, 136, 179, 180, 193–194, 257–259, 272, 400–401; rupture between Hotch and, 363–369; saving of life of, xxi–xxii, 120; sexual relationship between Ernest and, 97, 107, 134, 144, 153, 205, 213–214, 216–217, 252, 431; US-Cuba relations and, 340–342; Valerie and, 8, 178, 264, 270–271, 282, 300, 310–312, 315–316, 323, 324, 423, 425; as war correspondent, 25–34, 53–55, 61, 63–64; in wartime London, 19–23, 33–45, 51–53, 56–57, 97–98; wealth of, 313; wedding to Ernest, 116–119; at White House dinner, 340–346; will of, 427–429; work on *Islands in the Stream* by, 393; writing by, 397–399, 401, 410–411; during WWII, 11–32

Hemingway, Patrick, 101, 102, 110, 131, 164, 165, 192, 223–225, 284, 307, 424; African safari and, 346–348; on Baker, 387; Ernest's will and, 428–429; Hemingway's death and, 300, 301, 302, 308–309; Hemingway's will and, 185, 236; Mary and, 110, 115, 324; mental health issues of, 125–127, 245; mother and, 184; on *A Moveable Feast*, 354, 357; relationship between father and, 363; safari trip and, 201, 210, 212, 219, 347–348; visits to Finca by, 110, 116, 122, 123, 125–126

Hemingway, Seán, 354–358, 427

Hemingway, Ursula, 290, 352, 374

Hemingway, Valerie (Danby-Smith), 275, 322, 339, 382; Ernest and, 259–262, 265, 270–271, 273, 275–278, 309; on Ernest's suicide, 299, 300; at the Finca, 270–271; at funeral, 302; on Greg's relationship with father, 185; on *How It Was*, 416; marriage to Greg, 301; Mary and, 8, 178, 264, 282, 300, 310–311, 312, 315–316, 323, 324, 423, 425; *A Moveable Feast* and, 357; on Rice, 314, 430

Hemingway, Vanessa, 427
Hemingway Collection, 388–391
Hemingway in Love (Hotchner), 363
Hemingway in Spain (Castillo-Puche), 378
Hemingway Marlin-Fishing Tournament, 273
hemochromatosis, 285, 327–328
Hendrickson, Paul, 429
Herman, Jan, 415
Herrera, José Luis, 127, 175, 270, 319
Herrera, Roberto, 157, 168, 267, 317, 322
Herrera Sotolongo, José, 103
Herskovits, Melville, 5
Hewitt, Frank, 298, 299, 305–307
Higgins, Joan, 288
Hitler, Adolf, 10, 13, 19, 51, 64
Hoover, J. Edgar, 230, 284, 360–361
Hopkins, Harry, 28
horse racing, 159–160, 243
Hotchner, Ed, 164, 256, 259; Baker and, 380;
    Ernest and, 134, 228, 267, 277, 280, 293,
    309, 329–330, 333; at Ernest's birthday
    party, 261, 262; at the Finca, 156, 274; in
    France, 159–160; libel suit of, 378; Mary
    and, 255, 275, 362–363; *Papa Hemingway*,
    308, 363–371, 374–376; publishing of *A
    Moveable Feast* and, 352; rupture between
    Mary and, 363–369
Hotchner, Geraldine "Gerry," 156, 364, 365–366
Hotel Ritz, 78–80, 91–92, 96–97, 99, 159, 163,
    194, 227, 245, 262
Hotel Scribe, 63–64, 66, 70, 75
Howard, Leslie, 24
"How Do You Like it Now Gentlemen?"
    (Ross), 169–170
Howe, Irving, 169–170, 384
How It Was (Hemingway), 164, 184, 211, 302,
    351, 396, 407, 410–418; details left out of,
    417–418; Ernest's suicide in, 309–311; film
    rights of, 419; reviews of, 415–416; sales
    of, 416–417
Huertgen Forest battle, 85–91
Hunter, Kent A., 82
hunting trips, 121, 130, 141–142, 148–149,
    199–214, 253–255, 391–392
Huston, John, 221

I
Île-de-France, 243, 246

income streams, 119, 126, 290–291, 430–431
inheritance tax, 342
In the Company of Writers (Scribner), 393
Islands in the Stream (Hemingway), 185, 345,
    393, 422
Italy, 138–153, 160–162, 227
Ivancich, Adriana, 148–149, 152, 159–163,
    165, 171–181, 183, 190, 226–228, 356, 377
Ivancich, Dora, 162–163, 173–174, 179–180
Ivancich, Gianfranco, 174, 177, 178, 180, 194,
    197, 261

J
Jagiello, 135–138, 153
Jankow, Les, 297
John Fitzgerald Kennedy Presidential Library
    and Museum, 388–391, 422, 424, 427
Johnson, Lawrence, 289
Johnson, Lyndon, 361, 362
journalism, 5, 6
Joyce, James, 67, 318
Justice, Hilary, 73

K
Kamba people, 199, 210, 240
Karr, David, 398
Karsh, Solange, 248–249
Karsh, Yousuf, 248–249
Kechler, Carlos, 148
Kechler, Frederico, 139, 227
Kennedy, Jacqueline, 301, 340, 341, 343, 388,
    424, 427
Kennedy, John F., 286, 316, 322, 388, 389,
    422; Bay of Pigs and, 340–342, 344,
    346; inauguration of, 285; presidential
    campaign of, 266; statement on
    Hemingway's death by, 301; White House
    dinner by, 340–346
Kennedy, Joseph, Sr., 14
Kennedy, Robert, 276, 345, 361–362, 388
Kennedy, Ted, 390–391
Kennedy Library. *See* John Fitzgerald Kennedy
    Presidential Library and Museum
Kennish, Jacqui, 227
Kenya, 199–214, 219, 220, 231, 347; airplane
    crashes in, 220–225, 227, 231
Kenyan Wild Animals Protection Ordinance
    of 1951, 210

Kenyatta, Jomo "Burning Spear," 200, 347

Kert, Bernice, 176, 391, 415, 423

Ketchum, Idaho, 121, 253–255, 265–269, 279–
    280, 295, 323, 335, 373, 391, 426–427

Key West, 127, 132, 180, 240, 248, 275, 333

Kholey, Cucu, 111

Khrushchev, Nikita, 272, 341

Kikuyu people, 199–203, 210, 219, 347

"The Killers" (Hemingway), 340, 342

Kirkpatrick, Helen, 56–57

Klee, Paul, 318

Koyen, Kenneth, 14

L

La Consula, 257–264

Lanham, Charles "Buck" Truman, 78, 99,
    134–135, 333; Baker biography and,
    231, 380–387; at Ernest's brithday party,
    261–263; on Ernest's poems, 362–363; at
    the Finca, 112–114; WWII and, 57–60,
    75–76, 85, 86, 90, 96

Lanham, Mary "Pete," 112–115, 381–383,
    385, 387

Laski, Harold, 27

Leclerc, Philippe, 61–62, 65, 68

Lee, John, 57

Lehmann-Haupt, Christopher, 415

Leiber, Jerry, 430

Lewis, Sinclair, 345

Library of Congress, 343, 389

Life magazine, 150, 190–191, 264, 272, 276,
    277, 352, 364

lion hunting, 204, 207–208, 211–212, 347–
    348, 392

Lipscomb, Thomas, 358

literary critics, 402–409

literary executor, 239, 306, 313–314,
    429–430

literary reputation, 239

London, 7, 9, 11, 12, 27, 30; German bombing
    of, 19–23, 38, 43, 51, 56; trips to, 227, 245;
    during WWII, 19–23, 31, 33–45, 56–57,
    97–98

London Daily Express, 7–9, 11–12, 18

Look magazine, 194, 201, 202, 211, 218, 241–
    242, 322–323, 368, 371

Lookout Farm. *See* Finca Vigía (Lookout Farm)

The Lotos Club, 409, 414

Lowe, Bill, 194

Luce, Clare Boothe, 80, 414

Luce, Henry, 92

Luftwaffe, 13, 15, 19–20, 21, 38, 43

Lyons, Leonard, 296, 298, 311, 340

Lyson, Bill, 116

M

Machakos (dog), 246–247, 251

MacLeish, Archie, 245

MacMullan, Forrest "Duke," 303

Madinavieta, Juan Manuel, 244

Madrid, Spain, 197–198, 228, 244, 257, 264,
    275–276

Madura, 16

Maginot Line, 13–14

Maharaja of Jaipur, 261, 262

Mailer, Norman, 430

Main Street (Lewis), 345

Malibat, George, 160

Manges, Horace, 429

Mann, Charles W., 405

Maquis, 60–62

March, Frederic, 340, 342–345

Markel, Helen, 392

Marsh, Roy, 212, 218, 220–221, 223

Marshall, George, 343, 345

Martin, Judith, 384, 392, 394

Mason, Jane, 131

Masson, André, 133, 318

Matthews, Herbert, 190–191

Mau Mau, 200–203, 205, 210, 219

Mayo Clinic, 281–282, 284–286, 288–290,
    297–299, 308

McAdam, Ian, 221, 222

McClure, Robert, 27, 28, 34, 36, 53, 54,
    74–75, 98

McGoldrick, Ray, 298, 303

Menocal, Mayito, 204, 208, 209

Metro-Goldwyn-Mayer (MGM), 419

Meyer, Wallace, 190

Meyers, Jeffrey, 284–285

Miami, 116, 129, 244

Miguel, Luis, 274, 276

Mikoyan, Anastas, 272

Miller, Lee, 56, 70

Miller, Madelaine Hemingway "Sunny," 183,
    302–303

Milne, Joy, 227
Miró, Joan, 337–339, 389, 418, 424
Moddelmog, Debra, 217
Monks, John, 11
Monks, Noel, 9–13, 15, 16, 22, 25–32,
    43, 145; divorce from, 94, 98–99, 102,
    110, 112; marriage between Mary and,
    11, 25–26, 29–32, 43, 46, 48, 53–54,
    70–71, 417; return from Cairo, 46; as war
    correspondent, 25–26, 48, 56, 63
Montgomery, Bernard, 56
Moorehead, Alan, 145, 146, 151–152, 227
Moorehead, Caroline, 146
Moorehead, Lucy, 145–147, 151–152, 227
Moritz, John, 121, 130, 288
Morley, Robert, 399, 400
Mosby, Aline, 370
Mount Kilimanjaro, 348
A Moveable Feast (Hemingway), 73, 245, 280,
    349–358, 360, 382, 405
Mowrer, Paul, 105, 307, 330–332, 338–339,
    352
Murray, Albert, 395
Murrow, Ed, 50
Museo Hemingway, 318

N
Nairobi, 212, 219, 220, 223, 347
Nazis, 18
New York, 101, 158, 163–164, 191–192,
    247–248, 275–277, 279, 282, 359, 369–370,
    394–396
New York Post, 368
Nixon, Richard, 266
Nobel Prize for Literature, 232–234, 235, 340,
    362, 386
Non-Aggression Pact, 13
Normandy, invasion of, 49–50, 52, 53, 56
Northland, 3–4
Northwestern University, 5–6

O
Office of Strategic Services, 60
O'Hara, John, 171
The Old Man and the Sea (Hemingway), 179–
    183, 187, 188, 404, 407, 422; film version
    of, 236–237, 238, 241; publication of,
    181–183, 190–191; reaction to, 183, 192,

193–195, 205; success of, 264; writing of,
    179, 182, 335, 393
Olivares, Carlos, 315
Onassis, Jacqueline Kennedy. See Kennedy,
    Jacqueline
Operation Long Stop, 210
Operation Mongoose, 346
Operation Overlord, 44, 49
Operation Sea Lion, 19, 21
Order of Carlos Manuel de Céspedes, 229–230
Order of San Cristóbal, 240
Ordóñez, Antonio, 196–197, 243, 257–259,
    267, 274, 291, 350, 394, 395
Ordóñez, Carmen, 257, 259, 267

P
Page, Eleanor, 414
paintings: The Farm (Miró), 337–339, 369,
    389, 394, 424; from the Finca, 318–321
Pamplona, Spain, 376–377
Papa Hemingway (Hotchner), 308, 363–371,
    374–376
Paris, 7, 14, 15, 163; liberation of, 60–62; post-
    liberation, 63–69, 70, 78–81, 96–97; trips
    to, 159–160, 194–195, 227–228, 243, 245
Park, Colonel, 82
Park, Keith, 21
Parsons, Louella, 379
Patton, George S., 56
Paul, Steve, 357
Paul Bunyan, 1
Paz, Clara, 187
Pearl Harbor, 25, 26
Pei, I. M., 388, 389
Peirce, Waldo, 255–256, 369, 427
Pelkey, Archie "Red," 58, 59, 60, 62, 64, 66,
    74, 91
Peltellino, Ennio, 140
PEN/Hemingway prize, 427
Percival, Philip, 192, 198, 202–203, 205,
    207–208, 211, 219
perjury claim, 82
Perkins, Max, 101, 126–127, 158, 187–188,
    318
Pessino, Pedro Sanchez, 230
Pfeiffer, Pauline, 66, 105, 110, 113, 117, 123,
    125–128, 131, 132, 180, 183–184, 186,
    208, 355–357

Piaf, Edith, 414, 426
Picasso, Pablo, 68–69
Pilar, 41, 52, 53, 100, 106–107, 114, 135, 155, 170, 186–189, 230–231, 242, 246, 251, 273, 318, 321–322
plane crashes, 222–223, 231
Plimpton, George, 277
"Poem to Mary (Second Poem)" (Hemingway), 72
Poetics (Aristotle), 405, 406
poetry, 362–363
Poland, German invasion of, 13
Pollack, Sidney, 420
Polyandry May Come to Stay (Hemingway), 397–399
"Portrait of Mr. Papa" (Cowley), 150–151
Pound, Ezra, 67, 318
Prensa Latina, 266–267, 346
Prentice, P. I., 28, 33
Priestley, J. B., 23–24, 414
psychiatric standards, 325
psychosis, 328
psychotherapy, 328, 329, 330
publicity, 191, 192, 194, 201, 219, 267, 297
Public Relations Officer (PRO), 59
Pulitzer Prize, 193

Q
Quintana, Juanito, 196, 260

R
Rambouillet, France, 60–61, 385–386
Random House, 364, 365
reality-based psychotherapy, 328, 329, 330
Red Bull division, 26–27
Reid, Robert, 65
Restored Edition, 354–358
Reynolds, Mike, 391
Reynolds, Quentin, 360
Rice, Alfred, 136, 158, 238–239, 248, 277, 290, 306, 307, 313–315, 330–332, 339, 342, 389, 411, 418, 424–431
Rice, Felipe, 314
Rich, Motoko, 357
Richards, Lola, 238
Richardson, Hadley, 109, 113, 307, 334; *The Farm* painting and, 338–339, 418; loss of Hemingway's papers by, 72–73, 90;

marriage to Ernest of, 66, 67, 352–353, 355–357, 381; marriage to Mowrer, 331; Mary and, 105, 352; *A Moveable Feast* and, 352–354
Ritz, Charlie, 198
Robards, Jason, 255
Robinette, Martha, 392
Robinson, Sugar Ray, 247–248
Rome, Howard, 281, 282, 285, 290, 291, 293, 294, 296, 309, 310, 325–328, 431
"A Room of One's Own" (Woolf), 258
Roosevelt, Franklin Delano, 28, 31, 103–104
Roosevelt, Theodore, 202
Ross, Harold, 166
Ross, Lillian, 120, 135, 158, 164, 169–170, 191
Rossellini, Roberto, 164
Royal Air Force (RAF), 19, 21, 22, 26, 40
royalties, 126, 156, 261, 272, 291, 306, 313, 430–431
Rubinstein, Arthur, 177
Russia, 13

S
Sacrario Militaire, 139, 140
safari trip, 199–220, 229, 231, 346–348, 391, 392
Saint-Jean-de-Luz, 12
Salt, Waldo, 419, 420
Samuels, Lee, 292, 349
Sandburg, Carl, 5, 414
Sanford, Marcelline Hemingway, 107, 300
Sartre, Jean-Paul, 92–93, 155–156
Saturday Evening Post, 368, 372
Saviers, Fritz, 293, 295, 426
Saviers, George, 254, 259–261, 263, 268, 279, 281, 283, 286, 288–290, 292, 293, 295, 308, 309, 425, 426
Saviers, Pat, 259
Schell, Maria, 255
Scherman, Dave, 70
Schweitzer, Justice, 374–375
Scott, Edward "Ted," 230
Scott, Harry A., 248
Scribner, Charlie, 126, 128, 157, 163, 164, 172, 181–182, 184, 187–188, 191
Scribner, Charlie, Jr., 239, 248, 258, 307, 331, 350–352, 356, 391, 393, 412, 429

Scribner, Vera, 164, 181–182, 187
Seattle Post-Intelligencer, 304–305
"Second Poem to Mary" (Hemingway), 362–363
sexual relationship, 97, 107, 134, 144, 153, 205, 213–218, 252, 431
Shakespeare and Company, 67
Shank, J. M., 1
Shaw, George Bernard, 414
Shaw, Irwin, 35–39, 41–42, 44, 53, 54, 72, 75, 79, 83–84, 166–167, 394, 417
She Came to Stay (Beauvoir), 92
Shepherd, Richard, 419
Shipman, Evan, 338
Sicré, Ricardo, 261
Siegfried Line, 76, 85, 381, 385
Simpson, Wood, 397, 400, 411
Singer, Kurt, 330
Smith, Paul, 73
sodomy, 214–217
Somervell, Brehon, 27–28
Sotolongo, Herrera, 124
Spain, 191–192, 195–198, 228, 243–244, 257–264, 275–276, 376–377
Spatz, Carl "Tooey," 34, 95
Speiser, Maury, 136, 238
Spiegel, Clara, 301, 345–348, 424, 425
Spong, Edith, 12
SS *Constitution*, 257
Stais, John, 37, 41
Stalin, Joseph, 13
Stanfield, Agnes, 333–334
Stanley, Oliver, 23
Stein, Gertrude, 338, 349, 350
Stern, Ada, 123
Stewart, Allan, 256
Stimson, William, 384
St. Luke's Hospital, 425
St. Mary's Hospital, 281–285, 291–293
Stoneback, H. R., 379, 407–409
"The Strange Country" (Hemingway), 73
The Stranger (Camus), 93
Sudetenland, 10–11
suicide: accounts of Hemingway's, 366, 368, 372, 373, 374, 411–412; cover up of, 297–300, 310–312, 371, 418, 426; Dr. Rome on, 325–327; efforts to explain Hemingway's, 327–328; Hemingway's talk of, 273, 277,
282, 286–287, 290, 291, 294, 309–310; stigma of, 311–313; survivors of, 313
Summersby, Kay, 34, 95
The Sun Also Rises (Hemingway), 93, 195, 302, 339, 391
Sun Valley, Idaho, 120–121, 129–132, 135, 158, 300
Sun Valley Hospital, 253–254, 267, 288, 296, 308
Sweeney, Charlie, 255
symbolism, 191

T

Tagliapietra, Francesco, 147
Tavernier-Courbin, Jacqueline, 353–354
Taylor, Dorice, 296, 298
"That Magnificent Man and His Converter Machine" (Hemingway), 369
Theisen, Earl, 203, 208
Thiessen, Ty, 219, 241–242
This Week Magazine, 375
Thunder, Jim, 4
Time-Life, 18, 26, 27, 28, 54, 66, 80, 308, 432
Time magazine, 17–19, 26–29, 33–34, 73–74
Time Out, 25, 32, 43
T. J. Welsh Land and Lumber Company, 3
To Have and Have Not (Hemingway), 313
"To Mary in London" (Hemingway), 362–363
Torcello, 142–144, 147–149
Tracy, Spencer, 192, 193, 242, 253
Trogdon, Robert, 354
True at First Light (Hemingway), 216–217
Tucci, Maria, 416
Tucker, Lael, 32, 33
Turgenev, Ivan, 384
Twain, Mark, 409

U

United States: entrance into WWII, 25–27; relations between Cuba and, 267, 271, 274, 315, 340–342, 344
unpublished manuscripts, 307, 313, 345, 390, 393, 404–405
US Army, 26

V

Valium, 328, 329

Vanetti, Dolorès, 155–156
Venice, Italy, 140–144, 149, 160–162, 227
Verano, Juan, 175
Viertel, Jigee, 158–160, 194
Viertel, Peter, 158–160, 167, 194–195, 197, 236–237
Villa Aprile, 139, 149, 151
Villarreal, Raul, 318
Villarreal, René, 110, 238, 316–319
"The Voice of Ernest Hemingway," 362–363

W

Wagner, Linda, 391
Waldemann, Robert, 301–302
Walker, Jerry Jeff, 407–408
Walker, Minnesota, 1–2
Walton, William "Bill," 36, 41, 43, 46–47, 54, 55, 82, 84, 91, 96, 115, 186, 237, 284, 343, 376–377, 396, 402, 412, 427; Ernest and, 90, 94, 183; Hemingway's death and, 309, 310; on *How It Was*, 415–416; Kennedy and, 266, 276, 301, 316, 322, 340, 345–346; Kennedy library and, 388, 389; Martha Gellhorn and, 162; Mary and, 28–29, 32, 33, 277, 342, 395, 423–424; as war correspondent, 56, 85–86, 386
war correspondents, 9, 12, 17–24, 25–32, 33–34, 40, 54–62
Warren, Robert Penn, 409
Washburn, Susan, 394–396
Watson, Emmett, 304–308, 418
Wells, H. G., 414
Welsh, Adeline, 1–5, 29, 104, 121–122, 124–125, 132, 229, 234–235, 237, 241, 246, 250
Welsh, Mary. *See* Hemingway, Mary
Welsh, Otto, 2
Welsh, Thomas, 1–6, 29, 68, 104, 121–122, 124–126, 132, 133, 136, 182, 228–229, 233–234

Wertenbaker, Charles, 31–32, 44, 56, 64, 66, 70, 96–97
Wertenbaker, Leal, 44, 96
Weston, Jay, 419–420
White Tower, 34, 35, 37, 39, 41–42, 55, 73, 115
The White Tower (Ivancich), 181
Williams, Harris, 261
Williams, Taylor, 255, 287, 302, 426
Wilson, Earl, 277
Wolff, Geoffrey, 384
women's rights, 399–400
Wong, Ramón, 110
Woolf, Virginia, 258, 401
World War II: actions leading to, 9–13; Battle of the Bulge, 95; beginnings of, 13–16; D-Day, 49–50; end of, 70–77; England in, 15, 17–24, 30, 31, 34–45, 56–57, 97–98; Ernest Hemingway during, 49–53, 57–62, 85–91, 96, 385–386; Huertgen Forest battle, 85–91; London during, 31, 33–45, 51–53, 56–57, 97–98; Mary Hemingway during, 13–14, 17–32, 51–53, 56–57; US entrance into, 25–27; war correspondents in, 17–34, 40, 54–62

X
Xenophobia, 157–158, 168

Y
Young, Philip, 403–405
The Young Lions (Shaw), 36–37, 166–167

Z
Zaphiro, Denis, 203–206, 211, 223, 225, 246, 247, 248, 347, 392